Dynamic Term Structure Modeling

Founded in 1807, John Wiley & Sons is the oldest independent publishing company in the United States. With offices in North America, Europe, Australia, and Asia, Wiley is globally committed to developing and marketing print and electronic products and services for our customers' professional and personal knowledge and understanding.

The Wiley Finance series contains books written specifically for finance and investment professionals as well as sophisticated individual investors and their financial advisors. Book topics range from portfolio management to e-commerce, risk management, financial engineering, valuation, and financial instrument analysis, as well as much more.

For a list of available titles, visit our Web site at www.WileyFinance.com.

Dynamic Term Structure Modeling

The Fixed Income Valuation Course

SANJAY K. NAWALKHA
NATALIA A. BELIAEVA
GLORIA M. SOTO

John Wiley & Sons, Inc.

Published by John Wiley & Sons, Inc., Hoboken, New Jersey.
Published simultaneously in Canada.

Wiley Bicentennial Logo: Richard J. Pacifico.

Designations used by companies to distinguish their products are often claimed as trademarks. In all instances where John Wiley & Sons, Inc., is aware of a claim, the product names appear in initial capital or all capital letters. Readers, however, should contact the approprite companies for more complete information regarding trademarks and registration.

For general information on our other products and services or for technical support, please contact our Customer Care Department within the United States at (800) 762-2974, outside the United States at (317) 572-3993 or fax (317) 572-4002.

Wiley also publishes its books in a variety of electronic formats. Some content that appears in print may not be available in electronic books. For more information about Wiley products, visit our Web site at www.wiley.com.

Library of Congress Cataloging-in-Publication Data:

Nawalkha, Sanjay K.
    Dynamic term structure modeling : the fixed income valuation course /
Sanjay K. Nawalkha, Natalia A. Beliaeva, Gloria M. Soto.
        p. cm. — (Wiley finance series)
    Includes bibliographical references and index.
    ISBN 978-0-471-73714-8 (cloth/cd-rom)
1. Finance.   2. Stochastic processes.   I. Beliaeva, N. A. (Natal'ia
Anatol'evna)   II. Soto, Gloria M.   III. Title.
    HG101.N39 2007
    332.01'51923—dc22
                                                                2006037555

Printed in the United States of America.

10 9 8 7 6 5 4 3 2 1

To Sri Sri Ravi Shankar
—Sanjay K. Nawalkha

To my family
—Natalia A. Beliaeva

To my parents
—Gloria M. Soto

Preface

This is the second book of the trilogy on a fixed income valuation course by Wiley finance. This trilogy covers the following three areas of fixed income valuation:

1. Interest rate risk modeling
2. Term structure modeling
3. Credit risk modeling

Unlike other books in fixed income valuation, which are either too rigorous but mathematically demanding or easy-to-read but lacking in important details, our goal is to provide readability with sufficient rigor. In the first book, we gave a basic introduction to various fixed income securities and their derivatives. The principal focus of the first book was on measuring and managing interest rate risk arising from general nonparallel rate changes in the term structure of interest rates. Due to smoothness in the shapes of term structures, interest rate risk of straight bonds can be managed even without a proper valuation model simply by using empirical duration vectors or empirical key rate duration profiles. In fact, as demonstrated in the first book, *Interest Rate Risk Modeling, basic* interest rate risk management of financial institutions such as commercial banks, fixed income funds, insurance companies, and pension funds can be done without using the most sophisticated valuation models.

In this second book, we shift our focus to *valuation of fixed income securities and their derivatives*. A good valuation model is a key input not only for supporting the fixed income trading desks of financial institutions, but also for designing comprehensive risk management strategies for these institutions. The basic tools of fixed income valuation are "dynamic term structure models," which are also loosely referred to as "interest rate models." This second book in the trilogy aims to bridge the gap between the advanced technical books in the term structure area and the many elementary discussions of term structure models in the general fixed income trade books. By choosing basic mathematical rules with heuristic derivations over rigorous theoretical developments with technical proofs, we hope to make this difficult subject matter accessible to the wider audience of financial analysts, students, and academics. The readers will also benefit from Excel/VBA–based software, which runs C and C++ programs at the back-end, for valuing securities using the various term structure models given in this book.

Valuation of fixed income securities and their derivatives is of interest to many economic participants, including regular corporations funded with liabilities with embedded options, insurance companies and pension funds with fixed income assets and liabilities, investment banks dealing in swaps and other exotic interest rate products, hedge funds with long and short positions in credit derivatives, savings and commercial banks with prepayment options embedded in their mortgage portfolios, and many such institutions. The purpose of this book is to introduce a broad variety of term structure models, including the affine models, the quadratic models, the Heath, Jarrow, and Morton (HJM) models, and the LIBOR Market Model (LMM) and to show how to price basic interest rate and credit derivative products, such as Treasury futures, Eurodollar futures, bond options, forward rate agreements, interest rate swaps, interest rate caps, interest rate swaptions, credit default swaps, credit spread options, and the like, using some of these models.

UNIQUE FEATURES

This book distinguishes itself from other books in this area by making the following unique contributions:

A Comprehensive Classification Scheme for Term Structure Models

This book classifies all term structure models (TSMs) into four types:

1. Fundamental TSMs
2. Preference-Free Single-Plus TSMs
3. Preference-Free Double-Plus TSMs
4. Preference-Free Triple-Plus TSMs

All fundamental models (such as Vasicek [1977] and Cox, Ingersoll, and Ross (CIR) [1985]) assume a time-homogeneous short rate process and give explicit specifications of the market prices of risks. In contrast to fundamental models, preference-free models *do not require explicit specifications of the market prices of risks* for valuing bonds and interest rate derivatives. Hence, valuation can be done without knowing the risk preferences of the market participants under preference-free models. This book considers three types of preference-free TSMs, given as single-plus, double-plus, and triple-plus models. The risk-neutral stochastic processes of the state variables under any preference-free single-plus TSM are identical *in form* to the risk-neutral stochastic processes of the state variables under the corresponding fundamental TSM. However, the empirical estimates of the risk-neutral parameters are generally different under these two types of models, since the fundamental model imposes restrictive functional forms on the specifications of MPRs, while the corresponding single-plus model does not. The trick to deriving a single-plus TSM corresponding to a given fundamental TSM is to specify the stochastic bond price process exogenously using the same form of volatility function used under the given fundamental model. The exogenous stochastic bond price process is then combined with an exogenously given solution of the time 0 bond prices or forward rates, which leads to a time-homogeneous risk-neutral short rate process. This trick is explicitly demonstrated in Chapters 4 and 7. The introduction of single-plus TSMs in this book may appeal to both the econometrically inclined academics (who do not generally like time-inhomogeneous processes) and calibration-desiring practitioners (who must always "fit" a model to market prices!).

The preference-free double-plus TSMs are different from the corresponding fundamental TSMs in two ways. Not only are these models free of the market price of risk (MPR) specifications—similar to the single-plus models—but they also allow the model bond prices to exactly fit the initially observed bond prices. Unlike the single-plus TSMs that may require multiple factors to match the model prices with the observed prices, the double-plus TSMs can allow an exact fit even using a single factor. The initially observed bond prices are used as an input under the double-plus TSMs. These models exactly fit the initially observed bond prices by allowing time-inhomogeneity in the drift of the risk-neutral short rate process. Examples of double-plus TSMs include the models by Ho and Lee [1986], Hull and White [1990],[1] Heath, Jarrow, and Morton (HJM) [1992], and Brigo and Mercurio [2001].[2] This book derives double-plus TSMs corresponding to a variety of fundamental affine and quadratic models, in addition to those already given in the literature.

The preference-free triple-plus TSMs are different from the corresponding fundamental TSMs in three ways. Unlike the fundamental models, but similar to single-plus and double-plus models, these models are free of the MPR specifications. Unlike the fundamental and single-plus models but similar to double-plus models, these models allow an exact fit with the initially observed bond prices. However, unlike the fundamental, single-plus, and double-plus models, which all require a *time-homogeneous* specification of volatilities, the triple-plus TSMs allow time-inhomogeneous volatilities (i.e., time-inhomogeneous short rate volatility and/or time-inhomogeneous forward rate volatilities). Examples of triple-plus TSMs include extensions of the models of Hull and White [1990],[3] Black, Derman, and Toy [1990], and Black and Karasinski [1991] with time-inhomogeneous volatilities, and versions of the LIBOR market model with time-inhomogeneous volatilities (see Brigo and Mercurio [2001, 2006] and Rebonato [2002]).

The triple-plus models require a high number of parameters to obtain an exact fit with the chosen plain vanilla derivative instruments and may suffer from the criticism of "smoothing."

A detailed introduction to the four types of term structure models is given in the last section of Chapter 3, and various chapters explicitly consider fundamental models, single-plus models, and double-plus models. We generally do not consider triple-plus models in this book, except for the triple-plus extension of the Vasicek [1977] model in Chapter 4 and the triple-plus versions of the LIBOR market model in Chapter 12. The symbols +, ++, and +++ are used as suffixes after the name of the given fundamental model to denote the single-plus, double-plus, and triple-plus extensions, respectively, throughout the book.

Efficient Recombining Trees for Short Rate Models with State-Dependent Volatility, Stochastic Volatility, and Jumps

Chapter 6 extends the Nelson and Ramaswamy (NR)[1990] transform for generating efficient *recombining* trees under the square root model of Cox, Ingersoll, and Ross. As demonstrated by Nawalkha and Beliaeva [2007a], the equation for the movement of the short rate, when the short rate hits the zero boundary, has an error in the original transform proposed by NR. Nawalkha and Beliaeva (NB) correct this error and also truncate the NR tree at the zero boundary. NB show that using the NR tree keeps the short rate tree stuck at zero with a much higher probability than the CIR model requires, and as a result, the bond prices using the NR tree are significantly higher than the prices obtained from the closed-form solution (as reported in Table 2 of NR [1990]). NB's transform, based on a truncated tree, corrects these errors and obtains bond price approximations, which quickly converge to the closed-form solution with much fewer nodes.

Chapter 5 and 6 also demonstrate how to build recombining trees for *jump-extended* models of Vasicek and CIR, with both exponential and lognormal jumps for the jump-size distribution.

Further, building on the results in Nawalkha and Beliaeva [2007a], Beliaeva and Nawalkha [2007] introduce a two-dimensional transform for generating recombining trees for *stochastic-volatility-jump (SVJ)* models. Chapter 8 shows how to apply the two-dimensional transform to generate a recombining tree for the short rate under the stochastic volatility–based maximal model in the $A_1(2)$ subfamily.

The Fourier Inversion Method for Valuing Interest Rate Caps

Chapter 5 introduces the *Fourier inversion method* in the context of pricing interest rate caps (or portfolios of options on zero-coupon bonds) under the exponential jump-extended Vasicek model and its preference-free extensions. Chapter 9 extends the Fourier inversion method to value interest rate caps under the multifactor affine models and their preference-free extensions. Since these models nest most of the widely used one-, two-, and three-factor affine models (see Table 9.3), the solutions given in this chapter apply to all of these nested models. An advantage of the Fourier inversion method is that it only uses a single summation to obtain solutions even for models with multiple factors. Solutions under multiple-factor models typically require multiple-order summations using the traditional methods, such as Longstaff and Schwartz [1992]. Chapter 10 extends the Fourier inversion method to value interest rate caps under the multifactor quadratic models, and Chapter 12 uses this method to value interest caps under the LIBOR model extended with stochastic volatility and jumps.

The Cumulant Expansion Method for Valuing Swaptions

Chapter 9 demonstrates how to apply the *cumulant expansion method* of Collin-Dufresne and Goldstein [2001b] to price swaptions (or options on coupon bonds) under the simple $A_M(N)$ models and their preference-free extensions. This approach exploits the fact that the moments of a coupon bond also have affine closed-form solutions. Using these moments to uniquely identify the cumulants of the distribution of the coupon bond, the probability distribution of the coupon bond's future price at the option expiration date is obtained using an Edgeworth expansion technique. This approach is very fast, since no numerical integrations are performed. Our simulations find this approach to be faster than even the Fourier inversion approach, and hence, can be used to price options on zero-coupon bonds or caplets, as well. Chapter 10 generalizes the cumulant expansion method to multifactor quadratic models.

Analytical Solutions of Other Plain Vanilla Derivatives under Multifactor Affine and Quadratic Models

A variety of interest rate derivatives and credit derivatives can be priced using the analytical results and efficient trees given in this book. In addition to caps and swaptions (and related instruments), other plain vanilla derivatives such as Eurodollar futures and credit default swaps (CDS) are of significant interest to fixed income practitioners. We give solutions to both these derivatives under a variety of multifactor affine and quadratic models and their preference-free extensions. The solutions to Eurodollar futures are given with respect to virtually every fundamental and preference-free affine/quadratic model given in Chapters 4 though 10. The CDS solutions are given under multifactor affine models in Chapter 9 and multifactor quadratic models in Chapter 10. The CDS solutions in Chapter 9 nest the formulas of Longstaff, Mithal, and Neis [2003] and Pan and Singleton [2005] using a general multifactor affine model.

Introduction of Multifactor Explosive Square-Root Models

This book introduces *explosive* square-root processes for pricing interest rate and credit derivatives. Though all state variables should have stationary physical processes consistent with positive speeds of mean reversion, it is not economically unreasonable to expect some state variables to have *explosive risk-neutral processes* consistent with negative risk-neutral speeds of mean reversion. We show that if the product of the risk-neutral speed of mean reversion and the risk-neutral long-term mean of a given state variable remain positive, then the entire analytical apparatus of the square-root models remains valid, regardless of whether the risk-neutral speed of mean reversion is positive or negative. As a general rule, we find that square-root models do not allow sufficient volatility for the long-term forward rates. In order to add volatility at the longer end, lower risk-neutral speeds of mean reversion, including negative speeds, are required for some state variables. Curiously, the infinite-maturity forward rate remains constant over any finite interval of time, satisfying the arbitrage condition given in Dybvig, Ingersoll, and Ross [1996], even when one or more square-root state variables follow explosive risk-neutral processes. In the context of pricing credit default swaps, Pan and Singleton [2005] find default intensity to follow an explosive risk-neutral square-root process.

A Detailed Description of a USV Jump-Based LIBOR Model for Valuing Caps

The USV models arise more naturally under the forward rate models of Heath, Jarrow, and Morton (HJM) [1992] and the LIBOR market model (LMM). Chapter 12 gives a detailed description of the Jarrow, Li, and Zhao (JLZ) [2007] model for pricing interest rate caps. The JLZ model extends the LMM by adding USV processes and a jump process. JLZ note that a *symmetric* smile can be produced by the USV extension of the LFM model. In order to generate the asymmetric "hockey-stick shaped" smile, JLZ add a jump component that generates significantly negative jumps in the forward rates. A potential limitation of the JLZ model is that the term structure of risk premiums related to volatility and jump risks are *time-inhomogeneous*. Nawalkha, Beliaeva, and Soto (NBS) [2007b] extend the JLZ model by allowing the USV and jump parameters to be piecewise constant functions of the time to maturity of the forward rate under the respective forward measure. Using piecewise constant functions allows a time-homogeneous specification of the risk premiums.

Basic Software for Affine, Quadratic, and LIBOR Market Models

Similar to the first book in the trilogy, this book comes with software in a user-friendly Excel/VBA format, which covers a variety of models given in the 12 chapters of the book. The CD-ROM accompanying this book includes various Excel/VBA spreadsheets that allow the reader to explore a variety of term structure models given in the book. The software allows valuation of interest rate derivatives by building interest rate trees for low-dimensional affine models, as well as computing solutions using quasi-analytical formulas for higher-dimensional affine, quadratic, and LIBOR market models. Though most of the programs require coding in advanced scientific languages, such as C or C++, the final output is always presented in user-friendly Excel/VBA spreadsheets. These spreadsheets allow readers with basic Excel skills to instantly play with a variety of term structure models to price caps, swaptions, and other interest rate derivatives and credit derivatives.

Self-Empowering the Target Audience

This book is aimed both at the fixed income practitioners, as well as the graduate students of degree programs in mathematical finance, financial engineering, and MBA/MS/Ph.D. in finance. The writing style of this book has been deliberately chosen to self-empower readers who wish to develop quantitative skills required for valuation of fixed income securities and their derivatives. Though the new unifying framework presented in this book will appeal to the seasoned academics as well, it will be especially insightful for students and financial analysts who are new to this field. As in the first book of the trilogy, we expect that after reading chapters on given topics from the curent book, the reader should be able to follow the examples and be ready to apply these models. Since this books is part of the trilogy, it is integrated both conceptually and in terms of the mathematical notation with the next book, *Credit Risk Modeling*, which covers both the structural and reduced-form models for valuing credit derivatives.

As part of our mission of *Self Empowerment*, fifty percent of the royalties from this book will be donated to The Art of Living Foundation (ww.ArtOfLiving.org), which provide highly effective workshops for stress reduction and increased productivity for busy urban professionals (www.apexcourse.org).

Various aspects of this trilogy on the fixed income valuation course including the book descriptions, software details, online training seminars, and future updates are available on the website www.fixedincomerisk.com

CHAPTER CONTENTS

Chapter 1

This chapter introduces continuous-time diffusion and mixed jump-diffusion processes using heuristic derivations that serve to strengthen the mathematical intuition of the readers. The chapter gives some of the widely applied results from stochastic calculus, a field of mathematics that combines calculus with probability, and shows how these results can be used for modeling the term structure dynamics. The examples in this chapter highlight the mathematical intuition without worrying too much about the "regularity" conditions underlying the continuous-time framework. The results in this chapter may be skipped by readers who are well versed in continuous-time mathematics, but they could be helpful to readers unfamiliar with this branch of mathematics.

Chapter 2

The first half of this chapter gives an intuitive description of the martingale valuation theory using an example of a two-period discrete information structure. Using this example, the chapter gives a heuristic demonstration of the celebrated result that "absence of arbitrage guarantees the existence of an *equivalent* martingale measure under which discounted prices are martingales." Different types of martingale measures, such as the risk-neutral measure and the forward measure, are identified using different numeraires. The chapter also introduces other important concepts related to martingale valuation theory, such as the stochastic discount factor, the Radon-Nikodym derivative, and the Feynman-Kac theorem, in an intuitive manner. The continuous-time counterparts to the discrete-time results are given in the second half of the chapter.

Chapter 3

This chapter introduces basic pricing frameworks for valuing interest rate and credit derivatives, including futures on time deposits (e.g., Eurodollar and Euribor futures), bond futures (e.g., T-bill, T-note, and T-bond futures), bond options, forward rate agreements, interest rate swaps, interest rate options (e.g., caps, floors, and collars), swaptions, and credit default swaps. The chapter describes important features of these derivatives and highlights the underlying relationships among derivative prices. The final section of this chapter introduces a new taxonomy for term structure models that classifies all models as either fundamental models or preference-free models. The preference-free models are further classified as single-plus, double-plus, and triple-plus models.

Chapter 4

This chapter introduces the fundamental term structure model of Vasicek [1977] and derives the preference-free extensions of this model given as the Vasicek+ model, the Vasicek++ model (i.e., the extended Vasicek model), and the Vasicek+++ model (i.e., the fully extended Vasicek model). The chapter also obtains analytical results to price Eurodollar futures and European bond options and demonstrates the construction of binomial and trinomial trees for these models to price American bond options.

Chapter 5

This chapter extends the fundamental and preference-free Vasicek models by allowing Gaussian and exponentially distributed jumps. The chapter provides closed-form solutions for pricing zero-coupon bonds and Eurodollar futures and introduces the Fourier inversion method to price European bond options. The chapter also provides jump-diffusion trees by extending the work of Amin [1993] to price bond options with American features. These trees allow an arbitrarily large number of nodes at each step to capture the jump component, while two local nodes are used to capture the diffusion component. The chapter demonstrates how to calibrate jump-diffusion trees to fit an initial yield curve or initial zero-coupon bond prices by giving an analytical solution to the time-dependent drift of the short rate process. Finally, the chapter introduces the Fast Fourier Transform (FFT) and the fractional FFT for efficient pricing of options.

Chapter 6

This chapter begins with the derivation of formulas for bond prices, Eurodollar futures, and European bond options under the Cox, Ingersoll, and Ross

(CIR) [1985] model. Next, we show how to build binomial and trinomial trees to price derivatives with American features. As pointed out recently by Nawalkha and Beliaeva (NB) [2007a], the movement of the short rate tree when the short rate hits the zero boundary has an error in the original solution proposed by Nelson and Ramaswamy (NR) [1990]. NB correct this error using a truncated-tree transform, which is then used to generate binomial and trinomial trees to price American bond options. The final section of this chapter extends the CIR model to allow jumps and demonstrates the construction of truncated jump-diffusion trees for the CIR model extended with jumps under two jump-size distributions. Under the first case, the jumps in the short rate are distributed exponentially, allowing positive jumps only; while under the second case, jumps in the short rate are distributed lognormally, allowing both positive and negative jumps.

Chapter 7

This chapter gives preference-free extensions of the fundamental CIR model and derives the solutions to bond price, Eurodollar futures, and European bond options under these extensions. The chapter considers both stationary and explosive preference-free CIR models. The chapter also introduces the constant-elasticity-of-variance (CEV) models and their preference-free extensions. Further, the chapter derives Nelson-Ramaswamy–type transforms for generating recombining trees under preference-free CEV models. Finally, the preference-free CIR and CEV models are extended with jumps.

Chapter 8

This chapter considers the maximal versions of the three subfamilies of two-factor fundamental affine models (based on the Dai and Singleton [2000] classification) and derives their preference-free extensions. The solutions of Eurodollar futures and European bond options are derived only for the $A_1(2)$ subfamily. The corresponding solutions for the $A_0(2)$ and $A_2(2)$ subfamilies are nested under the simple $A_M(N)$ affine models and are given in Chapter 9. The preference-free single-plus extension of the fundamental $A_2(2)$ model, or the $A_2(2)+$ model, is shown to allow *negative* physical correlation between the state variables, even though negative physical correlation is disallowed under the fundamental model, thus demonstrating more realistic expected return relations under the preference-free models. Finally, this chapter demonstrates how to construct two-factor trees under all three subfamilies of the two-factor affine models and their preference-free extensions. The stochastic volatility–based maximal $A_1(2)$ model uses the two-dimensional transform of Nawalkha and Beliaeva [2007] for the tree construction.

Chapter 9

The first part of this chapter considers the maximal versions of two of the four subfamilies of three-factor fundamental affine models, given as the $A_1(3)$ model and the $A_2(3)$ model. The preference-free single-plus and double-plus models are derived corresponding to the maximal fundamental models in both these subfamilies. Next, the chapter gives a general derivation of the *simple* $A_M(N)$ model and its preference-free extensions. The N-M Gaussian processes are *uncorrelated* with the M square-root processes (though the Gaussian processes may be correlated among themselves) under the simple $A_M(N)$ model. The maximal versions of the $A_0(3)$ model and the $A_3(3)$ model are subsumed in the simple $A_M(N)$ model. The simple $A_M(N)$ model allows analytical closed-form solutions of the bond price and Eurodollar futures and quasi-analytical approximations to the prices of:

1. Options on zero-coupon bonds (or caplets) using the Fourier inversion method, and
2. Options on coupon bonds (or swaptions) using the cumulant expansion method.

An advantage of the Fourier inversion method for pricing caplets is that it uses only a single summation to obtain solutions for models with multiple factors. Solutions under multiple-factor models typically require multiple-order summations using the traditional methods, such as Longstaff and Schwartz [1992]. The cumulant expansion method also works extremely fast for pricing swaptions, since it does not require numerical integrations. In fact, we find that the cumulant expansion method works even faster than the Fourier inversion method, and hence, it can be used to price caplets as well. However, this method slows down for instruments with a large number payments, such as options on long maturity bonds, long maturity caps, or swaptions on long maturity swaps.

The final section of this chapter gives analytical solutions for valuing credit default swaps (CDS) using simple $A_M(N)$ models. These solutions allow an arbitrary number of factors for the short rate and the default intensity and nest the solutions of Longstaff, Mithal, and Neis [2003] and Pan and Singleton [2005].

Chapter 10

This chapter introduces single-and multifactor quadratic term structure models (QTSMs) with state variables that follow Gaussian processes. The short rate under the QTSMs is expressed as a quadratic function of the state variables. Unlike the affine models, in which an N-factor affine model can belong to $N + 1$ nonnested subfamilies, an N-factor quadratic model always leads to a single maximal model that nests all other N-factor quadratic models. The chapter considers both the fundamental and the preference-free QTSMs and obtains analytical closed-form solutions to the bond price and Eurodollar futures and quasi-analytical approximations to the prices of:

1. Options on zero-coupon bonds (or caplets) using the Fourier inversion method, and
2. Options on coupon bonds (or swaptions) using the cumulant expansion method.

The chapter also provides basic formulas of pricing credit derivatives, such as credit default swaps, using the fundamental and the preference-free N-factor QTSMs.

Chapter 11

Unlike affine and quadratic models, which first originated as fundamental models and were subsequently generalized as preference-free models, the forward rate models of Heath, Jarrow, and Morton (HJM) [1992] and the LIBOR market model (LMM) are preference-free by construction. Since these models exogenously specify the forward rate process, which uniquely determines the risk-neutral short rate process without requiring the specification of market prices of risks, preferences do not enter in the valuation process. Further, since the initially given forward rates are taken as the model input, these models are "double-plus" by construction.

This chapter introduces the equations for the bond price, the forward rates, and the short rate under the HJM forward rate model. The chapter shows how to construct nonrecombining explosive trees and demonstrates the advantages of using the *recursive* programming technique of Das [1998] for generating these trees. The chapter also demonstrates that the non-Markovian short rate process under the proportional volatility HJM model can be transformed into a *Markovian forward price process* by using the forward measure instead of the risk-neutral measure. The Markovian forward price process allows pricing of long-maturity caps using recombining trees under the forward measure.

Chapter 12

This chapter introduces the LIBOR market model[4] (LMM) and its extensions. We derive both the lognormal forward LIBOR model (LFM) for pricing caps and the lognormal forward swap model (LSM) for pricing swaptions. The LFM and LSM provide theoretical justifications for the widely used Black formulas for pricing caps and swaptions, respectively. The LFM assumes that the discrete forward LIBOR rate follows a lognormal distribution under the numeraire associated with the given caplet maturity, while the LSM assumes that the discrete forward swap rate follows a lognormal distribution under the swap numeraire. A joint framework is also considered by deriving the LFM using a single numeraire, which leads to an approximate Black formula for pricing swaptions. Different specifications of instantaneous volatilities and correlations are considered, consistent with the double-plus and the triple-plus versions of the LFM model.

The displaced-diffusion and the CEV extensions of the LFM are shown to capture the monotonically decreasing caplet smile, while the stochastic volatility–based extensions of the LFM are shown to capture the hockey-stick shaped caplet smile. The empirical results of the stochastic-volatility-jump extension of the LFM by Jarrow, Li, and Zhao (JLZ) [2007] are discussed for pricing caps, and the JLZ model is extended to allow *time-homogeneous* risk-premiums for volatility/jump risks.

SANJAY K. NAWALKHA
NATALIA A. BELIAEVA
GLORIA M. SOTO
www.fixedincomerisk.com

NOTES

1. See the extended Vasicek model of Hull and White [1990] or the Vasicek++ model in Chapter 4.
2. Brigo and Mercurio [2001] summarize various double-plus models, including the CIR++ model and the G2++ model. The G2++ model was originally derived by Hull and White [1996]. The CIR++ model was originally suggested by CIR [1985, bottom paragraph, p. 395] and derived formally by Dybvig [1988, 1997] and Scott [1995]. Chapter 7 derives the CIR++ model.
3. See the *fully extended* Vasicek model of Hull and White [1990] or the Vasicek+++ model given in Chapter 4.
4. The LMM model was discovered by Brace, Gatarek, and Musiela [1997] and is also referred to as the BGM model by many practitioners. Miltersen, Sandmann, and Sondermann [1997] also discovered this model independently, and Jamshidian [1997] contributed significantly to its initial development.

Acknowledgments

First and foremost, I would like to thank Iuliana Ismailescu and Chris Schwarz, who both took a special interest in this trilogy from the day they both entered the PhD program in finance at the University of Massachusetts, Amherst, in the Fall of 2003. Next, I would like to thank Aixin Ma and Karen Ma, who helped in the creation of the Web site www.fixedincomerisk.com, which contains information about all three books in the trilogy and the related online fixed income training seminars. The always-prompt assistance of Gong Zhan is also much appreciated. I would also like to acknowledge conversations with finance discipline colleagues, including Hossein Kazemi, Nikunj Kapadia, Sanjiv Das, Peter Ritchken, Ravi Jagannathan, and Dietmar Leisen. I feel especially grateful to my coauthors, Gloria Soto and Natalia Beliaeva, who have very patiently and steadfastly pursued this book with me over the past three years. A special thanks goes to Kim Nir for providing excellent editorial assistance. And finally, I would like to express my gratitude to my family, whose love and support has been essential in the completion of this book.

SANJAY K. NAWALKHA

I would like to express my gratitude to my family: my husband, Sergei, my daughter, Sasha, and my parents, Nina and Alexander, for their love and continuous support.

NATALIA A. BELIAEVA

I want to express my gratitude to my dear friends Tere and Yoyo for their continued friendship and love despite time and distance; my colleagues María and Paco, who have helped me to start every day with a smile on my face; and J. Alberto, who is my adviser, my soul mate, my husband, and my best friend.

GLORIA M. SOTO

About the Authors

Sanjay K. Nawalkha, Ph.D., is an Associate Professor at the Isenberg School of Management, University of Massachusetts, Amherst, where he teaches graduate courses in fixed income and financial theory. He has published extensively in academic and practitioner journals, especially in the areas of fixed income and asset pricing. His current research interests are in the areas of fixed income and equity derivatives. Dr. Nawalkha is also the president and founder of Nawalkha and Associates, a fixed-income training and consulting firm.

Natalia A. Beliaeva, Ph.D., is an Assistant Professor of Finance at the Suffolk University, Boston. She also holds an MS degree in computer science with a concentration in artificial intelligence. Dr. Beliaeva's expertise is in the area of applied numerical methods for pricing fixed income and equity derivatives.

Gloria M. Soto, Ph.D., is a Professor of Applied Economics and Finance at the University of Murcia, Spain, where she teaches courses in financial markets and institutions and applied economics. Dr. Soto has published extensively in both Spanish and international journals in finance and economics, especially in the areas of interest rate risk management and related fixed income topics.

Information about other fixed income books by the authors is available online at www.fixedincomerisk.com.

Contributors

Lixiong Guo
Ph.D. Candidate in Finance
Owen Graduate School of Management
Vanderbilt University
401 21st Avenue South
Nashville, TN 37203

Iuliana Ismailescu
Ph.D. Candidate in Finance
Isenberg School of Management
University of Massachusetts
Amherst, MA 01003

Jun Zhang
Manager of Quantitative Analysis
Enterprise Risk Management
SVB Financial Group Corporate Headquarters
3005 Tasman Drive
Santa Clara, CA 95054

Contents

CHAPTER 9
Fundamental and Preference-Free Multifactor Affine Models   413

List of Figures

List of Tables

A Simple Introduction to Continuous-Time Stochastic Processes

This chapter introduces continuous-time stochastic processes. Due to the applied focus of this book, we skip the proofs of the main results and provide heuristic derivations that serve to strengthen the mathematical intuition of the readers. The more rigorous proofs can be obtained from other sources.[1] Here, we simply give some of the widely applied results from stochastic calculus, a field of mathematics that combines calculus with probability, and show how these results can be used for modeling the term structure dynamics. The examples in this chapter highlight the mathematical intuition, without worrying too much about the "regularity" conditions underlying the continuous-time framework. The results in this chapter may be skipped by readers who are well versed in continuous-time mathematics, but they could be helpful to readers unfamiliar with this branch of mathematics.

Term structure modeling and derivative pricing are perhaps the most advanced areas of application of stochastic calculus in finance. Obviously, a comprehensive introduction to this mathematics is outside the scope of this chapter and this book. What we wish to accomplish here is to explain this difficult subject matter to the audience of fixed-income traders, analysts, and graduate students, using heuristic derivations and easy-to-read examples. We are well aware of the difficulty most non–mathematically inclined readers experience in comprehending advanced books in mathematical finance, and so this chapter puts together a basic toolbox of results from continuous-time stochastic processes to help those readers. More advanced mathematical ideas related to martingale valuation using absence of arbitrage are presented in Chapter 2.

We begin this chapter with an introduction to the continuous-time diffusion processes. A fundamental property of diffusion processes is that the magnitude of change over the next time interval is proportional to the length of the time interval. As the interval shrinks to zero, the change becomes continuous, but not differentiable. Since most prices and interest rates change randomly over very small time intervals (i.e., every day or minute by minute), modeling these processes as diffusion processes leads to good approximation for modeling uncertainty in the valuation process.

The basic tools of manipulating stochastic processes are Ito's lemma and the rules of stochastic differentiation and integration. Ito's lemma shows how to obtain the stochastic process of a variable that is a smooth (twice differentiable) function of another variable, whose stochastic process is known. For example, using Ito's lemma one can obtain the stochastic process of a bond price given the stochastic process of the short rate, assuming that the bond price is a twice differentiable function of the short rate. A stochastic differential equation shows how a variable changes stochastically over time. Specifically, it gives the probability distribution of the change in the variable over an infinitesimally small interval Δt. A stochastic integral is generally used to give the probability distribution of the change in the variable over a discrete interval. For example, a stochastic integral may give the distribution of the change in the bond price from time 0 to time t. We will cover some basic rules of stochastic differentiation and integration, without considering the precise mathematical regularity conditions. Most stochastic processes used in fixed income valuation generally satisfy the regularity conditions, and the reader will be alerted if violations of these conditions do occur.

Since stochastic processes are very general and may allow the instantaneous mean and variance of the underlying variable to change continuously over time, a stochastic integral can give a variety of distributions over discrete intervals, depending on the specific assumptions made about the parameters that define the stochastic process. In a multiple factor environment, modeling of stochastic processes allows dynamic conditional correlations and conditional volatilities that are more realistic than other simple approaches such as principal component analysis with a stationary variance-covariance matrix.

The final part of this chapter introduces the mixed jump-diffusion processes for modeling uncertainty. These processes use two components; one captures the diffusion element and the other captures the jump element. The jump element allows a sudden discontinuous movement in the underlying variable, the size of which is not restricted by the length of the time interval over which the jump occurs. However, the probability of the jump varies linearly with the length of the time interval, so the jumps occur with less likelihood over smaller time intervals. Many processes used in finance are a mix of a diffusion process and a jump process, such that the variable experiences a continuous change most of the time, while every once in a while the variable experiences a discontinuous change. We give examples of affine and quadratic term structure models with mixed jump-diffusion processes in Chapters 5, 6, 7, 9, 10, and 12.

CONTINUOUS-TIME DIFFUSION PROCESSES

A stochastic process is a variable whose value changes over time in a stochastic manner. If changes in the variable are measured over discrete intervals, the process is a discrete-time process. On the other hand, if the changes in the variable are measured over infinitesimally small intervals converging to zero, the process is a continuous-time process. Continuous-time diffusion processes display continuity such that the variable changes are infinitesimally small over infinitesimally small time intervals. A *Markov process* is a stochastic process in which only the present value of the variable is relevant for predicting the future evolution of the process. Most stochastic processes in finance are Markov processes, though some processes (such as the forward rate processes in the Heath, Jarrow, and Morton [1992] term structure model in Chapter 11) are non-Markovian processes.

Wiener Process

The simplest example of a continuous-time Markovian diffusion process is the well-known Brownian motion or the *Wiener process*. The behavior of a Wiener process $Z(t)$ can be understood by considering the change in its value $\Delta Z(t)$ over an infinitesimally small time interval Δt. Two basic assumptions that $\Delta Z(t)$ must satisfy for $Z(t)$ to be a Wiener process are as follows.

Assumption 1 The process $Z(t)$ is normally distributed and is given as:

$$\Delta Z(t) = Z(t + \Delta t) - Z(t) = \varepsilon_{t+\Delta t}\sqrt{\Delta t} \tag{1.1}$$

where $\varepsilon_{t+\Delta t}$ is a standardized normal variable with mean 0 and variance 1 at time t. By definition, the conditional mean and variance of $\Delta Z(t)$ are given as follows:

$$\begin{aligned} E_t(\Delta Z(t)) &= E_t(\varepsilon_{t+\Delta t}\sqrt{\Delta t}) = \sqrt{\Delta t} \times E_t(\varepsilon_{t+\Delta t}) = 0, \text{ and} \\ V_t(\Delta Z(t)) &= V_t(\varepsilon_{t+\Delta t}\sqrt{\Delta t}) = (\sqrt{\Delta t})^2 \times V_t(\varepsilon_{t+\Delta t}) = \Delta t \end{aligned} \tag{1.2}$$

Assumption 2 The values $\Delta Z(t)$ and $\Delta Z(s)$ are independently distributed for any $t \neq s$. Assumption 2 implies that $Z(t)$ is a Markov process.

A useful property of a Wiener process is that its unconditional variance grows proportionally with time. To see this, consider the change in the variable $Z(t)$ over a discrete interval from $t = 0$ to $t = T$. Divide T into N intervals of length Δt, or

$$\Delta t = \frac{T}{N}, \text{ or } T = N\Delta t \tag{1.3}$$

Then, using equation (1.1), it follows that,

$$\Delta Z((i-1)\Delta t) = Z(i\Delta t) - Z((i-1)\Delta t) = \varepsilon_{i\Delta t}\sqrt{\Delta t}, \text{ for } i = 1, 2, \ldots, N \tag{1.4}$$

Summing up from $i = 1$ to N, and assuming that the starting value of the Wiener process $Z(0) = 0$, we get:

$$\sum_{i=1}^{N} \Delta Z((i-1)\Delta t) = \sum_{i=1}^{N} Z(i\Delta t) - Z((i-1)\Delta t)$$

$$= Z(N\Delta t) - Z(0) = Z(T) - 0 = \sum_{i=1}^{N} \varepsilon_{i\Delta t}\sqrt{\Delta t} \tag{1.5}$$

Using *iterated* expectations, the mean and variance of $Z(T)$ can be given as:

$$E_0(Z(T)) = E_0\left(\sum_{i=1}^{N} \varepsilon_{i\Delta t}\sqrt{\Delta t}\right) = 0 \tag{1.6}$$

$$V_0(Z(T)) = V_0\left(\sum_{i=1}^{N} \varepsilon_{i\Delta t}\sqrt{\Delta t}\right) = \left(\sum_{i=1}^{N} 1 \times (\sqrt{\Delta t})^2\right) = N\Delta t = T \tag{1.7}$$

Note that the unconditional variance of $Z(T)$ grows proportionately with time because of the specific definition of $\Delta Z(t)$ in equation (1.1). Suppose instead of this definition we used the following more general definition:

$$\Delta Z(t) = Z(t + \Delta t) - Z(t) = \varepsilon_{t+\Delta t}(\Delta t)^{\alpha}, \text{ where } \varepsilon_{t+\Delta t} \sim N(0, 1) \tag{1.8}$$

Equation (1.8) is consistent with equation (1.1) only when $\alpha = 0.5$. Now consider a value of $\alpha \neq 0.5$ in equation (1.8). In this case equation (1.7) will change as follows:

$$V_0(Z(T)) = V_0\left(\sum_{i=1}^{N} \varepsilon_{i\Delta t}(\Delta t)^{\alpha}\right) = \left(\sum_{i=1}^{N} 1 \times (\Delta t)^{2\alpha}\right)$$

$$= N\Delta t(\Delta t)^{2\alpha-1} = T(\Delta t)^{2\alpha-1} \tag{1.9}$$

If $\alpha > 0.5$ in equation (1.9), then the variance of $Z(T)$ converges to zero as Δt converges to zero. On the other hand, if $\alpha < 0.5$ in equation (1.9), then the variance of $Z(T)$ converges to infinity as Δt converges to zero. Neither a zero variance nor an infinite variance are realistic, and hence $\alpha = 0.5$ is the only value that is reasonable to use in equation (1.8).

As a final observation, note that even though $\Delta Z(t)$ is a stochastic variable as defined in equation (1.1), *its square $(\Delta Z(t))^2$ is not stochastic* over an infinitesimally small time interval $\Delta t \to 0$. In fact, $(\Delta Z(t))^2$ is non-random and equals Δt. To understand this result we need to define what we mean by convergence.

A function of Δt is said to be of the order:

$$O(\Delta t) \quad \text{if} \quad \lim_{\Delta t \to 0} \frac{f(\Delta t)}{\Delta t} \to \text{constant, and}$$

$$o(\Delta t) \quad \text{if} \quad \lim_{\Delta t \to 0} \frac{f(\Delta t)}{\Delta t} \to 0 \tag{1.10}$$

In continuous-time mathematics, all terms that are of the order $o(\Delta t)$ can be ignored as $\Delta t \to 0$. Since these terms do not matter in convergence, from the definition of $\Delta Z(t)$ in equation (1.1), it follows that

$$E_t[(\Delta Z(t))^2] = E_t[(\varepsilon_{t+\Delta t})^2 \Delta t] = \Delta t \tag{1.11}$$

and

$$V_t[(\Delta Z(t))^2] = V_t[(\varepsilon_{t+\Delta t})^2 \Delta t] = \underbrace{[\Delta t]^2}_{o(\Delta t)} \overbrace{V[(\varepsilon_{t+\Delta t})^2]}^{\text{constant}} = o(\Delta t) \approx 0 \tag{1.12}$$

Since the variance of $(\Delta Z(t))^2$ is of the order $o(\Delta t)$, this term becomes insignificant as Δt becomes infinitesimally small, and it follows that $(\Delta Z(t))^2$ is not stochastic in the limit.[2] Since $(\Delta Z(t))^2$ is not stochastic, its value converges to its expectation given as:

$$(\Delta Z(t))^2 = E_t[(\Delta Z(t))^2] + o(\Delta t) = \Delta t + o(\Delta t) \approx \Delta t \tag{1.13}$$

Since $(\Delta Z(t))^2$ converges to Δt, it remains significant and leads to the celebrated Ito's lemma. But before we present Ito's lemma, we must define an Ito process, which is given next.

Ito Process

From now on we will consider only the limiting case when $\Delta t \to 0$, and use the notation $dZ(t)$ to represent $\Delta Z(t)$, and dt to represent $\Delta t \to 0$.

An Ito process is defined as follows:

$$dX(t) = X(t + dt) - X(t) = a(X, t) \, dt + b(X, t) \, dZ(t) \tag{1.14}$$

where $dX(t)$ gives the change in the X-process over the infinitesimal interval dt, and $a(X, t) = a(X(t), t)$ and $b(X, t) = b(X(t), t)$ are functions of the underlying variable $X(t)$ and time t. The expected value and the variance of $dX(t)$ are given as follows (using equation (1.2)):

$$E(dX(t)) = a(X,t)\,dt + b(X,t)E(dZ(t)) = a(X,t)\,dt \qquad (1.15)$$

$$V(dX(t)) = b^2(X,t)V(dZ(t)) = b^2(X,t)\,dt \qquad (1.16)$$

The X-process evolves with independent increments that are distributed normally with a mean equal to $a(X,t)dt$, and a conditional variance equal to $b^2(X,t)dt$ at any given time t. Since the X-process is stochastic, it could take a whole distribution of values $X(t)$ at a future time $t > 0$, given its value $X(0)$ at time 0. Obviously, at time 0, $X(t)$ is not known; and so it is a random variable with a probability distribution. This probability distribution is obtained using a *stochastic integral*. In fact, all stochastic integrals are probability distributions of some underlying variables over a discrete period.

The stochastic integral of the X-process given in equation (1.14) is given as:

$$\int_0^T dX(t) = \int_0^T a(X,t)\,dt + \int_0^T b(X,t)\,dZ(t) \qquad (1.17)$$

To understand the mathematical intuition of this integral (without a rigorous proof), divide the time T into N intervals as follows:

$$h = \frac{T}{N}, \text{ or } T = N \times h \qquad (1.18)$$

Now taking the stochastic integral of the expression on the left-hand side (L.H.S.) of equation (1.17) gives:

$$X(T) = X(0) + \int_0^T a(X,t)\,dt + \int_0^T b(X,t)\,dZ(t) \qquad (1.19)$$

The first stochastic integrals on the right-hand side (R.H.S.) of equation (1.19) are expressed as follows:

$$\int_0^T a(X,t)\,dt = \lim_{h \to 0} \begin{pmatrix} a(X(0),0)\,h \\ + a(X(h),h)\,h \\ + a(X(2h),\,2h)\,h \\ \vdots \\ + a(X(T-h),\,T-h)\,h \end{pmatrix} \qquad (1.20)$$

The second stochastic integral on the R.H.S. of equation (1.19) is expressed as follows:

$$\int_0^T b(X,t)\,dZ(t) = \lim_{h \to 0} \begin{pmatrix} b(X(0),\ 0)[Z(h) - Z(0)] \\ + b(X(h),\ h)[Z(2h) - Z(h)] \\ + b(X(2h),\ 2h)[Z(3h) - Z(2h)] \\ \vdots \\ + b(X(T-h),\ T-h)[Z(T) - Z(T-h)] \end{pmatrix} \qquad (1.21)$$

Using equation (1.4), the above stochastic integral in equation (1.21) can be expressed as follows:

$$\int_0^T b(X,t)\,dZ(t) = \lim_{h \to 0} \begin{pmatrix} b(X(0),\ 0)[\varepsilon_h\sqrt{h}] \\ + b(X(h),\ h)[\varepsilon_{2h}\sqrt{h}] \\ + b(X(2h),\ 2h)[\varepsilon_{3h}\sqrt{h}] \\ \vdots \\ + b(X(T-h),\ T-h)[\varepsilon_T\sqrt{h}] \end{pmatrix} \qquad (1.22)$$

The random variable $X(T)$ has a probability distribution at time 0, which can be obtained using the stochastic integrals on the R.H.S. of equation (1.19) and their approximations in equations (1.20) and (1.22), respectively. However, the probability distribution of the variable $X(T)$ is not always straightforward to derive analytically since both $a(X,t)$ and $b(X,t)$ are themselves stochastic and are functions of the stochastic variable $X(t)$, for $0 \leq t < T$. In the latter part of this chapter we investigate some special Gaussian cases for which it is easy to solve the first two moments of the stochastic integrals analytically. In other cases, the probability distribution implied by a stochastic integral is computed numerically using trees, Monte Carlo simulation, and other techniques. We are now ready to present Ito's lemma, but without a rigorous proof.

Ito's Lemma

Consider another function $Y(t) = Y(X,t)$, which depends both on $X(t)$ and t. If $Y(t)$ is twice differentiable in $X(t)$ and once differentiable in t, then the stochastic differential equation of the Y-process can be given using Ito's lemma as follows:

$$dY(t) = \frac{\partial Y}{\partial X}\,dX(t) + \frac{1}{2}\frac{\partial^2 Y}{\partial X^2}(dX(t))^2 + \frac{\partial Y}{\partial t}\,dt \qquad (1.23)$$

Note that the stochastic differential of $Y(t)$ in equation (1.23) is different from the differential of $Y(t)$ in ordinary calculus. In ordinary calculus, the term $(dX(t))^2$ goes to zero, and the differential is given as:

$$dY(t) = \frac{\partial Y}{\partial X} dX(t) + \frac{\partial Y}{\partial t} dt \qquad (1.24)$$

However in stochastic calculus, the term $(dX(t))^2$ contains $(dZ(t))^2$, which is of the order $O(dt)$ (see equations (1.10) and (1.13)), and so $(dX(t))^2$ remains significant. This is the main difference between ordinary calculus and stochastic calculus. By substituting the process for $dX(t)$ from equation (1.14) into equation (1.23), we get:

$$dY(t) = \frac{\partial Y}{\partial X}(a(X,t)\,dt + b(X,t)\,dZ(t))$$

$$+ \frac{1}{2}\frac{\partial^2 Y}{\partial X^2}(a(X,t)\,dt + b(X,t)\,dZ(t))^2 + \frac{\partial Y}{\partial t}\,dt \qquad (1.25)$$

Since dt^2 and $dZ(t) \times dt$ are both of the order $o(dt)$, these terms get eliminated; but the term $(dZ(t))^2 = dt$ remains of the order $O(dt)$, and equation (1.25) can be simplified to give Ito's lemma as follows:

$$dY(t) = \left(\frac{\partial Y}{\partial t} + a(X,t)\frac{\partial Y}{\partial X} + \frac{1}{2}b^2(X,t)\frac{\partial^2 Y}{\partial X^2} \right) dt + \frac{\partial Y}{\partial X}b(X,t)\,dZ(t) \quad (1.26)$$

Example 1.1 Reconsider the X-process given in equation (1.14), with $a(X,t) = aX(t)$, and $b(X,t) = bX(t)$, where a and b are two constants. The X-process can be given as:

$$dX(t) = aX(t)\,dt + bX(t)\,dZ(t) \qquad (1.27)$$

The above process is the well-known geometric Brownian motion followed by the stock price under the Black and Scholes [1973] option pricing model. Now consider a function $Y(t) = \ln(X(t))$. Since $Y(t)$ is only a function of $X(t)$, and not a function of t, we have:

$$\frac{\partial Y}{\partial t} = 0, \quad \frac{\partial Y}{\partial X} = \frac{\partial \ln X}{\partial X} = \frac{1}{X}, \quad \frac{\partial^2 Y}{\partial X^2} = \frac{\partial}{\partial X}\left(\frac{1}{X} \right) = -\frac{1}{X^2}$$

Substituting the above values of partial derivatives, and $a(X,t) = aX(t)$ and $b(X,t) = bX(t)$, in equation (1.26), the Y-process can be given as follows:

$$dY(t) = \left(\frac{aX(t)}{X(t)} - \frac{1}{2}\frac{(bX(t))^2}{X^2(t)} \right) dt + \frac{bX(t)}{X(t)}\,dZ(t) \qquad (1.28)$$

or

$$dY(t) = d\ln(X(t)) = (a - b^2/2)\,dt + b\,dZ(t) \qquad (1.29)$$

Simple Rules of Stochastic Differentiation and Integration

Two rules of stochastic differentiation and stochastic integration are given as follows. Both these rules hold regardless of the specification of the lower boundary of these integrals, even though we have put zero as the lower boundary.

Rule 1   Consider the following stochastic integral:

$$\int_0^t dX(v) = \int_0^t a(X,\, v)\, dv + \int_0^t b(X,\, v)\, dZ(v) \qquad (1.30)$$

The stochastic differential equation corresponding to equation (1.30) is given as:

$$dX(t) = a(X, t)\, dt + b(X, t)\, dZ(t) \qquad (1.31)$$

Rule 2   Consider the following stochastic integral:

$$\int_0^t dX(v) = \int_0^t a(X,\, v,\, t)\, dv + \int_0^t b(X,\, v,\, t)\, dZ(v) \qquad (1.32)$$

The stochastic differential equation corresponding to equation (1.32) is given as:

$$\left[a(X,\, t,\, t) + \int_0^t \frac{\partial a(X,\, v,\, t)}{\partial t}\, dv + \int_0^t \frac{\partial b(X,\, v,\, t)}{\partial t}\, dZ(v) \right] dt$$
$$+\, b(X,\, t,\, t)\, dZ(t) \qquad (1.33)$$

Though most finance applications require rule 1, certain applications such as the derivation of the short rate process under the Heath, Jarrow, Morton [1992] term structure model require rule 2.

Obtaining Unconditional Mean and Variance of Stochastic Integrals under Gaussian Processes

Many financial valuation problems require the computation of risk-neutral expectations of an underlying asset price. Since asset price distributions can be represented as stochastic integrals, computation of the expectations can be accomplished by knowing the probability distribution implied by the stochastic integral. For the case of Gaussian (i.e., normally distributed) processes, it is possible to obtain the mean and variance of the underlying variable by applying rules that give the mean and variance of a stochastic integral. These rules are given as follows:

Rule 3 Let $Z(t)$ be a Wiener process and $b(t)$ be a deterministic (i.e., nonrandom) function of time t. Then for all $T \geq t$, the stochastic integral:

$$g(t,\ T) = \int_t^T b(v)\, dZ(v) \tag{1.34}$$

is a Gaussian process with time t mean and variance given as follows:

$$E_t[g(t,\ T)] = 0$$

$$V_t[g(t,\ T)] = \int_t^T b^2(v)\, dv \tag{1.35}$$

It is easy to see why the expected value of $g(t,\ T)$ equals zero. However, to derive the expression of the variance of $g(t,\ T)$, divide $T - t$ into N intervals of length h, such as $(T - t)/N = h$. Using equation (1.4), we have,

$$g(t,\ T) = \int_t^T b(v)\, dZ(v) = \lim_{h \to 0} \begin{pmatrix} b(t)[\varepsilon_{t+h}\sqrt{h}] \\ + b(t + h)[\varepsilon_{t+2h}\sqrt{h}] \\ + b(t + 2h)[\varepsilon_{t+3h}\sqrt{h}] \\ \vdots \\ + b(T - h)[\varepsilon_T\sqrt{h}] \end{pmatrix} \tag{1.36}$$

where the N error terms ε on the R.H.S. of equation (1.36) are all standard normal variables with mean 0 and variance 1. Since all of the mean-zero error terms are independent, the variance of $g(t, T)$ is given by taking the time t expectation, given as follows:

$$V_t[g(t,\ T)] = \lim_{h \to 0} E_t \begin{pmatrix} b^2(t)[\varepsilon_{t+h}\sqrt{h}]^2 \\ + b^2(t + h)[\varepsilon_{t+2h}\sqrt{h}]^2 \\ + b^2(t + 2h)[\varepsilon_{t+3h}\sqrt{h}]^2 \\ \vdots \\ + b^2(T - h)[\varepsilon_T\sqrt{h}]^2 \end{pmatrix} \tag{1.37}$$

$$= \lim_{h \to 0} \begin{pmatrix} b^2(t)h \\ + b^2(t + h)h \\ + b^2(t + 2h)h \\ \vdots \\ + b^2(T - h)h \end{pmatrix} = \int_t^T b^2(v)\, dv$$

Rule 4   Let $Z(t)$ be a Wiener process and $b(t)$ and $c(t)$ be deterministic functions of time t. Define a new variable $h(t, T)$ as follows:

$$h(t, T) = \int_t^T c(v)g(t, v)\, dv$$

where $g(t, T)$ is a Gaussian variable defined in equation (1.34). Then $h(t, T)$ is a Gaussian process with time t mean and variance given as follows:

$$E_t[h(t, T)] = 0$$
$$V_t[h(t, T)] = \int_t^T b^2(v) \left(\int_v^T c(u)\, du \right)^2 dv \qquad (1.38)$$

The proof of equation (1.38) is more involved, but can be given using the same technique used for proving rule 3.

Rule 5   If a variable Y follows a Gaussian distribution with mean $E(Y)$ and variance $V(Y)$, then the mean of the variable $X = e^Y$ is given as follows:

$$E(X) = e^{E(Y)+(1/2)V(Y)} \qquad (1.39)$$

Examples of Gaussian Stochastic Integrals

As mentioned earlier, the probability distributions of stochastic integrals are not easy to solve analytically. For example, as shown in equation (1.19), since both $a(X, t)$ and $b(X, t)$ are stochastic and depend upon $X(t)$, the probability distribution of the stochastic integral is not easy to obtain. However, for certain specific functional forms of $a(X, t)$ and $b(X, t)$, transformations of the function X can be represented as stochastic integrals with Gaussian distributions. The mean and variance of these Gaussian-distributed stochastic integrals can be derived using the results in the previous section. The following two examples demonstrate this transform technique. The first example obtains the stochastic integral of the log of the stock price when stock price follows a geometric Brownian motion (as in the model of Black and Scholes [1973]), and the second example obtains the stochastic integral of the short rate, when the short rate follows the Ornstein-Uhlenbeck process under the term structure model of Vasicek [1977].

Example 1.2   This example derives the log stock price distribution under the geometric Brownian motion. Let the variable $X(t)$ represent the price of a stock in equation (1.27) in Example 1.1. Consider the stochastic integral of the X-process given as follows:

$$X(T) = X(t) + \int_t^T a\, X(v)\, dv + \int_t^T b\, X(v)\, dZ(v) \tag{1.40}$$

As mentioned earlier, since the X-variable appears as a part of the integrand, an analytical solution for the probability distribution of this integral does not seem feasible. However, we show that the log transform $Y(T) = \ln(X(T))$ is Gaussian, and hence the mean and variance of $Y(T)$ can be computed using the results given in equations (1.34) and (1.35). The stochastic differential equation of the Y-process was obtained in equation (1.29) in Example 1.1, using Ito's lemma. Taking the stochastic integral of the Y-process, we get:

$$Y(T) = Y(t) + \int_t^T (a - b^2/2)\, dv + \int_t^T b\, dZ(v) \tag{1.41}$$

or

$$Y(T) = Y(t) + (a - b^2/2)(T - t) + \int_t^T b\, dZ(v) \tag{1.42}$$

Applying equations (1.34) and (1.35) to the stochastic integral on the R.H.S. of equation (1.42), the time t mean and variance of the $Y(T)$ are given as follows:

$$E_t(Y(T)) = Y(t) + (a - b^2/2)(T - t) \tag{1.43}$$

$$V_t(Y(T)) = \int_t^T b^2\, dv = b^2(T - t) \tag{1.44}$$

The variable $Y(T) = \ln(X(T))$ is distributed normally, implying that the stock price $X(T)$ is distributed *lognormally*. The mean of the stock price $X(T)$ can be computed as follows: Since $Y(T) = \ln(X(T))$, it follows that $X(T) = e^{Y(T)}$. Further, since $Y(T)$ is a Gaussian process, the mean of $X(T)$ can be given using rule 5 (equation (1.39)) as follows:

$$\begin{aligned} E_t(X(T)) &= e^{E_t(Y(T)) + (1/2)V_t(Y(T))} \\ &= e^{Y(t) + (a - b^2/2)(T-t) + (1/2)b^2(T-t)} = e^{Y(t) + a(T-t)} = X(t)e^{a(T-t)} \end{aligned} \tag{1.45}$$

Hence, the current value of the stock is given as its future expected value, discounted by the drift rate a, or:

$$X(t) = \frac{E_t(X(T))}{e^{a(T-t)}} \tag{1.46}$$

Example 1.3 This example derives the short rate distribution under the Ornstein-Uhlenbeck process. Let the variable $r(t)$ represent the instantaneous short rate following the Ornstein-Uhlenbeck process given by Vasicek [1977] as follows:

$$dr(t) = \alpha(m - r(t)) \, dt + \sigma \, dZ(t) \tag{1.47}$$

where the parameters α, m, and σ are constants. The stochastic integral of equation (1.47) is given as:

$$r(T) = r(t) + \int_t^T \alpha(m - r(v)) \, dv + \int_t^T \sigma \, dZ(v) \tag{1.48}$$

To remove the variable r from the first integrand, consider the transform $Y(t) = r(t) \exp(\alpha t)$. Using Ito's lemma, the stochastic differential equation of Y-process can be obtained. To apply Ito's lemma, we need the following three partial derivatives:

$$\frac{\partial Y}{\partial t} = \alpha e^{\alpha t} r(t), \quad \frac{\partial Y}{\partial r} = e^{\alpha t}, \quad \frac{\partial^2 Y}{\partial r^2} = \frac{\partial}{\partial r}(e^{\alpha t}) = 0 \tag{1.49}$$

Using the above partial derivatives and Ito's lemma given in equation (1.26), we get:

$$\begin{aligned} dY(t) &= e^{\alpha t} \, dr(t) + \alpha e^{\alpha t} r(t) \, dt \\ &= e^{\alpha t}(\alpha(m - r(t)) \, dt + \sigma \, dZ(t)) + \alpha e^{\alpha t} r(t) \, dt \\ &= e^{\alpha t} \alpha m dt + e^{\alpha t} \sigma \, dZ(t) \end{aligned} \tag{1.50}$$

The stochastic integral of $Y(T)$ can be written as:

$$\begin{aligned} Y(T) &= Y(t) + \int_t^T (e^{\alpha v} \alpha m) \, dv + \int_t^T (e^{\alpha v} \sigma) \, dZ(v) \\ &= Y(t) + m(e^{\alpha T} - e^{\alpha t}) + \int_t^T (e^{\alpha v} \sigma) \, dZ(v) \end{aligned} \tag{1.51}$$

Substituting $Y(T) = e^{\alpha T} r(T)$ and $Y(t) = e^{\alpha t} r(t)$ in equation (1.51) and simplifying we get:

$$r(T) = e^{-\alpha(T-t)} r(t) + m(1 - e^{-\alpha(T-t)}) + e^{-\alpha T} \sigma \int_t^T e^{\alpha v} \, dZ(v) \tag{1.52}$$

Applying equation (1.34) to equation (1.52), the mean of $r(T)$ is given as follows:

$$E_t(r(T)) = e^{-\alpha(T-t)} r(t) + m(1 - e^{-\alpha(T-t)}) \tag{1.53}$$

As T goes to infinity, the long-term mean of $r(T)$ converges to m. By applying equation (1.35) to the stochastic integral on the R.H.S. of equation (1.52), the variance of $r(T)$ is given as follows:

$$
\begin{aligned}
V_t(r(T)) &= e^{-2\alpha T} \int_t^T (e^{2\alpha v} \sigma^2)\, dv = e^{-2\alpha T} \sigma^2 \left(\frac{e^{2\alpha T} - e^{2\alpha t}}{2\alpha} \right) \\
&= \sigma^2 \left(\frac{1 - e^{-2\alpha(T-t)}}{2\alpha} \right)
\end{aligned}
\tag{1.54}
$$

MIXED JUMP-DIFFUSION PROCESSES

As mentioned earlier, diffusion processes display continuity such that the variable changes are infinitesimally small over infinitesimally small time intervals. Jump processes display discontinuity such that the variable changes are non-infinitesimally large even over infinitesimally small time intervals. Jump processes experience no change with a probability $1 - \lambda\, dt$ and a discontinuous change with an infinitesimally small probability λdt, over the infinitesimally small time interval dt, where λ defines the intensity of the process. Many processes used in finance are a mix of a diffusion process and a jump process, such that the variable experiences a continuous change most of the time, while every once in a while the variable experiences a discontinuous change.

The Jump-Diffusion Process

Consider the mixed jump-diffusion process given as follows:

$$
dX(t) = a(X, t)\, dt + b(X, t)\, dZ(t) + h(J, X, t)\, dN(\lambda)
\tag{1.55}
$$

Equation (1.55) is identical to the diffusion process given in equation (1.14), except for the last term. This term has two components. The term $dN(\lambda)$ represents the Poisson process, which is independent of $dZ(t)$, and is given as follows:

$$
dN(\lambda) = \left\{ \begin{array}{l} 0, \text{ with probability } 1 - \lambda\, dt, \text{ and} \\ 1, \text{ with probability } \lambda\, dt \end{array} \right\}
\tag{1.56}
$$

When $dN(\lambda)$ equals 1 (with probability $\lambda\, dt$), then the magnitude of jump equals $h(J, X, t)\, dN(\lambda) = h(J, X, t)$. The variable $h(J, X, t)$ is a function of the random variable J that can have some arbitrarily specified distribution (i.e., binomial, Gaussian, etc.), $X(t)$, and t. The variable J is independent of both $dZ(t)$ and $dN(\lambda)$.

Ito's Lemma for the Jump-Diffusion Process

Let $Y(t) = Y(X,t)$ be a twice-differentiable function of $X(t)$ (where the X-process is given by equation (1.55)) and once differentiable function of t. Then, the stochastic differential equation of Y-process is given as follows:

$$dY(t) = \left(\frac{\partial Y}{\partial t} + a(X,t)\frac{\partial Y}{\partial X} + \frac{1}{2}b^2(X,t)\frac{\partial^2 Y}{\partial X^2} \right) dt + \frac{\partial Y}{\partial X}b(X,t)\,dZ(t)$$

$$+ [Y((X+h(J,\ X,\ t)),\ t) - Y(X,t)]\,dN(\lambda) \tag{1.57}$$

Equation (1.57) generalizes Ito's lemma to jump-diffusion processes. The top line on the R.H.S. of equation (1.57) gives the terms of Ito's lemma with respect to the diffusion process. The expression in the bottom line of the R.H.S. of equation (1.57) gives the additional term due to the jump component.

Example 1.4 Reconsider the X-process given in equation (1.27), but with an added jump component as follows:

$$dX(t) = aX(t)\,dt + bX(t)\,dZ(t) + JX(t)\,dN(\lambda) \tag{1.58}$$

Equation (1.58) is used by Merton [1976] to derive option prices under the jump-diffusion process. Now, consider the stochastic differential of the variable $Y(t) = \ln(X(t))$. Using equations (1.55) and (1.57), the Y-process is given as:

$$dY(t) = d\ln(X(t)) = (a - b^2/2)\,dt + b\,dZ(t)$$

$$+ \left(\ln(X(t) + JX(t)) - \ln X(t) \right) dN(\lambda) \tag{1.59}$$

Since $\ln(X(t)+JX(t)) = \ln(X(t)(1+J)) = \ln(X(t)) + \ln(1+J)$, equation (1.59) simplifies to the following equation:

$$dY(t) = d\ln(X(t)) = (a - b^2/2)\,dt + b\,dZ(t) + \ln(1+J)\,dN(\lambda) \tag{1.60}$$

The Ito's lemma for jumps given in equation (1.57) is very useful and is applied in Chapters 5, 6, 7, and 10 of this book to obtain the stochastic jump-diffusion process for the bond price when the interest rate or the state variable is driven by a jump-diffusion process.

NOTES

1. For example, Duffie [2001].
2. It is easy to show that skewness, kurtosis, and all other higher moments of $(\Delta Z(t))^2$ also are of the order $o(\Delta t)$.

CHAPTER 2

Arbitrage-Free Valuation

Arbitrage-free valuation using martingale theory is one of the most important discoveries in finance. Harrison and Kreps [1979] introduced the elegant mathematics of martingales in a widely cited paper on financial valuation.[1] A martingale measure is a probability measure associated with a variable, under which the current value of the variable is always equal to the expectation of its future value. The main result of the martingale valuation theory is that *absence of arbitrage guarantees the existence of an equivalent martingale measure under which discounted prices are martingales.* The equivalent martingale measure is not an actual or physical probability measure, but a pseudo probability measure that is useful for obtaining simple pricing rules based upon the mathematics of martingales. Different types of equivalent martingale measures exist, such as the risk-neutral measure (e.g., Black and Scholes [1973] and Cox and Ross [1976]) and the forward measure (e.g., Geman [1989], Geman, Karoui, and Rochet [1995], and Jamshidian [1989]). The martingale valuation result obtained by Harrison and Kreps [1979] is very general, and unlike the option valuation results of Black and Scholes [1973], Merton [1973], and Cox and Ross [1976], *it does not depend upon market completeness.*

A complete market is characterized by the feature that every state dependent payoff is attainable in the market using some trading strategy. An example of a complete market is the Black and Scholes [1973] economy in which continuous trading in the underlying stock and a default-free bond can exactly replicate the payoff of an option written on the stock. An example of an incomplete market is the Heston [1993] economy in which volatility is stochastic. In absence of an asset that is perfectly correlated with changes in the volatility, all states of nature cannot be spanned by a trading strategy using traded securities. Hence, all state dependent payoffs are not attainable in the Heston economy using traded securities, making it an incomplete market. The beauty of martingale pricing is that it applies both to the complete and the incomplete markets as "absence of arbitrage" and is the only assumption required for martingale pricing.

The traditional approach to valuation is based upon obtaining a partial differential equation (PDE) for a given security or contingent claim using the absence of arbitrage. For most fixed-income problems, the analytical solution to the PDE is obtained in two steps. In the first step the particular form of the solution is guessed and the PDE is broken into two or more ordinary differential equations (ODEs) using the guessed solution. In the second step, the ODEs resulting from the guessed solution to the PDE are solved explicitly. Generally, one must solve linear first-order ODEs, as well as nonlinear first-order ODEs known as the Riccati equations that appear often in fixed-income valuation problems. The methodology of solving the PDEs is discussed in detail in Chapters 4 through 10.

The bridge between the martingale valuation approach and the PDE approach is given by the famous *Feynman-Kac theorem*. This theorem allows for the conversion of the problem given under one approach to an equivalent problem under the other approach by just a simple inspection of the terms. So, for example, a given PDE can be converted into a discounted expectation and a given discounted expectation can be converted into a PDE. This is a very useful property as different analytical and numerical methods apply to the two approaches, and the most efficient methods of computation can be chosen by transforming the problem into the appropriate format. For example, the finite difference approximations require that the problem be stated in the PDE format, while the binomial and multinomial tree methods require that the problem be stated in the discounted expectation format.

ARBITRAGE-FREE VALUATION: SOME BASIC RESULTS

Arrow [1964] and Debreu [1959] gave the first formal treatment of contingent claims valuation by dividing the future into a finite number of states. Arrow-Debreu securities are the atomistic building blocks of the modern contingent claims valuation theory. An Arrow-Debreu security is defined as a security that pays \$1 only if one of the states occurs, and 0 in every other state. These securities play a key role in martingale valuation, and so we provide some intuition about these securities using a discrete-time example.

Consider a probability space given by $\{\Omega, \mathcal{F}, p\}$, where sample space Ω is the set of all possible states of nature, the filtration $\mathcal{F}$ represents those subsets of Ω whose probabilities we can determine using the measure p. For example, the information structure tree in Figure 2.1 has three trading dates, 0, 1, and 2. The filtration $\mathcal{F} = \{\mathcal{F}_t; t = 0, 1, \text{and } 2\}$ describes how the information about security prices is revealed to the market over the three

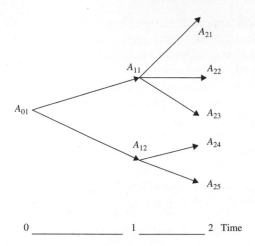

FIGURE 2.1 Information Structure

points in time, $t = 0$, 1, and 2. An example of the events with possibilities of different states can be given as follows:

$$A_{01} = \{\omega_1, \omega_2, \omega_3, \omega_4, \omega_5\}$$

$$A_{11} = \{\omega_1, \omega_2, \omega_3\} \quad \text{and} \quad A_{12} = \{\omega_4, \omega_5\} \tag{2.1}$$

$$A_{21} = \{\omega_1\}, A_{22} = \{\omega_2\}, A_{23} = \{\omega_3\}, A_{24} = \{\omega_4\}, \text{and } A_{25} = \{\omega_5\}$$

At $t = 0$, all states are possible and the event $A_0 = \Omega$. At $t = 1$ either event A_{11} or A_{12} can occur. Finally, at $t = 2$, any one of the five events can occur. The three events A_{21}, A_{22}, or A_{23}, can occur at $t = 2$, *only if* event A_{11} occurs at $t = 1$. Similarly, the two events A_{24} and A_{25} can occur at $t = 2$ *only if* event A_{12} occurs at $t = 1$. The tree in Figure 2.1 and the events defined in equation (2.1) capture the sequential information structure of the occurrence of events. Using set theory we can say that the event set A_{23} is a subset of the event set A_{11}, which in turn is a subset of the event set A_0. A fundamental property of the information structure is that the subsets of any event are disjointed (which means that subsets of the given event cannot contain any common occurrences of the states of nature) and the union of the subsets of a given event is the event itself. Though the tree must be nonrecombining to capture this information structure, it does not imply that the values of the variables have to be different at different nodes. For example, the price of a two-year bond may be $100 at all nodes at time 2, even though it may be different at the two nodes at time 1.

Let $p_0(z_t)$ be the time-zero probability of an event Az_t in Ω. For example, the probabilities $p_0(z_1)$ corresponding to the two events $z_1 = A_{11}$

and $z_1 = A_{12}$ are given as $p_0(11)$ and $p_0(12)$. Similarly, the probabilities $p_0(z_2)$ corresponding to the events $A_{21}, A_{22}, A_{23}, A_{24}$, and A_{25} are given as $p_0(21)$, $p_0(22)$, $p_0(23)$, $p_0(24)$, and $p_0(25)$.

Let $AD_0(z_t)$ be the time-zero price of the Arrow-Debreu (AD) security that pays \$1 if event Az_t occurs at time t, and zero in every other state. We can define the time-zero prices of all seven AD securities as follows: $AD_0(11)$, $AD_0(12)$, $AD_0(21)$, $AD_0(22)$, $AD_0(23)$, $AD_0(24)$, and $AD_0(25)$. We now show some relationships among AD security prices, bond prices, and the term structure of interest rates.

A Simple Relationship between Zero-Coupon Bond Prices and Arrow-Debreu Prices

Let the continuously compounded one-period riskless rate be given as $r(0)$ at time 0, and $r_{11}(1)$ and $r_{12}(1)$ at time 1, under events A_{11} and A_{12}, respectively, in Figure 2.1. Consider the value of a default-free zero-coupon bond that pays \$1 at time 1. Since the bond is *default-free*, it pays \$1 in both events A_{11} and A_{12}. The sum of the price of an AD security that pays \$1 when event A_{11} occurs and the price of another AD security that pays \$1 when event A_{12} occurs gives the price of this default-free bond, since holding these two AD securities is equivalent to holding this bond. Hence,

$$P(0,\ 1) = AD_0(11) + AD_0(12) \tag{2.2}$$

Similarly, the price of a two-year default-free zero-coupon bond that pays \$1 at maturity can be given as the sum of five AD securities that pay \$1 in each of the five events at time 2:

$$P(0,\ 2) = AD_0(21) + AD_0(22) + AD_0(23) + AD_0(24) + AD_0(25) \tag{2.3}$$

We can state equation (2.3) as a general result.

Result 1.   The price of a \$1 face-value default-free zero-coupon bond equals the sum of the AD securities that pay \$1 in different events at the maturity of the bond.

The Bayes Rule for Conditional Probabilities of Events

We now derive the future conditional probabilities of the events using the Bayes rule. Since the event A_{21} can occur at time 2 *only if* A_{11} occurs at time 1, we have:

$$p_0(21) = p_0(11) \times p_1(21) \tag{2.4}$$

where $p_0(21)$ is the time 0 unconditional probability of event A_{21}, $p_0(11)$ is the time 0 unconditional probability of event A_{11}, and $p_1(21)$ is the time 1 conditional probability of event A_{21}.

Similarly, we have the following relationships between time 1 conditional probabilities and time 0 unconditional probabilities of other events:

$$p_0(z_2) = p_0(11) \times p_1(z_2), \text{ for } z_2 = 21, 22, \text{ and } 23, \text{ and}$$
$$p_0(z_2) = p_0(12) \times p_1(z_2), \text{ for } z_2 = 24 \text{ and } 25 \tag{2.5}$$

By cross multiplication and generalizing the preceding result, the time t conditional probabilities of the occurrence of events at time T are given as ratios of the time 0 unconditional probabilities of those events, using the Bayes rule, as follows:

$$p_t(z_T) = p_0(z_T)/p_0(z_t)\big|\mathcal{F}_t \tag{2.6}$$

where the filtration $\mathcal{F}_t$ selects the events at time T that can occur *only if* a given event has occurred at time t, $p_0(z_T)$ is the time 0 unconditional probability of z_T occurring at time T, $p_0(z_t)$ is the time 0 unconditional probability of z_t occurring at time t, and $p_t(z_T)$ is the time t conditional probability of z_T occurring at time T.

The Relationship between Current and Future AD Prices

We can show that for the market equilibrium to be internally consistent, future prices of AD securities have an arbitrage relationship with time 0 prices of AD securities. Since event A_{21} can occur at time 2 *only if* A_{11} occurs at time 1, the following relationship must hold:

$$AD_0(21) = AD_0(11) \times AD_1(21) \tag{2.7}$$

where $AD_0(21)$ is the time 0 price of the AD security that pays \$1 in event A_{21} at time 2, $AD_0(11)$ is the time 0 price of the AD security that pays \$1 in event A_{11} at time 1, and $AD_1(21)$ is the time 1 price of the AD security that pays \$1 in event A_{21} at time 2.

By cross multiplication, the time 1 price of the AD security that pays \$1 in event A_{21} at time 2 is given as the ratio of two AD security prices observable at time 0, or:

$$AD_1(21) = AD_0(21)/AD_0(11) \tag{2.8}$$

Similar relationships hold for all time 1 prices of AD securities that pay \$1 in different events at time 2, or:

$$AD_1(z_2) = AD_0(z_2)/AD_0(11), \text{ for } z_2 = 21, \ 22, \text{and } 23, \text{ and}$$
$$AD_1(z_2) = AD_0(z_2)/AD_0(12), \text{ for } z_2 = 24 \text{ and } 25$$
$$(2.9)$$

In general, time t prices of AD securities that pay \$1 in different events at time T are given as ratios of the time 0 prices of AD securities, or:

$$AD_t(z_T) = AD_0(z_T)/AD_0(z_t)\big|\mathcal{F}_t \qquad (2.10)$$

where the filtration $\mathcal{F}_t$ selects the events at time T that can occur only if a given event has occurred at time t.

The Relationship between Cross-Sectional AD Prices and Intertemporal Term Structure Dynamics

Consider the price of the two-year zero-coupon bond at time 1. The bond has two prices $P_{11}(1, 2)$ and $P_{12}(1, 2)$ corresponding to events A_{11} and A_{12}, respectively. Suppose event A_{11} occurs at time 1. Conditional on the occurrence of A_{11}, only one of the three events A_{21}, A_{22}, and A_{23} can occur at time 2. Hence, the price $P_{11}(1, 2)$ should equal the sum of the prices observable at time 1 of the three AD securities corresponding to the events A_{21}, A_{22}, and A_{23}, which by using equation (2.9) is given as:

$$P_{11}(1, \ 2) = [AD_0(21) + AD_0(22) + AD_0(23)]/AD_0(11) \qquad (2.11)$$

Similarly, $P_{12}(1, 2)$, the price of a two-year default-free zero-coupon bond in event A_{12} at time 1, can be given as:

$$P_{12}(1, \ 2) = [AD_0(24) + AD_0(25)]/AD_0(12) \qquad (2.12)$$

Using the definitions of the bond prices, the one-period short rates in events A_{11} and A_{12} at time 1 can be given as follows:

$$r_{11}(1) = -\ln P_{11}(1, \ 2)$$
$$= \ln[AD_0(11)] - \ln[AD_0(21) + AD_0(22) + AD_0(23)] \qquad (2.13)$$
$$r_{12}(1) = -\ln P_{12}(1, \ 2) = \ln[AD_0(12)] - \ln[AD_0(24) + AD_0(25)] \qquad (2.14)$$

These equations demonstrate that the time 0 cross section of AD prices for two periods are sufficient for capturing the intertemporal dynamics of bond prices and short rate over the two periods. In a similar fashion, it can be shown that the time 0 cross-section of AD prices for N periods can give the intertemporal term structure dynamics of bond prices and short rate over N periods.

Existence of the Risk-Neutral Probability Measure

The time 0 AD prices can be used to construct a new variable given as follows:

$$\tilde{p}_0(z_t) = AD_0(z_t) \times B(z_t) \tag{2.15}$$

where $B(z_t)$ is the value of a money market account realized at time t. The money market account is reinvested period by period at the prevailing riskless short rate, and its starting value at time 0 equals $B(0) = \$1$.

Result 2. *In absence of arbitrage, the variable $\tilde{p}_0(z_t)$ is zero (positive) if and only if the probability $p_0(z_t)$ is zero (positive).*

In absence of arbitrage, if the probability of an event is zero, its AD price must also be zero. Otherwise, one can lock in a sure gain by selling short the AD security if it is worth a positive value or buying the AD security if it is worth a negative price. Similarly, if the probability of an event is positive, its AD price must also be positive. If the AD price is nonpositive, one can buy the AD security without losing anything, and then lock in a gain of \$1, if the event corresponding to the AD security is realized. Finally, using equation (2.15), note that since the value of the money market account is always positive, the price of the AD security is zero (positive), *if and only if* the variable $\tilde{p}_0(z_t)$ is also zero (positive). Harrison and Kreps [1979] demonstrate an important result related to the variable $\tilde{p}_0(z_t)$, given as follows:

Result 3. *Absence of arbitrage implies that the variable $\tilde{p}_0(z_t)$ is a probability measure. Further, the probability measures $p_0(z_t)$ and $\tilde{p}_0(z_t)$ are "equivalent" probability measures.*

Equivalent probability measures have the property that if one probability measure is zero (positive), then the other probability measure must also be zero (positive). We have already shown in result 2 that absence of arbitrage implies that the variable $\tilde{p}_0(z_t)$ is zero (positive) *if and only if* the probability $p_0(z_t)$ is zero (positive). Hence, if we can show that $\tilde{p}_0(z_t)$ is a probability measure, then $p_0(z_t)$ and $\tilde{p}_0(z_t)$ are "equivalent" probability measures.

To show that $\tilde{p}_0(z_t)$ is a probability measure, note that in absence of arbitrage, $\tilde{p}_0(z_t)$ can never be negative (result 2). Further, we show that the values of $\tilde{p}_0(z_t)$ corresponding to all events at time t add up to 1. However, instead of giving a rigorous proof of this result, we show that it holds for the two-period information structure tree given in Figure 2.1. The proof can be easily derived by generalizing the results based upon the two-period tree, to an N-period tree with an arbitrary number of states.

To demonstrate that the probabilities $\tilde{p}_0(z_t)$ do indeed add up to 1, reconsider the two-period tree given in Figure 2.1. Let the value of the money market in different states in Figure 2.1 be given as:

$$
\begin{aligned}
B(0) &= 1 \\[4pt]
B(11) &= B(12) = \exp(r(0)) \\
B(21) &= B(22) = B(23) = \exp(r(0) + r_{11}(1)) \\
B(24) &= B(25) = \exp(r(0) + r_{12}(1))
\end{aligned}
\tag{2.16}
$$

When $t = 1$, $B(11) = B(12) = \exp(r(0))$ at time 1, therefore, equation (2.15) implies the following equality:

$$
\tilde{p}_0(11) + \tilde{p}_0(12) = [AD_0(11) + AD_0(12)] \times \exp(r(0)) \tag{2.17}
$$

But since by equation (2.2), the sum of Arrow-Debreu prices equals $AD_0(11) + AD_0(12) = P(0, \ 1) = \exp(-r(0))$, hence, substituting this in equation (2.17) implies:

$$
\tilde{p}_0(11) + \tilde{p}_0(12) = 1 \tag{2.18}
$$

Hence $\tilde{p}_0(z_t)$ can be considered a probability measure for $t = 1$. Using similar logic, we show that $\tilde{p}_0(z_t)$ is a probability measure for $t = 2$, also. To see this, note that since $B(21) = B(22) = B(23) = \exp(r(0) + r_{11}(1))$, and using equations (2.11), (2.13), and (2.15), we have:

$$
\begin{aligned}
\tilde{p}_0(21) &+ \tilde{p}_0(22) + \tilde{p}_0(23) \\
&= [AD_0(21) + AD_0(22) + AD_0(23)] \exp[r(0) + r_{11}(1)] \\
&= P_{11}(1, \ 2)AD_0(11) \exp[r(0) + r_{11}(1)] \\
&= AD_0(11) \exp[r(0)]
\end{aligned}
\tag{2.19}
$$

Similarly, since $B(24) = B(25) = \exp(r(0) + r_{12}(1))$, and using equations (2.12), (2.14), and (2.15), we have:

$$
\begin{aligned}
\tilde{p}_0(24) + \tilde{p}_0(25) &= [AD_0(24) + AD_0(25)] \exp[r(0) + r_{12}(1)] \\
&= P_{12}(1, \ 2)AD_0(12) \exp[r(0) + r_{12}(1)] \\
&= AD_0(12) \exp[r(0)]
\end{aligned}
\tag{2.20}
$$

Summing up equations (2.19) and (2.20), and then using equations (2.17) and (2.18), we have:

$$
\begin{aligned}
\tilde{p}_0(21) &+ \tilde{p}_0(22) + \tilde{p}_0(23) + \tilde{p}_0(24) + \tilde{p}_0(25) \\
&= [AD_0(11) + AD_0(12)] \times \exp(r(0)) \\
&= \tilde{p}_0(11) + \tilde{p}_0(12) = 1
\end{aligned}
\tag{2.21}
$$

Hence, $\tilde{p}_0(z_t)$ is a probability measure for $t = 2$, also. In general, it can be shown that absence of arbitrage is equivalent to $\tilde{p}_0(z_t)$ being a probability measure for all $t > 0$. Harrison and Kreps [1979] show another important result given as follows:

Result 4. *Under the equivalent probability measure $\tilde{p}_0(z_t)$, all asset prices discounted by the money market account are martingales. An equivalent probability measure that uses the money market account as the numeraire asset is called the "risk-neutral" measure.*

A martingale is a variable such that the current expectation of the future value of the variable is always equal to the current value of the variable. Hence, if $Y_t = E(Y_T/\mathcal{F}_t)$, for all $0 \leq t \leq T$, and filtration $\mathcal{F}$, then the probability measure associated with the expectation is a martingale measure with respect to this variable.

A simple demonstration of result 4 can be given using a two-period example. Suppose a non-dividend-paying asset is worth $X(z_t)$ at time t. Define the discounted asset price process as the asset price divided by the money market account, or $X(z_t)/B(z_t)$. For the two-period example, we show the following:

$$
\frac{X(0)}{B(0)} = \tilde{E}_0\left(\frac{X(z_1)}{B(z_1)}\right) = \tilde{E}_0\left(\frac{X(z_2)}{B(z_2)}\right)
\tag{2.22}
$$

The first part of the equality follows since $B(0) = 1$, and:

$$
\begin{aligned}
\tilde{E}_0\left(\frac{X(z_1)}{B(z_1)}\right) &= \tilde{p}_0(11)\frac{X(11)}{B(11)} + \tilde{p}_0(12)\frac{X(12)}{B(12)} \\
&= AD_0(11)X(11) + AD_0(12)X(12) = X(0)
\end{aligned}
\tag{2.23}
$$

The second equality follows, since:

$$
\begin{aligned}
\tilde{E}_0\left(\frac{X(z_2)}{B(z_2)}\right) = &\ \frac{\tilde{p}_0(21) \times X(21)}{B(21)} + \frac{\tilde{p}_0(22) \times X(22)}{B(22)} \\
&+ \frac{\tilde{p}_0(23) \times X(23)}{B(23)} + \frac{\tilde{p}_0(24) \times X(24)}{B(24)} + \frac{\tilde{p}_0(25) \times X(25)}{B(25)}
\end{aligned}
$$

$$= AD_0(21)X(21) + AD_0(22)X(22) + AD_0(23)X(23)$$
$$+ AD_0(24)X(24) + AD_0(25)X(25) = X(0) \tag{2.24}$$

In general, it can be shown that discounted prices are always martingales under the equivalent probability measure $\tilde{p}_0(z_t)$, or

$$\frac{X(z_t)}{B(z_t)} = \tilde{E}_t\left(\frac{X(z_T)}{B(z_T)}\right) \tag{2.25}$$

for all $t \le T$. Hence, under the equivalent probability measure $\tilde{p}_0(z_t)$, all asset prices discounted by the money market account are martingales. According to result 3, absence of arbitrage guarantees the existence of this measure. Equation (2.25) implies the following solution for any non-dividend-paying asset or zero-coupon bond, at a given time t:

$$X(t) = \tilde{E}_t\left(\frac{X(T)}{B(T)}\right) B(t) \tag{2.26}$$

where for notational simplicity we have expressed $X(z_t)$ as $X(t)$ and $B(z_t)$ as $B(t)$. Equation (2.26) can be extended to assets that pay dividends or coupon bonds by using the value additivity principle. As a special case, the time t price of a zero-coupon bond that gives \$1 at time T can be given as follows:

$$P(t, T) = \tilde{E}_t\left(\frac{1}{B(T)}\right) B(t) \tag{2.27}$$

Until now in this chapter, we have assumed that we know the prices of the AD securities. However, in real markets the AD securities don't exist and so the prices of AD securities must be discovered by either using market completeness or by imposing some equilibrium on the market. In a complete market, even though AD securities don't exist, all of them can be replicated by trading existing securities with complex payoffs. For example, in the model of Black and Scholes [1973], Merton [1973], and Cox and Ross [1976], all AD securities can be replicated by continuous trading of the underlying stock and a default-free bond. Since the prices of complex securities are observable, the prices of AD securities can be obtained as functions of these observable prices. A complete market guarantees that the equivalent martingale measure (which must exist due to absence of arbitrage) is also unique. Another interesting property of complete markets is that market prices of risks do not explicitly enter into the valuation process, and valuation can be done as if investors have risk-neutral preferences.

We now state our final result regarding the multiplicity of risk-neutral measures when markets are incomplete.

Result 5. *All of the results given from equation (2.2) through equa-tion (2.27) continue to hold even when markets are incomplete, except that under incomplete markets the risk-neutral measure $\tilde{p}_0(z_t)$ is not uniquely determined by absence of arbitrage. In a complete market, the risk-neutral measure $\tilde{p}_0(z_t)$ is unique.*

In other words, if the market is incomplete, then absence of arbitrage may be consistent with the existence of two or more risk-neutral mea-sures. However, all AD prices, bond prices, the money market account, and so forth, will remain internally consistent such that given a particular risk-neutral measure, equations (2.2) through (2.27) will be satisfied. But, absence of arbitrage alone is no longer sufficient for obtaining valuation results in an incomplete market. One must make additional assumptions about investors' risk preferences, which enter the risk-neutral valuation equations (2.26) and (2.27). On the other hand, when the market is com-plete, then the risk-neutral measure $\tilde{p}_0(z_t)$ is uniquely determined by absence of arbitrage alone. Later in this chapter we give additional results on how the risk-neutral measure can be identified in a complete market by using absence of arbitrage in a continuous-time economy.

Because the historical origins of the "risk-neutral measure" are based upon complete market models (Black and Scholes [1973], Merton [1973], and Cox and Ross [1976]), the name of this measure is associated with doing valuation *as if investors have risk-neutral preferences.* However, this mea-sure is no longer identified by the complete market property. The concept of risk-neutral measure has evolved to mean an equivalent martingale measure that uses the money market account as the appropriate numeraire asset for valuation. The so called "risk-neutral measure" may use information related to the risk-aversion behavior of investors in an incomplete mar-ket, in order to uniquely identify a specific preference-dependent measure, from an infinite number of potential equivalent martingale measures. For example, the market price of volatility risk enters the Heston [1993] option pricing formula, and so information regarding *risk aversion* enters in the risk-neutral measure for obtaining unique preference-dependent solutions of contingent claims.

Hence, despite its origins, the risk-neutral measure is now used in the finance literature to denote the more general concept of the Harrison and Kreps–type "equivalent martingale measure," in the context of incom-plete markets, when the money market account is used as the appropriate numeraire asset for valuation. Consistent with this general practice, through-out this book we will use the expression "risk-neutral measure" to denote the more general equivalent martingale measure, which uses the money market account as the appropriate numeraire asset for valuation. As shown later in this chapter, the money market account is not the only numeraire asset choice for martingale valuation. Geman [1989] and Jamshidian [1989] identify zero-coupon bonds as numeraire assets, which lead to "forward" equivalent martingale measures for valuation of fixed income claims.

Stochastic Discount Factor

Because asset markets are generally incomplete due to the existence of jumps and stochastic volatility in asset prices (since no traded securities can dynamically replicate these risks), the identification of the risk-neutral measure from the set of all potential risk-neutral measures is problematic. Hansen and Richard [1987] and Constantinidies [1992] suggest estimating the risk-neutral measure empirically, exploiting a more direct approach based upon the *stochastic discount factor* or the *pricing kernel*. The stochastic discount factor is defined as the ratio of the AD price of an event to the physical probability of that event, or:

$$M(z_t) = \frac{AD_0(z_t)}{p_0(z_t)} \tag{2.28}$$

It can be shown that the product of the price of any asset and stochastic discount factor follows a martingale under the physical probability measure $p_0(z_t)$, or:

$$M(z_t)X(t) = E_t(M(z_T)X(T)) \tag{2.29}$$

where for notational simplicity $X(z_t)$ and $X(z_T)$ are expressed as $X(t)$ and $X(T)$, respectively. Equation (2.29) can be proven as follows. We know that the time t price of the asset can be given as the summation of the product of the time T values of the asset under different events (under filtration $\mathcal{F}_t$) and time t prices of the AD securities corresponding to those events, or:

$$X(t) = \sum_{z_T} AD_t(z_T)X(T)\big|\mathcal{F}_t \tag{2.30}$$

By multiplying and dividing the terms in the summation with time t probabilities and rewriting equation (2.30) as a time t expectation under filtration $\mathcal{F}_t$, we get:

$$X(t) = E_t\left(\frac{AD_t(z_T)}{p_t(z_T)}X(T)\right) \tag{2.31}$$

Expressing the time t price of an AD security as a ratio of time 0 prices of two AD securities using equation (2.10), and the corresponding time t probability as a ratio of two time 0 probabilities using equation (2.6), we get:

$$X(t) = E_t\left(\frac{AD_0(z_T)}{AD_0(z_t)}\frac{p_0(z_t)}{p_0(z_T)}X(T)\right) \tag{2.32}$$

Finally, using the definition of the stochastic discount factor in equation (2.28):

$$X(t) = E_t \left(\frac{M(z_T)}{M(z_t)} X(T) \right) \qquad (2.33)$$

and hence, equation (2.29) follows.

Equation (2.33) is very useful as it can be used to value any asset under the physical probability measure. One can empirically estimate the process for $M(z_t)$ under the physical probability measure $p_0(z_t)$, and then use it for valuation purposes. For the special case of complete markets, a unique process for $M(z_t)$ exists, which is determined by absence of arbitrage alone. To get additional intuition regarding the stochastic discount factor, consider how discounting is done under a simpler setting using a constant discount factor:

$$X(t) = E_t(X(T)) \times Constant \ discount \ factor \qquad (2.34)$$

In basic finance textbooks, the constant discount factor is typically given as $1/(1 + k)^{T-t}$, where k is some risk-adjusted discount rate. Comparing equations (2.33) and (2.34), note that the ratio $M(z_T)/M(z_t)$ replaces the role of discounting, but that this discounting term is inside the expectation operator in equation (2.33). Since the term $M(z_T)$ stochastically varies with events at time T (under the filtration $\mathcal{F}_t$), it is called the *stochastic discount factor*.

In a complete market, with observable asset return distributions the stochastic discount factor can be determined uniquely; however, in an incomplete market, even with observable asset return distributions, additional assumptions about risk preferences are needed to estimate the stochastic discount factor.[2] To get more insight into how the stochastic discount factor varies, consider a market equilibrium resulting from the maximization of a time-additive separable utility function with a constant time preference. Using the first-order conditions, it can be shown that:

$$\frac{U'(C(z_T))}{U'(C(z_t))} = \frac{M(z_T)}{M(z_t)} \bigg| \mathcal{F}_t \qquad (2.35)$$

where $U'(.)$ is the marginal utility of consumption. Since the marginal utility of consumption at time T is high under those events in which consumption is low, the stochastic discount factor is high when the economy does poorly and consumption is low. This explains much of the intuition of models such as the Consumption CAPM (see Breeden [1979]), in which the returns of stocks that co-vary more with future aggregate consumption have higher consumption betas and are discounted more.

Now, consider a special case of equation (2.33), when $X(T) = \$1$. This gives the time t price of a \$1 face-value zero-coupon bond maturing at time

T, as follows:

$$P(t, T) = E_t \left(\frac{M(z_T)}{M(z_t)} \right) \tag{2.36}$$

Hence, the process for the stochastic discount factor completely determines the evolution of all zero-coupon bond prices.

Radon-Nikodym Derivative

The Radon-Nikodym derivative is defined as the ratio of risk-neutral probability $\tilde{p}_0(z_t)$ to the physical probability $p_0(z_t)$, or:

$$\xi(z_t) = \frac{\tilde{p}_0(z_t)}{p_0(z_t)} \tag{2.37}$$

Knowing the Radon-Nikodym derivative is useful, as it allows us to obtain the risk-neutral probability measure from the physical probability measure. In a complete market, the Radon-Nikodym derivative can be uniquely identified. The Radon-Nikodym derivative allows the conversion of an expectation under the physical probability measure to the expectation under the risk-neutral probability measure, as follows:

$$\tilde{E}_t[X(T)] = \frac{E_t[X(T)\xi(z_T)]}{\xi(z_t)} \tag{2.38}$$

To prove this equality, substitute equation (2.37) to express the right-hand side of equation (2.38) as follows:

$$\frac{E_t[X(T)\xi(z_T)]}{\xi(z_t)} = \frac{\sum\limits_{z_T} p_t(z_T)X(T)\tilde{p}_0(z_T)/p_0(z_T)}{\tilde{p}_0(z_t)/p_0(z_t)}|\mathcal{F}_t \tag{2.39}$$

Using the definition of conditional probability from equation (2.6), equation (2.39) simplifies to:

$$\frac{E_t[X(T)\xi(z_T)]}{\xi(z_t)} = \frac{\sum\limits_{z_T} X(T)\tilde{p}_0(z_T)}{\tilde{p}_0(z_t)}|\mathcal{F}_t$$

$$= \sum\limits_{z_T} X(T)\tilde{p}_t(z_T)|\mathcal{F}_t = \tilde{E}_t[X(T)] \tag{2.40}$$

If $X(T) = 1$, equation (2.40) implies that the Radon-Nikodym derivative follows a martingale under the physical probability measure, or:

$$\xi(z_t) = E_t[\xi(z_T)] \tag{2.41}$$

Since by definition $\xi(z_0) = 1$ (see equation (2.37)), we also have:

$$E_0[\xi(z_T)] = 1, \quad \text{for all } T > 0 \tag{2.42}$$

A simple relationship exists between the Radon-Nikodym derivative and the stochastic discount factor. Using equations (2.15), (2.28), and (2.37), it can be seen that the stochastic discount factor is always equal to the Radon-Nikodym derivative discounted by the money market account, or:

$$M(z_t) = \frac{\xi(z_t)}{B(z_t)} \tag{2.43}$$

Though the intuition of the results until now was built with the aid of the two-period information structure tree, all of these results continue to hold even in continuous-time models.

In the next section we consider arbitrage-free valuation in a continuous-time setup. We first give an example of how the probability measures can be changed under processes with continuous density. Then we introduce the Girsanov theorem, which gives conditions under which we can switch the probability measures for continuous-time stochastic processes. We give some examples of commonly used continuous-time processes and identify the risk-neutral probability measures corresponding to these processes. We also introduce another arbitrage-free measure known as the *forward measure*, which is more convenient to apply for pricing bond options and yield options (i.e., caps, etc.) under various term structure models. And finally, we show how risk premiums under the physical measure are related to the process for the stochastic discount factor.

ARBITRAGE-FREE VALUATION IN CONTINUOUS TIME

In this section we outline the basic framework for the results derived in the previous section to hold in a continuous-time setup. Like the previous section, we do not provide rigorous proofs of these results, but provide a heuristic-based intuitive understanding of the results.

Until now we used the notation $p_0(z_t)$ and $\tilde{p}_0(z_t)$ for the time 0 physical and risk-neutral probability measures.[3] We now change the notation as follows. Since under continuous-time stochastic processes the events can occur over a continuous range of values, we define the physical probability space as $\{\Omega, \mathcal{F}, \mathcal{P}\}$, where filtration $\mathcal{F} = \{\mathcal{F}_t, 0 \le t \le T\}$ gives the information structure of events over a *continuous* interval [0, T]. The cumulative probability is now defined as $\mathcal{P}(z_t)$, where z_t belongs to the N-dimensional continuous sample space of real numbers $\Re^N = \{-\infty, \infty\}$. The differential of $\mathcal{P}(z_t)$ is given as $d\mathcal{P}(z_t)$, which can be used to obtain the time 0 probability density function of events at time t. Though $dP(z_t)$ gives the time 0 probability density, we do not explicitly mention the subscript for time 0, as was done using the discrete time setup.

Let a stochastic process $X(t)$ be *adapted*, which means that it is observable on $\mathcal{F}_t$. In other words, it is possible to deduce all possible values of $X(t)$ based on events in $\mathcal{F}_t$. For notational convenience, we assume that the expectation of a variable $X(T)$ under the probability measure $\mathcal{P}$ and filtration $\mathcal{F}_t$ can be expressed as $E_t(X(T)) = E(X(T)|\mathcal{F}_t)$.

The process $X(t)$ is a martingale under the probability measure $\mathcal{P}$ and filtration $\mathcal{F}_t$, if:

$$X(t) = E_t[X(t+s)], \text{for all } s \geq 0 \qquad (2.44)$$

We define the equivalent risk-neutral cumulative probability as $\tilde{P}(z_t)$, and the differential of $\tilde{P}(z_t)$ is given as $d\tilde{P}(z_t)$, which can be used to obtain the time 0 risk-neutral probability density function of events at time t. The martingale approach to contingent claims pricing exploits the martingale property in a sense that it requires computing the following expectation under the risk-neutral measure $\tilde{P}(z_t)$:

$$f(X(t), \ t) = \tilde{E}_t \left[\frac{F(X(T), \ T)}{B(T)} \right] B(t) \qquad (2.45)$$

where the function $F(X(T), \ T)$ gives the terminal payoff of the contingent claim, $f(X(t), \ t)$ gives the arbitrage-free price of the claim, and $B(t)$ is the value of the money market account at time t. The computation of the previous expectation requires that we obtain the equivalent risk-neutral probability measure from the physical probability measure. This can be done through the application of the Girsanov theorem for continuous-time processes. But before we do that, we show how probability measures can be changed for continuous densities.

Change of Probability Measure under a Continuous Probability Density

Let Z be a normally distributed random variable with mean 0 and variance 1. The probability density function of Z is given by:

$$f(z) = \frac{1}{\sqrt{2\pi}} e^{-\frac{1}{2}z^2} \qquad (2.46)$$

Let $dP(z)$ be the probability that the random variable Z will fall within a small interval of length dz centered around some z:

$$dP(z) = P(z - 0.5\,dz < Z < z + 0.5\,dz) \qquad (2.47)$$

Probabilities are often called *measures* because they are mappings from arbitrary sets to the set of nonnegative real numbers. Therefore, $d\mathcal{P}(z)$ is a probability measure. We can compute the expression in equation (2.47) as follows:

$$\mathcal{P}(z - 0.5\,dz < Z < z + 0.5\,dz) = \int_{z-0.5dz}^{z+0.5dz} \frac{1}{\sqrt{2\pi}} e^{-\frac{1}{2}x^2}\,dx \cong \frac{1}{\sqrt{2\pi}} e^{-\frac{1}{2}z^2}\,dz$$

(2.48)

or:

$$d\mathcal{P}(z) = \frac{1}{\sqrt{2\pi}} e^{-\frac{1}{2}z^2}\,dz$$

(2.49)

To show how probability measures can be changed, consider the following example. Let function $\xi(z) > 0$ be defined as follows:

$$\xi(z) = e^{z \times 2 - \frac{1}{2} \times 2^2}$$

(2.50)

Now compute the product of $d\mathcal{P}(z)$ and $\xi(z)$:

$$d\mathcal{P}(z) \times \xi(z) = \frac{1}{\sqrt{2\pi}} e^{-\frac{1}{2}z^2 + z \times 2 - \frac{1}{2} \times 2^2}\,dz$$

(2.51)

After grouping some terms, we obtain:

$$d\tilde{\mathcal{P}}(z) = \frac{1}{\sqrt{2\pi}} e^{-\frac{1}{2}(z-2)^2}\,dz$$

(2.52)

Clearly, $d\tilde{\mathcal{P}}(z)$ is a new probability measure, and it is associated with a normally distributed random variable with the mean 2 and variance 1. By multiplying $d\mathcal{P}(z)$ by $\xi(z)$, we have transformed the original distribution from $\mathcal{N}(0, 1)$ to $\mathcal{N}(2, 1)$; that is, the mean of the distribution was shifted, while the variance remained unchanged. To visualize this process, consider Figure 2.2.

The preceding example demonstrates how a new probability measure, $d\tilde{\mathcal{P}}(z)$, can be obtained by transforming some given probability measure, $d\mathcal{P}(z)$. This is achieved by multiplying the original probability measure by a function $\xi(z)$:

$$d\tilde{\mathcal{P}}(z) = \xi(z) \times d\mathcal{P}(z)$$

(2.53)

Note, that we can also go from probability measure $d\tilde{\mathcal{P}}(z)$ to $d\mathcal{P}(z)$ by simply multiplying $d\tilde{\mathcal{P}}(z)$ by the inverse of $\xi(z)$:

$$d\mathcal{P}(z) = \xi^{-1}(z) \times d\tilde{\mathcal{P}}(z)$$

(2.54)

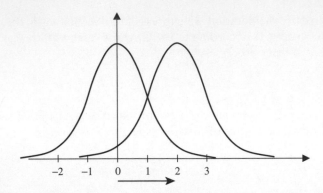

FIGURE 2.2   Transformation of Probability Distribution

If we rewrite equation (2.53) as follows:

$$\xi(z) = \frac{d\tilde{\mathcal{P}}(z)}{d\mathcal{P}(z)} \tag{2.55}$$

then $\xi(z)$ can be thought of as a derivative of $\tilde{\mathcal{P}}$ with respect to $\mathcal{P}$. Such derivatives are called *Radon-Nikodym derivatives* under continuous densities. Equation (2.55) implies that the Radon-Nikodym derivative would exist only if $d\mathcal{P}(z) > 0$. Alternatively, using the inverse $\xi^{-1}(z)$, the Radon-Nikodym derivative would exist only if $d\tilde{\mathcal{P}}(z) > 0$. Formally, the existence of $\xi(z)$ and its inverse are guaranteed if $\mathcal{P}$ and $\tilde{\mathcal{P}}$ satisfy the following condition:

$$d\tilde{\mathcal{P}}(z) > 0 \text{ if and only if } d\mathcal{P}(z) > 0 \tag{2.56}$$

If the above condition is satisfied, then $\mathcal{P}$ and $\tilde{\mathcal{P}}$ are called *equivalent probability measures*, and we can go back and forth between them using equations (2.53) and (2.54). The Girsanov theorem provides conditions under which the Radon-Nikodym derivative exists and is considered next.

The Girsanov Theorem and the Radon-Nikodym Derivative

Let $Z_1(t)$, $Z_2(t)$, ..., $Z_N(t)$ be a set of N independent Wiener processes under the probability measure $\mathcal{P}$. Now, define a zero-drift process given as follows:

$$\frac{d\xi(t)}{\xi(t)} = -\gamma_1(t)dZ_1(t) - \gamma_2(t)dZ_2(t) \cdots - \gamma_N(t)dZ_N(t) \tag{2.57}$$

where to simplify the notation we express $\xi(z_t) = \xi(t)$, and by definition we have $\xi(z_0) = \xi(0) = 1$. According to the Girsanov theorem, the following N processes are Wiener processes:

$$d\tilde{Z}_j(t) = dZ_j(t) + \gamma_j(t)\, dt \tag{2.58}$$

for $j = 1, 2, \ldots, N$, under the new probability measure $\tilde{\mathcal{P}}$, where the Radon-Nikodym derivative of $\tilde{\mathcal{P}}$ with respect to $\mathcal{P}$ is given as:

$$\xi(t) = \frac{d\tilde{\mathcal{P}}(z_t)}{d\mathcal{P}(z_t)} \tag{2.59}$$

For the Radon-Nikodym derivative to exist, the following Novikov condition must be satisfied, which ensures that $\gamma_j(t)$'s, for all $j = 1, 2, \ldots, N$, do not explode, or:

$$E\left[e^{\int_0^t \gamma_j^2(s)\, ds} \right] < \infty, \quad \text{for } j = 1, 2, \ldots, N, \text{ and } t \in [0, T] \tag{2.60}$$

By taking the stochastic integral of equation (2.57), the Radon-Nikodym derivative can be given as follows:

$$\xi(t) = \exp\left(-\sum_{j=1}^{N} \int_0^t \gamma_j(v)\, dZ_j(v) - \frac{1}{2} \sum_{j=1}^{N} \int_0^t \gamma_j^2(v)\, dv \right) \tag{2.61}$$

The Radon-Nikodym derivative allows the conversion of an expectation under the physical probability measure to the expectation under the risk-neutral probability measure, as follows:

$$\tilde{E}_t[X(T)] = \frac{E_t[X(T)\xi(T)]}{\xi(t)} \tag{2.62}$$

If $X(T) = 1$, equation (2.62) implies that the Radon-Nikodym derivative follows a martingale under the physical probability measure, or:

$$\xi(t) = E_t[\xi(T)] \tag{2.63}$$

where by definition $\xi(0) = 1$ in equation (2.61).

Equivalent Martingale Measures

The Girsanov theorem can be used to obtain equivalent martingale measures for various term structure models given in this book. Two types of equivalent martingale measures are generally used for pricing fixed-income securities and their derivatives. Under the traditional risk-neutral measure, all asset prices discounted by the money market account are martingales. This measure is used to price basic fixed-income securities such as zero-coupon bonds and coupon bonds. This measure can also price zero-investment contingent claims such as forwards/futures contracts written on bonds or on yields (e.g., T-bond futures, Eurodollar futures, etc.). The second type of equivalent martingale measure is called the "forward" measure. This measure is used to price various types of options written on fixed income securities, including options on bonds (i.e., calls and puts), options on yields (i.e., caps, floors, and collars), and options on swaps (i.e., swaptions).

The Risk-Neutral Measure   Virtually all term structure models in the various chapters in this book can be represented as special cases of the following bond price process with N independent Wiener processes:

$$\frac{dP(t,\ T)}{P(t,\ T)} = r(t)\,dt - \sum_{j=1}^{N} \sigma_{Pj}(\mathbf{Y},\ t,\ T)\gamma_j(t)\,dt$$

$$- \sum_{j=1}^{N} \sigma_{Pj}(\mathbf{Y},\ t,\ T)\,dZ_j(t) \tag{2.64}$$

where $P(t,\ T)$ is the time t price of a \$1 face-value zero-coupon bond maturing at time T, $\sigma_{Pj}(\mathbf{Y},\ t,\ T)$ is the bond volatility function associated with the jth Wiener process $dZ_j(t)$, $\gamma_j(j)$ is the market price of risk associated with the jth factor, and $\mathbf{Y}$ is the vector of state variables (which may include the short rate $r(t)$).

Now, define N new Wiener processes as follows:

$$d\tilde{Z}_j(t) = dZ_j(t) + \gamma_j(t)\,dt \tag{2.65}$$

for $j = 1,\ 2,\ \ldots,\ N$, under the probability measure $\tilde{\mathcal{P}}$, where the Radon-Nikodym derivative of $\tilde{\mathcal{P}}$ with respect to $\mathcal{P}$ is given as:

$$\xi(t) = \xi(z_t) = \frac{d\tilde{\mathcal{P}}(z_t)}{d\mathcal{P}(z_t)} \tag{2.66}$$

Using the Girsanov theorem, the Radon-Nikodym derivative in equation (2.66) is given by equation (2.61), assuming that the Novikov condition in equation (2.60) is satisfied.

The bond price process under the risk-neutral measure is obtained by substituting equation (2.65) into equation (2.64), as follows:

$$\frac{dP(t,\ T)}{P(t,\ T)} = r(t)\,dt - \sum_{j=1}^{N} \sigma_{Pj}(\mathbf{Y},\ t,\ T)\,d\tilde{Z}_j(t) \qquad (2.67)$$

Let the bond price discounted by the money market account be defined as follows:

$$\overline{P}(t,\ T) = P(t,\ T)/B(t) \qquad (2.68)$$

where

$$B(t) = \exp\left(\int_0^t r(v)\,dv\right)$$

Using Ito's lemma on equation (2.68), the stochastic process for the discounted bond price is given as follows:

$$\frac{d\overline{P}(t,\ T)}{\overline{P}(t,\ T)} = - \sum_{j=1}^{N} \sigma_{Pj}(\mathbf{Y},\ t,\ T)\,d\tilde{Z}_j(t) \qquad (2.69)$$

Since the discounted price has zero-drift, it is a martingale under the risk-neutral measure and is given as follows:

$$\overline{P}(t,\ T) = \tilde{E}_t[\overline{P}(t,\ T)] = \tilde{E}_t\left(\frac{1}{B(T)}\right) \qquad (2.70)$$

Substituting equation (2.68), the bond price is given by the following risk-neutral expectation:

$$P(t,\ T) = \tilde{E}_t\left(\frac{1}{B(T)}\right) B(t) \qquad (2.71)$$

The risk-neutral measure is used throughout this book to obtain the price of a zero-coupon bond (and a coupon bond) under various term structure models. In some cases, expectation under the risk-neutral measure is computed directly (e.g., see Appendix 4.1 in Chapter 4), while in others, the partial differential equation corresponding to this expectation is solved based upon the Feynman-Kac theorem given in the last section of this chapter. The risk-neutral measure is also used to price futures contracts on T-bonds and Eurodollar futures, as demonstrated in the next chapter. However, since futures contracts require zero initial investment, and marking to market is done daily, discounting by the money market account is not required to obtain the martingale pricing result.

Forward Measure Under the risk-neutral measure $\tilde{\mathcal{P}}$, any asset price discounted by the money market account follows a martingale. The martingale pricing result is, however, a lot more general. It can be shown that corresponding to every traded asset with a positive price, an asset-specific equivalent martingale measure exists, such that all other asset prices discounted by the chosen asset price are also martingales, simply by the absence of arbitrage. Hence, we could have used the net asset value (NAV) of a PIMCO bond fund instead of the money market account and shown that a PIMCO-specific martingale measure $\mathcal{P}^{PIMCO}$ exists under which all other asset prices in the financial markets discounted by the NAV of the PIMCO fund are martingales.

However, for solving fixed-income option valuation problems, it is more convenient to use a martingale measure known as the *forward* measure $\tilde{\mathcal{P}}^S$ discovered by Geman [1989] and Jamshidian [1989]. Under this martingale measure, all asset prices discounted by the price of a zero-coupon bond maturing at time S are martingales. This measure is used to price various types of options written on fixed-income securities, including options on bonds (i.e., calls and puts) and options on yields (i.e., caps, floors, and collars). The LIBOR market model given in Chapter 12 uses a sequence of forward measures to price a sequence of caplets of different maturities. The forward measure $\tilde{\mathcal{P}}^S$ can be obtained as a transformation of the risk-neutral measure $\tilde{\mathcal{P}}$. Consider the Radon-Nikodym derivative $\xi^S(t)$ for doing this transformation, defined as follows:

$$\xi^S(t) = \frac{d\tilde{\mathcal{P}}^S(z_t)}{d\tilde{\mathcal{P}}(z_t)} = \frac{P(t, S)}{P(0, S)B(t)} \tag{2.72}$$

where, $P(t, S)$ is the time t price of a zero-coupon bond that pays \$1 at the maturity date S, and $B(t)$ is the time t value of the money market account.

Note that $\xi^S(t)$ satisfies the basic properties of being a Radon-Nikodym derivative. It is always positive, it is a martingale under the measure $\tilde{\mathcal{P}}$, and by definition $\xi^S(0) = 1$. To see the martingale property note that:

$$\begin{aligned}
\tilde{E}_t[\xi^S(T)] &= \tilde{E}_t\left(\frac{P(T, S)}{P(0, S)B(T)}\right) = \frac{1}{P(0, S)}\tilde{E}_t\left(\frac{P(T, S)}{B(T)}\right) \\
&= \frac{1}{P(0, S)}\frac{P(t, S)}{B(t)} = \xi^S(t)
\end{aligned} \tag{2.73}$$

Now consider a discounted contingent claim price given as $X(t)/P(t, S)$, at time $t \leq S$. The above Radon-Nikodym derivative allows the conversion of an expectation under the risk-neutral measure to the expectation under the forward measure, as follows:

$$\tilde{E}_0^S \left(\frac{X(t)}{P(t,\,S)} \right) = \frac{\tilde{E}_0 \left(\dfrac{X(t)}{P(t,\,S)} \xi^S(t) \right)}{\xi^S(0)} \tag{2.74}$$

Substituting the value of $\xi^S(t)$ from equation (2.72), noting that $\xi^S(0) = 1$ and $B(0) = 1$, and further simplifying equation (2.74), we have:

$$
\begin{aligned}
\tilde{E}_0^S \left(\frac{X(t)}{P(t,\,S)} \right) &= \tilde{E}_0 \left(\frac{X(t)}{P(t,\,S)} \frac{P(t,\,S)}{P(0,\,S)B(t)} \right) \\
&= \frac{1}{P(0,\,S)} \tilde{E}_0 \left(\frac{X(t)}{B(t)} \right) = \frac{1}{P(0,\,S)} \left(\frac{X(0)}{B(0)} \right) \\
&= \frac{X(0)}{P(0,\,S)}
\end{aligned}
\tag{2.75}
$$

Hence, all contingent claims prices discounted by the zero-coupon bond maturing at time S are martingales under the forward measure $\tilde{\mathcal{P}}^S$. The dollar price of any contingent claim can be obtained under the forward measure as follows:

$$X(0) = P(0,\,S) \times \tilde{E}_0^S \left(\frac{X(t)}{P(t,\,S)} \right) \tag{2.76}$$

Though we have identified the Radon-Nikodym derivative in equation (2.72) that allows us to transform the traditional risk-neutral measure to the forward measure, we have not yet shown how the drifts of the zero-coupon bond price processes change under such transformation. Obviously, such transformation depends upon the nature of stochastic processes used (i.e., diffusion, jump process, etc.). As an example, we consider the specific case of an N-factor model driven by a set of N *independent* Wiener processes, specified under the risk-neutral measure $\tilde{\mathcal{P}}$ in equation (2.67). We demonstrate how the transformed Wiener processes under the forward measure $\tilde{\mathcal{P}}^S$ can be derived from the Wiener processes specified under the risk-neutral measure $\tilde{\mathcal{P}}$ using the Girsanov theorem, and how the drifts of the bond price processes must be adjusted under the measure $\tilde{\mathcal{P}}^S$.

The stochastic bond price process of a bond maturing at time S, for the general N-factor diffusion-based term structure models is given using equation (2.67), as follows:

$$\frac{dP(t,\,S)}{P(t,\,S)} = r(t)\,dt - \sum_{j=1}^{N} \sigma_{Pj}(\mathbf{Y},\,t,\,S)\,d\tilde{Z}_j(t) \tag{2.77}$$

Using Ito's lemma, the stochastic integral of the bond price can be given as follows:

$$P(t, S) = P(0, S)B(t)$$

$$\times \exp\left(-\sum_{j=1}^{N} \int_0^t \sigma_{Pj}(\mathbf{Y}, v, S)\, d\tilde{Z}_j(v) - \frac{1}{2}\sum_{j=1}^{N} \int_0^t \sigma_{Pj}^2(\mathbf{Y}, v, S)\, dv\right)$$

(2.78)

Using equation (2.78), the Radon-Nikodym derivative defined in equation (2.72) can be given as:

$$\xi^S(t) = \frac{P(t, S)}{P(0, S)B(t)}$$

$$= \exp\left(-\sum_{j=1}^{N} \int_0^t \sigma_{Pj}(\mathbf{Y}, v, S)\, d\tilde{Z}_j(v) - \frac{1}{2}\sum_{j=1}^{N} \int_0^t \sigma_{Pj}(\mathbf{Y}, v, S)^2\, dv\right)$$

(2.79)

Using the Girsanov theorem (see equations (2.57), (2.58), and (2.61)) and the definition of the Radon-Nikodym derivative given above, it follows that the N Wiener processes under the forward measure are given as follows:

$$d\tilde{Z}_j^S(t) = d\tilde{Z}_j(t) + \sigma_{Pj}(\mathbf{Y}, t, S)\, dt$$

(2.80)

Substituting equation (2.80) in equation (2.67), the bond price process can be given under the forward measure $\tilde{\mathcal{P}}^S$ as follows:

$$\frac{dP(t, T)}{P(t, T)} = \left(r(t) + \sum_{j=1}^{N} \sigma_{Pj}(\mathbf{Y}, t, S)\sigma_{Pj}(\mathbf{Y}, t, T)\right) dt - \sum_{j=1}^{N} \sigma_{Pj}(\mathbf{Y}, t, T)\, d\tilde{Z}_j^S(t)$$

(2.81)

As shown by the following example, the transformation of the bond price process under the forward measure $\tilde{\mathcal{P}}^S$ allows certain contingent claims (like call and put options on zero-coupon bonds) to be valued using the martingale pricing result given in equation (2.76).

Example 2.1 We now show how the forward measure can be used to solve the price of a European option written on a zero-coupon bond under deterministic volatility N-factor term structure models. Deterministic volatility models assume that the volatility functions $\sigma_{Pj}(\mathbf{Y}, t, T)$ in equation (2.77) are deterministic functions of time and do not depend upon the state variable vector $\mathbf{Y}$.

Assume that the volatility functions $\sigma_{Pj}(Y, t, T)$ in equation (2.77) are of the following form:

$$\sigma_{Pj}(Y, t, T) = \sigma_j(t)B_j(t, T) \tag{2.82}$$

where, $\sigma_j(t)$ is a function of time t, and $B_j(t, T)$ depends only on t and T. The above process is very general and applies to virtually all known deterministic volatility models, including those of Merton [1973], Vasicek [1977], extended Vasicek models of Hull and White [1993], and multiple factor extensions of these models.

Substituting equation (2.82) into equation (2.81), the bond price process in equation (2.77) can be given under the forward measure $\tilde{\mathcal{P}}^S$ as follows:

$$\frac{dP(t, T)}{P(t, T)} = r(t)\,dt + \sum_{j=1}^{N} \sigma_j^2(t)B_j(t, T)B_j(t, S)\,dt - \sum_{j=1}^{N} \sigma_j(t)B_j(t, T)\,d\tilde{Z}_j^S(t)$$

$$\tag{2.83}$$

When $T = S$, equation (2.83) becomes:

$$\frac{dP(t, S)}{P(t, S)} = r(t)\,dt + \sum_{j=1}^{N} \sigma_j^2(t)B_j^2(t, S)\,dt - \sum_{j=1}^{N} \sigma_j(t)B_j(t, S)\,d\tilde{Z}_j^S(t) \tag{2.84}$$

Now consider a European call option expiring at time S, written on a zcro-coupon bond maturing at time T with a face value of \$1. The terminal payoff of the call option at its expiration date S, can be given as follows:

$$c(S) = Max\,(P(S, T) - K, 0) \tag{2.85}$$

where K is the strike price of the call option.

To value this call option using the forward measure, define a new variable $y(t) = P(t, T)/P(t, S)$. Using equation (2.75), we know that $y(t)$ is a martingale under the measure $\tilde{\mathcal{P}}^S$. Since $P(S, S) = 1$, the call price in equation (2.85) can be expressed in terms of the variable $y(S)$, as follows:

$$c(S) = Max(P(S, T) - K, 0) = Max(P(S, T)/P(S, S) - K, 0)$$

$$= Max(y(S) - K, 0) \tag{2.86}$$

Since the discounted value of any contingent claim with a payoff given as a function of $y(S)$ is a martingale under the measure $\tilde{\mathcal{P}}^S$, the time t value of the call can be given as follows:

$$\frac{c(t)}{P(t, S)} = \tilde{E}_t^S(Max(y(S) - K, 0)) \tag{2.87}$$

To evaluate the above expectation, we need the stochastic process followed by the variable $y(t)$, under the measure $\tilde{\mathcal{P}}^S$. Since $y(t) = P(t, T)/P(t, S)$, and the stochastic processes for $P(t, T)$ and $P(t, S)$ are given in equations (2.83) and (2.84), respectively, under the measure $\tilde{\mathcal{P}}^S$, the process followed by $y(t)$ can be obtained by using Ito's lemma as follows:

$$\frac{dy(t)}{y(t)} = \sum_{j=1}^{N} (\sigma_j(t)B_j(t, T) - \sigma_j(t)B_j(t, S))\, d\tilde{Z}_j^S(t) \tag{2.88}$$

The above process has a zero drift. This is not a coincidence, since we already know that $y(t)$ is a martingale under the measure $\tilde{\mathcal{P}}^S$. By using Ito's lemma, the stochastic process for $\ln(y(t))$ is given as:

$$
\begin{aligned}
d\ln(y(t)) = &-\tfrac{1}{2} \sum_{j=1}^{N} \left(\sigma_j(t)B_j(t, T) - \sigma_j(t)B_j(t, S)\right)^2 dt \\
&+ \sum_{j=1}^{N} \left(\sigma_j(t)B_j(t, T) - \sigma_j(t)B_j(t, S)\right) d\tilde{Z}_j^S(t)
\end{aligned}
\tag{2.89}
$$

Since the bond volatilities are deterministic, the variable $\ln(y(S))$ is normally distributed for any $S > t$. To value the call option in equation (2.87), we need the time t variance of $\ln(y(S))$. By taking the stochastic integral of equation (2.89), and then applying rule 3 from Chapter 1, the time t variance of $\ln(y(S))$ is given as follows:

$$V = \sum_{j=1}^{N} \int_t^S \left(\sigma_j(v)B_j(v, T) - \sigma_j(v)B_j(v, S)\right)^2 dv \tag{2.90}$$

The call option price in equation (2.87) can be written as follows:

$$c(t) = P(t, S) \times \tilde{E}_t^S\left(Max(y(S) - K, 0)\right) \tag{2.91}$$

To evaluate the expectation on the R.H.S. of equation (2.91), we will use the following result. If $\ln(y(S))$ is normally distributed with the time t variance given as V, then:

$$\tilde{E}_t^S\left[Max\left(y(S) - K, 0\right)\right] = \tilde{E}_t^S\left[y(S)\right] \mathcal{N}(d_1) - K\mathcal{N}(d_2) \tag{2.92}$$

where $\mathcal{N}(x)$ is the value of cumulative normal distribution evaluated at x and

$$d_1 = \frac{\ln\left(\tilde{E}_t^S\left[y(S)\right]/K\right) + V/2}{\sqrt{V}}$$

$$d_2 = \frac{\ln\left(\tilde{E}_t^S\left[y(S)\right]/K\right) - V/2}{\sqrt{V}}$$

Since $y(t)$ is a martingale under the measure $\tilde{\mathcal{P}}^S$, the time t expectation of $y(S)$ must equal $y(t) = P(t, T)/P(t, S)$. Substituting this expectation in equation (2.92), we get:

$$\tilde{E}_t^S\left[Max\left(y(S) - K, 0\right)\right] = \frac{P(t, T)}{P(t, S)}\mathcal{N}(d_1) - K\mathcal{N}(d_2) \qquad (2.93)$$

where

$$d_1 = \frac{\ln\left(\left[P(t, T)\right]/\left[P(t, S)K\right]\right) + V/2}{\sqrt{V}}$$

$$d_2 = \frac{\ln\left(\left[P(t, T)\right]/\left[P(t, S)K\right]\right) - V/2}{\sqrt{V}} \qquad (2.94)$$

Substituting equation (2.93) into equation (2.91), the call price is given as follows:

$$c(t) = P(t, T)\mathcal{N}(d_1) - P(t, S)K\mathcal{N}(d_2) \qquad (2.95)$$

where d_1 and d_2 are defined in equation (2.94), and V is given in equation (2.90). The above solution holds for all deterministic single and multifactor term structure models. Examples of these models are given in Chapters 4 and 8.

Stochastic Discount Factor and Risk Premiums

We know that all asset prices discounted by the money market account are martingales under the risk-neutral measure $\tilde{\mathcal{P}}$, or

$$X(t)/B(t) = \tilde{E}_t\left[X(T)/B(T)\right] \qquad (2.96)$$

By applying the result in equation (2.62) to equation (2.96), we can switch from the risk-neutral expectation to the expectation under the physical probability measure as follows:

$$X(t)/B(t) = \tilde{E}_t\left[X(T)/B(T)\right] = \frac{E_t[X(T)\xi(T)/B(T)]}{\xi(t)} \qquad (2.97)$$

Define a new variable given as follows:

$$M(T) = \frac{\xi(T)}{B(T)} \qquad (2.98)$$

Substituting equation (2.98) into equation (2.97), we have:

$$X(t) = E_t \left(\frac{M(T)}{M(t)} X(T) \right) \tag{2.99}$$

The ratio $M(T)/M(t)$ can be used under the physical probability measure to discount the asset stochastically; that is, asset prices in different states are discounted by different values. Hence, the variable $M(T)$ is called the *stochastic discount factor*. As can be seen from equation (2.98), the stochastic discount factor is defined as the Radon-Nikodym derivative discounted by the money market account.

If the stochastic process for the stochastic discount factor is known, it immediately gives the risk premiums on the underlying asset return process. To see this reconsider equation (2.99) as follows:

$$Y(t) = E_t[Y(T)], \quad Y(t) = X(t)M(t) \tag{2.100}$$

Using iterated expectations, we have:

$$E_t[dY(t)] = E_t[Y_{t+dt} - Y(t)] = E_t[E_{t+dt}(Y(T)) - E_t(Y(T))] = 0 \tag{2.101}$$

Using Ito's lemma, and then taking the physical expectation, we have:

$$E_t(dY(t)) = E_t[X(t)\,dM(t) + M(t)\,dX(t) + dX(t)\,dM(t)] = 0 \tag{2.102}$$

Dividing equation (2.102) by $X(t)M(t)$, and rearranging the terms, we get:

$$E_t \left(\frac{dX(t)}{X(t)} \right) = -E_t \left(\frac{dM(t)}{M(t)} \right) - E_t \left(\frac{dM(t)}{M(t)} \frac{dX(t)}{X(t)} \right) \tag{2.103}$$

Since equation (2.103) holds for any asset, it must also hold for $X(t) = B(t)$, where $B(t)$ is the money market account. The differential of $B(t)$ given as $dB(t) = B(t)r(t)dt$ does not contain any stochastic term. Hence, for the special case of the money market account, the last term in equation (2.103) drops out, and the equation simplifies to:

$$E_t \left(\frac{dM(t)}{M(t)} \right) = -r(t)\,dt \tag{2.104}$$

Substituting equation (2.104) into equation (2.103), we get:

$$E_t \left(\frac{dX(t)}{X(t)} \right) = r(t)\,dt - E_t \left(\frac{dM(t)}{M(t)} \frac{dX(t)}{X(t)} \right) \tag{2.105}$$

The above relationship between expected return on an asset with the covariation between the return on that asset and the stochastic discount factor can be used to obtain the equivalent martingale measures (both the risk-neutral measure and the forward measure) for pricing of contingent claims, if the process for the stochastic discount factor can be exogenously specified. The only condition required is that the stochastic discount factor always remains positive, which precludes the existence of arbitrage opportunities. This approach is used in Chapters 5 and 10, which apply the stochastic discount factor either implicitly or explicitly, to obtain the risk-neutral measure.

The Feynman-Kac Theorem

Throughout this chapter we have focused on how to value assets using the risk-neutral valuation method. This method requires the identification of the "risk-neutral" measure under which all discounted prices are martingales. For example, the value of a zero-coupon bond can be solved by taking the discounted risk-neutral expectation of its terminal value (this is explicitly demonstrated in Appendix 4.1 in Chapter 4). However, the value of a zero-coupon bond can also be solved using the partial differential equation (PDE) approach.

The Feynman-Kac theorem connects the risk-neutral approach to the PDE approach. It gives very general conditions under which a risk-neutral expectation can be converted into a PDE and a PDE can be converted into a risk-neutral expectation. Though we do not show how to derive and solve the PDEs (these are shown in various chapters), we demonstrate how a risk-neutral expectation can be converted into a PDE, and vice versa, in this section.

Consider a variable $X(t)$ that follows a mixed jump-diffusion process given as follows (see Chapter 1 for a definition of this process):

$$dX(t) = \mu(X, t)\, dt + \sigma(X, t)\, dZ(t) + h(J, X, t)\, dN(\lambda) \qquad (2.106)$$

The variable $h(J, X, t)$ is a function of the random variable J that can have some arbitrarily specified distribution (i.e., binomial, Gaussian, etc.), $X(t)$, and t. The variable $dN(\lambda)$ is a Poisson process with intensity λ. The variable J is independent of both $dZ(t)$ and $dN(\lambda)$. According to the Feynman-Kac theorem, the solution $f(X(t), t)$ of the expectation given in the following equation:

$$f(X(t), t)) = E_t\left[e^{-\int_t^T g(X(v),v)\, dv} F(X(T), T)\right] \qquad (2.107)$$

is determined by the following partial differential difference equation:

$$g(X(t),\ t)f(X(t),\ t) = \frac{\partial f(X(t),\ t)}{\partial t} + \mu(X(t),\ t)\frac{\partial f(X(t),\ t)}{\partial X(t)}$$

$$+ \tfrac{1}{2}\sigma^2(X(t),\ t)\frac{\partial^2 f(X(t),\ t)}{\partial X(t)^2} \tag{2.108}$$

$$+ \lambda E_t\big[f\big((X(t)+h(J,\ X,\ t)),\ t\big) - f\big(X(t),\ t\big)\big]$$

subject to the boundary condition $f(X(T),\ T) = F(X(T),\ T)$.

Example 2.2   Let's assume that the riskless short rate follows the Ornstein-Uhlenbeck process given by Vasicek [1977]:

$$dr(t) = \alpha(m - r(t))\,dt + \sigma\,dZ(t) \tag{2.109}$$

where α is the speed of mean reversion, m is the long-term mean of the short rate, σ is the volatility of the short rate. As shown in Chapter 4, the risk-neutral process corresponding to the above short-rate process is given as follows:

$$dr(t) = \tilde{\alpha}(\tilde{m} - r(t))\,dt + \sigma\,d\tilde{Z}(t) \tag{2.110}$$

where

$$\tilde{\alpha} = \alpha + \gamma_1$$

$$\tilde{m} = \frac{\alpha m - \gamma_0}{\alpha + \gamma_1} \tag{2.111}$$

and γ_0 and γ_1 are the market prices of interest rate risk.

Let $P(t,\ T)$ represent the time t price of a zero-coupon bond that matures at time T and pays \$1 at maturity. Since the discounted bond price must be a martingale under the risk-neutral measure, we have:

$$P(t,\ T) = \tilde{E}_t\left[\frac{1}{B(T)}\right]B(t) \tag{2.112}$$

where the money market account is defined as follows:

$$B(t) = \exp\left[\int_0^t r(v)\,dv\right] \tag{2.113}$$

Substituting equation (2.113) into equation (2.112), we get:

$$P(t,\ T) = \tilde{E}_t\left[\exp\left(-\int_t^T r(v)\,dv\right)\right] \tag{2.114}$$

By applying the Feynman-Kac theorem to equation (2.114), we get the following PDE:

$$\frac{\partial P}{\partial t} + \tilde{\alpha}(\tilde{m} - r(t))\frac{\partial P}{\partial r} + \frac{1}{2}\sigma^2\frac{\partial^2 P}{\partial r^2} - r(t)P(t,\ T) = 0 \qquad (2.115)$$

subject to the boundary condition $P(r(T),\ T,\ T) = 1$. In Chapter 4, we show how to solve this PDE.

NOTES

1. Cox and Ross [1976] motivated the idea of using "risk-neutral distribution" for valuing contingent claims in complete markets. Harrison and Pliska [1981, 1983] and Back and Pliska [1991] extend the results in Harrison and Kreps [1979].

2. The problem is more complex, of course, as true asset return distributions are seldom observable.

3. The results in this chapter continue to hold if probability measures are defined at any future time, too, using the definitions of conditional probabilities under the filtration $\mathcal{F}_t$.

CHAPTER 3

Valuing Interest Rate and Credit Derivatives: Basic Pricing Frameworks

T he use of interest rate derivatives and credit derivatives has grown at a staggering pace over the past decade. Used by virtually all market participants, from large corporations to universal banks to hedge funds, these derivatives allow corporations and financial institutions to hedge unwanted risks and to diversify asset holdings in an efficient manner. Table 3.1 gives the total outstanding notional amounts of single-currency interest rate derivatives in the over-the-counter (OTC) market from June 1998 until June 2006. Over the past eight years, the total notional amount has grown from approximately $42 trillion to $262 trillion at the annual growth rate of 25.59 percent. Table 3.2 gives the breakdown of the notional value of the single-currency interest rate derivatives by instrument, counterparty, and currency at the end of June 2006. The top four currencies that dominate the OTC interest rate derivative market are euro, U.S. dollar, yen, and pound sterling.

Though credit derivatives entered the financial markets at least a decade after interest rate derivatives, they have also grown at an extremely rapid pace. More than half of the credit derivative market is dominated by credit default swaps. Table 3.3 gives the total outstanding notional value of credit default swaps broken down by the long and short positions held by the type of institutions and by the maturity of the contract at the end of June 2006. In the past five years, the total notional value of credit default swaps has grown from less than $1 trillion in 2001 to more than $20 trillion at the end of June 2006. The $20 trillion notional amount is divided as approximately two-thirds in single-name credit default swaps and approximately one-third in multiname credit default swaps.

This chapter introduces basic pricing frameworks for valuing interest rate and credit derivatives. We consider both the exchange-traded and the OTC derivatives, including futures on time deposits (e.g., Eurodollar and Euribor futures), bond futures (e.g., T-bill, T-note, and T-bond futures), bond options, forward rate agreements, interest rate swaps, interest rate

TABLE 3.1 Total Outstanding Notional
Amounts of Single-Currency Interest Rate
Derivatives (in millions of U.S. dollars)

Jun 98	$ 42,368,396
Dec 98	$ 50,014,688
Jun 99	$ 54,071,504
Dec 99	$ 60,090,932
Jun 00	$ 64,124,688
Dec 00	$ 64,667,584
Jun 01	$ 67,465,400
Dec 01	$ 77,567,656
Jun 02	$ 89,954,608
Dec 02	$101,657,672
Jun 03	$121,799,272
Dec 03	$141,990,560
Jun 04	$164,626,336
Dec 04	$190,501,952
Jun 05	$204,795,264
Dec 05	$211,970,496
Jun 06	$262,296,160

Source: The web site of the Bank for International
Settlements. http://www.bis.org/statistics/
derdetailed.htm.

options (e.g., caps, floors, and collars), swaptions, and credit default swaps. The chapter describes important features of these derivatives and highlights the underlying relationships among derivative prices. The chapter also demonstrates the use of the risk-neutral measure and the forward measure for pricing these derivatives and provides general results that hold under all term structure models.

For example, we show how a futures contract on a coupon bond can be considered a portfolio of futures contracts on zero-coupon bonds. Though formulas to price the futures on a zero-coupon bond are given in various chapters under different term structure models, this chapter demonstrates how these prices can be combined to obtain the quoted price of the T-bond futures in the presence of features like accrued interest, conversion factor, and so forth. As another example, we show how the price of a futures contract on a time deposit (such as Eurodollar and Euribor futures) can be obtained by using the risk-neutral expectation of the *inverse* of a zero-coupon bond price. Since this expectation can be derived in closed-form for affine and quadratic term structure models, it allows for obtaining the analytical solution to the price of futures on a time deposit under these

TABLE 3.2 Notional Amounts Outstanding at End of June 2006 of Interest Rate Derivatives by Instrument, Counterparty, and Currency (in millions of U.S. dollars)

Instrument/ Counter-party	Total	U.S. Dollar	Euro	Japanese Yen	Pound Sterling	Swiss Franc	Canadian Dollar	Swedish Krona	Australian Dollar	Hong Kong Dollar	Norwegian Krone	Danish Krone	New Zealand Dollar	Residual
Forward rate agreements	18,117,140	7,290,265	4,808,519	273,978	1,587,816	423,963	52,567	1,540,437	123,552	425	347,699	28,204	0	1,639,715
with reporting dealers	9,653,372	3,474,095	3,129,293	195,640	952,714	344,821	23,902	763,776	47,690	0	126,950	23,426	0	571,065
with other financial institutions	7,692,043	3,379,594	1,536,863	59,661	623,303	72,926	23,675	693,553	75,131	425	173,392	4,603	0	1,048,917
with nonfinancial institutions	771,726	436,573	142,364	18,676	11,798	6,216	4,990	83,108	730	0	47,357	175	0	19,739
Interest rate swaps	207,323,200	65,156,932	83,698,016	28,833,098	15,321,758	3,092,455	1,856,919	1,759,213	815,786	300,267	207,125	200,408	18,831	6,062,392
with reporting dealers	87,329,792	28,150,828	33,565,760	13,396,182	6,214,589	1,249,378	797,527	793,131	244,602	135,351	96,979	108,339	8,014	2,569,112
with other financial institutions	92,981,872	27,288,786	39,673,352	12,133,533	6,981,393	1,438,917	811,904	780,481	509,396	140,948	84,207	51,495	10,817	3,076,643
with nonfinancial institutions	27,011,526	9,717,315	10,458,912	3,303,385	2,125,776	404,159	247,490	185,601	61,788	23,968	25,939	40,574	0	416,619
Options sold	28,071,072	12,501,670	11,312,526	2,118,196	1,575,929	89,907	89,980	84,952	26,082	12,662	4,819	3,188	718	250,443
with reporting dealers	17,579,320	7,658,757	7,495,208	1,285,642	910,786	37,915	37,005	23,886	4,445	7,659	3,392	2,009	112	112,494
with other financial institutions	7,615,226	3,355,719	2,981,204	576,400	471,144	34,476	45,032	31,293	17,809	2,979	633	672	596	97,269

(continued)

TABLE 3.2 (*continued*)

Instrument/Counterparty	Total	U.S. Dollar	Euro	Japanese Yen	Pound Sterling	Swiss Franc	Canadian Dollar	Swedish Krona	Australian Dollar	Hong Kong Dollar	Norwegian Krone	Danish Krone	New Zealand Dollar	Residual
with nonfinancial institutions	2,876,527	1,487,194	836,116	256,153	194,000	17,516	7,943	29,775	3,828	2,024	794	507	0	40,677
Options bought with reporting dealers	26,275,172	10,590,261	11,396,557	2,269,972	1,518,551	76,733	84,866	102,144	20,735	12,900	5,638	2,674	414	193,727
with other financial institutions	17,401,476	7,232,209	7,722,423	1,276,091	939,095	33,872	38,034	44,786	2,788	7,965	3,013	1,555	0	99,645
with nonfinancial institutions	6,799,812	2,589,052	2,948,952	671,134	399,497	34,833	40,687	16,340	14,641	2,997	1,456	287	414	79,522
with nonfinancial institutions	2,073,885	769,001	725,185	322,744	179,960	8,028	6,145	41,018	3,306	1,938	1,169	832	0	14,559
Total options	36,855,848	15,646,454	15,100,271	3,107,308	2,169,544	130,752	137,330	152,764	43,202	17,751	7,255	4,081	1,071	338,065
Total contracts	262,296,160	88,093,632	103,606,808	32,214,372	19,079,112	3,647,163	2,046,808	3,452,404	982,537	318,442	562,079	232,691	19,902	8,040,210

While data on total options are shown on a net basis, separate data on options sold and options bought are recorded on a gross basis, i.e., not adjusted for interdealer double counting.

Source: The web site of the Bank for International Settlements. http://www.bis.org/statistics/derdetailed.htm.

TABLE 3.3 Credit Default Swaps Market Notional Amounts Outstanding at End of June 2006 (in millions of U.S. dollars)

	Notional Amounts Outstanding Bought	Notional Amounts Outstanding Sold	Total
Total CDS Contracts	15,728,650	15,232,121	20,352,240
Reporting dealers	10,669,920	10,547,142	10,608,531
Other financial institutions	4,656,774	4,360,374	9,017,148
Banks and security firms	22,555,167	2,469,618	5,024,785
Insurance and financial guaranty firms	228,580	68,164	296,749
Other	1,873,020	1,822,592	3,695,614
Nonfinancial institutions	401,954	324,607	726,561
Maturity of 1 year or less	1,326,477	1,167,745	1,573,542
Maturity over 1 year and up to 5 years	9,994,347	9,910,173	13,019,081
Maturity over 5 years	4,407,825	4,154,201	5,759,336
Single-name instruments	10,646,238	10,447,877	13,873,444
Multiname instruments	5,082,412	4,784,244	6,478,796

Source: The website of Bank of International Settlements. http://www.bis.org/statistics/derdetailed.htm.

models. As another example, though we provide the formulas for the prices of options on zero-coupon bonds in Chapters 4 through 10 under different affine and quadratic term structure models, this chapter demonstrates how yield options such as caps and floors can be considered portfolios of options on zero-coupon bonds and, thus, can be valued using the formulas of options on zero-coupon bonds given in Chapters 4 through 10.

Hence, this chapter provides important links between the theoretical formulas (and discrete-time interest rate trees given in various chapters) and the valuation of interest derivatives used in practice. Though many exotic products exist in the interest rate derivative market, our main focus here is the pricing of *basic* interest rate derivatives using a variety of term structure models and interest rate trees. A good understanding of the valuation of basic derivatives products is essential before pricing more exotic products with appropriate modifications and extensions.

This chapter also introduces the reduced-form pricing approach for pricing credit derivatives, such as credit default swaps, spread options, total return swaps, and others.[1] Unlike the structural models of risky debt, the reduced-form approach can be used to directly model default probabilities without requiring an endogenous relationship with the firm's underlying asset price process. This chapter presents some basic pricing results that are applied later in Chapters 9 and 10 to price credit default swaps using multifactor affine and quadratic models.

As shown by Duffie and Singleton [2003], the reduced-form approach allows using much of the modern technology of dynamic term structure theory for valuing a variety of credit derivative instruments. Though this is the core subject matter of the third book in this trilogy, a basic introduction given here and some applications shown in Chapters 9 and 10 demonstrate how the main results in this book, including analytical solutions and interest rate trees, can be applied for valuing credit derivatives.

The final section of this chapter introduces a new taxonomy for term structure models that classifies all models as either fundamental models or preference-free models. The preference-free models are further classified as single-plus models, double-plus models, and triple-plus models. The new classification allows making subtle distinctions between time-homogeneous models and preference-free models. Though preference-free models are generally also time-inhomogeneous (e.g., Heath, Jarrow, and Morton [1992]/LIBOR market model[2]/String model[3]), we introduce a new class of *single-plus* models that are both preference-free and time-homogeneous.

EURODOLLAR AND OTHER TIME DEPOSIT FUTURES

For centuries, futures contracts traded primarily on physical commodities such as precious metals, agriculture, wood products, and oil. The introduction of exchange-traded derivative contracts on financial securities in the 1970s coincided with the publications of highly influential papers on how to value these derivatives. A futures contract is an agreement between two parties to trade an asset at some future date for a fixed price agreed upon today. Due to features such as standardization and marking to market, futures contracts are more liquid and easier to trade than forward contracts. Popular interest-rate futures contracts in the United States and Europe include Eurodollar futures and futures on Treasury bonds, notes, and bills. Short-term interest-rate futures contracts, such as T-bills and Eurodollars, trade on the Chicago Mercantile Exchange (CME), while long-term contracts, such as T-notes and T-bonds, trade on the Chicago Board of Trade (CBOT). Table 3.4 displays the denomination, the name of the exchange, and the open interest (the number of contracts outstanding) on December 13, 2005, for the different interest rate futures contracts. As can be seen from this table, the explosive growth of the Eurodollar futures contract has come at the expense of the T-bill futures contract, which has virtually

TABLE 3.4 Interest Rate Futures

Contract	Denomination	Exchange	Open Interest December 12, 2005
U.S. T-Bills	$1,000,000	CME	0
Eurodollars	$1,000,000	CME	9,477,654
U.S. T-Bonds	$ 100,000	CBOT	547,263
U.S. T-Notes	$ 100,000	CBOT	3,219,171

Note: CME = Chicago Mercantile Exchange; CBOT = Chicago Board of Trade.
Source: CME and CBOT web sites.

faded to extinction, even though the T-bill cash market continues to be the most liquid short-term fixed-income market in the world. The number of contracts outstanding on T-notes and T-bonds are more than 3 million and half a million, respectively, while the number of contracts outstanding on Eurodollars was 9.5 million on December 13, 2005.

Interest rate futures can be classified into two types. The first type of futures contracts is based on some time deposit, such as the Eurodollar futures based on the Eurodollar deposits. The second type of futures contracts is based on zero-coupon bonds and coupon bonds (these are described in the next three sections). These contracts include T-bill, T-note, and T-bond futures and similar bill/bond futures denominated in other currencies. The basic difference between futures on time deposits and futures on bills/bonds is that the former are based upon add-on instruments, while the latter are based upon discount instruments. This difference becomes crucial in the way these contracts are priced, as we demonstrate later in this chapter.

This section focuses on the first type of futures contracts, based on time deposits. Large banks in different countries offer time deposits in selected currencies over a range of maturities. The most liquid and actively traded futures contract on a time deposit is the Eurodollar futures contract, based upon deposits denominated in U.S. dollars in a U.S. or foreign bank located outside the United States. Other important futures contracts on time deposits include the Euribor futures, based on euro currency time deposits; Euroyen futures, based on Japanese yen time deposits; and Short Sterling futures, based on sterling time deposits.

The interest rates on the Eurodollar deposits are given as the London Interbank Offer Rates (LIBOR), which are the *ask* rates at which large international banks lend U.S. dollar deposits of various maturities to each other.[4] The three-month Eurodollar futures contract is based upon a hypothetical three-month Eurodollar deposit with a face value of $1 million. The contract expires in the months of March, June, September, and December, as well as all four nearest months, with maturities extending up to ten years into the future. The Eurodollar futures contract is settled in cash on the second London business day prior to the third Wednesday of the delivery month. The huge success of the three-month Eurodollar futures contract has largely resulted from complimentary growth of the over-the-counter LIBOR-based derivative products, such as interest rate swaps, interest rate options (caps, floors, etc.), and forward rate agreements (FRAs). Traders often use Eurodollar futures to hedge against the exposure in interest rate swaps and other LIBOR-based products.

Virtually all futures on time deposits are cash settled and are based upon a hypothetical investment in the time deposit at time S, where S is the expiration date of the futures contract. Let $L(S, T)$ be the discretely compounded rate on a time deposit that invests the money for $U = T - S$ years at time S. Since $L(S, T)$ is quoted as a discrete rate using the day-count basis applicable to money market rates, the relationship between $L(S, T)$ and a hypothetical \$1 face-value zero-coupon bond price can be given as follows:

$$1 + L(S, T)\hat{U} = \frac{1}{P(S, T)} \tag{3.1}$$

where $\hat{U} =$ the accrual factor calculated using actual/360 day-count basis.

For example, assuming that the three-month time deposit has 91 days to maturity in a year with 365 days, $U = 91/365 = 0.2493$, and $\hat{U} = 91/360 = 0.2528$. Typically for money market instruments, $\hat{U} = U \times 365/360$, where $U = T - S$.

At the expiration date S, the quoted settlement price of the futures contract on a time deposit is calculated as follows:

$$P_F^{TD}(S, S, T) = 100(1 - L(S, T)) \tag{3.2}$$

The current futures price $P_F^{TD}(t, S, T)$ is calculated by the application of the risk-neutral valuation method and is demonstrated later in this section. Using the current futures price, the current futures *rate* is given by the following equation:

$$P_F^{TD}(t, S, T) = 100(1 - L_F(t, S, T)) \tag{3.3}$$

subject to the boundary condition $L_F(S, S, T) = L(S, T)$. Before we show how to solve the current futures price $P_F^{TD}(t, S, T)$, and hence, the current futures rate $L_F(t, S, T)$, let us understand the mechanism of incurring gains and losses on a futures position. The gains and losses are computed using the change in the *contract price*. The contract price is related to the current futures price, as follows:

$$\text{Contract Price} = CP(t, S, T) = \frac{F}{100}(100 - 0.25(100 - P_F^{TD}(t, S, T))$$

(3.4)

where F is the notional principal of the futures contract.

Example 3.1 Consider a Eurodollar futures contract expiring in S years, with a time t ($t < S$) futures price quoted at $P_F^{TD}(t, S, T) = 96$. Eurodollar futures have a notional principal, or $F = \$1,000,000$. The time t quarterly compounded futures rate $L_F(t, S, T)$ is calculated using equation (3.3) and equals 0.04, or 4 percent. Consider a change in the futures price after an infinitesimally small interval h to $P_F^{TD}(t + h, S, T) = 96.01$. The futures rate $L_F(t + h, S, T)$ becomes 0.0399, or 3.99 percent, using equation (3.3). The change in the contract price due to the change in the futures price equals:

$$\Delta\text{Contract Price} = \Delta CP(t, S, T)$$

$$= \frac{1,000,000}{100}(100 - 0.25(100 - 96.01))$$

$$- \frac{1,000,000}{100}(100 - 0.25(100 - 96)) \qquad (3.5)$$

$$= \$990,025 - \$990,000$$

$$= \$25$$

Hence, the gain on the futures position equals $25, when the futures price moves up by 0.01, or by one tick.

Next we describe the notional principal, the tick size, the change in value of the contract price due to one tick change in the value of the futures price (computed using equation (3.4)), and the definition of the three-month time deposit rate at time S for four different futures contracts on time deposits.

Eurodollar Futures
$F = \$1,000,000$
Tick size $= 0.01$
Change in $CP(t, S, T)$ due to 0.01 (or one tick) change in futures price $= \$25$.
$L(S, T) =$ three-month LIBOR rate observed on two business days prior to the third Wednesday of the contract month.

Euribor Futures
$F = €1,000,000$
Tick size $= 0.005$
Change in $CP(t, S, T)$ due to 0.005 (or one tick) change in futures price $=$
€12.50.
$L(S, T) =$ three-month Euribor offered rate by the European Bankers Federation on two business days prior to the third Wednesday of the contract month.

Euroyen Futures
$F = ¥100,000,000$
Tick size $= 0.005$
Change in $CP(t, S, T)$ due to 0.005 (or one tick) change in futures price $=$
¥1,250.
$L(S, T) =$ three-month TIBOR (Tokyo Interbank Offered Rate) observed on two business days prior to the third Wednesday of the contract month.

Short Sterling Futures
$F = £500,000$
Tick size $= 0.01$
Change in $CP(t, S, T)$ due to 0.01 (or one tick) change in futures price $=$
£12.50.
$L(S, T) =$ LIBOR rate for three-month sterling deposits observed on the third Wednesday of the contract month.

Valuing Futures on a Time Deposit

Futures on time deposits can be priced using the risk-neutral valuation method introduced in the previous chapter. As shown in the previous chapter, all assets provide the *same* expected return equal to the riskless rate, under the risk-neutral measure. An immediate corollary to this statement is that any zero investment portfolio must provide a zero *expected* gain (or loss), regardless of the risk it contains, under the risk-neutral measure. If a zero investment portfolio allowed a nonzero expected gain (or loss), then adding this portfolio to any security with a nonzero price will allow making a new portfolio with the expected return different from the riskless rate under the risk-neutral measure.

Now consider initiating a position in a futures contract at any time t and holding it for an infinitesimal interval dt. Since initiating a futures position is always *costless*, the time t investment is zero. Under the assumption of continuous marking to market, the expected change in the contract position (which defines the expected gain or loss on the futures position) must be zero under the risk-neutral measure, or:

$$\tilde{E}_t\big(dCP(t,\ S,\ T)\big) = \tilde{E}_t\big(CP(t+dt,\ S,\ T) - CP(t,\ S,\ T)\big) = 0 \qquad (3.6)$$

Equation (3.6) implies:

$$CP(t,\ S,\ T) = \tilde{E}_t\big(CP(t+dt,\ S,\ T)\big) \qquad (3.7)$$

Due to the linear relationship between the contract price and the quoted futures price in equation (3.4), equation (3.7) immediately implies the following:

$$P_F^{TD}(t,\ S,\ T) = \tilde{E}_t\big(P_F^{TD}(t+dt,\ S,\ T)\big) \qquad (3.8)$$

Using iterated expectations, equation (3.8) implies that the futures price is a martingale under the risk-neutral measure, or:

$$P_F^{TD}(t,\ S,\ T) = \tilde{E}_t\big(P_F^{TD}(S,\ S,\ T)\big) \qquad (3.9)$$

Using equations (3.1) and (3.2), the futures price at the expiration date S can be given as follows:

$$P_F^{TD}(S,\ S,\ T) = \frac{100}{\hat{U}}\left(1 + \hat{U} - \frac{1}{P(S,\ T)}\right) \qquad (3.10)$$

where $\hat{U}$ is the accrual factor calculated using actual/360 day-count basis. Typically for money market instruments, $\hat{U} = U \times 365/360$ and $U = T - S$.

Substituting equation (3.10) in equation (3.9), we get:

$$P_F^{TD}(t,\ S,\ T) = \frac{100}{\hat{U}}\left(1 + \hat{U} - \tilde{E}_t\left(\frac{1}{P(S,\ T)}\right)\right) \qquad (3.11)$$

The time t risk-neutral expectation of the inverse of the zero-coupon bond price plays a key role in the valuation of the futures on time deposits. Note that this equation applies to all major futures contracts on time deposits including Eurodollar futures, Euribor futures, Euroyen futures, and Short Sterling futures.

Equation (3.11) can be given another interpretation by rewriting it as follows:

$$P_F^{TD}(t,\ S,\ T) = \frac{100}{\hat{U}}\big(1 + \hat{U} - P_F^I(t,\ S,\ T)\big) \qquad (3.12)$$

where

$$P_F^I(t,\ S,\ T) = \tilde{E}_t\left(\frac{1}{P(S,\ T)}\right) \qquad (3.13)$$

The price $P_F^I(t, S, T)$ can be interpreted as the current price of a futures contract written on a hypothetical asset, which at the expiration date S is worth the *inverse* of a $1 face-value zero-coupon bond maturing at time T, or $1/P(S, T)$. Since the futures price on this hypothetical asset also must be a martingale under the risk-neutral measure, equation (3.13) follows that logic.

As we demonstrate in Chapters 4 through 10 of this book, the risk-neutral expectation of the inverse of the zero-coupon bond price is quite easy to compute for virtually all affine and quadratic classes of models. In general, if the bond price solution exists, so does the solution for the risk-neutral expectation of the inverse of the zero-coupon bond price. We derive the futures price solutions for all affine and quadratic term structure models in the literature using equation (3.11).

Convexity Bias

Convexity bias is the difference between the futures rate and the forward rate on a time deposit. Equating (3.3) and (3.11), the time t futures rate for the term S to T is given as follows:

$$
\begin{aligned}
L_F(t, S, T) &= \frac{1}{\hat{U}} \left(\tilde{E}_t \left(\frac{1}{P(S, T)} \right) - 1 \right) \\
&= \frac{1}{\hat{U}} (P_F^I(t, S, T) - 1)
\end{aligned}
\tag{3.14}
$$

The time t forward rate between time S and T can be defined using the ratio of two zero-coupon bond prices as follows:

$$
P(t, T)(1 + L_f(t, S, T)\hat{U}) = P(t, S)
\tag{3.15}
$$

or

$$
L_f(t, S, T) = \frac{1}{\hat{U}} \left(\frac{P(t, S)}{P(t, T)} - 1 \right)
\tag{3.16}
$$

The convexity bias is given as the difference between the futures rate and the forward rate as follows:

$$
\begin{aligned}
Convexity\ Bias &= L_F(t, S, T) - L_f(t, S, T) \\
&= \frac{1}{\hat{U}} \left(\tilde{E}_t \left(\frac{1}{P(S, T)} \right) - \frac{P(t, S)}{P(t, T)} \right) \\
&= \frac{1 + L_F(t, S, T)\hat{U}}{\hat{U}} \left(1 - \frac{P(t, S)}{P(t, T)P_F^I(t, S, T)} \right)
\end{aligned}
\tag{3.17}
$$

We compute the convexity bias for different affine and quadratic term structure models given in Chapters 4 through 10 of this book. In general, convexity bias is positive and it depends on a number of factors, including the length to the expiration date, speed of mean reversion, volatility of the state variables, and so forth.

TREASURY BILL FUTURES

The asset underlying a Treasury bill futures contract is the 13-week Treasury bill worth $1,000,000 in face value. Treasury bill futures trade on the CME, with contract expiration months in March, June, September, and December, and the nearest two months. Despite the large size of the U.S. T-bill market, the T-bill futures market has shrunk considerably, losing market share to the Eurodollar futures market. In recent years, T-bill futures have settled via cash, rather than physical delivery, which used to be the norm when these contracts were first introduced. Unlike the futures on time deposits, which do not converge to any underlying instrument, the price of the T-bill futures converges to the 13-week Treasury bill. This simplifies some of the calculations for valuing T-bill futures.

Let $R(S, T)$ be the 13-week quarterly compounded T-bill yield observed at time S. The relationship between $R(S, T)$ and the price of the 13-week T-bill is given as follows:

$$1 - R(S, T)\hat{U} = P(S, T) \tag{3.18}$$

whereas in the previous section, $\hat{U}$ is the accrual factor calculated using actual/360 day-count basis, and $U = T - S$. As an example, assuming that the 13-week T-bill has 91 days to maturity in a year with 365 days, $U = 91/365 = 0.2493$, and $\hat{U} = 91/360 = 0.2528$.

At the expiration date S, the quoted settlement price of the futures contract is calculated as follows:

$$P_F^{T-bill}(S, S, T) = 100(1 - R(S, T)) \tag{3.19}$$

The current futures price $P_F^{T-bill}(t, S, T)$ is calculated by the application of the risk-neutral valuation method and is demonstrated later in this section. Using the current futures price, the current futures *rate* is given by:

$$P_F^{T-bill}(t, S, T) = 100(1 - R_F(t, S, T)) \tag{3.20}$$

subject to the boundary condition $R_F(S, S, T) = R(S, T)$. The gains and losses on T-bill futures occur exactly as they do for futures on time deposits.

The contract price for T-bill futures is calculated as follows:

$$Contract\ Price = CP(t,\ S,\ T) = 10,000\big(100 - 0.25(100 - P_F^{T-bill}(t,\ S,\ T))\big) \tag{3.21}$$

For example, on July 2, 2003, the quoted futures price for the September T-bill futures contract was $P_F^{T-bill}(t, S, T) = 99.14$. According to equation (3.20), the quoted futures rate $R_F(t, S, T)$ equals $100 - 99.14 = 0.86$. Also, the contract price is given as $10,000(100 - 0.25 \times (100 - 99.14)) = \$997,850$. The tick size for the T-bill futures equals 0.005. The gain or loss on the T-bill futures is given by a change in the contract price. The change in the contract price $CP(t, S, T)$ due to 0.005 (or one tick) change in futures price equals \$12.50.

Valuing T-Bill Futures

Using the same argument used for the case of futures on time deposits, the futures price of a T-bill is a martingale under the risk-neutral measure, or:

$$P_F^{T-bill}(t,\ S,\ T) = \tilde{E}_t\big(P_F^{T-bill}(S,\ S,\ T)\big) \tag{3.22}$$

Using equations (3.18) and (3.19), the futures price at the expiration date S can be given as follows:

$$P_F^{T-bill}(S,\ S,\ T) = \frac{100}{\hat{U}}\big(\hat{U} - 1 + P(S,\ T)\big) \tag{3.23}$$

where $\hat{U}$ is the accrual factor calculated using actual/360 day-count basis and $U = T - S$. Substituting equation (3.23) in equation (3.22), we get:

$$P_F^{T-bill}(t,\ S,\ T) = \frac{100}{\hat{U}}\big(\hat{U} - 1 + \tilde{E}_t(P(S,\ T))\big) \tag{3.24}$$

The time t risk-neutral expectation of the zero-coupon bond price plays a key role in valuation of T-bill futures. As we demonstrate in Chapters 4 through 10 of this book, the risk-neutral expectation of the zero-coupon bond price is easy to compute for the affine and quadratic term structure models. In general, if the bond price solution exists, so does the solution for the risk-neutral expectation of the zero-coupon bond price.

Equation (3.24) can be given another interpretation by rewriting it as follows:

$$P_F^{T-bill}(t,\ S,\ T) = \frac{100}{\hat{U}}\big(\hat{U} - 1 + P_F(t,\ S,\ T)\big) \tag{3.25}$$

where

$$P_F(t, S, T) = \tilde{E}_t(P(S, T)) \qquad (3.26)$$

The price $P_F(t, S, T)$ can be interpreted as the current price of a futures contract written on a \$1 face-value zero-coupon bond maturing at time T, as demonstrated later in equations (3.40) through (3.42). Since a futures price must be a martingale under the risk-neutral measure, equation (3.26) follows immediately. The solutions of the futures price based on a \$1 face-value zero-coupon bond under alternative term structure models from various chapters of this book can be used to obtain the price of T-bill futures in equation (3.25).

Convexity Bias

Convexity bias is the difference between the futures rate and the forward rate on T-bills. Equating (3.20) and (3.24), the time t futures rate for T-bills for the term S to T is given as follows:

$$R_F(t, S, T) = \frac{1 - \tilde{E}_t(P(S, T))}{\hat{U}} \qquad (3.27)$$

The time t forward rate for T-bills between time S and T can be defined using the ratio of two zero-coupon bond prices as follows:

$$P(t, S)\left(1 - R_f(t, S, T)\hat{U}\right) = P(t, T) \qquad (3.28)$$

or

$$R_f(t, S, T) = \frac{1}{\hat{U}}\left(1 - \frac{P(t, T)}{P(t, S)}\right) \qquad (3.29)$$

The convexity bias is given as the difference between the futures rate and the forward rate as follows:

$$\begin{aligned}
\textit{Convexity Bias} &= R_F(t, S, T) - R_f(t, S, T) \\
&= \frac{1}{\hat{U}}\left(\frac{P(t, T)}{P(t, S)} - \tilde{E}_t(P(S, T))\right) \qquad (3.30) \\
&\frac{1 - R_F(t, S, T)\hat{U}}{\hat{U}}\left(\frac{P(t, T)}{P(t, S)P_F(t, S, T)} - 1\right)
\end{aligned}$$

Similar to the case of futures on time deposits, the convexity bias for futures on T-bills is generally positive, and it depends on a number of factors, including the length until the expiration date, the volatility of the state variables, and so forth.

TREASURY BOND FUTURES

Treasury bond futures are the most popular long-term interest rate futures. These futures trade on the Chicago Board of Trade and expire in the months of March, June, September, and December in addition to extra months scheduled by the CBOT based upon the demand for these contracts. The last trading day for these contracts is the business day prior to the last seven days of the expiration month. Delivery can take place any time during the delivery month, and the party on the short side of the contract initiates it. The first delivery day is the first business day of the delivery month. As with most other futures contracts, delivery seldom takes place. The uncertainty about the delivery date poses a risk to the futures buyer that cannot be hedged away.

The underlying asset in a Treasury bond futures contract is any $100,000 face-value government bond that has more than 15 years to maturity on the first day of delivery month and that is noncallable for 15 years from this day. The quoted price of the T-bond futures contract is based on the assumption that the underlying bond has a 6 percent coupon rate, but the CBOT also permits delivery of bonds with coupon rates other than 6 percent. In fact, a wide range of coupons and maturities qualify for delivery. To put all eligible bonds on a more or less equal footing, the CBOT has developed comprehensive tables to compute an adjustment factor, called the *conversion factor*, that converts the quoted futures price to an invoice price applicable for delivery. The invoice price for the deliverable Treasury bond (not including accrued interest) at the future's expiration date S is the bond's conversion factor times the futures price.

$$Invoice\ Price = P_F^{T\text{-}bond}(S,\ S) \times CF \qquad (3.31)$$

where

$P_F^{T\text{-}bond}(S,\ S) =$ quoted T-bond futures price at time S, with expiration
　　　　　　　　date S
　　$CF =$ conversion factor

The T-bond futures price quotes do not include accrued interest. Therefore, the delivery cash price is always higher than the invoice price by the amount of the accrued interest on the deliverable bond.

$$\begin{aligned} Delivery\ Cash\ Price &= Invoice\ Price + Accrued\ Interest \\ &= P_F^{T\text{-}bond}(S,\ S) \times CF + AI \end{aligned} \qquad (3.32)$$

where AI is the accrued interest.

Example 3.2 Suppose on November 12, 2005, the quoted price of the 10 percent coupon bond maturing on August 5, 2019, is 97-08 (or $97,250 on a $100,000 face value). Since government bonds pay coupons semiannually, a coupon of $5,000 would be paid on February 5 and August 5 of each year. The number of days between August 5, 2005, and November 12, 2005 (not including August 5, 2005 and including November 12, 2005), is 99, whereas the number of days between August 5, 2005, and February 5, 2006 (not including August 5, 2005, and including February 5, 2006), is 181 days. Therefore, with the actual/actual day-count convention used for Treasury bonds, the accrued interest from August 5, 2005, to November 12, 2005, is:

$$AI = \$5,000 \times \frac{99}{181} = \$2,734.81$$

If the preceding bond is the deliverable bond underlying the futures contract, then the cash price in equation (3.32) will be greater than the invoice price by an amount equal to the accrued interest of $2,734.81.

Conversion Factor

A bond's conversion factor is the price at which the bond would yield 6 percent to maturity or to first call date (if callable) on the first delivery date of the T-bond futures expiration month. The bond maturity is rounded down to the nearest zero, three, six, or nine months. If the maturity of the bond is rounded down to zero months, then the conversion factor is:

$$CF_0 = \frac{c}{2}\left[\frac{1}{0.03} - \frac{1}{0.03(1.03)^{2n}}\right] + \frac{1}{(1.03)^{2n}} \qquad (3.33)$$

where c is the coupon *rate* and n is the number of years to maturity. If the maturity of the bond is rounded down to three months, then the conversion factor is:

$$CF_3 = \frac{CF_0 + \frac{c}{2}}{(1.03)^{\frac{1}{2}}} - \frac{c}{4} \qquad (3.34)$$

If the maturity of the bond is rounded down to six months, then the conversion factor is:

$$CF_6 = \frac{c}{2}\left[\frac{1}{0.03} - \frac{1}{0.03(1.03)^{2n+1}}\right] + \frac{1}{(1.03)^{2n+1}} \qquad (3.35)$$

And, finally, if the maturity of the bond is rounded down to nine months, then the conversion factor is:

$$CF_9 = \frac{CF_6 + \dfrac{c}{2}}{(1.03)^{\frac{1}{2}}} - \frac{c}{4} \tag{3.36}$$

The formulas for CF_0 and CF_6 have the same format, as do the formulas for CF_3 and CF_9. Therefore, we can combine equations (3.33) and (3.35) into one single equation that has the following form:

$$CF_0 = \frac{c}{2}\left[\frac{1}{0.03} - \frac{1}{0.03(1.03)^m}\right] + \frac{1}{(1.03)^m} \tag{3.37}$$

where m is the number of semiannual periods to maturity.

Thus, instead of rounding the bond's maturity down to zero, three, six, or nine months, we can just round it down to zero or three months. If the result is zero, then use equation (3.37); otherwise, use equation (3.34). The conversion factor always increases with the coupon rate, holding the maturity constant. If the coupon rate is more than 6 percent, then the conversion factor increases with maturity; but if the coupon rate is less than 6 percent, then the conversion factor decreases with maturity. The conversion factor equals 1 when the coupon rate equals 6 percent, regardless of the maturity.

Example 3.3   Consider a futures contract expiring in the month of December with the underlying deliverable bond given in Example 3.2. Assume that the bond is delivered on the first day of the expiration month, December 1, 2005. On this day, the bond has 13 years 8 months 5 days to maturity. Rounding the bond's maturity on the delivery day down to the nearest zero or three months, the maturity is 13 years 6 months. We treat this as 27 six-month periods. Applying equation (3.37) for $m = 27$, we get:

$$CF_0 = \frac{0.10}{2}\left[\frac{1}{0.03} - \frac{1}{0.03(1.03)^{27}}\right] + \frac{1}{(1.03)^{27}} = 1.4$$

Suppose the quoted futures price on this bond is 98-04 (or $98,125 on a $100,000 face value contract). The time elapsed since the previous coupon payment date, August 5, 2005, to the expiration date of the futures contract, December 1, 2005, equals 118 days. Hence, the accrued interest on the bond equals:

$$\$5,000 \times \frac{118}{181} = \$3,259.67$$

Using equation (3.32), the delivery cash price of the T-bond futures contract is:

$$Delivery\ Cash\ Price = \$98,125 \times 1.4 + \$3,259.67 = \$140,634.67$$

Cheapest-to-Deliver Bond

The party with the short position in the T-bond futures contract can deliver any government bond that has more than 15 years to maturity and that is noncallable for 15 years from the delivery date. At any given day of the delivery month, there are about 30 bonds that the short side can deliver. So, which bond should the seller choose to deliver? The answer to this question can be understood as follows. On the delivery date, the seller receives:

$$Quoted\ Futures\ Price \times Conversion\ Factor + Accrued\ Interest$$

The cost of purchasing a bond to deliver is:

$$Quoted\ Bond\ Price + Accrued\ Interest$$

Hence, the seller will choose the *cheapest-to-deliver* bond, which is the bond for which the cost of delivery is lowest, where *cost of delivery* is defined as:

$$Cost\ of\ Delivery = Quoted\ Bond\ Price - Quoted\ Futures\ Price$$

$$\times Conversion\ Factor$$

$$= P - P_F^{T\text{-}bond}(S,\ S) \times CF \tag{3.38}$$

Example 3.4 illustrates the selection of the cheapest-to-deliver bond.

Example 3.4 Assume that the T-bond quoted futures price on the delivery day is 94.825 and that the party with the short position in the contract can choose to deliver from the bonds given in Table 3.5. The cost of delivering each of these bonds is given in Table 3.6.

Both tables give quoted bond price and quoted futures price in decimal form. Using equation (3.38), the cheapest-to-deliver bond is bond 4.

TABLE 3.5 Deliverable Bonds for the T-Bond Futures Contract

Bond	Maturity (years)	Coupon(%)	Quoted Bond Price P	Conversion Factor CF
1	$15\frac{1}{2}$	6.38	98.97	1.0375
2	18	6.00	97.50	1.0000
3	$16\frac{3}{4}$	7.00	99.38	1.0356
4	20	6.25	97.75	1.0289

TABLE 3.6   Cost of Delivery

Bond	Quoted Bond Price P	Quoted Futures Price FP	Conversion Factor CF	Cost of Delivery $P - (FP \times CF)$
1	98.97	94.825	1.0375	0.59
2	97.50	94.825	1.0000	2.68
3	99.38	94.825	1.0356	1.17
4	97.75	94.825	1.0289	0.19

Options Embedded in T-Bond Futures

A variety of options are embedded in T-bond futures. We have already discussed the cheapest-to-deliver option. The seller of the futures contract can also choose when to deliver the bond on the designated days in the delivery month, which is known as the *timing option*. Another option, known as the *wild card option*, makes the T-bond futures price lower than it would be without this option. This option arises from the fact that the T-bond futures market closes at 2:00 P.M. Chicago time, while the bonds continue trading until 4:00 P.M. Moreover, the individual on the short side of the futures contract does not have to notify the clearinghouse about her intention to deliver until 8:00 P.M. Thus, if the bond price declines between 2 and 4 P.M., the seller can notify the clearinghouse about her intention to deliver using the 2:00 P.M. futures price and make the delivery by buying the cheapest-to-deliver bond at a lower price after 2 P.M. Otherwise, the party with the short position keeps the position open and applies the same strategy the next day.

Valuing T-Bond Futures

Futures on a Zero-Coupon Bond   Just as zero-coupon bonds can be considered the building blocks of coupon bonds and bond portfolios, futures on zero-coupon bonds can be considered the building blocks of the CBOT's Treasury futures contracts on coupon bonds. Hence, even though futures on zero-coupon bonds don't exist, they must be modeled in order to price the other more complex futures contracts. A short (long) position in a futures contract on a zero-coupon bond gives the contract holder a right and an obligation to deliver (take delivery of) the underlying zero-coupon bond, unless the futures position is canceled before delivery by taking an opposite position. A futures contract is different from a forward contract in that it requires daily settlement of cash flows or *marking to market* the account every day. Before deriving the price of a futures contract, consider the price of a forward contract expiring at time S, written on a zero-coupon bond maturing at time T. The forward contract gives the holder of the short (long) position a right and an obligation to deliver (take delivery of) at date S the underlying zero-coupon bond maturing at time T. Since there are no intermediate cash flows related to a forward contract, it can be priced by using an arbitrage argument, as follows:

$$P_f(t, S, T) = \frac{P(t, T)}{P(t, S)} \qquad (3.39)$$

This relationship can be obtained by constructing a simple arbitrage portfolio that *replicates* the zero-coupon bond maturing at time T as follows: At time t, one buys $P_f(t, S, T)$ number of zero-coupon bonds maturing at time S and simultaneously enters into a long position into a forward contract expiring at time S, written on a zero-coupon bond maturing at time T. The initial dollar investment equals $P_f(t, S, T) \times P(t, S)$, which grows to equal $P_f(t, S, T)$ at time S. Since the amount $P_f(t, S, T)$ exactly equals the forward price, this amount is paid to take delivery of a zero-coupon bond maturing at time T. Hence, by the law of one price, the current price $P(t, T)$ of the zero-coupon bond maturing at time T must equal $P_f(t, S, T) \times P(t, S)$, which proves equation (3.39).

The intermediate cash flows related to marking to market of futures contracts make the price of futures contracts different from the price of corresponding forward contracts. Though this difference is small for short expiration dates, it can be substantial for longer expiration dates. The futures price can be determined by the application of risk-neutral valuation. Under the risk-neutral measure, all assets provide the *same* expected return equal to the riskless rate. An immediate corollary to this statement is that any zero-investment portfolio must provide a zero *expected* gain (or loss), regardless of the risk it contains. If a zero-investment portfolio allowed a nonzero expected gain (or loss), then adding this portfolio to any security with a nonzero price will result in a new portfolio with the expected return different from the riskless rate, under the risk-neutral measure.

Now consider initiating a position in a futures contract at any time t and holding it for an infinitesimal interval dt. Since initiating a futures position is always *costless*, the time t investment is zero. The expected gain on this position must be zero under the risk-neutral measure, or:

$$\tilde{E}_t[P_F(t + dt, S, T) - P_F(t, S, T)] = 0 \qquad (3.40)$$

where $P_F(t, S, T)$ equals time t price of a futures contract with delivery date S, written on a zero-coupon bond maturing on date T.

Equation (3.40) implies that the current futures price is the risk-neutral expectation of the futures price at the end of the next interval, or:

$$P_F(t, S, T) = \tilde{E}_t(P_F(t + dt, S, T)) \qquad (3.41)$$

We know that the futures price at the delivery date S must converge to the price of the underlying zero-coupon bond maturing at time T, or $P_F(S, S, T) = P(S, T)$. This, together with the law of iterated expectations, implies that current futures price is the risk-neutral expectation of the bond price $P(S, T)$, or:

$$P_F(t, S, T) = \tilde{E}_t(P_F(S, S, T)) = \tilde{E}_t(P(S, T)) \qquad (3.42)$$

Hence, the futures price is a martingale under the risk-neutral measure. The derivation of equation (3.42) did not require any assumptions about the stochastic processes underlying the bond market, so it remains valid in all economies in which the risk-neutral probability measure exists, or in all economies that do not allow riskless arbitrage.

Note that even though the futures price follows a martingale under the risk-neutral measure, the forward price defined in equation (3.39) does not follow a martingale under the risk-neutral measure. Though a forward contract is costless at the initiation time, due to the absence of marking to market over the next interval, the expected change in the value of a forward contract from time t to $t + dt$ under the risk-neutral measure is not given by the expected change in the forward price, but by the expected discounted value (discounted back from the delivery date S to $t + dt$) of the change in the forward price.

In equation (3.42), we give the time t price of a futures contract written on a zero-coupon bond as the risk-neutral expectation of the bond price $P(S, T)$. The delivery cash price of a futures contract on a coupon can be given as follows:

$$Delivery\ Cash\ Price = \sum_{i=1}^{n} C_i \times P(S, T_i) \qquad (3.43)$$

where C_i is the cash flow from the coupon bond at time T_i.

If the T-bond futures price was based upon a single coupon bond, then equation (3.43) could be used to get the futures price. Since equation (3.43) would give the delivery cash price of the coupon bond at time $t = S$, equation (3.32) would hold at time $t = S$, or:

$$Delivery\ Cash\ Price = \sum_{i=1}^{n} C_i P(S, T_i) = P_F^{T\text{-}bond}(S, S) \times CF + AI \qquad (3.44)$$

Taking the time t risk-neutral expectation of equation (3.44), the T-bond futures price would be given as follows:

$$
\begin{aligned}
P_F^{T\text{-}bond}(t,\ S) &= \frac{\sum_{i=1}^n C_i \tilde{E}_t(P(S,\ T_i)) - AI}{CF} \\
&= \frac{\sum_{i=1}^n C_i P_F(t,\ S,\ T_i) - AI}{CF}
\end{aligned}
\tag{3.45}
$$

Hence, if the T-bond futures were based upon a single deliverable bond, then equation (3.45) could be used to get the quoted futures price, which is given as a function of the corresponding zero-coupon futures prices, and is adjusted for both the accrued interest and the conversion factor.

Equation (3.45) ignores the delivery options owned by the seller of the futures contract. In the presence of multiple deliverable bonds, the futures price must account for the cheapest-to-deliver option held by the seller of the futures contract. By indexing all of the deliverable bonds from $j = 1, 2, \ldots, K$, the formula shown in equation (3.45) can be modified to obtain the futures price as follows:

$$
P_F^{T\text{-}bond}(t,\ S) = \tilde{E}_t \left(\min_j \left(\frac{\sum_{i=1}^{n_j} C_{ij} P(S,\ T_{ij}) - AI_j}{CF_j} \right) \right)
\tag{3.46}
$$

where subscript j has been added to denote the variables related to the jth deliverable Treasury bond. The formula shown in equation (3.46) assumes that the cheapest-to-deliver bond must be delivered on a fixed date S, and hence, ignores the value of both the *timing option* and the *wild card option*. The formula inside the minimization operator calculates the futures price at time S, as if the jth bond is the cheapest to deliver and has a zero cost of delivery. The minimization operator selects the cheapest-to-deliver bond by selecting the bond that minimizes the futures price at time S.

In general, closed-form formulas cannot be derived for the T-bond futures price since the deliverable bond is different in different states. However, we demonstrate how to construct one-factor and two-factor trinomial trees for the one-factor and two-factor term structure models, respectively, in Chapters 4 through 8 of this book. These trees can be used to solve for the futures price given in equation (3.46) by a simple backward recursion under the risk-neutral measure. The cheapest-to-deliver bonds have to be selected only at the terminal nodes of the tree in order to determine the terminal values of the T-bond futures price on these nodes. Once the terminal values are determined, the futures price is obtained by computing the risk-neutral expectation, using a simple backward recursion.

Though the formula shown in equation (3.46) accounts for the seller exercising the cheapest-to-deliver option, it ignores both the timing option, which applies in the delivery month, and the wild card option, which applies on the delivery day. Though the wild card option may have negligible value, the timing option can retain significant value. The timing option is an American option; hence, the tree can be modified to evaluate the optimal exercise time numerically.

A special case can be considered under which an approximate rule of thumb formula could be derived for the T-bond futures price without any of the delivery options. Assuming that the cheapest-to-deliver bond remains the same throughout the life of the contract, the futures price in equation (3.46) can be simplified by bringing the expectation operator inside the minimization operator to give:

$$
\begin{aligned}
P_F^{T\text{-}bond}(t,\ S) &= \min_j \left(\tilde{E}_t \left(\frac{\sum_{i=1}^{n_j} C_{ij} P(S,\ T_{ij}) - AI_j}{CF_j} \right) \right) \\
&= \min_j \left(\tilde{E}_t \left(\frac{\sum_{i=1}^{n_j} C_{ij} P_F(t,\ S,\ T_{ij}) - AI_j}{CF_j} \right) \right)
\end{aligned}
\tag{3.47}
$$

Since prices of futures on zero-coupon bonds are solved in closed form in Chapters 4 through 12 of this book, these formulas can be used to get the approximate formula for the futures price given in equation (3.47). In general, the difference between the futures prices in equations (3.46) and (3.47) is the value of the cheapest-to-deliver option owned by the seller of the futures contract. The value of this option depends on the range of deliverable bonds and the nature of economic uncertainty.

TREASURY NOTE FUTURES

Three kinds of Treasury note (T-note) futures are transacted on the Chicago Board of Trade given as two-year, five-year, and ten-year T-note futures. The two-year T-note futures are not as actively traded as the five-year and the ten-year T-note futures, because both T-bill futures and short-term Eurodollar futures are close competitors of the two-year T-note futures. The asset underlying the ten-year T-note futures contract is any $100,000 face-value Treasury note that matures between six and a half to ten years from the first calendar day of the delivery month. The asset underlying the five-year T-note futures contract is any $100,000 face-value T-note maturing between four and a quarter to five and a quarter years from the first calendar day of the delivery month. The five-year Treasury note issued after the last trading day of the contract month is not eligible for delivery into that month's contract. The least active of the three T-note futures, the two-year Treasury note futures contract, is based on a $200,000 face-value U.S. Treasury note with an original maturity of not more than five and one-quarter years and a remaining maturity of not less than one and three-quarter years from the first day of the delivery month but not more than two years from the last day of the delivery month.

Delivery months for the T-note futures are March, June, September, and December; and the first delivery day is the first business day of the delivery month. While five-year and ten-year T-note futures can be delivered any time during the delivery month, the delivery day of the two-year T-note futures contract is any day up to the third business day following the last trading day. The last trading day for the two-year T-note futures is the earlier of either (1) the second business day prior to the issue day of the two-year note auctioned in the current month or (2) the last business day of the calendar month, whereas for the other two futures contracts, it is the seventh business day preceding the last business day of the delivery month.

Since Treasury notes with different maturities and coupons are eligible for delivery on the T-note futures contract, the CBOT adjusts the invoice price and the deliverable cash price of the T-note futures in the same manner as it adjusts those for T-bond futures (see equations (3.31) and (3.32)). Even the definition of the conversion factor is similar for T-note futures as for T-bond futures, and is given by equations (3.33) through (3.36). The only difference between T-note futures and T-bond futures is the range of maturities of the deliverable bonds. Hence, all results derived for pricing of T-bond futures hold for T-note futures by considering the appropriate range of maturities of deliverable bonds applicable to the specific T-note futures.

FORWARD RATE AGREEMENTS

Unlike swaps, which are exchanges of two streams of multiple cash flows (where some of the exchanges may not even occur on the same date), a forward rate agreement (FRA) between two counterparties is an exchange of a single floating amount for a single fixed amount at a given future date. A typical FRA in the Eurodollar market requires an exchange of a LIBOR-based floating cash flow (known as the floating leg of the FRA) for a fixed cash flow (known as the fixed leg of the FRA), at a future time

T, based upon the LIBOR rate observed at the future time S ($S \leq T$). The payoff of an FRA based upon a notional principal of F, on the expiration date T, is given as follows:

$$F[L(S, T) - K]\hat{U} = L(S, T)F\hat{U} - KF\hat{U} \qquad (3.48)$$

where $\hat{U}$ is the accrual factor calculated using actual/360 day-count basis and $U = T - S$. The two expressions on the right-hand side (R.H.S.) of equation (3.48) represent a long position in the floating leg and a short position in the fixed leg of the FRA, respectively.

The payoff of the floating leg of the FRA can be replicated as a portfolio of two zero-coupon bonds, which expire at times S and T. The portfolio is given as a long position in the zero-coupon bond maturing at time S and a short position in the zero-coupon bond maturing at time T, where both bonds have their face values equal to the FRA's notional principal F. The time S proceeds from the portfolio's long position are reinvested for U years, from time S until time T, at the prevailing LIBOR rate $L(S, T)$. The payoff from this portfolio at time T is given as $[1 + L(S, T)\hat{U}]F - F$, or:

$$Portfolio\ Payoff = L(S, T)F\hat{U} \qquad (3.49)$$

The expression proves that the time T payoff from the portfolio in equation (3.49) equals the payoff of the floating leg of the FRA given in equation (3.48). Therefore, using the law of one price, the time t value of the floating leg of the FRA equals the time t price of the replicating portfolio. The value of the bond portfolio at time t is given as follows:

$$[P(t, S) - P(t, T)]F \qquad (3.50)$$

Hence, the time t price of the FRA payoff in equation (3.48), is given as follows:

$$\begin{aligned} P_{FRA}(t) &= [P(t, S) - P(t, T)]F - (KF\hat{U})P(t, T) \\ &= P(t, S)F - P(t, T)F(1 + K\hat{U}) \end{aligned} \qquad (3.51)$$

Hence, the FRA is equivalent to a long position in an \$$F$ face-value zero-coupon bond maturing at time S and to a short position in an \$$F(1 + K\hat{U})$ face-value zero-coupon bond maturing at date T.

INTEREST RATE SWAPS

The explosive growth of interest rate swaps over the last quarter century suggests that managing interest rate risk remains a chief concern for many financial institutions and other market participants, even as U.S. interest rates have gone down significantly since reaching their peak in 1980–1981. At the end of June 2006, the notional amount of interest rate swaps was about $207 trillion, which represented approximately 80 percent of the notional amount of all single-currency interest rate derivatives traded in the over-the-counter market (see Table 3.2).

An interest rate swap is a contractual agreement between two counterparties under which each agrees to make periodic payments to the other for a prespecified time period based upon a notional amount of principal. The principal amount is called *notional* because this amount is not exchanged, but is used as a notional figure to determine the cash flows that are exchanged periodically. In a plain vanilla interest rate swap, fixed cash flows computed using a fixed interest rate on the notional amount are exchanged for floating cash flows computed using a floating interest rate on the notional amount. The most common floating interest rate used for computing the floating leg of the cash flows is the three-month LIBOR. Most interest rate swaps exchange the floating cash flows every quarter and the fixed cash flows every six months. The stream of floating cash flows in a swap agreement is called the *floating leg*, whereas the stream of fixed cash flows constitute the *fixed leg*. The dates at which the floating rates are observed are called *resets*.

We begin this section with an example of a plain vanilla interest rate swap. For expositional simplicity, we assume that the counterparties exchange fixed and floating cash flows every six months.[5]

Example 3.5 Consider a two-year interest rate swap between firms A and B, initiated on September 1, 2005, with an annualized rate of 5 percent compounded semiannually for the fixed leg, and the six-month LIBOR for the floating leg. The notional principal of the swap equals $10 million. The LIBOR rates and the exchange of cash flows are displayed in Table 3.7.

TABLE 3.7 Cash Flows Exchanged by Firm A

Date	LIBOR Rate(%)	Floating Cash Flow Received	Fixed Cash Flow Paid	Net Cash Flow
September 1, 2005	4.50			
March 1, 2006	4.75	$225,000	$250,000	−$25,000
September 1, 2006	5.00	$237,500	$250,000	−$12,500
March 1, 2007	5.20	$250,000	$250,000	0
September 1, 2007	5.50	$260,000	$250,000	+$10,000

Every six months, firm A pays $0.025 \times \$10$ million $= \$250,000$ to firm B and receives the six-month LIBOR $\times \$10$ million from firm B, observed at the *beginning* of each six-month period. The first exchange occurs on March 1, 2006, six months after the agreement is initiated. Since the annualized six-month LIBOR rate observed six months earlier on September 1, 2005, is 4.5 percent, firm A receives from firm B a floating cash flow equal to $\frac{1}{2} \times 4.5\% \times 10,000,000 = \$225,000$ and pays to firm B a fixed cash flow equal to $\frac{1}{2} \times 5\% \times 10,000,000 = \$250,000$. Since the net difference between these two cash flows is $-\$25,000$, firm A sends $\$25,000$ to firm B on March 1, 2006. The second exchange of cash flows takes place on September 1, 2006. Since the six-month LIBOR rate observed six months earlier on March 1, 2006, is 4.75 percent, firm A receives from firm B a floating cash flow equal to $4.75\% \times \frac{1}{2} \times 10,000,000 = \$237,500$ on September 1, 2006, and in return pays the fixed cash flow of $\$250,000$, resulting in a net cash flow payment from firm A to firm B of $\$12,500$. The cash flow exchanges on other dates are shown in Table 3.7.

Another way to look at this swap transaction is to assume that firm A gives to firm B a fixed coupon bond in exchange for receiving a floating coupon bond, where both bonds have a redemption face value equal to the notional principal of $\$10$ million. Hence, a plain vanilla swap can be considered equivalent to a long position in the floating rate bond together with a short position in the fixed coupon bond (or vice versa). If one or both counterparties involved in the swap transaction decide to terminate the contract, they must negotiate the cancellation of the contract, called the "unwind," which requires one of the counterparties to make a payment based upon the mark-to-market value of the swap contract. Another way to terminate the original contract is to enter into a new swap contract by taking exactly opposite positions in the fixed and floating legs in order to neutralize the interest rate risk of the original swap contract.

For expositional simplicity, the previous example abstracted from the many real-world features of interest rate swap contracts. For example, one must consider day-count conventions used for computing the cash flows corresponding to the floating rates and fixed rates. Also, often the number of payments on the floating leg is not necessarily equal to the number of payments on the fixed leg, and cash flows are not exchanged on the same dates. We address all of these issues in the following sections.

Day-Count Conventions

In Example 3.5, we assumed that the floating rate for a six-month period is half as much as the annual rate. In doing this we disregarded that, as a money market instrument, LIBOR is quoted on an actual/360 basis.

However, between March 1 and September 1 there are 184 days, thus the second cash flow received by firm A should be:

$$4.75\% \times \frac{184}{360} \times \$10,000,000 = \$242,778$$

The fixed-rate payments in a plain vanilla swap are quoted on a 30/360 day-count basis, which generally assumes that every month has 30 days, and that the whole year has 360 days. Hence, using 30/360 basis, the second cash flow paid by firm A in Example 3.5 is correct. Hence, firm A's net cash outflow should be $250,000 - $242,778 = $7,222.

The fixed rate and the floating rate may come with different day-count conventions. If the fixed rate comes from a Treasury note or Treasury bond, it is quoted on an actual/365 basis and it cannot be directly compared with LIBOR, which is quoted on an actual/360 basis. To make the two rates comparable, we multiply the fixed rate by 360/365. Generally, for plain vanilla swaps, the fixed payments are quoted using the 30/360 basis, and floating payments are quoted using the actual/360 basis.

The Financial Intermediary

Originally, interest rate swaps were brokered transactions in which the financial intermediary would match customers interested in a swap transaction. Once the transaction was completed, the role of the intermediary ceased as the swap counterparties exchanged payments directly. Today, the swap market is more or less a dealer market dominated by large international banks and financial institutions that act as market makers—they become a counterparty to a swap transaction before a swap player for the other side of the transaction is found.

The plain vanilla swaps on U.S. interest rates usually yield 2 to 4 basis points to the financial intermediary on a pair of offsetting transactions. Figure 3.1 illustrates the role of the financial intermediary in a transaction similar to that described in Example 3.5.

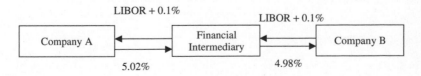

FIGURE 3.1 Interest Rate Swap with a Financial Intermediary

Note that the simple plain vanilla swap transaction in Example 3.5 is structured as a pair of offsetting transactions: one between the dealer and firm A and the other between the dealer and firm B. In most instances, firms A and B will never know that the financial institution has engaged in a swap transaction with the other firm. If either of the two firms defaults, it is the financial intermediary that assumes the loss, as it still must honor its agreement with the other firm. The 4 basis points fee partly compensates the intermediary against the risk of default. To further control this risk, some swap dealers require counterparties to post collateral, usually high-grade securities, that can be used in the case of default.

Significant efforts to ensure smooth trading of swaps have been made by the International Swaps and Derivatives Association (ISDA), a global organization representing leading participants in the swaps and derivatives markets. The ISDA recommends a standardized master agreement for counterparties interested in conducting derivatives business. The master agreement specifies many details, including how the mark-to-market of transactions are calculated, what mutual collateral thresholds apply, and the types of derivatives that are netted out for margins.

Motivations for Interest Rate Swaps

Interest swaps are motivated by either the existence of what is known as "comparative cost advantage" or by the need to hedge interest rate risk. The concept of comparative cost advantage can be understood using the following example.

Example 3.6 Consider issuance of debt by two firms. Firm A needs to issue fixed-coupon debt maturing in T years, while firm B needs to issue floating-coupon debt maturing in T years. The yield or the cost of debt for both these firms in the fixed-coupon debt market and the floating-coupon debt market are given in Table 3.8.

TABLE 3.8 Cost of Debt in Fixed and Floating Debt Markets

Firm	Fixed-Coupon Debt	Floating-Coupon Debt
A	5.5%	LIBOR + 0.50%
B	5.0%	LIBOR + 0.25%
Cost advantage for B	0.5%	0.25%

Due to its better credit rating, firm B gets cheaper financing in both the fixed-rate market and the floating-rate market. However, its advantage in the fixed-rate market is 0.5 percent, which is higher than its advantage in the floating-rate market of 0.25 percent. The difference between the cost advantages in the two markets is called the *comparative cost advantage* of firm B over firm A in the fixed-rate market compared to the floating-rate market and is given as:

$$Comparative\ Cost\ Advantage = 0.5\% - 0.25\% = 0.25\% \qquad (3.52)$$

If the comparative cost advantage is not zero, then both firms could benefit by issuing debt securities in the market in which they are relatively better off and still obtaining their choice of financing by doing an interest rate swap. Specifically, firm A needs to issue fixed-coupon debt but could issue floating-coupon debt instead, since in the floating-rate market its disadvantage is only 0.25%. Similarly, firm B needs to issue floating-coupon debt but could issue fixed-coupon debt instead, since in the fixed-rate market its advantage is 0.5%. Simultaneously, the two firms execute an interest rate swap, which converts firm A's financing from floating rate to fixed rate and firm B's financing from fixed rate to floating rate.

The issuance of securities by the two firms and the simultaneous execution of the interest rate swap through an intermediary are shown in Figure 3.2. Based upon the information in Figure 3.2, we can compute the cost of financing to each firm if they simply obtained the type of financing they needed without doing the swap, and then compare it to the cost of financing to each firm if they obtained financing from the markets in which they are relatively better off with a simultaneous execution of an interest rate swap. We assume that the intermediary charges an annual fee of 4 basis

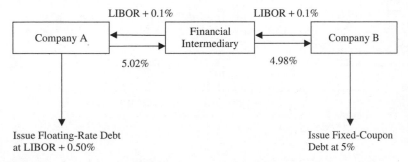

FIGURE 3.2 Issuance of Fixed-Coupon Debt and Floating-Rate Debt with a Simultaneous Execution of a Swap

points (or $0.04\% = 0.0004$), which is divided and paid equally by firms A and B.

The cost of financing to the two firms, using the type of financing they need without using a swap, is given as follows:

Firm A's cost of financing without the swap = 5.5%
Firm B's cost of financing without the swap = LIBOR + 0.25%

The cost of financing to the two firms, using the financing from the markets in which they are relatively better off with a simultaneous execution of an interest rate swap, is given as follows:

Firm A's cost of financing with the swap (see Figure 3.2):

Payments to financial intermediary = swap rate + fee = 5.0% + 0.02%
  + Payments to the investors in the floating-rate debt= LIBOR + 0.5%
  − Payments received from the financial intermediary= −(LIBOR + 0.1%)
  _____
                                                          5.42%

Firm B's cost of financing with the swap (see Figure 3.2):

Payments to financial intermediary   = LIBOR + 0.1%
  + Payments to the investors in the fixed-rate debt   = 5%
  − Payments received from the financial intermediary
    = −(swap rate − fee)   = −(5% − 0.02%)
  _____
                                                        LIBOR + 0.12%

The savings from using the swap are given as the firms' cost of financing without the swap minus the firms' cost of financing with the swap, as shown in Table 3.9.

The savings of firms A and B and the 4 basis points given to the intermediary add up to the comparative cost advantage of 0.25 percent as shown below:

Savings for firm A   = 0.08%
Savings for firm B   = 0.13%
Fee to the intermediary = 0.04%
_____
Total   = 0.25%

The fact that the annual savings to the two firms and the fee to the intermediary add up to 0.25 percent is not a coincidence. This was the annual comparative cost advantage computed earlier in equation (3.52).

TABLE 3.9   Cost of Financing and Savings for Firm A and Firm B

Cost of Financing	A	B
Without the swap	5.50%	LIBOR + 0.25%
With the swap	5.42%	LIBOR + 0.12%
Savings	0.08%	0.13%

As a general principal, the comparative cost advantage represents the pie that can be shared among all swap participants, including the fee paid to the intermediary. Of course, the existence of comparative cost advantage should not be necessarily viewed as arbitrage opportunities in the market. The intermediary will require collateral or may engage in better monitoring, some of which can explain a reduction in cost of financing to the swap participants. Occasionally, discrepancies in the relative pricing in different markets may exist temporarily, such that all swap participants can benefit as shown in this example.

The example demonstrates how comparative cost advantage can be exploited by the execution of an interest rate swap. Though intuitively appealing, the idea of comparative cost advantage rests upon the existence of market inefficiencies, which lead to arbitrage opportunities. The execution of interest rate swaps should eventually eliminate the arbitrage opportunities or the "comparative cost advantage." A more direct motivation for the use of interest rate swaps is managing interest rate risk. Interest rate swaps are used by financial institutions and other market participants, including corporations with interest rate sensitive assets or liabilities, for hedging interest rate risk arising from the maturity mismatches between the asset and the liabilities. For example, a mortgage bank with a high asset duration resulting from holding longer maturity fixed-rate loans and a low liability duration resulting from short maturity deposits may initiate an interest rate swap in which it pays the fixed leg of the cash flows and receives the floating leg of the cash flows. The swap-adjusted duration gap of the mortgage bank would be reduced considerably, though this would also mean lower return on its net worth. However, since the mortgage bank specializes in the business of profiting from the services provided in the home-loan business market, and not predicting the future direction of interest rates, initiating such a swap may be consistent with its business model. Similarly, very highly leveraged institutions, such as Fannie Mae and Freddie Mac, often use interest rate swaps to fine-tune their duration gaps. Virtually all financial institutions and many corporations with nonfinancial businesses use interest rate swaps to manage the effects of unwanted interest rate risk on their net worth.

Pricing Interest Rate Swaps

An interest rate swap is defined by a periodic exchange of fixed and floating cash flows. The fixed leg of the swap is represented by the set of fixed cash flows, and the floating leg of the swap is represented by the set of floating cash flows. A *payer swap* requires making fixed payments and receiving floating payments, and a *receiver swap* requires receiving fixed payments and making floating payments. The frequency of the fixed and floating payments may or may not be the same. For example, in the Eurodollar swap market, the fixed payments are made semiannually, and floating payments are made quarterly. To understand the basic valuation procedure for swaps, assume that the first reset date of the swap is given as S_0. The fixed leg makes N fixed payments at times S_1, $S_2, \ldots$, S_N, where $S_i < S_{i+1}$ for all i. The floating leg makes n floating payments at times T_1, T_2, $\ldots$, T_n, based upon the floating interest rates that are reset at times $S_0 = T_0$, T_1, T_2, $\ldots, T_{n-1}$, respectively, where $T_i < T_{i+1}$ for all i.[6] The last payment date of both the floating leg and the fixed leg are the same, or $S_N = T_n$.

Given the notional principal of F and the discretely compounded money market rate $L(T_i, T_{i+1})$ observed at time T_i, the payment from the floating leg of the swap at the time T_{i+1} is given as:

$$Floating\ Leg\ Payment = F \times \hat{U}_i \times L(T_i, T_{i+1}) \tag{3.53}$$

where $U_i = T_{i+1} - T_i$ and $\hat{U}_i$ is the corresponding accrual factor, generally calculated using actual/360 day-count basis. The present value of all the floating payments at time T_0 is given as follows:

$$P_{Floating\ Leg}(T_0) = F \sum_{i=0}^{i=n-1} \hat{U}_i \times L(T_i, T_{i+1}) \times P(T_0, T_{i+1}) \tag{3.54}$$

By definition, the LIBOR rate has the following relationship with the price of a default-free zero-coupon bond:

$$1 + L(T_i,\ T_{i+1})\hat{U}_i = \frac{1}{P(T_i, T_{i+1})} \tag{3.55}$$

Substituting equation (3.55) in equation (3.54), we get:

$$P_{Floating\ Leg}(T_0) = F \sum_{i=0}^{i=n-1} \left(\frac{1 - P(T_i,\ T_{i+1})}{P(T_i,\ T_{i+1})} \right) P(T_0,\ T_{i+1}) \tag{3.56}$$

Since by definition $P(T_0, \ T_i) \times P(T_i, \ T_{i+1}) = P(T_0, \ T_{i+1})$, equation (3.56) simplifies to:

$$P_{Floating\ Leg}(T_0) = F \sum_{i=0}^{i=n-1} \big(1 - P(T_i, \ T_{i+1})\big)P(T_0, \ T_i)$$

$$= F \sum_{i=0}^{i=n-1} \big(P(T_0, \ T_i) - P(T_0, \ T_{i+1})\big)$$

$$= F\big(P(T_0, \ T_0) - P(T_0, \ T_n)\big)$$

$$= F\big(1 - P(T_0, \ T_n)\big) \tag{3.57}$$

At any time t prior to the first reset date T_0, the value of the floating leg can be given by discounting equation (3.57) from T_0 to t, as follows:

$$P_{Floating\ Leg}(t) = F\big(P(t, \ T_0) - P(t, \ T_n)\big), \quad t \leq T_0 \tag{3.58}$$

The fixed leg of a swap makes fixed payments at dates S_j, $i = 1, \ 2, \ \ldots, \ $ N. Let $s_j = S_{j+1} - S_j$ define the length of the period between time S_j and S_{j+1}. Recall that by construction, $T_0 = S_0$ and $T_n = S_N$. The general notation allows the number of fixed payments N to be different from the number of floating payments n. For example, the Eurodollar interest rate swaps allow quarterly payments from the floating leg and semiannual payments from the fixed leg, such that $n = 2N$. The payment from the fixed leg of the swap at the time S_{j+1} is given as:

$$Fixed\ Leg\ Payment = F \times K \times \hat{s}_j \tag{3.59}$$

where $\hat{s}_j$ is the accrual factor corresponding to the period $s_j = S_{j+1} - S_j$ and K is the fixed rate applicable to the fixed leg of the swap. The accrual factors $\hat{s}_j$ for the fixed leg of the swap are based on a 30/360 basis, and hence, generally of the same length, even though the actual lengths of the corresponding periods s_j may be slightly different.

The present value of the fixed payments at time $S_0 = T_0$ is given as follows:

$$P_{Fixed\ Leg}(S_0) = F \times K \times \sum_{j=0}^{N-1} \hat{s}_j P(S_0, \ S_{j+1}) \tag{3.60}$$

At any time t prior to the first reset date S_0, the value of the fixed leg can be given by discounting equation (3.60) from S_0 to t, as follows:

$$P_{Fixed\ Leg}(t) = F \times K \times \sum_{j=0}^{N-1} \hat{s}_j P(t, \ S_{j+1}), \quad \text{for all } t \leq S_0 \tag{3.61}$$

An interest rate swap can also be considered an exchange of a fixed-coupon bond and a floating-rate bond with face values of both bonds equal to the notional principal of the swap. A payment of the notional value of F can be added to both the fixed leg and the floating leg at time $S_N = T_n$ to convert these to a fixed-coupon bond and a floating-rate bond, respectively. The coupon rate on the floating-rate bond can be considered as the floating rate that is used for obtaining the floating leg of the swap, while coupon rate on the fixed-coupon bond can be considered as the fixed rate that is used for obtaining the fixed cash flows of the swap. The price of the floating-rate bond at time $t \le T_0$ can be given as:

$$
\begin{aligned}
P_{Floating\text{-}Rate\ Bond}(t) &= P_{Floating\ Leg}(t) + FP(t, T_n) \\
&= F\big(P(t, T_0) - P(t, T_n)\big) + FP(t, T_n) \\
&= FP(t, T_0)
\end{aligned}
\tag{3.62}
$$

The price of the floating-rate bond converges to its face value F at the reset date T_0.

The price of the fixed-coupon bond at time $t \le S_0 = T_0$ can be given as follows:

$$
\begin{aligned}
P_{Fixed\text{-}Coupon\ Bond}(t) &= P_{Fixed\ Leg}(t) + FP(t, S_N) \\
&= F \times \left(K \times \sum_{j=0}^{N-1} \hat{s}_j P(t, S_{j+1}) + P(t, S_N) \right)
\end{aligned}
\tag{3.63}
$$

Since by definition $S_N = T_n$, a swap between the fixed leg and the floating leg is equivalent to the swap between the fixed-coupon bond and the floating-rate bond, as can be seen from equations (3.62) and (3.63). Mathematically, the time t value of a payer swap (i.e., pay fixed/receive floating swap) is given as follows:

$$
\begin{aligned}
P_{Payer\ Swap}(t) &= P_{Floating\ Leg}(t) - P_{Fixed\ Leg}(t) \\
&= F\big(P(t, T_0) - P(t, T_n)\big) - F \times K \times \sum_{j=0}^{N-1} \hat{s}_j P(t, S_{j+1}) \\
&= F \times P(t, T_0) - F \times \left(K \times \sum_{j=0}^{N-1} \hat{s}_j P(t, S_{j+1}) + P(t, S_N) \right) \\
&= P_{Floating\text{-}Rate\ Bond}(t) - P_{Fixed\text{-}Coupon\ Bond}(t)
\end{aligned}
\tag{3.64}
$$

Similarly, the time t $(t \leq S_0 = T_0)$ value of a receiver swap (i.e., receive fixed/pay floating swap) is given as follows:

$$P_{Receiver\ Swap}(t) = P_{Fixed\ Leg}(t) - P_{Floating\ Leg}(t)$$

$$= F \times K \times \sum_{j=0}^{N-1} \hat{s}_j P(t,\ S_{j+1}) - F\big(P(t,\ T_0) - P(t,\ T_n)\big)$$

$$\text{(3.65)}$$

$$= F \times \left(K \times \sum_{j=0}^{N-1} \hat{s}_j P(t,\ S_{j+1}) + P(t,\ S_N) \right) - FP(t,\ T_0)$$

$$= P_{Fixed\text{-}Coupon\ Bond}(t) - P_{Floating\text{-}Rate\ Bond}(t)$$

INTEREST RATE SWAPTIONS

An interest rate swaption is an option written on an interest rate swap. A *payer swaption* gives the option holder the right to initiate a payer swap. Similarly, a *receiver swaption* gives the option holder the right to initiate a receiver swap. The payer swaption gives the buyer the right to pay a fixed rate, known as the *strike rate* of the swaption, and receive the floating rate. The receiver swaption gives the buyer the right to pay the floating rate and receive the fixed strike rate. The payer swaption is exercised only if the market-observed *swap rate* is higher than the strike rate at the swaption's expiration date. The opposite is true for the receiver swaption.

When two counterparties enter a swaption, they agree upon the strike rate, length of the option period, the swap's maturity, notional amount, amortization, and frequency of the settlement. Depending on the exercise rights of the buyer, swaptions fall into three main categories:

1. A *European swaption* gives the buyer the right to exercise the option only at the expiration date.
2. An *American swaption* gives the buyer the right to exercise the option at any time until the expiration date.
3. A *Bermudan swaption* gives the buyer the right to exercise the option on specific dates until the expiration date.

The American and Bermudan swaptions must be priced using numerical methods (e.g., using the trinomial trees given for different term structure models in Chapters 4 through 10 of this book) or quasi-analytical methods.

Interestingly, a European payer (receiver) swaption can be shown to be equivalent to a European put (call) option on a coupon bond. This can be shown as follows. Evaluating equation (3.64) at time S_0, the terminal payoff of a European payer swaption can be given as follows:

$$P_{Payer\ Swaption}(S_0) = Max(P_{Payer\ Swap}(S_0), 0)$$

$$= Max(P_{Floating\text{-}Rate\ Bond}(S_0) - P_{Fixed\text{-}Coupon\ Bond}(S_0), 0)$$

$$(3.66)$$

$$= Max(F - P_{Fixed\text{-}Coupon\ Bond}(S_0), 0)$$

$$= Max\left(F - \left(F \times K \sum_{j=0}^{N-1} \hat{s}_j P(S_0,\ S_{j+1}) + F \times P(S_0,\ S_N)\right), 0\right)$$

where the last expression in equation (3.66) is obtained by noting that $S_N = T_n$ and the price of the floating-rate bond at the reset date $S_0 = T_0$ equals its face value F (using equation (3.62)). Hence, a payer swaption is equivalent to a put option with a strike rate equal to the notional value F, written on a default-free coupon bond with face value F, maturing at time S_N, with coupons of size $F \times K \times \hat{s}_j$, payable at times S_{j+1} (for $j = 0, 1, 2, \ldots, N - 1$).

Similarly, evaluating equation (3.65) at time S_0, the terminal payoff of a European receiver swaption can be given as follows:

$$P_{Receiver\ Swaption}(S_0) = Max(P_{Receiver\ Swap}(S_0),\ 0)$$

$$= Max(P_{Fixed\text{-}Coupon\ Bond}(S_0) - P_{Floating\text{-}Rate\ Bond}(S_0), 0)$$

$$(3.67)$$

$$= Max(P_{Fixed\text{-}Coupon\ Bond}(S_0) - F,\ 0)$$

$$= Max\left(\left(F \times K \sum_{j=0}^{N-1} \hat{s}_j P(S_0,\ S_{j+1}) + F \times P(S_0,\ S_N)\right) - F, 0\right)$$

Hence, a receiver swaption is equivalent to a call option with a strike rate equal to the notional value F, written on a default-free coupon bond with face value F, maturing at time S_N, with coupons of size $F \times K \times \hat{s}_j$, payable at times S_{j+1} (for $j = 0, 1, 2, \ldots, N - 1$).

Hence, swaptions can be valued as options on coupon bonds. Further, as shown by Jamshidian [1989], European options on coupon bonds can be priced as portfolios of European options on zero-coupon bonds, with appropriate adjustments to the exercise prices of the zero-coupon options, under all single-factor term structure models. We demonstrate Jamshidian's trick in Chapters 4, 6, and 7 on single-factor term structure models. The

European coupon-bond option formulas in these chapters can be used to price European swaptions using the framework given above.

Collin-Dufresne and Goldstein [2001b] also show how to price European swaptions under *multiple*-factor affine term structure models, using an Edgeworth expansion technique to estimate the probability distribution of the coupon bond's future price. The estimation requires using the cumulants of the distributions, which are given in approximate closed forms. Collin-Dufresne and Goldstein show very rapid convergence of the model swaption prices to the true prices using their method. We apply the Edgeworth expansion technique in Chapters 9 and 10 to price swaptions under multiple-factor affine models using the framework given in this section.

Though the payoffs given in equations (3.66) and (3.67) can be used for valuing swaptions under all continuous-time term structure models, including Gaussian, square root, generalized affine, quadratic, and HJM models given in Chapters 4 through 11, the LSM version of the LIBOR model given in Chapter 12 (more specifically, the lognormal forward swap model) expresses the same payoffs in a slightly different manner. The LSM model uses what is known as the *swap rate* prevailing at the swap initiation time S_0 to express the swaption payoffs. The swap rate is defined as the rate that makes the value of the interest rate swap zero at the initiation of the swap. Using equations (3.64) and (3.65), the swap rate $f^s(S_0)$ is the value of the fixed rate K at time $S_0 = T_0$ that makes the value of the fixed leg equal to the value of the floating leg such that the value of both the payer swap and the receiver swap are zero. By setting either equation (3.64) or equation (3.65) to zero at time $S_0 = T_0$, the swap rate is obtained as follows:

$$f^s(S_0) = \frac{1 - P(S_0, S_N)}{A(S_0)} \qquad (3.68)$$

where $T_n = S_N$ and

$$A(S_0) = \sum_{j=0}^{N-1} \hat{s}_j P(S_0, S_{j+1}) \qquad (3.69)$$

Equation (3.68) gives the time S_0 value of a traded portfolio in the units of the numeraire asset price $A(S_0)$. Considering the value of the portfolio at time $t \le S_0$ defines the *forward swap rate* as follows:

$$f^s(t) = \frac{P(t, S_0) - P(t, S_N)}{A(t)} \qquad (3.70)$$

The terminal payoffs of payer swaption and receiver swaption given in equations (3.66) and (3.67) can be expressed using the swap rate by substituting equation (3.68) as follows:

$$P_{Payer\ Swaption}(S_0) = Max\left(F - \left(F \times K \sum_{j=0}^{N-1} \hat{s}_j P(S_0,\ S_{j+1}) + F \times P(S_0,\ S_N)\right), 0\right)$$

$$= F \times Max\left(f^s(S_0) \times A(S_0) - K \times A(S_0), 0\right) \tag{3.71}$$

$$= F \times A(S_0) \times Max\left(f^s(S_0) - K, 0\right)$$

and

$$P_{Receiver\ Swaption}(S_0) = Max\left(\left(F \times K \sum_{j=0}^{N-1} \hat{s}_j P(S_0,\ S_{j+1}) + F \times P(S_0,\ S_N)\right) - F, 0\right)$$

$$= F \times Max\left(K \times A(S_0) - f^s(S_0) \times A(S_0),\ 0\right) \tag{3.72}$$

$$= F \times A(S_0) \times Max\left(K - f^s(S_0),\ 0\right)$$

Now consider an economy with $A(S_0)$ as the numeraire. Since in this economy all asset prices are measure in the units of $A(S_0)$, the terminal payoffs of the payer swaption and the receiver swaption can be given by dividing both sides of equations (3.71) and (3.72) by $A(S_0)$ as follows:

$$\frac{P_{Payer\ Swaption}(S_0)}{A(S_0)} = F \times Max\left(f^s(S_0) - K,\ 0\right) \tag{3.73}$$

and

$$\frac{P_{Receiver\ Swaption}(S_0)}{A(S_0)} = F \times Max\left(K - f^s(S_0),\ 0\right) \tag{3.74}$$

Hence, a payer (receiver) swaption measured in the units of the asset $A(S_0)$ is equivalent to F number of call (put) options written on the swap rate with a strike rate equal to K. Obviously, the stochastic dynamics of the forward swap rate under the numeraire asset price $A(t)$ are required to value swaptions at any time $t \leq S_0$. These dynamics are considered in Chapter 12, which derives the LSM version of the LIBOR model developed by Jamshidian [1997].

CAPS AND FLOORS

Caps and floors are options written on interest rates. Since generally these options are written on discretely compounded interest rates, they can be converted into options written on zero-coupon bonds. Unlike a swaption, which gives a right to initiate a swaption, a cap (floor) can limit the losses on an existing position in a receiver (payer) swap when interest rates go up (down) sharply. Though caps and floor are often used in conjunction with a swap position, these instruments are useful whenever one is exposed to either a long or a short position in variable interest rate securities, such as floating-rate bonds, adjustable-rate mortgages, floating-rate liabilities of a bank (e.g., time deposit accounts), and the like. Though mostly these instruments are used by financial institutions and corporations to hedge interest rate risk, they are also used by speculative hedge funds that bet on the direction or on the volatility of interest rate movements. Individual borrowers and lenders who want to protect themselves from sudden increases or decreases in interest rates are also frequent users of these instruments.[7]

For example, a corporation may wish to reduce the duration of its liabilities by converting one of its fixed-rate liabilities into a floating-rate liability using a receiver swap. The corporation may also desire to protect itself from a statistically small but economically significant possibility of a sharp increase in the interest rates that would make its synthetically created floating-rate liability expensive to support. Thus, the corporation may purchase an interest rate cap, which pays off when interest rates go above the *cap rate* (where the cap rate is set higher than the current level of interest rate). This allows the corporation to limit the cost of financing of the synthetically created floating-rate liability under scenarios with sharp increases in the interest rate. Further, to partially fund the purchase of the cap, the corporation may simultaneously write an interest rate floor, which obliges the corporation to make payments if interest rates go below the *floor rate* (where the floor rate is set below the current level of interest rate). If interest rates decrease sharply, then the corporation would be benefiting from low interest rates to fund its operations; hence, making payments on the floor would pose minimal risk. The long position in the cap and the short position in the floor may be embedded in the swap transaction itself as an interest rate *collar* in order to reduce transactions costs.

A cap can be given as a sum of a series of caplets, and a floor can be given as a sum of a series of floorlets. We first show how to price a caplet and a floorlet by converting these discrete rate options into options on zero-coupon bonds. Since prices of options on zero-coupon bonds are solved in various chapters under different term structure models, these formulas can be used to price caps and floors under a variety of different assumptions. In this chapter, we do not discuss the LIBOR market model in detail for pricing caps and floors, as the main focus here is to present results that hold under most term structure models given in the various chapters of the book. The LFM (lognormal forward rate model) version of the LIBOR model is discussed at length in Chapter 12 for pricing caps and floors.

The formulas given in the following sections hold only for caps and floors that pay *in arrears* (that is, they pay one period after the rate on which these options are based is realized). The formulas for caps and floors that pay *in advance* (that is, they pay exactly when the rate on which these options are based is realized) can be solved numerically or using other quasi-analytical methods such as the Fourier inversion method. Since the more common payment method is in arrears, this chapter focuses on caps and floors that pay in arrears.

Caplet

The underlying interest rate for the interest rate options in the LIBOR and other similar markets is defined using discrete compounding as follows:

$$1 + L(T_i, T_{i+1})\hat{U}_i = \frac{1}{P(T_i, T_{i+1})} \tag{3.75}$$

where, $L(T_i, T_{i+1})$ is the LIBOR rate observed at time T_i for the term $U_i = T_{i+1} - T_i$; the timeline is given as $t \leq T_0 < T_1 < T_2 < \ldots < T_n$; and $\hat{U}_i$ is the accrual factor for the period T_i to T_{i+1}, calculated using actual/360 day-count basis. Using equation (3.75), the zero-coupon bond price at time T_i can be given as follows:

$$P(T_i, T_{i+1}) = \frac{1}{1 + L(T_i, T_{i+1})\hat{U}_i} \tag{3.76}$$

The actual tenor length $U_i = T_{i+1} - T_i$ is typically close to 0.25 since most caps make quarterly payments. The payoff of a caplet at time T_{i+1} is defined as follows:

$$\textit{Caplet Payoff at } T_{i+1} = F \times \hat{U}_i \times \max[L(T_i, T_{i+1}) - K_i, 0] \tag{3.77}$$

where, F is the notional value of the caplet and K_i is the caplet strike rate. Notice that even though the payment is made at time T_{i+1}, the amount to be paid is known with certainty at time T_i. Hence, the option expires at time T_i, even though payment comes at time T_{i+1}. If we discount the payoff given in equation (3.77) by $1 + L(T_i, T_{i+1})\hat{U}_i$, we obtain the payoff at time T_i as follows:

$$\left(\frac{F\hat{U}_i}{1 + L(T_i, T_{i+1})\hat{U}_i} \right) \max[L(T_i, T_{i+1}) - K_i, 0] \tag{3.78}$$

Bringing all terms inside the maximum operator, we get:

$$\max\left[\frac{F\hat{U}_iL(T_i,\ T_{i+1})}{1+L(T_i,\ T_{i+1})\hat{U}_i} - \frac{F\hat{U}_iK_i}{1+L(T_i,\ T_{i+1})\hat{U}_i},\ 0\right] \qquad (3.79)$$

By adding and subtracting F in the numerator of the first expression in the bracket and then simplifying, equation (3.79) simplifies to the following:

$$\max\left[F - \frac{F(1+\hat{U}_iK_i)}{1+L(T_i,T_{i+1})\hat{U}_i},\ 0\right] \qquad (3.80)$$

Substituting equation (3.76) and rearranging the terms, equation (3.80) gives the caplet payoff at time T_i as follows:

$$Equivalent\ Caplet\ Payoff\ at\ Time\ T_i = \frac{F}{\hat{K}_i}\left(\max[\hat{K}_i - P(T_i,\ T_{i+1}),\ 0]\right)$$

$$(3.81)$$

where

$$\hat{K}_i = \frac{1}{(1+\hat{U}_iK_i)} \qquad (3.82)$$

Equation (3.81) gives the payoff from $F/\hat{K}_i$ number of European put options written on a \$1 face-value zero-coupon bond maturing at time T_{i+1}. The put options expire at time T_i with a strike price equal to $\hat{K}_i$, defined in equation (3.82). Hence, the payoff from a caplet at time $T_{i+1} = T_i + U_i$, given in equation (3.77), is equivalent to the payoff from $F/\hat{K}_i$ number of European put options expiring on T_i, written on a T_{i+1} maturity zero-coupon bond. Assuming that the current price of each put option equals $p_i(t)$, the price of the caplet can be obtained as follows:

$$P_{Caplet_i}(t) = \frac{F}{\hat{K}_i}p_i(t), \qquad t \le T_i \qquad (3.83)$$

Floorlet

The floorlet payoff at time T_{i+1} is given in a similar way as the caplet payoff, as follows:

$$Floorlet\ Payoff\ at\ T_{i+1} = F \times \hat{U}_i \times \max[K_i - L(T_i,\ T_{i+1}),\ 0] \qquad (3.84)$$

where K_i is the floor rate and all other variables are as defined earlier. Using similar logic as for the case of a caplet, the floorlet payoff at time T_{i+1} can be converted to an equivalent payoff at time T_i as follows:

$$\textit{Equivalent Floorlet Payoff at Time } T_i = \frac{F}{\hat{K}_i} \left(Max[P(T_i, T_{i+1}) - \hat{K}_i, 0] \right)$$

(3.85)

where

$$\hat{K}_i = \frac{1}{(1 + \hat{U}_i K_i)}$$

(3.86)

Equation (3.85) gives the payoff from $F/\hat{K}_i$ number of European call options written on a \$1 face-value zero-coupon bond maturing at time T_{i+1}. The call options expire at time T_i with a strike price equal to $\hat{K}_i$ defined in equation (3.86). Hence, the payoff from a floorlet at time $T_{i+1} = T_i + U_i$, given in equation (3.84), is equivalent to the payoff from $F/\hat{K}_i$ number of European call options expiring on T_i, written on a T_{i+1} maturity zero-coupon bond. Assuming that the current price of the call option equals $c_i(t)$, the price of the floorlet can be obtained as follows:

$$P_{Floorlet_i}(t) = \frac{F}{\hat{K}_i} c_i(t), \quad t \le T_i$$

(3.87)

Since virtually all chapters in this book give solutions of European puts and calls on zero-coupon bonds, these can be used to price the caplet and the floorlet using equations (3.83) and (3.87), respectively, under a variety of term structure models.

Collarlet

A collarlet is a long position in a caplet and a short position in a floorlet, where typically the cap rate is higher than the floor rate. The price of a collarlet can be given as follows:

$$P_{Collarlet_i}(t) = P_{Caplet_i}(t) - P_{Floorlet_i}(t), \quad t \le T_i$$

(3.88)

where all variables are as defined earlier.

Caps, Floors, and Collars

The price of an interest rate cap (with payments in arrears) with the first payoff on date T_1 and the last payoff on date $T_j(j = 1, 2, \ldots n)$ can be given as the sum of j number of caplets as follows:

$$P_{CAP}(t, T_j) = \sum_{i=0}^{j-1} P_{Caplet_i}(t)$$

(3.89)

where the time line is as defined earlier, $t \leq T_0 < T_1 < T_2 < \ldots < T_n$, and the price of the ith caplet is given in equation (3.83). The notional value and the cap rate are identical for all caplets.

Similarly, the price of an interest rate floor (with payments in arrears) with the first payoff on date T_1 and the last payoff on date $T_j (j = 1, 2, \ldots, n)$ can be given as the sum of j number of floorlets as follows:

$$P_{FLOOR}(t, \ T_j) = \sum_{i=0}^{j-1} P_{Floorlet_i}(t) \tag{3.90}$$

where the price of the ith floorlet is given in equation (3.87). The notional value and the floor rate are identical for all floorlets.

And finally, the price of an interest rate collar (with payments in arrears) with the first payoff on date T_1 and the last payoff on date $T_j (j = 1, 2, \ldots, n)$ can be given as the sum of j number of collarlets as follows:

$$P_{COLLAR}(t, \ T_j) = \sum_{i=0}^{j-1} P_{Collarlet_i}(t) \tag{3.91}$$

where the price of the ith collarlet is given in equation (3.88).

BLACK IMPLIED VOLATILITIES FOR CAPS AND SWAPTIONS

A lasting legacy of Fisher Black is the widespread adoption of his formulas as the industry benchmarks (given in Black and Scholes [1973], Black [1976], and other similar formulas) for computing implied volatilities in different derivative product markets ranging from basic equity options to commodity futures to vanilla interest rate options, such as caps and swaptions. The implied volatility of an equity option is defined as the value of volatility that makes the price of the option computed using the Black and Scholes model equal to the market-observed price of the option. The values of implied volatilities corresponding to different option strikes give the well-known volatility *smile* (or *smirk*), and values of implied volatilities corresponding to the combinations of option strikes and option expiration dates give the two-dimensional volatility surface.

Though Fischer Black did not develop the more popular term structure models, the benchmark formulas for measuring implied volatilities in the caps and swaptions markets are based upon heuristic generalizations of the original Black [1976] formula. By calibrating Black's formulas to the market-observed prices of caps and swaptions, one obtains the Black implied *market* volatilities of these instruments. These volatilities are quoted routinely by many data vendors including Bloomberg and Datastream.

A direct relation exists between Black implied volatilities and the volatility functions used in the LIBOR market models given in Chapter 12. However, the relationship between Black implied volatilities and the volatility parameters used in the standard affine and quadratic models is rather complex and nonlinear. Since Black implied volatilities have become the industry standard, these volatilities must be obtained for any term structure model to make meaningful comparisons across models. This is done using Black implied *model* volatilities, which are obtained by equating the prices of caps and swaptions computed using a specific term structure model to the Black formulas. For example, the Black implied *Vasicek* volatility of an interest rate cap is the value of volatility in the Black formula that makes the Vasicek [1977] model price of the cap equal to the price of the cap computed using the Black formula. Once Black implied *model* volatilities have been obtained for a given term structure model, it is easy to evaluate the model by comparing these volatilities to the Black implied *market* volatilities.

We clarify these concepts further by giving Black formulas for pricing caps and swaptions and then showing the difference between Black implied model volatilities and Black implied market volatilities. To obtain Black implied volatilities we need to first give Black's formulas for pricing caps and swaptions. This is done by a practically motivated extension of the Black [1976] option formula for pricing Eurodollar-based interest rate derivatives. Specifically, using the LIBOR rate as the underlying asset and the current forward rate as the expectation of the future LIBOR rate and assuming constant volatility gives the Black formula for pricing European options written on the future LIBOR rate. Similarly, using the prevailing swap rate as the underlying asset and the forward swap rate as the expectation of the future swap rate and assuming constant volatility gives the Black formula for pricing swaptions.

Initially, the theoretical underpinnings of this approach seemed dubious, even though practitioners used it routinely to price caps and swaptions. How could LIBOR rate and swap rate be considered traded assets? Under what measure could the expectation of the LIBOR rate be the current forward rate? Similarly, under what measure could the expectation of the swap rate be the current forward swap rate? And, how could one assume constant volatility? All of these assumptions seemed not to have much theoretical justification. Yet, as shown in Chapter 12, all of these assumptions can be justified by using the appropriate forward measures for pricing caps and swaptions. In the following section, we simply give the Black formulas of caps and swaptions for computing Black implied volatilities. The theoretically robust derivations of these formulas are the subject of Chapter 12, which presents the LIBOR market models.

We now consider three interest rate derivative securities: a swaption, a caplet, and a cap. The results for a floorlet and a floor are similar to that for a caplet and a cap, respectively.

Black Implied Volatilities: Swaptions

Market Volatilities   The Black implied market volatility of a payer swaption at time t with an expiration date S_0, strike rate K, and notional value equal to F can be obtained by equating the market-observed swaption price to the Black formula of the swaption price, as follows:

$$P^{Market}_{Payer\ Swaption}(t) = A(t) \times F \times \left(f^s(t)\mathcal{N}(d_1) - K\mathcal{N}(d_2)\right) \qquad (3.92)$$

where

$$A(t) = \left(\sum_{j=0}^{N-1} \hat{s}_j P(t,\ S_{j+1})\right)$$

$$d_1 = \frac{\ln(f^s(t)/K) + \vartheta^2_{S,Market}(S_0 - t)/2}{\vartheta_{S,Market}\sqrt{S_0 - t}}$$

$$d_2 = \frac{\ln(f^s(t)/K) - \vartheta^2_{S,Market}(S_0 - t)/2}{\vartheta_{S,Market}\sqrt{S_0 - t}}$$

The only unknown in equation (3.92) is the Black implied market volatility, $\vartheta_{S,Market}$, which can be solved for different values of S_0 and $S_N - S_0$, giving a two-dimensional surface of implied volatilities for a given strike price K. The theoretical justification of equation (3.92) is given in Chapter 12 using the LSM version of the LIBOR market model.

The price of the receiver swaption is given as follows:

$$P^{Market}_{Receiver\ Swaption}(t) = A(t) \times F \times \left(K\mathcal{N}(-d_2) - f^s(t)\mathcal{N}(-d_1)\right) \qquad (3.93)$$

where all variables are as defined previously. Using the same method as given for a payer swaption, gives the Black implied market volatility of a receiver swaption.

Model Volatilities   As discussed earlier (see equation (3.66)), a payer swaption is equivalent to a put option with a strike rate equal to the notional value F, written on a default-free coupon bond with face value F, maturing at time S_N, with coupons of size $F \times K \times \hat{s}_j$, payable at times S_{j+1} (for $j = 0, 1, 2, \ldots, N - 1$). The value of the put option can be obtained using the various term structure models in the various chapters of this book. Equating the *model price* obtained using a given term structure model to the Black formula given on the right-hand side of equation (3.92), and using $\vartheta_{S, \, Model}$ instead of $\vartheta_{S, \, Market}$, solves the Black implied model volatility of the payer swaption corresponding to that term structure model. Solving $\vartheta_{S, \, Model}$ for different values of S_0 and $S_N - S_0$ gives a two-dimensional surface of model volatilities for the given strike price K. The usefulness of a term structure model for pricing swaptions can be assessed by how well the two-dimensional surface of Black implied model volatilities fits the corresponding surface of Black implied market volatilities. Applying the same method to equation (3.93) solves the Black implied model volatility of a receiver swaption.

Black Implied Volatilities: Caplet

Market Volatilities   The Black implied market volatility of the *i*th (for $i = 0, 1, 2, 3, \ldots, n - 1$) caplet with the payoff defined in equation (3.77) can be obtained by equating the market-observed caplet price to the Black formula of the caplet price, as follows:

$$P^{Market}_{Caplet_i}(t) = F \times \hat{U}_i \times P(t, T_{i+1}) \left(f(t, T_i, T_{i+1}) \mathcal{N}(d_{1,i}) - K_i \mathcal{N}(d_{2,i}) \right) \qquad (3.94)$$

where

$\mathcal{N}(.) = $ cumulative normal distribution function

$$d_{1,i} = \frac{\ln(f(t, T_i, T_{i+1})/K_i) + \vartheta^2_{i, Market}(T_i - t)/2}{\vartheta_{i, \, Market} \sqrt{T_i - t}}$$

$$d_{2,i} = \frac{\ln(f(t, T_i, T_{i+1})/K_i) - \vartheta^2_{i, Market}(T_i - t)/2}{\vartheta_{i, Market} \sqrt{T_i - t}}$$

The only unknown in equation (3.94) is the Black implied market volatility, $\vartheta_{i, Market}$, which can be solved for different values of T_i, giving the term structure of Black implied market volatilities for a given strike price K_i.

Model Volatilities   As shown in equation (3.83), the model price of the *i*th caplet can be given as follows:

$$P^{Model}_{Caplet_i}(t) = \frac{F}{\hat{K}_i} p_i^{Model}(t), \quad t \leq T_i \qquad (3.95)$$

where $p_i^{Model}(t)$ is the model price of a European put option with a strike price $\hat{K}_i$, expiring on date T_i, written on a \$1 face-value zero-coupon bond maturing at time T_{i+1}, obtained using a given term structure model (the analytical solutions of European puts under various single and multiple-factor term structure models are given in various chapters of the book). Equating the *model price* of the caplet obtained using a specific term structure model to the Black formula given on the right-hand side of equation (3.94) and using $\vartheta_{i,Model}$ instead of $\vartheta_{i,Market}$ solves the Black implied model volatility of the caplet. The model volatility can be solved for different values of T_i, giving the term structure of Black implied model volatilities for a given strike price K_i.

Black Implied Volatilities: Caps

Market Volatilities   Individual caplets don't trade in interest rate derivative markets. Since an interest rate cap is a sum of interest rate caplets with increasing expiration dates (see equation (3.89)), a caplet with the payoff defined in equation (3.77) can be replicated as the difference between two caps with successive expiration dates T_i and T_{i+1}. However, caps with successive expiration dates are not generally observable, so it is not always possible to replicate the individual caplets from the market observable caps. In absence of data on individual caplet prices, practitioners frequently look at Black implied volatilities of caps. The Black implied market volatility of the *j*th (for $j = 1, 2, 3, \ldots, n$) cap with the last payment date T_j can be defined by equating the market-observed cap price to the sum of caplet prices using the Black formula, as follows:

$$
P_{Cap}^{Market}(t,\ T_j) = F \times \sum_{i=0}^{j-1} \hat{U}_i \times P(t,\ T_{i+1}) \left(f(t,\ T_i,\ T_{i+1}) \mathcal{N}(d_{1,i}) - K \mathcal{N}(d_{2,i}) \right)
$$

$$(3.96)$$

where

$$
d_{1,i} = \frac{\ln(f(t,\ T_i,\ T_{i+1})/K) + \vartheta_{j,CAP,Market}^2 (T_i - t)/2}{\vartheta_{j,CAP,Market}\sqrt{T_i - t}}
$$

$$
d_{2,i} = \frac{\ln(f(t,\ T_i,\ T_{i+1})/K) - \vartheta_{j,CAP,Market}^2 (T_i - t)/2}{\vartheta_{j,CAP,Market}\sqrt{T_i - t}}
$$

The only unknown in equation (3.96) is the Black implied market volatility, $\vartheta_{j,CAP,Market}$, which can be solved for different values of T_j (for $j = 1, 2, 3, \ldots, n$), giving the term structure of Black implied market volatilities for caps for a given strike price K. Note that equation (3.96) uses the same level of market volatility, $\vartheta_{j,CAP,Market}$, for all individual caplets comprising the cap. Of course, this does not imply that individual caplets have the same level of market volatility, but that the market volatility of a cap is quoted as some nonlinear average of the market volatilities of the individual caplets. Solving $\vartheta_{j,CAP,Market}$ for different values of $j = 1, 2, \ldots, n$ gives the term structure of Black implied market volatilities of caps.

Model Volatilities   The Black implied model volatility of the jth (for $j = 1, 2, 3, \ldots, n$) cap with the last payment date on T_j can be defined by equating the cap price obtained using a given term structure model (see equation (3.89)) to the Black formula given on the right-hand side of equation (3.96) and then solving for $\vartheta_{j,CAP,Model}$ instead of $\vartheta_{j,CAP,Market}$. Solving $\vartheta_{j,CAP,Model}$ for different values of $j = 1, 2, \ldots, n$ gives the term structure of Black implied model volatilities of caps.

The usefulness of a term structure model can be assessed by how well the term structure of Black implied model volatilities $\vartheta_{j,CAP,Model}$ fits the term structure of Black implied market volatilities $\vartheta_{j,CAP,Market}$. A good term structure model must display stability in parameters over time while allowing a good fit between the model and the market volatilities.

Black Implied Volatilities: Difference Caps

Since caps are portfolios of caplets, the Black implied volatilities of two very long maturity caps with adjacent maturities will be virtually identical using the proposed method given in the previous section, which may lead to estimation problems. Jarrow, Li, and Zhao [2007] suggest another method for computing Black implied volatilities using *difference caps*, which are given as the difference between two adjacent maturity cap prices. If caps of all maturities are available to span caplet prices, then a difference cap is simply an individual caplet. However, when caps of all maturities are not available, a difference cap will be given as a sum of just a few caplets, allowing a better differentiation of implied volatilities that correspond to caplets in different maturity ranges. For example, a difference cap given as the difference between two caps maturing on dates 9.5 years and 10 years, with quarterly payments, is the sum of two caplets with payment dates on 9.75 years and 10 years. The methodology for computing Black implied market volatilities and model volatilities for difference caps is similar to that for caps given earlier, except one uses the *difference* between two adjacent cap prices instead of cap prices themselves.

PRICING CREDIT DERIVATIVES USING THE REDUCED-FORM APPROACH

The past quarter century has witnessed an explosive growth in the notional value of over-the-counter (OTC) interest rate derivatives, from virtually nothing in 1980 to almost $262 trillion at the end of June 2006. The most optimistic of forecasters in 1980 could not have predicted even a fraction of this growth. The fundamental principle underlying the widespread use of interest rate derivatives is that firms should manage risks related to economic activities in which they *specialize* and should hedge unwanted risks. As the global financial markets get more integrated and firms compete more fiercely to add value by becoming more specialized, the definition of "unwanted risks" has become broader.

An unwanted risk for many financial institutions is the credit risk exposure resulting from *high concentration* of loans and/or securities in only a few sectors. As financial lending firms become more specialized in certain sectors, the concentration of funds in those sectors rises, increasing the overall credit risk exposure of these firms. The recent innovations in credit derivatives offer a natural way to eliminate the concentration risk, while simultaneously allowing efficiencies resulting from specialization in certain sectors. The lending institutions can do this by buying protection in the sectors in which they are heavily concentrated and selling protection (or insurance) in sectors in which they have little risk exposure. In addition to traditional lending institutions, security houses and hedge funds are also able to hedge some of the unwanted risks in their portfolios using credit derivatives. Though insurance companies and large banks have traditionally been the major sellers of credit derivatives, recent estimates of the British Bankers' Association survey suggest that hedge funds have also joined in as major sellers, in addition to being the major buyers.

Though the size of the credit derivatives market is much smaller than the size of the interest rate derivatives market, most of the growth in this market is yet to be realized. According to the Bank for International Settlements (BIS) the notional value of the credit default swaps grew from less than $1 trillion in June 2001 to more than $20 trillion at the end of June 2006. At present, credit default swaps dominate the credit derivatives market, comprising more than half of the notional value. Though book three in the trilogy on the Fixed Income Valuation Course covers the valuation of credit derivatives in more detail, this section gives the basic "reduced-form approach" for pricing credit derivatives. The reduced-form approach allows a direct application of the term structure technology from the interest rate derivatives area to the credit derivatives area. As an example, this section presents a formula for pricing credit default swaps, and Chapters 9 and 10 provide full analytical solutions of this formula using multiple-factor affine and quadratic models, respectively.

Unlike the structural models of Merton [1974] and Longstaff and Schwartz [1995], in which default process is modeled endogenously by specifying the underlying asset return process and the default regions, the reduced-form approach is based upon an exogenous modeling of the default process. The default process, with specific assumptions about the recovery rate in default combined with a term structure model for the default-free short rate, leads to parsimonious formulas for pricing risky bonds and associated credit derivatives. The preference-free framework presented in this book is especially suited for the reduced-form approach, as this framework allows calibrating virtually any affine or quadratic term structure model to initial default-free zero-coupon bond prices and initial risky zero-coupon bond prices.

Default Intensity and Survival Probability

To grasp the intuition underlying the reduced-form approach, consider a risky zero-coupon bond maturing at time T with a *promised* face value of $1. The risky bond may default at any time until maturity for various reasons including bankruptcy, restructuring, and so forth. Let the default probability process, also known as the intensity process, be defined by the variable $\lambda(t)$, where $\lambda(t)\Delta t$ gives the probability of default by time $t + \Delta t$, given that default has not occurred until time t. Suppose $\lambda(t) = \lambda$ is a constant. Then the survival probability from time 0 until time $S(0 \leq S \leq T)$, which is the probability of default not occurring from time 0 until time S, can be computed as a product of N probabilities, given as follows:

$$\underbrace{(1 - \lambda\Delta t)(1 - \lambda\Delta t)(1 - \lambda\Delta t)\cdots(1 - \lambda\Delta t)}_{N \text{ times}} \qquad (3.97)$$

where $N = S/\Delta t$ is the total number of intervals of size Δt over the period 0 to S. As Δt becomes infinitesimally small, $(1 - \lambda\Delta t)$ converges to $\exp(-\lambda\Delta t)$, and the survival probability can be expressed as follows:

$$\lim_{\Delta t \to 0} \underbrace{(e^{-\lambda\Delta t})(e^{-\lambda\Delta t})(e^{-\lambda\Delta t})\cdots(e^{-\lambda\Delta t})}_{S/\Delta t \text{ number of times}} = \lim_{\Delta t \to 0} e^{-\sum_{i=1}^{S/\Delta t} \lambda\Delta t} = e^{-\int_0^S \lambda\, dt} = e^{-\lambda S}$$

$$(3.98)$$

If the variable τ represents the *default time*, then the probability that the default time is *after* time S equals the survival probability until time S, or:

$$P(\tau > S) = e^{-\lambda S} \qquad (3.99)$$

The assumption of a constant intensity λ is unrealistic for the default process because firm-specific variables, such as financial leverage, operating leverage, and industry- and economy-wide factors, make λ change over time. Hence, consider the first generalization of the survival probability, where the default intensity is assumed to be a deterministic function of time given as $\lambda(t)$. Under this case, the survival probability is obtained following the same steps given in equations (3.97) to (3.99), as follows:

$$\mathcal{P}(\tau > S) = \lim_{\Delta t \to 0} e^{-\sum_{i=1}^{S/\Delta t} \lambda((i-1)\Delta t)\Delta t} = e^{-\int_0^S \lambda(t)\,dt} \qquad (3.100)$$

As a second and more realistic generalization of the survival probability, assume that the intensity process itself evolves stochastically over time in response to the stochastic changes in firm, industry, and economy-wide variables. Since both the default intensity and the probability of default are stochastic, the models arising from this assumption are also called doubly stochastic models. Under this case, the survival probability is given as the time-zero expectation of the expression in equation (3.100) given as follows:

$$\mathcal{P}(\tau > S) = E\left(e^{-\int_0^S \lambda(t)\,dt}\right) \qquad (3.101)$$

The expression for the survival probability reminds us of a familiar expression from the continuous-time term structure theory for default-free bonds. If the intensity process can be thought of as the short-rate process, the survival probability is analogous to the price of a default-free zero-coupon bond (see equation (2.114) in Chapter 2). Since analytical solutions exist for the price of a zero-coupon bond under a variety of affine, quadratic, and HJM term structure models (given in Chapters 4 through 11 in this book), by modeling the stochastic dynamics of the intensity process similar to those of the short-rate process, we immediately obtain analytical solutions to the survival probability from the term structure literature.

Recovery Assumptions

To move further in our analysis, we must now make some assumptions regarding the recovery value of the risky bonds upon default. Lando [1998] makes the "recovery of face value" (RFV) assumption, according to which a bondholder recovers a fraction $1 - L_F$ of the face value of the bond in the event of default. Duffie and Singleton [1999] make a "recovery of market value" (RMV) assumption, according to which the value of a risky zero-coupon bond that defaults at any time is a fraction $1 - L_M$ of its nondefaulted market value at that time. We now provide the basic frameworks for risk-neutral valuation under both the RMV and the RFV assumptions.[8] Though both assumptions can be used for pricing risky bonds, neither of them is suited for pricing all credit derivatives. For example, credit default swaps are priced more naturally using the RFV assumption, while credit spread options are priced more easily using the RMV assumption.

Risk-Neutral Valuation under the RMV Assumption

Let $D(t, T)$ be the nondefaulted market value of a $1 face-value risky zero-coupon bond at time t. Let $\tilde{L}_M$ be the risk-neutral loss rate, such that if the bond defaults at time t, its market value equals $D(t, T)(1 - \tilde{L}_M)$. Using the arbitrage-free pricing results in Chapter 2, the current price of the bond is given as the risk-neutral expectation of its value in the next period, or:

$$D(t, T) = \tilde{E}_t \left(\frac{D(t + dt, T)(1 - \tilde{L}_M)\tilde{\lambda}(t)\, dt + D(t + dt, T)(1 - \tilde{\lambda}(t)\, dt)}{e^{r(t)dt}} \right)$$

(3.102)

where $\tilde{\lambda}(t)dt$ is the risk-neutral probability of default occurring at time $t + dt$, given no default has occurred until time t. The risk-neutral default intensity $\tilde{\lambda}(t)$ and the physical default intensity $\lambda(t)$ will be generally different since investors demand a risk premium related to the risk of default. Similarly, the risk-neutral loss $\tilde{L}_M$ rate will be different from the physical loss rate L_M, due to a risk premium related to the loss given default. In general, $\tilde{\lambda}(t)$ and $\tilde{L}_M$ cannot be observed separately using the market data under the RMV approach.[9]

Simplifying equation (3.102) gives:

$$D(t, T) = \tilde{E}_t \left(\frac{D(t + dt, T)(1 - \tilde{\lambda}(t)\tilde{L}_M\, dt)}{e^{r(t)dt}} \right) = \tilde{E}_t \left(\frac{D(t + dt, T)(e^{-\tilde{\lambda}(t)\tilde{L}_M dt})}{e^{r(t)dt}} \right)$$

(3.103)

Define a new variable called the risk-neutral *mean* loss rate, given as the product of the risk-neutral default intensity and the risk-neutral loss rate given default, as follows:

$$s(t) = \tilde{\lambda}(t)\tilde{L}_M$$

(3.104)

Rearranging the terms in equation (3.103), we get:

$$D(t, T) = \tilde{E}_t \left(\frac{D(t + dt, T)}{e^{(r(t)+s(t))dt}} \right) = \tilde{E}_t \left(\frac{D(t + dt, T)}{e^{R(t)dt}} \right)$$

(3.105)

where $R(t)$ is defined as the instantaneous *risky* short rate, given as:

$$R(t) = r(t) + s(t)$$

(3.106)

By taking iterative expectations, equation (3.105) immediately gives:

$$D(t, T) = \tilde{E}_t \left(\frac{\$1}{e^{\int_t^T R(v)dv}} \right)$$

(3.107)

Hence, the nondefaulted risky zero-coupon bond is priced exactly as a default-free bond, except that the default-free short rate $r(t)$ is replaced by the risky short rate $R(t)$. The significance of this discovery by Madan and Unal [1998] and Jarrow, et al. cannot be overstated. It makes the entire technology of modern term structure theory, with analytical solutions and numerical applications, available for pricing risky bonds and many types of credit derivatives. The risky short rate is given as a sum of two variables in equation (3.106). By appropriately redefining the variables, analytical formulas are derived in Chapters 9 and 10 for pricing risky bonds.

Since risk-neutral default intensity is modeled as an exogenous process and the risk-neutral loss rate affects the market value of all cash flows from a bond in the same proportion, a coupon bond can be priced as a portfolio of zero-coupon bonds as follows:

$$D_{Coup}(t) = \tilde{E}_t \left(\sum_{i=1}^{n} \frac{C}{e^{\int_t^{T_i} R(v)\,dv}} + \frac{F}{e^{\int_t^{T_n} R(v)\,dv}} \right) \qquad (3.108)$$

where C is the promised coupon payment at time $T_i (i = 1, 2, \ldots, n)$ and F is the face value of the bond.

Risk-Neutral Valuation under the RFV Assumption

Under the recovery of face-value assumption, a bondholder recovers a fraction $1 - \tilde{L}_F$ of the face value of the bond in the event of default. Though risky bonds can be priced using either the RMV or the RFV assumption, certain credit derivatives such as spread options are easier to value using the RMV assumption, while other derivatives such as credit default swaps (CDS) are easier to value using the RFV assumption. We now demonstrate the valuation of risky bonds and CDS using the RFV assumption.

We again apply the principle of risk-neutral valuation from Chapter 2. Consider a coupon bond, with coupons C occurring at time T_i $(i = 1, 2, \ldots, n)$, and face value F occurring at time T_n. This bond can be valued as the risk-neutral expectation of the sum of two sets of cash flows. The first set of cash flows assumes *zero* recovery under default; hence, the market value of the bond goes to zero in the event of default. The second set of cash flows represents the cash flows recovered in the event of a default. The first set of cash flows can be valued using the mathematical setup of the RMV approach by simply assuming that the risk-neutral loss rate $\tilde{L}_M$ is 100 percent, or equal to 1. Using this approach, $s(t) = \tilde{\lambda}(t)$ in equation (3.104) and $R(t) = r(t) + \tilde{\lambda}(t)$ in equation (3.106). Substituting these expressions in equation (3.108), the risk-neutral expectation of the first set of cash flows from the bond is given as follows:

$$\tilde{E}_t\left(\sum_{i=1}^{n}\frac{C}{e^{\int_t^{T_i}(r(v)+\tilde{\lambda}(v))\,dv}}+\frac{F}{e^{\int_t^{T_n}(r(v)+\tilde{\lambda}(v))\,dv}}\right) \qquad (3.109)$$

To compute the present value of the second set of cash flows, we use the RFV assumption that a bondholder recovers a fraction $1-\tilde{L}_F$ of the face value of the bond at the *default time* τ. However, computing this requires the time t risk-neutral probability density of default time, which is the time t probability that default will occur in the infinitesimal interval τ to $\tau+d\tau$, where $\tau\in[t,T_n]$. This density must equal the time t risk-neutral probability of survival until time τ, multiplied by the time τ probability of default in the next instantaneous interval. Hence, this density can be obtained using the results derived earlier as follows:

$$\textit{Probability Density of Default Time}=e^{-\int_t^{\tau}\tilde{\lambda}(v)\,dv}\tilde{\lambda}(\tau)\,d\tau \qquad (3.110)$$

Note that this probability density is a random variable at time t. The risk-neutral discounted value of the recovery cash flow can be given as follows:

$$\tilde{E}_t\left(\int_t^{T_n}\left(\frac{F(1-\tilde{L}_F)e^{-\int_t^{\tau}\tilde{\lambda}(v)\,dv}\tilde{\lambda}(\tau)}{e^{\int_t^{\tau}r(v)\,dv}}\right)d\tau\right)$$

$$=F(1-\tilde{L}_F)\tilde{E}_t\left(\int_t^{T_n}\tilde{\lambda}(\tau)e^{-\int_t^{\tau}(r(v)+\tilde{\lambda}(v))\,dv}\,d\tau\right) \qquad (3.111)$$

Adding the risk-neutral expected values of the two sets of cash flows in equations (3.109) and (3.111), respectively, we get the price of the risky coupon bond as follows:

$$D_{Coup}(t)=\tilde{E}_t\left(\sum_{i=1}^{n}\frac{C}{e^{\int_t^{T_i}(r(v)+\tilde{\lambda}(v))\,dv}}+\frac{F}{e^{\int_t^{T_n}(r(v)+\tilde{\lambda}(v))\,dv}}\right)$$

$$+F(1-\tilde{L}_F)\tilde{E}_t\left(\int_t^{T_n}\tilde{\lambda}(\tau)e^{-\int_t^{\tau}(r(v)+\tilde{\lambda}(v))\,dv}\,d\tau\right) \qquad (3.112)$$

Valuing Credit Default Swaps Using the RFV Assumption

A single-name credit default swap between two parties can be illustrated as follows. The first party wants to protect itself from the risk of default on a bond issued by a company or a government, and so it buys insurance from the second party, the protection seller who is willing to insure the bond and bear the risk of default by the given company or the government. The protection buyer pays a periodic fee called the default swap premium to the protection seller. In the event of default, the protection seller buys the bond from the protection buyer for the full face value of the bond, and the protection buyer discontinues making periodic payments to the protection seller. If default does not occur, then the protection buyer continues to make periodic payments until the contract expires. As opposed to single-name credit default swaps, more general credit default swaps may allow the protection buyer to deliver the cheapest-to-deliver bond from a pool of prespecified bonds.

Consider a single-name credit default swap that requires the protection buyer to pay p $(p = N/(T - t))$ number of premiums each year until the bond defaults, for a maximum number of N periods over $T - t$ years. Let the annualized credit default swap spread (or premium) be given as $CDS(t)$ for every \$1 of the face value of the bond. The premium leg of the credit default swap makes payments in those states in which the underlying bond does not default and makes zero payments in those states in which the bond defaults. Hence, using the results given earlier, the present value of the premium leg is given by the following risk-neutral expectation:

$$\tilde{E}_t \left(\sum_{i=1}^{N} \frac{CDS(t)/p}{e^{\int_t^{t+i/p} (r(v) + \tilde{\lambda}(v))\, dv}} \right) \tag{3.113}$$

The protection seller must pay the difference between the face value of the bond and the market value of the bond when the bond defaults. This loss is exogenously specified as $\tilde{L}_F$ under the RFV assumption, which is why a CDS is priced more naturally under this assumption than under the RMV assumption. Using the probability density of default time given in equation (3.110), the present value of the protection leg for every \$1 of face value of the bond is given by the following risk-neutral expectation:

$$\tilde{L}_F \tilde{E}_t \left(\int_t^T \tilde{\lambda}(\tau) e^{-\int_t^\tau (r(v) + \tilde{\lambda}(v))\, dv}\, d\tau \right) \tag{3.114}$$

Equating the present value of the premium leg to the present value of the protection leg solves the default swap premium as follows:

$$CDS(t) = \frac{p \tilde{L}_F \tilde{E}_t \left(\int_t^T \tilde{\lambda}(\tau) e^{-\int_t^\tau (r(v) + \tilde{\lambda}(v))\, dv}\, d\tau \right)}{\tilde{E}_t \left(\sum_{i=1}^{N} e^{-\int_t^{t+i/p} (r(v) + \tilde{\lambda}(v))\, dv} \right)} \tag{3.115}$$

In Chapters 9 and 10, we give analytical solutions to the formula in equation (3.115) using a variety of multifactor affine and quadratic term structure models.

A NEW TAXONOMY OF TERM STRUCTURE MODELS

The origins of term structure models can be traced back to a footnote in the Nobel prize–winning work of Merton [1973], in which he related the dynamics of the bond price to that of the instantaneous default-free short rate. Like other famous footnotes in finance, this footnote was extended in many directions, eventually leading to the whole subfield of finance known as "term structure models." These models translate the uncertainty in interest rates into the uncertainty in traded securities in an arbitrage-free setting, thus allowing a rational determination of the prices of financial derivatives whose value depends upon the evolution in interest rates.

Though Merton *conceived* the idea of term structure modeling, Vasicek can be called the real father of term structure theory. From the earliest term structure models to the latest innovations, all use the basic arbitrage-free framework introduced by Vasicek [1977]. Though Vasicek is now associated with the specific example of the Ornstein-Uhlenbeck process for the instantaneous short rate, his original paper can be used to model virtually any Markovian term structure model in which zero-coupon yields are the underlying drivers of uncertainty. For example, all short-rate models, from the square root model of Cox, Ingersoll, and Ross (CIR) [1985] to the multifactor ATSMs of Dai and Singleton [2000] are solved using the partial differential equation known as the *term structure equation* originally derived by Vasicek. Additional restrictions can be imposed on the market price of interest rate risk (reward for bearing risk) using the equilibrium frameworks developed by CIR and others. Of course, these restrictions are consistent with Vasicek's term structure equation since "absence of arbitrage" conditions are weaker than the "equilibrium" conditions.

The Vasicek and CIR models are *fundamental* term structure models (TSMs), which, like all other fundamental TSMs, share two properties, as follows:

1. A time-homogenous short-rate process
2. An explicit specification of the market prices of risks

Fundamental TSMs value default-free zero-coupon bonds using the information related to investors' risk aversion and expected movements in the interest rates, similar to how fundamental equity models value stocks using the information related to earnings, systematic risk, and growth rate in earnings. A variety of multifactor fundamental TSMs have been derived in the past decade, chief among them being models in the affine and quadratic classes.[10] Fundamental models are applied by traders interested in *relative arbitrage* among default-free bonds of different maturities. These models are estimated using econometric techniques such as maximum likelihood, generalized method of moments, simulated method of moments, and so forth, using time-series data on zero-coupon yields. The intrinsic model prices implied by fundamental models may or may not converge to the market prices of bonds.

In contrast to fundamental models, preference-free models *do not require explicit specifications of the market prices of risks* for valuing bonds and interest rate derivatives. Hence, valuation can be done without knowing the risk preferences of the market participants under preference-free models.

This book considers three types of preference-free TSMs given as single-plus, double-plus, and triple-plus models. We show that a preference-free single-plus TSM exists corresponding to every fundamental TSM. The only difference between the fundamental TSM and the corresponding preference-free single-plus TSM is that the former requires an explicit specification of the market prices of risks (MPRs), while the latter does not require MPRs for valuing bonds and interest rate derivatives. In effect, since the latter does not require MPRs, it is consistent with general, nonlinear specifications of MPRs, which allows it to fit better with the market prices of bonds and interest rate derivatives. Though preference-free single-plus models may not fit the observed bond prices using only one or two factors, these models can be calibrated well to the observed bond prices with three or more factors.

The risk-neutral stochastic processes of the state variables under any single-plus TSM are identical *in form* to the risk-neutral stochastic processes of the state variables under the corresponding fundamental TSM. However, the empirical estimates of the risk-neutral parameters are generally different under these two models, as the latter model imposes restrictive functional forms on the specifications of MPRs. The restrictive MPRs under the latter model also imply that the stochastic processes of the state variables under these two models are different under the physical measure.

The trick to the derivation of a single-plus TSM corresponding to a given fundamental TSM is to specify the stochastic bond price process exogenously using the same form of volatility function used under the given fundamental model. The exogenous stochastic bond price process is then combined with an exogenously given solution of the time-zero bond prices or forward rates, which leads to a time-homogenous risk-neutral short-process. By fitting the prices implied by the single-plus TSM to the time-zero observed prices of bonds and interest rate derivatives, the risk-neutral parameters and state variable values are determined. Since single-plus TSMs obtain the short-rate process endogenously using an exogenous stochastic bond price process, these models allow independence from the MPRs. On the other hand, since fundamental TSMs assume the short-rate process under the physical measure and since the short rate does not trade, these models require explicit dependence on the MPRs for obtaining valuation formulas of bonds and interest rate derivatives.

The preference-free double-plus TSMs are different from the corresponding fundamental TSMs in two ways. These models are not only free of the MPR specifications—similar to the single-plus models—but they also allow the model bond prices to exactly fit the initially observed bond prices. Unlike the single-plus TSMs that may require multiple factors to match the model prices with the observed prices, the double-plus TSMs can allow an exact fit even using a single factor. The initially observed bond prices are used as an input under the double-plus TSMs. These models exactly fit the initially observed bond prices by allowing time inhomogeneity in the drift of the risk-neutral short rate process. This is unlike the single-plus models, which require a time-homogeneous drift for the risk-neutral short-rate process. Examples of double-plus TSMs include the models by Ho and Lee [1986], Hull and White [1990],[11] Heath, Jarrow, and Morton (HJM) [1992], and Brigo and Mercurio [2001].[12] Though double-plus models can be derived corresponding to all fundamental TSMs (or corresponding to all single-plus TSMs), the reverse is not necessarily true. For example, no fundamental TSM or single-plus TSM may exist corresponding to the non-Markovian double-plus HJM models.[13]

The preference-free triple-plus TSMs are different from the corresponding fundamental TSMs in three ways. Unlike the fundamental models, but similar to single-plus and double-plus models, these models are free of the MPR specifications. Unlike the fundamental and single-plus models, but similar to double-plus models, these models allow an exact fit with the initially observed bond prices. However, unlike the fundamental, single-plus and double-plus models, which all require a *time-homogeneous* specification of volatilities, the triple-plus TSMs allow time-inhomogeneous volatilities (i.e., time-inhomogeneous short-rate volatility and/or time-inhomogeneous forward-rate volatilities). Examples of triple-plus TSMs include extensions of the models of Hull and White [1990],[14] Black, Derman, and Toy [1990], and Black and Karasinski [1991] with time-inhomogeneous volatilities, and versions of LIBOR market model with time-inhomogeneous volatilities (see Brigo and Mercurio [2001, 2006] and Rebonato [2002]). These models originated from the work of practitioners interested in pricing exotic interest rate derivatives, relative to the pricing of some plain vanilla derivative benchmarks, such as caps and/or swaptions. The triple-plus models are motivated by the need to *exactly* fit the initial prices of the chosen set of plain vanilla derivatives, in addition to exactly fitting the initial bond prices. However, the triple-plus models require a high number of parameters to obtain an exact fit with the chosen plain vanilla derivative instruments and may suffer from the criticism of "smoothing."

Figure 3.3 depicts our Bayesian priors regarding the usefulness of various classes of term structure models using an inverted U-curve that plots the usefulness of the TSMs against the number of plusses, with zero-plus denoting the fundamental TSMs. Going from zero-plus to one-plus, the marginal benefit may be significant, as allowing flexibility in the specifications of MPRs is known to significantly enhance the performance of term structure models (see Duffee [2002] and Duarte [2004]). Hence, allowing TSMs to be completely independent of MPRs makes these models consistent with very general, nonlinear MPRs and allows more realistic stochastic processes under the physical measure. For example, as shown in Chapter 8, the two-factor single-plus affine model, or the $A_2(2)+$ model, can allow *negative* unconditional correlation between the two state variables under the physical measure, even though it must disallow negative correlation under the risk-neutral measure. In contrast, the two-factor fundamental affine model, or the $A_2(2)$ model, must disallow negative correlation under both the physical measure and the risk-neutral measure (see Dai and Singleton [2000]). The bond pricing formulas and the entire analytical apparatus for pricing derivatives is identical under the fundamental TSMs and single-plus TSMs, except that the empirical estimates of the risk-neutral parameters may be different under these two classes of models.

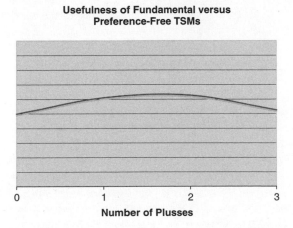

FIGURE 3.3 The Usefulness of Fundamental versus Preference-Free Models

Though single-plus models allow a time-homogeneous short-rate process, these models may not allow a good fit between the model bond prices and the observed bond prices when using a very small number of factors (e.g., only one or two factors). Hence, double-plus models may be useful, as these models allow exact calibration to the initially observed bond prices, even with a low number of factors, by allowing a time-inhomogeneous short-rate process. Further, since double-plus models are preference free, they share the same advantage of the single-plus models over the fundamental models, as mentioned earlier. However, as the number of factors increases, the advantage of having a time-homogeneous short rate process may dominate the disadvantage of not *exactly* fitting the initially observed bond prices, using single-plus models. This is because with a higher number of factors, single-plus models can fit the observed bond prices almost perfectly, if not exactly.

Though the triple-plus models may at first appear more general than single-plus or double-plus models, these models suffer from the criticism of "smoothing." In the discussion to follow, we define the term "smoothing" to imply fitting financial models to a set of observed prices without an underlying economic rationale. The concept of smoothing is different from overfitting in that the former implies fitting without an economic rationale, while the latter implies fitting based upon some economic rationale but using more parameters than needed to obtain a good fit. Smoothing may overlook some important relationships that could potentially be modeled endogenously, while overfitting fits to the noise present in the data. In other words, smoothing allows the modeler to ignore some important economic relationships by making entirely ad hoc adjustments to fit the model to observed prices (thus failing to deal with the misspecification error caused by some hidden variables), while overfitting allows the modeler to invent economic relationships that don't exist but are artifacts of the noise present in the observed prices.

A simple example of smoothing is using the Black and Scholes model for pricing equity call options of different strikes and using different volatilities corresponding to different strikes to fit the "smile" with a third-order polynomial function. If the dynamics of the smile are not modeled based on some economic fundamentals, then a trader may not know why and how the option smile changes over time. The option smile obviously represents some systematic economic factor(s), but incorporating these factor(s) into the option prices is beyond the scope of the Black and Scholes model. Perhaps a stochastic volatility/jump model is needed to fit the smile. Yet, if traders continue to use the Black and Scholes model to price options by adjusting the implied volatilities across different strikes to fit the smile using a third-order polynomial, then they are smoothing. Smoothing basically allows the option trader to price an option of a given strike, given the observed prices of options with strikes surrounding the given strike. However, traders can achieve such smoothed prices even by performing a giant Taylor series expansion without any knowledge of stochastic processes that drive the stock price movements.

Similarly, it would be wise to be aware of the dangers of smoothing while considering triple-plus TSMs with a high degree of time-inhomogeneity in the volatility process. Though some level of smoothing is present even under the double-plus models, the extent of smoothing under triple-plus models can make these models highly unreliable. The use of time-inhomogeneous volatilities as smoothing variables can be traced to the extended versions of the models of Black, Derman, and Toy [1990], Black and Karasinski [1991], and Hull and White [1990]. Though practitioners have mostly discarded these earlier generation models, triple-plus versions of the LIBOR market models remain quite popular. Rebonato [2002], recognizing the danger of this approach, recommends a three-step process that puts most of the burden of capturing the forward-rate volatilities on the time-homogeneous component of the forward-rate volatilities (see Chapter 12). However, since this alleviates the smoothing problem only partially, it is unclear how well the LIBOR model will perform over time, especially since little research exists on the *hedging effectiveness* of this model using the approach of Fan, Gupta, and Ritchken [2003].

This book takes a balanced approach and discusses all models, including fundamental, single-plus, double-plus, and triple-plus TSMs. Though various chapters discuss the fundamental, single-plus, and double-plus TSMs in the affine and quadratic class, we limit our attention to the triple-plus TSMs only to the case of the Vasicek+++ model and the LIBOR market model. These models may not be as useful as deemed by their users, given the high degree of smoothing resulting from two sources of time-homogeneity, one required to fit the initial bond prices and the other required to fit the given set of plain vanilla derivative prices. On the other hand, fundamental TSMs may be too narrowly defined due to the restrictive assumptions about the market prices of risks. The single-plus and double-plus TSMs may offer the best of both worlds, allowing preference-free pricing that appeals to practitioners interested in calibration without a high degree of smoothing. Finally, the usefulness of a given class of term structure model also depends upon the trading horizon. For relatively long horizons, time-homogeneous models such as the fundamental models and the preference-free single-plus models are preferred; for intermediate horizons, the time-inhomogeneous double-plus models are preferred; and for very short horizons (including applications such as daily marking to market of derivative securities), the time-inhomogenous triple-plus models are preferred.

NOTES

1. The reduced-form approach was developed by Madan and Unal [1998], Lando [1998], Jarrow, Lando, and Turnbull [1997], and Duffie and Singleton [1999], among others.
2. See Rebonato [2002].
3. See Santa-Clara and Sornette [2001].
4. The bid rate is known as the London Interbank Bid Rate, or LIBID.
5. In reality, most interest rate swaps exchange the floating cash flows every quarter, and the fixed cash flows every six months.
6. We consider the *spot-start* swap under which the first reset occurs at the same time as the initiation date of the swap.
7. Often individuals put an upper limit on the interest rate applicable to their borrowing through adjustable-rate mortgages using a cap or invest in interest rate products with embedded caps and floors.
8. Jarrow, Lando, and Turnbull [1997] and Lando [1998] assume that default probabilities are related to changes in credit ratings driven by a Markov transition probability matrix, while Madan and Unal [1998] and Duffie and Singleton [1999] do not use probability information from credit ratings changes.
9. See Duffie and Singleton [1997] and Houweling and Vorst [2005]. Pan and Singleton [2005] demonstrate that using the *recovery of face value* approach of Lando [1998] does allow a separate identification of risk-neutral loss variable $\tilde{L}_F$ from the data on sovereign CDS spreads.
10. See the general multifactor affine models of Dai and Singleton [2000, 2002], Duffee [2002], and Duarte [2004], and the multifactor quadratic models of Ahn, Dittmar, and Gallant [2002].
11. See the extended Vasicek model of Hull and White [1990] in Chapter 4.
12. Brigo and Mercurio [2001] summarize various double-plus models, including the CIR++ model and the G2++ model. The G2++ model was originally derived by Hull [1997]. The CIR++ model was originally suggested by CIR [1985, bottom paragraph, p. 395], and derived formally by Dybvig [1988, 1997] and Scott [1995]. Chapter 7 derives the CIR++ model.
13. Throughout this book, we assume that HJM models must imply (1) an exact fit with initially observed bond prices and (2) preference-free valuation independent of MPRs. Since using our classification, these two properties define a preference-free double-plus model, all HJM models are preference-free double-plus TSMs.
14. See the *fully extended* Vasicek model of Hull and White [1990] or the Vasicek+++ model given in Chapter 4.

CHAPTER 4

Fundamental and Preference-Free Single-Factor Gaussian Models

This chapter introduces the fundamental term structure model of Vasicek [1977] and derives the preference-free extensions of this model given as the Vasicek+ model, the Vasicek++ model (i.e., the extended Vasicek model), and the Vasicek+++ model (i.e., the fully extended Vasicek model). The taxonomy of fundamental models and the preference-free models with single-plus, double-plus, and triple-plus classification is given in the previous chapter and applies to all models in this book. The Ho and Lee [1986] model is shown to be a special case of the preference-free Vasicek++ model, without the mean reversion for the short rate.

The Gaussian example in Vasicek [1977] assumes that the short rate follows an Ornstein-Uhlenbeck process. Though the Gaussian assumption simplifies the analysis, it allows interest rates to become negative with a nonzero probability. However, this probability remains small, unlike the case of Merton's arithmetic random walk model of the short rate. Vasicek assumed a constant market price of interest rate risk in his original derivation. This leads to a constant sign of risk premiums on default-free bonds, regardless of the shape of the yield curve. However, recent research by Duffee [2002] suggests that market risk premiums tend to switch signs over time. We derive the Vasicek model with more general specifications of MPRs given by Duffee. The specifications of market prices of risk (MPRs) affect the empirical estimation of the risk-neutral parameters, since MPRs are estimated jointly with the risk-neutral parameters.

The empirical strategy of the estimation of risk-neutral parameters defines whether a term structure model is a fundamental model or a preference-free model. If econometric estimation (using maximum likelihood, generalized method of moments, etc.) obtains physical parameters, MPRs, and risk-neutral parameters jointly, then the model is a fundamental model. All fundamental term structure models require a parametric or a nonparametric estimation of the MPRs and typically impose simple parametric forms on the MPRs.

Preference-free term structure models, on the other hand, do not require the specification of MPRs. These models invert the risk-neutral parameters from the cross section of prices of bonds and interest rate derivatives, without requiring the estimation of the physical parameters or the MPRs. However, since the preference-free models do not require the specification of MPRs, these models implicitly allow general nonlinear MPRs consistent with general nonlinear specifications of market risk premiums on bonds. We introduce both the time-homogeneous preference-free Vasicek+ model and the time-inhomogeneous preference-free Vasicek++ and Vasicek+++ models.

The Vasicek+ model, like all other one-plus models in this book, is a time-homogeneous model. The formulas of the prices of bonds and interest rate derivatives under the Vasicek+ model are identical to these formulas under the fundamental Vasicek model, except that the empirical estimates of the risk-neutral parameters may be different under the two models, as the latter model imposes restrictive linear forms on the MPRs. Due to direct fitting of the Vasicek+ model to the cross section of prices of bonds and interest rate derivatives, it may lead to a more accurate estimation of risk-neutral parameters than the fundamental Vasicek model, if the nonlinear MPRs are the cause of the poor performance of the fundamental model.

Using only one factor is typically not sufficient to fit the prices of bonds and interest rate derivatives, hence neither the fundamental Vasicek model, nor the preference-free Vasicek+ model can fit these prices effectively. Derivative traders, who take initial bond prices as given, are interested in models that can fit the initial bond prices *exactly*. The first such model to be introduced was given by Ho and Lee [1986]. This was quickly followed by general models of this type by Hull and White [1990] and Heath, Jarrow, and Morton [1990, 1992]. These models are also preference-free models, as they do not require an explicit estimation of the physical parameters or the MPRs. However, these models require a time-inhomogeneous process for the short rate to exactly fit the initial bond prices. Using the taxonomy introduced in the previous chapter, we call the preference-free, time-inhomogeneous extension of the Vasicek model the Vasicek++ model, with one plus representing independence from MPRs and the other plus representing time-inhomogeneity required for obtaining an exact fit with the initial bond prices. The Vasicek++ model was introduced by Hull and White [1990] and is also known as the *extended Vasicek model*.

Finally, a more general class of models that not only fits the initial bond prices exactly but also the initial prices of a chosen set of plain vanilla derivatives such as interest rate caps, can be derived by introducing another source of time-inhomogeneity. These models introduced by Hull and White [1990], Black and Karasinzki [1991], Black, Derman, and Toy [1990], and some variations of the LIBOR Market Model (e.g., Rebonato [2002]) allow the short-rate volatility and/or forward-rate volatilities to be time-inhomogeneous. Using the taxonomy introduced in Chapter 3, we denote the preference-free, doubly time-inhomogeneous extension of the Vasicek model as the Vasicek+++ model, with one plus representing independence from MPRs, the second plus representing the time-inhomogeneity required for obtaining an exact fit with the initial bond prices, and the third plus representing the time-inhomogeneity required for fitting the initial prices of the chosen plain vanilla interest rate derivatives, such as caps. The Vasicek+++ model can be used to price other exotic interest rate derivatives using the chosen plain vanilla derivative as the valuation benchmark.

This chapter derives the Vasicek+++ model only for the purpose of exposition of the triple-plus models. As a general rule, based on the critical appraisal of the triple-plus models in the previous chapter, we do not consider these models. The Vasicek+++ model was originally introduced by Hull and White [1990] and is also known as the *fully extended Vasicek model*.

THE ARBITRAGE-FREE PRICING FRAMEWORK OF VASICEK

Vasicek [1977] developed a general arbitrage-free framework for short-rate models of the term structure. Vasicek assumed that the short rate (defined as the rate of return on the instantaneously maturing riskless debt) follows a continuous Markovian diffusion process given as follows:

$$dr(t) = \mu_r(r, t) \, dt + \sigma_r(r, t) \, dZ(t) \qquad (4.1)$$

where $dZ(t)$ is the Wiener process, and $\mu_r(r, t) = \mu_r(r(t), t)$ and $\sigma_r(r, t) = \sigma_r(r(t), t))$ are functions of the short rate $r(t)$ and time t. The function $\mu_r(r, t)$ is called the drift of the short rate, and the function $\sigma_r(r, t)$ is called the volatility of the short rate. The conditional mean and variance of $dr(t)$ (i.e., the change in $r(t)$ over an infinitesimally short interval of time dt conditional on the information available at time t) are given as follows:

$$E_t[\, dr(t)] = \mu_r(r, t) \, dt$$
$$V_t[\, dr(t)] = \sigma_r^2(r, t) \, dt \qquad (4.2)$$

If both functions $\mu_r(r, t)$ and $\sigma_r(r, t)$ are independent of time, the diffusion process is said to be *time-homogeneous*, and the distribution of the short rate $r(T)$ at a future date T will depend only on the current value of $r(t)$

and the time remaining to the future date, $T - t$. Otherwise, the diffusion process is said to be *time-inhomogeneous*, and the distribution of the future short rate $r(T)$ will depend on $r(t)$, $T - t$, and t. As will be shown later, time-homogeneous models disallow perfect calibration with the observed bond prices, while time-inhomogeneous models allow perfect calibration. Vasicek further assumed all riskless zero-coupon bond prices are functions of the short rate $r(t)$, the current time t, and the bond maturity date T, or:

$$P(t, T) = P(r(t), t, T) \tag{4.3}$$

Given this assumption, the entire term structure of zero-coupon yields $y(t, T)$ can be determined as follows:

$$y(t, T) = -\frac{\ln P(r(t), t, T)}{T - t} \tag{4.4}$$

The Term Structure Equation

Vasicek obtained his famous term structure equation using Ito's lemma and absence of arbitrage between riskless bonds. The term structure equation is derived as follows. Using Ito's lemma (see Chapter 1), the stochastic differential equation of the bond price given in equation (4.3) can be obtained from the short-rate process given in equation (4.1), as follows:

$$dP(t, T) = \left(\frac{\partial P}{\partial t} + \mu_r(r, t)\frac{\partial P}{\partial r} + \frac{1}{2}\sigma_r^2(r, t)\frac{\partial^2 P}{\partial r^2} \right) dt + \frac{\partial P}{\partial r}\sigma_r(r, t)\, dZ(t)$$
$$\tag{4.5}$$

By defining the drift and the volatility of the instantaneous bond return as:

$$\mu_p(r, t, T) = \frac{1}{P} \left(\frac{\partial P}{\partial t} + \mu_r(r, t)\frac{\partial P}{\partial r} + \frac{1}{2}\sigma_r^2(r, t)\frac{\partial^2 P}{\partial r^2} \right)$$

$$\sigma_p(r, t, T) = -\frac{1}{P}\sigma_r(r, t)\frac{\partial P}{\partial r} \tag{4.6}$$

the dynamics of the bond price can be expressed as:

$$\frac{dP(t, T)}{P(t, T)} = \mu_p(r, t, T)\, dt - \sigma_p(r, t, T)\, dZ(t) \tag{4.7}$$

where $\mu_p(r, t, T)$ and $\sigma_p(r, t, T)$ are the time t drift and volatility, respectively, of the instantaneous rate of return on the zero-coupon bond.

The term $\sigma_p(r, t, T)$ in equation (4.6) is defined to be positive. This is because bond price is inversely related to the short rate, which makes the partial derivative $\partial P/\partial r$ negative.

Since all bond prices are determined by a single stochastic variable, $r(t)$, the instantaneous returns on all bonds of varying maturities are perfectly correlated. The perfect correlation between any two bonds can be used to create a riskless portfolio comprising these bonds. Further, since the rate of return on a riskless portfolio must equal the riskless return, Vasicek's term structure equation follows immediately. The argument is similar to that used by Black and Scholes to derive the partial differential equation for pricing an option, which is assumed to be perfectly correlated with the underlying stock.

Specifically, consider an investor who at time t issues (or takes a short position) W_1 dollars of a bond maturing at time T_1 and simultaneously buys W_2 dollars of a bond maturing at time T_2. The change in the portfolio net worth is $W = W_2 - W_1$; and, using equation (4.7), it is given as follows:

$$dW(t) = \big(W_2\mu_p(r, t, T_2) - W_1\mu_p(r, t, T_1)\big)\,dt$$
$$- \big(W_2\sigma_p(r, t, T_2) - W_1\sigma_p(r, t, T_1)\big)\,dZ(t) \qquad (4.8)$$

Now consider making the following dollar investments in the two bonds:

$$W_1 = \frac{W\sigma_p(r, t, T_2)}{\sigma_p(r, t, T_1) - \sigma_p(r, t, T_2)}$$

$$W_2 = \frac{W\sigma_p(r, t, T_1)}{\sigma_p(r, t, T_1) - \sigma_p(r, t, T_2)} \qquad (4.9)$$

Substituting these values for W_1 and W_2 in equation (4.8) we get:

$$dW(t) = \frac{W[\mu_p(r, t, T_2)\sigma_p(r, t, T_1) - \mu_p(r, t, T_1)\sigma_p(r, t, T_2)]}{\sigma_p(r, t, T_1) - \sigma_p(r, t, T_2)}\,dt \quad (4.10)$$

Since the choice of W_1 and W_2 in equation (4.9) removes the stochastic terms, the investor's portfolio is riskless in equation (4.10); and, hence it must yield the risk-free rate $r(t)$, or:

$$dW(t) = Wr(t)\,dt \qquad (4.11)$$

By equating equations (4.10) and (4.11), we get:

$$\frac{[\mu_p(r, t, T_2)\sigma_p(r, t, T_1) - \mu_p(r, t, T_1)\sigma_p(r, t, T_2)]}{\sigma_p(r, t, T_1) - \sigma_p(r, t, T_2)} = r(t) \qquad (4.12)$$

Rearranging the terms, we obtain the following important result:

$$\frac{\mu_p(r,\ t,\ T_2) - r(t)}{\sigma_p(r,\ t,\ T_2)} = \frac{\mu_p(r,\ t,\ T_1) - r(t)}{\sigma_p(r,\ t,\ T_1)} \tag{4.13}$$

Since the maturities T_1 and T_2 were chosen arbitrarily, equation (4.13) holds for all terms of maturity $T \geq 0$, giving the *market price of interest rate risk* as follows:

$$\gamma(r,\ t) = -\frac{\mu_p(r,\ t,\ T) - r(t)}{\sigma_p(r,\ t,\ T)} \tag{4.14}$$

where $\gamma(r,\ t)$ is independent of T.

Substituting the formulas for $\mu_p(r,\ t,\ T)$ and $\sigma_p(r,\ t,\ T)$ from equation (4.6) into equation (4.14) and rearranging terms gives Vasicek's term structure equation for the bond price:

$$\frac{\partial P}{\partial t} + [\mu_r(r,\ t) - \sigma_r(r,\ t)\gamma(r,\ t)]\frac{\partial P}{\partial r} + \frac{1}{2}\sigma_r^2(r,\ t)\frac{\partial^2 P}{\partial r^2} - r(t)P(t,\ T) = 0 \tag{4.15}$$

The partial differential equation (4.15) can be solved by using specific functional forms for the drift, the volatility, and the market price of risk, subject to the boundary condition $P(T,\ T) = 1$. The derivation of the term structure equation is quite general, and it applies not only to zero-coupon bonds, but to any security whose value is a function of only $r(t)$ and t. For example, the price of a call option on a zero-coupon bond follows the same term structure equation given previously, except the call price replaces the bond price and the boundary condition changes to the payoff from the call option at time T.

Risk-Neutral Valuation

As shown in Chapter 2, in any complete market, the absence of arbitrage guarantees the existence of an equivalent probability measure under which the value of any security is obtained by discounting its expected future value (at some terminal date) using the riskless rate. The new probability measure is called the *risk-neutral probability measure*, and valuation under this measure is called *risk-neutral valuation*. This is a very powerful result as it allows valuation by simply discounting by the riskless rate once the stochastic processes are expressed under the risk-neutral probability measure. To express the bond-price process and the short-rate process under the risk-neutral measure, reconsider the stochastic differential equation of the bond price by substituting the value of $\mu_p(r, t, T)$ from equation (4.14) into equation (4.7) as follows:

$$\frac{dP(t, T)}{P(t, T)} = \left(r(t) - \gamma(r, t)\sigma_p(r, t, T)\right) dt - \sigma_p(r, t, T) \, dZ(t) \qquad (4.16)$$

Now define a transformation of the Wiener process $dZ(t)$ as follows:

$$d\tilde{Z}(t) = dZ(t) + \gamma(r, t) \, dt \qquad (4.17)$$

According to the Girsanov theorem (see equations (2.57) and (2.58)), under mild regularity conditions related to the Novikov condition, a new equivalent probability measure exists under which the process in equation (4.17) is a Wiener process. The expected value of the new Wiener process is zero *under the new probability measure*, even though its expected value under the original probability measure is nonzero as can be seen from equation (4.17).

Substituting equation (4.17) into equation (4.16), the stochastic bond-price process can be given under the new probability measure as follows:

$$\frac{dP(t, T)}{P(t, T)} = r(t) \, dt - \sigma_p(r, t, T) \, d\tilde{Z}(t) \qquad (4.18)$$

The new probability measure is called the *risk-neutral measure* since the expected return on all bonds under this measure is equal to the riskless short rate. Using the results of Harrison and Kreps [1979], absence of arbitrage guarantees the existence of this probability measure, and the value of any security is obtained by discounting its future value at some terminal date by the short rate.

For valuation, we need the stochastic process for the short rate under the risk-neutral measure. By substituting equation (4.17) into equation (4.1), the short-rate process under the risk-neutral measure is given as:

$$dr(t) = \tilde{\mu}_r(r, t) \, dt + \sigma_r(r, t) \, d\tilde{Z}(t) \qquad (4.19)$$

where $\tilde{\mu}_r(r, t) = \mu_r(r, t) - \gamma(r, t)\sigma_r(r, t)$.

The current price of a zero-coupon bond can be obtained by taking the risk-neutral expectation of the discounted future value, or:

$$P(t, T) = \tilde{E}_t \left[\exp\left[-\int_t^T r(v) \, dv \right] P(T, T) \right] \qquad (4.20)$$

Since the terminal value of a zero-coupon bond at its maturity date T is given by $P(T, T) = 1$, equation (4.20) simplifies to:

$$P(t, T) = \tilde{E}_t \left[\exp \left[- \int_t^T r(v) \, dv \right] \right] \qquad (4.21)$$

The last section of Chapter 2 shows how to solve the expectation of a stochastic integral indirectly by solving a partial differential equation using the Feynman-Kac theorem. We can now apply the Feynman-Kac theorem to obtain the partial differential equation followed by the bond price in equation (4.20), using the risk-neutral short-rate process given in equation (4.19). By making appropriate substitutions in equations (2.107) and (2.108), we obtain the following partial differential equation for the bond price:

$$\frac{\partial P}{\partial t} + \tilde{\mu}_r(r, t) \frac{\partial P}{\partial r} + \frac{1}{2} \sigma_r^2(r, t) \frac{\partial^2 P}{\partial r^2} - r(t)P(t, T) = 0 \qquad (4.22)$$

where, as shown in equation (4.19), $\tilde{\mu}_r(r, t) = \mu_r(r, t) - \gamma(r, t)\sigma_r(r, t)$.

Note that partial differential equation (4.22) is identical to equation (4.15), which was obtained directly by Vasicek to solve for the bond price. Hence, the Feynman-Kac theorem acts as a bridge between the risk-neutral expectations approach (also known as the martingale approach) given in equation (4.21) and the partial differential equation (PDE) approach given in equation (4.22).

Both these approaches are useful, though occasionally one is preferred over the other. The Gaussian examples of short-rate processes lead to solutions for the bond price using both approaches. On the other hand, it is easier to solve the bond price under the Cox, Ingersoll, and Ross model using the PDE approach. Numerical techniques such as finite differencing are applied using the PDE approach, while other numerical methods such as interest rate trees (binomial, trinomial, etc.) are applied using the risk-neutral expectations approach.

THE FUNDAMENTAL VASICEK MODEL

Though Vasicek's main contribution was the development of a robust theoretical framework for modeling the term structure of interest rates, he has become associated more with a specific example of the short-rate process known as the Ornstein-Uhlenbeck process. This process removes a number of shortcomings of the arithmetic random walk model of Merton by allowing the short rate to be mean-reverting. This process is specified as:

$$dr(t) = \alpha(m - r(t)) \, dt + \sigma \, dZ(t) \qquad (4.23)$$

where α, m, and σ are positive constants. Similar to the Merton model, the dynamics of the short rate incorporates random shocks through the diffusion term $\sigma dZ(t)$, which causes the short rate to move randomly from its deterministic trend. However, unlike the Merton model, the specification of the drift allows the short rate to be mean-reverting as the short rate is pulled back to its long-term mean, m, whenever it moves away from it. As shown in Figure 4.1, when the short rate goes below its long-term mean (i.e., $r(t) < m$), the short-rate drift becomes positive and the short-rate is pulled upward. On the other hand, when the short rate goes above its long-term mean (i.e., $r(t) > m$), the short-rate drift becomes negative and the short rate is pulled downward. The speed at which the drift is pulled upward or downward is given by the positive valued parameter α, which measures the speed of mean reversion.[1] The greater the speed, the faster the process reverts toward the long-term mean and the tighter the process is bound to the long-term mean.

Using Monte Carlo simulation, the Ornstein-Uhlenbeck process given by equation (4.23) is illustrated in Figure 4.2 for four different combinations of the parameters α, m, and σ. The initial short rate is set to $r(0) = 4\%$. The first graph in Figure 4.2 corresponds to the base case with values of the parameters given as $\alpha = 0.01$, $m = 2\%$, and $\sigma = 0.5\%$. In the remaining graphs, only one of these parameters is changed.

The top two graphs in Figure 4.2 show that the short rate is pulled toward its long-term mean, toward 2 percent in the first graph, and toward 6 percent in the second graph. The bottom-left graph shows that a higher speed of mean reversion makes the short rate bound more tightly to its long-term mean, thereby reducing the unconditional variance of the future

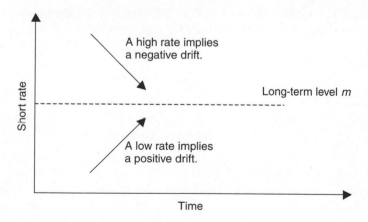

FIGURE 4.1 The Effect of Mean Reversion

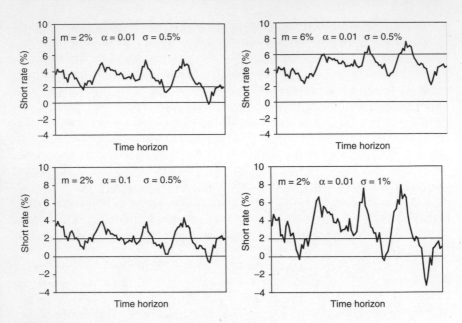

FIGURE 4.2 Sample Paths for Vasicek's Model

short rate. Mean reversion also reduces the probability of attaining negative rates, which is a big advantage of the Vasicek model over Merton's [1973] arithmetic random walk model. Finally, the bottom-right graph shows that higher volatility leads to higher fluctuations of the short rate around its long-term mean.

Using the result in example 1.3 from Chapter 1, the stochastic integral of the short-rate process in equation (4.23) is given as:

$$r(S) = m + (r(t) - m)e^{-\alpha(S-t)} + e^{-\alpha S}\sigma \int_t^S e^{\alpha v}\, dZ(v) \qquad (4.24)$$

Using rule 3 in Chapter 1, the short rate has a Gaussian distribution with the time t mean and variance of the future short rate $r(S)$, given as follows:

$$E_t(r(S)) = m + (r(t) - m)e^{-\alpha(S-t)}$$

$$V_t(r(S)) = e^{-2\alpha S}\sigma^2 \int_t^S e^{2\alpha v}\, dv = e^{-2\alpha S}\sigma^2 \left[\frac{e^{2\alpha S}}{2\alpha} - \frac{e^{2\alpha t}}{2\alpha}\right] = \frac{\sigma^2}{2}\left[\frac{1 - e^{-2\alpha(S-t)}}{\alpha}\right]$$

$$(4.25)$$

Unlike Merton's [1973] simple arithmetic random walk model, in which both the mean and the variance of the future short rate become infinite at the infinite horizon, the Vasicek model allows a finite long-term mean m and a finite variance equal to $\sigma^2/(2\alpha)$ at the infinite horizon. When the speed of mean reversion α becomes infinite, the variance of the future short rate (for any future date) becomes zero, and the future short rate gets quickly absorbed at its long-term mean m. The distance between the current short rate and its long-term level is expected to become half over the period $\ln(2)/\alpha$.

Given the stated properties, the Vasicek model captures the empirical behavior of interest rate movement significantly better than the arithmetic random walk model of Merton. Though the Vasicek model may lead to negative interest rates in the future, this probability is generally small. This probability can be obtained by using the mean and the variance of the future short rate as follows:

$$P_t[r(S) < 0] = \mathcal{N}\left[-\frac{m + (r(t) - m)e^{-\alpha(S-t)}}{\frac{\sigma}{\sqrt{2\alpha}}\sqrt{1 - e^{-2\alpha(S-t)}}} \right] \qquad (4.26)$$

where $\mathcal{N}(x)$ is the cumulative standard normal distribution evaluated at x.

For realistic parameter values, the probability in equation (4.26) is significantly lower under the Vasicek model than under the Merton model. This probability increases with the horizon date S and the interest rate volatility σ and decreases with the current level of the short rate $r(t)$, the long-term mean m, and the speed of mean reversion α. Figure 4.3 illustrates these relationships by showing the probability distribution of the future short rate for the four sets of parameter combinations that are used in Figure 4.2, over three different time horizons.

To obtain the bond price solution under Vasicek's model, consider the more general definition of the market price of risk by Duffee [2002]:

$$\gamma(r, t) = \frac{\gamma_0 + \gamma_1 r(t)}{\sigma} \qquad (4.27)$$

The definition in equation (4.27) allows market risk premiums on bonds to switch signs over time, consistent with observed behavior of bond prices. The bond-price solution under Vasicek's model is obtained by substituting $\mu_r(r, t) = \alpha(m - r(t)), \sigma_r(r, t) = \sigma$, and $\gamma(r, t)$ from equation (4.27) into equation (4.22), which gives the following PDE:

$$\frac{\partial P}{\partial t} + \tilde{\alpha}(\tilde{m} - r(t))\frac{\partial P}{\partial r} + \frac{1}{2}\sigma^2 \frac{\partial^2 P}{\partial r^2} - r(t)P(t, T) = 0 \qquad (4.28)$$

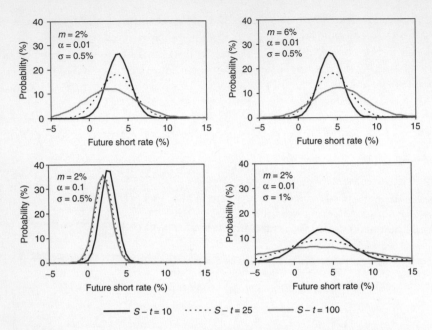

FIGURE 4.3 The Distribution of the Future Short Rate in Vasicek's Model

where

$$\tilde{\alpha} = \alpha + \gamma_1$$

$$\tilde{m} = \frac{\alpha m - \gamma_0}{\alpha + \gamma_1} \tag{4.29}$$

subject to the boundary condition $P(T, T) = 1$. The risk-neutral short-rate process consistent with the PDE given in equation (4.28) is given as:

$$dr(t) = \tilde{\alpha}(\tilde{m} - r(t))\,dt + \sigma\,d\tilde{Z}(t) \tag{4.30}$$

where, using equation (4.17) and (4.27), the change of measure is given as follows:

$$d\tilde{Z}(t) = dZ(t) + \left(\frac{\gamma_0 + \gamma_1 r(t)}{\sigma}\right)dt \tag{4.31}$$

Bond Price Solution

In order to relate the fundamental Vasicek model to its preference-free extensions given later in this chapter, we solve for the bond price after redefining the short rate as a sum of a constant and a mean-zero state variable given as follows:

$$r(t) = \tilde{m} + Y(t) \tag{4.32}$$

where

$$dY(t) = -\tilde{\alpha} Y(t)\,dt + \sigma\,d\tilde{Z}(t) \tag{4.33}$$

Using Ito's lemma, it is easy to confirm that the short-rate process given in equation (4.30) is consistent with the state variable process given in equation (4.33). Equation (4.33) also expresses the Vasicek model in the *Ay* form of the Gaussian models given by Dai and Singleton [2000]. Using a change of variable, the bond price can be expressed as a function of $Y(t)$ and t, and the PDE in equation (4.28) can be alternatively expressed as follows:

$$\frac{\partial P}{\partial t} - \tilde{\alpha} Y(t) \frac{\partial P}{\partial Y} + \frac{1}{2}\sigma^2 \frac{\partial^2 P}{\partial Y^2} - (\tilde{m} + Y(t))P(t,\ T) = 0 \tag{4.34}$$

Now consider the following form for the solution of the bond price:

$$P(t,\ T) = e^{A(\tau) - B(\tau)Y(t) - H(t,T)} \tag{4.35}$$

where $\tau = T - t$, subject to the boundary conditions $A(0) = 0$ and $B(0) = 0$, and $H(t,\ T)$ is defined as follows:

$$H(t,\ T) = \int_t^T \tilde{m}\,du = \tilde{m}(T - t) = \tilde{m}\tau \tag{4.36}$$

Using the above solution, the three partial derivatives in equation (4.34) can be solved as:

$$\frac{\partial P}{\partial t} = \left[-Y(t)\frac{\partial B(\tau)}{\partial t} + \frac{\partial A(\tau)}{\partial t} \right] P(t,\ T)$$

$$\frac{\partial P}{\partial Y} = -B(\tau)P(t,\ T) \tag{4.37}$$

$$\frac{\partial^2 P}{\partial Y^2} = B^2(\tau)P(t,\ T)$$

Substituting these partial derivatives in equation (4.34), using a change of variable $\tau = T - t$, and simplifying, we get:

$$\left[-\frac{\partial A(\tau)}{\partial \tau} + \frac{1}{2}\sigma^2 B^2(\tau) \right] P(t,\ T)$$

$$+ \left[-1 + \frac{\partial B(\tau)}{\partial \tau} + \tilde{\alpha} B(\tau) \right] Y(t)P(t,\ T) = 0 \tag{4.38}$$

Equation (4.38) can be solved as a sum of two ordinary differential equations (ODEs). The first ODE is obtained by equating the sum of all the terms multiplied by $Y(t)P(t, T)$ in equation (4.38) to zero, which gives:

$$\frac{\partial B(\tau)}{\partial \tau} = 1 - \tilde{\alpha}B(\tau) \tag{4.39}$$

This ODE subject to the boundary condition $B(0) = 0$ has a solution given as:

$$B(\tau) = \frac{1 - e^{-\tilde{\alpha}\tau}}{\tilde{\alpha}} \tag{4.40}$$

The second ODE is obtained by equating the sum of all the terms multiplied by $P(t, T)$ in equation (4.38) to zero, which gives:

$$\frac{\partial A(\tau)}{\partial \tau} = \frac{1}{2}\sigma^2 B^2(\tau) \tag{4.41}$$

Substituting $B(\tau)$ from equation (4.40) into equation (4.41) and subjecting it to the boundary condition $A(0) = 0$, the ODE in equation (4.41) has the following solution:

$$A(\tau) = (\tau - B(\tau))\frac{\sigma^2}{2\tilde{\alpha}^2} - \frac{\sigma^2 B^2(\tau)}{4\tilde{\alpha}} \tag{4.42}$$

Though the solution (in equation (4.42)) to the bond price is obtained by solving the partial differential equation given in equation (4.28), Appendix 4.1 demonstrates that the same solution can also be obtained by solving the discounted risk-neutral expectation of the terminal bond price.

Using Ito's lemma on the bond-price solution given in equation (4.35), the stochastic process for the bond price is given as:

$$\frac{dP(t, T)}{P(t, T)} = \big(r(t) - (\gamma_0 + \gamma_1 r(t))B(T - t)\big)\,dt - \sigma B(T - t)\,dZ(t) \tag{4.43}$$

The bond volatility $\sigma B(T - t)$ increases with bond maturity, though at a decreasing rate, attaining a maximum value of σ/α for the infinite maturity bond. The risk premiums on bonds can switch signs. For example, if γ_0 is positive and γ_1 is negative, then the risk premiums are low (high) when the short rate is low (high) and positive (negative) when the short rate is higher (lower) than $-\gamma_0/\gamma_1$.

The term structure of spot rates can be obtained using the expression:

$$y(t, T) = \frac{-\ln P(t, T)}{\tau} \tag{4.44}$$

The limiting values of the zero-coupon yields for zero and infinite maturities are:

$$\lim_{T \to t} y(t, \ T) = r(t)$$

$$\lim_{T \to \infty} y(t, \ T) = y^* = \tilde{m} - \frac{\sigma^2}{2\tilde{\alpha}^2}$$

(4.45)

The term structure begins at the intercept $r(t)$ and attains an asymptotic value y^* at the long end, which is independent of the current value of the short rate. The term structure is upward sloping if:

$$r(t) < y^* - \frac{\sigma^2}{4\tilde{\alpha}^2}$$

and downward sloping if:

$$r(t) > y^* + \frac{\sigma^2}{2\tilde{\alpha}^2}$$

For all intermediate values of $r(t)$, the term structure is humped, that is, increasing until a given term and then decreasing for longer maturities. Figure 4.4 illustrates the rising, humped, and falling shapes of the term structure for different values of the short rate ranging from 2 percent to 10 percent.

Figure 4.5 summarizes the differences in the volatilities structures (measured by the instantaneous standard deviations) of bond returns, zero-coupon yields, and instantaneous forward rates for the Merton and Vasicek models. The differences arise solely due to the mean reversion in the latter model, which makes the volatilities lower under the latter model.

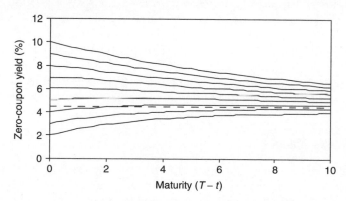

FIGURE 4.4 The Term Structure of Zero-Coupon Yields in Vasicek's Model

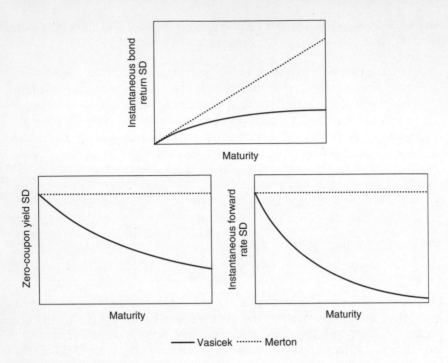

FIGURE 4.5 Volatilities Structures in the Vasicek and Merton Models

PREFERENCE-FREE VASICEK+, VASICEK++, AND VASICEK+++ MODELS

This section introduces preference-free extensions of the fundamental Vasicek model. These models use the implied volatility methodology to invert the risk-neutral parameters from the cross-sectional data on the prices of bonds and interest rate derivatives. Though the Vasicek++ model (i.e., extended Vasicek model) and the Vasicek+++ model (i.e., fully extended Vasicek model) have been derived by Hull and White [1990], we introduce the Vasicek+ model in the following section.

The Vasicek+ Model

The fundamental Vasicek model is typically estimated using the time-series dynamics of the changes in the yield of a given maturity (e.g., three-month yield or one-year yield). By matching the moments of yield changes, both the physical parameters and the risk-neutral parameters are obtained, consistent with some assumed form (typically linear) of market prices of risks. However, this strategy has three potential limitations:

1. The econometric estimation (using maximum likelihood, generalized method of moments, simulated methods of moments, etc.) under the fundamental model obtains physical parameters, MPRs, and risk-neutral parameters jointly. To the extent the functional form of MPRs is misspecified, the model will obtain incorrect estimates of the risk-neutral parameters. For example, the recent investigations by Duffee [2002] and Durate [2004] have found that more general specifications of MPRs significantly improve the fitting of the multifactor affine models to the observed cross-sectional and time-series dynamics of yield curve changes. However, even these authors use linear or simple nonlinear specifications of MPRs. To the extent MPRs contain a higher degree of nonlinearities, the fundamental Vasicek model will be misspecified.

2. Being a single-factor model, the fundamental Vasicek model is typically estimated using a single yield series. Much information in the time series evolution of the entire yield curve is ignored, and, hence, the methodology does not make optimal use of the information available.

3. Since the econometric estimation is based on historical data of yield series, it is backward looking, and ignores the forward looking information contained in current bond prices and interest rate derivative prices.

Being a preference-free model, the Vasicek+ model avoids these limitations by directly inverting the risk-neutral parameters from the cross sections of prices of bonds and interest rate derivatives without requiring the estimation of the physical parameters or the MPRs. Since MPRs are not explicitly specified, the Vasicek+ model is consistent with general nonlinear specifications of MPRs. In general, to understand the motivation underlying the single-plus models, consider the Vasicek+ model, which is the single-plus model corresponding to the fundamental Vasicek [1977] model. Let the stochastic bond-price process under the physical probability measure be given exogenously as follows:

$$\frac{dP(t,\ T)}{P(t,\ T)} = \mu(t,\ T)\,dt - \sigma B(T - t)\,dZ(t) \qquad (4.46)$$

where

$$B(T - t) = \frac{1}{a}(1 - e^{-a(T-t)}) \qquad (4.47)$$

and where $Z(t)$ is a Wiener process; $\mu(t,\ T)$ is the instantaneous expected return on the bond; $B(T - t)$ is the instantaneous bond volatility, which is a function of time remaining to maturity; and a and σ are constants greater than zero. Unlike the fundamental Vasicek model, which specifies the short-rate process under the physical measure, the Vasicek+ model specifies the bond-price process exogenously under the physical measure. Term structure models with an exogenous specification of a stochastic bond price have been given by Merton [1973], Ball and Torous [1983], Schaefer and Schwartz [1987], Nawalkha [1995], and others.[2] The Heath, Jarrow, and Morton [1992] model can also be specified using an exogenous stochastic bond-price process instead of the forward-rate process. The stochastic process in equation (4.46) assumes a *single* factor for bonds maturing at all dates T, such that $0 \le t \le T \le \infty$. As shown earlier, under the single-factor assumption, a hedge portfolio consisting of two zero-coupon bonds can be constructed to replicate the riskless return over the next instant. An immediate implication of the construction of such a hedge portfolio is that excess returns measured in the units of bond volatility are equal across all bonds, or:

$$-\frac{\mu(t,\ T) - r(t)}{\sigma B(T-t)} = -\frac{\mu(t,\ S) - r(t)}{\sigma B(S-t)} = \gamma(z,\ t) \qquad (4.48)$$

where $r(t)$ is the default-free instantaneous short rate and $\gamma(z,t)$ is the market price of interest rate risk with z defined in a general manner to include nonlinear functions of $r(t)$ and/or any other state variable values at time t; but $\gamma(z,t)$ must remain independent of the maturity term T for all $T \ge t$. Substituting equation (4.48) in equation (4.46), we get:

$$\frac{dP(t,\ T)}{P(t,\ T)} = \big(r(t) - \sigma B(T-t)\gamma(z,\ t)\big)\,dt - \sigma B(T-t)\,dZ(t) \qquad (4.49)$$

Using the Girsanov theorem, the Wiener process under the risk-neutral probability measure is given as:[3]

$$d\tilde{Z}(t) = dZ(t) + \gamma(z,\ t) \qquad (4.50)$$

Substituting equation (4.50) into equation (4.49), the risk-neutral bond-price process is obtained as follows:

$$\frac{dP(t,\ T)}{P(t,\ T)} = r(t)\,dt - \sigma B(T-t)\,d\tilde{Z}(t) \qquad (4.51)$$

Let $f(t,\ T) = -\partial \ln P(t,\ T)/\partial T$ define the time t instantaneous forward rate for date T. Taking the stochastic integral of equation (4.51) and then taking the partial derivative of the log of bond price with respect to bond maturity, the time t instantaneous forward rate is given as follows:

$$f(t,\ T) = f(0,\ T) + \int_0^t \sigma^2 e^{-a(T-v)} B(T-v)\, dv + \int_0^t \sigma e^{-a(T-v)}\, d\tilde{Z}(v) \quad (4.52)$$

where $f(0,\ T)$ is the instantaneous forward rate defined at time 0. Since the short rate $r(t) = f(t,\ t)$, evaluating equation (4.52) for $T = t$ gives:

$$r(t) = f(t,\ t) = f(0,\ t) + \int_0^t \sigma^2 e^{-a(t-v)} B(t-v)\, dv + \int_0^t \sigma e^{-a(t-v)}\, d\tilde{Z}(v) \quad (4.53)$$

Note that the market price of risk $\gamma(z,\ t)$ *does not appear* in equation (4.53) if it does not appear in the definition of $f(0,\ t)$. Various functions forms can be used to estimate the function $f(0,\ t)$ from the forward rates implied by the bonds trading at time zero. For example, Nelson and Siegel [1987] suggest a parsimonious parameterization of the instantaneous forward rate curve given as follows:

$$f(0,\ t) = \alpha_1 + \alpha_2 e^{-t/\beta} + \alpha_3 \frac{t}{\beta} e^{-t/\beta} \quad (4.54)$$

where the constants α and β are used for fitting the term structure using the observed bond prices at time zero. Using the function in equation (4.54), however, leads to a time-inhomogeneous short-rate process. Since the Vasicek+ model requires a time-homogeneous short-rate process under the risk-neutral measure (and, generally, also under the physical measure, if $\gamma(z,\ t)$ is independent of t), the functional form of $f(0,\ t)$ must be chosen to meet this criterion. It can be shown that the solution form under the fundamental Vasicek model is the only solution for $f(0,\ t)$ that allows a time-homogeneous risk-neutral short-rate process.[4] Hence, the following functional form is fitted to the forward rates implied by the bond prices observed at time 0:

$$f(0,\ t) = b + e^{-at} Y(0) - \frac{1}{2}\sigma^2 B^2(t) \quad (4.55)$$

where $Y(0) = r(0) - b$. Though both functional forms in equations (4.54) and (4.55) allow dependence on four parameters, the latter uses two parameters, a and σ, that also define the shape of the bond volatility function in equation (4.46). The interdependence of the shape of the forward-rate curve and the volatility curve is a characteristic of all time-homogeneous term structure models. Substituting the functional form of the forward rate given in equation (4.55) into equation (4.53) and then taking the stochastic differential of the short rate using rule 2 in Chapter 1, the risk-neutral short-rate process simplifies as follows:

$$dr(t) = a(b - r(t)) \, dt + \sigma \, d\tilde{Z} \qquad (4.56)$$

Expressing the short rate as the sum of parameter b and the state variable $Y(t)$:

$$r(t) = b + Y(t) \qquad (4.57)$$

the risk-neutral state variable process is given as follows:

$$dY(t) = -aY(t) \, dt + \sigma \, d\tilde{Z} \qquad (4.58)$$

Though equations (4.56) and (4.58) give the short rate and the state variable processes under the risk-neutral measure, the constants a and σ were specified exogenously under the physical measure as the parameters related to the bond volatility function. These parameters, together with exogenous specification of parameter b and the state variable value $Y(0)$, were used to fit the initial forward-rate curve at time zero. Unlike the case of the fundamental Vasicek model, the parameters a and b *do not contain the information related to market price of risk function* $\gamma(z, t)$. Hence, even though the risk-neutral process for the short rate has the same functional form under the Vasicek and Vasicek+ models, valuation under the Vasicek model is preference-dependent (since parameters $\tilde{\alpha}$ and $\tilde{m}$ in equation (4.30) contain market prices of risks), while valuation under the Vasicek+ model is preference-free. All of the valuation formulas and numerical algorithms for computing bond-price and interest rate derivatives under the Vasicek+ model are identical to the corresponding formulas and algorithms under the Vasicek model, and can be obtained by substituting $\tilde{\alpha} = a$, and $\tilde{m} = b$ in the equations given in the previous section under the Vasicek model.

The rest of this section uses a generalized framework for both Vasicek and Vasicek+ models, using the notation $\tilde{\alpha}$ and $\tilde{m}$, instead of a and b, respectively, even under the Vasicek+ model. Of course, the parameters $\tilde{\alpha}$ and $\tilde{m}$ are interpreted differently depending upon whether we are using the Vasicek model or the Vasicek+ model. Under the Vasicek model, these parameters are related to the physical parameters α and m of the short rate process through the market prices of risks as shown in equation (4.29). Since the Vasicek model is based upon an exogenous specification of the short-rate process under the physical measure and since the short rate does not trade, market prices of risk must enter the valuation formulas. On the other hand, the Vasicek+ model is based upon an exogenous specification of the bond-price process under the physical measure. The parameters $\tilde{\alpha} = a$ and $\tilde{m} = b$ (together with parameters σ and $Y(0)$) under the Vasicek+ model are used to 1) define the bond volatility function and 2) fit the initially observable bond prices at time zero. Since the Vasicek+ model assumes an exogenous stochastic bond price process and bonds are traded securities, market prices of risks do not enter the valuation formulas.

Unlike the Vasicek model that uses time-series econometric techniques to determine the risk-neutral parameters using yield data, the Vasicek+ model uses cross-sectional data on bond prices and interest rate derivatives to determine these parameters. For example, the parameters $\tilde{\alpha}$, $\tilde{m}$, σ, and $Y(0)$ can be determined by minimizing the deviations of the prices of bonds implied by the Vasicek+ model from the corresponding market prices, using time-zero cross-sectional price data, as follows:

$$\underset{\tilde{\alpha}, \tilde{m}, \sigma, Y(0)}{Min} \left(\sum_{j=1}^{n} \left(P_j^{Model} - P_j^{Market} \right)^2 \right) \tag{4.59}$$

where the index $j = 1, 2, \ldots, n$ sums up the deviations squared over n bonds of different maturities/coupons. The minimization routine in equation (4.59) may be sensitive to the specification of initial parameters and may not result in an accurate solution of the bond volatility function, even though it fits the cross sections of bond prices. Also, due to the absence of market prices of bonds on the *entire* continuum of maturity spectrum and bid-ask errors, and so forth, the minimization routine may be prone to errors. Hence, the cross-sectional prices of a given set of n_2 number of plain vanilla derivatives such as interest rate caps or interest rate swaptions could be used together with n_1 number of bond prices to give more accurate estimates of the four parameters, as follows:

$$\underset{\tilde{\alpha}, \tilde{m}, \sigma, Y(0)}{Min} \left(w_1 \left(\sum_{j=1}^{n_1} \left(P_j^{Model} - P_j^{Market} \right)^2 \right) + w_2 \left(\sum_{j=1}^{n_2} \left(c_j^{Model} - c_j^{Market} \right)^2 \right) \right) \tag{4.60}$$

The weights w_1 and w_2 can be used to normalize the dollar investments in bonds versus the interest rate derivatives (such as caps or swaptions).

Since Vasicek+ is a time-homogeneous model, the previous optimization does not have to be done using only one day of data (which is often the case for time-inhomogeneous models). By using the past k days of cross-sectional price data on bond and interest rate derivatives, the parameters $\tilde{\alpha}$, $\tilde{m}$, σ, and $Y(t_i)$, for $i = 1, 2, \ldots, k$, can be determined by minimizing the deviations of the prices of bonds implied by the Vasicek+ model from the corresponding market prices, as follows:

$$
\underset{\tilde{\alpha},\tilde{m},\sigma,Y(t_i)}{Min}\left(w_1\left(\sum_{i=1}^{k}\sum_{j=1}^{n_1}\left(P_{i,j}^{Model}-P_{i,j}^{Market}\right)^2\right)\right.
$$

$$
\left.+w_2\left(\sum_{i=1}^{k}\sum_{j=1}^{n_2}\left(c_{i,j}^{Model}-c_{i,j}^{Market}\right)^2\right)\right)
\tag{4.61}
$$

where the index $i = 1, 2, \ldots, k$ sums up the sum of deviations squared over n_1 bonds and n_2 interest rate derivatives over k days. The above optimization solves for $3 + k$ parameters and state variable values, given as the three parameters, $\tilde{\alpha}$, $\tilde{m}$, and σ and k values of the state variables, $Y(t_1)$, $Y(t_2)$, $\ldots$, $Y(t_k)$, over k days at times t_1, t_2, $\ldots$, t_k. In general, the above optimization may not work so well, since the Vasicek+ model is a single-factor model. A single-factor model cannot generally fit both the shape of the bond volatility function and the cross-sectional term structures of forward rates. Hence, significant deviations of model prices from market prices may imply *arbitrage opportunities* in either the bond market or the interest rate derivative market. The arbitrage opportunities could be minimized using two approaches. Using the first approach, the time-inhomogeneous Vasicek++ model (or the extended Vasicek model) can be used, as this model takes initial bond prices as given, as shown in the next section. The second approach for reducing the deviations of model prices from market prices is to use multiple factors. The general methodology given above can be applied under single-plus models corresponding to the multiple-factor affine and quadratic models given in Chapters 8, 9, and 10.

Though the Vasicek+ model may not perform as well as the multiple-factor single-plus models, it is likely to outperform the fundamental Vasicek model because:

1. It uses forward-looking information contained in the current prices of bonds and interest rate derivatives.
2. It allows general, nonlinear specifications of MPRs, which do not have to be estimated empirically.

The second observation is highly relevant as many recent studies (see Duffee [2002] and Duarte [2004]) find that using more general forms of MPRs can significantly enhance the ability of term structure models in capturing important yield dynamic relations. Consistent with this observation, consider the following example where the MPR function $\gamma(z,\ t)$ in equation (4.50) is defined as follows:

$$\gamma(z,\ t) = \frac{\gamma_0 + \gamma_1 r(t) + \gamma_2 r(t)^2 + \gamma_3 r(t)^3 + \gamma_4 X_1(t)}{\sigma} \qquad (4.62)$$

where $X_1(t)$ is another state variable that may be correlated with the short rate.

Substituting equation (4.62) in equation (4.50), the change of measure is given as follows:

$$d\tilde{Z}(t) = dZ(t) + \left(\frac{\gamma_0 + \gamma_1 r(t) + \gamma_2 r(t)^2 + \gamma_3 r(t)^3 + \gamma_4 X_1(t)}{\sigma}\right) dt \qquad (4.63)$$

Substituting equation (4.63) in equation (4.56), the short-rate process under the physical measure is given as follows:

$$dr(t) = \left(\tilde{\alpha}\tilde{m} + \gamma_0 - (\tilde{\alpha} - \gamma_1)\, r(t) + \gamma_2 r(t)^2 + \gamma_3 r(t)^3 + \gamma_4 X_1(t)\right) dt + \sigma\, dZ(t) \qquad (4.64)$$

where $\tilde{\alpha} = a$, and $\tilde{m} = b$, using the generalized notation. Since the drift under the physical measure is nonlinear and depends upon a second state variable $X_1(t)$, the short-rate process in equation (4.64) is obviously inconsistent with the fundamental Vasicek [1977] model.

Recently, Ait-Sahalia [1996a, 1996b], Stanton [1997], Conley and others [1997], and Boudoukh and Richardson [1999], using nonparametric techniques, have shown nonlinearities in the drift function of the short rate. These studies show mean reversion at high rates to be much stronger than in normal ranges of the short rate, where the mean reversion is close to zero. However, Pritsker [1998] and Chapman and Pearson [2000] criticize the small sample properties of these nonparametric studies and show that such nonlinearities can result even under linear drift models, simply due to small sample biases. Even if linearity in the affine models cannot be rejected due to small sample properties of the nonparametric tests, *these tests do not imply that nonlinear drifts do not exist.* Due to low power of these tests, we simply don't know if the alternative hypothesis of the existence of nonlinear drifts is true or false. Bali and Wu [2006], using a quasi-maximum likelihood estimation method and flexible parametric specifications of the drift and volatility, found that nonlinearities are strong in the federal funds rate and the seven-day Eurodollar rate but weaker in the three-month Treasury yield.

Regardless of whether nonlinear drifts exist, the preference-free Vasicek+ model is robust to such nonlinearities under the physical measure and restricts the drift to be linear only under the risk-neutral measure. The

Vasicek+ model obtains the risk-neutral parameters directly from the cross-sectional data on the prices of bonds and interest rate derivatives. More generally, this insight is useful in the context of all preference-free single-plus affine and quadratic models introduced in Chapters 4 through 10 of this book.

The stochastic bond-price process under the physical measure consistent with equations (4.62) and (4.64) is given as follows:

$$\frac{dP(t,\ T)}{P(t,\ T)} = \big(r(t) - (\gamma_0 + \gamma_1 r(t) + \gamma_2 r(t)^2 + \gamma_3 r(t)^3 + \gamma_4 X_1(t))B(T - t)\big)\, dt$$

$$- \sigma B(T - t)\, dZ(t) \tag{4.65}$$

The risk premium on the bond allows two state variables $r(t)$ and $X_1(t)$, which may be negatively correlated. Since prior research confirms the importance of negatively correlated state variables for explaining expected returns on bonds (see Dai and Singleton [2000] and Duffee [2002]), the bond-price process in equation (4.65) may be more realistic than the corresponding process under the fundamental Vasicek model.

Though the Vasicek+ model does not allow conditional volatilities to depend upon the short rate, the preference-free extension of the Cox, Ingersoll and Ross (CIR) model [1981] (i.e., the CIR+ model) does allow such dependence. In the context of the preference-free CIR+ model (introduced in Chapter 7), the specification of general MPRs, which include two state variables, $r(t)$ and $X_1(t)$, allows the breaking of tension between fitting conditional volatilities versus expected returns, while retaining the analytical properties of the fundamental CIR model for valuation of bond prices and interest rate derivatives.

The Vasicek++, or the Extended Vasicek Model

Hull and White [1990] introduced the "extended Vasicek model" by allowing a time-dependent risk-neutral drift for the short-rate process to fit the initially observed bond prices. The extended Vasicek model is obviously a preference-free model, since the risk-neutral parameters under this model are obtained using the cross section of prices of interest rate derivatives without the knowledge of MPRs or the physical parameters. This model also *implicitly* allows general nonlinear forms of MPRs given in the previous section. We denote this model as the Vasicek++ model, using the general terminology introduced in the previous chapter, with one plus denoting the independence from MPRs and the other plus denoting the time-dependent risk-neutral drift for the short-rate process, required to fit the initially observed bond prices.

The calibration of the preference-free Vasicek++ model to the initial zero-coupon bond prices can be done in two different but mathematically equivalent ways. The first approach allows the long-term mean of the short rate to become time-dependent, while keeping the speed of mean reversion constant. The short-rate process under this approach is given as follows:

$$dr(t) = \tilde{\alpha}\big(\tilde{m}(t) - r(t)\big)\, dt + \sigma\, d\tilde{Z}(t) \tag{4.66}$$

The time-dependent risk-neutral mean allows the model to be calibrated to the initial zero-coupon bond prices. The solution of $\tilde{m}(t)$ can be obtained by taking the stochastic differential of the short rate given in equation (4.53), using rule 2 in Chapter 1. This results in the short-rate process in equation (4.66) with the generalized notation $\tilde{\alpha} = a$, and $\tilde{m}(t)$ is defined as follows:

$$\tilde{m}(t) = f(0,\ t) + \frac{1}{\tilde{\alpha}}\frac{\partial f(0,\ t)}{\partial t} + \frac{\sigma^2}{2\tilde{\alpha}^2}(1 - e^{-2\tilde{\alpha}t}) \tag{4.67}$$

Only when $f(0,\ t)$ is specified as the time-homogeneous solution given by equation (4.55) does $\tilde{m}(t) = \tilde{m} = b$ (using the generalized notation) and the time-inhomogeneous Vasicek++ model reduces to the time-homogeneous Vasicek+ model. However, for all other specifications of $f(0,\ t)$, such as that given in equation (4.54), a time-inhomogeneous short-rate process with a time-dependent mean $\tilde{m}(t)$ is required to match the initial bond prices to the observed bond prices at time zero.

Equation (4.68) introduces the second approach to calibration by expressing the short rate as a sum of a time-homogeneous state variable process $Y(t)$ and a deterministic shift term $\delta(t)$ as follows:

$$r(t) = Y(t) + \delta(t) \tag{4.68}$$

Assume that the dynamics of $Y(t)$ are given under the risk-neutral measure as follows:

$$dY(t) = -\tilde{\alpha}Y(t)\, dt + \sigma\, d\tilde{Z}(t), \quad Y(0) = 0 \tag{4.69}$$

The state variable $Y(t)$ follows the Ornstein-Uhlenbeck process instead of the short rate $r(t)$, as in Vasicek's model. Applying Ito's lemma to equation (4.68) by using equation (4.69), the stochastic process for the short rate is given as:

$$dr(t) = \left(\frac{\partial \delta(t)}{\partial t} - \tilde{\alpha}Y(t)\right) dt + \sigma\, d\tilde{Z}(t) \tag{4.70}$$

By comparing the risk-neutral short rate in equation (4.66) with the risk-neutral short-rate process given in equation (4.70), we get:

$$\tilde{m}(t) = \delta(t) + \frac{1}{\tilde{\alpha}}\frac{\partial \delta(t)}{\partial t} \tag{4.71}$$

In equation (4.72), we use the second approach to calibration by explicitly using the relationship of the short rate with the state variable given in equation (4.68) and the state variable process given in equation (4.69). This approach to calibration is more natural when applied to other preference-free affine and quadratic models, and hence, provides a unified framework for considering all of these models.

Consider the time t price of a zero-coupon bond maturing at date T. Expressing the bond price as a function of $Y(t)$ and t, using Ito's lemma, and taking the risk-neutral expectation of the change in the bond price, the PDE for the bond price is given as follows:

$$\frac{\partial P}{\partial t} - \frac{\partial P}{dY}\alpha Y(t) + \frac{1}{2}\sigma^2\frac{\partial^2 P}{\partial Y^2} - Y(t)P(t,\ T) - \delta(t)P(t,\ T) = 0 \qquad (4.72)$$

subject to the boundary condition $P(T,\ T) = 1$. Assume that the solution to equation (4.72) has the following form:

$$P(t,\ T) = e^{A(\tau)-Y(t)B(\tau)-H(t,T)} \qquad (4.73)$$

where,

$$H(t,\ T) = \int_t^T \delta(u)\,du \qquad (4.74)$$

subject to $A(0) = B(0) = 0$, and by definition $H(T,\ T) = 0$.

Evaluating the partial derivatives of the bond price with respect to t and $Y(t)$, and substituting them in equation (4.72), and then using a separation of variables, we get the following two ordinary differential equations (after a change of variable $\tau = T - t$):

$$\begin{aligned}
\frac{\partial A(\tau)}{\partial \tau} &= \frac{1}{2}B^2(\tau)\sigma^2 \\
\frac{\partial B(\tau)}{\partial \tau} &= 1 - \tilde{\alpha}B(\tau)
\end{aligned} \qquad (4.75)$$

subject to the boundary conditions $A(0) = B(0) = 0$. The above ODEs are identical to the corresponding ODEs given in equations (4.41) and (4.39), under the fundamental Vasicek model, and so the solution directly follows from equations (4.42) and (4.40), as follows:

$$\begin{aligned}
A(\tau) &= \left(\tau - B(\tau)\right)\frac{\sigma^2}{2\tilde{\alpha}^2} - \frac{\sigma^2 B^2(\tau)}{4\tilde{\alpha}} \\
B(\tau) &= \frac{1 - e^{-\tilde{\alpha}\tau}}{\tilde{\alpha}}
\end{aligned} \qquad (4.76)$$

Let the initially observable zero-coupon bond-price function be given as $P(0, T)$. To calibrate the bond price in equation (4.73) to the initially observable bond-price function, consider the log of bond price evaluated at time 0 as follows:

$$\ln P(0, T) = A(T) - H(0, T) \qquad (4.77)$$

where by definition, $Y(0) = 0$. Differentiating equation (4.77) with respect to T and then replacing T with t, we get:

$$\delta(t) = f(0, t) + \frac{\sigma^2 B^2(0, t)}{2} \qquad (4.78)$$

where $f(0, t) = -\partial \ln P(0, t)/\partial t$ is the initial forward-rate curve at time 0.

The full closed-form solution of the bond price requires the solution of the function $H(t, T)$, which is given as an integral of the function $\delta(t)$ in equation (4.74). Using equations (4.76) and (4.77), the function $H(t, T)$ can be expressed as follows:

$$H(t, T) = H(0, T) - H(0, t)$$
$$= A(T) - A(t) - \ln P(0, T) + \ln P(0, t) \qquad (4.79)$$

Since $P(0, t)$ and $P(0, T)$ are the initially observed bond prices, equation (4.79) together with equation (4.76) gives the full closed-form solution of the bond price in equation (4.73).

Using Ito's lemma on equation (4.73), the stochastic bond-price process can be given under the risk-neutral measure as follows:

$$\frac{dP(t, T)}{P(t, T)} = r(t)\,dt - \sigma B(T - t)\,d\tilde{Z}(t) \qquad (4.80)$$

where $B(.)$ is defined in equation (4.76). The risk-neutral forward-rate process consistent with the bond-price process in equation (4.80) is given as:

$$df(t, T) = \sigma^2 B(T - t)e^{-\tilde{\alpha}\tau}\,dt + \sigma e^{-\tilde{\alpha}(T-t)}\,d\tilde{Z}(t) \qquad (4.81)$$

Since the Vasicek++ model takes current bond prices as given, it can be calibrated using time-zero prices of a given class of interest rate derivatives. The parameters $\tilde{\alpha}$, σ, and $Y(0)$ can be determined by minimizing the deviations of the prices of interest rate derivatives implied by the Vasicek++ model from the corresponding market prices, using time-zero cross-sectional price data, as follows:

$$\underset{\tilde{\alpha}, \sigma, Y(0)}{Min} \left(\sum_{j=1}^{n} (c_j^{Model} - c_j^{Market})^2 \right) \qquad (4.82)$$

where the index $j = 1, 2, \ldots, n$ sums up the deviations squared over n number of interest rate derivatives.

Ho and Lee [1986] Model The continuous-time version of the Ho and Lee [1986] model is nested in the Vasicek++ model. The Ho and Lee model was the first double-plus model that could be calibrated exactly to the initial zero-coupon bond prices. Originally, Ho and Lee [1986] derived their model using a discrete-time binomial tree. The continuous-time limit of the Ho and Lee [1986] model is equivalent to the Vasicek++ model with a zero mean reversion in the short rate under the risk-neutral measure, or $\tilde{\alpha} = 0$ in equation (4.69). The bond-price solution has the same form as in equation (4.73), but with simplified expressions for $A(\tau)$, $B(\tau)$, $H(t, T)$, and $\delta(t)$, for the special case of $\tilde{\alpha} = 0$, obtained using L'Hopital's rule, as follows:

$$A(\tau) = \frac{\sigma^2 \tau^3}{6}$$

$$B(\tau) = \tau \tag{4.83}$$

and

$$H(t, T) = \frac{\sigma^2 (T^3 - t^3)}{6} - \ln P(0, T) + \ln P(0, t)$$

$$\delta(t) = f(0, t) + \frac{\sigma^2 t^2}{2} \tag{4.84}$$

By substituting $\tilde{\alpha} = 0$ in equation (4.70), the risk-neutral short-rate process under the Ho and Lee model is given as follows:

$$dr(t) = \frac{\partial \delta(t)}{\partial t} dt + \sigma \, d\tilde{Z}(t) = \left(\frac{\partial f(0, t)}{\partial t} + \sigma^2 t \right) dt + \sigma \, d\tilde{Z}(t) \tag{4.85}$$

For most practical purposes, the Vasicek++ model is preferred over the Ho and Lee model, as a positive value of $\tilde{\alpha}$ is essential in fitting the model to the prices of interest rate derivatives.

The Vasicek+++, or the Fully Extended Vasicek Model

The models with two plusses, such as the Vasicek++ model, are calibrated to exactly fit the initial bond prices. However, if derivative traders prefer models that also fit the initial prices of some plain vanilla derivatives, such as interest rate caps, then another source of time-inhomogeneity can be introduced in the short-rate process. By either introducing time-dependence in the mean reversion and/or making the short-rate volatility time-dependent, the Vasicek++ model can be extended to fit an initial shape of bond volatility that is consistent with the initially observed prices of the given plain vanilla derivatives. The use of another plus symbol in the resulting Vasicek+++ model denotes that this model is calibrated to the initial prices of a given set of plain vanilla derivatives also. Similar to the preference-free Vasicek+ and Vasicek++ models, the Vasicek+++ model is also independent of MPRs and thus allows general, nonlinear MPRs, which do not have to be estimated.

Derivative traders, who want to price the more exotic interest rate derivatives in a way that is consistent with the prices of plain vanilla derivatives, may prefer models such as the Vaicek+++ model. However, as mentioned in the last section of Chapter 3, we do not recommend using the three-plus models generally, as these models imply a weird evolution of the bond-volatility function over time. We present the Vasicek+++ model in this chapter only to provide some intuition regarding such models; and as a general rule we will not consider other triple-plus models in this book.

Hull and White [1990] propose the Vasicek+++ model (i.e., the fully extended Vasicek model) by considering the following risk-neutral short-rate process with time-dependent parameters:

$$dr(t) = \tilde{\alpha}(t)\big(\tilde{m}(t) - r(t)\big)\, dt + \sigma(t)\, d\tilde{Z}(t) \tag{4.86}$$

where $\tilde{\alpha}(t)$ is the time-dependent risk-neutral speed of mean reversion, $\tilde{m}(t)$ is the time-dependent risk-neutral long-term mean of the short rate, and $\sigma(t)$ is the volatility of the short rate at time t. Equation (4.86) can be alternatively expressed as follows:

$$dr(t) = \big(\tilde{\beta}(t) - \tilde{\alpha}(t)r(t)\big)\, dt + \sigma(t)\, d\tilde{Z}(t) \tag{4.87}$$

where

$$\tilde{\beta}(t) = \tilde{\alpha}(t)\tilde{m}(t) \tag{4.88}$$

Since all three functions, $\tilde{\alpha}(t)$, $\tilde{\beta}(t)$, and $\sigma(t)$, evolve *deterministically* with time, the future values of these functions are known at time zero. The function $\tilde{\beta}(t)$ is used to calibrate the model to initially observable zero-coupon bond prices, while function $\tilde{\alpha}(t)$ is used to calibrate the model to the initial bond-volatility function implied by initially observable prices of some plain vanilla derivatives, such as interest rate caps. The short-rate process under the Vasicek+++ model can be alternatively expressed by defining the short rate as a sum of a mean-zero state variable and deterministic term as follows:

$$r(t) = Y(t) + \delta(t) \tag{4.89}$$

where the state variable $Y(t)$ follows this process:

$$dY(t) = -\tilde{\alpha}(t)Y(t)\, dt + \sigma(t)\, d\tilde{Z}(t), \quad Y(0) = 0 \tag{4.90}$$

Applying Ito's lemma to equation (4.89), the stochastic process for the short rate is given as:

$$dr(t) = \left(\frac{\partial \delta(t)}{\partial t} + \tilde{\alpha}(t)\delta(t) - \tilde{\alpha}(t)r(t) \right) dt + \sigma \, d\tilde{Z}(t) \qquad (4.91)$$

Comparing equation (4.86) with equation (4.91), it follows that the $\tilde{\beta}(t)$ function under the Hull and White framework is related to the $\delta(t)$ function given previously as follows:

$$\tilde{\beta}(t) = \frac{\partial \delta(t)}{\partial t} + \tilde{\alpha}(t)\delta(t) \qquad (4.92)$$

Using Ito's lemma and taking the risk-neutral expectation of the change in the bond price, the PDE for the bond price can be given as follows:

$$\frac{\partial P}{\partial t} - \tilde{\alpha}(t)Y(t)\frac{\partial P}{\partial Y} + \frac{1}{2}\sigma^2(t)\frac{\partial^2 P}{\partial Y^2} - \left(Y(t) + \delta(t)\right)P(t,\,T) = 0 \qquad (4.93)$$

subject to the boundary condition $P(T,\,T) = 1$. Consider the following solution to the bond price:

$$P(t,\,T) = e^{A(t,T) - Y(t)B(t,T) - H(t,T)} \qquad (4.94)$$

where

$H(t,\,T) = \int_t^T \delta(u)\,du$, subject to $A(T,\,T) = B(T,\,T) = 0$.

Note that functions $A(t,\,T)$ and $B(t,\,T)$ in equation (4.94) cannot be expressed only in terms of the time remaining to maturity, $\tau = T - t$. These functions depend both on t and T in a time-inhomogeneous manner. Evaluating the partial derivatives of the bond price with respect to t and $Y(t)$, and substituting them in equation (4.93), and then using a separation of variables, we get the following two ODEs:

$$\frac{\partial A(t,\,T)}{\partial t} = -\frac{1}{2}B^2(t,\,T)\sigma^2(t)$$

$$\frac{\partial B(t,\,T)}{\partial t} = -1 + \tilde{\alpha}(t)B(t,\,T) \qquad (4.95)$$

subject to the boundary conditions $A(T,\,T) = 0$ and $B(T,\,T) = 0$. The solutions to these ODEs are given as follows:

$$A(t,\,T) = \frac{1}{2}\int_t^T \sigma^2(v)B^2(v,T)\,dv \qquad (4.96)$$

$$B(t,\,T) = e^{k(t)}\int_t^T e^{-k(v)}\,dv \qquad (4.97)$$

where

$$k(t) = \int_0^t \tilde{\alpha}(u)\, du \qquad (4.98)$$

We wish to calibrate the above model to the *initial* bond volatilities given by the function $\sigma(0)B(0,\ t)$. It is assumed that the initial bond volatilities are implied from the calibration of the Vasicek+++ model to the initially observable prices of plain vanilla derivatives, such as interest rate caps. Using $B(0,\ t)$ as an exogenous input in equation (4.97), it is easy to show that:

$$\tilde{\alpha}(t) = -\left(\frac{\partial^2 B(0,\ t)}{\partial t^2}\right)\Big/\left(\frac{\partial B(0,\ t)}{\partial t}\right) \qquad (4.99)$$

Hence, by solving $\tilde{\alpha}(t)$ using equation (4.99), the Vasicek+++ model is calibrated to the initial bond-volatility function.

Consider the initially observable zero-coupon bond-price function given as $P(0,\ T)$. To calibrate the bond-price function in equation (4.79) to the initially observed bond-price function, the log of the bond price is evaluated at time 0 as follows:

$$\ln P(0,\ T) = A(0,\ T) - Y(0)B(0,\ T) - H(0,\ T) \qquad (4.100)$$

Substituting $Y(0) = 0$, differentiating equation (4.100) with respect to T, and then replacing T with t, we get:

$$\delta(t) = f(0,\ t) + e^{-k(t)}\int_0^t e^{k(v)}\sigma^2(v)B(v,\ t)\, dv \qquad (4.101)$$

The full closed-form solution of the bond price requires the solution of the function $H(t,\ T)$, which is given as an integral of the function $\delta(t)$ in equation (4.94). Using equation (4.100), the function $H(t,\ T)$ can be expressed as follows:

$$H(t,\ T) = H(0,\ T) - H(0,\ t) = A(0,\ T) - A(0,\ t) - \ln P(0,\ T) + \ln P(0,\ t) \qquad (4.102)$$

Since $P(0,\ t)$ and $P(0,\ T)$ are the initially observed bond prices, equation (4.102) together with equations (4.96) and (4.97) give the full closed-form solution of the bond price in equation (4.79).[5]

Using Ito's lemma on equation (4.94), the stochastic bond-price process can be given under the risk-neutral measure as follows:

$$\frac{dP(t,\ T)}{P(t,\ T)} = r(t)\, dt - \sigma(t)B(t,\ T)\, d\tilde{Z}(t) \qquad (4.103)$$

Though the parameter $\sigma(t)$ is also time-dependent, this parameter does not affect the shape of the time-zero term structure of bond volatilities. Instead, it affects the future evolution of the term structure of bond volatilities. Hence, keeping $\sigma(t) = \sigma$ as a constant allows the model to be calibrated to the initial shape of the bond-volatility function. However, the volatility of the bond returns is inhomogeneous since it cannot be expressed only as a function of the time remaining to maturity, $T - t$. This implies caution in using this model, as the future volatility may evolve in a strange manner.

The risk-neutral forward, rate process under the previous model can be given as follows:

$$df(t,\ T) = \sigma^2(t)B(t,\ T)e^{k(t)-k(T)}\,dt + \sigma(t)e^{k(t)-k(T)}\,d\tilde{Z}(t) \tag{4.104}$$

The forward-rate drift and volatilities are also time-inhomogeneous, as these cannot be expressed only as functions of $\tau = T - t$.

The mathematical framework given here is equivalent to the fully extended Vasicek framework given by Hull and White. This equivalence can be understood through equation (4.92), which gives the relationship between the term $\delta(t)$ and the term $\tilde{\beta}(t)$ related to the changing mean in the Hull and White framework. Using equations (4.92) and (4.101), the term $\tilde{\beta}(t)$ is solved as follows:

$$\tilde{\beta}(t) = \frac{\partial f(0,\ t)}{\partial t} + \tilde{\alpha}(t)f(0,\ t) + e^{-2k(t)}\int_0^t \sigma^2(v)e^{2k(v)}\,dv \tag{4.105}$$

Note that both $\tilde{\alpha}(t)$ given in equation (4.99) and $\tilde{\beta}(t)$ given in equation (4.105) are independent of the MPRs, since the Vasicek+++ model does not depend on the specific functional forms of MPRs, similar to the Vasicek+ and Vasicek++ models under the preference-free paradigm. The time-dependent risk-neutral long-term mean under the Vasicek+++ model is also independent of the MPRs, and can be obtained using equations (4.88) and (4.105), as follows:

$$\tilde{m}(t) = \frac{1}{\tilde{\alpha}(t)}\left(\frac{\partial f(0,\ t)}{\partial t} + \tilde{\alpha}(t)f(0,\ t) + e^{-2k(t)}\int_0^t \sigma^2(v)e^{2k(v)}\,dv\right) \tag{4.106}$$

VALUING FUTURES

This section provides formulas for pricing futures on a zero-coupon bond and futures on time deposits, such as Eurodollar futures and Euribor futures. The formula for the futures on a zero-coupon bond can be used to value T-Bill futures, as shown in equation (3.25) in Chapter 3. Further, if the cheapest-to-deliver option and other timing options can be ignored, then the price of futures contracts written on T-bonds and T-notes can be obtained using the formula for the price of a futures contract on a zero-coupon bond (see equation (3.47) in Chapter 3). We present the futures formulas in two sections. The first section presents these formulas for the fundamental Vasicek model and for the preference-free Vasicek+ and Vasicek++ models. Though the formulas look similar under these models, the empirical estimates of the risk-neutral parameters are generally different, and so the futures prices also will be different. The second section presents futures formulas for the Vasicek+++ model.

Valuing Futures under the Vasicek, Vasicek+, and Vasicek++ Models

Futures on a Zero-Coupon Bond   The time t price of a futures contract expiring at time S, written on a zero-coupon bond maturing at time T, under the Vasicek model can be obtained as follows. As shown in Chapter 3, the futures price is a martingale under the risk-neutral measure, or:

$$P_F(t, S, T) = \tilde{E}_t(P(S, T)) \qquad (4.107)$$

Due to continuous marking to market, the expected gain (or loss) in the futures position is zero under the risk-neutral measure (see Chapter 3 for more details), or:

$$\tilde{E}_t(dP_F(t, S, T)) = 0 \qquad (4.108)$$

Using Ito's lemma to solve the differential of the futures price and equating the risk-neutral expectation to zero, we get the PDE for the futures price as follows:

$$-\frac{\partial P_F}{\partial Y}\tilde{\alpha}Y(t) + \frac{1}{2}\sigma^2\frac{\partial^2 P_F}{\partial Y^2} + \frac{\partial P_F}{\partial t} = 0 \qquad (4.109)$$

subject to the boundary condition $P_F(S, S, T) = P(S, T)$, where $P(S, T)$ is defined by equation (4.35) under the Vasicek and Vasicek+ models and by equation (4.73) under the Vasicek++ model. We assume that the solution to equation (4.109) has the following form:

$$P_F(t, S, T) = e^{A_F(s)-B_F(s)Y(t)-H(S,T)}, \qquad s = S - t \qquad (4.110)$$

subject to $A_F(0) = A(U)$, $B_F(0) = B(U)$, and $U = T - S$, where $A(U)$ and $B(U)$ are given in equations (4.42) and (4.40), respectively. The formulas of $A(U)$ and $B(U)$ are the same under the Vasicek, Vasicek+, and Vasicek++

models.[6] The definition of $H(S, T)$ is given by equation (4.36) under the Vasicek and Vasicek+ models and by equation (4.79) under the Vasicek++ model.

Using a change of variable, $s = S - t$, the PDE in equation (4.109) becomes:

$$-\frac{\partial P_F}{\partial Y}\tilde{\alpha}Y(t) + \frac{1}{2}\sigma^2\frac{\partial^2 P_F}{\partial Y^2} - \frac{\partial P_F}{\partial s} = 0 \qquad (4.111)$$

Evaluating the partial derivatives of the futures price with respect to s and $Y(t)$, we have:

$$\frac{\partial P_F}{\partial Y} = -P_F(t, S, T)B_F(s)$$

$$\frac{\partial^2 P_F}{\partial Y^2} = P_F(t, S, T)B_F^2(s) \qquad (4.112)$$

$$\frac{\partial P_F}{\partial s} = P_F(t, S, T)\left(\frac{\partial A_F(s)}{\partial s} - \frac{\partial B_F(s)}{\partial s}Y(t)\right)$$

Substituting these partial derivatives in equation (4.111) and then using a separation of variables, we get the following two ODEs:

$$\frac{\partial B_F(s)}{\partial s} = -\tilde{\alpha}B_F(s)$$
$$\frac{\partial A_F(s)}{\partial s} = \frac{1}{2}\sigma^2 B_F^2(s) \qquad (4.113)$$

subject to $A_F(0) = A(U)$, $B_F(0) = B(U)$, and $U = T - S$. The solution is given as:

$$A_F(s) = A(U) + \frac{1}{4}\sigma^2 B^2(U)B(2s) \qquad (4.114)$$

$$B_F(s) = B(U)e^{-\tilde{\alpha}s} \qquad (4.115)$$

where $A(U)$ and $B(U)$ are as defined earlier in equations (4.42) and (4.40), respectively.

The futures price is lower than the forward price, as the asset underlying the futures contract is perfectly negatively correlated with the short rate (see Cox, Ingersoll, and Ross (CIR) [1981]). The futures-forward price discount, or FFPD, is given as:

$$FFPD = \frac{P_f(t, S, T) - P_F(t, S, T)}{P_f(t, S, T)} = 1 - P_F(t, S, T)\frac{P(t, S)}{P(t, T)}$$

$$= 1 - e^{\left(A_F(s)+A(s)-A(\tau)\right)-\left(B_F(s)+B(s)-B(\tau)\right)Y(t)}, \quad s = S - t, \quad \tau = T - t \qquad (4.116)$$

It is easy to show that the expression $B_F(s) + B(s) - B(\tau) = 0$, in the exponent of equation (4.116) and hence, the FFPD becomes:

$$FFPD = 1 - e^{\left(A_F(s)+A(s)-A(\tau)\right)}, \quad s = S - t, \quad \tau = T - t \quad (4.117)$$

The FFPD is always between 0 and 1 and depends upon the expiration date S, bond maturity T, the volatility parameter σ. and the speed of mean reversion α. Interestingly, the FFPD given in equation (4.117) does not depend upon the risk-neutral long-term mean, as the equation can be shown to simplify to the following:

$$FFPD = 1 - e^{-\frac{\sigma^2}{4\tilde{\alpha}}\left(\left(B(s)+B(U)\right)^2 - B^2(\tau) - \tilde{\alpha}B^2(U)B(2s)\right)},$$
$$s = S - t, \quad \tau = T - t, \quad U = T - S \quad (4.118)$$

In general, the FFPD is determined by the shape of the bond-volatility function given in equation (4.40) and is increasing in σ and decreasing in α. Since the asset underlying the futures contract is perfectly negatively correlated with the short rate, the futures price is lower than the forward price and the FFPD is always positive. The FFPD is zero, both when $t = S$ and when $S = T$.

Futures on a Time Deposit The price of a futures contract on a time deposit—such as Eurodollar and Euribor futures—can be obtained using equation (3.12) in Chapter 3:

$$P_F^{TD}(t, S, T) = \frac{100}{\hat{U}}\left(1 + \hat{U} - P_F^I(t, S, T)\right) \quad (4.119)$$

where S is the futures expiration date, $\hat{U}$ is the accrual factor typically calculated using actual/360 day-count basis, $U = T - S$, and $P_F^I(t, S, T)$ is the current price of a futures contract written on a hypothetical asset, which at the expiration date S is worth the inverse of a \$1 face-value zero-coupon bond maturing at time T. As shown in Chapter 3, the futures price, $P_F^I(t, S, T)$, is given by the following risk-neutral expectation:

$$P_F^I(t, S, T) = \tilde{E}_t\left(\frac{1}{P(S, T)}\right) \quad (4.120)$$

Using Ito's lemma to solve the differential of the futures price and equating the risk-neutral expectation to zero, we get the PDE for the futures price, as follows:

$$-\frac{\partial P_F^I}{\partial r}\tilde{\alpha}Y(t) + \frac{1}{2}\sigma^2\frac{\partial^2 P_F^I}{\partial r^2} + \frac{\partial P_F^I}{\partial t} = 0 \quad (4.121)$$

subject to the boundary condition $P_F^I(S, S, T) = 1/P(S, T)$, where $P(S, T)$ is defined by equation (4.35) under the Vasicek and Vasicek + models and by equation (4.73) under the Vasicek++ model. We assume that the solution to equation (4.121) has the following form:

$$P_F^I(t, S, T) = e^{a_F(s) - b_F(s)Y(t) + H(S,T)}, \qquad s = S - t \tag{4.122}$$

subject to $a_F(0) = -A(U)$, $b_F(0) = -B(U)$, and $U = T - S$. The definition of $H(S, T)$ is given by equation (4.36) under the Vasicek and Vasicek+ models, and given by equation (4.79) under the Vasicek++ model.

Note that the PDE in equation (4.121) is identical to the PDE in equation (4.109) and that the solution form in equation (4.122) is identical to the solution form in equation (4.110), except that the constants in the boundary conditions, $A(U)$ and $B(U)$ are of opposite signs in equation (4.122). Hence, the solutions of $a_F(s)$ and $b_F(s)$ immediately follow from equations (4.114) and (4.115), respectively, by switching the signs of the constants $A(U)$ and $B(U)$, and are given as follows:

$$a_F(s) = -A(U) + \frac{1}{4}\sigma^2 B^2(U)B(2s) \tag{4.123}$$

$$b_F(s) = -B(U)e^{-\tilde{\alpha}s} \tag{4.124}$$

where $A(U)$ and $B(U)$ are as defined earlier in equations (4.42) and (4.40), respectively. The solutions in equations (4.123) and (4.124) determine the futures price $P_F^I(t, S, T)$, and substituting this price in equation (4.119) gives the price of a futures contract on a time deposits such as Eurodollar futures and Euribor futures under the fundamental Vasicek model and the preference-free Vasicek+ and Vasicek++ models.

The convexity bias, given as the difference between the futures rate and the forward rate on a time deposit, is defined in equation (3.17) in Chapter 3 as follows:

$$Convexity\ Bias = L_F(t, S, T) - L_f(t, S, T)$$

$$= \frac{1 + L_F(t, S, T)\hat{U}}{\hat{U}} \left(1 - \frac{P(t, S)}{P_F^I(t, S, T)P(t, T)}\right) \tag{4.125}$$

where the futures rate and the forward rate are defined in Chapter 3 as follows:

$$L_F(t, S, T) = \frac{1}{\hat{U}}\left(P_F^I(t, S, T) - 1\right) \tag{4.126}$$

and

$$L_f(t, S, T) = \frac{1}{\hat{U}}\left(\frac{P(t, S)}{P(t, T)} - 1\right) \tag{4.127}$$

By substituting the appropriate formulas, we get:

$$Convexity\ Bias = L_F(t,\ S,\ T) - L_f(t,\ S,\ T)$$

$$= \frac{1 + L_F(t,\ S,\ T)\hat{U}}{\hat{U}} \left(1 - e^{A(s)-A(\tau)-a_F(s)-(B(s)-B(\tau)-b_F(s))Y(t)}\right)$$

(4.128)

$$s = S - t \ \text{ and } \ \tau = T - t$$

It is easy to show that the expression $B(s) - B(\tau) - b_F(s) = 0$ in the exponent of equation (4.128). Upon further simplification, the equation reduces to:

$$Convexity\ Bias = L_F(t,\ S,\ T) - L_f(t,\ S,\ T)$$

$$= \frac{1 + L_F(t,\ S,\ T)\hat{U}}{\hat{U}} \left(1 - e^{-\frac{\sigma^2}{4\tilde{\alpha}}\left((B(s)+B(U))^2 - B^2(\tau) + \tilde{\alpha}B^2(U)B(2s)\right)}\right)$$

(4.129)

$$s = S - t, \ \tau = T - t, \ U = T - S$$

The convexity bias depends upon the expiration date S, deposit maturity T, volatility σ, and the risk-neutral speed of mean reversion $\tilde{\alpha}$. In general, the convexity bias is determined by the shape of the bond volatility function given in equation (4.40) and is increasing in σ and decreasing in $\tilde{\alpha}$. Since the futures rate is perfectly positively correlated with the short rate, the futures rate is higher than the forward rate and the convexity bias is positive. The convexity bias is zero, both when $t = S$ and when $S = T$.

The convexity bias given previously is computed using the difference between the discretely compounded futures and forward rates, and hence, can be directly applied to futures on time deposits such as the Eurodollar futures and the Euribor futures in order to obtain the discrete forward LIBOR rates consistent with the observed futures prices. Further, using the discrete forward rates, the zero-coupon bond prices implied by Eurodollar futures can be obtained using equation (4.127).

Hull [1997, p. 566] computes the convexity bias using continuously compounded futures and forward rates, which is given as follows:

Hull's Convexity Bias with Continuously Compounded Rates under

$$Vasicek++Model = \frac{\sigma^2}{4\tilde{\alpha}U}B(U)\big(\tilde{\alpha}B(U)B(2s) + 2\tilde{\alpha}B^2(s)\big) \qquad (4.130)$$

Our simulations indicate that the convexity bias computed using the discretely compounded rates (such as quarterly compounded rates in the

Eurodollar futures market) is extremely close to Hull's convexity bias computed using the continuously compounded rates.

The convexity bias in equations (4.129) and (4.130) increases at a decreasing rate with the futures expiration date S, reaching a finite asymptotic value as S becomes infinite. Unlike the above result, the convexity bias increases *at an increasing rate* under the Ho and Lee model (this model is obtained as the special case of Vasicek++ model with $\tilde{\alpha} = 0$), becoming infinite as S becomes infinite. This can be shown by considering the special case of the convexity bias in equation (4.129) with $\tilde{\alpha} = 0$ and by applying the L'Hopital's rule to give:

$$Convexity\ Bias = L_F(t,\ S,\ T) - L_f(t,\ S,\ T)$$

$$= \frac{1 + L_F(t,\ S,\ T)\hat{U}}{\hat{U}} \left(1 - e^{-(\sigma^2 U^2 s + 0.5\sigma^2 s^2 U)}\right) \quad (4.131)$$

$$s = S - t \text{ and } U = T - S$$

The empirical data on Eurodollar futures does not support the convexity bias increasing at an increasing rate with S. Hence, the Vasicek++ model may represent a more realistic model for estimating the convexity bias than the Ho and Lee model does. Hull [1997] also computes the convexity bias under the Ho and Lee model using continuously compounded futures and forward rates, which is given as follows:

Hull's Convexity Bias with Continuously Compounded Rates under Ho

$$and\ Lee\ Model = \frac{1}{2}\sigma^2 s(s + U) \quad (4.132)$$

As shown in Appendix 4.2, Hull uses continuously compounded spot rates to derive the convexity bias. Again, our simulations indicate that the convexity bias computed under the Ho and Lee model using discretely compounded rates (such as quarterly compounded rates in the Eurodollar futures market) in equation (4.131) is quite close to Hull's convexity bias computed using continuously compounded rates in equation (4.132).

Valuing Futures under the Vasicek+++ Model

Futures on a Zero-Coupon Bond Following similar steps as for the case of the Vasicek, Vasicek+, and Vasicek++ models, we can derive the solution to the time t price of a futures contract $P_F(t,\ S,\ T)$, expiring at time S, written on a zero-coupon bond maturing at time T, under the Vasicek+++ model. Specifically, by noting that the futures price is a martingale under the risk-neutral measure and hence, equating the risk-neutral expectation of its differential to zero, we get the following PDE for the futures price under the Vasicek+++ model:

$$\frac{\partial P_F}{\partial t} - \tilde{\alpha}(t) Y(t) \frac{\partial P_F}{\partial Y} + \frac{1}{2}\sigma^2(t) \frac{\partial^2 P_F}{\partial Y^2} = 0 \tag{4.133}$$

subject to the boundary condition $P_F(S, S, T) = P(S, T)$. We assume that the solution to equation (4.133) has the following form:

$$P_F(t, S, T) = e^{A_F(t) - B_F(t)Y(t) - H(S,T)} \tag{4.134}$$

subject to the boundary conditions $A_F(S) = A(S, T)$ and $B_F(S) = B(S, T)$. The terms $A(S, T)$ and $B(S, T)$ are given in equations (4.96) and (4.97), and $H(S, T)$ is given in equation (4.102). Note that the terms $A_F(t)$ and $B_F(t)$ are expressed as functions of t, since these functions are not time-homogeneous under the Vasicek+++ model, and cannot be expressed solely as functions of $s = S - t$.

Evaluating the partial derivatives of the futures price with respect to t and $Y(t)$, and then substituting these back into equation (4.133), we obtain two ODEs as follows:

$$\frac{\partial B_F(t)}{\partial t} = \tilde{\alpha}(t) B_F(t)$$

$$\frac{\partial A_F(t)}{\partial t} = -\frac{1}{2} B_F^2(t)\sigma^2(t) \tag{4.135}$$

subject to $A_F(S) = A(S, T)$ and $B_F(S) = B(S, T)$. The solution to these ODEs is given as follows:

$$A_F(t) = \frac{1}{2} e^{-2k(S)} B^2(S, T) \left(\int_t^S e^{2k(v)} \sigma^2(v) \, dv \right) + A(S, T) \tag{4.136}$$

$$B_F(t) = e^{k(t) - k(S)} B(S, T) \tag{4.137}$$

where $k(t)$ is as defined in equation (4.98), and $A(S, T)$ and $B(S, T)$ are given in equations (4.96) and (4.97), respectively. The futures price is lower than the forward price, as the asset underlying the futures contract is perfectly negatively correlated with the short rate (see CIR [1981]). The futures-forward price discount is given as:

$$FFPD = \frac{P_f(t, S, T) - P_F(t, S, T)}{P_f(t, S, T)} = 1 - P_F(t, S, T)\frac{P(t, S)}{P(t, T)}$$

$$= 1 - e^{\left(A_F(t) + A(t,S) - A(t,T)\right) - \left(B_F(t) + B(t,S) - B(t,T)\right)Y(t)} \tag{4.138}$$

It is easy to show that the expression $B_F(t) + B(t, S) - B(t, T) = 0$ in the exponent of equation (4.138); hence, the FFPD becomes:

$$FFPD = 1 - e^{\left(A_F(t) + A(t,S) - A(t,T)\right)} \tag{4.139}$$

The FFPD is always between 0 and 1 and depends upon the expiration date S, bond maturity T, the volatility function $\sigma(t)$, and the speed of mean reversion function $\tilde{\alpha}(t)$. In general, $\sigma(t)$ is assumed to be a constant equal to the short-rate volatility at time 0, while $\tilde{\alpha}(t)$ is obtained through calibration to initial bond volatilities as specified in equation (4.84). Due to the time-inhomogeneity in future evolution of bond volatilities, the FFPD is also time-inhomogeneous, and is typically used only at time $t = 0$.

Futures on a Time Deposit   Similar to the earlier case, the price of a futures contract on a time deposit—such as Eurodollar and Euribor futures—can be given as follows:

$$P_F^{TD}(t, S, T) = \frac{100}{\hat{U}}\left(1 + \hat{U} - P_F^I(t, S, T)\right) \tag{4.140}$$

where $P_F^I(t, S, T)$ follows the same PDE followed by the futures on a zero coupon in equation (4.133), given as:

$$\frac{\partial P_F^I}{\partial t} - \tilde{\alpha}(t)Y(t)\frac{\partial P_F^I}{\partial Y} + \frac{1}{2}\sigma^2(t)\frac{\partial^2 P_F^I}{\partial Y^2} = 0 \tag{4.141}$$

subject to the boundary condition $P_F^I(S, S, T) = 1/P(S, T)$. Let the solution of $P_F^I(t, S, T)$ be given as:

$$P_F^I(t, S, T) = e^{a_F(t) - b_F(t)Y(t) + H(S,T)} \tag{4.142}$$

subject to the boundary conditions $a_F(S) = -A(S, T)$ and $b_F(S) = -B(S, T)$, where $A(S, T)$ and $B(S, T)$ are given in equations (4.96) and (4.97), respectively, and $H(S, T)$ is given in equation (4.102).

The solution form in equation (4.142) is identical to the solution form in equation (4.134) except that the constants in the boundary conditions, $A(S, T)$ and $B(S, T)$, have opposite signs in equation (4.142), and $H(S, T)$ has the opposite sign. Since solutions of $a_F(t)$ and $b_F(t)$ are not affected by the sign of $H(S, T)$, these solutions immediately follow from equations (4.136) and (4.137), respectively, by switching the signs of the constants $A(S, T)$ and $B(S, T)$, and are given as follows:

$$a_F(t) = \frac{1}{2} e^{-2k(S)} B^2(S, T) \left(\int_t^S e^{2k(v)} \sigma^2(v)\, dv \right) - A(S, T) \qquad (4.143)$$

$$b_F(t) = -e^{k(t)-k(S)} B(S, T) \qquad (4.144)$$

where $k(t)$ is as defined in equation (4.98).

The convexity bias, given as the difference between the futures rate and the forward rate on a time deposit, can be given under the Vasicek+++ model as follows:

$$Convexity\ Bias = L_F(t, S, T) - L_f(t, S, T)$$

$$(4.145)$$

$$= \frac{1 + L_F(t, S, T)\hat{U}}{\hat{U}} \left(1 - e^{A(t,S)-A(t,T)-a_F(t)-(B(t,S)-B(t,T)-b_F(t))Y(t)} \right)$$

It is easy to show that the expression $B(t, S) - B(t, T) - b_F(t) = 0$ in the exponent of equation (4.145). Hence, the equation reduces to:

$$Convexity\ Bias = L_F(t, S, T) - L_f(t, S, T)$$

$$= \frac{1 + L_F(t, S, T)\hat{U}}{\hat{U}} \left(1 - e^{A(t,S)-A(t,T)-a_F(t)} \right) \qquad (4.146)$$

where the futures and forward rates are as defined earlier. The convexity bias is positive and depends upon current time t, the expiration date S, bond maturity T, the volatility function $\sigma(t)$, and the speed of mean reversion function $\tilde{\alpha}(t)$. Due to the time-inhomogeneity in the future evolution of bond volatilities, the convexity bias is also time-inhomogeneous, and is typically calibrated at the current time using $t = 0$.

VALUING OPTIONS

Options on Zero-Coupon Bonds

Chapter 2 presented a general framework for pricing options on zero-coupon bonds under all multifactor Gaussian models using the forward measure $\tilde{\mathcal{P}}^S$. Specifically, Example 2.1 in Chapter 2 gives the time t price of a European call option and a European put option maturing at time S with an exercise price K, written on a \$1 face-value zero-coupon bond maturing at time T, under all Gaussian models. As a special case of this example, the call (c) and put (p) formulas can be given as follows:

$$c(t) = P(t, T)\mathcal{N}(d_1) - KP(t, S)\mathcal{N}(d_2)$$
$$p(t) = KP(t, S)\mathcal{N}(-d_2) - P(t, T)\mathcal{N}(-d_1)$$

$$(4.147)$$

where $\mathcal{N}(x)$ is the cumulative standard normal distribution evaluated at x. The variables d_1 and d_2 are given as:

$$d_1 = \frac{\ln([P(t, T)]/[P(t, S)K]) + V/2}{\sqrt{V}}$$

$$d_2 = \frac{\ln([P(t, T)]/[P(t, S)K]) - V/2}{\sqrt{V}}$$

$$(4.148)$$

and V is as given in equation (2.90) in Chapter 2. For the special case of Vasicek, Vasicek+, and Vasicek++ models, the bond volatility is given as $\sigma B(\tau)$, where $B(\tau)$ is as given by equation (4.40). Substituting this bond volatility in equation (2.90) in Chapter 2, V is given as:

$$V = \int_t^S \left(\sigma B(T - u) - \sigma B(S - u)\right)^2 du$$

$$= \int_t^S \left(\frac{\sigma}{\alpha}(1 - e^{-\alpha(T-u)}) - \frac{\sigma}{\alpha}(1 - e^{-\alpha(S-u)})\right)^2 du \qquad (4.149)$$

$$= \sigma^2 \left(\frac{1 - e^{-\alpha(T-S)}}{\alpha}\right)^2 \left(\frac{1 - e^{-2\alpha(S-t)}}{2\alpha}\right)$$

The empirical estimates of the risk-neutral parameters and the definition of the bond price are different under the Vasicek, Vasicek+, and Vasicek++ models, even though they use the same formulas for V given in equation (4.149). The fundamental Vasicek model will require estimates of the risk-neutral parameters through an econometric estimation using historical data. The specification of the functional form of MPRs, together with either the physical parameters or the risk-neutral parameters, is necessary to close the empirical estimation system under the fundamental Vasicek model.

The formulas of bond price and interest rate derivatives under the time-homogeneous preference-free Vasicek+ model are identical to those under the fundamental Vasicek model. However, the MPRs have to be neither specified theoretically nor estimated empirically under the Vasicek+ model, since the risk-neutral parameters are directly obtained from the cross-sectional data on the prices of bonds and interest rate derivatives.

Unlike the fundamental Vasicek model, which is estimated using historical data on the yield series of only a single maturity (e.g., 1 week or 3 months), the Vasicek+ model is estimated by performing a constrained nonlinear optimization using cross-sectional daily data on the prices of bonds and interest rate derivatives spanning a full spectrum of maturities and expiration dates, respectively. For example, using the most recent k days of cross-sectional data on the prices of bonds and interest rate derivatives requires inverting the $3 + k$ number of unknowns, given as three risk-neutral parameters $\tilde{\alpha}$, $\tilde{m}$, and σ, and the k values of the state variable $Y(t)$ on k different days (over which the cross-sectional data of prices of bonds and plain vanilla interest rate derivatives such as interest rate caps, swaptions, and/or Eurodollar futures exist). By minimizing the sums of squared deviations of actual bond prices and interest rate derivatives from the corresponding prices implied by the Vasicek+ model, the $3 + k$ number of parameters and state variable values can be inverted from the data. The objective function may give less or more weight to a particular class of security (such as caps or swaptions) in the optimization process, depending on the relative importance of that security using the subjective economic criteria set by the trading firm. For example, if a firm wishes to price derivatives that use interest rate caps as the pricing benchmark, then the weight given to swaptions and Eurodollar futures may be set to zero in the objective function.

The formula of bond price is different under the time-inhomogeneous preference-free Vasicek++ model, since this model uses the initially observable bond-price function as an input to the model. By using the observable zero-coupon bond prices, the option formulas in equation (4.147) also apply to the Vasicek++ model at time $t = 0$. Of course, since this is a time-inhomogeneous model that fits the initial bond prices *exactly*, typical inversion methods under this model only use a single day of cross-sectional price data on interest rate derivatives to obtain the two risk-neutral parameters $\tilde{\alpha}$ and σ. The parameter $\tilde{m}$ is not required under this model, and by construction, the time-zero value of the state variable $Y(0)$ equals 0.

The different methods used for obtaining the risk-neutral parameters under the Vasicek, Vasicek+, and Vasicek++ models, and the different formula for bond price under the Vasicek++ model will generally give different values of options under these models. The call and put option formulas in equation (4.147) apply to the time-inhomogenous preference-free Vasicek+++ model also, but with the following specification of V:

$$V = \int_t^S (\sigma(u)B(u,\ T) - \sigma(u)B(u,\ S))^2\, du \qquad (4.150)$$

where $B(t, T)$ is given in equation (4.82), with $\sigma(t)$ generally assumed to be a constant, though it can be made deterministic. The integral in equation (4.150) is computed numerically.

The Vasicek+++ model uses both the initially observable bond price function $P(0, T)$, and the initial bond volatility function, $\sigma B(0, T)$ implied by the initially observed prices of a given set of plain vanilla interest rate derivatives, such as interest rate caps, or swaptions, or Eurodollar futures. Such calibration performed over a single day gives an estimate of σ, and the estimates of the parameters related to some assumed functional form, such as polynomial, exponential, and so forth, of the speed of mean reversion function $\tilde{\alpha}(t)$ ($\tilde{\alpha}(t)$ is related to the bond volatility function, $\sigma B(0, T)$ through equation (4.99)). Once $P(0, T)$, $\tilde{\alpha}(t)$, and σ are inverted, the prices of all other interest rate derivatives can be computed under the Vasicek+++ model.

As a final observation, note that the call and put formulas under the Ho and Lee [1986] model can be obtained as a special case of the Vasicek++ model, with $\tilde{\alpha} = 0$, which simplifies the formula for V as follows:

$$V = \int_t^S (\sigma(T - u) - \sigma(S - u))^2 \, du$$

$$= \int_t^S (\sigma(T - S))^2 \, du = \sigma^2 (T - S)^2 (S - t) \tag{4.151}$$

Example 4.1 Consider a one-year European call option written on a \$100 face-value zero-coupon bond that matures in three years. The exercise price of the option equals \$85. The call option can be considered equivalent to 100 call options on \$1 face-value zero-coupon bonds that mature in three years, with a call exercise price of \$0.85. The short rate evolves according to Vasicek's model with risk-neutral parameters given as $\tilde{\alpha} = 0.3, \tilde{m} = 7\%$, and $\sigma = 0.5\%$. Assume that short rate equals 5 percent, which implies that $Y(0) = r(0) - \tilde{m} = -2\%$. Using equation (4.147), the value of the call option at time $t = 0$ can be computed as follows:

$$c(0) = 100 \times (P(0, 3)\mathcal{N}(d_1) - 0.85 \times P(0, 1)\mathcal{N}(d_2))$$

The two zero-coupon bond prices are computed using the bond-pricing equation (4.35), which gives:

$$P(0, 1) = \$0.95$$

$$P(0, 3) = \$0.84$$

The volatility, given as the square root of variance V, is computed using equation (4.149) as follows:

$$\sqrt{V} = 0.652\%$$

The values d_1 and d_2 are calculated using equation (4.148):

$$d_1 = 1.563 \qquad d_2 = 1.557$$

And finally, the cumulative standard normal distribution function at points d_1 and d_2, give:

$$\mathcal{N}(1.563) = 0.941 \qquad \mathcal{N}(1.557) = 0.940$$

Substituting these results in the first expression, the value of the option at the present time is computed as follows:

$$c(0) = 100 \times (0.84 \times 0.941 - 0.85 \times 0.95 \times 0.940) = \$0.87$$

Options on Coupon Bonds

A default-free coupon bond can be considered a portfolio of default-free zero-coupon bonds. However, an option on a coupon bond cannot be generally priced as a portfolio of options on the underlying zero-coupon bonds, because the portfolio will generally have less volatility than the weighted average of the volatilities of the individual components in the portfolio. It is well known that obtaining closed-form solutions for European options on coupon bonds is generally difficult.

However, for single-factor models, such as Vasicek and its one-plus, two-plus, and three-plus, preference-free extensions, bond prices are uniformly decreasing functions of the short rate. For these models, Jamshidian demonstrates a mathematical trick to obtain the European solution of an option on a coupon bond from the European solutions of options on the underlying zero-coupon bonds. Since European options on coupon bonds are equivalent to European swaptions (see Chapter 3), the analytical results that follow can be used for pricing European swaptions, also. Jamshidian's result can be demonstrated as follows.

Consider a European call option on a coupon bond, with an expiration date S and exercise price K. The coupon bond has n cash flows maturing *after* the option expiration date S, given as C_i at time $T_i > S$, for $i = 1, 2, \ldots, n$. The present value of these n cash flows is given as:

$$\sum_{i=1}^{n} C_i \times P(t, T_i) \tag{4.152}$$

where $P(t, T_i) = P(r(t), t, T_i)$ is the time t price of a zero-coupon bond that pays \$1 at date T_i. The value of the call option at expiration date S equals:

$$c(S) = Max\left[\left(\sum_{i=1}^{n} C_i \times P(S, T_i)\right) - K, 0\right] \tag{4.153}$$

where $P(S, T_i) = P(r(S), S, T_i)$ is the time S price of a zero-coupon bond maturing at date T_i. Since the zero-coupon bond price $P(S, T_i)$ is assumed to be a monotonically decreasing function of the short rate $r(S)$, the sum given in the inside brackets on the R.H.S. of equation (4.153) also decreases in $r(S)$. Consequently, the option will be exercised only if $r(S)$ is below the specific value of short rate equal to r^*, which makes the following equation hold:

$$\sum_{i=1}^{n} C_i \times P(r^*, S, T_i) = K \tag{4.154}$$

Now define n new constants given as follows:

$$K_i = P(r^*, S, T_i), \text{ for } i = 1, 2, \ldots, n \tag{4.155}$$

Substituting equation (4.155) into equation (4.154), we get:

$$\sum_{i=1}^{n} C_i K_i = K \tag{4.156}$$

By substituting equation (4.156) into equation (4.153), the payoff of the option on the coupon bond at time S can be expressed as:

$$Max\left[\left(\sum_{i=1}^{n} C_i \times P(S, T_i)\right) - K, 0\right] = Max\left[\sum_{i=1}^{n} C_i \times (P(S, T_i) - K_i), 0\right] \tag{4.157}$$

If $r(S) < r^*$, then $P(S, T_i) = P(r(S), S, T_i)$ will be higher than K_i for each i, and thus the payoff of the option becomes:

$$\sum_{i=1}^{n} C_i \times (P(S, T_i) - K_i) = \sum_{i=1}^{n} C_i \times Max[P(S, T_i) - K_i, 0] \tag{4.158}$$

If $r(S) \geq r^*$, then each term $P(S, T_i) - K_i$ will be nonpositive, and so the option is not exercised and its payoff equals zero. Hence, for all possible values of $r(S)$, the payoff of the option on the coupon bond is given as:

$$\sum_{i=1}^{n} C_i \times Max[P(S, T_i) - K_i, 0] \qquad (4.159)$$

Hence, the payoff of the option on the coupon bond equals the payoff on a portfolio of options on zero-coupon bonds comprising the coupon bond, and the time t price of the call option on the coupon bond equals the price of the portfolio of call options on zero-coupon bonds, or:

$$c(t) = \sum_{i=1}^{n} C_i \times c_i(t) \qquad (4.160)$$

where $c_i(t)$ is the price of the European call option with expiration date S and exercise price K_i, written on a \$1 face-value zero-coupon bond maturing at time T_i.

A similar argument can be applied to get the price of a European put option on a coupon bond as:

$$p(t) = \sum_{i=1}^{n} C_i \times p_i(t) \qquad (4.161)$$

where the put options are based upon the same variables as the call options.

Example 4.2 Assume that the risk-neutral parameters for the preference-free Vasicek+ model are given as $\tilde{\alpha} = 0.3$, $\tilde{m} = 7\%$, and $\sigma = 0.5\%$ and that the current value of the state variable $Y(0) = -2\%$. Since $r(t) = \tilde{m} + Y(t)$, the implied value of the current short rate equals $7\% - 2\% = 5\%$. Recall that the preference-free Vasicek+ model inverts the three risk-neutral parameter values and k state variable values using the cross-sectional data on the prices of bonds and plain vanilla interest rate derivatives over the most recent k days. Since the most recent k days include the current day 0, the value of $Y(0)$ is available. The implied value of $Y(0) = -2\%$ may not be consistent with the current short rate implied by the extremely short maturity bonds. Hence, the implied short rate of $5\% = 7\% - 2\%$ in this example may not exactly equal the actual short rate. Though the fundamental Vasicek model may use the actual short rate, the fundamental model is almost always inconsistent with the observable prices of longer maturity bonds. The inconsistency with the current short rate will diminish under the preference-free single-plus paradigm as more factors are added (see Chapters 8, 9, and 10). In general, the fit with the observed prices of

bonds and interest rate derivatives will be better under the preference-free
Vasicek+ model, since this model allows general nonlinear MPRs, while the
fundamental Vasicek model imposes restrictive linear functional forms on
the MPRs.

Now consider a one-year European call option with a strike price of
$96, written on a three-year 4 percent annual coupon bond with a $100 face
value. At the option expiration date of one year, the bond makes its first
coupon payment of $4, and the bond has two cash flows remaining. Hence,
at the end of one year, the bond can be regarded as a portfolio consisting of
four $1 face-value zero-coupon bonds maturing at time $T_1 = 2$ years, and
104 $1 face-value zero-coupon bonds maturing at time $T_2 = 3$ years. The
coupon bond can be valued as follows:

$$4 \times P(1,\ 2) + 104 \times P(1,\ 3)$$

To determine the strike prices of the options on the zero-coupon bonds, we
need to find r^*, which is that value of $r(1)$ that makes the coupon bond price
at the end of one year equal to the strike price of $96 (see equation (4.154)).
Substituting the Vasicek bond-price formulas, we estimate r^* from the
following equation:

$$4 \times P(1,\ 2) + 104 \times P(1,\ 3) = \$85 \qquad (4.162)$$

Using the solver function in Excel, $r^* = 5.680\%$. Substituting $r^* = 5.680\%$
for the short rate, the zero-coupon bond prices $P(1,\ 2)$ and $P(1,\ 3)$ are
given as:

$$P(1,\ 2) = \$0.94 \ \text{ and } \ P(1,\ 3) = \$0.89$$

Using Jamshidian's trick, the value of the option on the coupon bond equals
the value of the portfolio consisting of:

- 4 one-year European options with strike price $0.94 on a zero-coupon
  that pays $1 at year 2.
- 104 one-year European options with strike price $0.89 on a zero-coupon
  that pays $1 at year 3.

The calculations needed for valuing each of the two European options are
shown in Table 4.1.

The value of the option on the coupon bond is given as:

$$c(0) = (4 \times 0.0021) + (104 \times 0.0033) = \$0.36$$

TABLE 4.1 Calculations for Separate Zero-Coupon European Calls

	Option 1	Option 2
Bond face value	$1	$1
Bond maturity	2 years	3 years
Option strike price	$0.94	$0.89
Option maturity	1 year	1 year
$\sqrt{V}$	0.375%	0.652%
d_1	0.379	0.382
d_2	0.376	0.376
$\mathcal{N}(d_1)$	0.648	0.649
$\mathcal{N}(d_2)$	0.646	0.646
Option price	$0.0021	$0.0034

VALUING INTEREST RATE CONTINGENT CLAIMS USING TREES

Unlike European contingent claims, which generally have analytical solutions, American interest rate contingent claims must be solved using some numerical techniques. Two popular numerical methods for solving American claims are trees and finite difference methods. Finite difference methods represent a numerical approximation to the "partial differential equation approach" for valuing American claims. Trees represent a numerical approximation to the "risk-neutral expectations approach" (or martingale approach) for valuing American claims. Trees are also the simplest and perhaps the best expositional method for demonstrating the valuation of a variety of interest rate contingent claims. Occasionally, trees are also used to value European claims that do not have analytical solutions (e.g., options on coupon bonds in a *multifactor* interest rate model, or option valuation when the underlying interest process does not have a known distribution).

To demonstrate the tree method, first consider the value of any *European* contingent claim, such as a European call option, given using the discounted risk-neutral expectation of its terminal value, as follows (see Chapter 2 for more details):

$$c(t) = \tilde{E}_t \left(\frac{c(S)}{e^{\int_t^S r(v)\,dv}} \right) \tag{4.163}$$

where $c(S)$ is the terminal payoff at time S, and $r(t)$ is the short rate. The expectation in equation (4.163), using the risk-neutral probability measure

$\tilde{\mathcal{P}}$, can be generally solved analytically in closed form when interest rates are constant (i.e., call option on a stock, under the Black and Scholes [1973] model). When interest rates are stochastic, the risk-neutral measure $\tilde{\mathcal{P}}$ still provides solutions to basic claims such as the prices of zero-coupon bonds and futures on zero-coupon bonds (and futures on time deposits); but the forward measure $\tilde{\mathcal{P}}^{S}$ is more convenient to obtain prices of options written on these claims. Chapter 2 demonstrates how to obtain an analytical solution to the price of an option on a zero-coupon bond using the forward measure $\tilde{\mathcal{P}}^{S}$ under multifactor Gaussian models. However, very often, neither measure $\tilde{\mathcal{P}}$ nor measure $\tilde{\mathcal{P}}^{S}$ will provide an analytical solution (e.g., analytical solutions don't exist for bond prices or other contingent claims for some affine models of the short rate in Chapter 9). In such cases, trees may be used to compute the risk-neutral expectation given in equation (4.163).

Now consider the value of any *American* contingent claim, such as an American call option. American options give the holder the right to exercise the option at any point of time before the expiration date S. The early exercise feature makes the price of an American option greater than or equal to the price of the corresponding European option. Early exercise opportunities arise when the intrinsic value of the option (i.e., the value of the option exercised immediately) becomes greater than the discounted expected value of holding the option. When this happens, the value-maximizing option-holder optimally stops holding the option by immediately exercising it. The random time at which an option holder optimally stops holding the option is called the *optimal stopping time*. Optimal stopping time is a *random variable*, since the option may be exercised in some states and not exercised in other states at any given time in the future. Since the option-holder selects optimal stopping time from all possible stopping times, the value of the American option can be expressed as the discounted risk-neutral expectation, given as follows:

$$c^{*}(t) = \underset{t \leq S^{*} \leq S}{Max}\ \tilde{E}_{t} \left[\frac{c(S^{*})}{e^{\int_{t}^{S^{*}} r(v)\,dv}} \right] \qquad (4.164)$$

where the maximum is taken over all possible stopping times S^{*}. Though approximations have been derived to solve equation (4.164) analytically for the case of constant interest rates, virtually no analytical solution has been proposed for the case of stochastic interest rates. Hence, trees may be used to compute the risk-neutral expectation given in equation (4.164).

The tree construction for solving both European claims and American claims requires that the short-rate process be given under the risk-neutral measure. For all Gaussian models, the risk-neutral process for the short rate is generally given as follows:

$$dr(t) = \tilde{\mu}_r(r,\ t)\,dt + \sigma\,d\tilde{Z}(t) \qquad (4.165)$$

Equation (4.165) is consistent with the fundamental Vasicek model, as well as the preference-free Vasicek+, Vasicek++, and Vasicek+++ models. In the following section, we demonstrate how to build a binomial tree as well as a trinomial tree consistent with the process given in equation (4.165). The trinomial tree has been found to be computationally more efficient than the binomial tree for valuing interest rate derivatives. The trinomial tree also allows the valuation of certain exotic derivatives (e.g., various kinds of barrier options), which cannot be easily valued using a binomial tree.

Binomial Trees

The binomial tree can be built by dividing the time to expiration (or time to maturity) of any given contingent claim into n discrete periods of length Δt. Over any given time interval Δt, the short rate either moves up or moves down by a constant magnitude $\Delta r = \sigma \sqrt{\Delta t}$. The probability of the short rate moving up is given as p_u, and the probability of the short rate moving down is given as $p_d = 1 - p_u$. Figure 4.6 illustrates a one-period binomial tree assuming that the short rate starts at time 0, at the starting value of $r(0)$.

Figure 4.7 shows a two-period binomial tree. Since the tree is recombining, the down node followed by the up node gives the same value for the short rate as the up node followed by the down node. The two-period tree gives three different values of the short rate. Continuing in this manner, the n-period tree gives $n + 1$ different values of the short rate. If we had

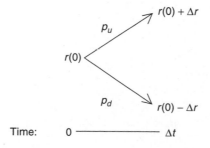

FIGURE 4.6 One-Period Binomial Tree

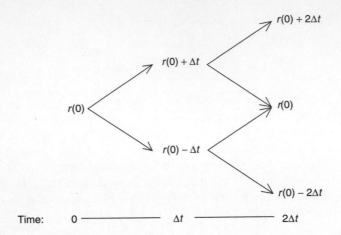

FIGURE 4.7 Two-Period Binomial Tree

used a nonrecombining tree instead, it would have resulted in 2^n different values of the short rate after n periods, making the tree computationally very expensive.

Let the value of the short rate at time t be given as $r(t)$ on a given node on the tree. The up and down probabilities at this node can be computed as follows:

$$p_u + p_d = 1$$

$$p_u \Delta r(t) + p_d(-\Delta r(t)) = (\tilde{\mu}_r(r, t))\Delta t \tag{4.166}$$

The probability values in equation (4.166) allow the approximation of the drift of the short rate to its continuous-time limit as Δt becomes infinitesimally small. Since the up move in the short rate equals $r(t) + \sigma\sqrt{\Delta t}$ and the down move in the short rate equals $r(t) - \sigma\sqrt{\Delta t}$, the instantaneous variance of the short rate always equals $\sigma^2 \Delta t$, regardless of the probability values in equation (4.166).[7]

Equation (4.166) gives the following solution to the up and down probabilities:

$$p_u = \frac{1}{2} + \frac{1}{2}\frac{\tilde{\mu}_r(r, t)}{\sigma}\sqrt{\Delta t}$$

$$p_d = \frac{1}{2} - \frac{1}{2}\frac{\tilde{\mu}_r(r, t)}{\sigma}\sqrt{\Delta t} \tag{4.167}$$

Trinomial Trees

Trinomial trees allow three branches at each node. The branches represent up movement, middle movement, and down movement. The three probabilities associated with the three movements are defined as p_u, p_m, and p_d, respectively. Figure 4.8 illustrates these movements over the first period.

The three probabilities can be computed by matching the moments as follows:[8]

$$p_u + p_m + p_d = 1$$

$$p_u \Delta r + 0 + p_d(-\Delta r) = (\tilde{\mu}_r(r, t))\Delta t \qquad (4.168)$$

$$p_u(\Delta r)^2 + 0 + p_d(\Delta r)^2 = \sigma^2 \Delta t$$

In the binomial model, the value of Δr must equal $\sigma\sqrt{\Delta t}$ in order to obtain probabilities that allow both the instantaneous mean and the variance of the short-rate process to be matched. In the trinomial model, an additional degree of freedom exists because of one extra probability. Hence, the Δr can be chosen in a more general way, as follows:

$$\Delta r = b\sigma\sqrt{\Delta t} \qquad (4.169)$$

If $b = 1$, the value of the middle probability p_m must equal 0, and hence, the up and down trinomial probabilities become identical to the binomial probabilities given earlier. If $b > 1$, the middle probability p_m becomes greater than 0 and converges to 1 if b becomes very large. If b is between 0 and 1, the value of the middle probability p_m is negative.

Hence, the value of b must be chosen to be greater than 1. Hull and White [1994a] find that using $b = \sqrt{3}$ leads to good approximations when

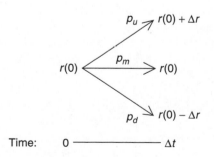

FIGURE 4.8 One-Period Trinomial Tree

using trinomial trees. Using this value for b, the three probabilities are given as follows:

$$p_u = \frac{1}{6} + \frac{1}{6}\frac{\tilde{\mu}_r(r,\ t)}{\sigma}\sqrt{3\Delta t}$$

$$p_m = \frac{2}{3}$$ (4.170)

$$p_d = \frac{1}{6} - \frac{1}{6}\frac{\tilde{\mu}_r(r,\ t)}{\sigma}\sqrt{3\Delta t}$$

Contingent claims can be priced by starting at the terminal nodes, taking discounted risk-neutral expectations at each step, and moving back through the tree to the current time. By appropriately identifying the parameters for the specific Gaussian short-rate models, the binomial probabilities (see equation (4.167)) and the trinomial probabilities (see equation (4.170)) can be used to construct trees for these models. For example, the following substitution can be made in equations (4.167) and (4.170) for the preference-free Vasicek+ model:

$$\tilde{\mu}_r(r,\ t) = \tilde{\alpha}(\tilde{m} - r(t))$$ (4.171)

The following examples demonstrate the construction of trinomial trees for the Vasicek+ model.

Example 4.3 Consider a zero-coupon bond that pays \$100 ($F = 100$) in 2.5 years. Assume the following risk-neutral parameters for the Vasicek+ model: $\tilde{\alpha} = 0.1$, $\tilde{m} = 6\%$, $\sigma = 0.5\%$. Let the current value of the state variable $Y(0) = -1\%$, giving the current estimated short-rate value equal to $6\% - 1\% = 5\%$ (see equation (4.32)). Consider using a five-step trinomial tree to compute the present value of this bond. The time step equals $\Delta t = 2.5/5 = 0.5$ years.

The trinomial tree for this example is shown in Figure 4.9. The number in the top row of each node gives the price of the zero-coupon bond, and the number in the bottom row gives the value of the short rate.

The short rate increases or decreases every period by a constant amount given as:

$$\Delta r = b\sigma\sqrt{\Delta t} = \sqrt{3} \times 0.005 \times \sqrt{0.5} = 0.612\%$$

Hence, at the end of the first period, the short rate either moves up to 5.612% (at node N_{11}), remains at 5% (at node N_{12}), or moves down to 4.388% (at node N_{13}). The probabilities change over time, since the

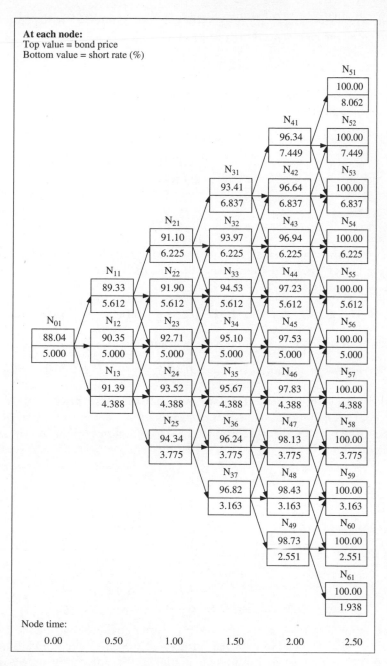

At each node:
Top value = bond price
Bottom value = short rate (%)

Node time:

0.00   0.50   1.00   1.50   2.00   2.50

FIGURE 4.9 Tree for a Bond for the Vasicek+ Model

risk-neutral drift varies with time in the Vasicek+ model. For the assumed parameters, the risk-neutral drift is given as:

$$\tilde{\alpha}\big(\tilde{m} - r(t)\big) = 0.1 \times \big(0.06 - r(t)\big)$$

For example, at node N_{11} the value of the short rate is 5.612%, and the drift and the probability values are given as:

$$\tilde{\alpha}\big(\tilde{m} - r(t)\big) = 0.1 \times (0.06 - 0.056) = 0.00039$$

$$p_u = \frac{1}{6} + \frac{1}{6} \times \frac{0.00039}{0.005}\sqrt{3 \times 0.5} = 0.182$$

$$p_m = 0.667$$

$$p_d = 1 - p_u - p_m = 0.151$$

The bond's current value is computed by taking the risk-neutral discounted expectation of the bond's terminal value of $100. For example, the bond price one period earlier, at node N_{41}, is computed as follows:

$$(0.107 \times 100 + 0.667 \times 100 + 0.226 \times 100)e^{-0.074 \times 0.5} = \$96.34$$

Similarly, at node N_{31}, the bond price is computed as follows:

$$(0.132 \times 96.34 + 0.667 \times 96.64 + 0.176 \times 96.94)e^{-0.068 \times 0.5} = \$93.41$$

Working back through the tree, we find that the bond price at time 0 is $88.04. This value is a numerical approximation to the true price of the bond. Using the closed-form formula given in equation (4.35), the true price of the bond is given as:

$$P(0,\ 2.5) = e^{A(2.5) - B(2.5)Y(0) - H(0,2.5)}$$

where

$$Y(0) = -0.01$$
$$B(2.5) = \frac{1 - e^{-0.1 \times 2.5}}{0.1} = 2.21199$$
$$A(2.5) = (2.5 - 2.212)\left(\frac{0.005^2}{2 \times 0.1^2}\right) - \frac{0.005^2 \times 2.212^2}{4 \times 0.1} = 0.00004671$$
$$H(0,\ 2.5) = 0.06 \times 2.5 = 0.15$$

Substituting the above values, the true bond price equals $88 using the bond-price formula. As we increase the number of steps, the tree price quickly converges to the true price as shown in Figure 4.10. Generally, using between 50 and 200 steps gives a good approximation of the bond price.

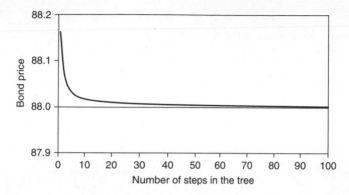

FIGURE 4.10 Convergence of the Tree Solution

Example 4.4 Now we show how to price European and American options using the tree in Example 4.3. Consider valuing two different options on the zero-coupon bond given in Example 4.3. The first option is a European call option with a strike price of $96.50 maturing at the end of two years. The second option is an American put option with the same characteristics.

The tree for the European call is shown in Figure 4.11. Each node of the tree consists of three different rows. The number in the top row gives the value of the option. The number in the middle row gives the price of the zero-coupon bond. The number in the bottom row gives the value of the short rate. The numbers in the middle row and the bottom row are obtained from Example 4.3. The probabilities of the up, middle, and down movements and the drift of the short rate are as given in Example 4.3. Since the option matures in two years, the number of steps in the option tree is $2/0.5 = 4$.

Since the call option is European, it can be exercised only at the expiration date of the option. The terminal value of the option at node N_{41} is:

$$Max[96.34 - 96.5, \ 0] = 0$$

and so the option is not exercised at this node. However, at node N_{42}, the call option is exercised, since the payoff is positive, and given as follows:

$$Max[96.64 - 96.5, \ 0] = \$0.14$$

Option prices at earlier nodes are computed by taking discounted risk-neutral expectations. For example, at node N_{31}, the option value is computed as follows:

$$(0.132 \times 0 + 0.667 \times 0.14 + 0.201 \times 0.44)e^{-0.068 \times 0.5} = \$0.17$$

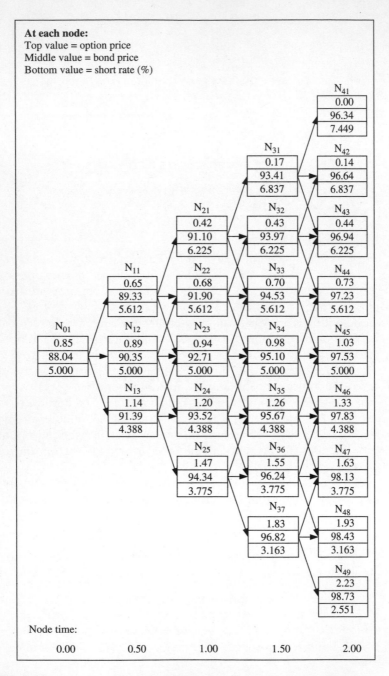

At each node:
Top value = option price
Middle value = bond price
Bottom value = short rate (%)

FIGURE 4.11   Tree for a European Call Option for the Vasicek+ Model

Working backward through the tree, we obtain the value of the European call option at time 0 as $0.85. The value of the option using the closed-form solution is $0.84. With 200 steps, the option value using the tree converges to the value using the closed-form solution.

Now consider the trinomial tree for valuing the American put option as shown in Figure 4.12. At the terminal node N_{41}, the value of the put option is given as:

$$Max[96.5 - 96.34, \ 0] = \$0.16$$

At node N_{42}, the option is not exercised, and its value is given as:

$$Max[96.5 - 96.64, \ 0] = 0$$

Since the American option allows early exercise, we must check at each node whether exercise is preferable to holding the option for another period. The value of the option if held for another period is obtained by discounting its expected value from the next period. This value can be compared to the intrinsic value (i.e., value of the option upon immediate exercise) of the option to determine whether exercising the option is optimal.

For example, at node N_{36}, the intrinsic value of the option is $96.5 - 96.24 = \$0.26$. This is more than the discounted expected value of 0. Therefore, at this node the option is exercised and its value equals $0.26. Now, consider the option value at node N_{37}. At this node, the discounted expected value is also 0; but if the option is exercised, it gives a negative payoff ($96.5 - 96.82 = -0.32$). Hence the value of the option at this node is the discounted expected value of 0.[9]

Trinomial Tree under the Vasicek++ Model: An Example

We now show some additional considerations that become relevant when we construct trinomial trees for pricing American options under the time-inhomogeneous Vasicek++ model. Potentially, three methods exist for constructing trinomial trees for the Vasicek++ model:

1. Use a discrete trinomial approximation for the stochastic process for the short rate given by equations (4.66) and (4.67). This method requires estimating the initial forward-rate curve and its first derivative from the initial bond prices at time 0, and then using this information for obtaining the deterministically changing risk-neutral long-term mean.
2. Use a discrete trinomial approximation for the stochastic process for the state variable $Y(t)$ given by equation (4.69). After obtaining the discrete

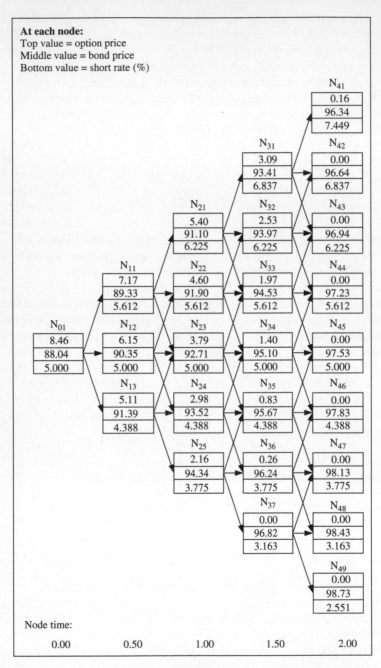

At each node:
Top value = option price
Middle value = bond price
Bottom value = short rate (%)

Node time:

0.00   0.50   1.00   1.50   2.00

FIGURE 4.12 Tree for an American Put Option for the Vasicek+ Model

trinomial tree for $Y(t)$, add the deterministic function $\delta(t)$ given in equation (4.78) at every node of the tree to obtain the tree for the short rate $r(t)$. This method requires using the initial forward-rate function, but not its first derivative as required by 1 method.

3. Directly shift either the risk-neutral long-term mean or the level of the short rate at every step of the discrete trinomial tree, such that the initial prices of zero-coupon bonds (with increasing maturities) exactly match the prices obtained from the tree at every step.

Methods 1 and 2 allow the prices obtained from the tree to match the time 0 prices used for calibration only as the number of steps becomes large, since the functional forms of either $\tilde{m}(t)$ or $\delta(t)$ are valid only in the continuous-time limit. However, the advantage of these two methods is that they do not require forward recursion, as backward recursion is sufficient to value interest rate derivatives. The main advantage of method 3 is that it allows the zero-coupon bond prices obtained from the tree to exactly match the initial prices used for calibration, for an arbitrarily small number of steps. However, this method requires a search method to obtain the exact magnitude of the shift at every step, thus also requiring forward recursion to build the tree. Hence, the advantage of obtaining *exactly matched* initial bond prices must be traded off against the disadvantage of requiring forward recursion at every step to build the tree for pricing interest rate derivatives.

The trinomial trees using the first two methods are quite similar to the trinomial trees constructed earlier, except that either the long-term mean $\tilde{m}(t)$ or the deterministic term $\delta(t)$ also changes at every step in a deterministic manner. Instead of focusing on these two methods, we demonstrate the construction of a trinomial tree using method 3 in the following example.

Example 4.5 Assume that the current short rate is 5%, $\tilde{\alpha} = 0.1$, and $\sigma = 0.5\%$. Also, assume that zero-coupon bonds with maturity of 0.5, 1, 1.5, 2, and 2.5 years and a face value of \$100 are traded in the marketplace at prices $P(0, 0.5) = \$97.49, P(0, 1) = \$94.98, P(0, 1.5) = \$92.50, P(0, 2) = \$90.06$, and $P(0, 2.5) = \$87.69$, respectively.

Now consider a trinomial tree for each of these bonds. The change in the short rate is approximated as follows under a trinomial tree:

$$\Delta r = \sigma\sqrt{3\Delta t}$$

and the probabilities of movements to the up, down, and middle nodes are given as:

$$p_u = \frac{1}{6} + \frac{1}{6}\frac{\tilde{\alpha}\big(\tilde{m}(t) - r(t)\big)}{\sigma}\sqrt{3\Delta t}$$

$$p_m = \frac{2}{3}$$

$$p_d = \frac{1}{6} - \frac{1}{6} \frac{\tilde{\alpha}(\tilde{m}(t) - r(t))}{\sigma} \sqrt{3\Delta t}$$

where Δt is the length of the time-step, which is assumed to be 0.5. Substituting the assumed parameters in these equations, we get:

$$\Delta r = 0.005\sqrt{3 \times 0.5} = 0.612\%$$

$$p_u = \frac{1}{6} + \frac{1}{6} \times \frac{0.1 \times (\tilde{m}(t) - r(t))}{0.005} \sqrt{3 \times 0.5}$$

$$p_m = \frac{2}{3}$$

$$p_d = \frac{1}{6} - \frac{1}{6} \times \frac{0.1 \times (\tilde{m}(t) - r(t))}{0.005} \sqrt{3 \times 0.5}$$

The tree for the zero-coupon bond with a maturity of 0.5 years is shown in Figure 4.13. Each node consists of two rows. The number in the top row gives the bond price, and the number in the bottom row gives the value of the short rate. Starting from the initial node N_{01}, the short rate can increase

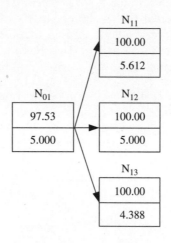

Node time:

0.00   0.50

FIGURE 4.13 Tree for the 0.5-Year Zero-Coupon Bond for the Vasicek++ Model

by 0.612 percent, decrease by 0.612 percent, or stay at the same level. The bond price at node N_{01} is obtained as follows:

$$P_{01} = (100 \times p_u + 100 \times p_m + 100 \times p_d) \times e^{-0.05 \times 0.5}$$

Since probabilities sum up to unity, the bond price is given as:

$$P_{01} = 100 \times e^{-0.05 \times 0.5} = \$97.53$$

Since we do not know the long-term mean of the short rate at time 0, the tree for the 1-year zero-coupon bond is incomplete, as illustrated in Figure 4.14.

However, $\tilde{m}(0)$ can be estimated by using the market price of the 1-year bond given as \$94.98. The value of this bond at node N_{01} is given as:

$$P_{01} = (97.23 \times p_u + 97.53 \times p_m + 97.83 \times p_d) \times e^{-0.05 \times 0.5}$$

where the three probabilities are given as:

$$p_u = \frac{1}{6} + \frac{1}{6} \times \frac{0.1 \times (\tilde{m}(0) - 0.05)}{0.005} \sqrt{3 \times 0.5}$$

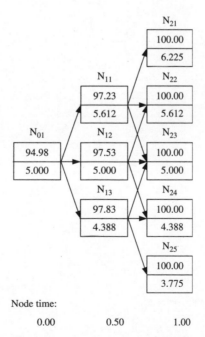

Node time:

           0.00   0.50   1.00

FIGURE 4.14 Tree for the 1-Year Zero-Coupon Bond for the Vasicek++ Model

$$p_m = \frac{2}{3}$$

$$p_d = \frac{1}{6} - \frac{1}{6} \times \frac{0.1 \times (\tilde{m}(0) - 0.05)}{0.005} \sqrt{3 \times 0.5}$$

Substituting $P_{01} = \$94.98$ and the three probabilities, the value of $\tilde{m}(0) = 9.082\%$. The three probabilities are then given as $p_u = 0.333$, $p_m = 0.667$, and $p_d = 0$.

Next, consider the 1.5-year zero-coupon bond. The tree for this bond is shown in Figure 4.15.

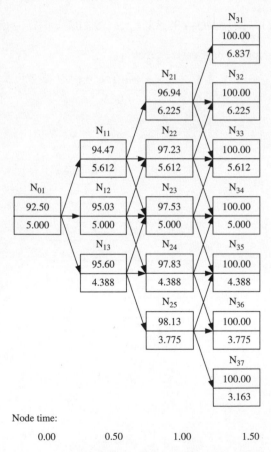

Node time:

        0.00   0.50   1.00   1.50

FIGURE 4.15 Tree for the 1.5-Year Zero-Coupon Bond for the Vasicek++ Model

This 1.5-year bond allows the estimation of $\tilde{m}(0.5)$ by matching its price at node N_{01} to the market price of \$92.50. The price of this bond is calculated as follows:

$$P_{01} = (P_{11} \times 0.333 + P_{12} \times 0.667 + P_{13} \times 0) \times e^{-0.05 \times 0.5}$$

The prices P_{11}, P_{12}, and P_{13} are functions of $\tilde{m}(0.5)$. The price P_{11} is given as:

$$P_{11} = \left[96.94 \times \left(\frac{1}{6} + \frac{1}{6} \times \frac{0.1 \times (\tilde{m}(0.5) - 0.05612)}{0.005} \sqrt{3 \times 0.5} \right) \right.$$
$$+ 97.23 \times 0.667 + 97.53$$
$$\left. \times \left(\frac{1}{6} - \frac{1}{6} \times \frac{0.1 \times (\tilde{m}(0.5) - 0.05612)}{0.005} \sqrt{3 \times 0.5} \right) \right] \times e^{-0.05612 \times 0.5}$$

The price P_{12} is given as:

$$P_{12} = \left[97.23 \times \left(\frac{1}{6} + \frac{1}{6} \times \frac{0.1 \times (\tilde{m}(0.5) - 0.05)}{0.005} \sqrt{3 \times 0.5} \right) \right.$$
$$+ 97.53 \times 0.667 + 97.83$$
$$\left. \times \left(\frac{1}{6} - \frac{1}{6} \times \frac{0.1 \times (\tilde{m}(0.5) - 0.05)}{0.005} \sqrt{3 \times 0.5} \right) \right] \times e^{-0.05 \times 0.5}$$

The price P_{13} is given as:

$$P_{13} = \left[97.53 \times \left(\frac{1}{6} + \frac{1}{6} \times \frac{0.1 \times (\tilde{m}(0.5) - 0.04388)}{0.005} \sqrt{3 \times 0.5} \right) \right.$$
$$+ 97.83 \times 0.667 + 98.13$$
$$\left. \times \left(\frac{1}{6} - \frac{1}{6} \times \frac{0.1 \times (\tilde{m}(0.5) - 0.04388)}{0.005} \sqrt{3 \times 0.5} \right) \right] \times e^{-0.04388 \times 0.5}$$

Substituting these prices in the expression for P_{01} and equating P_{01} to \$92.50, we obtain $\tilde{m}(0.5) = 8.767\%$.

Using this method iteratively and using the market prices of 2-year and 2.5-year zero-coupon bonds, we obtain the values of $\tilde{m}(1)$ and $\tilde{m}(1.5)$ as 3.850 percent and 5.449 percent, respectively.

Trinomial Tree under the Vasicek+++ Model: An Example

Example 4.6 This example shows how to construct a trinomial tree to price an American option using the Vasicek+++ model. The previous example used initially given zero-coupon bond prices and used an iterative procedure to determine the risk-neutral drift of the short-rate process that allowed an exact matching with the given bond prices. This example shows how to apply the initially given forward-rate function and uses the time-dependent functions related to the continuous-time drift of the short-rate process specified in equations (4.87), (4.88), (4.99), and (4.105) to match both the initial forward-rate curve and the initial bond-volatility function under the Vasicek+++ model.

Assume that the instantaneous forward rates are given by the Nelson and Siegel exponential model as follows (see Chapter 3 in the first book of the Fixed Income Valuation Course, *Interest Rate Risk Modeling*):

$$f(0,\ t) = \alpha_1 + \alpha_2 e^{-t/b} + \alpha_3 \frac{t}{b} e^{-t/b} \tag{4.172}$$

Further, assume that the parameters are given as: $\alpha_1 = 0.052$, $\alpha_2 = -0.002, \alpha_3 = 0.006$, and $b = 2$. Also assume that the volatility of the short rate is 0.5 percent, or 0.005.

The first derivative of the instantaneous forward-rate function is given as follows:

$$\frac{\partial f(0,\ t)}{\partial t} = -\frac{1}{b^2} e^{-t/b}(\alpha_2 b + \alpha_3(t - b)) \tag{4.173}$$

The forward-rate function and its first derivative are required to compute the function $\tilde{\beta}(t)$ given in equation (4.105). Also consider the market volatility of zero-coupon bonds with maturities ranging from 0.5 years to 2.5 years given in Table 4.2.

We first fit a cubic spline to the volatility data in order to solve for the function $\tilde{\alpha}(t)$ given in equation (4.99). Then $\tilde{\beta}(t)$, given in equation (4.105), is solved using $\tilde{\alpha}(t)$ and the forward-rate function and its first derivative given in equations (4.172) and (4.173), respectively, are solved. Next, we use the transformation $\tilde{m}(t) = \tilde{\beta}(t)/\tilde{\alpha}(t)$ to solve for the drift of the short-rate process defined as:

$$dr(t) = \tilde{\alpha}(t)(\tilde{m}(t) - r(t))\ dt + \sigma(t)\ d\tilde{Z}(t)$$

TABLE 4.2   Volatilities of Zero-Coupon
Bonds for the Vasicek+++ Model

Bond Maturity (years)	Volatility (%)
0.5	14.56
1	28.27
1.5	41.32
2	53.91
2.5	66.23

Although the formulas for the parameters are not reproduced here because
they depend on the intervals of the spline and are cumbersome to report,
Figure 4.16 shows the shapes of these functions.

These functions can be used to value any interest rate contingent claim
using a trinomial tree. Figure 4.17 illustrates the tree for an American call
option expiring in two years with strike price of $95, written on a 2.5-year
zero-coupon bond with face value $100, using time-step $\Delta t = 0.5$ years.
Each node consists of three different rows. The number in the top row gives
the value of the option, the number in the middle row gives the price of the
zero-coupon bond, and the number in the bottom row gives the value of
the short rate. Using the five-step tree, the current value of the zero-coupon
bond equals $87.65, and the current value of the option equals $2.09. A
100-step trinomial tree gives the value of the zero-coupon bond as $87.68
and the value of the option as $2.12.

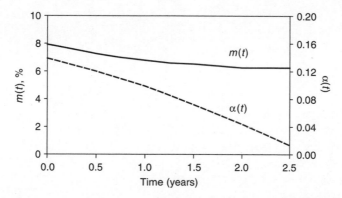

FIGURE 4.16   Time-Dependent Drift-Related Functions of the Short-Rate Process
for the Vasicek+++ Model

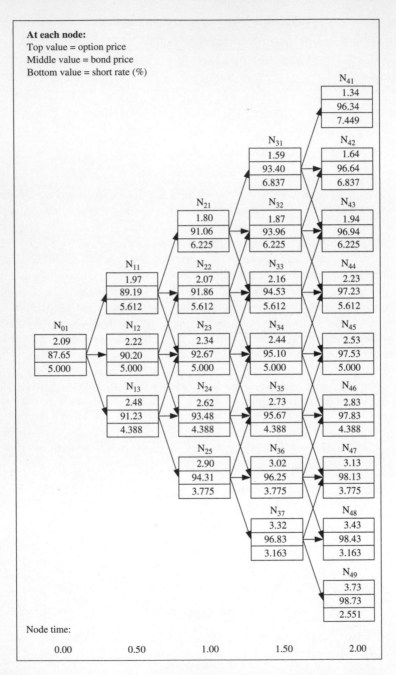

At each node:
Top value = option price
Middle value = bond price
Bottom value = short rate (%)

Node time:

0.00   0.50   1.00   1.50   2.00

FIGURE 4.17 Tree for an American Call Option for the Vasicek+++ Model

APPENDIX 4.1. BOND PRICE SOLUTION USING THE RISK-NEUTRAL VALUATION APPROACH UNDER THE FUNDAMENTAL VASICEK MODEL AND THE PREFERENCE-FREE VASICEK+ MODEL

Equation (4.30) gives the short-rate process for the Vasicek model under the risk-neutral measure as follows:

$$dr(t) = \tilde{\alpha}(\tilde{m} - r(t))\, dt + \sigma\, d\tilde{Z}(t) \tag{4.174}$$

The stochastic integral of equation (4.174) is given as:

$$r(T) = r(t) + \int_t^T \tilde{\alpha}(\tilde{m} - r(v))\, dv + \int_t^T \sigma\, d\tilde{Z}(v) \tag{4.175}$$

To remove the variable r from the first integrand, consider the transform $X(t) = e^{\tilde{\alpha}t}r(t)$. Using Ito's lemma, the stochastic differential equation of the X-process can be obtained. To apply Ito's lemma, we need the following three partial derivatives:

$$\frac{\partial X}{\partial t} = \tilde{\alpha}e^{\tilde{\alpha}t}r(t), \quad \frac{\partial X}{\partial r} = e^{\tilde{\alpha}t}, \quad \frac{\partial^2 X}{\partial r^2} = \frac{\partial}{\partial r}(e^{\tilde{\alpha}t}) = 0 \tag{4.176}$$

Using these partial derivatives and Ito's lemma, we get:

$$\begin{aligned}
dX(t) &= e^{\tilde{\alpha}t}\, dr(t) + \tilde{\alpha}e^{\tilde{\alpha}t}r(t)\, dt \\
&= e^{\tilde{\alpha}t}\left(\tilde{\alpha}(\tilde{m} - r(t))\, dt + \sigma\, d\tilde{Z}(t)\right) + \tilde{\alpha}e^{\tilde{\alpha}t}r(t)\, dt \\
&= e^{\tilde{\alpha}t}\tilde{\alpha}\tilde{m}\, dt + e^{\tilde{\alpha}t}\sigma\, d\tilde{Z}(t)
\end{aligned} \tag{4.177}$$

The stochastic integral of $X(T)$ can be written as:

$$\begin{aligned}
X(T) &= X(t) + \int_t^T (e^{\tilde{\alpha}v}\tilde{\alpha}\tilde{m})\, dv + \int_t^T (e^{\tilde{\alpha}v}\sigma)\, d\tilde{Z}(v) \\
&= X(t) + \tilde{m}(e^{\tilde{\alpha}T} - e^{\tilde{\alpha}t}) + \int_t^T (e^{\tilde{\alpha}v}\sigma)\, d\tilde{Z}(v)
\end{aligned} \tag{4.178}$$

Substituting $X(T) = e^{\tilde{\alpha}T}r(T)$ and $X(t) = e^{\tilde{\alpha}t}r(t)$ in equation (4.178) and simplifying, we get:

$$r(T) = e^{-\tilde{\alpha}\tau}r(t) + \tilde{m}(1 - e^{-\tilde{\alpha}\tau}) + e^{-\tilde{\alpha}T}\sigma \int_t^T e^{\tilde{\alpha}v}\, d\tilde{Z}(v), \tau = T - t \tag{4.179}$$

Applying rule 3 from Chapter 1 to equation (4.179), $r(T)$ has a Gaussian distribution with risk-neutral mean and variance given as follows:

$$\tilde{E}_t(r(T)) = e^{-\tilde{\alpha}\tau}r(t) + \tilde{m}(1 - e^{-\tilde{\alpha}\tau}) \tag{4.180}$$

$$V_t(r(T)) = e^{-2\tilde{\alpha}T} \int_t^T (e^{2\tilde{\alpha}v}\sigma^2)\, dv$$

$$= e^{-2\tilde{\alpha}T}\sigma^2 \left(\frac{e^{2\tilde{\alpha}T} - e^{2\tilde{\alpha}t}}{2\tilde{\alpha}} \right) = \sigma^2 \left(\frac{1 - e^{-2\tilde{\alpha}(T-t)}}{2\tilde{\alpha}} \right) \tag{4.181}$$

The time t price of a \$1 face-value zero-coupon bond maturing at time T is given by the following risk-neutral expectation:

$$P(t,\ T) = \tilde{E}_t \left[\exp\left(-\int_t^T r(v)\, dv \right) \right] \tag{4.182}$$

Since $r(t)$ has a Gaussian distribution, using rule 4 in Chapter 1, the stochastic integral given inside the exponential function in equation (4.182) also has a Gaussian distribution. Hence, applying rule 5 in Chapter 1 to equation (4.182), we obtain the following result:

$$P(t,\ T) = \exp \left[\tilde{E}_t \left(-\int_t^T r(v)\, dv \right) + (1/2)V_t \left(-\int_t^T r(v)\, dv \right) \right] \tag{4.183}$$

Now define the two variables $g(t,\ T)$ and $h(t,\ T)$ as follows:

$$g(t,\ T) = \int_t^T \sigma e^{\tilde{\alpha}v}\, d\tilde{Z}(v)$$

$$\tag{4.184}$$

$$h(t,\ T) = \int_t^T e^{-\tilde{\alpha}v} g(t,\ v)\, dv$$

Using these two definitions and equation (4.175), we get:

$$\int_t^T r(v)\, dv = \int_t^T \left(e^{-\tilde{\alpha}(v-t)}r(t) + \tilde{m}(1 - e^{-\tilde{\alpha}(v-t)}) \right) dv + \underbrace{\int_t^T e^{-\tilde{\alpha}v} g(t,\ v)\, dv}_{h(t,T)}$$

$$\tag{4.185}$$

or

$$\int_t^T r(v)\, dv = \tilde{m}(\tau - B(\tau)) + r(t)B(\tau) + h(t,\ T) \tag{4.186}$$

where $B(\tau)$ is defined as follows:

$$B(\tau) = \frac{1 - e^{-\tilde{\alpha}\tau}}{\tilde{\alpha}}, \quad \tau = T - t \qquad (4.187)$$

Using the definitions in equation (4.184) and rule 4 in Chapter 1, the mean and the variance of $h(t, T)$ are given as follows:

$$\tilde{E}_t[h(t, T)] = 0 \qquad (4.188)$$

and

$$V_t[h(t, T)] = \int_t^T \sigma^2 e^{2\tilde{\alpha}v} \left(\int_v^T e^{-\tilde{\alpha}u} \, du \right)^2 dv$$

$$= \frac{\sigma^2}{\tilde{\alpha}^2} \left(\tau + \left(\frac{1 - e^{-2\tilde{\alpha}\tau}}{2\tilde{\alpha}} \right) - 2B(\tau) \right) \qquad (4.189)$$

Equation (4.189) can be simplified by noting the following equality:

$$\frac{1 - e^{-2\tilde{\alpha}\tau}}{2\tilde{\alpha}} = B(\tau) - \frac{\tilde{\alpha}}{2} B^2(\tau) \qquad (4.190)$$

Substituting equation (4.190) into equation (4.189), we get:

$$V_t[h(t, T)] = \frac{\sigma^2}{\tilde{\alpha}^2} \left(\tau - \frac{\tilde{\alpha}}{2} B^2(\tau) - B(\tau) \right) \qquad (4.191)$$

Using the mean and the variance of $h(t, T)$ in equations (4.188) and (4.191), respectively, for computing the mean and the variance of the stochastic integral in equation (4.186) and simplifying, we get:

$$\tilde{E}_t \left(-\int_t^T r(v) \, dv \right) = -\tilde{m}(\tau - B(\tau)) - r(t)B(\tau) \qquad (4.192)$$

and

$$V_t \left(-\int_t^T r(v) \, dv \right) = V_t[-h(t, T)] = V_t[h(t, T)]$$

$$= \frac{\sigma^2}{\tilde{\alpha}^2} \left(\tau - \frac{\tilde{\alpha}}{2} B^2(\tau) - B(\tau) \right) \qquad (4.193)$$

Substituting these values into equation (4.183), we get the bond price as follows:

$$P(t, T) = e^{A(\tau) - B(\tau)Y(t) - H(t,T)} \qquad (4.194)$$

where $Y(t) = r(t) - \tilde{m}$ is as defined in equation (4.32), $B(\tau)$ is as defined in equation (4.187), and $A(\tau)$ and $H(t, T)$ are given as follows:

$$A(\tau) = \left(\tau - B(\tau)\right)\frac{\sigma^2}{2\tilde{\alpha}^2} - \frac{\sigma^2 B^2(\tau)}{4\tilde{\alpha}} \tag{4.195}$$

$$H(t, T) = \tilde{m}(T - t) = \tilde{m}\tau \tag{4.196}$$

APPENDIX 4.2. HULL'S APPROXIMATION TO CONVEXITY BIAS UNDER THE HO AND LEE MODEL

Hull [1997] approximates the convexity bias in the Eurodollar time deposit market using continuously compounded rates. Let $y(S, T)$ be the U ($U = T - S$) period continuously compounded spot rate observed at time S. Consider a futures contract with a delivery date S, based upon some linear function of the spot rate $y(S, T)$. Let $F(t, S, T)$ be the corresponding futures rate observed at time t. As shown in Chapter 3, futures prices are martingales under the risk-neutral measure, and hence, the futures rate can be given as:

$$F(t, S, T) = \tilde{E}_t\big(Y(S, T)\big) = -\tilde{E}_t\left(\frac{\ln P(S, T)}{U}\right) \tag{4.197}$$

where $U = T - S$. By substituting the bond-price formula from equation (4.73) for the special case of the Ho and Lee model (i.e., $\tilde{\alpha} = 0$), we get:

$$\begin{aligned}
F(t, S, T) &= \frac{-\tilde{E}_t\big(A(U) - Y(S)B(U) - H(S, T)\big)}{U} \\
&= \frac{-A(U) + Y(t)B(U) + H(S, T)}{U}
\end{aligned} \tag{4.198}$$

Using the definitions of $A(U)$ and $B(U)$ from equations (4.83) and of $H(S, T)$ from equation (4.84), respectively, equation (4.198) simplifies to:

$$F(t, S, T) = \frac{1}{2}\sigma^2 s(s + U) + f(t, S, T) \tag{4.199}$$

where $f(t, S, T)$ is the forward rate observed at time 0, for the term S to T, defined as follows:

$$f(t, S, T) = \frac{-\ln P(t, T) + \ln P(t, S)}{U}$$

$$= \frac{-\big(A(\tau) - B(\tau)Y(t) - H(t,\ T)\big) + \big(A(s) - B(s)Y(t) - H(t,\ S)\big)}{U}$$

$$= \frac{-A(\tau) + A(s) + B(U)Y(t) + H(S,\ T)}{U} \tag{4.200}$$

where $\tau = T - t$ and $s = S - t$. Hence, Hull's approximation to the convexity bias under the Ho and Lee model, using continuously compounded rates, equals:

$$F(t,\ S,\ T) - f(t,\ S,\ T) = \frac{1}{2}\sigma^2 s(s + U), \quad s = S - t \tag{4.201}$$

A similar method can be used to derive Hull's convexity bias under the Vasicek++ model using continuously compounded rates, given in equation (4.130).

NOTES

1. A negative value for α would make the short-rate process *mean-averting*, and the drift of the short rate would cause it to be pulled away even more from its mean whenever it is away from its mean.
2. The models of Merton [1973] and Nawalkha [1995] do not violate the Girsanov theorem for performing the change of measure; however, the models of Ball and Torous [1983] and Schaefer and Schwartz [1987] violate this theorem and, hence, imply arbitrage opportunities.
3. The function $\gamma(t,\ z)$ must satisfy certain boundedness conditions related to the Novikov condition of the Girsanov theorem and to the Lipschitz and growth conditions for obtaining unique solutions given in Appendix D of Duffie [2001].
4. Though the solution form under the Vasicek+ model is identical to the solution form under the fundamental Vasicek model, the empirical estimates of the risk-neutral parameters under the two models will be generally different due to the restrictive nature of MPRs under the latter model.
5. The outlined calibration procedure requires the functions $B(0,\ t)$, $A(0,\ t)$, and $\ln P(0,\ t)$ to be twice differentiable. Therefore, it might be necessary to fit discrete market data by functions that are at least twice differentiable, such as cubic splines.
6. Since the empirical estimates of the risk-neutral parameters under the Vasicek, Vasieck+, and Vasicek++ models are generally different, the same formulas for $A(U)$ and $B(U)$ under these three models will lead to different numerical values.
7. This assumes that terms of the order Δt^2 can be ignored, assuming that Δt is sufficiently small.
8. See endnote number 7.

9. The zero value for an option cannot occur in continuous-time limit, but may occur when using discrete-time trees, on the nodes from which there is zero probability of ever obtaining a positive payoff from the option. If we increase the number of steps in the tree sufficiently, then zero option values will not occur before the option expiration date is reached.

CHAPTER 5

Fundamental and Preference-Free Jump-Extended Gaussian Models

C hapter 4 assumed that the Gaussian-distributed interest rate undergoes only local changes—changes due to the diffusion component of the interest rate process. However, interest rate changes can also occur due to rare events associated with the arrival of lumpy information, which makes interest rates suddenly jump to higher or lower levels. *Jumps* can be defined as infrequent events that displace interest rates by discrete magnitudes, the size of which does not depend upon the length of the infinitesimal intervals over which the events take place. Interest rate jumps can be caused by market crashes, interventions by the Federal Reserve, economic surprises, shocks in the foreign exchange markets, and other rare events. Though the size of the jumps does not depend upon the length of the time interval over which the jumps occur, the probability of jumps is assumed to be directly proportional to the length of the time interval. The size of the jumps is generally assumed to be a random variable with some probability distribution.

A number of empirical studies have found jumps to play a significant role in explaining the dynamics of interest rate changes.[1] Empirical studies have found the short-rate to exhibit significant leptokurtosis, which is consistent with the occurrence of jumps. Das [2002] finds that a mix of ARCH processes with jumps explains the behavior of short-rate changes well. The ARCH features are required to capture the high persistence in short-rate volatility, and jump features are required to explain the sudden large movements that lead to leptokurtosis. Das finds jumps to be more pronounced during the two-day meeting dates of the Federal Open Market Committee and, curiously, also on many Wednesdays due to the option expiry effects on that day.

This chapter extends the fundamental and preference-free Vasicek models by allowing Gaussian and exponentially distributed jumps (see Baz and Das [1996], Das and Foresi [1996], and Chacko and Das [2002]). Closed-form solutions are derived for pricing zero-coupon bonds with the jump component. The chapter also provides jump-diffusion trees by extending the work of Amin [1993] to price interest rate options with American features. These trees allow an arbitrarily large number of nodes at each step to capture the jump component, while two local nodes are used to capture the diffusion component. Finally, the chapter demonstrates how to calibrate the jump-diffusion trees to fit an initial yield curve or initial zero-coupon bond prices by allowing a time-dependent drift for the short-rate process.

A limitation of using the Vasicek models extended with Gaussian-distributed jumps (Vasicek-GJ models, hereafter) is that interest rates can become negative with a significant probability, since jumps of the same magnitude (and frequency) occur in *both* directions. This problem is somewhat alleviated by using the Vasicek models with exponentially distributed jumps (Vasicek-EJ models, hereafter). The advantage of the latter model is that it allows separate distributions for the upward jumps and downward jumps. This can significantly reduce the probability of negative interest rates by allowing more flexibility in estimating parameters for different interest rate regimes. For example, in a regime with a lower value for the speed of mean reversion of the short rate, downward jumps may have a lower size and a lower frequency of occurrence than upward jumps.

The jump-diffusion trees developed in this chapter can also be useful as numerical pricing tools for other non-Gaussian models that disallow negative interest rates. For example, the quadratic term structure models (QTSMs) in Chapter 10 assume Gaussian-distributed state variables. Since the short rate is a quadratic function of the state variable under the Gaussian-quadratic model, it always remains positive. The jump-diffusion trees developed in this chapter can be used to obtain a jump-diffusion tree for a Gaussian-quadratic model extended with jumps with very slight modifications.[2]

FUNDAMENTAL VASICEK-GJ MODEL

Consider the short-rate process given by Vasicek [1977] with an added Poisson-jump component given as follows:

$$dr(t) = \alpha(m - r(t))\, dt + \sigma\, dZ(t) + J dN(\lambda) \qquad (5.1)$$

where α, m, and σ define the speed of mean reversion, the long-term mean, and the diffusion volatility, respectively, as in Chapter 4. The variable $Z(t)$ is the Wiener process distributed independently of $N(\lambda)$. The variable $N(\lambda)$ represents a Poisson process with an intensity λ. The variable λ gives the mean number of jumps per unit of time. The variable J denotes the size of the jump and is assumed to be distributed independently of both $Z(t)$ and $N(\lambda)$. The choice of jump distribution has a significant effect on the pricing of bonds. For example, the jump size can follow a Gaussian, a lognormal, or an exponential distribution. This chapter considers jumps that follow Gaussian and exponential distributions. In this section, we assume that the jump size, J, follows a Gaussian distribution with mean μ_J and variance σ_J^2. We denote the Gaussian jump-extended fundamental Vasicek model as the "Vasicek-GJ" model, with the subscript GJ representing Gaussian jumps.

The probability of the occurrence of one Poisson event over the infinitesimal time interval dt is given as λdt. Upon the occurrence of the Poisson event, the change in the Poisson variable, $dN(\lambda)$, equals 1, otherwise $dN(\lambda)$ equals 0 as shown in Figure 5.1. The probability that more than one jump occurs during the interval dt is less than $o(dt)$, hence as dt converges to an infinitesimally small number, only one jump with probability λdt needs to be modeled for numerical applications (since the variable λ gives the mean number of jumps per unit of time).[3]

In the absence of the jump component, it is possible to derive the term structure equation for the Vasicek model by constructing a riskless portfolio of two bonds of different maturities and imposing the absence of arbitrage condition (see equation (4.15) in Chapter 4). However, in the presence of a jump component, the absence of arbitrage argument can no longer be applied, as jump risk cannot be diversified away using traded bonds. This leaves two alternatives for the derivation of the term structure equation for pricing default-free bonds. The first alternative is to impose some market equilibrium as in Cox, Ingersoll, and Ross [1985] to derive the term structure equation. The second alternative is to directly specify the process for the stochastic discount factor introduced in Chapter 2. The stochastic discount factor captures all information needed to price a security and as shown below, it can be used directly to obtain the term structure equation consistent with the short-rate process given in equation (5.1).

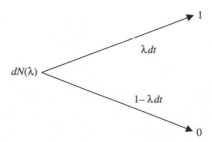

FIGURE 5.1 The Poisson Process over an Infinitesimally Small Interval dt

Since $Z(t)$ and $N(\lambda)$ are the two factors driving interest rate movements in equation (5.1), we propose the following process for the stochastic discount factor:

$$\frac{dM(t)}{M(t)} = -r(t)\,dt - \left(\frac{\gamma_0 + \gamma_1 r(t)}{\sigma}\right)dZ(t) - \gamma_J\,dN(\lambda) + \gamma_J \lambda\,dt \qquad (5.2)$$

where, γ_0 and γ_1 are coefficients for the market price of diffusion risk (consistent with Duffee [2002]) and γ_J is the market price of jump risk. Since $E_t[\gamma_J\,dN(\lambda)] = \gamma_J \lambda\,dt$, the last term in equation (5.2) is needed to ensure that the expected value of $E_t[dM(t)/M(t)] = -r(t)\,dt$. Using equation (2.105) in Chapter 2, the instantaneous expected return on any security has the following relationship with the stochastic discount factor:

$$E_t\left(\frac{dP(t)}{P(t)}\right) = r(t)\,dt - E_t\left(\frac{dM(t)}{M(t)}\frac{dP(t)}{P(t)}\right) \qquad (5.3)$$

where $P(t)$ is the current price of the security and the expectation is taken under the physical measure. Now, suppose the security is a default-free zero-coupon bond, which gives \$1 at its maturity T. Hence, the instantaneous expected return on this bond is given as follows:

$$E_t\left(\frac{dP(t,\,T)}{P(t,\,T)}\right) = r(t)\,dt - E_t\left(\frac{dM(t)}{M(t)}\frac{dP(t,\,T)}{P(t,\,T)}\right) \qquad (5.4)$$

Equation (5.4) gives:

$$E_t\big(dP(t,\,T)\big) = r(t)P(t,\,T)\,dt - E_t\left(\frac{dM(t)}{M(t)}\,dP(t,\,T)\right) \qquad (5.5)$$

To evaluate the expectation of equation (5.5), we first express the bond price $P(t,\,T) = P(r(t),\,t,\,T)$ as a function of the short rate $r(t)$ and time t. Using Ito's lemma for jump-diffusion processes given in equation (1.57) in Chapter 1, we have:

$$
\begin{aligned}
dP(t,\,T) = {}& \left(\frac{\partial P}{\partial t} + \alpha(m - r(t))\frac{\partial P}{\partial r} + \frac{1}{2}\sigma^2\frac{\partial^2 P}{\partial r^2}\right)dt + \frac{\partial P}{\partial r}\sigma\,dZ(t) \\
& + \big[P(r(t) + J,\,t,\,T) - P(r(t),\,t,\,T)\big]\,dN(\lambda)
\end{aligned} \qquad (5.6)
$$

Taking the expectation of equation (5.6) under the physical measure gives:

$$
\begin{aligned}
E_t\big(dP(t,\,T)\big) = {}& \left(\frac{\partial P}{\partial t} + \alpha(m - r(t))\frac{\partial P}{\partial r} + \frac{1}{2}\sigma^2\frac{\partial^2 P}{\partial r^2}\right)dt \\
& + E_t\big[P(r(t) + J,\,t,\,T) - P(r(t),\,t,\,T)\big]\lambda\,dt
\end{aligned} \qquad (5.7)
$$

Also, using equations (5.2) and (5.6), we have:

$$
E_t\left(\frac{dM(t)}{M(t)}\,dP(t,\ T)\right) = -\frac{\partial P}{\partial r}\big(\gamma_0 + \gamma_1 r(t)\big)\,dt
$$
$$
- E_t\big[P\big(r(t)+J,t,T\big) - P\big(r(t),t,T\big)\big]\gamma_J\lambda\,dt \tag{5.8}
$$

Substituting equations (5.7) and (5.8) into equation (5.5) gives the term structure equation as follows:

$$
\frac{\partial P}{\partial t} + \tilde{\alpha}(\tilde{m} - r(t))\frac{\partial P}{\partial r} + \frac{1}{2}\sigma^2\frac{\partial^2 P}{\partial r^2} - r(t)P(t,\ T)
$$
$$
+ E_t\big[P\big(r(t)+J,\ t,\ T\big) - P\big(r(t),\ t,\ T\big)\big]\tilde{\lambda} = 0 \tag{5.9}
$$

where

$$
\tilde{\alpha} = \alpha + \gamma_1
$$
$$
\tilde{m} = \frac{\alpha m - \gamma_0}{\alpha + \gamma_1} \tag{5.10}
$$
$$
\tilde{\lambda} = \lambda(1 - \gamma_J)
$$

subject to the boundary condition $P(T,\ T) = 1$.

The partial differential difference equation (PDDE), equation (5.9), generalizes the Vasicek term structure equation to the case when the short rate experiences jump risk in addition to diffusion risk. Both the diffusion risk and jump risk are priced through the market prices of these risks. The PDDE of bond price given in equation (5.9) is consistent with the following risk-neutral short-rate process:

$$
dr(t) = \tilde{\alpha}(\tilde{m} - r(t))\,dt + \sigma\,d\tilde{Z}(t) + JdN(\tilde{\lambda}) \tag{5.11}
$$

Due to the specific nature of the process assumed for the stochastic discount factor, we do not model a separate risk premium for the jump-size variable J and assume that all risk premium related to jump risk is artificially absorbed by the change in the intensity of jump from λ under the physical measure to $\tilde{\lambda}$ under the risk-neutral measure.

Bond Price Solution

In order to relate the fundamental Vasicek-GJ model to its preference-free extensions given later, we solve for the bond price after redefining the short rate as a sum of a constant and a mean-zero state variable given as follows:

$$
r(t) = \tilde{m} + Y(t) \tag{5.12}
$$

where

$$dY(t) = -\tilde{\alpha}Y(t)\, dt + \sigma\, d\tilde{Z}(t) + J\, dN(\tilde{\lambda}) \tag{5.13}$$

Using Ito's lemma, it is easy to confirm that the short-rate process given in equation (5.11) is consistent with the state variable process given in equation (5.13). Using a change of variable, the bond price can be expressed as a function of $Y(t)$ and t, and the partial differential equation (PDE) in equation (5.9) can be alternatively expressed as follows:

$$\frac{\partial P}{\partial t} - \tilde{\alpha}Y(t)\frac{\partial P}{\partial Y} + \frac{1}{2}\sigma^2\frac{\partial^2 P}{\partial Y^2} - (\tilde{m} + Y(t))P(t, T)$$

$$+ E_t\big[P(Y(t) + J, t, T) - P(Y(t), t, T)\big]\tilde{\lambda} = 0 \tag{5.14}$$

subject to the boundary condition $P(T, T) = 1$. Now consider the following form for the solution of the bond price:

$$P(t, T) = e^{A(\tau) - B(\tau)Y(t) - H(t,T)} \tag{5.15}$$

where $\tau = T - t$, subject to the boundary conditions $A(0) = 0$ and $B(0) = 0$, and $H(t, T)$ is defined as follows:

$$H(t, T) = \int_t^T \tilde{m}\, du = \tilde{m}(T - t) = \tilde{m}\tau \tag{5.16}$$

The partial derivatives of bond price can be given as follows:

$$\frac{\partial P}{\partial t} = \left[-Y(t)\frac{\partial B(\tau)}{\partial t} + \frac{\partial A(\tau)}{\partial t}\right]P(t, T)$$

$$\frac{\partial P}{\partial Y} = -B(\tau)P(t, T) \tag{5.17}$$

$$\frac{\partial^2 P}{\partial Y^2} = B^2(\tau)P(t, T)$$

Also, using equation (5.15), we have:

$$E_t\big[P(Y(t) + J, t, T) - P(Y(t), t, T)\big]$$

$$= P(Y(t), t, T)\big[E_t(e^{-B(\tau)J}) - 1\big] \tag{5.18}$$

Since the variable J is normally distributed with mean μ_J and variance $\sigma_J{}^2$, we have:

$$E_t(e^{-B(\tau)J}) = e^{-\mu_J B(\tau) + \frac{1}{2}\sigma_J^2 B^2(\tau)} \tag{5.19}$$

Substituting equation (5.19) into equation (5.18), we get:

$$E_t\left[P\big(Y(t)+J,\ t,\ T\big) - P\big(Y(t),\ t,\ T\big)\right] = P\big(Y(t),\ t,\ T\big)L(\tau) \qquad (5.20)$$

where $L(\tau)$ is the expected return on the bond, conditional on the realization of the jump, or $dN(\tilde{\lambda}) = 1$, in the state variable process given in equation (5.13), or:

$$
\begin{aligned}
L(\tau) &= \frac{E_t\left[P\big(Y(t)+J,\ t,\ T\big) - P\big(Y(t),\ t,\ T\big)\right]}{P\big(Y(t),\ t,\ T\big)} \\
&= \left[e^{-\mu_J B(\tau) + \frac{1}{2}\sigma_J^2 B^2(\tau)} - 1 \right]
\end{aligned}
\qquad (5.21)
$$

Note that since we do not model a separate risk premium for the jump-size variable J, the conditional expectation in equation (5.21) is the same under the physical and the risk-neutral measures. Substituting the expressions in equations (5.17) and (5.20) into equation (5.14) and then using a separation of variables, the PDDE for the bond price simplifies to the following two ODEs after using a change of variable $\tau = T - t$:

$$
\begin{aligned}
\frac{\partial B(\tau)}{\partial \tau} &= 1 - \tilde{\alpha}B(\tau) \\
\frac{\partial A(\tau)}{\partial \tau} &= \frac{1}{2}\sigma^2 B^2(\tau) + \tilde{\lambda}L(\tau)
\end{aligned}
\qquad (5.22)
$$

subject to the boundary conditions $A(0) = 0$ and $B(0) = 0$. The solutions to the ODEs are given as:

$$B(\tau) = \left(\frac{1 - e^{-\tilde{\alpha}\tau}}{\tilde{\alpha}} \right) \qquad (5.23)$$

and

$$A(\tau) = \big(\tau - B(\tau)\big)\frac{\sigma^2}{2\tilde{\alpha}^2} - \frac{\sigma^2 B^2(\tau)}{4\tilde{\alpha}} + \tilde{\lambda}\int_0^\tau L(v)\,dv \qquad (5.24)$$

A full analytical solution to the expression for $A(\tau)$ cannot be obtained since the integral in equation (5.24) contains the term $L(.)$, which is a double-exponential (see equations (5.21) and (5.23)). However, a simple numerical solution to the integral given in equation (5.24) can be obtained within a fraction of a second using any standard programming languages. The solution of bond price in equation (5.15) under the Vasicek-GJ model is identical to the solution under the Vasicek model given in equation (4.35) in Chapter 4, except for the addition of the last term on the right-hand side of equation (5.24), which accounts for the effect of jumps on the bond price.

Since the PDDE for the bond price under the Vasicek-GJ model does have a quasi-analytical solution, the Fourier inversion method (see Duffie, Pan, and Singleton [2000] and Chacko and Das [2002]) can be used to obtain analytical solutions of options. Due to space constraints, we derive solutions to futures and options only under the Vasciek model extended with exponential jumps later in this chapter. The same methods also can be used to derive solutions of futures and options under the Vasicek-GJ model.

Jump-Diffusion Tree

This section explains how to build a jump-diffusion tree for the Vasicek-GJ model for pricing American options.[4] The diffusion component and the jump component of the risk-neutral short-rate process in equation (5.11) can be expressed using two variables as follows:

$$r(t) = r_1(t) + r_2(t) \tag{5.25}$$

where $r_1(0) = r(0)$ and $r_2(0) = 0$, and the stochastic differential of the short rate is given as follows:

$$dr(t) = dr_1(t) + dr_2(t) \tag{5.26}$$

where

$$
\begin{aligned}
dr_1(t) &= \tilde{\alpha}(\tilde{m} - r(t))\,dt + \sigma\,d\tilde{Z}(t) \\
dr_2(t) &= J dN(\tilde{\lambda})
\end{aligned}
\tag{5.27}
$$

The joint Markovian system represented by the previous equations can be modeled as a combination of two trees: one tree for the continuous diffusion process $dr_1(t)$, and another tree for the jump process $dr_2(t)$. The joint probabilities can be then obtained by multiplying the probabilities of the nodes of the first tree by the probabilities of the nodes of the second tree (since the two processes are independent). However, the jump-diffusion tree can be modeled more efficiently (i.e., with fewer nodes) with the following approximation of the jump-diffusion process:

$$
dr(t) = \left\{
\begin{aligned}
&\tilde{\alpha}(\tilde{m} - r(t))\,dt + \sigma\,d\tilde{Z}(t), \text{ with probability } 1 - \tilde{\lambda}\,dt \\
&\tilde{\alpha}(\tilde{m} - r(t))\,dt + J, \text{ with probability } \tilde{\lambda}\,dt
\end{aligned}
\right\}
\tag{5.28}
$$

Equation (5.28) deviates from equation (5.26) only in the order $o(dt)$; and, hence, the two equations converge in the limit as dt goes to zero. To approximate the jump-diffusion process in equation (5.28), we will use a single *n*-step *recombining* tree with M branches, where M is always an odd number. This is more efficient than the approximation of the jump-diffusion process in equation (5.26), which would have required two independent trees. This tree is displayed in Figure 5.2. Given that the initial value of the short rate is $r(0)$, the short rate can either undergo a local change due to the diffusion component shown through two local branches (represented by the segmented lines) or experience a jump shown through $M - 2$ remaining branches, including the central branch, where the short rate does not change (represented by the solid lines). As mentioned earlier, the jump size J is assumed to be normally distributed with mean equal to μ_J and variance equal to σ_J^2.

To keep the analysis general, we consider an arbitrary node $r(t)$, at time $t = i\Delta t$, for $i = 0, 1, 2, \ldots, n-1$, where length of time T is divided into n equal intervals of Δt. At time $(i + 1)\Delta t$, the M different values for the interest rate are given as follows:

$$r(t) \pm j\sigma\sqrt{\Delta t}, \; j = 0, 1, \ldots, \frac{M-1}{2}$$

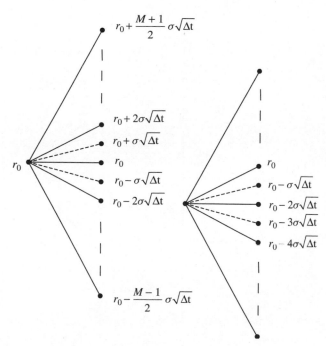

FIGURE 5.2 Jump-Diffusion Interest Rate Tree

We need to specify the M probabilities associated with the M nodes. At time $(i+1)\Delta t$, the short rate can either undergo a local change with probability $1 - \tilde{\lambda}\Delta t$ or experience a jump with probability $\tilde{\lambda}\Delta t$.

The two local probabilities are computed as follows:

$$P[r(t) + \sigma\sqrt{\Delta t}] = \left(\frac{1}{2} + \frac{1}{2}\frac{\tilde{\alpha}(\tilde{m} - r(t))}{\sigma}\sqrt{\Delta t}\right)(1 - \tilde{\lambda}\Delta t)$$

$$P[r(t) - \sigma\sqrt{\Delta t}] = \left(\frac{1}{2} - \frac{1}{2}\frac{\tilde{\alpha}(\tilde{m} - r(t))}{\sigma}\sqrt{\Delta t}\right)(1 - \tilde{\lambda}\Delta t)$$

(5.29)

Since the total probability of jump occurrence is $\tilde{\lambda}\Delta t$, this probability is allocated to M nonoverlapping intervals of a normal distribution with mean μ_J and variance σ_J^2. The normal distribution over the entire real line from negative infinity to positive infinity with M nonoverlapping intervals is displayed in Figure 5.3. The probability mass over each of these M intervals is assigned to the point at the center of each of these intervals in the following three steps:

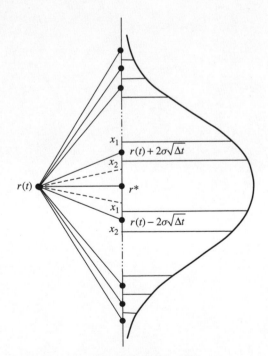

FIGURE 5.3   Approximation of the Jump Distribution

Step 1. The first step computes the probabilities of all jump nodes except the central node, the top node, and the bottom node, as follows:

$$P[r(t) + k\sigma\sqrt{\Delta t}] = [\mathcal{N}(x_1) - \mathcal{N}(x_2)]\tilde{\lambda}\Delta t,$$

$$k = -\frac{M-3}{2}, \ldots, -4, -3, -2, 2, 3, 4, \ldots, \frac{M-3}{2} \qquad (5.30)$$

where

$$x_1 = \frac{(k+0.5)\sigma\sqrt{\Delta t} - \mu_J - \tilde{\alpha}(\tilde{m} - r(t))\Delta t}{\sigma_J}$$

$$x_2 = \frac{(k-0.5)\sigma\sqrt{\Delta t} - \mu_J - \tilde{\alpha}(\tilde{m} - r(t))\Delta t}{\sigma_J}$$

The expression $\mathcal{N}(x_1) - \mathcal{N}(x_2)$ gives the difference between two cumulative normal distributions, and hence it gives the area under the normal curve over one of the nonoverlapping regions in Figure 5.3. Multiplication of this probability by the risk-neutral jump probability $\tilde{\lambda}\Delta t$ gives the probability of the short-rate node at the point in the center of x_1 and x_2.

Step 2. Since the normal distribution covers the whole real line from negative infinity to positive infinity, but we only consider a finite number of nodes in the region:

$$\left(r(t) - \frac{M-1}{2}\sigma\sqrt{\Delta t}, r(t) + \frac{M-1}{2}\sigma\sqrt{\Delta t} \right)$$

probabilities for the end nodes may be adjusted to account for the probability mass outside this region. Probability for the top node is computed as:

$$P\left(r(t) + \frac{M-1}{2}\sigma\sqrt{\Delta t} \right) = (1 - \mathcal{N}(x_2))\tilde{\lambda}\Delta t \qquad (5.31)$$

where,

$$x_2 = \frac{\left(\frac{M-1}{2} - 0.5\right)\sigma\sqrt{\Delta t} - \mu_J - \tilde{\alpha}(\tilde{m} - r(t))\Delta t}{\sigma_J}$$

Similarly, the probability for the bottom node is computed as:

$$P\left(r(t) - \frac{M-1}{2}\sigma\sqrt{\Delta t} \right) = \mathcal{N}(x_1)\tilde{\lambda}\Delta t \qquad (5.32)$$

where

$$x_1 = \frac{\left(-\dfrac{M-1}{2} + 0.5\right)\sigma\sqrt{\Delta t} - \mu_J - \tilde{\alpha}(\tilde{m} - r(t))\Delta t}{\sigma_J}$$

Step 3. The central area corresponding to the center node covers a wider region; and, hence, the probability for the central node is computed as follows:

$$P\big(r(t)\big) = \big(\mathcal{N}(x_1) - \mathcal{N}(x_2)\big)\tilde{\lambda}\Delta t \qquad (5.33)$$

where

$$x_1 = \frac{1.5\sigma\sqrt{\Delta t} - \mu_J - \tilde{\alpha}(\tilde{m} - r(t))\Delta t}{\sigma_J}$$

$$x_2 = \frac{-1.5\sigma\sqrt{\Delta t} - \mu_J - \tilde{\alpha}(\tilde{m} - r(t))\Delta t}{\sigma_J}$$

Equation (5.29) defines the probabilities at two nodes that give the local change due to the diffusion; process, and equations (5.30), (5.31), (5.32), and (5.33) define the probabilities at the remaining $M - 2$ nodes that give the change due to the jump process. Together, all of these probabilities sum up to one.

Using the probabilities given, the jump tree can be built in a recombining fashion as shown in Figure 5.2. At every node of the tree, there exist M branches; and the probabilities of these branches are as given in the preceeding equations. Example 5.1 demonstrates how the jump-diffusion tree can be used to price a bond.

Example 5.1   Consider a bond that pays \$100 in two months ($T = 2/12 = 0.167$). Current riskless interest rate $r_0 = 5\%$, volatility of the interest rate $\sigma = 1\%$, risk-neutral mean reversion speed $\tilde{\alpha} = 0.5$, risk-neutral long-term mean $\tilde{m} = 6\%$, risk-neutral intensity $\tilde{\lambda} = 1$, mean of the jump process $\mu_J = 0$, and volatility of the jump process $\sigma_J = 3\%$. For expositional purposes, we use a two-period tree ($\Delta t = T/2 = 1/12 = 0.083$) with $M = 5$ branches.

Figure 5.4 shows the five node values at the end of the first period with the five corresponding probabilities. The last column also gives the five probabilities of the five node values at the end of the second period.

Consider the top node of the tree. The short rate at this node is computed as follows:

$$r_0 + 2\sigma\sqrt{\Delta t} = 0.05 + 2 \times 0.01 \times \sqrt{0.083} = 0.056$$

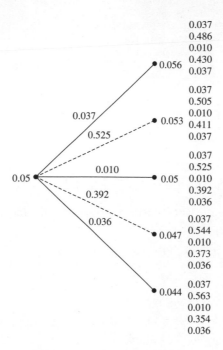

FIGURE 5.4 Inerest Rate Tree

Now let's compute the set of five probabilities at this node corresponding to the five node values at the end of the second period. These are shown in the last column of Figure 5.4. The first probability value corresponds to the top jump node; therefore, equation (5.31) is applied as follows:

$$p_1 = \left(1 - \mathcal{N}\left(\frac{1.5 \times 0.01\sqrt{0.083} - 0.5 \times (0.06 - 0.056) \times 0.083}{0.03}\right)\right)$$

$$\times 1 \times 0.083$$

$$= \left(1 - \mathcal{N}(0.138)\right) \times 1 \times 0.083 = 0.037$$

The second probability value corresponds to the diffusion node; therefore, equation (5.29) is applied as follows:

$$p_2 = \left(0.5 + 0.5\frac{(0.5 \times (0.06 - 0.056))\sqrt{0.083}}{0.01}\right) \times (1 - 1 \times 0.083)$$

$$= 0.529 \times (1 - 1 \times 0.083) = 0.486$$

The third probability value corresponds to the middle jump node; therefore, equation (5.33) is applied as follows:

$$p_3 = \left(\mathcal{N} \left(\frac{1.5 \times 0.01\sqrt{0.083} - 0.5 \times (0.06 - 0.056) \times 0.083}{0.03} \right) \right.$$

$$\left. - \mathcal{N} \left(\frac{-1.5 \times 0.01\sqrt{0.083} - 0.5 \times (0.06 - 0.056) \times 0.083}{0.03} \right) \right)$$

$$\times 1 \times 0.083$$

$$= \big(\mathcal{N}(0.138) - \mathcal{N}(-0.150) \big) \times 1 \times 0.083 = 0.010$$

The fourth probability value corresponds to the diffusion node; therefore, equation (5.29) is applied as follows:

$$p_4 = \left(0.5 - 0.5 \frac{(0.5 \times (0.06 - 0.056))\sqrt{0.083}}{0.01} \right) \times (1 - 1 \times 0.083)$$

$$= 0.471 \times (1 - 1 \times 0.083) = 0.430$$

The fifth probability value corresponds to the bottom jump node; therefore, equation (5.32) is applied as follows:

$$p_5 = \mathcal{N} \left(\frac{-1.5 \times 0.01\sqrt{0.083} - 0 - 0.5 \times (0.06 - 0.056) \times 0.083}{0.03} \right)$$

$$\times 1 \times 0.083$$

$$= \mathcal{N}(-0.150) \times 1 \times 0.083 = 0.037$$

Figure 5.5 prices the zero-coupon bond by taking risk-neutral expectations of the bond values at different nodes. The bond pays $100 at the end of the second time period. To compute the bond values at each node at the end of the first time period, we use the short-rate values and the probability values corresponding to each of these nodes.

For example, consider the value of the bond at the top node at the end of the first period, computed as follows:[5]

$$(100.00 \times 0.037 + 100.00 \times 0.486 + 100.00 \times 0.010$$

$$+ \, 100.00 \times 0.430 + 100.00 \times 0.037) \times e^{-0.056 \times 0.083} = \$99.54$$

Similarly, the value of the bond at time 0 is computed as follows:

$$P_0 = (99.54 \times 0.037 + 99.56 \times 0.525 + 99.58 \times 0.010 + 99.61 \times 0.392$$

$$+ \, 99.63 \times 0.036) \times e^{-0.05 \times 0.083} = \$99.17$$

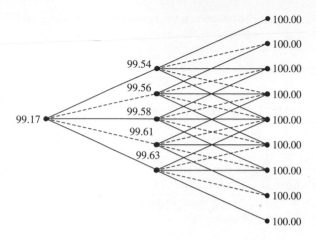

FIGURE 5.5 Bond-Value Calculation

where the time 0 probabilities of the five nodes at time 1 are computed in a similar way as demonstrated earlier.

Using a 100-step tree with $M = 101$, the price of the bond equals $99.16. The closed-form solution of the bond price using equation (5.15) also equals $99.16.

PREFERENCE-FREE VASICEK-GJ+ AND VASICEK-GJ++ MODELS

Preference-free extensions of the fundamental Vasicek-GJ model, given as the Vasicek-GJ+, Vasicek-GJ++, and Vasicek-GJ+++ models, can be derived using the approach outlined in Chapter 4. Since this book does not focus on triple-plus models, this section gives only the Vasicek-GJ+ and Vasicek-GJ++ models. The preference-free Vasicek-GJ+ model can be derived assuming an exogenous stochastic bond-price process and fitting the bond-price to the specific bond-price solution that leads to a time-homogeneous risk-neutral short-rate process implied by this model. This approach allows the Vasicek-GJ+ model to be *preference-free*. Since this approach is equivalent to an exogenous specification of the risk-neutral short-rate process (instead of an exogenous specification of the physical short-rate process), the next section begins by specifying the short-rate process directly under the risk-neutral measure. A similar argument applies to the preference-free Vasicek-GJ++ model, which also specifies the short-rate process directly under the risk-neutral measure. Unlike the

Vasicek-GJ+ model, the short-rate process under the Vasicek-GJ++ model is time-inhomogeneous.

The Vasicek-GJ+ Model

The Vasicek-GJ+ model begins with an exogenous specification of the risk-neutral short-rate process as follows:

$$dr(t) = \tilde{\alpha}(\tilde{m} - r(t))\, dt + \sigma\, d\tilde{Z}(t) + J dN(\tilde{\lambda}) \qquad (5.34)$$

Though the risk-neutral short-rate process is identical to the corresponding process under the fundamental Vasicek-GJ model, the preference-free Vasicek-GJ+ model allows general nonlinear MPRs that are consistent with the following change of measure:

$$dZ̃(t) = dZ(t) + \gamma(z, t)\, dt$$

$$\frac{\tilde{\lambda}}{(1 - \gamma_J(z, t))} = \lambda(z, t) \qquad (5.35)$$

where $dZ(t)$ is the Wiener process under the physical measure, and $\lambda(z, t)$ is the intensity of the Poisson process under the physical measure. In general, as shown in Chapter 4 (see equation (4.62)), function $\gamma(z, t)$ can allow the short-rate drift and the expected bond return under the physical measure to have arbitrary nonlinearities, and also allow dependence on multiple state variables. Similarly, even though the risk-neutral intensity $\tilde{\lambda}$ is a constant by assumption, the function $\gamma_J(z, t)$ allows the physical intensity $\lambda(z, t)$ to have nonlinear dependence on the state variables. For example, physical intensity could increase with an increase in the absolute level of the short rate. Certain regularity conditions to guarantee the existence of unique strong solutions (see Duffie [2001, Appendix D]), and the conditions related to the Girsanov theorem must be satisfied by functions $\gamma(z, t)$ and $\gamma_J(z, t)$. Also, function $\gamma_J(z, t)$ must always remain less than one in order for the risk-neutral intensity in equation (5.35) to remain positive.

The stochastic discount factor consistent with the change of measure shown in equation (5.35) can be given as follows:

$$\frac{dM(t)}{M(t)} = -r(t)\, dt - \gamma(z, t)\, dZ(t) - \gamma_J(z, t)\, dN(\lambda) + \gamma_J(z, t)\lambda\, dt \qquad (5.36)$$

Since the specification of the risk-neutral short-rate process under the preference-free Vasicek-GJ+ model given in equation (5.34) has an identical form as the corresponding process under the fundamental Vasicek-GJ model, the formulas of the bond price and interest rate derivatives under the

Vasicek-GJ+ model are identical to those under the Vasicek-GJ model given earlier. However, the empirical estimates of the risk-neutral parameters may be different under the two models, since the latter model imposed restrictive linear functional form on the MPRs.

The Vasicek-GJ++ Model

The Vasicek-GJ++ model can be derived in two different ways. Baz and Das [1996] make the long-term mean time dependent in equation (5.34) and specify the risk-neutral short-rate process as follows:

$$dr(t) = \tilde{\alpha}(\tilde{m}(t) - r(t))\, dt + \sigma\, d\tilde{Z}(t) + J dN(\tilde{\lambda}) \qquad (5.37)$$

Baz and Das suggest a numerical solution for the time-dependent risk-neutral long-term mean in equation (5.37). We suggest an alternative but equivalent approach that expresses the short rate as a sum of a time-dependent term and a mean-zero state variable. Our approach allows an analytical solution to the time-dependent risk-neutral long-term mean in the equation (5.37). We express the short rate as follows:

$$r(t) = \delta(t) + Y(t) \qquad (5.38)$$

where $\delta(t)$ is the deterministic term used for calibration to the initial bond prices, and the risk-neutral stochastic process for the state variable $Y(t)$ is given as follows:

$$dY(t) = -\tilde{\alpha}Y(t)\, dt + \sigma\, d\tilde{Z}(t) + J dN(\tilde{\lambda}), \quad Y(0) = 0 \qquad (5.39)$$

Using Ito's lemma, the short-rate process can be given as:

$$dr(t) = \tilde{\alpha}\left(\delta(t) + \frac{1}{\tilde{\alpha}}\frac{\partial\delta(t)}{\partial t} - r(t)\right) dt + \sigma\, d\tilde{Z}(t) + J dN(\tilde{\lambda}) \qquad (5.40)$$

Comparing equations (5.37) and (5.40), we get:

$$\tilde{m}(t) = \delta(t) + \frac{1}{\tilde{\alpha}}\frac{\partial\delta(t)}{\partial t} \qquad (5.41)$$

Expressing the bond price as a function of $Y(t)$ and t, using Ito's lemma, and taking the risk-neutral expectation of the bond price, the PDDE for the bond price can be given as follows:

$$\frac{\partial P}{\partial t} - \tilde{\alpha}Y(t)\frac{\partial P}{\partial Y} + \frac{1}{2}\sigma^2\frac{\partial^2 P}{\partial Y^2} + E_t\big[P\big(Y(t)+J,\ t,\ T\big) - P\big(Y(t),\ t,\ T\big)\big]\tilde{\lambda}$$
$$= r(t)P(t,\ T) = \big(Y(t)+\delta(t)\big)P(t,\ T) \qquad (5.42)$$

Consider the following solution to the PDDE in equation (5.42):

$$P(t, T) = e^{A(\tau) - B(\tau)Y(t) - H(t, T)} \qquad (5.43)$$

where $\tau = T - t$ and

$$H(t, T) = \int_t^T \delta(u)\, du \qquad (5.44)$$

subject to $A(0) = B(0) = 0$ and by definition $H(T, T) = 0$. The solutions of $A(\tau)$ and $B(\tau)$ are identical to the corresponding solutions under the Vasicek-GJ model and are obtained following the same steps as in the previous section, as follows:

$$A(\tau) = (\tau - B(\tau)) \left(\frac{\sigma^2}{2\tilde{\alpha}^2} \right) - \frac{\sigma^2 B^2(\tau)}{4\tilde{\alpha}} + \tilde{\lambda} \int_0^\tau L(v)\, dv \qquad (5.45)$$

$$B(\tau) = \left(\frac{1 - e^{-\tilde{\alpha}\tau}}{\tilde{\alpha}} \right) \qquad (5.46)$$

$$L(\tau) = e^{-\mu_J B(\tau) + \frac{1}{2}\sigma_J^2 B^2(\tau)} - 1 \qquad (5.47)$$

Now consider the initially observable zero-coupon bond-price function given as $P(0, T)$. To calibrate the bond price in equation (5.43) to the initially observable bond-price function, consider the log of the bond price evaluated at time 0 as follows:

$$\ln P(0, T) = A(T) - H(0, T) \qquad (5.48)$$

where, by definition, $Y(0) = 0$. Differentiating equation (5.48) with respect to T, we get:

$$\delta(T) = \frac{\partial A(T)}{\partial T} + f(0, T) \qquad (5.49)$$

where $f(0, T) = -\partial \ln P(0, T)/\partial T$ is the initial forward-rate curve at time 0. Simplifying equation (5.49) and then replacing T with t, we get:

$$\delta(t) = f(0, t) + \frac{1}{2}\sigma^2 B^2(t) + \tilde{\lambda}L(t) \qquad (5.50)$$

The full closed-form solution of the bond price requires the solution of the function $H(t, T)$, which is given as an integral of the function $\delta(t)$ in equation (5.44). Using equation (5.44) and (5.48), the function $H(t, T)$ can be directly obtained as follows:

$$H(t, T) = H(0, T) - H(0, t)$$

$$= A(T) - A(t) - \ln P(0, T) + \ln P(0, t) \qquad (5.51)$$

Since $P(0, t)$ and $P(0, T)$ are the initially observed bond prices, equation (5.51) plus equations (5.45) and (5.46) give the full closed-form solution of the bond price in equation (5.43). The solution requires only one numerical integral in equation (5.45).

Note that the closed-form solution of $\delta(t)$ in equation (5.50) also provides a closed-form solution to the time-dependent long-term mean in equation (5.37), as follows:

$$
\begin{aligned}
\tilde{m}(t) &= \delta(t) + \frac{1}{\tilde{\alpha}} \frac{\partial \delta(t)}{\partial t} \\
&= f(0,\ t) + \frac{1}{\tilde{\alpha}} \frac{\partial f(0,\ t)}{\partial t} + \frac{\sigma^2}{2\tilde{\alpha}^2}(1 - e^{-2\tilde{\alpha}t}) \\
&\quad + \frac{\tilde{\lambda}}{\tilde{\alpha}} L(t) \left[\tilde{\alpha} + (1 - \tilde{\alpha}B(t)) (-\mu_J + \sigma_J^2 B(t)) \right]
\end{aligned}
\tag{5.52}
$$

Jump-Diffusion Tree

A slight modification of the jump-diffusion tree derived earlier immediately gives the jump-diffusion tree for the Vasicek-GJ++ model. Consider the short-rate process and the state-variable process given in equations (5.11) and (5.39), respectively, given as follows:

$$
dr(t) = \tilde{\alpha}(\tilde{m} - r(t))\, dt + \sigma\, d\tilde{Z}(t) + J dN(\tilde{\lambda})
\tag{5.53}
$$

$$
dY(t) = \tilde{\alpha}(0 - Y(t))\, dt + \sigma\, d\tilde{Z}(t) + J dN(\tilde{\lambda}), \quad Y(0) = 0
\tag{5.54}
$$

The processes in equations (5.53) and (5.54) have identical forms except that the risk-neutral long-term mean is zero for the Y-process and the starting value for the Y-process is given as $Y(0) = 0$. Hence, the jump-diffusion tree for the Y-process can be built exactly as it was built for the short rate earlier, by equating $\tilde{m}$ to 0 and using the starting value $Y(0) = 0$. Once the jump-diffusion tree for the Y-process has been built, the jump-diffusion tree for the short rate $r(t)$ can be obtained by adding the deterministic term $\delta(t)$ to $Y(t)$ at each node of the tree (see equation (5.38)). The term $\delta(t)$ can be solved using two different methods. Using the first method, $\delta(t)$ is solved analytically using equation (5.50). However, this solution is valid only in the continuous-time limit, and so it allows an exact match with the initial zero-coupon bond prices only when using a large number of steps in the tree. If an exact match is desired for an arbitrarily small number of steps, then $\delta(t)$ can be obtained numerically for $0 \le t < T$ by defining a pseudo bond price $P^*(0,\ t)$ as follows:

$$
P(0,\ t) = P^*(0,\ t)e^{-H(0,t)} = P^*(0,\ t)e^{-\int_0^t \delta(v)\, dv}
\tag{5.55}
$$

where $P(0, t)$ is the initially observed bond price and $P^*(0, t)$ is the pseudo bond price obtained by taking discounted risk-neutral expectation using the Y-process as the pseudo short rate. The jump-diffusion tree for the Y-process can be used to obtain $P^*(0, t)$ for different values of t (such that $0 \leq t < T$). Given the values of $P(0, t)$ and $P^*(0, t)$ for different values of t, $\delta(t)$ can be obtained numerically, as follows:

$$H(0, t) = \sum_{j=0}^{t/\Delta t - 1} \delta(j\Delta t)\Delta t = \ln P^*(0, t) - \ln P(0, t) \qquad (5.56)$$

where $\Delta t = t/n$ and the integral in $H(0, t)$ is approximated as a discrete sum by dividing t into $t/\Delta t$ number of steps. The values of $\delta(j\Delta t)$, for $j = 0, 1, 2, \ldots, n-1$, can be obtained iteratively by using successive values of t as $\Delta t, 2\Delta t, \ldots, n\Delta t$, such that an exact match is obtained with the initial bond-price function $P(0, T)$. The values of $\delta(t)$ can be then added to the appropriate nodes on the n-step $Y(t)$-tree to obtain the corresponding tree for the short rate.

FUNDAMENTAL VASICEK-EJ MODEL

Chacko and Das [2002] extend the fundamental Vasicek model with two exponential jump processes, such that the jump size and the jump intensity of the upward jumps can be different from those of the downward jumps. Unlike the Vasicek-GJ model, the double exponential jump model allows an analytical closed-form solution to the bond price. As mentioned earlier, denote the double exponential jump-extended Vasicek model as the "Vasicek-EJ" model, with EJ representing exponential jumps.

Consider the short-rate process with one diffusion variable and two jump variables, given as follows:

$$dr = \alpha(m - r(t))\,dt + \sigma\,dZ(t) + J_u\,dN_u(\lambda_u) - J_d\,dN_d(\lambda_d) \qquad (5.57)$$

where the diffusion part of the process in equation (5.57) is as defined in the previous section. The up-jump variable J_u and the down-jump variable J_d are exponentially distributed with positive means $1/\eta_u$ and $1/\eta_d$, respectively. The two Poisson variables, $dN_u(\lambda_u)$ and $dN_d(\lambda_d)$, are distributed independently, with intensities λ_u and λ_d, respectively. The probability density of the exponential variable J is defined as follows:

$$f(J) = \eta \times e^{-J \times \eta}, \text{for } 0 \leq J \leq \infty \qquad (5.58)$$

The advantage of this model over the Vasicek-GJ is that it allows separate distributions for the upward jumps and downward jumps. This can significantly reduce the probability of negative interest rates caused by downward jumps by allowing more flexibility in choosing the parameters under different interest rate regimes. For example, in a regime with a lower value for the speed of mean reversion, downward jumps in interest rates can be chosen to be lower, in both the magnitude and the frequency of occurrence, than the upward jumps.

As in the previous section, we assume that the stochastic discount factor is given as follows:

$$\frac{dM(t)}{M(t)} = -r(t)\,dt - \left(\frac{\gamma_0 + \gamma_1 r(t)}{\sigma}\right) dZ(t)$$
$$- \gamma_{uJ}\big(dN_u(\lambda_u) - \lambda_u\,dt\big) + \gamma_{dJ}\big(dN_d(\lambda_d) - \lambda_d\,dt\big) \tag{5.59}$$

where γ_0 and γ_1 are coefficients for the market prices of diffusion risk (consistent with Duffee [2002]) and γ_{uJ} and γ_{dJ} are market prices of upward and downward jump risks, respectively.

As in the previous sections in this chapter, the stochastic discount factor given in equation (5.59) can be used to obtain the risk premiums for the zero-coupon bond and then, by using a change of probability measure, obtain the risk-neutral process for the short rate as follows:

$$dr = \tilde{\alpha}(\tilde{m} - r(t))\,dt + \sigma\,d\tilde{Z}(t) + J_u\,dN_u(\tilde{\lambda}_u) - J_d\,dN_d(\tilde{\lambda}_d) \tag{5.60}$$

where

$$\tilde{\alpha} = \alpha + \gamma_1 r$$
$$\tilde{m} = \frac{\alpha m - \gamma_0}{\alpha + \gamma_1}$$
$$\tilde{\lambda}_u = \lambda_u(1 - \gamma_{uJ}) \tag{5.61}$$
$$\tilde{\lambda}_d = \lambda_d(1 - \gamma_{dJ})$$

Bond Price Solution

To derive the bond-price solution, we first express the short-rate process as a sum of a constant and a zero-mean state-variable process. This allows us to extend the results given here to the preference-free Vasicek-EJ+ and Vasicek-EJ++ models and to use a common framework to derive solutions of options and futures for Vasicek-EJ, Vasicek-EJ+, and Vasicek-EJ++ models. Let the short rate be given as follows:

$$r(t) = \tilde{m} + Y(t) \tag{5.62}$$

where the state variable $Y(t)$ follows the following risk-neutral process:

$$dY(t) = -\tilde{\alpha}Y(t)\,dt + \sigma\,d\tilde{Z}(t) + J_u\,dN_u(\tilde{\lambda}_u) - J_d\,dN_d(\tilde{\lambda}_d) \qquad (5.63)$$

Using Ito's lemma, it is easy to confirm that the short-rate process given in equation (5.60) is consistent with the state-variable process given in equation (5.63).

Expressing the bond price as a function of $Y(t)$ and t, using Ito's lemma, and taking the risk-neutral expectation of the bond price, the PDDE for the bond price can be given as follows:

$$\frac{\partial P}{\partial t} - \tilde{\alpha}Y(t)\frac{\partial P}{\partial Y} + \frac{1}{2}\sigma^2\frac{\partial^2 P}{\partial Y^2} + E_t[P(Y(t) + J_u, t, T) - P(Y(t), t, T)]\tilde{\lambda}_u$$
$$+E_t[P(Y(t) - J_d, t, T) - P(Y(t), t, T)]\tilde{\lambda}_d \qquad (5.64)$$
$$= r(t)P(t, T) = (\tilde{m} + Y(t))P(t, T)$$

Consider the following solution to the PDDE in equation (5.64):

$$P(t,\ T) = e^{A(\tau) - B(\tau)Y(t) - H(t, T)} \qquad (5.65)$$

where $\tau = T - t$ and,

$$H(t,\ T) = \int_t^T \tilde{m}\,du = \tilde{m}(T - t) = \tilde{m}\tau \qquad (5.66)$$

subject to $A(0) = B(0) = 0$, and by definition $H(T,\ T) = 0$.

It is easy to show that the expected return on the bond conditional on the occurrence of an up-jump is given as:

$$L_u(\tau) = \frac{E_t\big[P\big(Y(t) + J_u,\ t,\ T\big) - P\big(Y(t),\ t,\ T\big)\big]}{P\big(Y(t),\ t,\ T\big)} = E_t(e^{-B(\tau)J_u}) - 1 \quad (5.67)$$

Similarly, the expected return on the bond conditional on the occurrence of a down-jump is given as:

$$L_d(\tau) = \frac{E_t\big[P\big(Y(t) - J_d,\ t,\ T\big) - P\big(Y(t),\ t,\ T\big)\big]}{P\big(Y(t),\ t,\ T\big)} = E_t(e^{B(\tau)J_d}) - 1 \quad (5.68)$$

Since J_u and J_d are exponentially distributed with positive means $1/\eta_u$ and $1/\eta_d$, respectively, we have:

$$L_u(\tau) = E_t(e^{-B(\tau)J_u}) - 1 = \int_0^\infty e^{-B(\tau)J_u}\eta_u e^{-\eta_u J_u}\,dJ_u - 1$$
$$= \frac{\eta_u}{\eta_u + B(\tau)} - 1 = \frac{-B(\tau)}{\eta_u + B(\tau)} \qquad (5.69)$$

and

$$
\begin{aligned}
L_d(\tau) = E_t(e^{B(\tau)J_d}) - 1 &= \int_0^\infty e^{B(\tau)J_d} \eta_d e^{-\eta_d J_d} \, dJ_d - 1 \\
&= \frac{\eta_d}{\eta_d - B(\tau)} - 1 = \frac{B(\tau)}{\eta_d - B(\tau)}
\end{aligned}
\tag{5.70}
$$

Using equation (5.65) to obtain the partial derivatives of the bond price, the PDDE given in equation (5.64) can be shown to reduce to the following two ODEs (the steps are identical to those in the previous section for Gaussian jumps):

$$
\begin{aligned}
\frac{\partial B(\tau)}{\partial \tau} &= 1 - \tilde{\alpha} B(\tau) \\
\frac{\partial A(\tau)}{\partial \tau} &= \frac{1}{2}\sigma^2 B^2(\tau) + \tilde{\lambda}_u L_u(\tau) + \tilde{\lambda}_d L_d(\tau)
\end{aligned}
\tag{5.71}
$$

Solving the two ODEs in equation (5.71) subject to the boundary condition $A(0) = B(0) = 0$, we get:

$$
\begin{aligned}
A(\tau) = (\tau - B(\tau))\left(\frac{\sigma^2}{2\tilde{\alpha}^2}\right) &- \frac{\sigma^2 B^2(\tau)}{4\tilde{\alpha}} - (\tilde{\lambda}_u + \tilde{\lambda}_d)\tau \\
&+ \frac{\tilde{\lambda}_u \eta_u}{\tilde{\alpha}\eta_u + 1} \ln\left|\left(1 + \frac{1}{\tilde{\alpha}\eta_u}\right) e^{\tilde{\alpha}\tau} - \frac{1}{\tilde{\alpha}\eta_u}\right| \\
&+ \frac{\tilde{\lambda}_d \eta_d}{\tilde{\alpha}\eta_d - 1} \ln\left|\left(1 - \frac{1}{\tilde{\alpha}\eta_d}\right) e^{\tilde{\alpha}\tau} + \frac{1}{\tilde{\alpha}\eta_d}\right|
\end{aligned}
\tag{5.72}
$$

$$
B(\tau) = \left(\frac{1 - e^{-\tilde{\alpha}\tau}}{\tilde{\alpha}}\right)
\tag{5.73}
$$

Jump-Diffusion Tree

The following approximation is used to model the short-rate tree with exponential jumps:

$$
dr(t) = \left\{
\begin{array}{l}
\tilde{\alpha}(\tilde{m} - r(t))\, dt + \sigma \, d\tilde{Z}(t), \text{ with probability } 1 - \tilde{\lambda}_u \, dt - \tilde{\lambda}_d \, dt \\
J_u, \text{ with probability } \tilde{\lambda}_u \, dt \\
-J_d, \text{ with probability } \tilde{\lambda}_d \, dt
\end{array}
\right\}
\tag{5.74}
$$

It can be shown that equation (5.74) deviates from equation (5.60) only in the order $o(dt)$, and hence, the two equations converge in the limit as dt goes to zero. The methodology of constructing an exponential jump tree is very similar to the methodology of constructing a Gaussian jump tree. To keep the analysis general, we consider an arbitrary node $r(t)$, at time $t = i\Delta t$, for $i = 0, 1, 2, \ldots, n-1$, where length of time T is divided into n equal intervals of Δt. At time $(i+1)\Delta t$, the M different values for the interest rate are given as follows:

$$r(t) \pm j\sigma\sqrt{\Delta t}, \quad j = 0, 1, \ldots, \frac{M-1}{2}$$

We specify M probabilities associated with the M nodes. The short rate can either undergo a local change with probability $1 - \tilde{\lambda}_u \, dt - \tilde{\lambda}_d \, dt$, or experience an up-jump with probability $\tilde{\lambda}_u \, dt$, or experience a down-jump with probability $\tilde{\lambda}_d \, dt$.

The two local probabilities are computed as follows:

$$P\left(r(t) + \sigma\sqrt{\Delta t}\right) = \left(\frac{1}{2} + \frac{1}{2}\frac{\tilde{\alpha}(\tilde{m} - r(t))}{\sigma}\sqrt{\Delta t}\right)(1 - \tilde{\lambda}_u\Delta t - \tilde{\lambda}_d\Delta t)$$

$$P\left(r(t) - \sigma\sqrt{\Delta t}\right) = \left(\frac{1}{2} - \frac{1}{2}\frac{\tilde{\alpha}(\tilde{m} - r(t))}{\sigma}\sqrt{\Delta t}\right)(1 - \tilde{\lambda}_u\Delta t - \tilde{\lambda}_d\Delta t)$$

(5.75)

The major difference arises in the way jump distribution is approximated (see Figure 5.6). The upward-jump nodes and the downward-jump nodes are approximated separately with two exponential curves.

The total risk-neutral probability of upward jumps is $\tilde{\lambda}_u\Delta t$, and the total risk-neutral probability of downward jumps is $\tilde{\lambda}_d\Delta t$. The upward-jump probability and the downward-jump probability are allocated to two separate exponential distributions, one drawn from zero to infinity above the center point, and the other drawn from zero to negative infinity below the center point in Figure 5.6. The entire line from negative infinity to positive infinity in Figure 5.6 consists of M points and M nonoverlapping intervals that cover both the exponential distributions for upward and downward jumps. The probability mass over each of these M intervals is assigned to the point in between each of these intervals using the following three steps:

Step 1. The first step computes the probabilities of all jump nodes except the central node, the top node, and the bottom node, as follows. The probability mass for the intervals corresponding to the upward-jump nodes is assigned to the points at the center of these intervals as follows:

$$P\left(r(t) + k\sigma\sqrt{\Delta t}\right) = (F_u(x_1) - F_u(x_2))\tilde{\lambda}_u\Delta t,$$

$$k = 2, \ldots, \frac{M-3}{2}$$

(5.76)

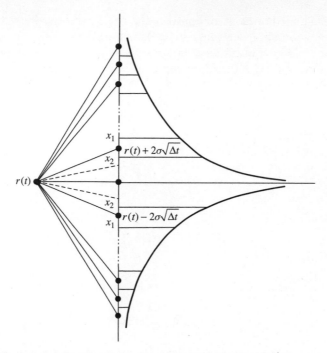

FIGURE 5.6 Approximation of the Jump Distribution Using Two Exponential Curves

where $F_u(x)$ is the cumulative exponential distribution for upward jumps defined as follows:

$$F_u(x) = \int_0^x \eta_u e^{-\eta_u J_u} \, dJ_u = 1 - e^{-\eta_u x} \tag{5.77}$$

and

$$x_1 = (k + 0.5)\sigma\sqrt{\Delta t}$$

$$x_2 = (k - 0.5)\sigma\sqrt{\Delta t}$$

The expression $F_u(x_1) - F_u(x_2)$ gives the difference between two cumulative exponential distribution functions, and hence, it gives the probability measured by the area under the exponential curve over one of the regions corresponding to the upward jumps in Figure 5.6. Multiplication of this probability by the total risk-neutral jump probability of upward jumps $\tilde{\lambda}_u \Delta t$ gives the probability of the short-rate node at the point between of x_1 and x_2 as shown in equation (5.76)

Similarly, the probability mass for the intervals corresponding to the downward-jump nodes is assigned to the points at the center of the following intervals as follows:

$$P\left(r(t) - k\sigma\sqrt{\Delta t}\right) = (F_d(x_1) - F_d(x_2))\tilde{\lambda}_d \Delta t$$
$$k = 2, \ldots, \frac{M-3}{2} \tag{5.78}$$

where $F_d(x)$ is the cumulative exponential distribution for downward jumps defined as follows:

$$F_d(x) = \int_0^x \eta_d e^{-\eta_d J_d} \, dJ_d = 1 - e^{-\eta_d x} \tag{5.79}$$

where

$$x_1 = (k + 0.5)\sigma\sqrt{\Delta t}$$
$$x_2 = (k - 0.5)\sigma\sqrt{\Delta t}$$

Step 2. Since we only consider the nodes in the range

$$\left[r(t) + \frac{M-1}{2}\sigma\sqrt{\Delta t}, r(t) - \frac{M-1}{2}\sigma\sqrt{\Delta t}\right]$$

in Figure 5.6, the probability mass outside this region should be assigned to the end nodes. The probability mass assigned to the top node corresponding to the upward jump is given as:

$$P\left(r(t) + \frac{M-1}{2}\sigma\sqrt{\Delta t}\right) = [(1 - F_u(x_2))]\tilde{\lambda}_u \Delta t \tag{5.80}$$

where

$$x_2 = \left(\frac{M-1}{2} - 0.5\right)\sigma\sqrt{\Delta t}$$

Similarly, the probability mass assigned to the bottom node corresponding to the downward jump is given as:

$$P\left(r(t) - \frac{M-1}{2}\sigma\sqrt{\Delta t}\right) = (1 - F_d(x_2))\tilde{\lambda}_d \Delta t \tag{5.81}$$

where

$$x_2 = \left(\frac{M-1}{2} - 0.5\right)\sigma\sqrt{\Delta t}$$

Step 3. The remaining probabilities from both exponential distributions for upward jumps- and downward-jumps are allocated to the central node as follows:

$$P\big(r(t)\big) = \big(F_u(x_1)\big)\tilde{\lambda}_u \Delta t + \big(F_d(x_1)\big)\tilde{\lambda}_d \Delta t \qquad (5.82)$$

where

$$x_1 = 1.5\sigma\sqrt{\Delta t}$$

Equation (5.75) defines the probabilities at two nodes that give the local change due to the diffusion process; and equations (5.76), (5.78), (5.80), (5.81), and (5.82) define the probabilities at the remaining $M - 2$ nodes that give the change due to the two exponential jumps. Together, all of these probabilities sum up to 1. Example 5.2 demonstrates how the exponential jump-diffusion tree can be used to price a bond.

Example 5.2   Consider a bond that pays \$100 in two months ($T = 2/12 = 0.167$). Current riskless interest rate $r_0 = 5\%$, volatility of the interest rate $\sigma = 1\%$, risk-neutral mean reversion speed $\tilde{\alpha} = 0.5$, risk-neutral long-run mean $\tilde{m} = 6\%$, risk-neutral intensity for the up-jump $\tilde{\lambda}_u = 0.75$, risk-neutral intensity for the down-jump $\tilde{\lambda}_d = 0.25$, and the exponential distribution parameters $\eta_u = \eta_d = 100$. Assume that a two-period tree with $M = 5$ branches is used and that the length of each period is $\Delta t = 1/12 = 0.083$.

Figure 5.7 shows a one-period interest rate tree with corresponding probabilities.

Consider the top node of the tree at time Δt. The interest rate value for this node is computed as follows:

$$r(t) = r_0 + 2\sigma\sqrt{\Delta t} = 0.05 + 2 \times 0.01 \times \sqrt{0.083} = 0.056$$

Lets compute the set of probabilities corresponding to this node. The first probability value corresponds to the top up-jump node; therefore, equation (5.80) is applied as follows:

$$p_1 = \big(1 - (1 - e^{-1.5 \times 0.01 \times \sqrt{0.083} \times 100})\big) \times 0.75 \times 0.083$$

$$= 0.649 \times 1 \times 0.75 \times 0.083 = 0.041$$

The second probability value corresponds to the diffusion node; therefore, equation (5.75) is applied as follows:

$$p_2 = \left(0.5 + 0.5\frac{(0.5 \times (0.06 - 0.056))\sqrt{0.083}}{0.01}\right)$$

$$\times (1 - 0.75 \times 0.083 - 0.25 \times 0.083)$$

$$= 0.529 \times (1 - 1 \times 0.083) = 0.486$$

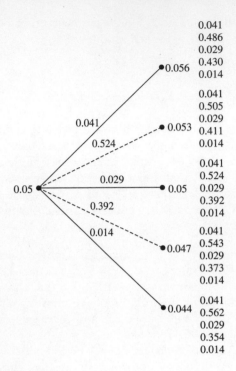

0.041
0.486
0.029
0.430
0.014

0.041
0.505
0.029
0.411
0.014

0.041
0.524
0.029
0.392
0.014

0.041
0.543
0.029
0.373
0.014

0.041
0.562
0.029
0.354
0.014

FIGURE 5.7 Interest Rate Tree

The third probability value corresponds to the middle jump node; therefore, equation (5.82) is applied as follows:

$$p_3 = (1 - e^{-1.5 \times 0.01 \times \sqrt{0.083} \times 100}) \times 0.75 \times 0.083$$

$$+ (1 - e^{-1.5 \times 0.01 \times \sqrt{0.083} \times 100}) \times 0.25 \times 0.083$$

$$= 0.029$$

The fourth probability value corresponds to the diffusion node; therefore, equation (5.75) is applied as follows:

$$p_4 = \left(0.5 - 0.5 \frac{(0.5 \times (0.06 - 0.056))\sqrt{0.083}}{0.01} \right)$$

$$\times (1 - 0.75 \times 0.083 - 0.25 \times 0.083)$$

$$= 0.471 \times (1 - 1 \times 0.083) = 0.430$$

The fifth probability value corresponds to the bottom down-jump node; therefore, equation (5.81) is applied as follows:

$$p_5 = \left(1 - (1 - e^{-1.5 \times 0.01 \times \sqrt{0.083} \times 100})\right) \times 0.25 \times 0.083$$

$$= 0.649 \times 1 \times 0.25 \times 0.083 = 0.014$$

As shown in Figure 5.8, we work backward through the tree to determine the current value of the bond. At the end of the second time period, the bond pays $100. To compute bond values for each node at the end of the first time period, we use interest rate and probability values corresponding to each node.

For example, consider the top node at the end of the first period. The bond value for this node is computed as follows:

$$(100.00 \times 0.041 + 100.00 \times 0.486 + 100.00 \times 0.029 + 100.00 \times 0.430$$

$$+ 100.00 \times 0.014) \times e^{-0.056 \times 0.083} = \$99.54$$

Similarly, the value of the bond at time 0 is computed as follows:

$$P_0 = (99.54 \times 0.041 + 99.56 \times 0.524 + 99.58 \times 0.029 + 99.61 \times 0.392$$

$$+ 99.63 \times 0.014) \times e^{-0.05 \times 0.083} = \$99.17$$

Using a 100-step tree with $M = 101$, the price of the bond equals $99.16. The price using the closed-form solution also equals $99.16.

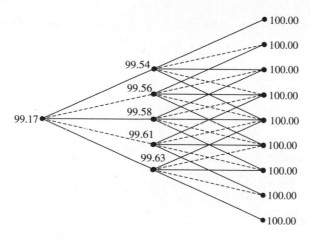

FIGURE 5.8   Bond-Value Calculation

PREFERENCE-FREE VASICEK-EJ++ MODEL

Preference-free extensions of the Vasicek-EJ model can be derived following the same approach as those derived for the Vasicek-GJ model. The formulas of bond price and interest rate derivatives under the Vasicek-EJ+ model are identical to the corresponding formulas under the Vasicek-EJ model given in the previous section. However, the empirical estimates of the risk-neutral parameters may be different under the two models, since the latter model imposed restrictive linear functional form on the MPRs. To derive the preference-free Vasicek-EJ++ model, consider the following definition of the short-rate process:

$$r(t) = \delta(t) + Y(t) \tag{5.83}$$

where $\delta(t)$ is the deterministic term used for calibration to the initial bond prices, and the risk-neutral stochastic process for the state variable $Y(t)$ is given as follows:

$$dY(t) = -\tilde{\alpha}Y(t)\,dt + \sigma\,d\tilde{Z}(t) + J_u\,dN_u(\tilde{\lambda}_u) - J_d\,dN_d(\tilde{\lambda}_d), \quad Y(0) = 0 \tag{5.84}$$

Expressing the bond price as a function of $Y(t)$ and t, using Ito's lemma, and taking risk-neutral expectation of the bond price, the PDDE for the bond price can be given as follows:

$$\frac{\partial P}{\partial t} - \tilde{\alpha}Y(t)\frac{\partial P}{\partial Y} + \frac{1}{2}\sigma^2\frac{\partial^2 P}{\partial Y^2} + E_t\big[P\big(Y(t) + J_u,\ t,\ T\big) - P\big(Y(t),\ t,\ T\big)\big]\tilde{\lambda}_u$$

$$+ E_t\big[P\big(Y(t) - J_d,\ t,\ T\big) - P\big(Y(t),\ t,\ T\big)\big]\tilde{\lambda}_d = r(t)P(t,\ T) \tag{5.85}$$

$$= \big(Y(t) + \delta(t)\big)P(t,\ T)$$

Consider the following solution to the PDDE in equation (5.85):

$$P(t,\ T) = e^{A(\tau) - B(\tau)Y(t) - H(t,T)} \tag{5.86}$$

where $\tau = T - t$ and

$$H(t,\ T) = \int_t^T \delta(u)\,du \tag{5.87}$$

subject to $A(0) = B(0) = 0$, and by definition $H(T,\ T) = 0$. Following similar steps as in the previous section, the PDDE can be broken into two ODEs, which are given as follows:

$$\frac{\partial B(\tau)}{\partial \tau} = 1 - \tilde{\alpha}B(\tau)$$

$$\frac{\partial A(\tau)}{\partial \tau} = \frac{1}{2}\sigma^2 B^2(\tau) + \tilde{\lambda}_u L_u(\tau) + \tilde{\lambda}_d L_d(\tau) \tag{5.88}$$

where

$$L_u(\tau) = E_t\left(e^{-B(\tau)J_u}\right) - 1 = \frac{-B(\tau)}{\eta_u + B(\tau)}$$

$$L_d(\tau) = E_t\left(e^{B(\tau)J_d}\right) - 1 = \frac{B(\tau)}{\eta_d - B(\tau)}$$

and J_u and J_d are exponentially distributed with positive means $1/\eta_u$ and $1/\eta_d$, respectively. The solutions to the ODEs in equation (5.88) are given as:

$$
\begin{aligned}
A(\tau) = \left(\tau - B(\tau)\right)\frac{\sigma^2}{2\tilde{\alpha}^2} - \frac{\sigma^2 B^2(\tau)}{4\tilde{\alpha}} - (\tilde{\lambda}_u + \tilde{\lambda}_d)\tau \\
+ \frac{\tilde{\lambda}_u \eta_u}{\tilde{\alpha}\eta_u + 1} \ln\left|\left(1 + \frac{1}{\tilde{\alpha}\eta_u}\right)e^{\tilde{\alpha}\tau} - \frac{1}{\tilde{\alpha}\eta_u}\right| \\
+ \frac{\tilde{\lambda}_d \eta_d}{\tilde{\alpha}\eta_d - 1} \ln\left|\left(1 - \frac{1}{\tilde{\alpha}\eta_d}\right)e^{\tilde{\alpha}\tau} + \frac{1}{\tilde{\alpha}\eta_d}\right|
\end{aligned}
\tag{5.89}
$$

and,

$$B(t,\ T) = \left(\frac{1 - e^{-\tilde{\alpha}\tau}}{\tilde{\alpha}}\right) \tag{5.90}$$

Consider the initially observable zero-coupon bond-price function given as $P(0,\ T)$. To calibrate the bond price in equation (5.86) to the initially observable bond-price function, consider the log of a bond price evaluated at time 0 as follows:

$$\ln P(0,\ T) = A(T) - H(0,\ T) \tag{5.91}$$

where, by definition, $Y(0) = 0$. Differentiating equation (5.91) with respect to T, we get:

$$\delta(T) = f(0,\ T) + \frac{\partial A(T)}{\partial T} \tag{5.92}$$

where $f(0,\ T) = -\partial \ln P(0,\ T)/\partial T$ is the initial forward-rate curve at time 0. Substituting the partial derivative of $A(T)$ from equation (5.88) and then replacing T with t, we get:

$$\delta(t) = f(0,\ t) + \tfrac{1}{2}\sigma^2 B^2(t) + \tilde{\lambda}_u L_u(t) + \tilde{\lambda}_d L_d(t) \tag{5.93}$$

Using equations (5.87) and (5.91), the function $H(t, T)$ can be expressed as follows:

$$
\begin{aligned}
H(t,\ T) &= H(0,\ T) - H(0,\ t) \\
&= A(T) - A(t) - \ln P(0,\ T) + \ln P(0,\ t)
\end{aligned}
\tag{5.94}
$$

Since $P(0, t)$ and $P(0, T)$ are the initially observed bond prices, the equation (5.94) plus equations (5.89) and (5.90) give the full closed-form solution of the bond price in equation (5.86).

Jump-Diffusion Tree

A slight modification of the jump-diffusion tree derived for the Vasicek-EJ model immediately gives the jump-diffusion tree for the Vasicek-EJ++ model. Consider the short-rate process and the state-variable process given in equations (5.60) and (5.84), respectively, given as follows:

$$dr = \tilde{\alpha}(\tilde{m} - r(t))\, dt + \sigma\, d\tilde{Z}(t) + J_u\, dN_u(\tilde{\lambda}_u) - J_d\, dN_d(\tilde{\lambda}_d) \qquad (5.95)$$

$$dY(t) = \tilde{\alpha}(0 - Y(t))\, dt + \sigma\, d\tilde{Z}(t) + J_u\, dN_u(\tilde{\lambda}_u) - J_d\, dN_d(\tilde{\lambda}_d),\ Y(0) = 0 \qquad (5.96)$$

The processes in equations (5.95) and (5.96) have identical forms except that the risk-neutral long-term mean $\tilde{m}$ equals 0 for the $Y(t)$ process and the starting value for the $Y(t)$ process is given as $Y(0) = 0$. Hence, the jump-diffusion tree for the $Y(t)$ process can be built exactly as it was built for the short rate under the Vasiciek-EJ model, by equating $\tilde{m}$ to 0 and using the starting value $Y(0) = 0$. Once the jump-diffusion tree for $Y(t)$ process has been built, the jump-diffusion tree for the short rate $r(t)$ can be obtained by adding the deterministic term $\delta(t)$ to $Y(t)$ at each node of the tree. The term $\delta(t)$ can be solved using two different methods. Using the first method, $\delta(t)$ is solved analytically using equation (5.93). However, this solution is valid only in the continuous-time limit, and so it allows an exact match with the initial zero-coupon bond prices only when using a large number of steps in the tree. If an exact match is desired for an arbitrarily small number of steps, then $\delta(t)$ can be obtained numerically using the same method as proposed in equations (5.55) and (5.56) for tree construction under the Vasicek-GJ++ model.

VALUING FUTURES AND OPTIONS

Recall that we expressed the bond-price solution in a slightly nontraditional form in this chapter and in the previous chapter as follows:

$$P(t, T) = e^{A(\tau) - B(\tau)Y(t) - H(t,T)} \qquad (5.97)$$

where $A(\tau)$ and $B(\tau)$ are time-homogeneous functions of $\tau = T - t$. The motivation for using this form is that it allows a common framework for obtaining the formulas for interest rate derivatives such as futures and options under the fundamental and preference-free versions of Vasicek models and jump-extended Vasicek models. For example, note that the formulas for $A(\tau)$ and $B(\tau)$ are given by equations (5.72) and (5.73), respectively, under the Vasicek-EJ/Vasicek-EJ+ models. These formulas are identical to the corresponding formulas under the Vasicek-EJ++ model given by equations (5.89) and (5.90), respectively (of course, the values of the risk-neutral parameters may be different under different models). The only difference between the formulas for Vasicek-EJ/Vasicek-EJ+ models and the Vasicek-EJ++ is due to the term $H(t, T)$, which is defined by equation (5.66) under the former models and by equation (5.94) under the latter model.

In this section, we derive formulas for futures and options under the Vasicek-EJ/Vasicek-EJ+ and Vasicek-EJ++ models and show that differences in the formulas between these models result only from the $H(t, T)$ term. Though we don't provide futures and options formulas under the Vasicek-GJ/Vasicek-GJ+ and Vasicek-GJ++ models, a similar argument applies to these models also, and formulas under these models can be obtained by following the same approach as outlined next.

Valuing Futures

Futures on a Zero-Coupon Bond   The time t price of a futures contract expiring at time S, written on a zero-coupon bond maturing at time T, under the extended Vasicek model with exponentially distributed jumps can be obtained as follows. As shown in Chapter 3, futures price is a martingale under the risk-neutral measure, or:

$$P_F(t, S, T) = \tilde{E}_t\big(P(S, T)\big) \tag{5.98}$$

Due to continuous marking to market, the expected gain (or loss) in the futures position is zero under the risk-neutral measure, or:

$$\tilde{E}_t\big(dP_F(t, S, T)\big) = 0 \tag{5.99}$$

The current futures price is a function of $Y(t)$ and t. Using Ito's lemma to solve the differential of the futures price and equating the risk-neutral expectation to zero, we get the PDDE for the futures price, as follows:

$$
\begin{aligned}
&\frac{\partial P_F}{\partial t} - \tilde{\alpha}Y(t)\frac{\partial P_F}{\partial Y} + \frac{1}{2}\sigma^2\frac{\partial^2 P_F}{\partial Y^2} \\
&+ E_t[P_F(Y(t) + J_u, t, S, T) - P_F(Y(t), t, S, T)]\tilde{\lambda}_u \\
&+ E_t[P_F(Y(t) - J_d, t, S, T) - P_F(Y(t), t, S, T)]\tilde{\lambda}_d = 0
\end{aligned}
\tag{5.100}
$$

subject to the boundary condition $P_F(S, S, T) = P(S, T)$. We assume that the solution to equation (5.100) has the following form:

$$P_F(t, S, T) = e^{A_F(s) - B_F(s)Y(t) - H(S,T)}, \quad s = S - t \tag{5.101}$$

subject to $A_F(0) = A(U)$, $B_F(0) = B(U)$, and $U = T - S$. Since the formulas for $A(U)$ and $B(U)$ are the same under the Vasicek-EJ, Vasicek-EJ+, and Vasicek-EJ++ models, the formulas of $A_F(s)$ and $B_F(s)$ are also the same under these models, as shown next. The formula for $H(S, T)$ is given by equation (5.66) under the Vasicek-EJ/Vasicek-EJ+ models and by equation (5.94) under the Vasicek-EJ++ model.

Using equation (5.101), and a change of variable $s = S - t$, the PDDE in equation (5.100) can be expressed as follows:

$$
-\frac{\partial P_F}{\partial s} - \tilde{\alpha} Y(t) \frac{\partial P_F}{\partial Y} + \frac{1}{2}\sigma^2 \frac{\partial^2 P_F}{\partial Y^2}
$$
$$
+ \left(L_u^F(s)\tilde{\lambda}_u + L_d^F(s)\tilde{\lambda}_d \right) P_F(t, S, T) = 0
\tag{5.102}
$$

subject to the boundary condition $P_F(S, S, T) = P(S, T)$, where $L_u^F(s)$ and $L_d^F(s)$ are the expected returns on the futures contract, conditional on the occurrence of an up-jump and a down-jump, respectively, given as follows:

$$
L_u^F(s) = E_t(e^{-B_F(s)J_u}) - 1 = \int_0^\infty e^{-B_F(s)J_u} \eta_u e^{-\eta_u J_u}\, dJ_u - 1
$$
$$
= \frac{\eta_u}{\eta_u + B_F(s)} - 1 = \frac{-B_F(s)}{\eta_u + B_F(s)}
\tag{5.103}
$$

and,

$$
L_d^F(s) = E_t(e^{B_F(s)J_d}) - 1 = \int_0^\infty e^{B_F(s)J_d} \eta_d e^{-\eta_d J_d}\, dJ_d - 1
$$
$$
= \frac{\eta_d}{\eta_d - B_F(s)} - 1 = \frac{B_F(s)}{\eta_d - B_F(s)}
\tag{5.104}
$$

Taking the partial derivatives of the futures price in equation (5.101) with respect to $Y(t)$ and s and substituting these in equation (5.102) leads to two ODEs given as follows:

$$
\frac{\partial B_F(s)}{\partial s} = -\tilde{\alpha} B_F(s)
$$
$$
\frac{\partial A_F(s)}{\partial s} = \frac{1}{2}\sigma^2 B_F^2(s) + \tilde{\lambda}_u L_u^F(s) + \tilde{\lambda}_d L_d^F(s)
\tag{5.105}
$$

subject to $A_F(0) = A(U), B_F(0) = B(U)$, and $U = T - S$. The solution is given as:

$$A_F(s) = A(U) + \frac{1}{4}\sigma^2 B^2(U)B(2s) + \frac{\tilde{\lambda}_u}{\tilde{\alpha}}\ln\left|\frac{\eta_u + B(U)e^{-\tilde{\alpha}s}}{\eta_u + B(U)}\right|$$

$$+ \frac{\tilde{\lambda}_d}{\tilde{\alpha}}\ln\left|\frac{\eta_d - B(U)e^{-\tilde{\alpha}s}}{\eta_d - B(U)}\right|$$

(5.106)

$$B_F(s) = B(U)e^{-\tilde{\alpha}s}$$

(5.107)

The futures-forward price discount (FFPD) is given as follows:

$$FFPD = \frac{P_f(t, S, T) - P_F(t, S, T)}{P_f(t, S, T)} = 1 - P_F(t, S, T)\frac{P(t, S)}{P(t, T)}$$

$$= 1 - e^{A_F(s)+A(s)-A(\tau)}$$

(5.108)

$$s = S - t, \text{ and } \tau = T - t$$

Futures on a Time Deposit The price of a futures contract on a time deposit—such as Eurodollar and Euribor futures—can be obtained using equation (3.12) in Chapter 3:

$$P_F^{TD}(t, S, T) = \frac{100}{\hat{U}}(1 + \hat{U} - P_F^I(t, S, T))$$

(5.109)

where S is the futures expiration date, $\hat{U}$ is the accrual factor typically calculated using actual/360 day-count basis, $U = T - S$, and $P_F^I(t, S, T)$ is the current price of a futures contract written on a hypothetical asset, which at the expiration date S is worth the inverse of a \$1 face-value zero-coupon bond maturing at time T. As shown in Chapter 4, the futures price, $P_F^I(t, S, T)$, follows the same PDE as followed by $P_F(t, S, T)$, except that the constants in the boundary conditions are of the opposite signs. Hence, the solution to $P_F^I(t, S, T)$ can be written by a simple inspection of the solution to $P_F(t, S, T)$ a given in equations (5.101), (5.106), and (5.107), as follows:

$$P_F^I(t, S, T) = e^{a_F(s)-b_F(s)Y(t)+H(S,T)}, \quad s = S - t$$

(5.110)

where

$$a_F(s) = -A(U) + \frac{1}{4}\sigma^2 B^2(U)B(2s) + \frac{\tilde{\lambda}_u}{\alpha}\left(\frac{\eta_u - B(U)e^{-\alpha s}}{\eta_u - B(U)}\right)$$

$$+ \frac{\tilde{\lambda}_d}{\alpha}\left(\frac{\eta_d + B(U)e^{-\alpha s}}{\eta_d + B(U)}\right) \tag{5.111}$$

$$b_F(s) = -B(U)e^{-\alpha s} \tag{5.112}$$

where the formula for $H(S, T)$ is given by equation (5.66) under the Vasicek-EJ/Vasicek-EJ+ models, and by equation (5.94) under the Vasicek-EJ++ model.

The convexity bias, given as the difference between the futures rate and the forward rate on a time deposit, can be given as follows (see equation (3.17), Chapter 3):

$$Convexity\ Bias = L_F(t, S, T) - L_f(t, S, T)$$

$$= \frac{1 + L_F(t, S, T)\hat{U}}{\hat{U}}\left(1 - e^{A(s)-A(\tau)-a_F(s)}\right) \tag{5.113}$$

$$s = S - t,\ \text{and}\ \tau = T - t$$

Valuing Options: The Fourier Inversion Method

Heston [1993] introduced the "Fourier inversion method" to solve the price of an option when the underlying stock follows a stochastic volatility process. Recently, a number of researchers, including Duffie, Pan, and Singleton [2000], Bakshi and Madan [2000], and Chacko and Das [2002], have shown this method to be versatile in obtaining quasi-analytical formulas for a variety of more difficult option-pricing problems. For example, this method can be used to solve option prices when the underlying price processes include jumps and stochastic volatility, as well as to solve the prices of more complex derivatives, like the Asian options. We now demonstrate this method to solve the price of an option on a zero-coupon bond under the Vasicek model with exponential jumps. This method is also applied in Chapters 6, 7, 9, 10, and 12 for solving option prices under affine, quadratic, and LIBOR market models.

The Fourier inversion method guarantees a quasi-analytical solution to the price of an option written on a zero-coupon bond if a closed-form solution exists for the underlying bond price. Since bond-price solutions do exist for many affine and quadratic models, solutions to option prices can be derived under these models. Further, regardless of the number of factors in the underlying model, the Fourier inversion method requires computation of only a single-dimensional numerical integral, even when using a multiple-factor model, making it more efficient than the traditional solutions that require computing a multiple-dimensional integral under a multifactor model (e.g., option price under the two-factor model of Longstaff and Schwartz [1992] requires a two-dimensional integral).

We now demonstrate this method using the following four steps. Much of this exposition is quite general and applies to virtually every affine and quadratic term structure model, even though we introduce it in the context of the Vasicek-EJ/Vasicek-EJ+ and Vasicek-EJ++ models.

Step 1. Probability Transformations The price of a call option expiring on date S, written on a \$1 face-value zero-coupon bond maturing at time T, can be given as follows:

$$c(t) = \tilde{E}_t\left[e^{-\int_t^S r(u)\,du}c(S)\right] = \tilde{E}_t\left[e^{-\int_t^S r(u)\,du}\max\left(P(S,\,T) - K,\,0\right)\right]$$
(5.114)

The call option can be alternatively expressed as follows:

$$c(t) = P(t,\,T)\Pi_{1t} - KP(t,\,S)\Pi_{2t}$$
(5.115)

where

$$\Pi_{1t} = \tilde{E}_t\left[\frac{e^{-\int_t^S r(u)\,du}P(S,\,T)1_{\{P(S,T)\geq K\}}}{P(t,\,T)}\right]$$
(5.116)

$$\Pi_{2t} = \tilde{E}_t\left[\frac{e^{-\int_t^S r(u)\,du}1_{\{P(S,T)\geq K\}}}{P(t,\,S)}\right]$$
(5.117)

$1_{\{P(S,T)\geq K\}}$ is the indicator function, which equals 1 when $P(S,\,T) \geq K$ and 0 otherwise and when the zero-coupon bond prices $P(t,\,T)$ and $P(t,\,S)$ are given as the discounted risk-neutral expectations as follows:

$$P(t,\,T) = \tilde{E}_t\left[e^{-\int_t^T r(u)\,du}\right] = \tilde{E}_t\left[e^{-\int_t^S r(u)\,du}P(S,\,T)\right]$$
(5.118)

$$P(t,\,S) = \tilde{E}_t\left[e^{-\int_t^S r(u)\,du}\right]$$
(5.119)

As we show next, the terms Π_{1t} and Π_{2t} can be interpreted as *forward probabilities* using the definition of zero-coupon bond prices in equations (5.118) and (5.119). Since the condition $P(t,\,T) \geq K$ is the same as the condition $\ln P(t,\,T) \geq \ln K$, the probabilities

Π_{1t} and Π_{2t} can be rewritten as follows:

$$\Pi_{1t} = \int_{\ln K}^{\infty} \left[\frac{e^{-\int_t^S r(u)\,du} P(S,\,T)}{P(t,\,T)} f_t(y) \right] dy \qquad (5.120)$$

$$\Pi_{2t} = \int_{\ln K}^{\infty} \left[\frac{e^{-\int_t^S r(u)\,du}}{P(t,\,S)} f_t(y) \right] dy \qquad (5.121)$$

where $y = \ln P(S,\,T)$ and $f_t(y)$ is the time t risk-neutral probability density of y. Equations (5.120) and (5.121) can be rewritten as follows:

$$\Pi_{1t} = \int_{\ln K}^{\infty} f_{1t}(y)\,dy \qquad (5.122)$$

$$\Pi_{2t} = \int_{\ln K}^{\infty} f_{2t}(y)\,dy \qquad (5.123)$$

where

$$f_{1t}(y) = \left[\frac{e^{-\int_t^S r(u)\,du} P(S,\,T)}{P(t,\,T)} f_t(y) \right] \qquad (5.124)$$

$$f_{2t}(y) = \left[\frac{e^{-\int_t^S r(u)\,du}}{P(t,\,S)} f_t(y) \right] \qquad (5.125)$$

Note that $f_{1t}(y)$ and $f_{2t}(y)$, obtained as transformations of the risk-neutral probability density $f_t(y)$, are probability densities under the *forward* measures associated with maturities T and S, respectively. The forward measures Π_{1t} and Π_{2t} are equivalent to the risk-neutral probability measure $\tilde{\mathcal{P}}(t)$, with the Radon-Nikodym derivatives (see Chapter 2) given as follows:

$$\xi_1(t) = \frac{d\Pi_{1t}}{d\tilde{\mathcal{P}}(t)} = \frac{e^{-\int_t^S r(u)\,du} P(S,\,T)}{P(t,T)} \qquad (5.126)$$

$$\xi_2(t) = \frac{d\Pi_{2t}}{d\tilde{\mathcal{P}}(t)} = \frac{e^{-\int_t^S r(u)\,du}}{P(t,S)} \qquad (5.127)$$

Step 2. Characteristic Function and the Fourier Inverse For many stochastic processes, even though the probability density $f(y)$ cannot be solved in closed form, the associated characteristic function is given in closed form. Since there is a unique one-to-one relationship between any probability density function and the associated characteristic function, the probability density can be obtained by Fourier inversion of the characteristic function. The *characteristic function* associated with a probability density $f(y)$ of a variable y is defined as follows:

$$g(\omega) = E[e^{i\overline{\omega}y}] = \int_{-\infty}^{\infty} e^{i\omega y} f(y) \, dy \qquad (5.128)$$

where i is the imaginary number given as the square root of -1. The probability density $f(y)$ can be obtained from its characteristic function by using the inverse relationship, known as the *Fourier inverse*, given as follows:

$$f(y) = \frac{1}{2\pi} \int_{-\infty}^{\infty} e^{-i\omega y} g(\omega) \, d\omega \qquad (5.129)$$

Also, if Π is the probability of the variable y being greater than or equal to a constant C, then Π can be obtained by the following Fourier inversion formula:

$$\Pi = \int_{C}^{\infty} f(y) \, dy = \frac{1}{2} + \frac{1}{\pi} \int_{0}^{\infty} \text{Re} \left[\frac{e^{-i\omega C} g(\omega)}{i\omega} \right] d\omega \qquad (5.130)$$

where the Re(.) function denotes the *real part* of the expression contained in the brackets. The expression inside the bracket of Re(.) contains complex numbers. All complex numbers can be written $a + bi$, where i is the imaginary number. The real part of $a + bi = \text{Re}(a + bi)$ is a, the number that is not multiplied by i. Though equation (5.130) looks a bit intimidating, computer languages like C or C++ can easily solve the real part and then perform the numerical integration using a truncated summation.

Step 3. Quasi-Analytical Solutions to the Option Price under Vasicek-EJ, Vasicek-EJ+, and Vasicek-EJ++ Models Consider a European call option expiring at time S, written on a zero-coupon bond maturing at time T. The solution of the option price basically requires the solutions to the probabilities Π_{1t} and Π_{2t} in equation (5.115). To solve these probabilities, we need to obtain the characteristic functions of the corresponding probability densities $f_{1t}(y)$ and $f_{2t}(y)$, defined in equations (5.124) and (5.125), respectively, and then, using the Fourier inversion formula in equation (5.130), invert the characteristic functions to obtain Π_{1t} and Π_{2t}.

The characteristic functions of $f_{1t}(y)$ and $f_{2t}(y)$ can be given using equations (5.124) and (5.125) as follows:

$$g_{1t}(\omega) = \int_{-\infty}^{\infty} e^{i\omega y} f_{1t}(y)\, dy = \int_{-\infty}^{\infty} e^{i\omega y} \left[\frac{e^{-\int_t^S r(u)\, du} P(S, T)}{P(t, T)} f_t(y) \right] dy \tag{5.131}$$

$$g_{2t}(\omega) = \int_{-\infty}^{\infty} e^{i\omega y} f_{2t}(y)\, dy = \int_{-\infty}^{\infty} e^{i\omega y} \left[\frac{e^{-\int_t^S r(u)\, du}}{P(t, S)} f_t(y) \right] dy \tag{5.132}$$

Substituting $y = \ln P(S, T)$ and $P(S, T) = \exp(\ln P(S, T))$ and using the risk-neutral expectation, we get:

$$g_{1t}(\omega)P(t, T) = \tilde{E}_t \left[e^{\ln(P(S,T))(1+i\omega)} e^{-\int_t^S r(u)\, du} \right] \tag{5.133}$$

$$g_{2t}(\omega)P(t, S) = \tilde{E}_t \left[e^{\ln(P(S,T))(i\omega)} e^{-\int_t^S r(u)\, du} \right] \tag{5.134}$$

Multiplying both sides of equations (5.133) and (5.134) by $\exp(H(t, S))$, and expressing the bond price $P(S, T)$ using the formulas given under the Vasicek-EJ/Vasicek-EJ+ and Vasicek-EJ++ models (given in equations (5.65) and (5.86), respectively), we get:

$$\begin{aligned} P_1^*(Y(t), t, \omega) &= g_{1t}(\omega)P(t, T)e^{H(t,S)} \\ &= \tilde{E}_t \left[e^{\ln(P(S,T))(1+i\omega)} e^{-\int_t^S Y(u)\, du} e^{-H(t,S)} \right] e^{H(t,S)} \\ &= \tilde{E}_t \left[e^{(A(U)-B(U)Y(S)-H(S,T))(1+i\omega)} e^{-\int_t^S Y(u)du} \right] \end{aligned} \tag{5.135}$$

and

$$\begin{aligned} P_2^*(Y(t), t, \omega) &= g_{2t}(\omega)P(t, S)e^{H(t,S)} \\ &= \tilde{E}_t \left[e^{\ln(P(S, T))(i\omega)} e^{-\int_t^S Y(u)du} e^{-H(t,S)} \right] e^{H(t,S)} \\ &= \tilde{E}_t \left[e^{(A(U)-B(U)Y(S)-H(S,T))(i\omega)} e^{-\int_t^S Y(u)du} \right] \end{aligned} \tag{5.136}$$

where $H(t, S)$ and $H(S, T)$ are defined by equation (5.66) under the Vasicek-EJ/Vasicek-EJ+ models and by equation (5.94) under the Vasicek-EJ++ model.

Using the Feynman-Kac theorem in Chapter 2, the expectations given in equations (5.135) and (5.136) are consistent with the following PDDE. For $i = 1$ and 2:

$$\frac{\partial P_i^*}{\partial t} - \tilde{\alpha}Y(t)\frac{\partial P_i^*}{\partial Y} + \frac{1}{2}\sigma^2\frac{\partial^2 P_i^*}{\partial Y^2}$$

$$+ E_t[P_i^*(Y(t) + J_u, \ t, \ T) - P_i^*(Y(t), \ t, \ T)]\tilde{\lambda}_u \qquad (5.137)$$

$$+ E_t[P_i^*(Y(t) - J_d, \ t, \ T) - P_i^*(Y(t), \ t, \ T)]\tilde{\lambda}_d = Y(t)P_i^*(Y(t), \ t, \ T)$$

subject to the boundary conditions $P_1^*\big(Y(S), \ S, \ \omega\big) = \exp\big[(A(U) - B(U)Y(S) - H(S, \ T))(1 + i\omega)\big]$ and $P_2^*\big(Y(S), \ S, \ \omega\big) = \exp\big[(A(U) - B(U)Y(S) - H(S, \ T))(i\omega)\big]$.

Now consider the following solutions for $P_1^*\big(Y(t), \ t, \ \omega\big)$ and $P_2^*\big(Y(t), t, \ \omega\big)$:

$$P_1^*\big(Y(t), \ t, \ \omega\big) = e^{A_1^*(s) - B_1^*(s)Y(t) - H(S,T)(1+i\omega)}, \quad s = S - t \qquad (5.138)$$

$$P_2^*\big(Y(t), \ t, \ \omega\big) = e^{A_2^*(s) - B_2^*(s)Y(t) - H(S,T)(i\omega)}, \quad s = S - t \qquad (5.139)$$

with the following boundary conditions:

$$\begin{aligned} A_1^*(0) &= a_1 = A(U)(1 + i\omega) \\ B_1^*(0) &= b_1 = B(U)(1 + i\omega) \end{aligned} \qquad (5.140)$$

and

$$\begin{aligned} A_2^*(0) &= a_2 = A(U)(i\omega) \\ B_2^*(0) &= b_2 = B(U)(i\omega) \end{aligned} \qquad (5.141)$$

By taking the partial derivatives of $P_1^*\big(Y(t), \ t, \ \omega\big)$ and $P_2^*\big(Y(t), \ t, \ \omega\big)$ using equations (5.138) and (5.139), respectively, and then substituting these partial derivatives in the PDDE in (5.137) and using a separation of variables, we get the following ODEs. For $i = 1$ and 2:

$$\frac{\partial B_i^*(s)}{\partial s} = 1 - \tilde{\alpha}B_i^*(s)$$

$$\frac{\partial A_i^*(s)}{\partial s} = \frac{1}{2}\sigma^2\big(B_i^*(s)\big)^2 + \tilde{\lambda}_u L_{iu}^*(s) + \tilde{\lambda}_d L_{id}^*(s) \qquad (5.142)$$

where

$$L_{iu}^*(s) = E_t\big(e^{-B_i^*(s)J_u}\big) - 1 = \frac{-B_i^*(s)}{\eta_u + B_i^*(s)}$$

$$L_{id}^*(s) = E_t\big(e^{B_i^*(s)J_d}\big) - 1 = \frac{B_i^*(s)}{\eta_d - B_i^*(s)}$$

Note that the ODEs in equation (5.142) are identical to the ODEs for $A(.)$ and $B(.)$ terms corresponding to the bond-price solution under the Vasicek-EJ, Vasicek-EJ+, and Vasicek-EJ++ models, but with nonzero boundary conditions given by equations (5.140) and (5.141). The solutions to the ODEs are given as follows. For $i = 1$ and 2:

$$
\begin{aligned}
A_i^*(s) = a_i &+ \frac{1}{2}\frac{\sigma^2}{\tilde{\alpha}^2}\left(s - 2(1 - \tilde{\alpha}b_i)B(s) + \frac{1}{2}(1 - \tilde{\alpha}b_i)^2 B(2s)\right) \\
&+ \frac{\tilde{\lambda}_u \eta_u}{\tilde{\alpha}\eta_u + 1}\ln\left|\frac{(\tilde{\alpha}\eta_u + 1)e^{\tilde{\alpha}s} - (1 - \tilde{\alpha}b_i)}{\tilde{\alpha}(\eta_u + b_i)}\right| \\
&+ \frac{\tilde{\lambda}_d \eta_d}{\tilde{\alpha}\eta_d - 1}\ln\left|\frac{(\tilde{\alpha}\eta_d - 1)e^{\tilde{\alpha}s} + (1 - \tilde{\alpha}b_i)}{\tilde{\alpha}(\eta_d - b_i)}\right| \\
&- (\tilde{\lambda}_u + \tilde{\lambda}_d)s
\end{aligned} \tag{5.143}
$$

and

$$
B_i^*(s) = B(s) + b_i e^{-\tilde{\alpha}s} \tag{5.144}
$$

where a_i and b_i for $i = 1$ and 2 are defined in equations (5.140) and (5.141).

The characteristic functions can be now given using equations (5.135) and (5.136) as follows:

$$
g_{1t}(\omega) = \frac{e^{A_1^*(s) - B_1^*(s)Y(t) - H(S,T)(1+i\omega) - H(t,S)}}{P(t,\ T)}, \quad s = S - t \tag{5.145}
$$

$$
g_{2t}(\omega) = \frac{e^{A_2^*(s) - B_2^*(s)Y(t) - H(S,T)(i\omega) - H(t,S)}}{P(t, S)}, \quad s = S - t \tag{5.146}
$$

where, as mentioned earlier, $H(t, S)$ and $H(S, T)$ are defined by equation (5.66) under the Vasicek-EJ/Vasicek-EJ+ models and by equation (5.94) under the Vasicek-EJ++ model.

The call option price in equation (5.115) can be now solved using the probabilities Π_{1t} and Π_{2t} given in equations (5.122) and (5.123), respectively. The solutions to these probabilities are obtained using the Fourier inversion formula given in equation (5.130) as follows:

$$
\begin{aligned}
\Pi_{1t} &= \int_k^\infty f_{1t}(y)\,dy = \frac{1}{2} + \frac{1}{\pi}\int_0^\infty \mathrm{Re}\left[\frac{e^{-i\omega k}g_{1t}(\omega)}{i\omega}\right]d\omega \\
\Pi_{2t} &= \int_k^\infty f_{2t}(y)\,dy = \frac{1}{2} + \frac{1}{\pi}\int_0^\infty \mathrm{Re}\left[\frac{e^{-i\omega k}g_{2t}(\omega)}{i\omega}\right]d\omega
\end{aligned} \tag{5.147}
$$

where $k = \ln K$.

The solutions of the probabilities Π_{1t} and Π_{2t} can also be used to price a European put option by applying the put-call parity relation, as follows:

$$p(t) = KP(t,\ S)(1 - \Pi_{2t}) - P(t,\ T)(1 - \Pi_{1t}) \qquad (5.148)$$

Step 4. Numerical Solutions of the Probabilities Since the integrals contained in the probabilities in equation (5.147) do not have analytical solutions, they can be approximated numerically. For example, the solution of the probability Π_{1t} is approximated as follows:

$$\Pi_{1t} = \int_k^\infty f_{1t}(y)\,dy = \frac{1}{2} + \frac{1}{\pi}\int_0^\infty \text{Re}\left[\frac{e^{-i\omega k}g_{1t}(\omega)}{i\omega}\right]d\omega$$

$$\approx \frac{1}{2} + \frac{1}{\pi}\int_0^U \text{Re}\left[\frac{e^{-i\omega k}g_{1t}(\omega)}{i\omega}\right]d\omega \qquad (5.149)$$

$$\approx \frac{1}{2} + \frac{1}{\pi}\sum_{n=1}^N \text{Re}\left[\frac{e^{-i[(n-0.5)\Delta]k}g_{1t}[(n-0.5)\Delta]}{i[(n-0.5)\Delta]}\right]\Delta$$

where

Δ = step size
N = integer value of (U/Δ)
U = upper truncation boundary

The summation in the last equality of (5.149) uses the *midpoint rule* of integration, as other integration rules such as the trapezoidal rule and the Simpson's rule cannot be applied due to the singularity at point 0. The midpoint rule circumvents the singularity at 0 by evaluating the summation terms at $n - 0.5$, instead of at $n - 1$, for $n = 1, 2, \ldots, N$. The solution in equation (5.149) introduces two types of errors. The *discretization error* related to using the step size greater than zero, or $\Delta > 0$, and the *truncation error* related to using a *finite* upper integration boundary U. The truncation error remains small only if the characteristic function $g_{1t}(.)$ converges quickly toward zero above the upper truncation boundary U. In our simulations, we find that using $\Delta = 0.001$ and $U = 100$ is more than sufficient for producing accurate results for pricing caps, floors, and other fixed-income options under a wide range of parameter values.

The discrete summation in equation (5.149) does not fully exploit the computational power of the Fast Fourier Transform (FFT), which represents one of the fundamental advances in the field of scientific computing. Carr and Madan [1999] show how to use the FFT for pricing hundreds of options in real time. The *Fractional* FFT of Bailey and Swarztrauber [1991, 1994] can further enhance the efficiency of the traditional FFT by removing the excess computations performed by the FFT method.[6]

However, the probabilities in equation (5.147) do not allow the applications of either the FFT or the fractional FFT due to the singularity at 0. Carr and Madan propose a technique to remove this singularity by considering the Fourier transform of the option with a *damping* constant. Similar to Carr and Madan, we consider the Fourier transforms of the probabilities in equation (5.147), with a damping constant $\beta > 0$.[7] Using generalized notation, let $\Pi_{1t}(k)$ and $\Pi_{2t}(k)$ represent the two probabilities defined in equation (5.147), corresponding to the strike price K (where $k = \ln K$). Let:

$$\hat{\Pi}_{1t}(k) = e^{\beta k} \Pi_{1t}(k)$$

$$\hat{\Pi}_{2t}(k) = e^{\beta k} \Pi_{2t}(k)$$

(5.150)

As shown in Appendix 5.1, by taking the Fourier transforms of $\hat{\Pi}_{1t}(k)$ and $\hat{\Pi}_{2t}(k)$ and then using the inverse Fourier transforms, the probabilities $\Pi_{1t}(k)$ and $\Pi_{2t}(k)$ can be obtained as follows:

$$\Pi_{1t}(k) = \frac{e^{-\beta k}}{\pi} \int_0^\infty \frac{e^{-i\omega k} g_{1t}(\omega - \beta i)}{\beta + i\omega} \, d\omega$$

$$\Pi_{2t}(k) = \frac{e^{-\beta k}}{\pi} \int_0^\infty \frac{e^{-i\omega k} g_{2t}(\omega - \beta i)}{\beta + i\omega} \, d\omega$$

(5.151)

Since the damping constant β is greater than zero, the singularity at 0 is avoided, allowing the application of the FFT for the computation of the probabilities given in equation (5.151).[8]

The FFT algorithm is an efficient implementation of a *Discrete Fourier Transform*. The FFT returns an output vector Y_m (for $m = 1, 2, \ldots, N$), which is defined as the discrete Fourier transform of an input vector X_n (for $n = 1, 2, \ldots, N$), as follows:

$$Y_m = \sum_{n=1}^N e^{\left(-i\frac{2\pi}{N}(n-1)(m-1)\right)} X_n, \quad \text{for } m = 1, 2, \ldots, N$$

(5.152)

Note that for each value of m, the computation of Y_m requires a summation of N terms. Since m can also take N values, the total order of complexity to compute Y_m for all values of m is equal to $N \times N = N^2$.

The FFT algorithm reduces the complexity from the order of N^2 to $N\log_2(N)$, where $\log_2(.)$ is the log function with base 2. For example, if $N = 1,024$, then the complexity of the order of $1,024^2 = 1,048,576$ is reduced to $1,024 \times \log_2(1,024) = 1,024 \times 10 = 10,240$, a reduction in the order of about $1/100$ times. The reduction in complexity would be of a higher order for higher values of N.

Now, consider a range of log strike prices given as follows:

$$k_m = k_1 + d(m - 1) \qquad (5.153)$$

for $m = 1, 2, \ldots, N$, where k_1 and d are selected to consider the desired range of strike prices.

To compute the probabilities using the FFT algorithm, the integrals in equation (5.151) are expressed in the form of the discrete Fourier transform given in equation (5.152). For example, the first integral in (5.151) can be approximated by substituting $k = k_m$ from equation (5.153) as follows:

$$\int_0^\infty \frac{e^{-i\omega k_m} g_{1t}(\omega - \beta i)}{\beta + i\omega}\, d\omega \approx Y_m = \sum_{n=1}^N \frac{e^{-i((n-1)\Delta)k_m} g_{1t}((n-1)\Delta - \beta i)I_n}{\beta + i((n-1)\Delta)}\Delta$$

$$= \sum_{n=1}^N e^{\left(-i(\Delta d)(n-1)(m-1)\right)} X_n \qquad (5.154)$$

where

$$X_n = \frac{e^{-i((n-1)\Delta)k_1} g_{1t}((n-1)\Delta - \beta i)I_n}{\beta + i((n-1)\Delta)}\Delta \qquad (5.155)$$

and the variable I_n defines the integration rule such as the trapezoidal rule or Simpson's rule. Using the trapezoidal rule, $I_n = 0.5$, if either $n = 1$ or $n = N$, and $I_n = 1$, otherwise. Using Simpson's rule, $I_n = (1/3)[3 + (-1)^n - \delta_{n-1}]$, where δ_j is the Kronecker delta function, which equals 1 for $j = 0$ and equals 0 otherwise.

Note that the summation in equation (5.154) is given exactly in the form of the discrete Fourier transform defined in equation (5.152), with:

$$d = \frac{2\pi}{N\Delta} = \frac{2\pi}{U} \qquad (5.156)$$

where $U = N\Delta$. Hence, the integral in equation (5.154) can be approximated for $m = 1, 2, \ldots, N$, using the FFT algorithm and using standard scientific programming languages. Given the values of Y_m as the output from the FFT algorithm, the probabilities $\Pi_{1t}(k_m)$ are obtained by substituting equation (5.154) into equation (5.151) as follows:

$$\Pi_{1t}(k_m) = \frac{e^{-\beta k_m}}{\pi} Y_m, \text{ for } m = 1, 2, \ldots, N \qquad (5.157)$$

The probabilities $\Pi_{2t}(k_m)$ are obtained in a similar manner, using the characteristic function $g_{2t}(.)$ instead of $g_{1t}(.)$.

The relationship in equation (5.156) shows that the parameters d, Δ, and N are related such that any two of them determine the third parameter. Ensuring high accuracy in computing option prices requires a high truncation value $U = N\Delta$ and a low value of step size Δ. Using $U = 100$ is sufficient for obtaining accurate pricing of most fixed-income options. This value of U gives $d = 2\pi/100 = 0.0628$. Now consider call options on a \$1 face-value zero-coupon bond, with strikes ranging from 0.8 to 1.2. Since $\ln(0.8) = -0.2231$ and $\ln(1.2) = 0.1823$, using the value of $d = 0.0628$ gives only six options with strike prices in the range of 0.8 and 1.2 (see equation (5.153)). Hence, using $N \geq 2^{10}$, such that $\Delta = U/N$ remains small for ensuring high accuracy, implies that more than 99.99 percent of the strike prices of options will be outside the range of 0.8 to 1.2. This implies that most of the computation power of the FFT algorithm is wasted on considering strike prices that are either too high or too low, and hence, of little interest to option traders. Though this problem applies to equity options too, it is more serious for fixed-income options.[9]

The fractional FFT algorithm of Bailey and Swarztrauber [1991, 1994] can be used to break the relation between d and U for a given step size Δ. This algorithm allows a reduction in the size of d, without changing either U or Δ, such that many more strike prices can be considered in the desired range using equation (5.153). The fractional FFT returns an output vector Y_m (for $m = 1, 2, \ldots, N$), which is defined as the discrete Fourier transform of an input vector X_n (for $n = 1, 2, \ldots, N$), as follows:

$$Y_m = \sum_{n=1}^{N} e^{(-i(2\pi c)(n-1)(m-1))} X_n, \quad \text{for } m = 1, 2, \ldots, N \qquad (5.158)$$

The traditional FFT can be obtained as a special case of the fractional FFT by setting the constant c equal to $1/N$. Note that the summation in equation (5.154) is given exactly in the form of the discrete Fourier transform defined in equation (5.158), with:

$$d = \frac{2\pi c}{\Delta} \qquad (5.159)$$

Since c is an extra parameter, the implementation of the fractional FFT allows all three parameters, d, Δ, and N, to be chosen independently of each other. Hence, the grid spacing of log strikes (given by the parameter d) can be made as dense as possible in a given range by choosing a sufficiently small value of the parameter c in equation (5.159), without restricting the size of either Δ or N. The fractional FFT can be implemented using the algorithm given by Bailey and Swarztrauber [1991].

The four steps given, in the previous section can be used to solve for the prices of European calls and puts (and, thus, prices of caplets/floorlets and caps/floors), not only under the Vasicek-EJ/Vasicek-EJ+ and Vasicek-EJ++ models, but also under a variety of affine and quadratic models. Any term structure model that has analytical solutions of the characteristic functions $g_{1t}(\omega)$ and $g_{2t}(\omega)$, given in equations (5.131) and (5.132), respectively, allows the use of these four steps to solve option prices. We provide analytical solutions of the characteristic functions $g_{1t}(\omega)$ and $g_{2t}(\omega)$ under a variety of affine and quadratic models in Chapters 6 through 10.

Finally, note that the $H(t, T)$ term under the Vasicek-EJ++ model is given in closed form by equation (5.94). Hence, our method has an analytical advantage over the calibration method suggested by Chacko and Das [2002], under which the time-dependent long-term mean is determined numerically using an iterative method. As shown in the chapters that follow, this advantage becomes even more powerful in the context of models with state variable dependent volatilities such as the square root affine models or quadratic models, under which using our framework allows calibration to an arbitrarily specified initial zero-coupon bond-price function, while shifting the long-term mean in an iterative manner does not allow calibration to all shapes of the initial zero-coupon bond-price function.

APPENDIX 5.1: PROBABILITY TRANSFORMATIONS WITH A DAMPING CONSTANT

Consider the Fourier transform of $\hat{\Pi}_{1t}(k)$, given as follows:

$$h_{1t}(\omega) = \int_{-\infty}^{\infty} e^{i\omega k} \hat{\Pi}_{1t}(k) \, dk \qquad (5.160)$$

Then using the inverse Fourier transform:

$$\hat{\Pi}_{1t}(k) = \frac{1}{2\pi} \int_{-\infty}^{\infty} e^{-i\omega k} h_{1t}(\omega)\, d\omega \qquad (5.161)$$

Using equation (5.150), equation (5.161) becomes:

$$\Pi_{1t}(k) = \frac{e^{-\beta k}}{2\pi} \int_{-\infty}^{\infty} e^{-i\omega k} h_{1t}(\omega)\, d\omega \qquad (5.162)$$

The solution of $h_{1t}(\omega)$ can be obtained by substituting equations (5.122) and (5.150) into (5.160) as follows:

$$h_{1t}(\omega) = \int_{-\infty}^{\infty} e^{i\omega k} e^{\beta k} \int_{k}^{\infty} f_{1t}(y)\, dy\, dk \qquad (5.163)$$

Changing the order of integration, we get:

$$h_{1t}(\omega) = \int_{-\infty}^{\infty} f_{1t}(y) \int_{-\infty}^{y} e^{k(\beta + i\omega)}\, dk\, dy \qquad (5.164)$$

Integrating the inside integral, we get:

$$h_{1t}(\omega) = \int_{-\infty}^{\infty} f_{1t}(y) \left(\frac{e^{y(\beta + i\omega)}}{\beta + i\omega} \right) dy \qquad (5.165)$$

Multiplying the terms in the exponent by $-i^2 = 1$ and rearranging terms we get:

$$h_{1t}(\omega) = \frac{1}{\beta + i\omega} \int_{-\infty}^{\infty} e^{iy(\omega - \beta i)} f_{1t}(y)\, dy \qquad (5.166)$$

Using equation (5.131), equation (5.166) can be rewritten as follows:

$$h_{1t}(\omega) = \frac{g_{1t}(\omega - \beta i)}{\beta + i\omega} \qquad (5.167)$$

Since $\Pi_{1t}(k)$ is real, equation (5.162) can be rewritten as:

$$\Pi_{1t}(k) = \frac{e^{-\beta k}}{\pi} \int_{0}^{\infty} e^{-i\omega k} h_{1t}(\omega)\, d\omega \qquad (5.168)$$

Substituting equation (5.167) into equation (5.168), we get the first equation in (5.151). The second equation in (5.151) can be proven in a similar manner.

NOTES

1. See Backus, Foresi, and Wu [1997], Das [2002], Das and Foresi [1996], and Piazzesi [1998, 2005].
2. See Ahn, Dittmar, and Gallant [2002] for a comprehensive theoretical framework for Gaussian quadratic models.
3. See Chapter 1 for the definitions of $o(dt)$ and $O(dt)$.
4. The jump-diffusion tree for the short rate is adapted from Amin [1993].
5. Since the bond pays $100 always at end of the second period, we could have simply used the formula $100/e^{-0.096 \times 0.083} = \$99.20$. Our demonstration is more general and applies to any node of the tree, and not just at the maturity of the bond.
6. See Chourdakis [2004] and Cassasus, Collin-Dufresne, and Goldstein [2004].
7. Using the Fourier transforms of the probabilities with a damping constant allows us to use the solutions of the characteristic functions $g_{1t}(\omega)$ and $g_{2t}(\omega)$ in the FFT application.
8. See Carr and Madan [1999] for the discussion of an upper bound on β.
9. See Chourdakis [2004] for an explanation of this issue in the context of equity options.

The Fundamental Cox, Ingersoll, and Ross Model with Exponential and Lognormal Jumps

A significant limitation of the Gaussian models is that these models allow the short rate to become negative with a positive probability. Though allowing the short rate to be mean-reverting significantly reduces the probability of negative rates, traders still prefer models that can preclude the occurrence of negative rates. Negative interest rates also become statistically more probable—despite the presence of mean-reversion—during economic regimes characterized by unusually low levels of the short rate (e.g., for a few years after the events of September 11, 2001).

Another limitation of Gaussian models is that conditional volatility of the interest rates is independent of the level of the interest rates. A casual look at the interest rate data (a good visual demonstration of this is given by the Excel-based term structure "movie" in Chapter 3 of the first book of the Fixed Income Valuation Course, *Interest Rate Risk Modeling*) reveals that interest rate volatility was much higher in the late 1970s and early 1980s, when interest rates were high. Chan, Karolyi, Longstaff, and Sanders (CKLS) [1992], using a Generalized Method of Moments (GMM) estimation, confirm this view and find that the volatility of conditional changes in the short rate is proportional to the level of the short rate raised to the power β (i.e., $r(t)^\beta$), where $\beta = 1.5$. However, other researchers using corrections to the data set used by CKLS, regime shift models, stochastic volatility models, and better discretisation schemes have found β to be a lot lower. Li and Xu [2002], using a regime shift model, confirm that a better estimate of β is closer to 0.5, as high (low) interest rate regimes may also have high (low) volatility.[1] These findings seem realistic as the period from September 1979 to October 1982 can be considered a distinct economic regime due to unusually high interest rates supported by the Federal Reserve policy and high inflation triggered by the oil supply shocks.[2]

Cox, Ingersoll, and Ross (CIR) [1985] assume $\beta = 0.5$ and use the following mean-reverting specification for the short rate process:

$$dr(t) = \alpha\big(m - r(t)\big)\, dt + \sigma\sqrt{r(t)}\, dZ(t) \tag{6.1}$$

where α is the speed of mean reversion, m is the long-term mean of the short rate, and σ is the volatility coefficient. Both α and m are assumed to be positive under the physical measure, which keep the short rate distribution stationary. The short rate remains above zero if $2\alpha m \geq \sigma^2$. When the short rate goes to zero (i.e., if $2\alpha m < \sigma^2$), the volatility also becomes zero, and the drift converges to αm in equation (6.1). The positive drift makes the short rate bounce back from the zero boundary and become positive again. Due to the continuity of the diffusion process, the short rate can never become negative under the CIR model. The short rate process under the CIR model leads to an affine solution for the bond price in which the log of the bond price is linear in the short rate.

The CIR model is derived using an equilibrium resulting from the utility-maximizing behavior of identical individuals with a log-utility function. The CIR model assumes that physical investment is performed by a single stochastic constant return-to-scale technology that produces a single good that is either consumed or reinvested in production. The state variable in this economy follows a square root process. CIR demonstrate that the bond market equilibrium in this economy is consistent with:

1. the square root process for the short rate given in equation (6.1), and
2. affine risk premiums on bonds.

Since the CIR model specifies the risk premiums on bonds explicitly using an underlying economic equilibrium, it is obviously a *fundamental* model. We derive preference-free CIR+ and CIR++ versions of this model in Chapter 7 that can allow general, nonlinear forms of market prices of risks consistent with general, nonlinear risk premiums on bonds.

This chapter begins with the derivation of formulas for bond price, futures, and options under the CIR model, with more generalized forms of market prices of risk given by Duffee [2002]. Next, we show how to build binomial and trinomial trees to price derivatives with American features. Building an interest rate tree for the CIR model is not straightforward because the volatility of the short rate is not constant. This makes the tree *nonrecombining*, as a down movement in the short rate followed by an up movement does not give the same value for the short rate as an up movement in the short rate followed by a down movement. It is well-known that the number of nodes on a nonrecombining tree increases exponentially, making it computationally expensive.

Nelson and Ramaswamy [1990] show how to generate recombining trees for state-dependent or time-dependent volatility-based processes, such as the square root model of CIR. The Nelson and Ramaswamy (NR) technique uses a transform of the short rate, which is a specific nonlinear function of the short rate that displays constant volatility. Using a recombining tree for the transform (since it has constant volatility), NR show how to generate the recombining tree for the short rate by inverting the transform.

However, as pointed out recently by Nawalkha and Beliaeva (NB) [2007a], the movement of the short rate tree when the short rate hits the zero boundary has an error in the original solution proposed by NR. NB correct this error and also truncate the NR tree at the zero boundary. NB show that using the NR tree keeps the short rate tree stuck at zero with a much higher probability than the CIR model requires and as a result, the bond prices using the NR tree are significantly higher than the prices obtained from the closed-form solution (as reported in the simulations of NR [1990]). The truncated tree corrects these problems and obtains bond price approximations, which quickly converge to the closed-form solution, while using fewer nodes. In this chapter, we demonstrate with examples how binomial and trinomial trees can be generated using the truncated tree method and use it to price American options on coupon bonds (or American swaptions).

The final section of this chapter extends the CIR model to allow jumps. Many researchers, including Das [2002], Johannes [2004], Piazzesi [2005], and Durham [2005], have found that jumps play a significant role in the movements of interest rates. Though jumps do not explain much of the cross-sectional differences in bond yields, their effects are significant for the pricing of interest rate derivatives. Jarrow, Li, and Zhao [2004] find that upward jumps in the interest rates played an important role in the pricing of long-term caps, while downward jumps played an important role in the pricing of short-term and medium-term caps after September 2001.

Finally, we demonstrate how to build truncated jump-diffusion trees for the CIR model extended with jumps, under two jump-size distributions. Under the first case, the jumps in the short rate are distributed exponentially, allowing positive jumps only; under the second case, jumps in the short rate are distributed lognormally, allowing both positive and negative jumps.

THE FUNDAMENTAL COX, INGERSOLL, AND ROSS MODEL

Before we derive the formulas for bond price, futures, and options under the fundamental CIR model, we give a brief introduction to the distribution properties of the short rate. The probability density of the interest rate at time S, conditional on its value at the current time t, is given by:

$$f\big(r(S),\ S; r(t),\ t\big) = ce^{-u-v}\left(\frac{v}{u}\right)^{q/2} I_q\big(2(uv)^{1/2}\big) \tag{6.2}$$

where

$$c \equiv \frac{2\alpha}{\sigma^2(1 - e^{-\alpha(S-t)})}$$

$$u \equiv cr(t)e^{-\alpha(S-t)}$$

$$v \equiv cr(S)$$

$$q \equiv \frac{2\alpha m}{\sigma^2} - 1$$

and where $I_q(\cdot)$ is the modified Bessel function of the first kind of order q. The distribution function is the noncentral chi-square, $\chi^2[2cr(S);\ 2q+2,\ 2u]$, with $2q+2$ degrees of freedom and parameter of noncentrality $2u$ proportional to the current spot rate.

The time t mean and variance of $r(S)$ are given as follows:

$$E_t[r(S)] = r(t)e^{-\alpha(S-t)} + m(1 - e^{-\alpha(S-t)})$$
$$V_t[r(S)] = r(t)\left(\frac{\sigma^2}{\alpha}\right)(e^{-\alpha(S-t)} - e^{-2\alpha(S-t)}) + m\left(\frac{\sigma^2}{2\alpha}\right)(1 - e^{-\alpha(S-t)})^2 \tag{6.3}$$

where the parameters α, m, and σ are greater than zero. The asymptotic mean and variance of the short rate are given as:

$$\lim_{S\to\infty} E_t[r(S)] = m$$
$$\lim_{S\to\infty} V_t[r(S)] = \frac{m\sigma^2}{2\alpha} \tag{6.4}$$

Unlike the Vasicek model (see equation (4.25)), in which the long-term mean does not appear in the expressions for unconditional volatilities, this parameter does determine unconditional volatilities for the CIR model.

As shown in Chapter 4 (equation (4.15)), Vasicek [1977] derived the term structure equation for the bond price under all single-factor Markovian short rate processes as follows:

$$\frac{\partial P}{\partial t} + [\mu_r(r,\ t) - \sigma_r(r,\ t)\gamma(r,\ t)]\frac{\partial P}{\partial r} + \frac{1}{2}\sigma_r^2(r,\ t)\frac{\partial^2 P}{\partial r^2} - r(t)P(t,T) = 0 \tag{6.5}$$

where t is the current time, T is the bond maturity date, and the drift and diffusion functions in equation (6.5) can be identified with the CIR process in equation (6.1), as follows:

$$\mu_r(r,\ t) = \alpha(m - r(t))$$

$$\sigma_r(r,\ t) = \sigma\sqrt{r(t)}$$

The market price of interest rate risk in the CIR model has the following form:

$$\gamma(r,\ t) = \frac{\gamma\sqrt{r(t)}}{\sigma} \tag{6.6}$$

where γ is a constant. Substituting equation (6.6), and using a change of variable from t to $\tau = T - t$, the PDE given in equation (6.5) becomes:

$$[\alpha m - (\alpha + \gamma)r(t)]\frac{\partial P}{\partial r} + \frac{1}{2}\sigma^2 r(t)\frac{\partial^2 P}{\partial r^2} - \frac{\partial P}{\partial \tau} - r(t)P(t,\ T) = 0 \tag{6.7}$$

It is important to note that even though equation (6.7) is a special case of Vasicek's general term structure equation (6.5), absence of arbitrage alone cannot identify the functional form of the market price of risk in equation (6.6) in the CIR model. This functional form results endogenously from the equilibrium framework assumed by CIR. This equilibrium framework keeps the model internally consistent because when the short rate becomes zero, both the risk and risk premium on a default-free bond go to zero.

The PDE in equation (6.7) can be alternatively expressed as follows:

$$[\tilde{\alpha}(\tilde{m} - r(t))]\frac{\partial P}{\partial r} + \frac{1}{2}\sigma^2 r(t)\frac{\partial^2 P}{\partial r^2} - \frac{\partial P}{\partial \tau} - r(t)P(t,\ T) = 0 \tag{6.8}$$

where

$$\tilde{\alpha} = \alpha + \gamma$$

$$\tilde{m} = \frac{\alpha m}{\alpha + \gamma} \tag{6.9}$$

The PDE in equation (6.8) is consistent with the following stochastic process for the short rate under the risk-neutral measure:

$$dr(t) = \tilde{\alpha}(\tilde{m} - r(t))\,dt + \sigma\sqrt{r(t)}\,d\tilde{Z}(t) \tag{6.10}$$

where the change of measure is given as:

$$d\tilde{Z}(t) = dZ(t) + \frac{\gamma\sqrt{r(t)}}{\sigma}\,dt \tag{6.11}$$

The PDE in equation (6.8) can be solved subject to the boundary condition $P(T, T) = 1$. Assume that the solution to equation (6.11) has the following form:

$$P(t, T) = e^{A(\tau) - B(\tau)r(t)} \qquad (6.12)$$

where $A(0) = 0$ and $B(0) = 0$.

Evaluating the partial derivatives of the bond price with respect to the short rate and bond maturity, we get:

$$\frac{\partial P}{\partial \tau} = P(t, T)\left[\frac{\partial A(\tau)}{\partial \tau} - \frac{\partial B(\tau)}{\partial \tau}r(t)\right]$$

$$\frac{\partial P}{\partial r} = -P(t, T)B(\tau) \qquad (6.13)$$

$$\frac{\partial^2 P}{\partial r^2} = P(t, T)B^2(\tau)$$

Substituting the expressions in equation (6.13) into equation (6.7) leads to the following two ordinary differential equations (ODEs) by collecting terms multiplied by $P(t, T)$ and $r(t)P(t, T)$, respectively:

$$\underbrace{\frac{\partial B(\tau)}{\partial \tau} = 1 - \tilde{\alpha}B(\tau) - \frac{1}{2}\sigma^2 B^2(\tau)}_{Riccati} \qquad (6.14)$$

$$\frac{\partial A(\tau)}{\partial \tau} = -\tilde{\alpha}\tilde{m}B(\tau)$$

subject to the boundary conditions $A(0) = 0$ and $B(0) = 0$.

The first equation in (6.14) is the well-known Riccati equation with constant coefficients. In fact, Riccati equations with constant coefficients are ubiquitous in finance, especially in the area of term structure modeling. In addition to the CIR model, many multifactor affine models in Chapters 8 and 9 and quadratic models in Chapter 10 use the solutions based on Riccati equations. We first provide a general solution to the Riccati equation with constant coefficients in the following section, which can be applied to solve not only the CIR model, but also many other multifactor affine and quadratic models given in other chapters.

Solution to Riccati Equation with Constant Coefficients

Let $Y(\tau)$ be a deterministic function of a variable τ. A Riccati equation with constant coefficients is defined as follows:

$$\frac{\partial Y(\tau)}{\partial \tau} = P + QY(\tau) + RY^2(\tau) \qquad (6.15)$$

where, P, Q, and R are constants. The solution to equation (6.15), given the boundary condition $Y(\tau = 0) = K$ (where K is a constant), is given as:

$$Y(\tau) = -\frac{b}{R}\left[\frac{\frac{a}{b}\left(\dfrac{b+RK}{a+RK}\right)e^{(a-b)\tau}-1}{\left(\dfrac{b+RK}{a+RK}\right)e^{(a-b)\tau}-1}\right] \qquad (6.16)$$

where

$$a = \frac{Q+\sqrt{Q^2-4PR}}{2}$$

$$b = \frac{Q-\sqrt{Q^2-4PR}}{2} \qquad (6.17)$$

The solution in equation (6.16) can be applied in many contexts, including solving the bond price and futures price under multifactor affine and quadratic models and solving other interest rate derivatives using Fourier inversion methods. Generally, solving the bond price requires that K equal zero, while solving futures and other derivatives (with Fourier inversion methods) requires that K be nonzero.

Substituting $K = 0$ in equation (6.16), the solution to the Riccati equation simplifies to the following:

$$Y(\tau) = -\frac{b}{R}\left[\frac{e^{(a-b)\tau}-1}{\dfrac{b}{a}e^{(a-b)\tau}-1}\right] \qquad (6.18)$$

CIR Bond Price Solution

To solve for the zero-coupon bond price in the CIR model, the Riccati equation in (6.14) can be expressed as follows:

$$\frac{\partial B(\tau)}{\partial \tau} = P + QB(\tau) + RB^2(\tau), \qquad (6.19)$$

subject to $B(\tau = 0) = 0$, where $P = 1$, $Q = -\tilde{\alpha}$, and $R = -(1/2)\sigma^2$.

The solution to equation (6.19) is given by equation (6.18), with $Y(\tau)$ replaced by $B(\tau)$. Substituting P, Q, and R in equation (6.17), and then substituting a and b from equation (6.17) into equation (6.18) and simplifying, the solution to $B(\tau)$ is given as follows:

$$B(\tau) = \frac{2(e^{\beta\tau}-1)}{(\beta+\tilde{\alpha})(e^{\beta\tau}-1)+2\beta} \qquad (6.20)$$

where

$$\beta = \sqrt{\tilde{\alpha}^2 + 2\sigma^2} \tag{6.21}$$

Integrating the second PDE in equation (6.14) after substituting equation (6.20), we obtain:

$$A(\tau) = -\tilde{\alpha}\tilde{m} \int_0^\tau B(u)\,du = \frac{2\tilde{\alpha}\tilde{m}}{\sigma^2} \ln\left[\frac{2\beta e^{\frac{1}{2}(\beta+\tilde{\alpha})\tau}}{(\beta+\tilde{\alpha})(e^{\beta\tau}-1)+2\beta}\right] \tag{6.22}$$

Using Ito's lemma, the stochastic differential equation for the bond price can be given as:

$$\frac{dP(t,\,T)}{P(t,\,T)} = [r(t) - \gamma r(t)B(T-t)]\,dt - \sigma\sqrt{r(t)}B(T-t)\,dZ(t) \tag{6.23}$$

where a negative value for γ implies positive risk premiums. The risk premiums remain of one sign regardless of the level of the short rate. The bond volatility increases with maturity, though at a decreasing rate.

General Specifications of Market Prices of Risk

Duffee [2002] generalizes the fundamental CIR model by introducing the "essentially affine" form of market prices of risk, which can be specified in a more general manner by using the following change of measure:

$$d\tilde{Z}(t) = dZ(t) + \frac{\gamma_0}{\sigma\sqrt{r(t)}} + \frac{\gamma_1\sqrt{r(t)}}{\sigma}\,dt \tag{6.24}$$

Substituting equation (6.24) in equation (6.1), the risk-neutral short rate process is given as:

$$dr(t) = \tilde{\alpha}(\tilde{m} - r(t))\,dt + \sigma\sqrt{r(t)}\,d\tilde{Z}(t) \tag{6.25}$$

where

$$\begin{aligned} \tilde{\alpha} &= \alpha + \gamma_1 \\ \tilde{m} &= \frac{\alpha m - \gamma_0}{\alpha + \gamma_1} \end{aligned} \tag{6.26}$$

The bond price solution remains of the same form, except the definitions of risk-neutral parameters is now given using equation (6.26) instead of equation (6.9).

The relationship between the risk-neutral process and the physical process given by the change of measure in equation (6.24) allows the market risk premiums on bonds to switch signs depending on the level of short rate. This can be seen by generalizing the stochastic bond price process under the physical measure given in equation (6.23), using the general form of market prices of risk given in equation (6.24), as follows:

$$\frac{dP(t,\ T)}{P(t,\ T)} = \left[r(t) - \left(\gamma_0 + \gamma_1 r(t)\right)B(T-t)\right]dt - \sigma\sqrt{r(t)}B(T-t)\,dZ(t) \quad (6.27)$$

If γ_0 and γ_1 are of opposite signs, then the bond risk premiums will switch signs depending on the level of short rate, a result confirmed in the empirical study of Fama and French [1993].

The change of measure in equation (6.24) does not satisfy the Novikov condition related to the Girsanov theorem given in Chapter 2, since the term with $r(t)$ in the denominator in equation (6.24) explodes as $r(t)$ approaches zero. However, as pointed out by Collin-Dufresne and Goldstein [2004], the Novikov condition is sufficient, but not necessary, and a simple application of Theorem 7.19 in Liptser and Shiryaev [1974, p. 294] shows that if the zero boundary is inaccessible by the short rate under both measures, then the probability measures are equivalent, and the change of measure can be used in an arbitrage-free manner. Hence, the conditions $2\alpha m \geq \sigma^2$ and $2\tilde{\alpha}\tilde{m} \geq \sigma^2$ must be met to allow the more general market price of risk specification in equation (6.24). Given that these conditions are met, all of the valuation results in this chapter continue to hold in an arbitrage-free setting, using the more general risk-neutral parameters defined by equation (6.26) under the fundamental CIR model.

A simple economic exposition of the necessity of a strictly positive short rate for precluding the existence of riskless arbitrage, when using generalized form of the market prices of risk, can be given by evaluating the bond risk premium in equation (6.27) with $r(t) = 0$. Taking the physical expectation gives $E_t[dP(t,\ T)/P(t,\ T)] = -\gamma_0 B(T-t)$. However, since bond volatility is zero when $r(t) = 0$, the bond is riskless and, therefore, should earn the riskless rate of return equal to zero. Hence, in absence of arbitrage, $r(t) = 0$ necessarily implies $\gamma_0 = 0$, which disallows the generalized form of market prices of risk given by Duffee. Thus, to allow the generalized form of market prices of risk in equation (6.24), $r(t)$ must remain strictly above zero.

Valuing Futures

Futures on a Zero-Coupon Bond   Following the same steps as in the previous chapters, the PDE for the price $P_F(t,\ S,\ T)$ of a futures contract expiring at time S and written on a zero-coupon bond maturing at time T under the CIR model can be given as follows:

$$\frac{\partial P_F}{\partial r}(\tilde{\alpha}(\tilde{m} - r(t))) + \frac{1}{2}\sigma^2 r(t)\frac{\partial^2 P_F}{\partial r^2} + \frac{\partial P_F}{\partial t} = 0 \qquad (6.28)$$

subject to the boundary condition $P_F(S, S, T) = P(S, T)$. We assume that the solution to equation (6.28) has the following form:

$$P_F(t, S, T) = e^{A_F(s) - B_F(s)r(t)}, \quad s = S - t \qquad (6.29)$$

subject to $A_F(0) = A(U)$, $B_F(0) = B(U)$, $U = T - S$.

Using a change of variable, $s = S - t$, the PDE in equation (6.28) becomes:

$$\frac{\partial P_F}{\partial r}(\tilde{\alpha}(\tilde{m} - r(t))) + \frac{1}{2}\sigma^2 r(t)\frac{\partial^2 P_F}{\partial r^2} - \frac{\partial P_F}{\partial s} = 0 \qquad (6.30)$$

Evaluating the partial derivatives of the futures price with respect to s and $r(t)$, we have:

$$\frac{\partial P_F}{\partial r} = -P_F(t, S, T)B_F(s)$$

$$\frac{\partial^2 P_F}{\partial r^2} = P_F(t, S, T)B_F(s)^2 \qquad (6.31)$$

$$\frac{\partial P_F}{\partial s} = P_F(t, S, T)\left(\frac{\partial A_F(s)}{\partial s} - \frac{\partial B_F(s)}{\partial s}r(t)\right)$$

Substituting these partial derivatives in equation (6.30), and then using a separation of variables, we get the following two ODEs:

$$\underbrace{\frac{\partial B_F(s)}{\partial s} + B_F(s)\tilde{\alpha} + \frac{1}{2}B_F^2(s)\sigma^2 = 0}_{Riccati} \qquad (6.32)$$

$$\frac{\partial A_F(s)}{\partial s} + B_F(s)\tilde{\alpha}\tilde{m} = 0$$

subject to $A_F(0) = A(U)$, $B_F(0) = B(U)$, $U = T - S$.

The solution is given as:

$$A_F(s) = A(U) - \frac{2\tilde{\alpha}\tilde{m}}{\sigma^2}\ln\left|\frac{\sigma^2 B(U)(e^{-\tilde{\alpha}s} - 1) - 2\tilde{\alpha}}{2\tilde{\alpha}}\right| \qquad (6.33)$$

$$B_F(s) = \frac{-2\tilde{\alpha}B(U)e^{-\tilde{\alpha}s}}{\sigma^2 B(U)(e^{-\tilde{\alpha}s} - 1) - 2\tilde{\alpha}} \qquad (6.34)$$

where $A(U)$ and $B(U)$ are as defined earlier in equations (6.22) and (6.20), respectively.

Similar to the Gaussian models, the futures price is lower than the forward price. This is because the asset underlying the futures contract is perfectly negatively correlated with the short rate. The futures-forward price discount (FFPD) is given as:

$$
\begin{aligned}
FFPD &= \frac{P_f(t,\ S,\ T) - P_F(t,\ S,\ T)}{P_f(t,\ S,\ T)} = 1 - P_F(t,\ S,\ T)\frac{P(t,\ S)}{P(t,\ T)} \\
&= 1 - e^{\left(A_F(s)+A(s)-A(\tau)\right)-\left(B_F(s)+B(s)-B(\tau)\right)r(t)}, \quad s = S-t, \quad \tau = T-t
\end{aligned}
\tag{6.35}
$$

The FFPD is always between 0 and 1. In general, everything else held constant, a higher value of the short rate implies a higher FFPD. This is because marking to market is dependent on the conditional volatility, which, in turn, is dependent on the level of the short rate under the CIR model. The FFPD is also an increasing function of $\tilde{m}$ and a decreasing function of $\tilde{\alpha}$.

Futures on a Time Deposit The price of a futures contract on a time deposit—such as Eurodollar and Euribor futures—can be obtained using equation (3.12) in Chapter 3:

$$
P_F^{TD}(t,\ S,\ T) = \frac{100}{\hat{U}}\left(1 + \hat{U} - P_F^I(t,\ S,\ T)\right)
\tag{6.36}
$$

where S is the futures expiration date, $U = T - S$ is the deposit time period calculated using the actual/actual day-count convention, $\hat{U}$ is the deposit time period calculated using actual/360 day-count convention, and $P_F^I(t,\ S,\ T)$ is the current price of a futures contract written on a hypothetical asset, which at the expiration date S is worth the inverse of a \$1 face-value zero-coupon bond maturing at time T. Following the same steps as in the previous chapters, the PDE for $P_F^I(t,\ S,\ T)$ under the CIR model is given as:

$$
\frac{\partial P_F^I}{\partial r}\left(\tilde{\alpha}(\tilde{m} - r(t))\right) + \frac{1}{2}\sigma^2 r(t)\frac{\partial^2 P_F^I}{\partial r^2} + \frac{\partial P_F^I}{\partial t} = 0
\tag{6.37}
$$

subject to the boundary condition $P_F^I(S,\ S,\ T) = 1/P(S,\ T)$. We assume that the solution to equation (6.37) has the following form:

$$
P_F^I(t,\ S,\ T) = e^{a_F(s)-b_F(s)r(t)}, \quad s = S-t
\tag{6.38}
$$

subject to $a_F(0) = -A(U)$, $b_F(0) = -B(U)$, and $U = T - S$.

Note that the PDE in equation (6.37) is identical to the PDE in equation (6.28) and that the solution form in equation (6.38) is identical to the solution form in equation (6.29), except that the constants in the boundary conditions, $A(U)$ and $B(U)$, are of opposite signs in equation (6.38). Hence, the solutions of $a_F(s)$ and $b_F(s)$ immediately follow from equations (6.33) and (6.34), respectively, by switching the signs of the constants $A(U)$ and $B(U)$ and are given as follows:

$$a_F(s) = -A(U) - \frac{2\tilde{\alpha}\tilde{m}}{\sigma^2} \ln \left| \frac{\sigma^2 B(U)(1 - e^{-\tilde{\alpha}s}) - 2\tilde{\alpha}}{2\tilde{\alpha}} \right| \qquad (6.39)$$

$$b_F(s) = \frac{2\tilde{\alpha}B(U)e^{-\tilde{\alpha}s}}{\sigma^2 B(U)(1 - e^{-\tilde{\alpha}s}) - 2\tilde{\alpha}} \qquad (6.40)$$

The convexity bias, given as the difference between the futures rate and the forward rate on a time deposit, is defined in equation (3.17) in Chapter 3 as follows:

$$Convexity\ Bias = L_F(t, S, T) - L_f(t, S, T)$$

$$= \frac{1 + L_F(t, S, T)\hat{U}}{\hat{U}} \left(1 - \frac{P(t, S)}{P(t, T)P_F^I(t, S, T)} \right)$$

$$= \frac{1 + L_F(t, S, T)\hat{U}}{\hat{U}} (1 - e^{A(s)-a_F(s)-A(\tau)-\left(B(s)-b_F(s)-B(\tau)\right)r(t)}), \qquad (6.41)$$

$$s = S - t \text{ and } \tau = T - t$$

The convexity bias is always positive; and, everything else held constant, a higher value of the short rate implies a higher convexity bias. This is because marking to market depends on the conditional volatility, which, in turn, depends on the level of the short rate under the CIR model. The convexity bias is also an increasing function of $\tilde{m}$ and a decreasing function of $\tilde{\alpha}$.

Valuing Options

CIR give the closed-form solution of a European call option on a zero-coupon bond by taking the following expectation at the current time t:

$$c_i(t) = \tilde{E}_t \left[\frac{c_i(S) = Max(P(S, T_i) - K_i, 0)}{e^{\int_t^S r(v)dv}} \right] \qquad (6.42)$$

where T_i is the maturity date of the \$1 face-value zero-coupon bond underlying the ith call option, S is the option expiration date, and K_i is the strike price. The subscript i is used in equation (6.42) so that the value of a call option on a coupon bond can be expressed without any alteration to the notation.

Taking the risk-neutral expectation, the European call price equals:

$$c_i(t) = P(t, \ T_i)\chi^2 \left(v_1; \ \frac{4\tilde{\alpha}\tilde{m}}{\sigma^2}, \ \frac{2\beta_3^2 r(t)e^{\beta_{1s}}}{\beta_2 + \beta_3 + B(U_i)} \right)$$

$$- K_i P(t, \ S)\chi^2 \left(v_2; \ \frac{4\tilde{\alpha}\tilde{m}}{\sigma^2}, \ \frac{2\beta_3^2 r(t)e^{\beta_{1s}}}{\beta_2 + \beta_3} \right) \qquad (6.43)$$

where

$$s = S - t$$

$$U_i = T_i - S$$

$$v_1 = 2(\beta_2 + \beta_3 + B(U_i)) \left(\frac{A(U_i) - \log(K_i)}{B(U_i)} \right)$$

$$v_2 = 2(\beta_2 + \beta_3) \left(\frac{A(U_i) - \log(K_i)}{B(U_i)} \right)$$

$$\beta_3 = \frac{2\beta_1}{\sigma^2(e^{\beta_{1s}} - 1)}$$

$$\beta_2 = \frac{\tilde{\alpha} + \beta_1}{\sigma^2}$$

$$\beta_1 = \sqrt{\tilde{\alpha}^2 + 2\sigma^2}$$

and $\chi(v; a, \ b)$ is the cumulative distribution of the noncentral chi-squared distribution with a degrees of freedom and parameter of noncentrality equal to b.

Using Jamshidian's trick, the value of a call option on a coupon bond can be given as a portfolio of call options on zero-coupon bonds as follows. Consider a European call option on a coupon bond with an expiration date S and exercise price K. The coupon bond has n cash flows maturing *after* the option expiration date S, given as C_i at time $T_i > S$, for $i = 1, \ 2, \ \dots, n$. The present value of these n cash flows is given as:

$$\sum_{i=1}^{n} C_i \times P(t, \ T_i) \qquad (6.44)$$

The value of the call option at expiration date S equals:

$$c(S) = Max \left[\left(\sum_{i=1}^{n} C_i \times P(S, \ T_i) \right) - K, \ 0 \right] \qquad (6.45)$$

Now find the rate $r^*(S)$, such that the following equality holds:

$$\sum_{i=1}^{n} C_i \times P(r^*(S), \ S, \ T_i) = K \qquad (6.46)$$

As demonstrated in Chapter 4, the current price of the call option on the coupon bond equals the price of the portfolio of call options on zero-coupon bonds, given as follows:

$$c(t) = \sum_{i=1}^{n} C_i \times c_i(t) \tag{6.47}$$

where $c_i(t)$ is the price of the European call option with expiration date S and exercise price K_i, written on a \$1 face-value zero-coupon bond maturing at time T_i, where $K_i = P(r^* (S), S, T_i)$. By computing the values of $c_i(t)$ using equation (6.43) for all $i = 1, 2, \ldots, n$ and substituting these in equation (6.47), the value of the call option on the coupon bond is obtained.

Using put-call parity, the closed-form solution of a European put option on a zero-coupon bond and a coupon bond can be immediately obtained. Also, using the equivalence relationships in Chapter 3, the closed-form solutions of caps and swaptions also follow from the solutions of options on zero-coupon bonds and coupon bonds, respectively.

INTEREST RATE TREES FOR THE COX, INGERSOLL, AND ROSS MODEL

Techniques such as analytical solutions, Fourier inversion methods, and Monte Carlo methods can compute prices of many European and path-dependent interest rate derivatives, but cannot generally be used for pricing derivatives with American features. In this section, we demonstrate how to build interest rate trees for pricing derivatives with American option features.

Binomial Tree for the CIR Model

The binomial interest rate tree for the CIR model is constructed using the risk-neutral short rate process given as follows:

$$dr(t) = \tilde{\alpha}(\tilde{m} - r(t))\, dt + \sigma\sqrt{r(t)}\, d\tilde{Z}(t) \tag{6.48}$$

Since the volatility of the interest rate is not constant, the tree for the interest rate process does not recombine. This happens because a down movement in the short rate followed by an up movement does not give the same value for the short rate as an up movement in the short rate followed by a down movement. Nelson and Ramaswamy (NR) [1990] provide a solution to this problem using a binomial tree framework. However, as we demonstrate later, the NR transform is not entirely satisfactory, and a simpler and more accurate approach has been recently provided by Nawalkha and Beliaeva [2007a] by modifying the original transform given by NR.

The basic idea underlying the NR approach is given next. Consider a general stochastic process for the short rate as follows:

$$dr(t) = \mu_r(r, t)\, dt + \sigma_r(r, t)\, dZ(t) \tag{6.49}$$

Since the volatility of short rate $\sigma_r(r, t)$ is a function of $r(t)$ and t, recombining trees cannot be constructed as easily as they were for the Gaussian models with constant short rate volatility in Chapters 4 and 5. NR suggest using a transform or a function of the short rate, such that the stochastic process of the transform has constant volatility. Let $X(t) = f(r(t), t)$ be this function, which is called the X-transform of the short rate. Using Ito's lemma:

$$dX(t) = \frac{\partial X(t)}{\partial r(t)}\, dr(t) + \frac{1}{2}\frac{\partial^2 X(t)}{\partial r(t)^2}(dr(t))^2 + \frac{\partial X(t)}{\partial t}\, dt \tag{6.50}$$

Substituting $dr(t)$ from equation (6.49) into equation (6.50), we get:

$$dX(t) = \mu(X, t)\, dt + \sigma(X, t)\, dZ(t) \tag{6.51}$$

where

$$\mu(X, t) = \frac{\partial X(t)}{\partial r(t)}\mu_r(r, t) + \frac{1}{2}\frac{\partial^2 X(t)}{\partial r(t)^2}(\sigma_r(r, t))^2 + \frac{\partial X(t)}{\partial t} \tag{6.52}$$

and

$$\sigma(X, t) = \frac{\partial X(t)}{\partial r(t)}\sigma_r(r, t) \tag{6.53}$$

In order to have constant volatility for the transform, NR set $\sigma(X, t)$ equal to 1 in equation (6.53), which implies:

$$\sigma(X, t) = \frac{\partial X(t)}{\partial r(t)}\sigma_r(r, t) = 1 \tag{6.54}$$

or

$$\frac{\partial X(t)}{\partial r(t)} = \frac{1}{\sigma_r(r, t)} \tag{6.55}$$

By solving the linear differential equation (6.55) using ordinary calculus, $X(t)$ is given as:

$$X(t) = \int^{r(t)} \frac{1}{\sigma_r(u, t)}\, du \tag{6.56}$$

Equation (6.56) gives a general formula for the X-transform. This formula applies to all processes for the short rate, when volatility is not constant.[3]

For the CIR model, the X-transform becomes:

$$X(t) = \int^{r(t)} \frac{1}{\sigma\sqrt{u}} \, du = \frac{2\sqrt{r(t)}}{\sigma} \tag{6.57}$$

By taking the inverse of equation (6.57), we get back the short rate as:

$$r(t) = \frac{X(t)^2 \sigma^2}{4} \tag{6.58}$$

The basic idea behind the NR approach is to obtain a recombining tree for the X-transform since it has constant volatility, and then use the inverse of the transform given by equation (6.58) to find the values of the short rate on the tree. Using Ito's lemma on equation (6.58) and using equation (6.57), the stochastic process for the $X(t)$ can be given as:

$$dX(t) = \mu(X, t) \, dt + d\tilde{Z}(t) \tag{6.59}$$

where

$$\mu(X, t) = \frac{1}{X(t)} \left(\frac{1}{2}\tilde{\alpha} \left(\frac{4\tilde{m}}{\sigma^2} - X(t)^2 \right) - \frac{1}{2} \right) \tag{6.60}$$

The diffusion element of equation (6.59) can be easily modeled using the tree shown in Figure 6.1. The $X(t)$ tree begins at $X(0) = [2\sqrt{r(0)}]/\sigma$; and then, using a discrete approximation Δt for the size of the time step dt, the up node is defined as $X_u = X(0) + \sqrt{\Delta t}$, and the down node is defined as $X_d = X(0) - \sqrt{\Delta t}$, and so on. However, the binomial probabilities cannot be easily obtained, as these probabilities depend upon the drift of $X(t)$ given in equation (6.60). Since $X(t)$ reaches zero boundary as shown in Figure 6.1 and $X(t)$ is in the denominator of equation (6.60), the drift $\mu(X, t)$ explodes as $X(t)$ goes to zero, which makes the probabilities explode. Li Ritchken and Sankarasubramanian [1995] use this approach by simply tweaking the $X(t)$ process slightly if $X(t)$ hits the zero boundary.[4] However, this is not an entirely satisfactory approach as the adjustment is quite arbitrary and may lead to slow convergence. Brigo and Mercurio [2001] suggest using a truncation level above zero, at which the tree is truncated. However, this is also arbitrary and cannot give proper solutions in high-volatility environments in which the zero boundary may be accessible by the short rate.[5]

Nelson and Ramaswamy Tree for the CIR Model   Unlike Li et al. [1995], Nelson and Ramaswamy [1990] use the X-tree in Figure 6.1 to only match the diffusion element of the the $X(t)$ process. For matching the drift of the short

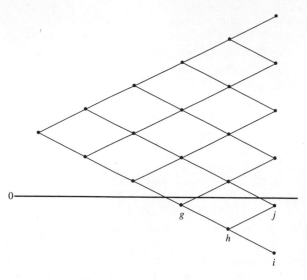

FIGURE 6.1   X-Process Tree

rate, NR first invert the short rate tree from the X-tree using the following inverse formula:

$$r(t) = \frac{X(t)^2 \sigma^2}{4} \text{ when } X(t) > 0, \text{ and}$$
$$= 0 \text{ when } X(t) \le 0 \qquad (6.61)$$

Hence, NR allows $r(t)$ to be positive only in the area where $X(t)$ is positive. When $X(t)$ becomes less than or equal to zero, $r(t)$ is set equal to zero. For example, $X(t)$ is negative in Figure 6.1 at nodes g, h, i, and j; and hence, $r(t) = 0$ at all these nodes. Using the inverse transform formula in equation (6.61), the node values for the tree for $r(t)$ are immediately computed from the node values of the tree for $X(t)$. NR match the drift of the short rate process using the tree for the short rate. However, a slight complication arises when the short rate is close to zero. For the binomial probabilities to remain between 0 and 1, a necessary condition is that the short rate plus its drift remain in between the short rate values at the up node and the down node, or:

$$r_d < r(t) + \tilde{\alpha}(\tilde{m} - r(t)) \, dt < r_u \qquad (6.62)$$

where r_d (r_u) is the value of the short rate at the down (up) node. Though this condition is generally met when short rate is far away from zero, it is violated when short rate is very close to zero, even as the time interval dt shrinks to zero. This is because the volatility of the short rate equals $\sigma\sqrt{r(t)}$ under the CIR model, and as $r(t)$ gets close to zero, the volatility goes to zero, too. An almost-zero volatility (at close-to-zero value of the short rate) implies that r_u and r_d cannot span the short rate plus its drift in equation (6.62), and hence, probabilities cannot remain between 0 and 1. When this happens, the only way to match the positive short rate drift is to make the up probability greater than 1 and the down probability less than 0, using the traditional binomial tree.

NR suggest a solution to the preceding problem by allowing the short rate to jump a *multiple* number of nodes when it reaches close to zero.

The multiple-node jumps occur from the nodes when either the short rate is below a certain critical positive value or when the short rate equals zero (note that the short rate is zero in the entire area below the zero line, including at nodes g, h, i, and j, in Figure 6.2). When the short rate is very small or equal to zero, then the volatility of short rate remains insignificantly different from zero and only the drift of the short rate—which remains significant—needs to be matched. However, since the volatility of the short rate is low at these levels, multiple-node jumps are required (as shown in Figure 6.2) to match the drift, without getting negative probabilities for the down moves (or greater than one probabilities for the up moves). For example, from node f, instead of moving up to node k, the upper branch moves to node m.

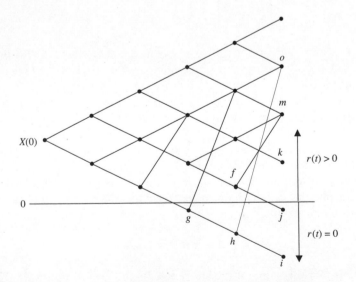

FIGURE 6.2 $X(t)$ Tree with Multiple-Node Jumps—NR Approach

In the region where $r(t)$ equals zero (i.e., nodes g, h, i, and j), the up branch must always go into the positive region, while the down branch stays in the zero region. For example, from node h, the up branch moves to node o. Without moving into positive region from the zero region, the short rate drift can never become positive. Recall that in the CIR model, the drift is always positive when the short rate is zero, since the risk-neutral speed of mean reversion and the risk-neutral long-term mean are either both positive or both negative (the latter occurs under the risk-neutral explosive process).

From the programming perspective, the main issue in building the short rate tree is to determine the path of the multiple-node jumps. Though NR provide a formula that at any given node determines exactly how many nodes to skip when multiple jumps occur, Nawalkha and Beliaeva (NB) [2007a] show that the NR formula is incorrect when the short rate is in the zero region (i.e., when the X-transform is less than or equal to zero). Using the NR formula for the multiple-node jumps in this case makes the variance of the change in the short rate significantly greater than zero, even though the short rate value is zero, which violates the condition that in the zero region, the short rate variance should be close to zero. Also, the short rate remains stuck in the zero-region with a higher probability. This inflates the prices of the bonds, consistent with the unusually large positive approximation errors reported by NR [1990] in many instances. In the following section, we describe the NB approach, which corrects the NR formula for determining the multiple jumps and also provides a *truncated tree* approach, which saves computation time.

Nawalkha and Beliaeva Tree for the CIR Model   NB truncate the X-tree at zero as shown in Figure 6.3. At any given time t, the value of $X(t)$ is forced to equal zero at the first node at which $X(t)$ is less than or equal to zero. The number of nodes to be stored reduces considerably since $r(t)$, which is computed using the inverse transform of $X(t)$, can take zero values only on a *single* path (as opposed to on multiple paths in the region below the zero line using the traditional NR approach as shown in Figure 6.2) shown with the arrows.

Using the NB approach, the inverse transform formula to obtain the short rate $r(t)$ given in equation (6.61) changes as follows:

$$r(t) = \frac{X(t)^2 \sigma^2}{4} \text{ when } X(t) > 0, \text{ and}$$
$$r(t) = 0 \text{ when } X(t) = 0 \tag{6.63}$$

The tree may be truncated even above zero using the NB approach, if the process requires this to be so (based on the discussion to follow), but not arbitrarily, as suggested by some researchers. This is shown in Figure 6.4.

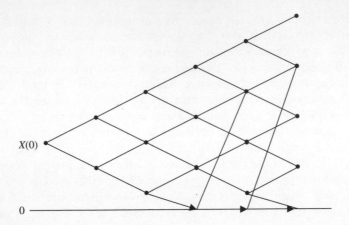

FIGURE 6.3 $X(t)$ Tree with Multiple-Node Jumps—NB Approach

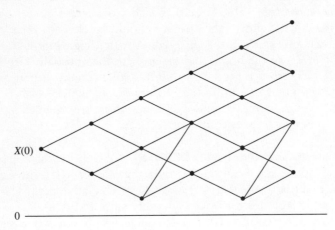

FIGURE 6.4 $X(t)$ Tree with Multiple-Node Jumps Truncated above Zero—NB Approach

The tree branches cannot go to zero in Figure 6.4 because from the second-to-last row from the zero line, both branches move up in order to match the drift of the short rate while keeping the probabilities positive. In fact, for certain parameter choices (e.g., when volatility parameter σ is very low), the CIR model can never allow the short rate to go to zero. An advantage to the truncated tree approach of NB illustrated in Figure 6.3 and Figure 6.4 is that it leads to significant savings in computation time, due to the reduction in the number of paths by the truncation process.

The construction of the truncated tree using the NB approach can be demonstrated using the following two steps. Similar to the NR approach, multiple-node jumps are required to match the drift of the short rate when it is close to zero or at zero. The first step determines the exact path of the tree, with or without multiple-node jumps, when the short rate is strictly positive; the second step determines the path of the tree, with or without multiple-node jumps, when the short rate is at zero.

Step 1. The value of X(t) > 0 and, hence, r(t) > 0. Under this case, the up and down moves are given as follows:

$$X_u = X(t) + (J+1)\sqrt{\Delta t}$$
$$X_d = Max\left(0, X(t) + (J-1)\sqrt{\Delta t}\right) \tag{6.64}$$

where J is an integer such that:

$$J = \begin{cases} Z & \text{if } Z \text{ is even} \\ Z+1 & \text{if } Z \text{ is odd} \end{cases} \tag{6.65}$$

and

$$Z = FLOOR\left(\frac{\sqrt{X(t)^2\sigma^2(1 - \tilde{\alpha}\Delta t) + 4\tilde{\alpha}\tilde{m}\Delta t} - X(t)\sigma}{\sigma\sqrt{\Delta t}}\right) \tag{6.66}$$

where $FLOOR(x)$ is the integer value of x, *rounded down* (e.g., $FLOOR(2.3) = 2$, and $FLOOR(-2.7) = -3$).

The value of Z in equation (6.66) is computed using the condition that the probabilities of the up and down nodes remain positive only if the mean value of the short rate remains in between its two realizations at the up and down nodes, or:

$$r_d < r(t) + \tilde{\alpha}(\tilde{m} - r(t))\, dt < r_u \tag{6.67}$$

Equations (6.64), (6.65), and (6.66) are obtained by imposing the restriction in equation (6.67) and by using the relationship of $r, r_u,$ and r_d, with the corresponding values of $X, X_u,$ and X_d given by the inverse transform in equation (6.63).

The probabilities of the up and down nodes can be now computed to match the drift of the short rate and are given as follows:

$$p_u = \frac{\tilde{\alpha}(\tilde{m} - r(t))\Delta t + r(t) - r_d}{r_u - r_d} \tag{6.68}$$

$$p_d = 1 - p_u$$

Equation (6.65) is needed to ensure that the up and down nodes *remain on the tree*. Equation (6.65) gives the closed-form solution of J, which specifies the path of the tree exactly at all nodes when both $X(t)$ and $r(t)$ are strictly positive. The value of J in equation (6.65) guarantees that the probabilities are well behaved, that is, $0 \leq p_u, p_d \leq 1$, in equation (6.68). The value of J also gives an *analytical solution* to equations (61) and (62) in NR [1990, p. 412] when both $X(t)$ and $r(t)$ are strictly positive. The bottom row of nodes corresponding to the NB truncated tree in Figure 6.3 has $X(t) = 0$ and $r(t) = 0$. This case is considered in step 2.

Step 2. The value of X(t) = 0 and hence, r(t) = 0. Under this case, the values of the up node and the down node must satisfy the following constraints. The up node is the node *closest* to the truncation line of zero in Figure 6.3, at which the inequality given in the following equation is satisfied:

$$X_u \geq \frac{2}{\sigma} \sqrt{\tilde{a}\tilde{m}\Delta t} \qquad\qquad (6.69)$$

Also, as shown in Figure 6.3, the down node simply moves horizontally and stays at zero, or:

$$X_d = 0 \qquad\qquad (6.70)$$

It can be shown that though equation (61) in NR [1990, p. 412] satisfies equation (6.69) *it does not select the node that is closest in value to zero.* In fact, it selects a node that is often far above zero value, which makes the variance of the change in the short rate significantly different from zero, violating the condition that the short rate variance converges to zero when the short rate converges to zero. Also, because the NR equation (61) selects the up node X_u far above zero, it gives a much higher probability to X_d in order to match the drift of the short rate. This keeps the short rate stuck at zero with a much higher probability than is needed and explains why the simulations by NR [1990] generate very high positive approximation errors for pricing bonds in some instances.

    The truncated binomial approach given here also has an advantage over approaches suggested by Li, Ritchken, and Sankarasubramanian [1995] and Acharya and Carpenter [2002]. These authors model the probabilities and multiple jumps using the drift of the X-transform itself, defined as $\mu(X, t)$ in equation (6.60). However, note that $\mu(X, t)$ as defined in equation (6.60) becomes very large as $X(t)$ approaches zero, becoming infinite if $X(t)$ hits exactly zero. This singularity at $X(t) = 0$ forces these authors to perturb the X-transform slightly in an ad-hoc manner.[6] Our approach does not require such perturbing since we use the drift of the short rate and not the drift of the X-transform for obtaining the probabilities in equation (6.68), for defining J for the multiple-node jumps in equation (6.65) in step 1, and for solving equation (6.69) in step 2.

An application of the truncated binomial tree methodology using the NB approach is given in the following example.

Example 6.1 Consider the valuation of a zero-coupon bond that pays $100 ($F = 100$) at the end of one year ($T = 1$). Assume that the risk-neutral parameters of the short rate process are given as: $r_0 = 6\%$, $\tilde{\alpha} = 0.5$, $\tilde{m} = 6\%$, and $\sigma = 40\%$. Consider using a five-step tree for pricing this bond (hence, $\Delta t = 1/5 = 0.2$). The binomial tree for this example is illustrated in Figure 6.5. Each node consists of three different rows. The number in the top row is the bond price obtained by discounting future bond values using the short rate at the given node. The number in the middle row is the value of $X(t)$ at that node. The number in the bottom row is the interest rate value at the node obtained using the inverse transform in equation (6.63). The tree is truncated at $X(t) = 0$.

Now consider a specific node, for example, the node N_{33}. At this node, $X(t = 0.6) = 0.778$. This corresponds to the interest rate of:

$$r(t = 0.6) = \frac{0.778^2 \times 0.4^2}{4} = 0.024$$

Next determine the value of J at this node using equation (6.65):

$$Z = FLOOR\left(\frac{\sqrt{(0.778)^2(0.4)^2(1 - (0.5)(0.2)) + 4(0.5)(0.06)(0.2)} - (0.778)(0.4)}{0.4\sqrt{0.2}}\right)$$

$$= FLOOR(0.124) = 0$$

Since Z is even, using equation (6.65), $J = Z = 0$. Therefore, the up and down nodes are N_{43} and N_{44}. At these nodes, the corresponding values of the short rate are $r_u = 0.06$ and $r_d = 0.004$ as shown in Figure 6.5. The binomial probabilities are computed using equation (6.68) as follows:

$$p_u = \frac{0.5 \times (0.06 - 0.024) \times 0.2 + (0.024 - 0.004)}{0.06 - 0.004} = 0.42$$

$$p_d = 1 - 0.42 = 0.58$$

The bond value at node N_{33} is computed as follows:

$$P_{33} = \frac{98.81 \times 0.42 + 99.91 \times 0.58}{e^{0.024 \times 0.2}} = 98.97$$

At each node:
Top value = bond price, $P(t, T)$
Middle value = transformed process, $X(t)$
Bottom value = interest rate process, $r(t)$

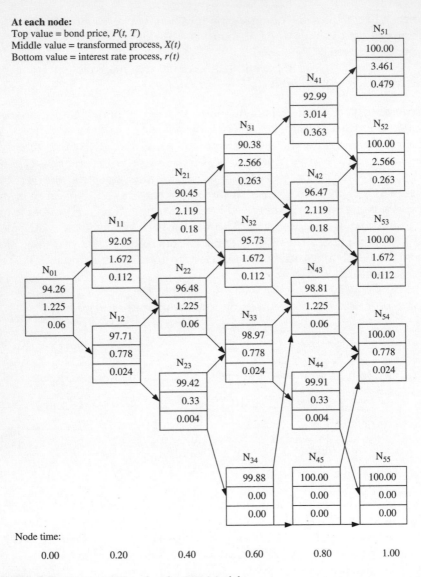

FIGURE 6.5 Binomial Tree for the CIR Model

Next consider one of the truncation nodes, N_{34}. At this node $X(t = 0.6) = 0$, and hence $r(t = 0.6) = 0$. This corresponds to step 2 given earlier, and the number of nodes to be skipped to get to the up node is determined by using equation (6.69). The down node just moves horizontally and stays at zero.

Using equation (6.69), the up node is that node at which the value of X_u is closest to the truncation line of zero and satisfies the following constraint:

$$X_u \geq \frac{2}{0.4}\sqrt{(0.5)(0.06)(0.2)} = 0.3873$$

By inspection of Figure 6.5, this node must be N_{43}. Hence, in this case, the transition will be to nodes N_{43} and N_{45} with $r_u = 0.06$ and $r_d = 0$. The binomial probabilities are computed using equation (6.68) as follows:

$$p_u = \frac{0.5 \times (0.06 - 0) \times 0.2 + (0 - 0)}{0.06 - 0} = 0.1$$

$$p_d = 1 - 0.1 = 0.9$$

And the bond value at node N_{34} is given as follows:

$$P_{34} = \frac{98.81 \times 0.1 + 100 \times 0.9}{e^{0 \times 0.2}} = 99.88$$

By following a similar procedure at all nodes, the bond price at time 0 is obtained as $P(0) = \$94.26$. With a 100-step tree, the price of the bond is $94.28, which is the same price given by the closed-form solution.

Table 6.1 examines the numerical accuracy of the truncated NB binomial tree in valuing discount bonds under the assumption that the short rate follows the CIR process. The parameter values are given as follows. The risk-neutral speed of mean reversion $\tilde{\alpha}$ is varied from 0.01 to 0.5, the risk-neutral long run mean $\tilde{m}$ is fixed at 8 percent, and the interest rate volatility σ is varied from 0.1 to 0.5. The maturity of bonds T is varied from one month to 5 years, the bond face value F is assumed to be $100. The zero-coupon bond prices are computed for two values of the short rate, given as 5 percent and 11 percent. The bond prices are solved using 50 steps and 200 steps.

Table 6.1 compares the bond prices obtained through the NB approach to the NR approach (see Table 2 in Nelson and Ramaswamy [1990]). NR use the same parameters given in Table 6.1 in their simulations. Bond prices from both approaches are compared to the closed-form solution of the bond price using the CIR model. In general, the accuracy of both trees decreases with an increase in interest rate volatility and a longer time to maturity, but increases with an increase in the number of steps used. But clearly, the errors from the NB truncated tree are lower than the corresponding errors from the NR approach. As mentioned earlier, the high errors using the NR approach result from the cases when the transformed X-process takes negative values;

TABLE 6.1 Prices of Zero-Coupon Bonds for the CIR Term Structure Model, Using the NB Approach versus the NR Approach (see Nelson and Ramaswamy, Table 2)

				N				CIR
		Maturity		50		200		True
$\tilde{\alpha}$	σ	(months)	r_0	NR	NB	NR	NB	Price
0.01	0.1	1	0.05	99.5841	99.5841	99.5841	99.5841	99.5841
0.01	0.1	1	0.11	99.0877	99.0876	99.0877	99.0876	99.0876
0.01	0.1	6	0.05	97.5290	97.5284	97.5285	97.5284	97.5284
0.01	0.1	6	0.11	94.6570	94.6542	94.6549	94.6542	94.6542
0.01	0.1	12	0.05	95.1192	95.1166	95.1173	95.1166	95.1166
0.01	0.1	12	0.11	89.6235	89.6123	89.6157	89.6129	89.6131
0.01	0.1	60	0.05	78.3999	78.3296	78.3665	78.3412	78.3451
0.01	0.1	60	0.11	59.2818	59.0976	59.1727	59.1262	59.1358
0.1	0.1	1	0.05	99.5832	99.5832	99.5832	99.5832	99.5832
0.1	0.1	1	0.11	99.0886	99.0885	99.0886	99.0886	99.0886
0.1	0.1	6	0.05	97.4973	97.4967	97.4963	97.4962	97.4960
0.1	0.1	6	0.11	94.6877	94.6848	94.6860	94.6853	94.6855
0.1	0.1	12	0.05	94.9975	94.9948	94.9937	94.9930	94.9924
0.1	0.1	12	0.11	89.7367	89.7258	89.7307	89.7279	89.7287
0.1	0.1	60	0.05	76.0941	76.0230	76.0236	76.0057	76.0000
0.1	0.1	60	0.11	60.5878	60.4174	60.4942	60.4515	60.4628
0.1	0.5	1	0.05	99.5833	99.5833	99.5833	99.5833	99.5833
0.1	0.5	1	0.11	99.0889	99.0888	99.0888	99.0888	99.0888
0.1	0.5	6	0.05	97.5287	97.5193	97.5293	97.5194	97.5194
0.1	0.5	6	0.11	94.7384	94.7327	94.7370	94.7343	94.7349
0.1	0.5	12	0.05	95.2503	95.1603	95.2535	95.1625	95.1632
0.1	0.5	12	0.11	90.0911	90.0635	90.1101	90.0730	90.0762
0.1	0.5	60	0.05	87.1194	83.3398	87.4445	83.4422	83.4832
0.1	0.5	60	0.11	75.1890	72.2953	74.7616	72.4837	72.5572
0.5	0.5	1	0.05	99.5793	99.5793	99.5792	99.5792	99.5792
0.5	0.5	1	0.11	99.0928	99.0928	99.0929	99.0928	99.0929
0.5	0.5	6	0.05	97.3993	97.3865	97.3959	97.3848	97.3843
0.5	0.5	6	0.11	94.8598	94.8523	94.8618	94.8552	94.8562
0.5	0.5	12	0.05	94.9097	94.6644	94.9745	94.6605	94.6592
0.5	0.5	12	0.11	90.5151	90.4130	90.5427	90.4234	90.4269
0.5	0.5	60	0.05	76.0322	74.7386	86.9128	74.8087	74.8289
0.5	0.5	60	0.11	75.1403	68.4997	77.4502	68.6001	68.6361

and, hence, the short rate is set to zero. In these cases, equation (61) in NR selects the up node for the short rate that is *significantly farther from zero* than required to simply match the drift of the short rate. This makes the variance of the change in the short rate significantly higher than required. Since the variance should be insignificantly different from zero when the short rate is zero, this error leads to upward biases in the bond prices caused by a significantly higher probability of the short rate remaining at zero.

The upward biases in the bond prices using the NR approach are especially large when the volatility of the short rate is high and when bond maturity is long. For example, for $T = 5$, $N = 200$, $\sigma = 0.5$, and $r_0 = 11\%$, the bond price computed using the NB approach is \$68.60, while the bond price using the NR approach is \$77.45, and the CIR closed-form solution is \$68.64.

Trinomial Tree for the CIR Model

Though trinomial trees have been constructed for Gaussian models by Hull and White [1994a, 1994b, 1996] and others, these trees have been difficult to create when the short rate follows a square process as in the CIR model. NB [2007a] provide a trinomial tree for the CIR model using the generalization of the truncated binomial tree approach given in the previous section. It is well known that trinomial trees are more accurate than binomial trees, when using fewer steps in the tree. As the number of steps increases, the binomial and trinomial trees converge rapidly.

A trinomial tree allows three branches from a given node $X(t)$. Typically, the up node is given as $X(t) + b\sigma\sqrt{\Delta t}$, the middle node stays at $X(t)$, and the bottom node is given as $X(t) - b\sigma\sqrt{\Delta t}$, where b is a parameter greater than 1. The parameter b cannot be less than 1 because a value of $b < 1$ makes the middle node probability negative, in order to match the instantaneous variance of the X process. If $b = 1$, then the trinomial model is similar to a binomial model,[7] since the middle node probability becomes zero. A typical value of b used by researchers is $\sqrt{3}$ for trinomial trees for the Gaussian models.

Using the traditional NR method, the stochastic process for the X-transform given in equation (6.59) can be approximated using the trinomial tree shown in Figure 6.6. The tree starts at $X(0) = 2\sqrt{r(0)}/\sigma$; then, using a discrete approximation Δt for the size of the time step dt, the up node is defined as $X_u = X(0) + b\sqrt{\Delta t}$, the down node is defined as $X_d = X(0) - b\sqrt{\Delta t}$, and the middle node is defined as the starting value $X(0)$. The tree recombines, as the up node followed by the down node is the same as the down node followed by the up node, or $X_{ud} = X_u - b\sqrt{\Delta t} = X(0) = X_d + b\sqrt{\Delta t} = X_{du}$.

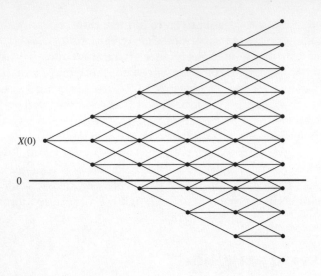

FIGURE 6.6 X-Process Trinomial Tree

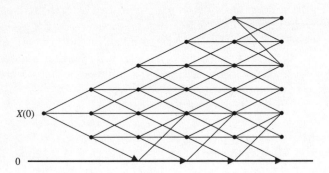

FIGURE 6.7 Truncated X-Process Trinomial Tree

Using the NB approach, the trinomial tree is truncated at zero as shown in Figure 6.7. Similar to the binomial tree, the trinomial tree must allow multiple-node jumps to match the drift when the short rate is at zero or close to zero. For the trinomial tree, we also allow multiple-node jumps in the top area of the tree, where the short rate becomes very high, making the short rate drift highly negative. Due to the occurrence of multiple-node jumps on both ends, the tree is truncated both from below and from above, which saves considerable computational time. To capture the drift using multiple-node jumps on a trinomial tree, the following restriction must apply on the parameter b given in the previous paragraph: $1 \le b \le \sqrt{2}$.

We show in the following discussion that if this restriction is violated, then multiple-node jumps cannot be modeled while simultaneously keeping all probabilities non negative. Hence, $b = \sqrt{3}$ cannot be used, as it is generally used in modeling of the trinomial trees for Gaussian models.

An important difference between the binomial tree given in the previous section and the trinomial tree modeled in this section is that the trinomial tree matches the mean and the variance of $dX(t)$ when $r(t) > 0$, but matches the mean of $dr(t)$ when $r(t) = 0$. The main reason behind using the mean and variance of $dX(t)$ instead of $dr(t)$ when $r(t) > 0$ is that when the parameter b is greater than one (which is required for the middle node probability to remain positive), it does not allow a straightforward computation of the path of multiple-node jumps by using the mean and variance of $dr(t)$.

Another difference between the binomial tree and the trinomial tree relates to the distance of the second to last row of nodes from the truncation line of zero. As shown in Figure 6.7, the nodes in the second to last row are exactly $b\sigma\sqrt{\Delta t}$ distance away from the truncation line. In fact, the value of the parameter b is selected such that the distance between any two adjacent rows in Figure 6.7 is equal to $b\sigma\sqrt{\Delta t}$. This is done to avoid the $X(t)$-process from coming extremely close to zero (e.g., $X(t)$ of the order $O(\Delta t^2)$), and still not hitting zero, which can create singularity problems due to the explosion of the drift of $X(t)$ in equation (6.60) (as in the model of Li et al. [1995]).

Due to the structure of the trinomial tree shown in Figure 6.7, the value of the parameter b must be defined properly. As shown later, in order to keep the probabilities nonnegative, when multiple-node jumps occur, b must be in the following range:

$$1 \leq b \leq \sqrt{2} \tag{6.71}$$

We choose the value of $b = \sqrt{1.5} +$ adjustment term. The adjustment term is small and keeps b between 1 and $\sqrt{2}$, as required by equation (6.71). As the number of steps becomes large, the adjustment term goes to zero. A negative adjustment term contracts the distance between any two adjacent nodes, while a positive adjustment term expands the distance between any two adjacent nodes. The tree contraction is illustrated in Figure 6.8. The tree expansion is illustrated in Figure 6.9.

Either contraction or expansion allows the nodes in the second to last row to be exactly $b\sigma\sqrt{\Delta t}$ distance away from the truncation line of zero. Substituting $X(t) = b\sigma\sqrt{\Delta t}$ in equation (6.60), it is easy to show that $\mu(X, t)\Delta t$ does not explode, and hence, X_u can be found on the tree, such that $0 = X_d < X(t) + \mu(X, t)\Delta t < X_u$. In other words, doing this avoids the $X(t)$-process from coming extremely close to zero and still not hitting zero,

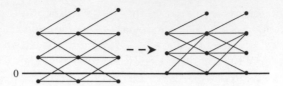

FIGURE 6.8 Trinomial Tree Contraction

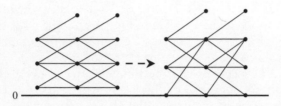

FIGURE 6.9 Trinomial Tree Expansion

which can create singularity problems due to the explosion of the drift of $X(t)$ in equation (6.60).

We choose between contraction and expansion by selecting that value of b that comes closest to the initial value of $\sqrt{1.5}$. This is done by first computing the values of b_e and b_c, where b_e corresponds to tree expansion and b_c corresponds to tree contraction:

$$b_e = \frac{X(0)/\sqrt{\Delta t}}{INT\left(\dfrac{X(0)}{\sqrt{1.5\Delta t}}\right)} \tag{6.72}$$

$$b_c = \frac{X(0)/\sqrt{\Delta t}}{INT\left(\dfrac{X(0)}{\sqrt{1.5\Delta t}}+1\right)} \tag{6.73}$$

where INT(.) gives the integer value. The final value of b is the value from equations (6.72) and (6.73) that is closest to the starting value of $\sqrt{1.5}$ in *absolute distance*. Hence:

$$b = \begin{cases} b_c \text{ if } |b_c - \sqrt{1.5}| < |b_e - \sqrt{1.5}| \\ b_e \text{ otherwise} \end{cases} \tag{6.74}$$

With this procedure, the value of b tends to its starting value of $\sqrt{1.5}$ as the number of steps in the tree becomes large and the step size Δt tends to zero.

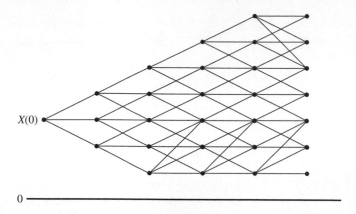

FIGURE 6.10 Multiple Jumps in a Trinomial Tree

Note that just knowing the value of $X(0)$ and the step size Δt are sufficient for obtaining the value of b in equation (6.74), using equations (6.72) and (6.73).

As in the binomial model, multiple-node jumps must be allowed to ensure that probabilities are well behaved. The multiple-node jumps may occur either when the tree reaches zero as in Figure 6.7 or even when the tree is above zero as in Figure 6.10. We now demonstrate how to determine the path of the tree with multiple-node jumps and how the probabilities are computed using the following two steps.

Step 1. The values of $r(t) > 0$ and $X(t) > 0$. Under this case, the up, middle, and down moves are given as follows:

$$X_u = X + b(J + 1)\sqrt{\Delta t}$$

$$X_m = X + bJ\sqrt{\Delta t} \qquad (6.75)$$

$$X_d = X + b(J - 1)\sqrt{\Delta t}$$

where b is computed as in equation (6.74) and J is given as follows:

$$J = FLOOR\left(\frac{\mu(X, t)\sqrt{\Delta t}}{b} + \frac{1}{b^2}\right) \qquad (6.76)$$

where $\mu(X, t)\Delta t$ is the drift of the $X(t)$ process. The trinomial probabilities for matching the drift $\mu(X, t)\Delta t$ and the variance Δt of the $X(t)$ process (see equations (6.59) and (6.60)), using the three nodes in equation (6.75), are given as follows:

$$p_u = \frac{1}{2b^2} - \frac{J}{2} + \frac{1}{2b}\mu(X, t)\sqrt{\Delta t}$$

$$p_d = \frac{1}{2b^2} + \frac{J}{2} - \frac{1}{2b}\mu(X, t)\sqrt{\Delta t} \qquad (6.77)$$

$$p_m = 1 - \frac{1}{b^2}$$

The probabilities in equation (6.77) are obtained as follows. First, setting $p_u = 1/(2b^2) + A$, $p_d = 1/(2b^2) - A$, and $p_m = 1 - 1/(b^2)$ ensures that the variance of $dX(t)$ using the three nodes in equation (6.75) equals Δt when $J = 0$. By solving for the mean of $dX(t)$, based upon X-tree values defined in equation (6.75), for any $J \geq 0$, gives $A = -J/2 + (1/(2b))\mu(X, t)\sqrt{\Delta t}$. Further, since only the mean and not the variance needs to be matched when $J > 0$, the probabilities in equation (6.77) remain valid even though they do not match the variance when $J > 0$. The variance remains insignificantly close to zero when $J > 0$, and hence, matching the mean is sufficient. Finally, since the tree is naturally truncated from above as soon as $J < 0$, the probabilities defined in equation (6.77) are sufficient for modeling the $X(t)$ process.

It can be seen that b must be greater than 1 in order to have a positive middle node probability p_m. Also, the up and down probabilities must also be positive and less than $1 - p_m$, or $1/b^2 \geq p_u, p_d \geq 0$. The last restriction implies the following inequality (based upon the definitions of p_u and p_d in equation (6.77)):

$$\frac{\mu(X, t)\sqrt{\Delta t}}{b} + \frac{1}{b^2} \geq J \geq \frac{\mu(X, t)\sqrt{\Delta t}}{b} - \frac{1}{b^2} \qquad (6.78)$$

Equation (6.78) is used to define the value of J in equation (6.76). To ensure that some integer value of J always exists, the value of b in equation (6.78) must be less than or equal to $\sqrt{2}$. If $b > \sqrt{2}$, then no integer value may exist, which would satisfy equation (6.78).[8] Hence, b must satisfy the following constraint:

$$1 \leq b \leq \sqrt{2} \qquad (6.79)$$

When $J = 0$, the short rate tree has no multiple-node jumps, and the branches move as shown in the middle section of Figure 6.10. When $J \geq 1$, the tree branches move upward, as shown at the bottom level of nodes in Figure 6.10. When $J \leq -1$, the tree branches move downward, as shown at the top level of nodes in Figure 6.10. Hence, the tree is truncated both from above and below. Often, truncation may not occur from below until the short rate becomes exactly equal to zero. This case is considered next.

Step 2. The values of X(t) = 0 and r(t) = 0. When $X(t)$ and $r(t)$ are equal to zero, only the mean of the short rate process needs to be matched. The up node is selected as the node *closest* to the truncation line of zero in Figure 6.7, at which the inequality given in equation (6.80) is satisfied:

$$X_u = X + b(J + 1)\sqrt{\Delta t} = b(J + 1)\sqrt{\Delta t} \geq \frac{2}{\sigma}\sqrt{\tilde{\alpha}\tilde{m}\Delta t} \qquad (6.80)$$

such that $J \geq 1$. As shown in Figure 6.7, the down node simply moves horizontally and stays at zero, or:

$$X_d = 0 \qquad (6.81)$$

We do not need the middle node, since the variance of the short rate is zero when $r = 0$ and only the mean of the short rate needs to be matched. The probabilities of the up and the down nodes are computed using the binomial method to match the drift of the short rate, and are given as follows:

$$p_u = \frac{\tilde{\alpha}(\tilde{m} - r)\Delta t + r - r_d}{r_u - r_d} = \frac{\tilde{\alpha}\tilde{m}\Delta t}{r_u} \qquad (6.82)$$

$$p_d = 1 - p_u$$

An application of the trinomial tree is illustrated by example 6.2.

Example 6.2 Consider the discount bond given in Example 6.1 ($F = 100$, $T = 1$, $r_0 = 6\%$, $\tilde{\alpha} = 0.5$, $\tilde{m} = 6\%$, and $\sigma = 40\%$). Consider using a five-step trinomial tree for pricing this bond ($\Delta t = 0.2$) depicted in Figure 6.11. Each node consists of three rows. The number in the top row is the bond price obtained as the discounted expected value of the future bond prices; the number in the middle row is the value of the transformed process, $X(t)$, and the number in the bottom row is the short rate. The tree is truncated at $X(t) = 0$.

The value of b is computed using equations (6.72), (6.73), and (6.74) to ensure that the X-process values at the last level of nodes are *exactly* zero.

$$b_e = \frac{1.225}{\left\lceil \dfrac{1.225}{\sqrt{1.5 \times 0.2}}\right\rceil \times \sqrt{0.2}} = \frac{1.225}{2 \times \sqrt{0.2}} = 1.369$$

$$b_c = \frac{1.225}{\left\lceil \dfrac{1.225}{\sqrt{1.5 \times 0.2}} + 1\right\rceil \times \sqrt{0.2}} = \frac{1.225}{3 \times \sqrt{0.2}} = 0.913$$

At each node:
Top value = bond price, $P(t, T)$
Middle value = transformed process, $X(t)$
Bottom value = interest rate process, $r(t)$

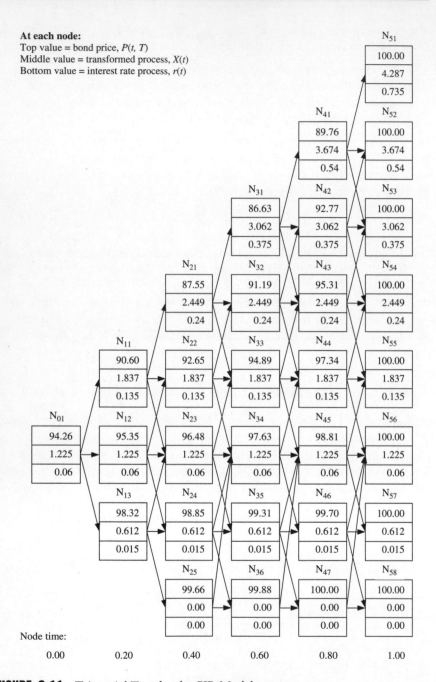

FIGURE 6.11 Trinomial Tree for the CIR Model

Since $b_e = 1.369$ is closer in absolute distance to $\sqrt{1.5}$, $b = 1.369$ is selected using equation (6.74).

Now consider a given node, for example, node N_{31}. At this node, $X(t = 0.6) = 3.062$. This corresponds to the short rate value of:

$$r = \frac{3.062^2 \times 0.4^2}{4} = 0.375$$

Since $r > 0$, the value of J at this node is computed using equation (6.76) in step 1 as follows:

$$\mu(X, t) = \frac{1}{3.062} \left(\frac{1}{2} \times 0.5 \left(\frac{4 \times 0.06}{0.4^2} - 3.062^2 \right) - \frac{1}{2} \right) = -0.806$$

$$J = FLOOR \left(\frac{-0.806 \times \sqrt{0.2}}{1.369} + \frac{1}{1.369^2} \right) = FLOOR(0.27) = 0$$

Since $J = 0$, the next step transitions will be to nodes N_{41}, N_{42}, and N_{43}. The trinomial probabilities are computed using equation (6.77) as follows:

$$p_u = \frac{1}{2 \times 1.369^2} - \frac{0}{2} + \frac{1}{2 \times 1.369} \times (-0.806) \times \sqrt{0.2} = 0.135$$

$$p_d = \frac{1}{2 \times 1.369^2} + \frac{0}{2} - \frac{1}{2 \times 1.369} \times (-0.806) \times \sqrt{0.2} = 0.398$$

$$p_m = 1 - \frac{1}{1.369^2} = 0.466$$

The bond price at node N_{31} is given as follows:

$$P_{31} = \frac{89.76 \times 0.135 + 92.77 \times 0.398 + 95.31 \times 0.467}{e^{0.375 \times 0.2}} = 86.63$$

Now consider one of the truncation nodes, for example, node N_{36}. At this node $X = 0$, and hence $r = 0$. Since this corresponds to the case in step 2, the middle node probability is zero, so that there are only two branches as shown in Figure 6.11. The number of nodes to be skipped to get to the up node is determined by using equation (6.80). The down node just moves horizontally and stays at zero. Using equation (6.80), the up node is the node at which the value of X_u is closest to the truncation line of zero and that satisfies the following constraint:

$$X_u = b(J + 1)\sqrt{\Delta t} \geq \frac{2}{0.4}\sqrt{(0.5)(0.06)(0.2)} = 0.3873$$

TABLE 6.2 Prices of Zero-Coupon Bonds for the CIR Term Structure Model, Using the Trinomial Tree versus the Binomial Tree, Using the NB Approach

				N				CIR
		Maturity		100		500		True
$\tilde{\alpha}$	σ	(years)	r_0	BIN	TRIN	BIN	TRIN	Price
0.1	0.1	0.5	0.05	97.4963	97.4963	97.4961	97.4961	97.4960
0.1	0.1	0.5	0.11	94.6851	94.6851	94.6854	94.6854	94.6855
0.1	0.1	1	0.05	94.9936	94.9936	94.9927	94.9937	94.9924
0.1	0.1	1	0.11	89.7272	89.7272	89.7284	89.7284	89.7287
0.1	0.1	5	0.05	76.0114	76.0114	76.0023	76.0023	76.0000
0.1	0.1	5	0.11	60.4401	60.4397	60.4583	60.4582	60.4628
0.1	0.1	10	0.05	56.7051	56.7127	56.6945	56.6954	56.6919
0.1	0.1	10	0.11	40.0995	40.0993	40.1351	40.1348	40.1440
0.1	0.5	0.5	0.05	97.5193	97.5193	97.5194	97.5194	97.5194
0.1	0.5	0.5	0.11	94.7338	94.7338	94.7347	94.7347	94.7349
0.1	0.5	1	0.05	95.1617	95.1615	95.1629	95.1629	95.1632
0.1	0.5	1	0.11	90.0698	90.0694	90.0749	90.0748	90.0762
0.1	0.5	5	0.05	83.4166	83.4203	83.4682	83.4688	83.4832
0.1	0.5	5	0.11	72.4238	72.3771	72.5290	72.5241	72.5572
0.1	0.5	10	0.05	75.1244	75.3726	75.2722	75.3189	75.3333
0.1	0.5	10	0.11	64.7359	64.8255	64.9397	64.9699	65.0224
0.5	0.5	0.5	0.05	97.3854	97.3854	97.3845	97.3845	97.3843
0.5	0.5	0.5	0.11	94.8543	94.8542	94.8558	94.8558	94.8562
0.5	0.5	1	0.05	94.6618	94.6617	94.6597	94.6597	64.6592
0.5	0.5	1	0.11	90.4199	90.4195	90.4255	90.4254	90.4269
0.5	0.5	5	0.05	74.7885	74.8230	74.8198	74.8227	74.8289
0.5	0.5	5	0.11	68.5585	68.5741	68.6211	68.6196	68.6361
0.5	0.5	10	0.05	55.6141	55.8913	55.7938	55.8077	55.8290
0.5	0.5	10	0.11	50.9397	51.0866	51.0918	51.1003	51.1349
0.5	0.8	0.5	0.05	97.4177	97.4177	97.4172	97.4172	97.4171
0.5	0.8	0.5	0.11	94.9201	94.9200	94.9224	94.9224	94.9230
0.5	0.8	1	0.05	94.8611	94.8610	94.8616	94.8617	94.8618
0.5	0.8	1	0.11	90.7980	90.7962	90.8072	90.8070	90.8096
0.5	0.8	5	0.05	78.2241	78.4128	78.3477	78.3773	78.3804
0.5	0.8	5	0.11	72.9841	73.1062	73.1307	73.1410	73.1629
0.5	0.8	10	0.05	61.8156	63.2809	62.1703	62.2726	62.2540
0.5	0.8	10	0.11	57.5318	58.2924	57.9930	58.0741	58.0983

such that $J \geq 1$. The previous equation is satisfied for $J = 1$, since:

$$X_u = 1.369(1 + 1)\sqrt{0.2} = 1.225 \geq 0.3873$$

Hence, $J = 1$ and the up node moves to N_{45}, at which $X_u = 1.225$ in Figure 6.11. The down node moves horizontally and stays at zero. In this case, the transition will be to nodes N_{45} and N_{47} with $r_u = 0.06$ and $r_d = 0$. The up and down probabilities in this case are given by equation (6.82):

$$p_u = \frac{0.5 \times 0.06 \times 0.2}{0.06} = 0.1$$

$$p_d = 1 - 0.1 = 0.9$$

The bond price at node N_{36} is:

$$P_{36} = \frac{98.81 \times 0.1 + 100 \times 0.9}{e^{0 \times 0.2}} = 99.88$$

By following a similar procedure at each node, the bond price at time zero is $P(0) = \$94.26$. If a 100-step tree is used, the price of the bond is \$94.28; the closed-form solution is also equal to \$94.28.

Table 6.2 compares the accuracy of the proposed binomial and trinomial trees in valuing zero-coupon bonds under the assumption that interest rate follows the CIR process. The parameter values are the same as in Table 6.1, and the results are shown using 100 and 500 steps. In general, the performance of the binomial tree is similar to that of the trinomial tree for bonds of low to medium maturities (i.e., one to five years) and interest rate volatility of less than 0.5. However, the trinomial tree outperforms the binomial tree when both bond maturity and interest rate volatility are high. For example, for $T = 10$, $\tilde{\alpha} = 0.5$, $\sigma = 0.8$, $r_0 = 11\%$, and $N = 100$, the error from the binomial tree is 57 cents, while the error from the trinomial tree is only 19 cents. The performance advantage of the trinomial tree reduces as the number of steps increases. With an increase in the number of steps to $N = 500$, the error reduces to 11 cents for the binomial tree and to 2 cents for the trinomial tree.

PRICING BOND OPTIONS AND INTEREST RATE OPTIONS WITH TRINOMIAL TREES

The accuracy of the trinomial tree procedure can also be assessed by computing the prices of call options on zero-coupon bonds using the tree and then comparing these values to those obtained using the closed-form solution of the call option given in equation (6.43). Table 6.3 demonstrates that a truncated trinomial tree with 500 steps leads to good convergence of the value of a call option on a zero-coupon bond to the solution obtained using the closed-form formula. The accuracy of the tree decreases with an increase in the volatility and an increase in the time to expiration of the option. Though the trinomial tree with 200 steps can have errors up to 5 percent or more, the errors from a tree with 500 steps are generally less than 1 percent. These results hold for a variety of parameter combinations of option expiration date, bond maturity, risk-neutral speed of mean reversion, and short rate volatility.

Table 6.4 gives the prices of European call options on an 8 percent coupon bond. The prices obtained from the tree are compared with the prices obtained using the formula given in equation (6.47), which gives the price of an option on a coupon bond as a sum of the prices of options on zero-coupon bonds. Similar to Table 6.3, the truncated trinomial tree with 500 steps leads to good convergence of the option prices based upon coupon bonds. Table 6.4 also gives the prices of American options on coupon bonds. These prices deviate significantly from the European counterparts, especially when the options are in the money and when the option expiration is long. Example 6.3, explaining the pricing American options, is given as follows.

Example 6.3   Consider a semi-annual coupon bond with a coupon rate of 6 percent and the other parameters given in Example 6.2 ($F = 100$, $T = 1$, $r_0 = 6\%$, $\tilde{\alpha} = 0.5$, $\tilde{m} = 6\%$, and $\sigma = 40\%$). Now consider an American call option on this bond with expiration of 0.6 and a strike price of 95. Consider using a five-step trinomial tree for pricing this option ($\Delta t = 0.2$). The trinomial tree for this example is depicted in Figure 6.12. Each node consists of three rows. The number in the top row is the value of the option, the number in the middle row is the bond price obtained as the discounted expected value of the future bond prices, and the number in the bottom row is the short rate. The tree is truncated at $X(t) = 0$.

Because the parameters of the CIR process are exactly as in Example 6.2 and the tree spans the entire life of the bond, the tree has the same truncation points and probabilities as in Example 6.2. We first demonstrate how to compute the price of the coupon bond. The terminal bond values are given as the face value of the bond plus the last coupon. Hence, the value of the bond at the final node is $103. The bond values for the rest of the nodes are computed by discounting in exactly the same way as in Example 6.2, except that the coupon value of the bond is added to the bond price around the time of the coupon payment. In this case, there is only one coupon period—when going from time 0.6 to time 0.4. The coupon could be added at either of these two nodes. Here, we add it to the bond value at time

TABLE 6.3 Prices of Zero-Coupon Bond Options under the CIR Term Structure Model, Using the NB Truncated-Tree Approach (with $\tilde{m} = 0.08$)[a]

$\tilde{\alpha}$	σ	T	S	K	r_0	N 500	N 1,000	Closed Form
0.01	0.1	2	0.25	91.6279	0.05	0.6868	0.6935	0.6937
0.01	0.1	2	0.25	82.6558	0.11	0.9036	0.9149	0.9146
0.1	0.1	2	0.25	91.1705	0.05	0.6291	0.6350	0.6341
0.1	0.1	2	0.25	83.0492	0.11	0.8303	0.8409	0.8402
0.1	0.5	2	0.25	92.2663	0.05	2.6653	2.6764	2.6753
0.1	0.5	2	0.25	85.1619	0.11	3.6634	3.6797	3.6780
0.5	0.5	2	0.25	90.4306	0.05	1.9137	1.9227	1.9204
0.5	0.5	2	0.25	85.5941	0.11	2.6345	2.6464	2.6451
0.5	0.8	2	0.25	91.3631	0.05	2.4713	2.4820	2.4822
0.5	0.8	2	0.25	87.1623	0.11	3.6007	3.6127	3.6125
0.01	0.1	2	1	95.1348	0.05	0.7885	0.7885	0.7885
0.01	0.1	2	1	89.7355	0.11	1.0410	1.0407	1.0406
0.1	0.1	2	1	94.7756	0.05	0.7288	0.7282	0.7281
0.1	0.1	2	1	90.0540	0.11	0.9519	0.9515	0.9515
0.1	0.5	2	1	95.7456	0.05	2.4810	2.4804	2.4804
0.1	0.5	2	1	91.9948	0.11	3.6864	3.6875	3.6873
0.5	0.5	2	1	94.3065	0.05	2.0050	2.0029	2.0016
0.5	0.5	2	1	92.1354	0.11	2.6317	2.6320	2.6312
0.5	0.8	2	1	95.0799	0.05	2.1820	2.1796	2.1775
0.5	0.8	2	1	93.4374	0.11	2.9583	2.9559	2.9556
0.01	0.1	10	1	67.1400	0.05	4.1825	4.1781	4.1753
0.01	0.1	10	1	43.4405	0.11	3.7705	3.7736	3.7749
0.1	0.1	10	1	59.6805	0.05	2.6099	2.6044	2.5983
0.1	0.1	10	1	44.7393	0.11	2.6736	2.6798	2.6769
0.1	0.5	10	1	79.1622	0.05	4.8744	4.8525	4.8480
0.1	0.5	10	1	72.1861	0.11	6.8685	6.8525	6.8551
0.5	0.5	10	1	58.9790	0.05	2.2994	2.2989	2.3027
0.5	0.5	10	1	56.5483	0.11	2.9571	2.9615	2.9622
0.5	0.8	10	1	65.6260	0.05	2.3023	2.2523	2.2454
0.5	0.8	10	1	63.9781	0.11	3.0290	3.0147	3.0068
0.01	0.1	10	5	81.5128	0.05	4.8288	4.8285	4.8284
0.01	0.1	10	5	65.8287	0.11	4.3922	4.3933	4.3957
0.1	0.1	10	5	74.5947	0.05	3.2249	3.2215	3.2184
0.1	0.1	10	5	66.3946	0.11	3.0621	3.0602	3.0584
0.1	0.5	10	5	90.2377	0.05	2.4208	2.4024	2.3917
0.1	0.5	10	5	89.6154	0.11	2.4450	2.4322	2.4227
0.5	0.5	10	5	74.6089	0.05	2.3609	2.3568	2.3562
0.5	0.5	10	5	74.5014	0.11	2.2082	2.2018	2.1993
0.5	0.8	10	5	79.4255	0.05	2.0438	1.9967	1.9851
0.5	0.8	10	5	79.4095	0.11	1.8871	1.8712	1.8611

a. The strike price K equals the forward price of the underlying bond, or $K = P(0, T)/P(0, S) \times 100$, assuming that the face value of the underlying bond equals \$100.

TABLE 6.4 Prices of Coupon Bond Options under the CIR Term Structure Model with 8 percent Coupon, Using the NB Truncated-Tree Approach (with $\tilde{m} = 0.08$ and $K = 100$)[a]

$\tilde{\alpha}$	σ	T	S	American Option $(n = 1,000)$	r_0	European N = 500	European N = 1,000	Closed Form
0.01	0.1	2	0.25	5.5190	0.05	4.7904	4.8007	4.8009
0.01	0.1	2	0.25	0.0187	0.11	0.0175	0.0185	0.0187
0.1	0.1	2	0.25	5.0248	0.05	4.3051	4.3151	4.3149
0.1	0.1	2	0.25	0.0175	0.11	0.0164	0.0173	0.0175
0.1	0.5	2	0.25	7.2886	0.05	6.7927	6.8073	6.8083
0.1	0.5	2	0.25	3.0116	0.11	2.8842	2.9072	2.9050
0.5	0.5	2	0.25	5.0334	0.05	4.5683	4.5775	4.5767
0.5	0.5	2	0.25	2.1301	0.11	2.0099	2.0274	2.0268
0.5	0.8	2	0.25	6.7212	0.05	6.1065	6.1171	6.1173
0.5	0.8	2	0.25	4.1982	0.11	3.9361	3.9488	3.9503
0.01	0.1	2	1	5.5190	0.05	2.8457	2.8456	2.8457
0.01	0.1	2	1	0.2640	0.11	0.2181	0.2181	0.2181
0.1	0.1	2	1	5.0248	0.05	2.4878	2.4876	2.4873
0.1	0.1	2	1	0.2600	0.11	0.2134	0.2133	0.2132
0.1	0.5	2	1	8.5648	0.05	5.2208	5.2204	5.2200
0.1	0.5	2	1	5.2909	0.11	3.6264	3.6261	3.6259
0.5	0.5	2	1	6.0710	0.05	3.4834	3.4821	3.4805
0.5	0.5	2	1	3.9809	0.11	2.6033	2.6016	2.5999
0.5	0.8	2	1	7.9817	0.05	4.4684	4.4661	4.4654
0.5	0.8	2	1	6.3601	0.11	3.8638	3.8613	3.8602
0.01	0.1	10	1	26.7705	0.05	24.4023	24.4093	24.4151
0.01	0.1	10	1	2.4288	0.11	2.3922	2.3877	2.3927
0.1	0.1	10	1	17.2605	0.05	15.0172	15.0136	15.0125
0.1	0.1	10	1	1.6127	0.11	1.5739	1.5718	1.5693
0.1	0.5	10	1	44.9603	0.05	41.4815	41.4823	41.4903
0.1	0.5	10	1	33.1085	0.11	31.3275	31.3280	31.3372
0.5	0.5	10	1	17.5063	0.05	14.7738	14.7645	14.7789
0.5	0.5	10	1	13.1141	0.11	11.6274	11.6218	11.6295
0.5	0.8	10	1	27.3816	0.05	23.6342	23.5692	23.5743
0.5	0.8	10	1	23.5732	0.11	20.8725	20.8499	20.8519
0.01	0.1	10	5	27.4054	0.05	15.4685	15.4710	15.4731
0.01	0.1	10	5	6.6832	0.11	4.7992	4.8006	4.8016
0.1	0.1	10	5	17.7237	0.05	8.5877	8.5257	8.5240
0.1	0.1	10	5	5.0692	0.11	3.3929	3.3897	3.3878
0.1	0.5	10	5	47.9560	0.05	24.5669	24.5577	24.5519
0.1	0.5	10	5	38.9651	0.11	21.0435	21.0393	21.0434
0.5	0.5	10	5	19.4982	0.05	8.3437	8.3359	8.3352
0.5	0.5	10	5	16.7306	0.11	7.6009	7.6014	7.6042
0.5	0.8	10	5	28.6177	0.05	12.8464	12.7934	12.7926
0.5	0.8	10	5	25.9081	0.11	11.9517	11.9405	11.9343

a. The face value of the coupon bond equals $100, and coupons are paid semi-annually.

At each node:
Top value = *American option price*
Middle value = bond value, $P(t)$
Bottom value = interest rate process, $r(t)$

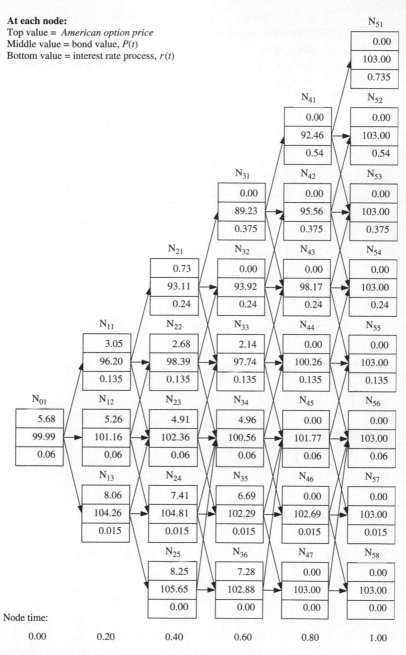

FIGURE 6.12 Trinomial Tree for the CIR Model for Pricing an American Call Option on a Coupon Bond

0.4. Since the $3 semi-annual coupon is added at time 0.4 and the actual payment is at 0.5, the coupon needs to be discounted back to 0.4 (note that if the coupons were added to the nodes at time 0.6, the coupon value would need to be compounded from time 0.5 to 0.6). For example, the bond price at node N_{24} is computed as follows. The short rate value at this node is 1.5 percent. Since $r > 0$, the value of J at this node is computed using equation (6.76) as follows:

$$\mu(X,\ t) = \frac{1}{0.612}\left(\frac{1}{2} \times 0.5\left(\frac{4 \times 0.06}{0.4^2} - 0.612^2\right) - \frac{1}{2}\right) = -0.357$$

$$J = FLOOR\left(\frac{-0.357 \times \sqrt{0.2}}{1.369} + \frac{1}{1.369^2}\right) = FLOOR(0.42) = 0$$

Since $J = 0$, the next step transitions are at nodes N_{34}, N_{35}, and N_{36}. The trinomial probabilities are computed using equation (6.77) as follows:

$$p_u = \frac{1}{2 \times 1.369^2} - \frac{0}{2} + \frac{1}{2 \times 1.369} \times (-0.357) \times \sqrt{0.2} = 0.208$$

$$p_d = \frac{1}{2 \times 1.369^2} + \frac{0}{2} - \frac{1}{2 \times 1.369} \times (-0.357) \times \sqrt{0.2} = 0.325$$

$$p_m = 1 - \frac{1}{1.369^2} = 0.466$$

The bond price at node N_{24} is given as follows:

$$P_{24} = \frac{100.56 \times 0.208 + 102.29 \times 0.467 + 102.88 \times 0.325}{e^{0.015 \times 0.2}}$$

$$+ \frac{3}{e^{0.015 \times 0.1}} = 104.81$$

Next, we demonstrate the pricing of the American call option. The option values at maturity, that is, at time 0.6, are calculated as the maximum of zero and the bond price at that node minus the strike adjusted for accrued interest (AI). Since we are in between coupons, the adjusted strike price is computed as follows:

$$Strike + AI = 95.0 + \frac{0.6 - 0.5}{0.5} \times 3.0 = 95.6$$

For example, an option value at node N_{34} is given as:

$$Max(0, 100.56 - 95.6) = 4.96$$

The option values for the rest of the nodes are computed as the maximum of the option continuation value obtained by discounting future option values and the option's immediate exercise value. For example, at node N_{24}, the price is computed as follows:

$$Continuation\ Value = \frac{4.96 \times 0.208 + 6.69 \times 0.467 + 7.28 \times 0.325}{e^{0.015 \times 0.2}}$$

$$= 6.50$$

The adjusted strike price is:

$$Strike + AI = 95.0 + \frac{0.4 - 0}{0.5} \times 3.0 = 97.4$$

The price if the option is exercised immediately is:

$$Immediate\ Exercise\ Value = 104.81 - 97.4 = 7.41$$

The value of the American call option at node N_{24} is then:

$$Call = Max(6.50, 7.41) = 7.41$$

Using this procedure recursively gives the time 0 price of the bond as $99.99 and the time 0 price of the American call option as $5.68. Using 500 steps gives the bond price as $100.02 and the American call option price as $5.80.

THE CIR MODEL EXTENDED WITH JUMPS

Unlike the jump extensions of the Vasicek model given by Baz and Das [1996], Das and Foresi [1996], Chacko and Das [2002], and Durham [2005], little work exists on the jump extensions of the CIR model. Though Ahn and Thomson [1988] add a jump component to the CIR short rate process, their model has two limitations. First, the short rate experiences *negative* jumps only, making their model somewhat unrealistic. Second, the jumps are limited to be of *constant* size and forced to be smaller than the positive drift of the short rate, so that the short rate remains positive after hitting the zero boundary.

Nawalkha and Beliaeva [2007b] propose two jump extensions of the CIR model, which can be specified using the following short rate process, given directly under the risk-neutral measure as:

$$dr(t) = \tilde{\alpha}(\tilde{m} - r(t))\, dt + \sigma\sqrt{r(t)}\, d\tilde{Z}(t) + f(r, J)\, dN(\tilde{\lambda}) \qquad (6.83)$$

As in Chapter 5, the relationship between the risk-neutral parameters and the physical parameters can be derived using the stochastic discount factor given in Chapter 2. The function $f(.)$ may depend on both the short rate $r(t)$ and the jump variable J, where the distribution of J is specified under the risk-neutral measure. Nawalkha and Beliaeva consider two special cases of $f(r, J)$, given as follows:

Case 1.

$$f(r, J) = J_E \tag{6.84}$$

where J_E is distributed exponentially with a positive mean $1/\eta$.

Case 2.

$$f(r, J) = r(t)(e^{J_N} - 1) \tag{6.85}$$

where J_N is distributed normally with mean μ_J and variance σ_J^2.

Case 1 does not allow negative jumps in the short rate, as an exponential distribution with a positive mean cannot allow negative outcomes. This process has been used by Duffie, Pan, and Singleton [2000] for modeling volatility jumps. This case is the opposite of that considered by Ahn and Thompson, which allows negative jumps and restricts positive jumps, but with the advantage that jump size is allowed to be random and can be of any size greater than zero. This case can be useful for pricing short-term options during periods in which positive jumps are expected to dominate negative jumps, for example, at the beginning phase of an economic boom or coming out of an economic crisis. In general, jumps in rates in only one direction can be useful in certain economic regimes; Jarrow, Li, and Zhao [2004] found that downward jumps after September 11, 2001, played an important role in the pricing of short-term and medium-term caps, a period in which the U.S. central bank accelerated the cuts in the key short rates. Though limited to only certain economic regimes, this case leads to a simple analytical solution for the bond price and also to quasi-analytical solutions for interest rate derivatives using the method of Fourier inversion.

Though case 1 cannot generate negative jumps under the single-factor case, it can generate both positive and negative jumps when using multiple square root processes with exponential jumps. For example, Nawalkha, Beliaeva, and Soto (NBS) [2007a] consider a mixed-sign model with short rate given as: $r(t) = \delta + Y_1(t) - Y_2(t) + Y_3(t)$, where δ is a constant and $Y_1(t)$, $Y_2(t)$, and $Y_3(t)$ are three state variables that follow square root processes with exponential jumps. Since $Y_2(t)$ appears with a negative sign in the definition of the short rate, the positive jumps in $Y_2(t)$ translate into negative jumps in the short rate. The preliminary results of NBS indicate that if δ is sufficiently greater than zero, if the state variable $Y_2(t)$ has a low mean and a high mean reversion, and if the jump probability is not too high, then the probability of getting a negative short remains quite low. Since case 1 allows analytical solutions, the mixed-sign multifactor extension given by NBS allows a realistic multifactor square root model with both positive and negative jumps, which can price interest rate derivatives analytically using the Fourier inversion method given in Chapter 5.

Case 2 gives the only known process in the literature that extends the CIR model to allow both positive and negative jumps. This is realistic, as it allows us to investigate how the interaction of the jumps in both directions affects the pricing of interest rate derivatives. To get more insight on case 2, consider the change in the short rate, conditional on the occurrence of a jump, as follows:

$$dr(t) = r(t)(e^{J_N} - 1), \quad \text{if } dN(\tilde{\lambda}) = 1 \tag{6.86}$$

The change in the log of the short rate is given as follows:

$$\begin{aligned} d\log r(t) &= \log\left(r(t) + r(t)(e^{J_N} - 1)\right) - \log r(t) \\ &= J_N, \quad \text{if } dN(\tilde{\lambda}) = 1 \text{ and } r(t) > 0 \end{aligned} \tag{6.87}$$

Hence, conditional on the jump occurrence, the change in the log of the short rate is normally distributed. Since negative infinity is an unattainable boundary for J_N, zero is an unattainable boundary for the short rate over the next interval if the current value of the short rate is greater than zero. Of course, the short rate may become zero over a finite period of time under the jump-extended CIR model, but the zero boundary is reached by the diffusion component of the short rate process. When the zero boundary is reached, the change in the short rate due to the jump component is zero in the next interval (see equation (6.86)). The short rate becomes positive after hitting zero, due to the positive drift from the diffusion component of the short rate process. Nawalkha and Beliaeva [2007b] show that the lognormal jump process in equation (6.85) is the only process within a larger family of CEV jump processes that can allow both positive and negative jumps for the CIR model. To see this, consider the family of CEV jump processes given as follows:

$$f(r, J) = (r(t))^p (e^{J_N} - 1) \tag{6.88}$$

where p is *not equal* to 1 and J_N is distributed normally with mean μ_J and variance σ_J^2. If p is less than 1, and if $r(t)$ is below 100 percent, then a large negative value for J_N can make the short rate process go below zero in equation (6.83). Similarly, if p is greater than 1, and if $r(t)$ is above 100 percent, then again a large negative value for J_N can make the short rate process go below zero in equation (6.83). Hence, $p = 1$ is the only value that allows the short rate to remain nonnegative while still allowing jumps in both directions, which demonstrates the usefulness of the lognormal jump model in equation (6.85).

Expressing bond price $P(t, T)$ as a twice differentiable function of $r(t)$ and once differentiable function of t, using Ito's lemma, and taking the risk-neutral expectation, the partial differential difference equation (PDDE) of the bond price can be given as follows:

$$\frac{\partial P}{\partial t} + \tilde{\alpha}(\tilde{m} - r(t))\frac{\partial P}{\partial r} + \frac{1}{2}\sigma^2 r(t)\frac{\partial^2 P}{\partial r^2} - r(t)P(t, T) + L(\tau)P(t, T)\,\tilde{\lambda} = 0$$

(6.89)

subject to $P(t, T) = 1$, where $L(\tau)$, the expected return on the bond conditional on the realization of the jump, given as follows:

$$L(\tau) = \frac{\tilde{E}_t\big[P\big(r(t) + f(r, J), t, T\big) - P\big(r(t), t, T\big)\big]}{P\big(r(t), t, T\big)}$$

(6.90)

The PDDE in equation (6.89) can be solved analytically for case 1, but not for case 2. Later in this chapter, we demonstrate how to construct jump-diffusion trees for both cases, which can be used to solve the PDDE numerically. Consider the solution for the PDDE, for case 1 with exponentially distributed jumps as follows:

$$P(t, T) = e^{A(\tau) - B(\tau)r(t)}$$

(6.91)

where $\tau = T - t$. The partial derivatives of bond price can be given as follows:

$$\frac{\partial P}{\partial t} = \left[-r(t)\frac{\partial B(\tau)}{\partial t} + \frac{\partial A(\tau)}{\partial t}\right]P(t, T)$$

$$\frac{\partial P}{\partial r} = -B(\tau)P(t, T)$$

(6.92)

$$\frac{\partial^2 P}{\partial r^2} = B^2(\tau)P(t, T)$$

Substituting $f(r, J) = J_E$, under case 1, and using equation (6.91), the expected return conditional on the realization of the jump is given as follows:

$$L(\tau) = \frac{\tilde{E}_t\big[P\big(r(t) + J_E, t, T\big) - P\big(r(t), t, T\big)\big]}{P\big(r(t), t, T\big)} = [\tilde{E}_t(e^{-B(\tau)J_E}) - 1]$$

(6.93)

Since variable J_E is exponentially distributed with a positive mean $1/\eta$, $L(\tau)$ can be solved as follows:

$$L(\tau) = \tilde{E}_t(e^{-B(\tau)J_E}) - 1 = \int_0^\infty e^{-B(\tau)J_E} \eta e^{-\eta J_E} dJ_E - 1$$

$$= \frac{\eta}{\eta + B(\tau)} - 1 = \frac{-B(\tau)}{\eta + B(\tau)} \tag{6.94}$$

Substituting the partial derivatives given in equations (6.92) and the solution of $L(\tau)$ from equation (6.94) into equation (6.89), and then using a separation of variables, the PDDE for the bond price simplifies to the following two ODEs, after using a change of variable $\tau = T - t$:

$$\underbrace{\frac{\partial B(\tau)}{\partial \tau} = 1 - \tilde{\alpha}B(\tau) - \frac{1}{2}\sigma^2 B^2(\tau)}_{\text{Riccati}}$$

$$\frac{\partial A(\tau)}{\partial \tau} = -\tilde{\alpha}\tilde{m}B(\tau) - \tilde{\lambda}\left(\frac{B(\tau)}{\eta + B(\tau)}\right) \tag{6.95}$$

subject to the boundary conditions $A(0) = 0$ and $B(0) = 0$. The solutions to the ODEs in equation (6.95) are similar to the solutions of the ODEs under the CIR model, except for one extra numerical integral in the solution of $A(\tau)$, and are given as follows:

$$A(\tau) = \frac{2\tilde{\alpha}\tilde{m}}{\sigma^2} \ln\left[\frac{2\beta e^{\frac{1}{2}(\beta+\tilde{\alpha})\tau}}{(\beta + \tilde{\alpha})(e^{\beta\tau} - 1) + 2\beta}\right] - \tilde{\lambda}\int_0^\tau \frac{B(u)}{\eta + B(u)} du \tag{6.96}$$

$$B(\tau) = \frac{2(e^{\beta\tau} - 1)}{(\beta + \tilde{\alpha})(e^{\beta\tau} - 1) + 2\beta} \tag{6.97}$$

where $\beta = \sqrt{\tilde{\alpha}^2 + 2\sigma^2}$

The extra integral term in the solution of $A(\tau)$ captures the effect of jumps on CIR bond prices. In general, jumps don't have a big effect on bond yields, but they can have significant effects on derivative prices, as shown by Johannes [2004].

VALUING FUTURES

Futures on a Zero-Coupon Bond

The time t price of a futures contract expiring at time S, written on a zero-coupon bond maturing at time T, under the CIR model extended with exponential jumps can be obtained in the same manner as already demonstrated in the previous chapters and the CIR model in this chapter. We give the final solution as follows:

$$P_F(t, \ S, \ T) = e^{A_F(s) - B_F(s)r(t)}, \qquad s = S - t \qquad (6.98)$$

where

$$A_F(s) = A(U) - \frac{2\tilde{\alpha}\tilde{m}}{\sigma^2} \ln \left| \frac{\sigma^2 B(U)(e^{-\tilde{\alpha}s} - 1) - 2\tilde{\alpha}}{2\tilde{\alpha}} \right| - \tilde{\lambda} \int_0^s \frac{B_F(u)}{\eta + B_F(u)} \, du \qquad (6.99)$$

$$B_F(s) = \frac{-2\tilde{\alpha}B(U)e^{-\tilde{\alpha}s}}{\sigma^2 B(U)(e^{-\tilde{\alpha}s} - 1) - 2\tilde{\alpha}} \qquad (6.100)$$

and where $A(U)$ and $B(U)$ are as defined earlier in equations (6.96) and (6.97), respectively. The futures-forward price discount, or FFPD, is given as:

$$FFPD = \frac{P_f(t, \ S, \ T) - P_F(t, \ S, \ T)}{P_f(t, \ S, \ T)} = 1 - P_F(t, \ S, \ T)\frac{P(t, \ S)}{P(t, \ T)}$$

$$= 1 - e^{\left(A_F(s) + A(s) - A(\tau)\right) - \left(B_F(s) + B(s) - B(\tau)\right)r(t)}, \qquad s = S - t, \quad \tau = T - t \qquad (6.101)$$

Futures on a Time Deposit The price of a futures contract on a time deposit—such as Eurodollar and Euribor futures—can be obtained using equation (3.12) in Chapter 3:

$$P_F^{TD}(t, \ S, \ T) = \frac{100}{\hat{U}} \left(1 + \hat{U} - P_F^I(t, \ S, \ T) \right) \qquad (6.102)$$

where S is the futures expiration date, $U = T - S$ is the deposit time period calculated using the actual/actual day-count convention, $\hat{U}$ is the deposit time period calculated using actual/360 day-count convention, and $P_F^I(t, \ S, \ T)$ is the current price of a futures contract written on a hypothetical asset, which at the expiration date S is worth the inverse of a \$1 face-value zero-coupon bond maturing at time T. As shown in Chapter 3, the futures price $P_F^I(t, \ S, \ T)$ is given by the following risk-neutral expectation:

$$P_F^I(t, \ S, \ T) = \tilde{E}_t \left(\frac{1}{P(S, T)} \right) \qquad (6.103)$$

Following the same method already demonstrated for a number of models in the earlier chapters, the solution of $P_F^I(t, , \ S, \ T)$ can be given as:

$$P_F^I(t, \ S, \ T) = e^{a_F(s) - b_F(s)r(t)}, \qquad s = S - t \qquad (6.104)$$

where the solutions of $a_F(s)$ and $b_F(s)$ immediately follow from equations (6.99) and (6.100), respectively, by switching the signs of the constants $A(U)$ and $B(U)$ and are given as follows:

$$a_F(s) = -A(U) - \frac{2\tilde{\alpha}\tilde{m}}{\sigma^2} \ln \left| \frac{\sigma^2 B(U)(1 - e^{-\tilde{\alpha}s}) - 2\tilde{\alpha}}{2\tilde{\alpha}} \right| - \tilde{\lambda} \int_0^s \frac{b_F(u)}{\eta + b_F(u)} \, du$$
(6.105)

$$b_F(s) = \frac{2\tilde{\alpha}B(U)e^{-\tilde{\alpha}s}}{\sigma^2 B(U)(1 - e^{-\tilde{\alpha}s}) - 2\tilde{\alpha}}$$
(6.106)

and $A(U)$ and $B(U)$ are defined earlier in equations (6.96) and (6.97), respectively. The convexity bias, given as the difference between the futures rate and the forward rate on a time deposit, is defined in equation (3.17) in Chapter 3 as follows:

$$\text{Convexity Bias} = L_F(t, S, T) - L_f(t, S, T)$$

$$= \frac{1 + L_F(t, S, T)\hat{U}}{\hat{U}} \left(1 - \frac{P(t, S)}{P(t, T)P_F^I(t, S, T)} \right)$$
(6.107)

By substituting the appropriate formulas we get:

$$\text{Convexity Bias} = L_F(t, S, T) - L_f(t, S, T)$$

$$= \frac{1 + L_F(t, S, T)\hat{U}}{\hat{U}} \left(1 - e^{A(s)-a_F(s)-A(\tau)-\left(B(s)-b_F(s)-B(\tau)\right)r(t)} \right),$$

$$s = S - t \quad \text{and} \quad \tau = T - t$$
(6.108)

Valuing Options

Since an analytical solution exists for the bond price under the CIR model extended with exponential jumps (i.e., under case 1), a quasi-analytical solution must exist for the price of an option on a zero-coupon bond under this model, using the Fourier inversion method introduced in Chapter 5. The solution provided in equation (6.109) follows the first three steps outlined in the last section of Chapter 5. Using the notation from Chapter 5, the price of a call option expiring at time S, written on a zero-coupon bond maturing at time T, is given as (see equation (5.115)):

$$c(t) = P(t, T)\Pi_{1t} - KP(t, S)\Pi_{2t}$$
(6.109)

where

$$\Pi_{1t} = \frac{1}{2} + \frac{1}{\pi} \int_0^\infty Re\left[\frac{e^{-i\omega \ln K}g_{1t}(\omega)}{i\omega}\right] d\omega \qquad (6.110)$$

$$\Pi_{2t} = \frac{1}{2} + \frac{1}{\pi} \int_0^\infty Re\left[\frac{e^{-i\omega \ln K}g_{2t}(\omega)}{i\omega}\right] d\omega \qquad (6.111)$$

The characteristic functions $g_{1t}(\omega)$ and $g_{2t}(\omega)$ are the solutions to the same PDDE followed by the bond price in equation (6.89), but with different boundary conditions, and are solved next.

Solution of $g_{1t}(\omega)$ Following the method given in step 3 of the last section in Chapter 5, the solution of $g_{1t}(\omega)$ can be given as:

$$g_{1t}(\omega) = \frac{e^{A_1^*(s)-B_1^*(s)r(t)}}{P(t,\ T)}, \qquad s = S - t \qquad (6.112)$$

where $A_1^*(s)$ and $B_1^*(s)$ follow the same ODEs that are followed by $A(s)$ and $B(s)$, respectively, in equation (6.95), but with the following boundary conditions:

$$A_1^*(0) = a_1 = A(U)(1 + i\omega)$$
$$B_1^*(0) = b_1 = B(U)(1 + i\omega) \qquad (6.113)$$

where i is the square root of minus one, $U = T - S$, and $A(U)$ and $B(U)$ are as given in equations (6.96) and (6.97), respectively. The ODEs for $A_1^*(s)$ and $B_1^*(s)$ with the given boundary conditions have the following solutions:

$$A_1^*(s) = a_1 - 2\frac{\tilde{\alpha}\tilde{m}}{\sigma^2}\left(\beta_3 s + \ln\left(\frac{1 - \beta_4 e^{\beta_1 s}}{1 - \beta_4}\right)\right) - \tilde{\lambda}\int_0^s \left(\frac{B_1^*(u)}{\eta + B_1^*(u)}\right) du \qquad (6.114)$$

$$B_1^*(s) = \frac{2}{\sigma^2}\frac{\beta_2 \beta_4 e^{\beta_1 s} - \beta_3}{\beta_4 e^{\beta_1 s} - 1} \qquad (6.115)$$

where

$$\beta_1 = \sqrt{\tilde{\alpha}^2 + 2\sigma^2}, \quad \beta_2 = \frac{-\tilde{\alpha} + \beta_1}{2}, \quad \beta_3 = \frac{-\tilde{\alpha} - \beta_1}{2}, \quad \beta_4 = \frac{-\tilde{\alpha} - \beta_1 - b_1\sigma^2}{-\tilde{\alpha} + \beta_1 - b_1\sigma^2}$$

Solution of $g_{2t}(\omega)$ Again, following the method given in step 3 of the last section in Chapter 5, the solution of $g_{2t}(\omega)$ can be given as:

$$g_{2t}(\omega) = \frac{e^{A_2^*(s) - B_2^*(s)r(t)}}{P(t, S)}, \quad s = S - t \qquad (6.116)$$

where $A_2^*(s)$ and $B_2^*(s)$ follow the same ODEs that are followed by $A(s)$ and $B(s)$, respectively, in equation (6.95), but with the following boundary conditions:

$$\begin{aligned} A_2^*(0) &= a_2 = A(U)(i\omega) \\ B_2^*(0) &= b_2 = B(U)(i\omega) \end{aligned} \qquad (6.117)$$

where $U = T - S$ and $A(U)$ and $B(U)$ are given in equations (6.96) and (6.97), respectively. The solutions of $A_2^*(s)$ and $B_2^*(s)$ are identical to the solutions of $A_1^*(s)$ and $B_1^*(s)$, respectively, except that a_1 is replaced with a_2 and b_1 is replaced with b_2 in equations (6.114) and (6.115), respectively.

Substituting the solutions of $g_{1t}(\omega)$ and $g_{2t}(\omega)$ into equations (6.110) and (6.111) and approximating the integrals in these two equations numerically by using a truncated summation (as demonstrated in equation (5.149) in Chapter 5) gives the solution to the price of the call option. The solution to a European put option can be obtained in a similar manner, or by applying the put-call parity relation.

JUMP-DIFFUSION TREES FOR THE CIR MODEL EXTENDED WITH JUMPS

Exponential Jumps

In this case, the short rate is assumed to follow the following process:

$$dr(t) = \tilde{\alpha}(\tilde{m} - r(t))\, dt + \sigma\sqrt{r(t)}\, d\tilde{Z}(t) + J_E\, dN(\tilde{\lambda}) \qquad (6.118)$$

where J_E is distributed exponentially with mean $1/\eta$.

The following approximation is used to model the short rate tree with exponential jumps:

$$dr(t) = \begin{cases} \tilde{\alpha}(\tilde{m} - r(t))\, dt + \sigma\sqrt{r(t)}\, d\tilde{Z}(t), & \text{with probability } 1 - \tilde{\lambda}\, dt \\ J_E, & \text{with probability } \tilde{\lambda}\, dt \end{cases}$$

$$(6.119)$$

To keep the analysis general, we consider an arbitrary node $r(t)$ at time $t = i\Delta t$ for $i = 0, 1, 2, \ldots, N - 1$, where time T is divided into N equal intervals of length Δt. At time $(i + 1)\Delta t$, the M different values for the interest rate are given as follows:

$$r(t) + \Delta_k, \qquad \text{where}$$

$$k = \begin{cases} J - 1, J, J + 1, J + 2, \ldots, J + M - 2 & \text{if } J \geq -2 \\ J - 1, J, J + 1, 0, 1, \ldots, M - 4 & \text{otherwise} \end{cases}$$

where J is computed according to equation (6.76).

A two-step general jump-diffusion tree is shown in Figure 6.13. The segmented lines in Figure 6.13 refer to the diffusion nodes, and the solid lines refer to the jump nodes.

We specify the M probabilities associated with the M nodes as follows. The short rate can either undergo a local diffusion change with probability $1 - \tilde{\lambda} dt$ (nodes corresponding to $k = J - 1, J, J + 1$), or it can experience an upward jump with probability $\tilde{\lambda} dt$ (the remaining nodes). We first give the local probabilities for the diffusion case.

Local (or Diffusion) Probabilities   Unlike the pure diffusion model, the integer value of the parameter J, which determines the number of nodes to jump on the tree, can be lessthan or equal to -1 under the CIR model extended with jumps. This happens when short rate jumps to some high value, and due to the mean reversion implicit in the drift of the short rate, the drift

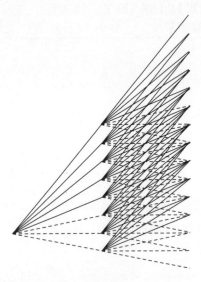

FIGURE 6.13   General Jump-Diffusion Tree

becomes highly negative, which makes J take on negative values. This makes the three diffusion node branches move downward significantly to match the negative drift. However, the three diffusion probabilities in equation (6.77) were derived under the assumption that J is greater than or equal to zero, and it can be shown that the variance computation of $dX(t)$ is no longer given by these three probabilities. For the case when J is less than or equal to -1, we derive three new diffusion probabilities that allow the matching of mean and variance of the diffusion part. Hence, we consider two separate cases corresponding to $J \geq 0$ and $J \leq -1$ for the diffusion probabilities. The first step is to compute both b and J using equations (6.74) and (6.76), respectively. Next, we give the diffusion probabilities corresponding to the two cases.

Case 1: $J \geq 0$. In this case, the local (or diffusion) probabilities are computed using equation (6.77) as follows:

$$P[r(t) + \Delta_{J+1}] = \left(\frac{1}{2b^2} - \frac{J}{2} + \frac{1}{2b}\mu(X,\ t)\sqrt{\Delta t} \right)(1 - \tilde{\lambda}\Delta t)$$

$$P[r(t) + \Delta_{J-1}] = \left(\frac{1}{2b^2} + \frac{J}{2} - \frac{1}{2b}\mu(X,\ t)\sqrt{\Delta t} \right)(1 - \tilde{\lambda}\Delta t) \qquad (6.120)$$

$$P[r(t) + \Delta_{J}] = \left(1 - \frac{1}{b^2} \right)(1 - \tilde{\lambda}\Delta t)$$

Case 2: $J < 0$. In this case, the value of J is recomputed as follows:

$$J = \text{Integer value closest in absolute distance to} \left(\frac{\mu(X,\ t)\sqrt{\Delta t}}{b} \right) \qquad (6.121)$$

The local (or diffusion) probabilities in this case are computed as follows:

$$P[r(t) + \Delta_{J+1}] = \frac{e_m e_d + \Delta t}{2b^2 \Delta t}(1 - \tilde{\lambda}\Delta t)$$

$$P[r(t) + \Delta_{J}] = \frac{-(e_d e_u + \Delta t)}{b^2 \Delta t}(1 - \tilde{\lambda}\Delta t) \qquad (6.122)$$

$$P[r(t) + \Delta_{J-1}] = \frac{e_u e_m + \Delta t}{2b^2 \Delta t}(1 - \tilde{\lambda}\Delta t)$$

where

$$e_u = b(J+1)\sqrt{\Delta t} - \mu(X,\ t)\Delta t$$

$$e_m = bJ\sqrt{\Delta t} - \mu(X,\ t)\Delta t \qquad (6.123)$$

$$e_d = b(J-1)\sqrt{\Delta t} - \mu(X,\ t)\Delta t$$

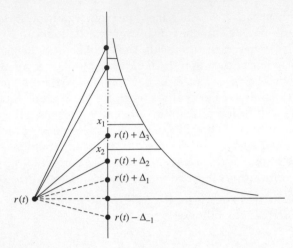

FIGURE 6.14 Approximation of the Jump Distribution Using an Exponential Curve

Jump Probabilities   The upward jump nodes are approximated with an exponential curve that goes from zero to positive infinity (see Figure 6.14).

The total risk-neutral probability of upward jumps is $\tilde{\lambda}\Delta t$. The entire line from zero to positive infinity in Figure 6.14 contains $M - 3$ jump nodes, and it is subdivided into $M - 3$ nonoverlapping intervals that cover the area under the exponential distribution curve for upward jumps. Note that the first three nodes are diffusion nodes. The area under the exponential curve that corresponds to the diffusion nodes is assigned to the first upward jump node. Therefore, the first of $M - 3$ intervals in such cases is wider than the remaining intervals. The probability mass over each of $M - 3$ intervals is assigned to the point inside of these intervals according the following two cases.

Case 1: $J \geq -1$. In this case, jump nodes lie right above the diffusion nodes. This case is illustrated in Figure 6.14, which assumes $J = 0$. If $J = 1$, then both the diffusion nodes and jump nodes shift up one level, such that jump nodes still remain above the diffusion nodes.[9] The probabilities of the jump nodes are given as:

$$P[(r(t) + \Delta_{J+2}] = F(x_1)\lambda\Delta t,$$

$$x_1 = \frac{(X + b(J + 2.5)\sqrt{\Delta t})^2\sigma^2}{4} - r(t)$$

$$P[(r(t) + \Delta_{J+3}] = (F(x_1) - F(x_2))\lambda\Delta t,$$

$$x_1 = \frac{(X + b(J + 3.5)\sqrt{\Delta t})^2 \sigma^2}{4} - r(t) \tag{6.124}$$

$$x_2 = \frac{(X + b(J + 2.5)\sqrt{\Delta t})^2 \sigma^2}{4} - r(t)$$

$$P[(r(t) + \Delta_{J+M-2}] = (1 - F(x_2))\lambda \Delta t,$$

$$x_2 = \frac{(X + b(J + M - 2.5)\sqrt{\Delta t})^2 \sigma^2}{4} - r(t)$$

where $F(x)$ is the cumulative exponential distribution for upward jumps defined as follows:

$$F(x) = \int_0^x \eta e^{-\eta J}\, dJ = 1 - e^{-\eta x} \tag{6.125}$$

Case 2: $J < -1$. Under this case, all three diffusion nodes are always below the current value of the interest rate. Therefore, all nodes under the exponential curve in Figure 6.15 will be the jump nodes. The probabilities of the jump nodes are given as follows:

$$P[(r(t)] = F(x_1)\lambda \Delta t,$$

$$x_1 = \frac{(X + 0.5b\sqrt{\Delta t})^2 \sigma^2}{4} - r(t)$$

$$P[(r(t) + \Delta_1] = (F(x_1) - F(x_2))\lambda \Delta t,$$

$$x_1 = \frac{(X + 1.5b\sqrt{\Delta t})^2 \sigma^2}{4} - r(t) \tag{6.126}$$

$$x_2 = \frac{(X + 0.5b\sqrt{\Delta t})^2 \sigma^2}{4} - r(t)$$

$$P[(r(t) + \Delta_{M-4}] = (1 - F(x_2))\lambda \Delta t,$$

$$x_2 = \frac{(X + (M - 4.5)b\sqrt{\Delta t})^2 \sigma^2}{4} - r(t)$$

where $F(x)$ is defined in equation (6.125).

Figure 6.15 illustrates the jump nodes assuming $J = -3$. In this case, the diffusion nodes are $r(t) + \Delta_{-4}$, $r(t) + \Delta_{-3}$, and $r(t) + \Delta_{-2}$; and the jump nodes are $r(t)$, $r(t) + \Delta_1$, ... , $r(t) + \Delta_{M-4}$. This implies that the node $r(t) + \Delta_{-1}$ is neither a diffusion node nor a jump node. Hence, the probability of this node is set to 0.

The number of nodes in a jump-diffusion tree is of the order $O(N^2 M)$. To increase the efficiency, we implement the following truncation methodology.

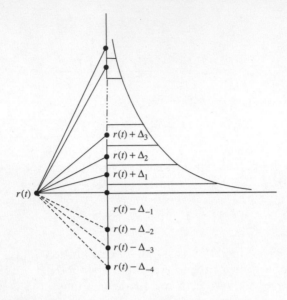

FIGURE 6.15 Approximation of the Jump Distribution Using an
Exponential Curve

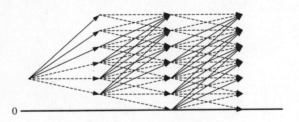

FIGURE 6.16 Exponential Jump-Diffusion Tree Truncation

First, since the short rate cannot assume negative values, the tree is automatically truncated at zero. However, we also truncate the tree from above
at $M - 1$ under the assumption that for a large enough M, the probability
of the short rate jumping to a higher node than $M - 1$ is low enough to not
affect bond and option prices. The truncation is illustrated in Figure 6.16.
The probability mass above the truncation line is assigned to the node on
the truncation line. Because of truncation, the number of nodes in the tree
is reduced to the order $O(N \times M)$.

Example 6.4 demonstrates how the untruncated exponential jump-
diffusion tree can be used to price a bond.

Example 6.4   Consider a discount bond with $F = 100$, $T = 1$, $r_0 = 6\%$, $\tilde{\alpha} = 0.5$, $\tilde{m} = 6\%$, and $\sigma = 7.5\%$. The intensity of the Poisson process is $\tilde{\lambda} = 1$, and the mean of the exponentially distributed jump is $1/\eta = 0.01$, giving $\eta = 100$. For pricing this bond, consider using a three-step tree ($N = 3$) with five branches ($M = 5$). The time step of the tree is $\Delta t = 0.33$. The tree for this example is illustrated in Figure 6.17. The solid lines correspond to jump nodes, and the segmented lines correspond to the diffusion nodes. Each node consists of two numbers. The number in the top row is the bond price obtained by discounting the future bond values. The number in the bottom row is the short rate.

To make sure that the X-process values at the bottom level of nodes are *exactly* zero, the value of $b = 1.257$ is computed using equations (6.72), (6.73), and (6.74).

Now consider a given node, for example, the uppermost node at time $t = 0.33$. At this node, $X(t = 0.33) = 8.709$. This corresponds to the short rate value of:

$$r = \frac{8.709^2 \times 0.075^2}{4} = 0.107$$

Since $r > 0$, the value of J at this node should be computed using equation (6.76) as follows:

$$\mu(X,\ t) = \frac{1}{8.709} \left(\frac{1}{2} \times 0.5 \left(\frac{4 \times 0.06}{0.075^2} - 8.709^2 \right) - \frac{1}{2} \right) = -1.01$$

$$J = FLOOR \left(\frac{-1.01 \times \sqrt{0.33}}{1.257} + \frac{1}{1.257^2} \right) = FLOOR(0.169) = 0$$

Since $J = 0$, the diffusion probabilities are computed using equation (6.120) as follows:

$$p_{-1} = \left(\frac{1}{2 \times 1.257^2} + \frac{0}{2} - \frac{1}{2 \times 1.257}(-1.01)\sqrt{0.33} \right)(1 - 1 \times 0.33)$$

$$= 0.366$$

$$p_0 = \left(1 - \frac{1}{1.257^2} \right)(1 - 1 \times 0.33) = 0.245$$

$$p_1 = \left(\frac{1}{2 \times 1.257^2} - \frac{0}{2} + \frac{1}{2 \times 1.257}(-1.01)\sqrt{0.33} \right)(1 - 1 \times 0.33)$$

$$= 0.056$$

At each node:
Top value = bond price, $P(t, T)$
Bottom value = interest rate process, $r(t)$

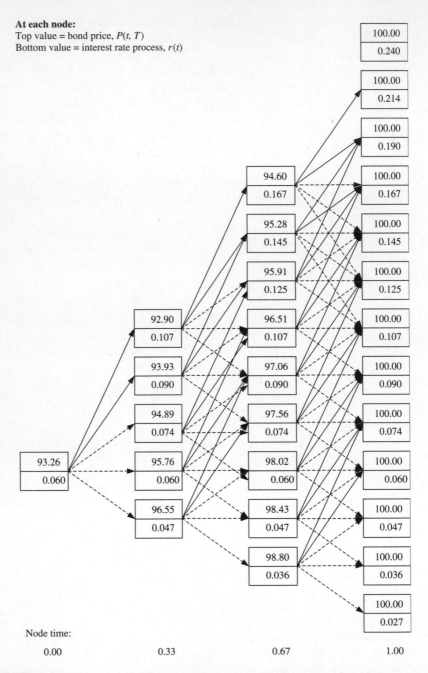

Node time:

0.00   0.33   0.67   1.00

FIGURE 6.17   Tree for the CIR Model Extended with Exponential Jumps

The jump probabilities are computed according to equation (6.124) as follows:

$$x_1 = \frac{(8.709 + 1.257 \times 2.5 \times \sqrt{0.33})^2 0.075^2}{4} - 0.107 = 0.049$$

$$p_2 = (1 - e^{-0.049/0.01}) \times 1 \times 0.33 = 0.331$$

$$x_2 = \frac{(8.709 + 1.257 \times 2.5 \times \sqrt{0.33})^2 0.075^2}{4} - 0.107 = 0.049$$

$$p_3 = e^{-0.049/0.01} \times 1 \times 0.33 = 0.002$$

The bond price at this node is given as follows:

$$P_{31} = \frac{\begin{array}{c} 94.60 \times 0.002 + 95.28 \times 0.331 + 95.91 \times 0.056 \\ + 96.51 \times 0.245 + 97.06 \times 0.366 \end{array}}{e^{0.107 \times 0.33}}$$

$$= \$92.90$$

By following a similar procedure at each node, the bond price at time 0 is $93.26. A 100-step tree gives the price of the bond as $93.75, only 3 cents away from the true price of $93.78 (obtained using the closed-form solution). The CIR bond price without jumps equals $94.18.

Lognormal Jumps

Under this case, the short rate is assumed to follow the following process:

$$dr(t) = \tilde{\alpha}(\tilde{m} - r(t)) \, dt + \sigma \sqrt{r(t)} \, d\tilde{Z}(t) + r(t)(e^{J_N} - 1) \, dN(\tilde{\lambda}) \qquad (6.127)$$

where J_N is normally distributed with mean μ_J and variance σ_J^2.

The following approximation is used to model the short rate tree with lognormal jumps:

$$\left\{ \begin{array}{l} dr(t) = \alpha(\tilde{m} - r(t)) \, dt + \sigma \sqrt{r(t)} \, d\tilde{Z}(t), \text{ with probability } 1 - \tilde{\lambda} \, dt, \\ d \ln r(t) = J_N, \text{ with probability } \tilde{\lambda} \, dt \end{array} \right\}$$

$$(6.128)$$

The tree is constructed by using the grid for the X-transform based on the truncated trinomial tree method of Nawalkha and Beliaeva [2007a] introduced in a previous section of this chapter. However, to accommodate jumps from any given node, we consider M nodes at the next step, with three nodes to capture the diffusion component and $M - 3$ nodes to capture the jump component. The diffusion component of the tree is built exactly as shown in the previous section of the chapter on building trinomial trees for the traditional CIR model. To model the jump component of the tree, the X-transform values are converted back to the short rate values using the formula $r(t) = X^2(t)\sigma^2/4$; and then $r(t)$ values are converted to $\ln r(t)$ values on the entire grid. To keep the analysis general, we consider an arbitrary node $r(t)$ at time $t = i\Delta t$, for $i = 0, 1, 2, \ldots, n-1$, where length of time T is divided into n equal intervals of Δt. At time $(i+1)\Delta t$, the M different values for the interest rate are given as follows:

$$r(t) + \Delta_k, \ k = -\frac{M-1}{2}, \ldots, -1, 0, 1, \ldots, \frac{M-1}{2}$$

A three-step jump-diffusion tree is shown in Figure 6.18. The segmented lines in this figure refer to the diffusion nodes, and solid lines refer to the jump nodes. Note that jumps cannot occur when $r(t) = 0$, and so the next step transitions are either straight or up. The M probabilities associated with the M nodes are given as follows: The short rate can either undergo a local (or diffusion) change with probability $1 - \tilde{\lambda}dt$ or experience a lognormal jump with probability $\tilde{\lambda}dt$. The diffusion probabilities are computed in exactly the same way as those under the exponential jump case (see equations (6.120) and (6.122)).

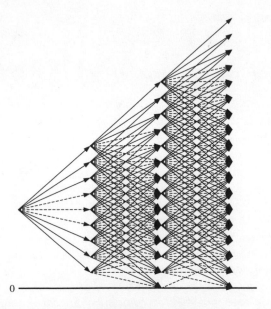

FIGURE 6.18 Three-Step Jump-Diffusion Tree with $M = 9$

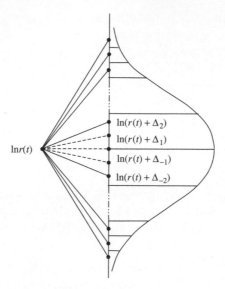

FIGURE 6.19 Approximation of the Lognormal Jump Distribution Using a Normal Curve

The jump nodes are approximated with a normal curve, which can take values between negative infinity and positive infinity (see Figure 6.19). The total risk-neutral probability of jumps is $\tilde{\lambda}\Delta t$. The entire line from negative infinity to positive infinity in Figure 6.19 contains $M - 3$ jump nodes, and it is subdivided into $M - 3$ nonoverlapping intervals that cover the area under the normal curve. The top half of the area under the normal curve that corresponds to three diffusion nodes is assigned to the first jump node above the diffusion nodes, and the bottom half is assigned to the first jump node below the diffusion nodes. The probability mass over each of these $M - 3$ intervals is assigned to the point at the center of each of these intervals in the following three steps.

Step 1. The first step computes the probabilities of all jump nodes except the following nodes: (1) the first jump node above and the first jump node below the three diffusion nodes, and (2) the top jump node and the bottom jump node. The probabilities of these remaining jump nodes are computed as follows:

$$P[r(t) + \Delta_k] = [\mathcal{N}(x_1) - \mathcal{N}(x_2)]\,\tilde{\lambda}\Delta t,$$

$$k = -\frac{M-3}{2}, \ldots, J-2, J+2, \ldots, \frac{M-3}{2} \qquad (6.129)$$

where

$$x_1 = \frac{\ln\left(\dfrac{(X + (k+0.5)b\sqrt{\Delta t})^2 \sigma^2}{4}\right) - \mu_J - \ln(r(t))}{\sigma_J}$$

$$x_2 = \frac{\ln\left(\dfrac{(X + (k-0.5)b\sqrt{\Delta t})^2 \sigma^2}{4}\right) - \mu_J - \ln(r(t))}{\sigma_J}$$

The expression $\mathcal{N}(x_1) - \mathcal{N}(x_2)$ gives the difference between two cumulative normal distributions. Multiplication of this probability with the risk-neutral jump probability $\tilde{\lambda}\Delta t$ gives the probability of the short rate node at the point in the middle of x_1 and x_2.

Step 2. Since the normal distribution covers the whole real line from negative infinity to positive infinity, but we only consider a finite number of nodes in the region, $[r(t) + \Delta_{-(M-1)/2}, r(t) + \Delta_{(M-1)/2}]$ probabilities for the end nodes are adjusted to account for the probability mass outside this region. The probability of the top node is computed as:

$$P\big(r(t) + \Delta_{(M-1)/2}\big) = [1 - \mathcal{N}(x_2)]\,\tilde{\lambda}\Delta t \tag{6.130}$$

where

$$x_2 = \frac{\ln\left(\dfrac{\left(X + \left(\frac{M-1}{2} - 0.5\right)b\sqrt{\Delta t}\right)^2 \sigma^2}{4}\right) - \mu_J - \ln(r(t))}{\sigma_J}$$

Similarly, the probability for the bottom node is computed as:

$$P\big(r(t) + \Delta_{-(M-1)/2}\big) = \mathcal{N}(x_1)\,\tilde{\lambda}\Delta t \tag{6.131}$$

where

$$x_1 = \frac{\ln\left(\dfrac{\left(X + \left(-\frac{M-1}{2} + 0.5\right)b\sqrt{\Delta t}\right)^2 \sigma^2}{4}\right) - \mu_J - \ln(r(t))}{\sigma_J}$$

Step 3. The probability for the first jump node above the diffusion nodes is computed as follows:

$$P\big(r(t) + \Delta_{J+2}\big) = [\mathcal{N}(x_1) - \mathcal{N}(x_2)]\,\tilde{\lambda}\Delta t \tag{6.132}$$

where

$$x_1 = \frac{\ln\left(\dfrac{(X + (J + 2.5)b\sqrt{\Delta t})^2\sigma^2}{4}\right) - \mu_J - \ln(r(t))}{\sigma_J}$$

$$x_2 = \frac{\ln\left(\dfrac{(X + Jb\sqrt{\Delta t})^2\sigma^2}{4}\right) - \mu_J - \ln(r(t))}{\sigma_J}$$

The probability for the first jump node below the diffusion nodes is computed as follows:

$$P\big(r(t) + \Delta_{J-2}\big) = [\mathcal{N}(x_1) - \mathcal{N}(x_2)]\,\tilde{\lambda}\Delta t \tag{6.133}$$

where

$$x_1 = \frac{\ln\left(\dfrac{(X + Jb\sqrt{\Delta t})^2\sigma^2}{4}\right) - \mu_J - \ln(r(t))}{\sigma_J}$$

$$x_2 = \frac{\ln\left(\dfrac{(X + (J - 2.5)b\sqrt{\Delta t})^2\sigma^2}{4}\right) - \mu_J - \ln(r(t))}{\sigma_J}$$

As in the case of exponentially distributed jumps, the number of nodes in a jump-diffusion tree is of the order $O(N^2 M)$. To increase the efficiency of computation, we also truncate the tree from below and above. Though the tree is automatically truncated at zero, we also truncate the tree from above at $(M - 1)/2$. This truncation is illustrated in Figure 6.20. Due to truncation, the number of nodes in a tree is reduced to $O(N \times M)$.

Example 6.5 demonstrates how the untruncated normal jump-diffusion tree can be used to price a bond.

Example 6.5 Consider a discount bond with $F = 100$, $T = 1$, $r_0 = 6\%$, $\tilde{\alpha} = 0.5$, $\tilde{m} = 6\%$, and $\sigma = 10\%$. The intensity of the Poisson process is $\tilde{\lambda} = 1$, and the jump parameters are $\mu_J = 0.144$ and $\sigma_J = 0.142$. Consider using a three-step tree ($N = 3$) with 13 branches ($M = 13$) for pricing this

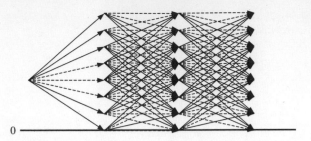

FIGURE 6.20   Lognormal Jump-Diffusion Tree Truncation

bond. The time step of the tree is $\Delta t = 0.33$. The first step of the tree for this example is illustrated in Figure 6.21. The segmented lines correspond to diffusion nodes, while the solid lines correspond to the jump nodes. Each node consists of two numbers. The number in the top row is the bond price obtained by discounting future bond values. The number in the bottom row is the short rate.

To ensure that the X-process values at the bottom level of nodes are *exactly* zero, the value of $b = 1.212$ is computed using equations (6.72), (6.73), and (6.74).

Now consider a given node, for example, the node at time $t = 0.0$. Since this is a starting node of the interest rate tree, $r(0) = 6\%$. The starting value of the X-process is:

$$X(0) = \frac{2\sqrt{0.06}}{0.1} = 4.899$$

Since $r(0) > 0$, the value of J at this node is computed using equation (6.76) as follows:

$$\mu(X,\ t) = \frac{1}{4.899}\left(\frac{1}{2} \times 0.5\left(\frac{4 \times 0.06}{0.1^2} - 4.899^2\right) - \frac{1}{2}\right) = -0.102$$

$$J = FLOOR\left(\frac{-0.102 \times \sqrt{0.33}}{1.212} + \frac{1}{1.212^2}\right) = FLOOR(0.632) = 0$$

Since $J = 0$, the diffusion probabilities are computed using equation (6.120) as follows:

$$p_s = \left(\frac{1}{2 \times 1.212^2} + \frac{0}{2} + \frac{1}{2 \times 1.212}(-0.102)\sqrt{0.33}\right)(1 - 1 \times 0.33)$$

$$= 0.2106$$

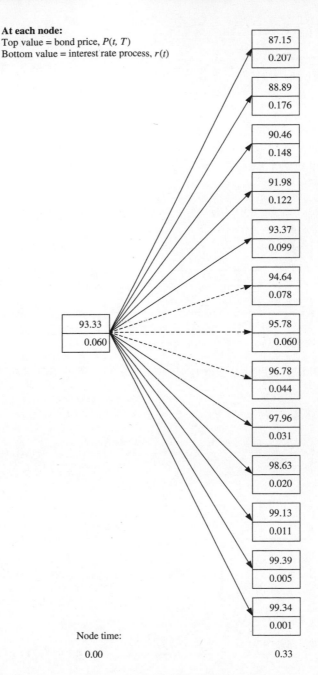

At each node:
Top value = bond price, $P(t, T)$
Bottom value = interest rate process, $r(t)$

Node time:

0.00   0.33

FIGURE 6.21 Tree for the CIR Model Extended with Lognormal Jumps

$$p_6 = \left(1 - \frac{1}{1.212^2}\right)(1 - 1 \times 0.33) = 0.2130$$

$$p_7 = \left(\frac{1}{2 \times 1.212^2} + \frac{0}{2} + \frac{1}{2 \times 1.212}(-0.102)\sqrt{0.33}\right)(1 - 1 \times 0.33)$$

$$= 0.2431$$

The jump probabilities $p_0, p_1, p_2, p_9, p_{10}, p_{11}$ and p_{12} are approximately zero. The computations of the remaining jump probabilities are shown as follows. The jump probability of node 3 is computed according to equation (6.129) as follows:

$$p_3 = (\mathcal{N}(4.697) - \mathcal{N}(3.287)) \times 1 \times 0.33 = 0.0002$$

$$x_1 = \frac{\ln\left(\frac{(4.899 + 3.5 \times 1.212\sqrt{0.33})^2 0.1^2}{4}\right) - 0.144 - \ln(0.06)}{0.142} = 4.697$$

$$x_2 = \frac{\ln\left(\frac{(4.899 + 2.5 \times 1.212\sqrt{0.33})^2 0.1^2}{4}\right) - 0.144 - \ln(0.06)}{0.142} = 3.287$$

The jump probability of node 4 is computed according to equation (6.132) as follows:

$$p_4 = (\mathcal{N}(3.287) - \mathcal{N}(-1.014)) \times 1 \times 0.33 = 0.2814$$

$$x_1 = \frac{\ln\left(\frac{(4.899 + 2.5 \times 1.212\sqrt{0.33})^2 0.1^2}{4}\right) - 0.144 - \ln(0.06)}{0.142} = 3.287$$

$$x_2 = \frac{\ln\left(\frac{(4.899 + 0 \times 1.212\sqrt{0.33})^2 0.1^2}{4}\right) - 0.144 - \ln(0.06)}{0.142} = -1.014$$

Finally, the jump probability of node 8 is computed according to equation (6.133) as follows:

$$p_8 = (\mathcal{N}(-1.014) - \mathcal{N}(-7.237)) \times 1 \times 0.33 = 0.0518$$

$$x_1 = \frac{\ln\left(\frac{(4.899 + 0 \times 1.212\sqrt{0.33})^2 0.1^2}{4}\right) - 0.144 - \ln(0.06)}{0.142} = -1.014$$

$$x_2 = \frac{\ln\left(\frac{(4.899 - 2.5 \times 1.212\sqrt{0.33})^2 0.1^2}{4}\right) - 0.144 - \ln(0.06)}{0.142} = -7.237$$

The time 0 bond price at this node is computed as follows:

$$P_0 = e^{-0.06 \times 0.33} \times \begin{pmatrix} 87.15 \times 0.0 + 88.89 \times 0.0 + 90.46 \times 0.0 \\ +91.98 \times 0.0002 + 93.37 \times 0.2814 \\ +94.64 \times 0.2106 + 95.78 \times 0.2130 \\ +96.78 \times 0.2431 + 97.96 \times 0.0518 \\ +98.63 \times 0.0 + 99.13 \times 0.0 \\ +99.39 \times 0.0 + 99.34 \times 0.0 \end{pmatrix}$$

$$= \$93.33$$

Therefore, the bond price at time 0 is \$93.33. A 100-step tree gives the price of the bond as \$93.76, only 1 cent away from the true price of \$93.77 (obtained using a Monte Carlo simulation). The CIR bond price without jumps equals 94.18.

In general, the number of steps required for accurate valuation of bonds increases with bond maturity. Our simulations suggest that truncating the jump trees from above significantly enhances the efficiency of these trees when using longer maturity bonds. Since the tree is naturally truncated at zero, allowing the truncation from above makes the tree move horizontally from both ends, leading to a significant reduction in computational time. For example, solving a 10-year bond price under a jump-diffusion process can require from 1,500 up to 2,000 steps. With truncation, a value of $M = 100$ to 150 is typically sufficient under realistic parameter values, though the appropriate number will depend upon the relative magnitudes of jump and diffusion variances. Hence, the total number of nodes is of the order $2,000 \times 125 = 250,000$. This is of the same order as a 500-node *pure diffusion* tree without truncation, which also uses $500 \times 500 = 250,000$ nodes.

NOTES

1. Also see Campbell, Lo, and MacKinlay [1997].
2. Also see Bliss and Smith [1998] and Ball and Torous [1995].
3. For example, it can be applied to the model of Ahn and Gao [1999], in which the volatility of the short rate is proportional to $r^{1.5}$.
4. Also see Acharya and Carpenter [2002].
5. Though zero is theoretically not accessible if risk-neutral parameters are defined using the more general market prices of risk (as in Collin-Dufresne Goldstein,

and Jones [2004]), it may be accessible under the traditional risk-neutral parameters given by CIR [1985], without violating arbitrage conditions.

6. Another unsatisfactory method is to disallow the short rate to reach zero by using an arbitrarily small truncation level above zero as suggested by Brigo and Mercurio [2001]. This can be problematic in certain high-volatility scenarios in which the short rate *can reach zero*. We have found that error can accumulate, and simply increasing the number of steps does not allow convergence in this case.

7. The binomial and trinomial models are similar but not identical, even when $b = 1$, due to the structure of node spacing.

8. For example, $5.8 \geq J \geq 5.2$, does not allow an integer value for J.

9. Due to the nature of our tree construction, J is either 0 or 1 when J is not negative and when the total number of steps in the tree is not too small.

CHAPTER 7

Preference-Free CIR and CEV Models with Jumps

This chapter gives preference-free extensions of the fundamental Cox, Ingersoll, and Ross (CIR) [1985] model introduced in Chapter 6. This chapter also introduces the constant elasticity of variance (CEV) models and their preference-free extensions. Fundamental models are useful in determining bond prices from the economic fundamentals reflected in the time-series dynamics of the state variable processes, while preference-free models are useful in valuing interest rate derivatives given the information contained in the cross section of bond prices and/or the prices of a chosen set of plain vanilla interest rate derivatives.

The single-plus models, such as the CIR+ and CEV+ models (i.e., time-homogeneous, preference-free models), invert the risk-neutral parameters by fitting the model prices to the cross sections of market prices of bonds and interest rate derivatives. Since the single-plus models do not require the market prices of risk (MPRs), these models are potentially consistent with general, nonlinear specifications of MPRs consistent with nonaffine state variable processes under the physical measure. The main theoretical appeal of the single-plus models is that the short rate process remains *time-homogeneous* under these models.[1]

The short rate under the preference-free extensions of the CIR and CEV models is given as follows:

$$r(t) = \delta(t) + Y(t) \qquad (7.1)$$

where $\delta(t)$ is a deterministic term and $Y(t)$ is the underlying state variable. The time-homogeneous CIR+ and CEV+ models require that $\delta(t) = \delta$ is a constant, while the time-inhomogeneous CIR++ and CEV++ models allow $\delta(t)$ to change deterministically in order to *exactly* fit the initial bond prices. Since the time-homogeneous CIR+ and CEV+ allow an extra parameter δ, the solutions of bond price and interest rate derivatives under these models nest the corresponding solutions under the fundamental CIR and CEV models.[2]

The first reference to the time-inhomogeneous CIR++ model is given in the original article of CIR [1985, bottom paragraph, p. 395]. However, under the CIR conceptualization, the physical process of the short rate is still affine, consistent with the traditional definition of market price of risk. The CIR approach has been followed by many authors, including Dybvig [1988, 1997], Scott [1995], and Brigo and Mercurio [2001], who use the deterministic term $\delta(t)$ for exact calibration to the initial zero-coupon bond prices. Unlike these papers, we allow the MPRs to be of general, nonlinear form in our derivation of the preference-free CIR++ model. Since Brigo and Mercurio [2001] do not model the MPRs and directly use the Black implied volatility data from caps for inverting the risk-neutral parameters, their approach is consistent with the *preference-free* CIR++ model.[3]

However, none of the authors, including CIR, Dybvig [1988, 1997], Scott [1995], and Brigo and Mercurio [2001], consider the *time-homogeneous* preference-free CIR+ model. Under this approach, the risk-neutral state variable process is specified as follows:

$$dY(t) = \tilde{\alpha}(\tilde{m} - r(t))\, dt + \sigma \, d\tilde{Z}(t) \qquad (7.2)$$

with short rate defined as $r(t) = \delta + Y(t)$. Similar to the derivation of the Vasicek+ model in Chapter 4, the risk-neutral state variable process in equation (7.2) under the CIR+ model can be derived by assuming an exogenous stochastic bond price process under the physical measure and a specific functional form for the cross section of zero-coupon bond prices. Since the parameters, δ, $\tilde{\alpha}$, $\tilde{m}$, and σ are exogenous inputs related to bond volatility and bond prices, these parameters are measured under the physical measure. However, since these parameters also define the risk-neutral state variable process, we allow $\tilde{\alpha}$ and $\tilde{m}$ to have tilde symbols for notational consistency with the fundamental CIR model.

This chapter derives the solutions of bond price and interest rate derivatives under the time-inhomogeneous CIR++ and CEV++ models. The corresponding solutions under the time-homogeneous CIR+ and CEV+ models can be obtained by considering the special case $\delta(t) = \delta$ as a constant. This chapter also considers extensions to these models with exponential and lognormal jumps. Before introducing the CIR++ and CEV++ models, we first summarize another method of calibration to initial zero-coupon bond prices known as the "mean calibration" method. More academic work has been done on the mean-calibrated CIR model since this model was suggested in the original paper of Cox, Ingersoll, and Ross [1985, equations 27 through 30, p. 395] and later formalized by Hull and White [1990, 1993]. This method calibrates the short rate process to initial prices by making the long-term mean of the short rate process time-dependent. Under the mean calibration method, the state variable continues to be the short rate itself, which is different from the CIR++ model in which the state variable is different from the short rate. Hull and White [1990] and Heath, Jarrow, and Morton (HJM) [1992] show that the mean calibration method does not allow calibration of the CIR model to *all* initial shapes of the forward rate curve.

The CIR++ model has a number of theoretical and computational advantages over the mean-calibrated CIR model. Though the mean-calibrated CIR model allows time-homogeneous conditional volatilities for the state variables, the unconditional volatilities are time-inhomogeneous using this method. In contrast, the CIR++ model allows both conditional and unconditional volatilities of the short rate and the forward rates to remain time-homogeneous. Further, the CIR++ model is naturally consistent with the HJM [1992] models, allowing model prices to be calibrated to any shape of the initial forward-rate curve. Another advantage of the CIR++ model is that analytical solutions to bond prices, option prices, and trinomial trees can be derived by simple modifications of these under the original CIR model, whereas analytical solutions do not exist for the mean-calibrated CIR model.

MEAN-CALIBRATED CIR MODEL

Hull and White [1990] apply the mean-calibration method by fitting the CIR model to initially observable bond prices (or forward rates) by making the risk-neutral long-term mean time dependent as follows:

$$dr(t) = \tilde{\alpha}\big(\tilde{m}(t) - r(t)\big)\,dt + \sigma\sqrt{r(t)}\,d\tilde{Z}(t) \qquad (7.3)$$

As we demonstrate now, depending on the shape of the initial forward-rate function, the long-term mean $\tilde{m}(t)$ may take on a negative value when $r(t)$ hits zero. This makes the short rate negative in the next interval. Since the square root of the negative short rate is not meaningful in defining the short rate volatility in the next interval, this method cannot be used for arbitrarily chosen shapes of the initial forward rate curve. To see this, consider the PDE for bond price obtained by using Ito's lemma on bond price and taking risk-neutral expectation as follows:

$$\frac{\partial P}{\partial t} + \tilde{\alpha}\big(\tilde{m}(t) - r(t)\big)\frac{\partial P}{\partial r} + \frac{1}{2}\sigma^2 r(t)\frac{\partial^2 P}{\partial r^2} - r(t)P(t,\,T) = 0 \qquad (7.4)$$

subject to the boundary condition $P(T,\,T) = 1$. Assume that the solution to equation (7.4) has the following form:

$$P(t,\,T) = e^{A(t,T) - r(t)B(\tau)} \qquad (7.5)$$

where $\tau = T - t$, subject to the boundary conditions, $A(T, T) = 0$ and $B(0) = 0$.

Evaluating the partial derivatives of bond price with respect to $r(t)$ and t and substituting them in equation (7.4) produces two ODEs that solve for $A(t, T)$ and $B(\tau)$ given as follows:

$$\underbrace{\frac{\partial B(\tau)}{\partial \tau} = 1 - \tilde{\alpha}B(\tau) - \frac{1}{2}\sigma^2 B^2(\tau)}_{Riccati}$$

(7.6)

$$\frac{\partial A(t, T)}{\partial t} = \tilde{\alpha}\tilde{m}(t)B(T - t)$$

The solution to $B(\tau)$ remains identical to that in the original CIR model and depends on the time remaining to maturity, or $\tau = T - t$. However, solution to $A(t, T)$ is no longer time-homogeneous and depends both on t and T. The solution to the ODE for $A(t, T)$ is given as follows:

$$A(t, T) = -\tilde{\alpha} \int_t^T \tilde{m}(u)B(T - u)\,du$$

(7.7)

Suppose the initial bond prices at time 0 are given by the function $P(0, T)$. To calibrate the bond price function in equation (7.5) to the initial prices, we must have:

$$P(0, T) = e^{A(0,T)-r(0)B(T)}$$

(7.8)

Taking the logarithm of equation (7.8) and substituting $A(0, T)$ from equation (7.7), we get:

$$\ln P(0, T) = -\tilde{\alpha} \int_0^T \tilde{m}(u)B(T - u)\,du - r(0)B(T)$$

(7.9)

Differentiating with respect to T, we get:

$$f(0, T) - r(0)\frac{\partial B(T)}{\partial T} = \tilde{\alpha} \int_0^T \tilde{m}(u)\frac{\partial B(T - u)}{\partial T}\,du$$

(7.10)

Since the derivative of $B(T - u)$ with respect to T is always positive, a necessary condition for $\tilde{m}(t)$ to be positive for all t such that $0 \leq t \leq T$ is that the initial forward-rate curve satisfies the following inequality:

$$f(0, T) \geq r(0)\frac{\partial B(T)}{\partial T}$$

(7.11)

for all $T > 0$. Not all initial forward-rate curves satisfy inequality (7.11); and, hence, the mean-calibration method of CIR [1985] and Hull and White [1990] cannot be always applied, and is inconsistent with the theoretical framework of Heath, Jarrow, and Morton (HJM) [1992]. Also, since no known analytical solution exists for $\tilde{m}(t)$ in equation (7.10), numerical methods are required for solving the bond price using the preceding approach. These methods are computationally expensive, as forward induction involving root-search algorithms must be used to obtain the value of the long-term mean $\tilde{m}(t)$ at each time step.

Finally, it can be shown that the *unconditional* volatilities of both the short rate and the forward rate over a finite horizon become time-inhomogeneous using the mean-calibration method. This is because even though the conditional volatilities of the short rate and the forward rates do not depend upon the long-term mean $\tilde{m}(t)$, the unconditional volatilities of these variables over a finite horizon do depend upon $\tilde{m}(t)$ under the mean-calibrated CIR model. Since interest derivative prices are highly sensitive to the unconditional volatility of the short rate over the option expiration date, a time-inhomogeneous unconditional volatility remains a potential problem for the mean-calibrated CIR model. This is true even when the mean-calibrated CIR model is calibrated to fit only the initial bond prices and not the shape of the initial bond volatility function.[4]

PREFERENCE-FREE CIR+ AND CIR++ MODELS

The single-plus model corresponding to the fundamental CIR model can be shown to be *preference free*, as this model exogenously specifies the stochastic bond price process under the physical measure, as follows:

$$\frac{dP(t, T)}{P(t, T)} = \mu(t, T)\, dt - \sigma\sqrt{Y(t)}B(T - t)\, dZ(t) \qquad (7.12)$$

where,

$$B(\tau) = \frac{2(e^{\beta\tau} - 1)}{(\beta + a)(e^{\beta\tau} - 1) + 2\beta}$$

$$\beta = \sqrt{a^2 + 2\sigma^2} \qquad (7.13)$$

$$Y(t) = r(t) - \delta$$

and where $Z(t)$ is a wiener process; $\mu(t, T)$ is the instantaneous expected return on the bond; and $\sigma\sqrt{Y(t)}B(T - t)$ is the instantaneous bond volatility, which is a function of time remaining to maturity, the state variable $Y(t)$, and nonnegative constants a and σ. The dependence of bond return volatility on the state variable $Y(t)$ instead of the short rate $r(t)$ allows the volatility to be proportional to state variable values that are less than or equal to the short rate by a positive constant equal to δ. Unlike the fundamental CIR model, which specifies the short rate process under the physical measure, the CIR+ model specifies the bond price process exogenously under the physical measure.[5]

The stochastic process in equation (7.12) assumes a *single* factor for bonds maturing at all dates T, such that $0 \leq t \leq T \leq \infty$. As shown in Chapter 4 under the single-factor assumption, a hedge portfolio consisting of two zero-coupon bonds can be constructed to replicate the riskless return over the next instant. An immediate implication of the construction of such a hedge portfolio is that excess returns measured in the units of bond volatility are equal across all bonds, or:[6]

$$-\frac{\mu(t,\ T) - r(t)}{\sigma\sqrt{Y(t)}B(T-t)} = -\frac{\mu(t,\ S) - r(t)}{\sigma\sqrt{Y(t)}B(S-t)} = \gamma(z,\ t) \qquad (7.14)$$

where $\gamma(z,\ t)$ is the market price of interest rate risk with z defined in a general manner to include nonlinear functions of $r(t)$, and/or any other state variable values at time t but $\gamma(z,\ t)$ must remain independent of the maturity term T for all $T \geq t$. Substituting equation (7.14) in equation (7.12) and then using a change of measure, we get:

$$\frac{dP(t,\ T)}{P(t,\ T)} = r(t)\,dt - \sigma\sqrt{Y(t)}B(T-t)\,d\tilde{Z}(t) \qquad (7.15)$$

where, using the Girsanov theorem, the Wiener process under the risk-neutral measure is given as:[7]

$$d\tilde{Z}(t) = dZ(t) + \gamma(z,\ t) \qquad (7.16)$$

Let $f(t,\ T) = -\partial \ln P(t,\ T)/\partial T$ define the time t instantaneous forward rate for date T. Taking the stochastic integral of equation (7.16) and then taking the partial derivative of the log of bond price with respect to bond maturity, the time t instantaneous forward rate is given as follows:

$$f(t,\ T) = f(0,\ T) + \int_0^t \sigma^2 Y(v)\big(\partial B(T-v)/\partial T\big)B(T-v)\,dv$$
$$+ \int_0^t \sigma\sqrt{Y(v)}\big(\partial B(T-v)/\partial T\big)\,d\tilde{Z}(v) \qquad (7.17)$$

where $f(0, T)$ is the instantaneous forward rate defined at time 0. Since the short rate $r(t) = f(t, t)$, evaluating equation (7.17) for $T = t$, gives:

$$
\begin{aligned}
r(t) = f(t, t) = f(0, t) &+ \int_0^t \sigma^2 Y(v)(\partial B(t - v)/\partial t) B(t - v)\, dv \\
&+ \int_0^t \sigma\sqrt{Y(v)}(\partial B(t - v)/\partial t)\, d\tilde{Z}(v)
\end{aligned}
\tag{7.18}
$$

Since the market price of risk $\gamma(z, t)$ *does not appear* in equation (7.18), valuation is preference free under the CIR+ model. Since the CIR+ model requires a *time-homogeneous* short rate process, it requires that the time 0 forward-rate curve is fitted to the following functional form:

$$
f(0, t) = \delta + abB(t) + \left(1 - aB(t) - \frac{1}{2}\sigma^2 B^2(t)\right) Y(0)
\tag{7.19}
$$

It is easy to show that only the specific functional form given in equation (7.19) leads to a time-homogeneous short rate process. Fitting an arbitrary functional form, such as that given by Nelson and Siegel [1987], to $f(0, t)$, leads to a time-inhomogeneous short rate process.

The functional form in equation (7.19) depends upon four parameters, δ, a, b, and σ and the time 0 value of the state variable $Y(0)$. The parameters a and σ and the state variable $Y(0)$ also define the initial bond volatility function in equation (7.12). The interdependence between the shape of the forward rate curve and the volatility curve is a characteristic of all time-homogeneous term structure models. Substituting equation (7.19) into equation (7.18), the risk-neutral short rate process is obtained as follows:

$$
dr(t) = a(b - Y(t))\, dt + \sigma\sqrt{Y(t)}\, d\tilde{Z}(t)
\tag{7.20}
$$

Since by assumption $r(t) = \delta + Y(t)$, the risk-neutral stochastic process of the state variable $Y(t)$ is given as follows:

$$
dY(t) = a(b - Y(t))\, dt + \sigma\sqrt{Y(t)}\, d\tilde{Z}(t)
\tag{7.21}
$$

The preference-free time-inhomogeneous CIR++ model can also be derived using an exogenous stochastic bond price process under the physical measure and an arbitrary initial forward rate curve $f(0, t)$, using the approach for the time-homogeneous CIR+ model, by replacing the parameter δ with a time-dependent function $\delta(t)$. The CIR++ model represents an alternative to the mean-calibrated CIR approach given in the earlier section for fitting *exactly* to any arbitrarily specified initial forward rate curve $f(0, t)$. All of the equations from (7.12) through (7.19) continue to hold under CIR++ model with $\delta(t)$ replacing the parameter δ. Replacing δ with $\delta(t)$, equation (7.19) gives the solution to $\delta(t)$ under the CIR++ model as follows:

$$\delta(t) = f(0,\ t) - abB(t) - \left(1 - aB(t) - \frac{1}{2}\sigma^2 B^2(t)\right)Y(0) \qquad (7.22)$$

where $f(0,\ t)$ is now specified using an arbitrary functional form, such as that given by Nelson and Siegel [1987].

The risk-neutral stochastic process of the state variable $Y(t)$ has the same form under the CIR++ model as under the CIR+ model and is given by equation (7.21). However, since $r(t) = \delta(t) + Y(t)$, using equations (7.21) and (7.22), the time-inhomogeneous risk-neutral short rate process under the CIR++ model is given by applying Ito's lemma, as follows:

$$dr(t) = \left(a\big(b - r(t)\big) + a\delta(t) + \frac{\partial\delta(t)}{\partial t}\right)dt + \sigma\sqrt{Y(t)}\,d\tilde{Z}(t) \qquad (7.23)$$

A Common Notational Framework

The rest of this chapter uses a common framework for the CIR, CIR+, and CIR++ models using the notation $\tilde{\alpha}$ and $\tilde{m}$ instead of a and b, respectively, even under the CIR+/CIR++ models. Of course, the parameters $\tilde{\alpha}$ and $\tilde{m}$ are interpreted differently depending upon whether we are using the fundamental CIR model or the preference-free CIR+/CIR++ models. Under the fundamental CIR model, these parameters are related to the physical parameters α and m of the short rate process through the market prices of risks as shown in equation (6.26) in Chapter 6. Since the fundamental CIR model is based upon an exogenous specification of the short rate process under the physical measure and since the short rate does not trade, market prices of risk must enter the valuation formulas. On the other hand, the preference-free CIR+/CIR++ models are based upon an exogenous specification of the bond price process under the physical measure. The parameters $\tilde{\alpha} = a$, $\tilde{m} = b$, δ, and σ and the initial state variable value $Y(0)$ under the CIR+ model are used to (1) define the bond volatility function and (2) fit the initially observable bond prices at time 0. The CIR++ model differs from the CIR+ model in that the parameter δ is replaced by the deterministic function $\delta(t)$, given in equation (7.22), which is used to fit an arbitrary shape of the initial forward rate curve $f(0,\ t)$.

In the following, we consider the risk-neutral process of $Y(t)$ in its most general form, using a common notational framework with $\tilde{\alpha}$ and $\tilde{m}$ instead of a and b, respectively.[8] Though economic reasons exist for requiring the stationarity of the state variable under the physical measure, a strong theoretical rationale does not exist for requiring stationarity under the risk-neutral measure. Hence, we allow the risk-neutral speed of mean reversion to even take negative values leading to an explosive state-variable process under the risk-neutral measure. As shown in Chapter 9, explosive square-root processes under the risk-neutral measure may be useful for pricing interest rate derivatives. Explosive state variables are quite useful for pricing credit derivatives using the reduced-form framework. For example, Pan and Singleton [2005] find that default intensities implied by the pricing of credit default swaps based on sovereign debt issues often display explosive risk-neutral processes under many different currencies.

Probability Density and the Unconditional Moments

Consider the risk-neutral process for the state variable $Y(t)$ defined in equation (7.2). The time t risk-neutral probability density of the state variable at time S is given as follows:

$$f\big(Y(S), \, S; \, Y(t), \, t\big) = ce^{-u-v}\left(\frac{v}{u}\right)^{q/2} I_q\big(2(uv)^{1/2}\big) \qquad (7.24)$$

where

$$c \equiv \frac{2\tilde{\alpha}}{\sigma^2(1 - e^{-\tilde{\alpha}(S-t)})}$$

$$u \equiv cr(t)e^{-\tilde{\alpha}(S-t)}$$

$$v \equiv cr(S)$$

$$q \equiv \frac{2\tilde{\alpha}\tilde{m}}{\sigma^2} - 1$$

and $I_q(\cdot)$ is the modified Bessel function of the first kind of order q. The distribution function is the noncentral chi-square $\chi^2[2cY(S); \, 2q+2, \, 2u]$, with $2q+2$ degrees of freedom and parameter of noncentrality $2u$ proportional to the current value of the state variable.

The time t mean and variance of $Y(S)$ are given as follows:

$$E_t[Y(S)] = Y(t)e^{-\tilde{\alpha}(S-t)} + \tilde{m}(1 - e^{-\tilde{\alpha}(S-t)})$$

$$V_t[Y(S)] = Y(t)\left(\frac{\sigma^2}{\tilde{\alpha}}\right)(e^{-\tilde{\alpha}(S-t)} - e^{-2\tilde{\alpha}(S-t)}) + \tilde{m}\left(\frac{\sigma^2}{2\tilde{\alpha}}\right)(1 - e^{-\tilde{\alpha}(S-t)})^2 \qquad (7.25)$$

where $\tilde{\alpha}\tilde{m} > 0$ and $\sigma > 0$. The density and moments in equation (7.25) are valid when either both $\tilde{\alpha}$ and $\tilde{m}$ are positive or *both* $\tilde{\alpha}$ and $\tilde{m}$ are negative. Under both cases, the moments remain finite *over a finite time interval*. Obviously, negative values of $\tilde{\alpha}$ and $\tilde{m}$ give infinite unconditional mean and variance at infinite time. This is not problematic in an economic sense, however, since the state variable is assumed to follow a stationary process under the physical measure. Further, unlike the explosive CIR+ and CIR++ models, which allow infinite mean and variance at infinite time, only under the risk-neutral measure, some commonly used preference-free models, such as those considered in Rebonato [2002] and HJM [1992], allow infinite mean and variance at infinite time under both the physical and the risk-neutral measure. For example, consider the proportional volatility forward rate process given by HJM as follows:

$$df(t, T) = \sigma(t, T, f(t, T)) \int_t^T \sigma(t, v, f(t, v)) \, dv + \sigma(t, T, f(t, T)) \, d\tilde{Z}$$

(7.26)

where

$$\sigma(t, T, f(t, T)) = \sigma Min(f(t, T), K)$$ (7.27)

and a finite positive value of K is required to ensure the absence of arbitrage. It can be shown that the asymptotic unconditional mean and variance of this process are infinite under both the physical and the risk-neutral measure. Further, as shown by Jeffrey [1997], the infinite maturity forward rate under the above model becomes infinite over any finite interval of time, which not only violates the results in Dybvig, Ingersoll, and Ross [1996], but seems intuitively quite unreasonable. Similar demonstration can be made regarding the assumed volatility functions for the LIBOR market models proposed by Rebonato [2002].[9] Interestingly, the infinite maturity forward rate under the explosive CIR+ and CIR++ models remains a constant *over any finite interval of time*, and hence, does not violate the arbitrage conditions given by Dybvig, Ingersoll, and Ross [1996].

Using the notation $\tilde{\alpha} = a$, and $\tilde{m} = b$, the risk-neutral stochastic process for the short rate under the CIR++ model can be expressed using equation (7.23), as follows:

$$dr(t) = \left(\tilde{\alpha}(\tilde{m} - r(t)) + \alpha\delta(t) + \frac{\partial\delta(t)}{\partial t} \right) dt + \sigma\sqrt{Y(t)} \, d\tilde{Z}(t)$$ (7.28)

The level of volatility of the short rate is determined by the level of the state variable $Y(t)$, and not the short rate, under the CIR++ model. Both the conditional volatility and the unconditional volatility of the short rate process remain *time-homogeneous* under the CIR++ model. The conditional volatility is time-homogeneous because $Y(t)$ follows a time-homogeneous process. The unconditional volatility of $r(S)$ given $r(t)$, for $S > t$, can be given using equation (7.1), as follows:

$$Var(r(S)|r(t)) = Var(Y(S)|Y(t))$$ (7.29)

Since $Y(t)$ follows a time-homogeneous process, the unconditional volatility of $Y(S)$ given $Y(t)$ is time-homogeneous. Hence, the unconditional volatility of $r(S)$ given $r(t)$ is also time-homogeneous. Note that unlike the CIR++ model, the mean-calibrated CIR model given in equation (7.3) does not allow time-homogeneous unconditional volatility for the short rate process, due to the changing long-term mean $\tilde{m}(t)$.

Bond Price Solution

We first derive the bond price formula using the CIR++ model, and then consider the CIR+ model under the assumption $\delta(t) = \delta$, a constant. Due to the assumed affine relation between $r(t)$ and the state variable $Y(t)$ under the CIR++ model, the solution to the bond price is assumed to be of the following form:

$$P(t,\ T) = e^{A(\tau) - Y(t)B(\tau) - H(t,T)} \qquad (7.30)$$

where

$$H(t,\ T) = \int_t^T \delta(u)\, du \qquad (7.31)$$

subject to $A(0) = B(0) = 0$ and, by definition, $H(t,\ T) = 0$.

Assuming the bond price is a function of $Y(t)$ and t, where the risk-neutral stochastic process of $Y(t)$ is given in equation (7.2) and the short rate is given in equation (7.1), the PDE of the bond price can be derived by the application of Ito's lemma. Taking the partial derivates of the bond price using equation (7.30) and then substituting the partial derivatives into the PDE, we get the following two ODEs:

$$\underbrace{\frac{\partial B(\tau)}{\partial \tau} = 1 - \tilde{\alpha}B(\tau) - \frac{1}{2}\sigma^2 B^2(\tau)}_{Riccati} \qquad (7.32)$$

$$\frac{\partial A(\tau)}{\partial \tau} = -\tilde{\alpha}\tilde{m}B(\tau)$$

Since the ODEs are identical to those under the fundamental CIR model, the solutions of $A(\tau)$ and $B(\tau)$ have the same form as under the CIR model and are given as follows:

$$A(\tau) = \frac{2\tilde{\alpha}\tilde{m}}{\sigma^2} \ln\left[\frac{2\beta e^{\frac{1}{2}(\beta + \tilde{\alpha})\tau}}{(\beta + \tilde{\alpha})(e^{\beta\tau} - 1) + 2\beta} \right] \qquad (7.33)$$

$$B(\tau) = \frac{2(e^{\beta\tau} - 1)}{(\beta + \tilde{\alpha})(e^{\beta\tau} - 1) + 2\beta} \qquad (7.34)$$

where

$$\beta = \sqrt{\tilde{\alpha}^2 + 2\sigma^2}$$

To calibrate the bond price in equation (7.30) to the initially observed bond price, consider the log of the initial price evaluated at time 0 as follows:

$$\ln P(0,\ T) = A(T) - Y(0)B(T) - H(0,\ T) \tag{7.35}$$

Differentiating equation (7.35) with respect to T and simplifying:

$$\delta(T) = \frac{\partial A(T)}{\partial T} - Y(0)\frac{\partial B(T)}{\partial T} - \frac{\partial \ln P(0,\ T)}{\partial T} \tag{7.36}$$

Substituting the partial derivatives of $A(T)$ and $B(T)$ from equation (7.32) in equation (7.36) and then replacing T with t, we get:

$$\delta(t) = f(0,\ t) - \tilde{\alpha}\tilde{m}B(t) - Y(0)\left(1 - \tilde{\alpha}B(t) - \frac{1}{2}\sigma^2 B^2(t)\right) \tag{7.37}$$

where $f(0,\ t) = -\partial \ln P(0,\ t)/\partial t$. Equation (7.37) is the same as obtained earlier in equation (7.22) using the generalized notation $\tilde{\alpha} = a$ and $\tilde{m} = b$.

Since $r(t) = Y(t) + \delta(t)$ and $Y(t)$ cannot be negative, the only way the short rate can become negative is through a negative value of $\delta(t)$ for some $t > 0$. In our simulations, we find that the function $\delta(t)$ remains positive for a range of realistic values of parameters used in the calibration. The most important determinants of whether $\delta(t)$ can be negative for some t is the starting value of the state variable $Y(0)$ and the shape of the initially observable forward rate curve $f(0,\ t)$. If $Y(0)$ is close to $r(0)$ and if $f(0,\ t)$ has an inverted shape, then it's easier for $\delta(t)$ to be negative. On the other hand, if $Y(0)$ is close to zero and if $f(0,\ t)$ has a normal rising shape, then $\delta(t)$ remains positive. We find through calibrations that fitting the CIR++ model to the prices of interest rate caps requires that $Y(0)$ be much smaller than $r(0)$. This, together with the fact that most of the time forward-rate curve displays a rising shape, ensures that $\delta(t)$ is generally positive for all t.

The function $H(t,\ T)$ given as the integral of $\delta(t)$ in equation (7.31) can be solved directly using equation (7.35) under the CIR++ model, as follows:

$$H(t,\ T) = \int_t^T \delta(u)\,du = H(0,\ T) - H(0,\ t) \tag{7.38}$$

$$= A(T) - A(t) - \ln P(0,\ T) + \ln P(0,\ t) - Y(0)\big(B(T) - B(t)\big)$$

Under the time-homogeneous CIR+ model, the function $\delta(t) = \delta$, a constant, and the counterpart to equation (7.37) are given as follows:

$$f(t, \ T) = \delta + \tilde{\alpha}\tilde{m}B(\tau) + Y(t)\left(1 - \tilde{\alpha}B(\tau) - \frac{1}{2}\sigma^2 B^2(\tau)\right), \quad \tau = T - t \quad (7.39)$$

In other words, the forward rate $f(t, \ T)$ implied by the CIR+ model is a time-homogeneous function of $\tau = T - t$ and the state variable $Y(t)$. Since the risk-neutral parameters under the CIR+ model are obtained using the cross sections of market prices of bonds and interest rate derivatives independently of MPR specifications, the time 0 forward-rate curve implied by the CIR+ model fits the observed forward-rate curve better than the forward-rate curve implied by the fundamental CIR model. Further, the fit between the implied forward-rate curve and the observed forward-rate curve improves significantly under the multiple-factor single-plus models with three or more factors.

The $H(t, \ T)$ function under the CIR+ model is given as follows:

$$H(t, \ T) = \int_t^T \delta \, dv = \delta(T - t) = \delta\tau \qquad (7.40)$$

Expected Bond Returns

As in the case of preference-free Gaussian models, the market price of risk can be of a general, nonlinear form under the preference-free CIR+ and CIR++ models, given by the following change of measure:

$$d\tilde{Z}(t) = dZ(t) + \gamma(z, \ t)\,dt \qquad (7.41)$$

where the variable z represents nonlinearities, multiple state variables, and the like. Substituting equation (7.41) into equation (7.2), the physical process followed by the state variable is given as:

$$dY(t) = \left(\tilde{\alpha}(\tilde{m} - Y(t)) + \sigma\gamma(z, \ t)\sqrt{Y(t)}\right)dt + \sigma\sqrt{Y(t)}\,dZ(t) \qquad (7.42)$$

Of course, certain regularity conditions to guarantee the existence of unique strong solutions (see Duffie [2001], Appendix D) and the conditions related to the Girsanov theorem must be satisfied by the function $\gamma(z, t)$ for allowing the change of measure in an arbitrage-free manner (for example, restrictions on the parameters such that $\gamma(z, \ t)$ does not explode to infinity are required to satisfy the Novikov condition related to Girsanov theorem). The stochastic bond price process under the physical measure is given as follows:

$$\frac{dP(t, T)}{P(t, T)} = [r(t) - \sigma\sqrt{Y(t)}B(T - t)\gamma(z, t)]\, dt - \sigma\sqrt{Y(t)}B(T - t)\, dZ(t)$$

$$(7.43)$$

A number of researchers have noted that the market price of risk under the traditional CIR model cannot explain the empirical behavior of expected returns on bonds. For example, expected returns are positive and tend to move in the same direction as the slope of the term structure. These two features contradict each other under the traditional CIR model. To allow richer empirical behavior in expected returns, Duffee [2002] proposes essentially affine extensions of the traditional affine models, while Duarte [2004] proposes semiaffine extensions of the affine models. Duarte's model is similar to the CIR+ model, as it allows nonaffine physical processes for the state variables. Though CIR+ is a preference-free model, it nests the fundamental CIR model, as well as the essentially affine and semiaffine extensions given by Duffee and Duarte, respectively. Future empirical research may identify a more general extension of the fundamental CIR model with even more general MPRs than given by Duffee and Duarte. Such a model will be still nested in the CIR+ model, which allows general specifications of the MPRs.

Though the specification of Duffee [2002] and Duarte [2004] are more realistic in capturing the behavior of expected returns, they still have difficulty in simultaneously fitting the cross-sectional and time-series properties of the yield curve. Both Duffee [2002] and Duarte [2004] find that affine models, even with generalized risk premiums, cannot simultaneously capture both the time variation in conditional variances and the expected return relation with the slope of the term structure. In contrast to these models, note that the expected return specification in equation (7.43) can allow arbitrary nonlinearities and even multiple state variables, similar to equation (4.65) given in Chapter 4 under the Vasicek+ model. Hence, the CIR+ model may introduce less misspecification bias in obtaining the risk-neutral parameters compared to the fundamental CIR model.

Constant Infinite-Maturity Forward Rate under Explosive CIR+ and CIR++ Models

In some instances, it is useful to consider an explosive risk-neutral process for the state variable. An explosive process requires that *both* $\tilde{\alpha}$ and $\tilde{m}$ are negative in equation (7.2), such that $\tilde{\alpha}\tilde{m} > 0$. For example, Pan and

Singleton [2005] find explosive default intensity processes implied by credit default swaps prices in the sovereign debt market. Though fitting the CIR+ and CIR++ models to bond prices and interest rate derivatives may or may not require an explosive risk-neutral process, we show that the explosive process is consistent with a constant infinite-maturity forward rate and hence, does not violate the arbitrage conditions given in Dybvig, Ingersoll, and Ross [1996].

The time t forward rate is an affine function of the state variable $Y(t)$ under the CIR+ and CIR++ models and can be derived by differentiating the logarithm of bond price with respect to T in equation (7.30), as follows:

$$f(t,\,T) = \tilde{\alpha}\tilde{m}B(T-t) + Y(t)\frac{\partial B(T-t)}{\partial T} + \delta(T) \qquad (7.44)$$

where $\delta(t)$ is defined by equation (7.37) under the CIR++ model and $\delta(T) = \delta$, a constant under the CIR+ model.

First, consider the infinite-maturity forward rate at any finite time t under the time-inhomogeneous CIR++ model. Substituting the expressions for $\partial B(T-t)/\partial T$ from equation (7.32) and $\delta(T)$ from equation (7.37) into equation (7.44) and simplifying, we get:

$$
\begin{aligned}
f(t,\,T) = {} & f(0,\,T) + \tilde{\alpha}\tilde{m}[B(T-t) - B(T)] - Y(0)\left[1 - \tilde{\alpha}B(T) - \frac{1}{2}\sigma^2 B^2(T)\right] \\
& + Y(t)\left[1 - \tilde{\alpha}B(T-t) - \frac{1}{2}\sigma^2 B^2(T-t)\right]
\end{aligned}
\qquad (7.45)
$$

Interestingly, the expressions inside the three square brackets in equation (7.45) go to zero as T tends to infinity, *both when $\tilde{\alpha} > 0$ and when $\tilde{\alpha} \leq 0$*. Hence, even when the state variable follows an explosive process (i.e., when $\tilde{\alpha} < 0$ and $\tilde{\alpha}\tilde{m} > 0$), the infinite-maturity forward rate remains a constant over any finite time interval given as:

$$f(t,\,\infty) = f(0,\,\infty) \quad \text{for all } 0 < t < \infty \qquad (7.46)$$

The infinite-maturity forward rate is equal to the initially observed infinite-maturity forward rate over any finite time interval under both a stationary and an explosive process for the state variable $Y(t)$.

Next, consider the infinite-maturity forward rate at any finite time t under the time-homogeneous CIR+ model. Substituting the expressions for $\partial B(T-t)/\partial T$ from equation (7.32) and $\delta(T) = \delta$ into equation (7.44) and simplifying, we get:

$$f(t,\,T) = \tilde{\alpha}\tilde{m}B(T-t) + Y(t)\left[1 - \tilde{\alpha}B(T-t) - \frac{1}{2}\sigma^2 B^2(T-t)\right] + \delta \quad (7.47)$$

Again, since the expression inside the three square brackets in equation (7.47) goes to zero as T tends to infinity, *both when $\tilde{\alpha} > 0$ and when $\tilde{\alpha} \leq 0$*, we have:

$$f(t, \infty) = \delta + \frac{2\tilde{\alpha}\tilde{m}}{\beta + \tilde{\alpha}}, \quad \text{for all } 0 < t < \infty \qquad (7.48)$$

Similar to the CIR++ model, the infinite-maturity forward rate is not stochastic even under the CIR+ model over any finite time interval under both a stationary and an explosive process for the state variable $Y(t)$.

More insight on the behavior of forward-rate volatility can be obtained by considering the risk-neutral stochastic process of the forward rate given as follows under the CIR+ and CIR++ models:

$$df(t, T) = \mu_f(t, T)\,dt + \sqrt{Y(t)}\sigma_f(t, T)\,d\tilde{Z}(t) \qquad (7.49)$$

where

$$\mu_f(t, T) = Y(t)\sigma^2 B(T - t)\left(1 - \tilde{\alpha}B(T - t) - \frac{1}{2}\sigma^2 B^2(T - t)\right), \text{ and}$$

$$\sigma_f(t, T) = \sigma\left(1 - \tilde{\alpha}B(T - t) - \frac{1}{2}\sigma^2 B^2(T - t)\right) \qquad (7.50)$$

It is easy to show that the cross-section shape of the function $\sigma_f(t, T)$ is humped only if the risk-neutral speed of mean reversion $\tilde{\alpha}$ is negative. Interestingly, even with a negative value of $\tilde{\alpha}$, the long-term forward rates are *less* volatile than short-term forward rates, consistent with the empirical behavior of interest rates. This implication does not hold for explosive risk-neutral Gaussian processes, under which the infinite-maturity forward rate has infinite first and second moments, violating the arbitrage conditions in Dybvig, Ingersoll, and Ross [1996].

Though the humped forward-rate volatility curve is consistent with the observed shape of forward-rate volatility curve in bond markets, in our simulations, we find that negative $\tilde{\alpha}$ does not always provide a good fit with the cross-section of interest rate derivative prices, such as interest rate caps and swaptions, under the CIR+ and CIR++ models. Though a negative value of $\tilde{\alpha}$ may not be so useful in the current context of pricing interest rate derivatives using the preference-free CIR+ and CIR++ models, it can be useful in a multifactor context, such as the affine models in Chapter 9 and Pan and Singleton's [2005] model for pricing credit default swaps prices in the sovereign debt market.[10] Our exposition here demonstrates that using an explosive risk-neutral square-root process creates no economic or computational difficulties for the multifactor models.

A Comparison with Other Markovian Preference-Free Models

The forward-rate process under the time-inhomogeneous CIR++ model given in equation (7.49) can be compared to other time-inhomogeneous forward-rate models in the HJM [1992] class. Since the CIR++ model allows a path-independent tree, we focus only on other path-independent models. As is well known, the nodes on a path-independent tree recombine, which reduces the computational burden significantly. Ritchken and Sankarasubramanian (RS) [1995a, 1995b] suggest the following form for the forward-rate volatility function, which allows a two-state variable model with a path-independent tree:

$$Vol[df(t, T)] = g(t, Y(.))k(t, T) \qquad (7.51)$$

where the function $g(t, Y(.))$ may depend upon the current time t and the past and present values of any state variables, such as the short rate (e.g., $Y(t) = r(t)$) but does not depend on T, while $k(t, T)$ is a deterministic function satisfying the following semigroup property:

$$k(t, T) = k(t, u)k(u, T),$$

for all $t \leq u \leq T$, and $k(u, u) = 1$ $\qquad (7.52)$

RS propose the following functional form for the deterministic function $k(t, T)$:

$$k(t, T) = e^{-\kappa(T-t)} \qquad (7.53)$$

Caverhill [1994], Hull and White [1993], RS, and Inui and Kijima [1998] show that it is both necessary and sufficient that the functional form of $k(t, T)$ is given by equation (7.53) in order to obtain a path-independent tree for all *deterministic* volatility models (i.e., $g(t, Y(.))$ is a constant in equation (7.51)). RS further show that for state-variable dependent volatility models (i.e., $g(t, Y(.))$ may depend on t and state variables), it is *sufficient* for the functional form of $k(t, T)$ to be specified by equation (7.53) in order to obtain a path-independent tree. The models that use the functional form of $k(t, T)$ given in equation (7.53) are referred to as the "generalized Vasicek" models in the term structure literature. RS show how to price interest rate derivatives using the generalized Vasicek models by constructing a two-state variable tree that grows in complexity of order N^2 with N steps. On the other hand, the typical HJM model trees grow in complexity of order 2^N with N steps.

Note that the functional form of $k(t, T)$ in equation (7.53) is sufficient, *but not necessary*, to obtain path, independent trees under the time-homogeneous state-variable dependent volatility models. For example, the forward-rate volatility of the CIR++ model given in equation (7.50) is not consistent with the generalized Vasicek models given by equations (7.51) through (7.53). Yet, the CIR++ model allows a statevariable dependent volatility and a path-independent tree. Also, since the CIR++ model only uses one state variable, it grows in complexity of the order N for an N-step tree. Further, not only is the complexity of the tree of a lower order under the CIR++ model, but also the forward-rate volatility curve allows more realistic cross-sectional shapes (including the humped shape) using two parameters versus the exponentially declining shapes under the RS model using only one parameter.

Calibration to the Market Prices of Bonds and Interest Rate Derivatives

Unlike the fundamental CIR model, which uses time-series econometric techniques to determine the risk-neutral parameters using yield data, the CIR+ model uses cross-sectional data on bond prices and interest rate derivatives to determine these parameters. The risk-neutral parameters and state variable values are estimated in the same manner as under the Vasicek+ model in Chapter 4. By using k days of cross-sectional price data on bond and interest rate derivatives, the parameters $\tilde{\alpha}$, $\tilde{m}$, σ, and δ and $Y(t_i)$, for $i = 1, 2, \ldots k$, can be determined by minimizing the deviations of the prices of bonds implied by the CIR+ model from the corresponding market prices as follows:

$$
\underset{\tilde{\alpha},\tilde{m},\sigma,\delta,Y(t_i)}{Min} \left(w_1 \left(\sum_{i=1}^{k} \sum_{j=1}^{n_1} (P_{i,j}^{Model} - P_{i,j}^{Market})^2 \right) \right.
$$
$$
\left. + w_2 \left(\sum_{i=1}^{k} \sum_{j=1}^{n_2} (c_{i,j}^{Model} - c_{i,j}^{Market})^2 \right) \right)
\tag{7.54}
$$

where the index $i = 1, 2, \ldots, k$ sums up the sum of deviations squared over n_1 bonds and n_2 interest rate derivatives over k days. The optimization solves for $4 + k$ parameters and state variable values, given as four parameters, $\tilde{\alpha}$, $\tilde{m}$, σ, and δ and k values of the state variables, $Y(t_1), Y(t_2), \ldots, Y(t_k)$, over k days at times $t_1, t_2, \ldots, t_k$. The weights w_1 and w_2 can be used to normalize the dollar investments in bonds versus the interest rate derivatives (such as caps or swaptions). The calibration in equation (7.54) is consistent with general, nonlinear MPRs, which may depend upon multiple state variables.

Since CIR++ is a time-inhomogeneous model, it takes current bond prices as given, and hence, it can be calibrated using time 0 prices of a given class of interest rate derivatives. The parameters $\tilde{\alpha}$, $\tilde{m}$, σ, and $Y(0)$ can be determined by minimizing the deviations of the prices of interest rate derivatives implied by the CIR++ model from the corresponding market prices, using time 0 cross-sectional price data, as follows.

$$\underset{\tilde{\alpha},\tilde{m},\sigma,Y(0)}{Min}\left(\sum_{j=1}^{n}(c_j^{Model}-c_j^{Market})^2\right) \tag{7.55}$$

where the index $j = 1, 2, \ldots, n$ sums up the deviations squared over n number of interest rate derivatives.

Valuing Futures

Futures on a Zero-Coupon Bond   The time t price of a futures contract expiring at time S written on a zero-coupon bond maturing at time T can be obtained in the same manner under the preference-free CIR+ and CIR++ models as under the fundamental CIR model in Chapter 6. The futures price $P_F(t, S, T)$ follows the following PDE:

$$\frac{\partial P_F}{\partial Y}\left(\tilde{\alpha}(\tilde{m}-Y(t))\right)+\frac{1}{2}\sigma^2 Y(t)\frac{\partial^2 P_F}{\partial Y^2}+\frac{\partial P_F}{\partial t}=0 \tag{7.56}$$

subject to $P_F(S, S, T) = P(S, T)$. Following steps similar to those in Chapter 6, the solution is given as:

$$P_F(t, S, T) = e^{A_F(s)-B_F(s)Y(t)-H(S,T)}, \qquad s = S - t \tag{7.57}$$

where

$$A_F(s) = A(U) - \frac{2\tilde{\alpha}\tilde{m}}{\sigma^2}\ln\left|\frac{\sigma^2 B(U)(e^{-\tilde{\alpha}s}-1)-2\tilde{\alpha}}{2\tilde{\alpha}}\right| \tag{7.58}$$

$$B_F(s) = \frac{-2\tilde{\alpha}B(U)e^{-\tilde{\alpha}s}}{\sigma^2 B(U)(e^{-\tilde{\alpha}s}-1)-2\tilde{\alpha}} \tag{7.59}$$

and $A(U)$ and $B(U)$ are as given in equations (7.33) and (7.34), respectively. The term $H(S, T)$ is defined by equation (7.38) under the CIR++ model and by equation (7.40) under the CIR+ model.

As in the CIR model, the futures price is lower than the forward price; and the futures-forward price discount (FFPD) is given as:

$$FFPD = \frac{P_f(t, S, T) - P_F(t, S, T)}{P_f(t, S, T)} = 1 - P_F(t, S, T)\frac{P(t, S)}{P(t, T)}$$

$$= 1 - e^{(A_F(s)+A(s)-A(\tau))-(B_F(s)+B(s)-B(\tau))Y(t)} \tag{7.60}$$

$$s = S - t \quad \text{and} \quad \tau = T - t$$

The FFPD is always between 0 and 1. In general, with everything else held constant, a higher value of $Y(t)$ implies a higher FFPD. This is because marking to market is dependent on the conditional volatility, which depends on the level of the state variable $Y(t)$. Other relationships are the same as under the fundamental CIR model.

Futures on a Time Deposit   The price of a futures contract on a time deposit—such as Eurodollar and Euribor futures—can be obtained using equation (3.12) in Chapter 3:

$$P_F^{TD}(t, S, T) = \frac{100}{\hat{U}}(1 + \hat{U} - P_F^I(t, S, T)) \tag{7.61}$$

where S is the futures expiration date, $U = T - S$ is the deposit time period calculated using the actual/actual day-count convention, $\hat{U}$ is the deposit time period calculated using actual/360 day-count convention, and $P_F^I(t, S, T)$ is the current price of a futures contract written on a hypothetical asset, which at the expiration date S is worth the inverse of a \$1 face-value zero-coupon bond maturing at time T. Following the same steps as in the previous chapters, the PDE for $P_F^I(t, S, T)$ under the CIR+ and CIR++ models is given as:

$$\frac{\partial P_F^I}{\partial Y}(\tilde{\alpha}(\tilde{m} - Y(t))) + \frac{1}{2}\sigma^2 Y(t)\frac{\partial^2 P_F^I}{\partial Y^2} + \frac{\partial P_F^I}{\partial t} = 0 \tag{7.62}$$

subject to the boundary condition $P_F^I(S, S, T) = 1/P(S, T)$. The solution to equation (7.62) has the following form:

$$P_F^I(t, S, T) = e^{a_F(s)-b_F(s)Y(t)+H(S,T)}, \qquad s = S - t \tag{7.63}$$

subject to $a_F(0) = -A(U)$, $b_F(0) = -B(U)$, and $U = T - S$.

Using the same logic as in Chapter 6, the solutions of $a_F(s)$ and $b_F(s)$ immediately follow from equations (7.58) and (7.59), respectively, by switching the signs of the constants $A(U)$ and $B(U)$ and are given as follows:

$$a_F(s) = -A(U) - \frac{2\tilde{\alpha}\tilde{m}}{\sigma^2} \ln \left| \frac{\sigma^2 B(U)(1 - e^{-\tilde{\alpha}s}) - 2\tilde{\alpha}}{2\tilde{\alpha}} \right| \tag{7.64}$$

$$b_F(s) = \frac{2\tilde{\alpha}B(U)e^{-\tilde{\alpha}s}}{\sigma^2 B(U)(1 - e^{-\tilde{\alpha}s}) - 2\tilde{\alpha}} \tag{7.65}$$

The convexity bias, given as the difference between the futures rate and the forward rate on a time deposit, is defined in equation (3.17) in Chapter 3 and is given as follows:

$$Convexity\ Bias = L_F(t,\ S,\ T) - L_f(t,\ S,\ T)$$

$$= \frac{1 + L_F(t,\ S,\ T)\hat{U}}{\hat{U}}(1 - e^{A(s)-a_F(s)-A(\tau)-\left(B(s)-b_F(s)-B(\tau)\right)Y(t)})$$

$$s = S - t \quad \text{and} \quad \tau = T - t \tag{7.66}$$

The convexity bias is always positive; and, with everything else held constant, a higher value of $Y(t)$ implies a higher convexity bias due to higher conditional volatility. Other relationships are the same as under the fundamental CIR model.

Valuing Options

The closed-form solution of a European call option on a zero-coupon bond under the CIR+ and CIR++ models can be given by taking the following expectation:

$$c_i(t) = \tilde{E}_t \left[\frac{c_i(S) = Max(P(S,\ T_i) - K_i,\ 0)}{e^{\int_t^S r(v)dv}} \right] \tag{7.67}$$

where S is the option expiration date, K_i is the strike price, and T_i is the maturity of the \$1 face-value zero-coupon bond on which the option is written $(T_i \geq S \geq t)$.

Taking the risk-neutral expectation, the European call price equals:

$$c_i(t) = P(t,\ T_i)\chi^2 \left(v_1;\ \frac{4\tilde{\alpha}\tilde{m}}{\sigma^2},\ \frac{2\beta_3^2 Y(t)e^{\beta_1 s}}{\beta_2 + \beta_3 + B(U_i)} \right)$$

$$- K_i P(t,\ S)\chi^2 \left(v_2;\ \frac{4\tilde{\alpha}\tilde{m}}{\sigma^2},\ \frac{2\beta_3^2 Y(t)e^{\beta_1 s}}{\beta_2 + \beta_3} \right) \tag{7.68}$$

where $U_i = T_i - S$

$$v_1 = 2(\beta_2 + \beta_3 + B(U_i)) \left(\frac{A(U_i) - H(S, \ T_i) - \log(K_i)}{B(U_i)} \right)$$

$$v_2 = 2(\beta_2 + \beta_3) \left(\frac{A(U_i) - H(S, \ T_i) - \log(K_i)}{B(U_i)} \right)$$

$$\beta_3 = \frac{2\beta_1}{\sigma^2(e^{\beta_1 s} - 1)}$$

$$\beta_2 = \frac{\tilde{\alpha} + \beta_1}{\sigma^2}$$

$$\beta_1 = \sqrt{\tilde{\alpha}^2 + 2\sigma^2}$$

and where $\chi(v; \ a, \ b)$ is the cumulative distribution of the noncentral chi-squared distribution with a degrees of freedom and parameter of non-centrality equal to b. The term $H(S, \ T_i)$ is defined by equation (7.38) under the CIR++ model and by equation (7.40) under the CIR+ model.

Now consider a European call option on a coupon bond with expiration date S and exercise price K. The coupon bond has n cash flows maturing *after* the option expiration date S, given as C_i at time $T_i > S$, for $i = 1, \ 2, \ \dots, n$. The value of the call option on the coupon bond at expiration date S equals:

$$c(S) = Max \left[\left(\sum_{i=1}^{n} C_i \times P(S, \ T_i) \right) - K, \ 0 \right] \tag{7.69}$$

With a slight alteration to Jamshidian's trick, find the value of the state variable $Y^*(S)$, such that the following equality holds:

$$\sum_{i=1}^{n} C_i \times P(Y^*(S), \ S, \ T_i) = K \tag{7.70}$$

where $P(S, \ T_i) = P(Y^*(S), \ S, \ T_i)$ is the bond price at time S given by equation (7.30). The current price of the call option on the coupon bond equals the price of the portfolio of call options on zero-coupon bonds, given as follows:

$$c(t) = \sum_{i=1}^{n} C_i \times c_i(t) \tag{7.71}$$

where $c_i(t)$ is the time t price of the European call option with expiration date S and exercise price K_i, written on a \$1 face-value zero-coupon bond maturing at time T_i, where $K_i = P(Y^*(S), S, T_i)$. By computing the values of $c_i(t)$ using equation (7.68) for all $i = 1, 2, \ldots, n$ and substituting these in equation (7.71), the value of the call option on the coupon bond is obtained.

Using put-call parity, the closed-form solution of a European put option on a zero-coupon bond and a coupon bond can be immediately obtained. Also, using the equivalence relationships in Chapter 3, the closed-form solutions of caps and swaptions also follow from the solutions of options on zero-coupon bonds and coupon bonds, respectively.

Interest Rate Trees

With a slight modification, the procedure to build binomial and trinomial short rate trees for the CIR+ and CIR++ models is very similar to that given in Chapter 6 for the CIR model. Instead of building the tree for the short rate, it is built for the state variable $Y(t)$. The risk-neutral process for $Y(t)$ given in equation (7.2) has the same form as the risk-neutral process for the short rate given in Chapter 6. Hence, by replacing $r(t)$ with $Y(t)$, the binomial and trinomial trees for the variable $Y(t)$ can be built exactly as they were built for the short rate $r(t)$ using the NB truncated-transform approach from Chapter 6. Once the tree has been built for the $Y(t)$ process and probabilities of all nodes have been computed, the tree for the short rate is obtained by simply adding the term $\delta(t)$ on every node, where $\delta(t)$ equals δ, a constant, under the CIR+ model and is given by equation (7.37) under the CIR++ model.

The term $\delta(t)$ under the CIR++ model can be computed using two different methods. Using the first method, $\delta(t)$ is solved analytically using equation (7.37). However, this solution is valid only in the continuous-time limit, and so it allows an exact match with the initial zero-coupon bond prices only when using a large number of steps in the tree. If an exact match is desired for an arbitrarily small number of steps, then $\delta(t)$ can be obtained numerically for $0 \le t < T$ by defining a pseudo bond price $P^*(0, t)$ as follows:

$$P(0, t) = P^*(0, t)e^{-H(0,t)} = P^*(0, t)e^{-\int_0^t \delta(v)\,dv} \qquad (7.72)$$

where $P(0, t)$ is the initially observed bond price, $P^*(0, t)$ is the pseudo bond price obtained by taking the discounted risk-neutral expectation using the state variable Y as the pseudo short rate. The tree for the Y-process can be used to obtain $P^*(0, t)$ for different values of t (such that $0 \le t < T$). Given the values of $P(0, t)$ and $P^*(0, t)$ for different values of t, $\delta(t)$ can be obtained numerically as follows:

$$H(0, \ t) = \sum_{j=0}^{t/\Delta t - 1} \delta(j\Delta t)\Delta t = \ln P^*(0, \ t) - \ln P(0, \ t) \qquad (7.73)$$

where $\Delta t = t/n$ and the integral in $H(0, \ t)$ is approximated as a discrete sum by dividing t into $t/\Delta t$ number of steps. The values of $\delta(j\Delta t)$, for $j = 0, \ 1, \ 2, \ \dots, n - 1$ can be obtained iteratively by using successive values of t as Δt, $2\Delta t$, $\dots$, and $n\Delta t$, such that an exact match is obtained with the initial bond price function $P(0, \ t)$. The values of $\delta(t)$ can then be added to the appropriate nodes on the n-step $Y(t)$-tree to obtain the corresponding tree for the short rate.

The second method's advantage of exact fitting to initial prices for an arbitrarily small number of steps must be traded off against the disadvantage of the more intensive computation that is required by this method. The choice of method to be used can be evaluated using simulations. Note that both methods given in this section are computationally more efficient than building trees under the Hull and White extension of the CIR model, which requires a forward induction method involving a root-search algorithm to obtain the value of the changing long-term mean $m(t)$ at each time step.

THE CIR+ AND CIR++ MODELS EXTENDED WITH JUMPS

We consider two types of extensions of the CIR+ and CIR++ models with exponential and lognormal jumps. We let the short rate process be defined as a sum of the state variable $Y(t)$ and the deterministic term $\delta(t)$ and allow the state variable to follow jump-diffusion processes, which are given under these two extensions, as follows:

CIR-EJ+ and CIR-EJ++ Models with Exponential Jumps

$$dY(t) = \tilde{\alpha}(\tilde{m} - Y(t)) \, dt + \sigma\sqrt{Y(t)} \, d\tilde{Z}(t) + J_E \, dN(\tilde{\lambda}) \qquad (7.74)$$

where J_E is the jump size distributed exponentially with a positive mean $1/\eta$ and $dN(\tilde{\lambda})$ is a Poisson process distributed with intensity $\tilde{\lambda}$.

CIR-LJ+ and CIR-LJ++ Models with Lognormal Jumps

$$dY(t) = \tilde{\alpha}(\tilde{m} - Y(t)) \, dt + \sigma\sqrt{Y(t)} \, d\tilde{Z}(t) + Y(t)(e^{J_N} - 1) \, dN(\tilde{\lambda}) \qquad (7.75)$$

where J_N is distributed normally with mean μ_J and variance σ_J^2 and $dN(\tilde{\lambda})$ is a Poisson process distributed with intensity $\tilde{\lambda}$.

The exponential jump-based CIR-EJ+ and CIR-EJ++ models allow analytical solutions of bond price, futures price, and options price. Though the prices of these securities must be solved using trees under the lognormal jump-based CIR-LJ+ and CIR-LJ++ models, these models are more realistic than the exponential jump models as they allow both positive and negative jumps, while the exponential jump models allow only positive jumps.

Preference-Free CIR-EJ+ and CIR-EJ++ Models

The bond price, futures price, and options price under the CIR-EJ+ and CIR-EJ++ models can be obtained with slight modifications to these prices under the CIR-EJ model given in Chapter 6. Since the approach is similar to how the CIR+ and CIR++ models are obtained as extensions of the original CIR model, we simply give the analytical solutions without the derivations. Also, since the solutions of the prices of bonds, futures, and options under the CIR-EJ+ and CIR-EJ++ models are very similar to the corresponding solutions under the CIR-EJ model given in Chapter 6, we reference some terms in the formulas that are already derived in Chapter 6. The reader should note that the parameters $\tilde{\alpha}$, $\tilde{m}$, and σ used for defining the short rate process in Chapter 6 should be now reinterpreted as parameters that define the risk-neutral process followed by the state variable $Y(t)$ in equation (7.74) whenever we directly use any terms from Chapter 6. Similarly, the jump parameters from Chapter 6 should be translated as jump parameters used here. Doing this avoids much repetition in rewriting of the similar-looking formulas. The solutions of bond price, futures price, and options price use the term $\delta(t)$ and $H(t, T)$, which are defined differently under the CIR-EJ+ model and the CIR-EJ++ model. Under the CIR-EJ+ model, $\delta(t) = \delta$ and $H(t, T) = \delta(T - t) = \delta\tau$, whereas under the CIR-EJ++ model, they are defined as follows:

$$\delta(t) = f(0, t) - \left(Y(0) + \tilde{\alpha}B(t)(\tilde{m} - Y(0)) - \frac{1}{2}\sigma^2 B^2(t)Y(0) \right) - \frac{\tilde{\lambda}B(t)}{\eta + B(t)}$$

(7.76)

$$H(t, T) = A(T) - A(t) - \ln P(0, T) + \ln P(0, t) - Y(0)\big(B(T) - B(t)\big) \quad (7.77)$$

The following sections give the analytical solutions of bond price, futures price, and options price under the CIR-EJ+ and CIR-EJ++ models.

Bond Price   The solution of the bond price is given as follows:

$$P(t, T) = e^{A(\tau) - Y(t)B(\tau) - H(t,T)} \quad (7.78)$$

and the functions $A(.)$ and $B(.)$ are given in equations (6.96) and (6.97), respectively, in Chapter 6.

Futures on a Zero-Coupon Bond The time t price of a futures contract expiring at time S written on a zero-coupon bond maturing at time T is given as follows:

$$P_F(t, S, T) = e^{A_F(s) - B_F(s)Y(t) - H(S,T)} \tag{7.79}$$

where $A_F(s)$ and $B_F(s)$ are given in equations (6.99) and (6.100), respectively.

Futures on a Time Deposit The time t price of a futures contract on a time deposit—such as Eurodollar and Euribor futures—can be obtained using equation (3.12) in Chapter 3:

$$P_F^{TD}(t, S, T) = \frac{100}{\hat{U}} \left(1 + \hat{U} - P_F^I(t, S, T) \right) \tag{7.80}$$

The solution to $P_F^I(t, S, T)$ is given as:

$$P_F^I(t, S, T) = e^{a_F(s) - b_F(s)Y(t) + H(S,T)} \tag{7.81}$$

where the solutions of $a_F(s)$ and $b_F(s)$ are given in equations (6.105) and (6.106), respectively.

Options Let the time t price of a call option expiring at time S written on a zero-coupon bond maturing at time T under case 1 be given as:

$$c(t) = \tilde{E}_t \left[e^{-\int_t^S r(u)du} max(P(S, T) - K, 0) \right] \tag{7.82}$$

Based upon the Fourier inversion method given in steps 1 through 4 in Chapter 5 (see equations (5.114) through (5.149)), the call price at time t can be given as follows:

$$c(t) = P(t, T)\Pi_{1t} - KP(t, S)\Pi_{2t} \tag{7.83}$$

where

$$\Pi_{1t} = \int_{\ln K}^{\infty} f_{1t}(y)\, dy = \frac{1}{2} + \frac{1}{\pi} \int_0^{\infty} \text{Re} \left[\frac{e^{-i\omega \ln K} g_{1t}(\omega)}{i\omega} \right] d\omega \tag{7.84}$$

$$\Pi_{2t} = \int_{\ln K}^{\infty} f_{2t}(y)\, dy = \frac{1}{2} + \frac{1}{\pi} \int_0^{\infty} \text{Re} \left[\frac{e^{-i\omega \ln K} g_{2t}(\omega)}{i\omega} \right] d\omega \tag{7.85}$$

where

$$g_{1t}(\omega) = \frac{e^{A_1^*(s) - B_1^*(s)Y(t) - H(S,T)(1+i\omega) - H(t,S)}}{P(t, T)}, \qquad s = S - t \tag{7.86}$$

$$g_{2t}(\omega) = \frac{e^{A_2^*(s) - B_2^*(s)Y(t) - H(S,T)(i\omega) - H(t,S)}}{P(t, S)}, \qquad s = S - t \tag{7.87}$$

where $A_1^*(s)$, $B_1^*(s)$, $A_2^*(s)$, and $B_2^*(s)$ are identical to the corresponding solutions given in Chapter 6 (see equations (6.114) through (6.117)). Step 4 in Chapter 5 also demonstrates how to compute the probabilities in equations (7.84) and (7.85) numerically.

Jump-Diffusion Trees

Case 1: CIR-EJ+ and CIR-EJ++ Models   The process for the state variable in equation (7.74) is identical to the short rate process in equation (6.118) in Chapter 6. Hence, the jump-diffusion tree for the $Y(t)$ process can be built exactly as it was built for the short rate in Chapter 6 under exponential jumps. The jump-diffusion tree for the short rate $r(t)$ can be obtained by adding the deterministic term $\delta(t)$ to $Y(t)$ at each node of the tree. The term $\delta(t) = \delta$ is a constant under the CIR-EJ+ model. Under the CIR-EJ++ model, $\delta(t)$ can be solved using two different methods. Using the first method, $\delta(t)$ is solved analytically using equation (7.76). However, this solution is valid only in the continuous-time limit, and so it allows an exact match with the initial zero-coupon bond prices only when using a large number of steps in the tree. If an exact match is desired for an arbitrarily small number of steps, then $\delta(t)$ must be obtained numerically by applying the technique demonstrated in equations (7.72) and (7.73) for the CIR++ model, given earlier.

Case 2: CIR-LJ+ and CIR-LJ++ Models   The process for the state variable in equation (7.75) is identical to the short rate process in equation (6.127) in Chapter 6. Hence, the jump-diffusion tree for the $Y(t)$ process can be built exactly as it was built for the short rate in Chapter 6 under lognormal jumps. The jump-diffusion tree for the short rate $r(t)$ can be obtained by adding the deterministic term $\delta(t)$ to $Y(t)$ at each node of the tree. The term $\delta(t) = \delta$ is a constant under the CIR-LJ+ model. Since the CIR-LJ++ model does not have an analytical solution, $\delta(t)$ cannot be solved analytically. Hence, $\delta(t)$ must be obtained numerically by applying the technique demonstrated in equations (7.72) and (7.73) for the CIR++ model, given earlier.

FUNDAMENTAL AND PREFERENCE-FREE CONSTANT-ELASTICITY-OF-VARIANCE MODELS

Consider the constant-elasticity-of-variance (CEV) process followed by the state variable under the risk-neutral measure, given as follows:

$$dY(t) = (\tilde{\mu} - \tilde{\alpha}Y(t))\,dt + \sigma Y(t)^p\,d\tilde{Z}(t) \tag{7.88}$$

where $\sigma > 0$ and $\tilde{\mu}$ and $p \geq 0$. The parameter $\tilde{\alpha}$ is generally nonnegative but may be negative *if* $p \geq 0.5$. When $\tilde{\alpha} < 0$, the state variable follows a risk-neutral explosive process, while the restriction $p \geq 0.5$ guarantees a unique solution and a nonstochastic infinite-maturity forward rate consistent with the results in Dybig, Ingersoll, and Ross [1996]. The short rate is given as the sum of the state variable and a deterministic term as follows:

$$r(t) = \delta(t) + Y(t) \tag{7.89}$$

The previous model nests the fundamental CEV models and preference-free CEV+ and CEV++ models. The fundamental CEV models generally assume that $\delta(t) = 0$ for all $t \geq 0$, such that $r(t) = Y(t)$, but can allow $\delta(t) = \delta$ to be a constant (e.g., the extension of fundamental CIR model in Duffie and Kan [1996]). The fundamental CEV model nests many models, including those of Merton [1973], Vasicek [1977], CIR [1985 and 1980], Dothan [1978], Marsh and Rosenfeld [1983], Brennan and Schwartz [1980], Courtadon [1982], and Cox and Ross [1976]. For example, assuming $\tilde{\alpha} = 0$ and $p = 0$ gives the Merton [1973] model; assuming $\tilde{\mu} = \tilde{\alpha}\tilde{m}$ and $p = 0$ gives the Vasicek model, where $\tilde{m}$ is the risk-neutral long-term mean of the short rate; and assuming $\tilde{\mu} = \tilde{\alpha}\tilde{m}$ and $p = 0.5$ gives the CIR [1985] model. Similarly, other models listed are nested in equation (7.88) and Table 7.1 gives the restrictions on different parameters required under these models.

Fundamental CEV models typically maintain an affine *drift* term under both measures; and hence, the physical process of the state variable can be given as follows:

$$dY(t) = \left(\mu - \alpha Y(t)\right) dt + \sigma Y(t)^p dZ(t) \tag{7.90}$$

where the physical parameters $\sigma > 0$ and $\alpha, \mu, p \geq 0$. The affine drift is not necessary under the fundamental CEV models, but it is assumed for

TABLE 7.1 Parameter Restrictions Imposed by Alternative Models of Short-Term Interest Rates

Model	μ	α	σ^2	p
Merton		0		0
Vasicek				0
CIR [1985]				1/2
Dothan	0	0		1
GBM	0			1
Brennan and Schwartz				1
CIR [1980]	0	0		3/2
Cox and Ross	0			

simplifying the econometric estimation of the parameters.[11] Chan, Karolyi, Longstaff, and Sanders (CKLS) [1992] use a GMM estimation to identify the physical parameters of the fundamental CEV models.

The preference-free CEV+ and CEV++ models do not require the estimation of MPRs, as these models directly use the cross sections of prices of bonds and interest rate derivatives to invert the risk-neutral parameters. The MPRs under the preference-free CEV+ and CEV++ models can be given by using the following change of measure:

$$d\tilde{Z}(t) = dZ(t) + \gamma(z, t)\, dt \qquad (7.91)$$

where, as under the preference-free affine models given earlier, the variable z may represent nonlinearities and multiple state variables. The physical process of the state variable under the preference-free CEV+ and CEV++ models can be given by substituting equation (7.91) into equation (7.88) to give:

$$dY(t) = (\tilde{\mu} - \tilde{\alpha}Y(t) + \sigma Y(t)^p \gamma(z, t))\, dt + \sigma Y(t)^p\, dZ(t) \qquad (7.92)$$

Certain regularity conditions to guarantee the existence of unique strong solutions (see Duffie [2001, Appendix D]) and the conditions related to the Girsanov theorem must be satisfied by function $\gamma(z,t)$ for allowing the change of measure in an arbitrage-free manner.

Though forward rate volatilities and bond return volatilities must be time-homogeneous under the CEV and CEV+ models, it is not clear whether they remain time-homogeneous under the CEV++ model, which allows a time-inhomogeneous short rate. The following section demonstrates that the volatilities under the CEV++ models also remain time-homogeneous.

Forward Rate and Bond Return Volatilities under the CEV++ Models

Using Ito's lemma, the stochastic process for the short rate is given under the CEV++ models as follows:

$$dr(t) = \tilde{\alpha}(\tilde{m}(t) - r(t))\, dt + \sigma Y(t)^p\, d\tilde{Z}(t) \qquad (7.93)$$

where

$$\tilde{m}(t) = \frac{\tilde{\mu}}{\tilde{\alpha}} + \delta(t) + \frac{1}{\alpha}\frac{\partial \delta(t)}{\partial t}$$

Similar to the CIR++ model, both the conditional and the unconditional volatility of the short rate remain time-homogeneous under the CEV++

models. The conditional volatility of the short rate is time-homogeneous in equation (7.93) since the $Y(t)$ process is time-homogeneous in equation (7.2). Also, using equation (7.89), the unconditional volatility of $r(S)$ given $r(t)$ is equal to:

$$Var(r(S)|r(t)) = Var(Y(S)|Y(t)) \qquad (7.94)$$

Since the unconditional volatility of $Y(S)$ is time-homogeneous, the unconditional volatility of $r(S)$ is time-homogeneous, too.

Expressing the bond price as a function of $Y(t)$ and t, using Ito's lemma, and taking the risk-neutral expectation, the PDE for the bond price under the CEV++ models is given as follows:

$$\frac{\partial P}{\partial t} + [\tilde{\mu} - \tilde{\alpha}Y(t)]\frac{\partial P}{\partial Y} + \frac{1}{2}\sigma^2 Y(t)^{2p}\frac{\partial^2 P}{\partial Y^2} = r(t)P(t, T) = (\delta(t) + Y(t))P(t, T)$$
$$(7.95)$$

subject to the boundary condition $P(T, T) = 1$. Using Ito's lemma and the PDE in equation (7.95), the stochastic bond price process under the risk-neutral measure can be given as follows:

$$\frac{dP(t, T)}{P(t, T)} = r(t)\,dt - \sigma Y(t)^p B(t, T, Y(t))\,d\tilde{Z}(t) \qquad (7.96)$$

where

$$B(t, T, Y(t)) = -\frac{1}{P(t, T)}\frac{\partial P}{\partial Y}$$

Note that unlike the case of the Vasicek++ and CIR++ models, the more general CEV++ models may allow the state variable $Y(t)$ to be contained in the duration of the bond given as $B(t, T, Y(t))$.

By substituting equation (7.91) in equation (7.96), the risk-premium on the bond can be obtained by specifying the bond return under the physical measure as follows:

$$\frac{dP(t, T)}{P(t, T)} = [r(t) - \sigma Y(t)^p B(t, T, Y(t))\gamma(z, t)]\,dt - \sigma Y(t)^p B(t, T, Y(t))\,dZ(t)$$
$$(7.97)$$

The risk premium may contain nonlinearities and may depend upon multiple state variables, as under the CIR++ model given earlier.

The risk-neutral bond price process in equation (7.96) implies the following risk-neutral forward rate process:

$$
\begin{aligned}
df(t,\ T) = {}& \sigma^2 Y(t)^{2p} \frac{\partial B(t,\ T,\ Y(t))}{\partial T} B(t,\ T,\ Y(t))\, dt \\
& + \sigma Y(t)^p \frac{\partial B(t,\ T,\ Y(t))}{\partial T}\, d\tilde{Z}(t)
\end{aligned}
\tag{7.98}
$$

It can be shown that the functions $B(t,\ T,\ Y(t))$ and $\partial B(t,\ T,\ Y(t))/\partial T$ that measure the cross-sectional shape of the bond return volatilities and forward rate volatilities in equations (7.96) and (7.98), respectively, are time-homogeneous. To see this, consider a special case of the PDE given in equation (7.95), which assumes that $\delta(t) = 0$ for all $t \geq 0$. Let $P^*(t,\ T)$ represent the pseudo price of the bond that solves this PDE by forcing $\delta(t)$ to equal 0 for all $t \geq 0$. The PDE of $P^*(t,\ T)$ can be given as follows:

$$
\frac{\partial P^*}{\partial t} + [\,\tilde{\mu} - \tilde{\alpha} Y(t)\,]\frac{\partial P^*}{\partial Y} + \frac{1}{2}\sigma^2 Y(t)^{2p} \frac{\partial^2 P^*}{\partial Y^2} - Y(t)P^*(T,\ T) = 0
\tag{7.99}
$$

subject to $P^*(T,\ T) = 1$. Since $Y(t)$ is a time-homogeneous process and the PDE in equation (7.99) does not contain any time-dependent terms, the solution of $P^*(t,\ T)$ will be time-homogeneous and hence, expressible as a function of $\tau = T - t$, or $P^*(t,\ T) = P^*(\tau)$. Also, since the true bond price $P(t,\ T)$ is given as the discounted risk-neutral expectation of the face value of the bond, the relationship between $P(t,\ T)$ and $P^*(t,\ T)$ must be given as:

$$
P(t,\ T) = P^*(t,\ T)e^{-H(t,T)} = P^*(\tau)e^{-H(t,T)}
\tag{7.100}
$$

where

$$
H(t,\ T) = \int_t^T \delta(u)\, du
\tag{7.101}
$$

It follows from equations (7.100) and (7.101) that the function $B(t,\ T,\ Y(t))$ defined in equation (7.96) is given as follows:

$$
B(t,\ T,\ Y(t)) = -\frac{1}{P(t,\ T)} \times \frac{\partial P(t,\ T)}{\partial Y(t)} = -\frac{1}{P^*(\tau)} \times \frac{\partial P^*(\tau)}{\partial Y(t)} = B(\tau, Y(t))
\tag{7.102}
$$

Hence, $B(t,\ T,\ Y(t)) = B(\tau,\ Y(t))$ and $\partial B(t,\ T,\ Y(t))/\partial T = \partial B(\tau,\ Y(t))/\partial \tau$ are time-homogeneous, as they can expressed as functions of $\tau = T - t$ and $Y(t)$. Also, since $Y(t)$ is also a time-homogeneous process, the conditional volatilities of bond return and the forward rate process are time-homogeneous in equations (7.96) and (7.98), respectively.

The forward rate volatility in equation (7.98) cannot be solved analytically since the bond price does not have an analytical solution. However, as shown next, the bond price can be solved using trinomial trees, similar to the ones introduced in Chapter 6. By using the bond price solution from trinomial trees, the forward rate volatility can be approximated using the definitions in equations (7.96) and (7.98), as follows:

$$\sigma Y(t)^p \frac{\partial B(t,\ T,\ Y(t))}{\partial T}$$

$$= \sigma Y(t)^p \lim_{\Delta T \to 0} \left(\lim_{\Delta Y \to 0} \left(\begin{array}{c} -\dfrac{\left(\begin{array}{c} P(t,\ T+\Delta T,\ Y(t)+\Delta Y) \\ -P(t,\ T+\Delta T,\ Y(t)) \end{array} \right)}{P(t,\ T+\Delta T,\ Y(t))\Delta Y} \\ +\dfrac{P(t,\ T,\ Y(t)+\Delta Y)-P(t,\ T,\ Y(t))}{P(t,\ T,\ Y(t))\Delta Y} \end{array} \right) \Big/ \Delta T \right)$$

$$(7.103)$$

Equation (7.103) requires solving the bond price for four different values using the trinomial trees given in the next section. By using very small values of $\Delta r \to 0$ and $\Delta T \to 0$, equation (7.103) gives a numerical solution of forward rate volatility for a given term T.[12] Solving equation (7.103) for a range of values of T, the forward rate volatility curve can be obtained. By allowing the value of $\tilde{\alpha}$ to be negative with $p \geq 0.5$ and varying other parameters, one could obtain humped shapes for the forward rate volatility curve.

Since analytical solutions don't exist for fundamental and preference-free CEV models, for general values of p, we need a fast and accurate numerical valuation method for these models.[13] We now demonstrate how trinomial trees can be applied for valuing bonds, futures, and options under these models.

Valuing Interest Rate Derivatives Using Trinomial Trees

Except for a few special cases, when $p = 0$ and $p = 0.5$ in equation (7.88), the CEV, CEV+, and CEV++ models do not have analytical solutions for the prices of bonds, futures, options, and other interest rate derivatives. The derivative prices are computed using trinomial trees by specifying the appropriate boundary conditions at the terminal payoff dates. We show how the trinomial tree derived in Chapter 6 can be generalized to apply to the CEV, CEV+, and CEV++ models nested in equations (7.88) and (7.89).

The procedure for valuing interest rate derivatives follows two steps. In the first step we obtain a trinomial tree for the time-homogeneous risk-neutral process followed by the state variable in equation (7.88). The second step obtains the trinomial tree for the short rate process by using the term $\delta(t)$. Though $\delta(t)$ is a constant equal to δ under the CEV and CEV+ models, it is time-dependent under the CEV++ models. Adding $\delta(t)$ to every node of the trinomial tree for $Y(t)$ gives the trinomial tree for the short rate, which is then applied for valuing bonds, futures, and options.

We consider the generalization under three different cases, given as $0.5 \le p < 1, p = 1$, and $p > 1$, which are given as follows:[14]

Case 1: $0.5 \le p < 1$

The Nelson and Ramaswamy transform given in Chapter 6 can be applied to the state variable process in equation (7.88), as follows:

$$X(t) = \int^{Y(t)} \frac{1}{\sigma u^p}\, du = \frac{(Y(t))^{1-p}}{\sigma(1 - p)} \tag{7.104}$$

By taking the inverse of equation (7.104), we obtain the short rate as follows:

$$Y(t) = \left(\sigma X(t)(1 - p)\right)^{1/(1-p)} \tag{7.105}$$

Applying Ito's lemma on equation (7.104), the stochastic process for the $X(t)$ can be given as:

$$dX(t) = \mu(X,\, t)\, dt + d\tilde{Z}(t) \tag{7.106}$$

where

$$\mu(X,\, t) = \frac{\tilde{\mu}}{\sigma}\left(\sigma X(t)(1 - p)\right)^{p/(p-1)} - \tilde{\alpha}X(t)(1 - p) - \frac{1}{2X(t)}\frac{p}{(1 - p)} \tag{7.107}$$

The procedure to obtain the trinomial trees is similar to the NB truncated-transform approach given in Chapter 6 and is described as follows: The nodes on the X-tree and the corresponding probabilities are given by following two steps.

Step 1: The Values of $Y(t) > 0$ and $X(t) > 0$ The up, middle, and down moves of the $X(t)$ process are given as follows:

$$X_u = X(t) + b(J + 1)\sqrt{\Delta t}$$

$$X_m = X(t) + bJ\sqrt{\Delta t} \tag{7.108}$$

$$X_d = X(t) + b(J - 1)\sqrt{\Delta t}$$

where b is computed using equation (6.74) in Chapter 6, $X(0)$ is computed from $Y(0)$ using equation (7.104), and J is given as follows:

$$J = FLOOR \left(\frac{\mu(X, t)\sqrt{\Delta t}}{b} + \frac{1}{b^2} \right) \tag{7.109}$$

and $\mu(X, t)$ is as defined in (7.107). To match the instantaneous mean $\mu(X, t)\Delta t$ and the variance Δt of the $X(t)$ process (see equations (7.106) and (7.107)), the trinomial probabilities are given as follows:

$$p_u = \frac{1}{2b^2} - \frac{J}{2} + \frac{1}{2b}\mu(X, t)\sqrt{\Delta t}$$

$$p_d = \frac{1}{2b^2} + \frac{J}{2} - \frac{1}{2b}\mu(X, t)\sqrt{\Delta t} \tag{7.110}$$

$$p_m = 1 - \frac{1}{b^2}$$

Step 2: The Values of $X(t) = 0$ and $Y(t) = 0$ When $X(t)$ and $Y(t)$ are equal to zero, only the drift of the state variable process needs to be matched. The up node is selected as the node *closest* to the truncation line of zero at which the inequality given in equation (7.111) is satisfied:

$$Y^u = \left(\sigma X^u (1 - p) \right)^{1/(1-p)} \geq \tilde{\mu}\Delta t$$

which implies:

$$X^u = b(J + 1)\sqrt{\Delta t} \geq \frac{(\tilde{\mu}\Delta t)^{1-p}}{\sigma(1 - p)} \tag{7.111}$$

such that $J \geq 1$. The down node simply moves horizontally and stays at zero, or:

$$X_d = 0 \tag{7.112}$$

We do not need the middle node since the variance of the state variable is zero when $Y = 0$, and only the drift of the state variable needs to be matched. The probabilities of the up and the down nodes are computed using the binomial method to match the drift of the state variable and are given as:

$$p_u = \frac{(\tilde{\mu} - \tilde{\alpha}Y)\Delta t + Y - Y_d}{Y_u - Y_d} = \frac{\tilde{\mu}\Delta t}{Y_u}$$

since $Y, Y_d = 0$ and

$$p_d = 1 - p_u \tag{7.113}$$

The trees obtained for these cases will generally exhibit multiple-node jumps, which are applied in the same manner as the trinomial tree method given in Chapter 6.

Case 2: p = 1 Under this case, the risk-neutral process for the state variable can be rewritten as follows:

$$dY(t) = \left(\tilde{\mu} - \tilde{\alpha} Y(t) \right) dt + \sigma Y(t) \, d\tilde{Z}(t) \tag{7.114}$$

The $X(t)$ transform given in Chapter 6 can be applied to the process in equation (7.114) as follows:

$$X(t) = \int^{Y(t)} \frac{1}{\sigma u} \, du = \frac{\ln(Y(t))}{\sigma} \tag{7.115}$$

By taking the inverse of equation (7.115), we get back the state variable as:

$$Y(t) = e^{X(t)\sigma} \tag{7.116}$$

Applying Ito's lemma on equation (7.115), the stochastic process for the $X(t)$ can be given as:

$$dX(t) = \mu(X, t) \, dt + d\tilde{Z}(t) \tag{7.117}$$

where

$$\mu(X, t) = \frac{\tilde{\mu}}{\sigma} e^{-\sigma X(t)} - \frac{\tilde{\alpha}}{\sigma} - \frac{\sigma}{2} \tag{7.118}$$

The values of the X-transform for the case when $0.5 \leq p < 1$ (see equation (7.104)) range from zero to less than infinity. In contrast, the X-transform given in equation (7.115) for the current case allows $X(t)$ values to range between negative infinity and positive infinity. A zero value for $Y(t)$ implies that $X(t)$ equals negative infinity, and a positive infinite value of $Y(t)$ implies that $X(t)$ equals positive infinity. Hence, the state variable $Y(t)$ remains strictly positive (zero is an unattainable boundary) and is always less than infinity over any finite interval. Since $Y(t)$ never hits zero, we can ignore the computation of the parameter b in equation (6.74) in Chapter 6, and simply use $b = \sqrt{1.5}$. The up, middle, and down moves in the X-process with $b = \sqrt{1.5}$ are given as follows:

$$X_u = X(t) + (J + 1)\sqrt{1.5}\sqrt{\Delta t}$$
$$X_m = X(t) + J\sqrt{1.5}\sqrt{\Delta t} \tag{7.119}$$
$$X_d = X(t) + (J - 1)\sqrt{1.5}\sqrt{\Delta t}$$

where J is given as follows:

$$J = FLOOR\left(\frac{\mu(X,\ t)\sqrt{\Delta t}}{\sqrt{1.5}} + \frac{2}{3}\right) \qquad (7.120)$$

and $\mu(X,\ t)$ is given in equation (7.118). To match the instantaneous mean $\mu(X,\ t)\Delta t$ and the variance Δt of the $X(t)$ process (see equations (7.117) and (7.118)), using the three nodes in equation (7.120), the trinomial probabilities are given as follows:

$$p_u = \frac{1}{3} - \frac{J}{2} + \frac{1}{\sqrt{6}}\mu(X,\ t)\sqrt{\Delta t}$$

$$p_m = \frac{1}{3} \qquad (7.121)$$

$$p_d = \frac{1}{3} + \frac{J}{2} - \frac{1}{\sqrt{6}}\mu(X,\ t)\sqrt{\Delta t}$$

Case 3: $p > 1$ For this case, the equations for the X-transform, the inverse to obtain the state variable, the stochastic process for $X(t)$, and the drift $\mu(X, t)$ are identical to case 1 and are given by equations (7.104), (7.105), (7.106), and (7.107), respectively. For this case, $X(t)$ equals negative infinity when the state variable $Y(t)$ equals zero, and $X(t)$ equals zero when the state variable $Y(t)$ equals positive infinity. The state variable can never become zero over a finite length of time.

The up, middle, and down moves of the $X(t)$ process are given as follows:

$$X_u = X(t) + (J+1)\sqrt{1.5}\sqrt{\Delta t}$$

$$X_m = X(t) + J\sqrt{1.5}\sqrt{\Delta t} \qquad (7.122)$$

$$X_d = X(t) + (J-1)\sqrt{1.5}\sqrt{\Delta t}$$

and J is given as follows:

$$J = FLOOR\left(\frac{\mu(X,\ t)\sqrt{\Delta t}}{\sqrt{1.5}} + \frac{2}{3}\right) \qquad (7.123)$$

where $\mu(X,\ t)$ is defined in (7.107). To match the instantaneous mean $\mu(X,\ t)\Delta t$ and the variance Δt of the $X(t)$ process (see equations (7.106) and (7.107)), using the three nodes in equation (7.123), the trinomial probabilities are given as follows:

$$p_u = \frac{1}{3} - \frac{J}{2} + \frac{1}{\sqrt{6}}\mu(X, t)\sqrt{\Delta t}$$

$$p_m = \frac{1}{3} \qquad\qquad\qquad (7.124)$$

$$p_d = \frac{1}{3} + \frac{J}{2} - \frac{1}{\sqrt{6}}\mu(X, t)\sqrt{\Delta t}$$

The previous three cases show how to build the trinomial tree for the $Y(t)$ process. The trinomial tree for the short rate under the CEV and CEV+ models can be obtained by adding a constant δ to the values on the tree for the $Y(t)$ process.[15] To obtain the trinomial tree for the short rate under the CEV++ models, we need to solve the deterministic term $\delta(t)$, which allows an exact fit with the initial zero-coupon bond prices. The $\delta(t)$ term can be computed by defining the pseudo bond price $P^*(t, T)$ using the state variable $Y(t)$ given in equation (7.88) as the pseudo short rate using the technique outlined in equations (7.72) and (7.73).

As a final observation, note that the path-independent nature of the tree allows extending the single-factor CEV, CEV+, and CEV++ models to two-factor versions of these models with correlated factors, providing a powerful set of alternatives to two-factor affine and quadratic models. The basic tree construction for this is similar to the procedure for two-factor trees given in Chapter 8, with the use of NB truncated-transform as explained in this chapter. The two-factor trees for CEV, CEV+, and CEV++ models are not only relevant for pricing interest rate derivatives, but with slight modifications, they are also relevant for pricing credit derivatives with American features using the reduced-form approach introduced in Chapter 9.

FUNDAMENTAL AND PREFERENCE-FREE CONSTANT-ELASTICITY-OF-VARIANCE MODELS WITH LOGNORMAL JUMPS

This section considers the fundamental and preference-free constant-elasticity-of-variance models with lognormal jumps, denoted as the CEV-LJ, CEV-LJ+, and CEV-LJ++ models. Since the analytical tractability allowed by the exponential jump process is of little use under general CEV models and since this process disallows negative jumps, we do not consider this process. Let the short rate be given as $r(t) = Y(t) + \delta(t)$, and let $Y(t)$

follow a CEV process with lognormal jumps, given under the risk-neutral measure as:

$$dY(t) = \left(\tilde{\mu} - \tilde{\alpha} Y(t) \right) dt + \sigma Y(t)^p \, d\tilde{Z}(t) + Y(t)(e^{J_N} - 1) \, dN(\tilde{\lambda}) \quad (7.125)$$

where $p \geq 0.5$, $\tilde{\mu} > 0$, J_N is distributed normally with mean μ_J and variance σ_J^2, and $dN(\tilde{\lambda})$ is a Poisson process distributed with intensity $\tilde{\lambda}$. To get more insight on the process in equation (7.125), consider the change in the state variable conditional on the occurrence of a jump, as follows:

$$dY(t) = Y(t)(e^{J_N} - 1), \text{ if } dN(\tilde{\lambda}) = 1 \quad (7.126)$$

The change in the log of the state variable is given as follows:

$$d \log Y(t) = \log \left(Y(t) + Y(t)(e^{J_N} - 1) \right) - \log Y(t) = J_N \quad \begin{cases} \text{if } dN(\tilde{\lambda}) = 1 \\ \text{and } Y(t) > 0 \end{cases}$$
$$(7.127)$$

and

$$d \log Y(t) = 0 \quad \{\text{if } dN(\tilde{\lambda}) = 1, \text{ and } Y(t) = 0 \quad (7.128)$$

Since negative infinity is an unattainable boundary for J_N, zero is an unattainable boundary for the state variable over the next interval *if* the current value of the state variable is greater than zero. Since we restrict our attention to models with $p \geq 0.5$, we can consider two special cases. When $0.5 \leq p < 1$, the state variable may become zero, but the zero boundary is reached by the diffusion component of the state variable process, since a jump by itself can never hit zero *if* the current value of the state variable is greater than zero. Of course, downward jumps can lead to the state variable hitting zero more quickly, but eventually the zero boundary is reached by the diffusion component and not the jump component. When the zero boundary is reached, the change in the state variable due to the jump component is zero in the next interval (see equation (7.128)). The state variable becomes positive after hitting zero, due to the positive drift (i.e., $\tilde{\mu} > 0$) from the diffusion component of the state variable process. When $p \geq 1$, neither the diffusion component nor the jump component can allow the state variable to hit the zero boundary.

The valuation of bonds and interest rate derivatives under the CEV-LJ, CEV-LJ+, and CEV-LJ++ models must be done using numerical techniques such as the jump-diffusion trees given in Chapter 6. We already demonstrated how the trinomial trees for the CIR model from Chapter 6 can be modified to generate the trinomial trees for the CEV, CEV+, and CEV++ models in this chapter (see equations (7.104) through (7.124)).

In Chapter 6, we also demonstrate how a multinomial jump tree can be superimposed on the trinomial diffusion tree under the CIR-LJ model (i.e., CIR model with lognormal jumps). Since the jump tree for the $Y(t)$ process under lognormal jumps is identical to the jump tree for the short rate process in Chapter 6, a similar multinomial jump tree can be superimposed on the trinomial diffusion tree given in this chapter for valuation under the CEV-LJ, CEV-LJ+, and CEV-LJ++ models.

The CEV-LJ, CEV-LJ+, and CEV-LJ++ models can be applied in a number of interest rate derivative markets. Though models without jumps may perform well in fitting at-the-money interest rate caps and swaptions, systematic biases may exist in fitting these models to deep-out-of-the-money caps and swaptions (see Jarrow, Li, and Zhao [2004]). In fact, jump-based models are typically useful in fitting model prices to market prices of instruments trading far from at-the-money strikes in most financial derivative markets. Using the additional flexibility allowed by both jumps and parameter p for the degree of dependence of conditional volatility on the state variable $Y(t)$, the CEV-LJ, CEV-LJ+, and CEV-LJ++ models can be fitted to a larger variety of humped shapes of the two-dimensional Black implied-volatility surfaces (with strike and expiration date as the two axes) in the interest rate cap and swaptions markets.

The pricing of credit derivatives using reduced form models is another area with potential applications. For example, the default spread process can be modeled using the CEV-LJ+ or CEV-LJ++ framework, while the short rate can follow a regular CEV+ or CEV++ process. With appropriate correlation between the spread process and the short rate process, a two-dimensional tree with jumps can be constructed to price a variety of credit derivatives. Some of these applications are illustrated in the third book in the trilogy on The Fixed Income Valuation Course, *Credit Risk Modeling*.

NOTES

1. General preference-free models in the HJM [1992] class do not allow a *time-homogeneous* short rate process.
2. Note that under the Gaussian case, the fundamental models and single-plus models have identical solutions (see Chapters 4 and 5).
3. The notation "CIR++" was invented by Brigo and Mercurio [2001]. However, the meaning given to the two plus signs, the first plus for independence from MPRs and the second plus for calibration to the initial bond prices, is our contribution. The CIR+ model (with only one plus sign) has been introduced in this book.
4. Calibrating to the shape of the initial bond volatility function obviously introduces time-inhomogeneous volatility.

5. Term structure models with an exogenous specification of a stochastic bond price have been given by Merton [1973], Ball and Torous [1983], Schaefer and Schwartz [1987], Nawalkha [1995], and others. The Heath, Jarrow, and Morton [1992] model also can be specified using an exogenous stochastic bond price process instead of the forward-rate process. The models of Merton [1973] and Nawalkha [1995] do not violate the Girsanov theorem for performing the change of measure; however, the models of Ball and Torous [1983] and Schaefer and Schwartz [1987] violate this theorem and hence, imply arbitrage opportunities.

6. This is formally shown in Chapter 4.

7. The function $\gamma(t, z)$ must satisfy certain boundedness conditions related to the Novikov condition of the Girsanov theorem and to the Lipschitz and growth conditions for obtaining unique solutions given in Appendix D of Duffie [2001].

8. Using the generalized notation, equation (7.2) is identical to equation (7.21). The risk-neutral state variable process in equation (7.21) is obtained endogenously using an exogenous specification of the stochastic bond price process under the CIR+/CIR++ models.

9. In contrast, the infinite maturity forward rate always has a zero instantaneous volatility under the CIR++ model (shown later in the chapter), even though it allows an explosive risk-neutral process.

10. Pan and Singleton [2005] find that default intensity follows a risk-neutral explosive process in the credit default swap markets of various currencies.

11. For certain forms of MPRs, additional restrictions may be required. For example, under the essentially affine form of MPRs in Duffee [2002], additional parameter restrictions are needed to guarantee that the state variable will remains strictly above zero under both the physical measure and the risk-neutral measure.

12. For example, using $\Delta r = 0.00001$ and $\Delta T = 0.0001$ gives accurate results.

13. Analytical solutions exist only when $p = 0$ and 0.5.

14. The case of $p = 0$ is already considered in Chapter 4, which gives trinomial trees for Vasicek [1977] and its preference-free extensions.

15. For all fundamental CEV models given in Table 7.1, $\delta = 0$.

CHAPTER 8

Fundamental and Preference-Free Two-Factor Affine Models

O ne of the aims of the trilogy in The Fixed Income Valuation Course is to provide basic analytical and software tools that can be used for building security valuation models in a diverse set of fixed income markets including, but not limited to, loans and bonds with embedded options (e.g., callable and convertible bonds) in the corporate bond markets, exchange-traded futures and options in the Treasury markets, standard and exotic interest rate derivative products in the over-the-counter Eurodollar/Euroyen markets, credit derivatives instruments in the over-the-counter credit markets, and prepayment options in the mortgage-backed securities markets. Many products in these markets require only a single interest rate factor, as other noninterest factors play a significant role in valuation. For example, pricing of a credit default spread may require only one interest rate factor in addition to the credit factor. Yet, other products may require two interest rate factors, and some may require more than three or four interest rate factors (e.g., the exotic interest rate derivative products).

This chapter introduces two-factor affine term structure models for pricing interest rate and credit derivatives. The demonstration of these models for pricing credit derivatives is given in Chapter 9. We consider both fundamental affine term structure models (ATSMs) and preference-free ATSMs. The assumptions made by the models in these two paradigms are guided by different objectives. The fundamental ATSMs are used for valuing default-free bonds given basic assumptions about the economic factors and preferences, while the preference-free ATSMs are used for valuing derivative securities that are consistent with a given set of observed bond prices. The fundamental ATSMs require a joint estimation of the physical parameters and the market prices of risks (MPRs), while preference-free ATSMs do not require MPRs as inputs and hence, allow general nonlinear specifications

---

This chapter was coauthored with Iuliana Ismailescu.

of the MPRs. The preference-free ATSMs can be further divided into time-homogeneous models and time-inhomogeneous models.

Dai and Singleton [2000, 2002] show that the N-factor fundamental ATSMs can be classified into $N + 1$ nonnested subfamilies by using the criteria of *admissibility* and *maximal flexibility*. The specification of an affine model is considered admissible if it allows a well-defined bond price that remains an exponentially affine function of the state variables. The specification of an affine model is maximally flexible if any additional flexibility in the model is not econometrically identifiable. The criteria given by Dai and Singleton can be used to determine whether a given affine model in the term structure literature is maximally flexible in its subfamily or is overidentified.

The notation $A_M(N)$ defines a distinct fundamental ATSM subfamily of N-factor models with conditional volatilities of the state variables depending on M number of state variables. Since the integer M can range from zero to N, there exist $N + 1$ nonnested subfamilies of N-factor fundamental ATSMs. For bond prices to meet the admissibility criteria and remain exponentially affine, some of the conditional correlations cannot be allowed for nested subfamilies with $M > 0$. Also, since models in the $A_M(N)$ subfamily require that the M state variables always remain nonnegative (since volatilities cannot be square roots of negative numbers), certain restrictions on the signs and magnitudes of drift parameters are also required to satisfy the admissibility criteria.

This chapter introduces nested subfamilies of two-factor fundamental ATSMs given as $A_0(2)$ (i.e., two-factor Gaussian), $A_1(2)$ (i.e., two-factor hybrid), and $A_2(2)$ (i.e., two-factor square-root) models. The fundamental models impose restrictive linear forms on the specifications of market prices of risks (MPRs), which are generally required for a joint econometric estimation of the physical parameters and the MPRs using the time-series data on bond yields.

This chapter also considers preference-free extensions of the fundamental two-factor ATSMs that allow general nonlinear specifications of the MPRs. Chapter 4 and Chapter 7 demonstrate how preference-free extensions of the Vasicek and CIR models, respectively, can be obtained by exogenous specifications of the stochastic bond price processes and specific bond price solutions at time zero. This technique allows obtaining the stochastic process for the short rate directly under the risk-neutral measure, circumventing the requirement of market prices of risks. Consistent with this approach, this chapter derives preference-free two-factor ATSMs by specifying the short rate process *directly under the risk-neutral measure*.

Extending the notation of Dai and Singleton [2000], the time-homogeneous preference-free two-factor ATSMs are denoted as $A_0(2)+$, $A_1(2)+$, and $A_2(2)+$ models. The risk-neutral parameters under these models are estimated directly using the cross sections of prices on bonds and interest rate derivatives. Since these models are consistent with general nonlinear MPRs, they can allow conditional correlations of any sign between the physical processes of the state variables under all three subfamilies of the two-factor ATSMs. The criteria of admissibility is applied only to the risk-neutral processes used for valuation of bonds and interest rate derivatives, and hence, the physical processes may be nonaffine and allow multiple state variables in the diffusion and drift coefficients under these models. Though the solutions of bond price and interest rate derivatives under the time-homogeneous preference-free ATSMs are identical to those under the corresponding fundamental models, the similarity is only in the form, as the empirical estimates of the risk-neutral parameters under the two paradigms are different because the latter models impose restrictive functional forms on the MPRs.

The time-inhomogeneous preference-free two-factor ATSMs corresponding to the fundamental two-factor ATSMs are denoted as $A_0(2)++$, $A_1(2)++$, and $A_2(2)++$ models. These models are not only consistent with general nonlinear MPRs, but also with an initially observed zero-coupon bond price function. The consistency with the initially observed zero-coupon bond price function is obtained by allowing a time-inhomogeneous process for the short rate under the risk-neutral measure. Some of the more common time-inhomogeneous preference-free models are easily classified using our generalized scheme. For example, the two-factor Hull and White [1996] model and the G2++ model of Brigo and Mercurio [2006] are both equivalent to the $A_0(2)++$ model. Similarly, the CIR2++ (Cox, Ingersoll, and Ross) model of Brigo and Mercurio [2006] is equivalent to the $A_2(2)++$ model.

Though its potentially feasible to derive the *triple-plus* time-inhomogeneous preference-free models given as $A_0(2)+++$, $A_1(2)+++$, and $A_2(2)+++$, which, in addition to the other characteristics of the double-plus models, also allow an *exact fit* with an initially observed shape of the bond volatility function, these models imply a time-inhomogeneous evolution of the future bond volatility function. Since in our view (see last section of Chapter 3), a time-inhomogeneous volatility function can lead to strange and unappealing behavior of future bond volatilities, we do not consider the triple-plus term structure models in this book.

Duffee [2002] and Duarte [2004] propose the "essentially affine" and "semiaffine" generalizations of the traditional affine models, highlighting the importance of more general specifications of MPRs in the context of the fundamental ATSMs. The semiaffine models even allow *nonaffine* state variable processes under the physical measure. Though these generalizations provide significant improvements over the completely affine models (see Dai and Singleton [2002]), they still impose restrictive functional forms on the MPRs.

The preference-free ATSMs simply do away with the need for a joint estimation of the physical parameters and the MPRs to obtain the risk-neutral parameters and hence, are consistent with general nonlinear specifications of MPRs. Since the risk-neutral parameters of the preference-free ATSMs are obtained directly from the cross sections of prices of bonds and interest rate derivatives, and since these parameters are estimated without specifying the MPRs, they are not exposed to the misspecification biases resulting from the restricted forms of MPRs under the fundamental models.

This chapter also demonstrates how to obtain two-factor trinomial trees for the three subfamilies of two-factor preference-free ATSMs. The tree construction for the $A_0(2)+$ and $A_0(2)++$ models is straightforward since both state variables follow Gaussian processes. The trees for the $A_2(2)+$ and $A_2(2)++$ models are obtained by extending the trinomial trees in the CIR+ and CIR++ frameworks to two-factor trees using Nawalkha and Beliaeva's [2007a] truncated-transform approach. The two-factor short rate trees under the models mentioned grow to the order of N^2 nodes at the Nth step. The trees for the stochastic volatility-based $A_1(2)+$ and $A_1(2)++$ models are more complex, as the second state variable's conditional variance depends on the first state variable, which makes the tree grow to the order of N^3 nodes at the Nth step.

TWO-FACTOR GAUSSIAN MODELS

The time-inhomogeneous preference-free two-factor Gaussian model, or the $A_0(2)++$ model, is perhaps the most widely used model in the fixed income derivative markets after the LIBOR market model. Introduced as the two-factor Hull and White [1996] model, this model has been renamed as the G2++ model by Brigo and Mercurio [2006], who give an extensive set of formulas for pricing a variety of interest rate derivatives using this model. We begin this section with an introduction to the fundamental $A_0(2)$ model and then consider the preference-free extensions of this model, given as then $A_0(2)+$ and $A_0(2)++$ models.

The $A_0(2)$, $A_0(2)+$, and $A_0(2)++$ models can also be expressed in three different forms, given as the Ac form, the Ay form, and the Ar form (see Dai and Singleton [2000]). The two state variables under the Ac, or the canonical, form are *conditionally* independent (i.e., the instantaneous changes in the state variables over the next instantaneous interval are independent) but may be unconditionally correlated. The state variables under the Ay form are *conditionally* correlated but do not have unconditional correlations.

Finally, one of the state variables under the *Ar* form is the short rate itself. Adding another subscript to denote whether the given model is expressed in *Ac*, *Ay*, or *Ar* form uniquely identifies not only the specific model, but also the form in which it is expressed. For example, $A_{0y}(2)+$ denotes the time-homogeneous preference-free two-factor Gaussian model expressed in the *Ay* form. Similarly, although both the Hull and White [1996] model and the Brigo and Mercurio [1996] G2++ model are equivalent forms of the $A_0(2)++$ model, the former model is classified as the $A_{0r}(2)++$ model, and the latter model is classified as the $A_{0y}(2)++$ model.

Due to much practitioner interest in the $A_0(2)++$ model, we demonstrate the main elements of this model in all three forms and show the equivalence relationships between the different forms. Doing this exercise illuminates the subtle relationships between conditional correlations, unconditional correlations, and conditional means of the state variables. This is also helpful in understanding the relationships between equivalent forms of ATSMs in other subfamilies with even a higher number of factors, given in Chapter 9.

The Canonical, or the *Ac*, Form: The Dai and Singleton [2002] Approach

The $A_{0c}(2)$ Model Consider the short rate defined as the sum of a constant and two state variables given as follows:

$$r(t) = \delta + X_1(t) + X_2(t) \tag{8.1}$$

The state variables follow Gaussian processes under the risk-neutral measure given as follows:

$$dX_1(t) = -\tilde{\alpha}_{11}X_1(t)\,dt + \sigma_1\,d\tilde{Z}_1(t), \quad X_1(0) = 0$$
$$dX_2(t) = [-\tilde{\alpha}_{21}X_1(t) - \tilde{\alpha}_{22}X_2(t)]\,dt + \sigma_2\,d\tilde{Z}_2(t), \quad X_2(0) = 0 \tag{8.2}$$

where the two Wiener processes are independent. Duffee [2002] and Dai and Singleton [2002] give more general forms of market prices of risks, under which the change of measure can be given as follows:

$$d\tilde{Z}_1(t) = dZ_1(t) + \left(\frac{\gamma_{10} + \gamma_{11}X_1(t) + \gamma_{12}X_2(t)}{\sigma_1} \right) dt$$
$$d\tilde{Z}_2(t) = dZ_2(t) + \left(\frac{\gamma_{20} + \gamma_{21}X_1(t) + \gamma_{22}X_2(t)}{\sigma_2} \right) dt \tag{8.3}$$

The physical processes followed by the state variables can be obtained by substituting the Wiener processes in equation (8.2). Dai and Singleton use the maximally flexible form in equation (8.2) to specify the physical processes, while we use it to specify the risk-neutral processes. Since our objective is to price securities using the risk-neutral measure, equation (8.2) allows using the least number of risk-neutral parameters for achieving this, while still allowing the maximal specification of the $A_{0c}(2)$ model. Alternatively, we could have used the form in equation (8.2) to specify the physical processes, substituted the Wiener processes from equation (8.3) into equation (8.2) to get the risk-neutral processes, and then used a rotation of factors to allow the maximally flexible specification given in the same reduced form with only six parameters.

The advantage of specifying MPRs in a general manner in equation (8.3) is that it allows the key empirical findings of Fama and Bliss [1987] and Campbell and Shiller [1991] related to the patterns of violations of "expectations theory" to be explained within the framework of fundamental ATSMs. Specifically, the parameters γ_{11}, γ_{12}, γ_{21}, and γ_{22} play a key role in explaining the conditional expected returns on bonds. Though Dai and Singleton [2002] recommend a three-factor Gaussian model, the general MPR specifications are relevant for better specifications of the two-factor Gaussian model, also.

By applying Ito's lemma to the bond price, equating the change in bond price to riskless return, and then taking the risk-neutral expectation, the PDE for the bond price is given as follows:

$$\frac{\partial P}{\partial t} - \frac{\partial P}{\partial X_1}\tilde{\alpha}_{11}X_1(t) - \frac{\partial P}{\partial X_2}\left(\tilde{\alpha}_{21}X_1(t) + \tilde{\alpha}_{22}X_2(t)\right) + \frac{1}{2}\frac{\partial^2 P}{\partial X_1^2}\sigma_1^2 + \frac{1}{2}\frac{\partial^2 P}{\partial X_2^2}\sigma_2^2$$

$$= r(t)P(t, T) \tag{8.4}$$

subject to $P(T, T) = 1$. Consider the following solution of the bond price:

$$P(t, T) = e^{A(\tau) - B_1(\tau)X_1(t) - B_2(\tau)X_2(t) - H(t,T)} \tag{8.5}$$

where

$$H(t, T) = \int_t^T \delta \, dv = \delta(T - t) = \delta\tau \tag{8.6}$$

and $\tau = T - t$. Taking the partial derivatives of the bond price using equation (8.5), substituting these in equation (8.4), and using a change of variable $\tau = T - t$, we get the following three ODEs:

$$\frac{\partial A(\tau)}{\partial \tau} = \frac{1}{2}\sigma_1^2 B_1^2(\tau) + \frac{1}{2}\sigma_2^2 B_2^2(\tau)$$

$$\frac{\partial B_1(\tau)}{\partial \tau} = 1 - \tilde{\alpha}_{11} B_1(\tau) - \tilde{\alpha}_{21} B_2(\tau) \tag{8.7}$$

$$\frac{\partial B_2(\tau)}{\partial \tau} = 1 - \tilde{\alpha}_{22} B_2(\tau)$$

subject to $A(0) = B_1(0) = B_2(0) = 0$. The closed-form solutions for $A(\tau)$, $B_1(\tau)$, and $B_2(\tau)$ are given as follows:

$$
A(\tau) = \frac{\sigma_1^2}{2} \left\{
\begin{aligned}
& \left(\frac{\tilde{\alpha}_{22} - \tilde{\alpha}_{11}}{\tilde{\alpha}_{11}\tilde{\alpha}_{22}}\right)^2 \left(\tau - 2\frac{e^{-\tilde{\alpha}_{11}\tau} - 1}{\tilde{\alpha}_{11}} - \frac{e^{-2\tilde{\alpha}_{11}\tau} - 1}{2\tilde{\alpha}_{11}}\right) \\
& + \left(\frac{\tilde{\alpha}_{21}}{\tilde{\alpha}_{22}(\tilde{\alpha}_{11} - \tilde{\alpha}_{22})}\right)^2 \left(-\frac{e^{-2\tilde{\alpha}_{22}\tau} - 1}{2\tilde{\alpha}_{22}}\right) \\
& + 2\frac{e^{-(\tilde{\alpha}_{11}+\tilde{\alpha}_{22})\tau} - 1}{\tilde{\alpha}_{11} + \tilde{\alpha}_{22}} - \frac{e^{-2\tilde{\alpha}_{11}\tau} - 1}{2\tilde{\alpha}_{11}}\right) \\
& + 2\frac{\tilde{\alpha}_{21}(\tilde{\alpha}_{22} - \tilde{\alpha}_{21})}{\tilde{\alpha}_{11}\tilde{\alpha}_{22}^2(\tilde{\alpha}_{11} - \tilde{\alpha}_{22})} \left(\frac{e^{-\tilde{\alpha}_{11}\tau} - 1}{\tilde{\alpha}_{11}} - \frac{e^{-\tilde{\alpha}_{22}\tau} - 1}{\tilde{\alpha}_{22}}\right. \\
& \qquad\qquad\qquad\qquad \left.+ \frac{e^{-(\tilde{\alpha}_{11}+\tilde{\alpha}_{22})\tau} - 1}{\tilde{\alpha}_{11} + \tilde{\alpha}_{22}} - \frac{e^{-2\tilde{\alpha}_{11}\tau} - 1}{2\tilde{\alpha}_{11}}\right)
\end{aligned}
\right\}
$$
$$
+ \frac{\sigma_2^2}{2\tilde{\alpha}_{22}^2} \left\{\tau + 2\frac{e^{-\tilde{\alpha}_{22}\tau} - 1}{\tilde{\alpha}_{22}} - \frac{e^{-2\tilde{\alpha}_{22}\tau} - 1}{2\tilde{\alpha}_{22}}\right\} \tag{8.8}
$$

$$B_1(\tau) = \left(1 - \frac{\tilde{\alpha}_{21}}{\tilde{\alpha}_{22}}\right)\left(\frac{1 - e^{-\tilde{\alpha}_{11}\tau}}{\tilde{\alpha}_{11}}\right) + \frac{\tilde{\alpha}_{21}}{\tilde{\alpha}_{22}}\left(\frac{e^{-\tilde{\alpha}_{22}\tau} - e^{-\tilde{\alpha}_{11}\tau}}{\tilde{\alpha}_{11} - \tilde{\alpha}_{22}}\right) \tag{8.9}$$

$$B_2(\tau) = \frac{1 - e^{-\tilde{\alpha}_{22}\tau}}{\tilde{\alpha}_{22}} \tag{8.10}$$

The $A_{0c}(2)+$ and $A_{0c}(2)++$ Models The preference-free $A_{0c}(2)+$ and $A_{0c}(2)++$ models obtain the risk-neutral parameters directly from the cross sections of prices on bonds and interest rate derivatives, and hence, do not require restrictive assumptions on the functional forms of MPRs. Using general nonlinear MPRs, the change of measure in equation (8.3) can be replaced with the following:

$$d\tilde{Z}_i(t) = dZ_i(t) + \gamma_i(z, t)\,dt, \quad \text{for all } i = 1 \text{ and } 2 \tag{8.11}$$

where it is assumed that the conditions related to the Girsanov theorem are satisfied by the functions $\gamma_i(z, t)$ for allowing the change of measure in an arbitrage-free manner (for example, restrictions on the parameters such that $\gamma_i(z, t)$ does not explode to infinity are required to satisfy the

Novikov condition related to Girsanov theorem). The functions $\gamma_i(z, t)$ can be nonlinear functions of $X_1(t)$ and $X_2(t)$ and may even depend on other state variables (for example, see equations (4.62) through (4.65) in Chapter 4).

The solutions of the bond price and interest rate derivatives under the time-homogeneous preference-free $A_{0c}(2)+$ model are identical to those under the fundamental $A_{0c}(2)$ model, except that the risk-neutral parameters estimated under the two models may be different, since the latter model imposes restrictive linear functional forms on the MPRs. The solution of the bond price under the time-inhomogeneous preference-free $A_{0c}(2)++$ model can be obtained by following the same steps as under the fundamental $A_{0c}(2)$ model, except that the constant δ in equation (8.1) is replaced with a deterministic function $\delta(t)$, the time 0 values of the state variables $X_1(0)$ and $X_2(0)$ are equated to zero, and $H(t, T)$ in equation (8.6) is replaced by the following:

$$H(t, T) = \int_t^T \delta(v)\, dv \qquad (8.12)$$

To give a full closed-form solution to the bond price under the $A_{0c}(2)++$ model, we now derive the solution to both functions $\delta(t)$ and $H(t, T)$. Consider the initially observable zero-coupon bond price function given as $P(0, T)$. To calibrate the bond price solution in equation (8.5) to the initial bond price function $P(0, T)$, consider the log of bond price evaluated at time 0 as follows:

$$\ln P(0, T) = A(T) - H(0, T) \qquad (8.13)$$

where, by definition, $X_1(0) = X_2(0) = 0$. Taking the partial derivative of equation (8.13) with respect to bond maturity and then substituting the first ODE given in equation (8.7), we get:

$$\delta(t) = f(0, t) + \frac{1}{2}B_1^2(t)\sigma_1^2 + \frac{1}{2}B_2^2(t)\sigma_2^2 \qquad (8.14)$$

where $f(0, t) = -\partial \ln P(0, t)/\partial t$ is the time 0 forward rate for term t. The solution to the term $H(t, T)$ can be given using equation (8.5), as follows:

$$H(t, T) = \int_t^T \delta(v)\, dv = H(0, T) - H(0, t)$$
$$= A(T) - A(t) - \ln P(0, T) + \ln P(0, t) \qquad (8.15)$$

where $A(t)$ and $A(T)$ are given by equation (8.8), and $P(0, t)$ and $P(0, T)$ are initial zero-coupon bond prices.

The *Ar* Form: The Hull and White [1996] Approach

Hull and White [1996] give the time-inhomogeneous preference-free $A_0(2)++$ model in the *Ar* form, or the $A_{0r}(2)++$ model, without deriving the fundamental $A_{0r}(2)$ model corresponding to it. The $A_{0r}(2)++$ model is equivalent to the canonical $A_{0c}(2)++$ model given in the previous section. We begin this section by directly introducing the $A_{0r}(2)++$ model, which nests both the time-homogeneous preference-free $A_{0r}(2)+$ model and the fundamental $A_{0r}(2)$ model. The short rate process under the $A_{0r}(2)++$ model is given as follows:

$$dr(t) = \left(\theta(t) + u(t) - \tilde{\alpha}_r r(t)\right) dt + \sigma_r \, d\tilde{Z}_r(t)$$

$$du(t) = -\tilde{\alpha}_u u(t) \, dt + \sigma_u \, d\tilde{Z}_u(t), \quad u(0) = 0 \tag{8.16}$$

where $d\tilde{Z}_r(t)d\tilde{Z}_u(t) = \rho_{ru}dt$.

The Hull and White model can be made consistent with the framework presented in this chapter by expressing the short rate as follows:

$$r(t) = Y(t) + \delta(t), \quad Y(0) = 0 \tag{8.17}$$

Then by defining $\theta(t)$ as:

$$\theta(t) = \tilde{\alpha}_r \delta(t) + \frac{\partial \delta(t)}{\partial t} \tag{8.18}$$

and using (8.16) and (8.17), we get:

$$dY(t) = \left(u(t) - \tilde{\alpha}_r Y(t)\right) dt + \sigma_r \, d\tilde{Z}_r(t), \qquad Y(0) = 0$$

$$du(t) = -\tilde{\alpha}_u u(t) \, dt + \sigma_u \, d\tilde{Z}_u(t), \qquad u(0) = 0 \tag{8.19}$$

Unlike equation (8.16), the formulation in equation (8.19) gives a *time-homogeneous* system of equations for the state variable processes. As in the previous section, the market prices of risks can be of a general, nonlinear form. By applying Ito's lemma to the bond price, equating the change in bond price to riskless return, and then taking risk-neutral expectation, we get the PDE for the bond price as follows:

$$\frac{\partial P}{\partial t} + \frac{\partial P}{\partial Y}\left(u(t) - \tilde{\alpha}_r Y(t)\right) - \frac{\partial P}{\partial u}\tilde{\alpha}_u u(t) + \frac{1}{2}\frac{\partial^2 P}{\partial Y^2}\sigma_r^2 + \frac{1}{2}\frac{\partial^2 P}{\partial u^2}\sigma_u^2$$

$$+ \frac{\partial^2 P}{\partial Y \partial u}\sigma_r \sigma_u \rho_{ru} = r(t)P(t, \, T) \tag{8.20}$$

subject to $P(T, T) = 1$. Since bond prices are exponentially affine in state variables, consider the following solution of the bond price:

$$P(t, T) = e^{A(\tau) - B_u(\tau)u(t) - B_r(\tau)Y(t) - H(t,T)} \tag{8.21}$$

where

$$H(t, T) = \int_t^T \delta(v)\, dv \tag{8.22}$$

and $\tau = T - t$. Taking the partial derivatives of the bond price using equation (8.21), substituting these in equation (8.20), and using a change of variable $\tau = T - t$, we get the following three ODEs:

$$\frac{\partial A(\tau)}{\partial \tau} = \frac{1}{2}B_u^2(\tau)\sigma_u^2 + \frac{1}{2}B_r^2(\tau)\sigma_r^2 + B_u(\tau)B_r(\tau)\sigma_u\sigma_r\rho_{ru}$$

$$\frac{\partial B_u(\tau)}{\partial \tau} = B_r(\tau) - B_u(\tau)\tilde{\alpha}_u \tag{8.23}$$

$$\frac{\partial B_r(\tau)}{\partial \tau} = 1 - B_r(\tau)\tilde{\alpha}_r$$

subject to $A(0) = B_u(0) = B_r(0) = 0$. The closed-form solutions for $A(\tau)$, $B_u(\tau)$, and $B_r(\tau)$ are given as follows:

$$
\begin{aligned}
A(\tau) = {} & \tau\left(\frac{\sigma_u^2}{2\tilde{\alpha}_r^2\tilde{\alpha}_u^2} + \frac{\sigma_r^2}{2\tilde{\alpha}_r^2} + \frac{\sigma_u\sigma_r\rho_{ru}}{\tilde{\alpha}_r^2\tilde{\alpha}_u}\right) \\
& - \frac{\sigma_u^2(\tilde{\alpha}_u^3 e^{-2\tilde{\alpha}_r\tau} + \tilde{\alpha}_r^3 e^{-2\tilde{\alpha}_u\tau})}{4\tilde{\alpha}_r^3\tilde{\alpha}_u^3(\tilde{\alpha}_r - \tilde{\alpha}_u)^2} + \frac{\sigma_u^2 e^{-(\tilde{\alpha}_r + \tilde{\alpha}_u)\tau}}{\tilde{\alpha}_r\tilde{\alpha}_u(\tilde{\alpha}_r - \tilde{\alpha}_u)^2(\tilde{\alpha}_r + \tilde{\alpha}_u)} \\
& - \frac{\sigma_u^2(\tilde{\alpha}_u^2 e^{-\tilde{\alpha}_r\tau} - \tilde{\alpha}_r^2 e^{-\tilde{\alpha}_u\tau})}{\tilde{\alpha}_r^3\tilde{\alpha}_u^3(\tilde{\alpha}_r - \tilde{\alpha}_u)} + \frac{\sigma_r^2(4e^{-\tilde{\alpha}_r\tau} - e^{-2\tilde{\alpha}_r\tau})}{4\tilde{\alpha}_r^3} \\
& + \frac{\sigma_u\sigma_r\rho_{ru}(\tilde{\alpha}_u^2 e^{-2\tilde{\alpha}_r\tau} - 2\tilde{\alpha}_u^2 e^{-\tilde{\alpha}_r\tau} + 2\tilde{\alpha}_r^2 e^{-\tilde{\alpha}_u\tau})}{2\tilde{\alpha}_r^3\tilde{\alpha}_u^2(\tilde{\alpha}_r - \tilde{\alpha}_u)} \\
& - \frac{\sigma_u\sigma_r\rho_{ru}e^{-(\tilde{\alpha}_u + \tilde{\alpha}_r)\tau}}{\tilde{\alpha}_r\tilde{\alpha}_u(\tilde{\alpha}_r^2 - \tilde{\alpha}_u^2)} + \frac{\sigma_u\sigma_r\rho_{ru}e^{-\tilde{\alpha}_r\tau}}{\tilde{\alpha}_r^3\tilde{\alpha}_u}
\end{aligned}
\tag{8.24}
$$

$$B_u(\tau) = \frac{e^{-\tilde{\alpha}_r\tau}}{\tilde{\alpha}_r(\tilde{\alpha}_r - \tilde{\alpha}_u)} - \frac{e^{-\tilde{\alpha}_u\tau}}{\alpha_u(\tilde{\alpha}_r - \tilde{\alpha}_u)} + \frac{1}{\tilde{\alpha}_r\tilde{\alpha}_u} \tag{8.25}$$

$$B_r(\tau) = \frac{1 - e^{-\tilde{\alpha}_r\tau}}{\tilde{\alpha}_r} \tag{8.26}$$

The solution of $\delta(t)$ is obtained by taking the partial derivative of the logarithm of the time 0 bond price (given in equation (8.21)) with respect to bond maturity and then substituting the ODEs given in equation (8.23) to get:

$$\delta(t) = f(0, \ t) + \frac{1}{2}B_u^2(t)\sigma_u^2 + \frac{1}{2}B_r^2(t)\sigma_r^2 + B_u(t)B_r(t)\sigma_u\sigma_r\rho_{ru} \qquad (8.27)$$

where $f(0, \ t) = -\partial \ln P(0, \ t)/\partial t$ is the time 0 forward rate for term t and, by definition, $Y(0) = u(0) = 0$. The solution to the term $H(t, \ T)$ is given using equation (8.21), as follows:

$$\begin{aligned} H(t, \ T) &= \int_t^T \delta(v)\, dv = H(0, \ T) - H(0, \ t) \\ &= \hat{A}(T) - A(t) - \ln P(0, \ T) + \ln P(0, \ t) \end{aligned} \qquad (8.28)$$

where $A(t)$ and $A(T)$ are given in equation (8.24) and $P(0, \ t)$ and $P(0, \ T)$ are initial zero-coupon bond prices.

The bond price solution in equation (8.21) is equivalent to the solution by Hull [2003], which is given as follows:

$$P(t, \ T) = \hat{A}(t, \ T)e^{-B_u(\tau)u(t) - B_r(\tau)r(t)} \qquad (8.29)$$

where $\tau = T - t$, $B_u(\tau)$ and $B_r(\tau)$ are given in equations (8.25) and (8.26), respectively, and $\ln \hat{A}(\tau)$ is given as follows:

$$\ln \hat{A}(t, \ T) = \ln P(0, \ T) - \ln P(0, \ t) + B_r(\tau)f(0, \ t) - \eta(t, \ T) \qquad (8.30)$$

where $\eta(t, \ T)$ is given in Appendix 8.1. The Hull and White bond price solution in equation (8.29) can be rewritten as follows:

$$P(t, \ T) = \hat{A}(t, \ T)e^{-B_u(\tau)u(t) - B_r(\tau)r(t)} = e^{\left(\ln \hat{A}(t,T) - B_r(\tau)\delta(t)\right) - B_u(\tau)u(t) - B_r(\tau)Y(t)} \qquad (8.31)$$

Comparing our bond price solution given in equation (8.21) with the Hull and White solution given in equation (8.31), we get:

$$\ln \hat{A}(t, \ T) - B_r(\tau)\delta(t) = A(\tau) - H(t, \ T) \qquad (8.32)$$

Substituting equations (8.27), (8.28), and (8.30) in equation (8.32) and simplifying, we get:

$$\eta(t, \ T) = A(T) - A(\tau) - A(t)$$

$$- B_r(\tau)\left(\frac{1}{2}B_u^2(t)\sigma_u^2 + \frac{1}{2}B_r^2(t)\sigma_r^2 + B_u(t)B_r(t)\sigma_u\sigma_r\rho_{ru}\right) \qquad (8.33)$$

Equation (8.33) gives an alternative solution to $\eta(t, T)$ that is equivalent to the original solution of Hull and White given in Appendix 8.1. The solution given in equation (8.33) uses the time homogeneous functions $A(.)$, $B_u(.)$, and $B_r(.)$, already solved in equations (8.24), (8.25), and (8.26), respectively.

The time-homogeneous preference-free $A_{0r}(2)+$ model can be obtained by making $\delta(t) = \delta$ a constant in equation (8.17) (which implies, $\theta(t) = \tilde{\alpha}_r \times \delta$, a constant, in equations (8.16) and (8.18)), allowing $Y(0)$ and $u(0)$ to be free parameters not equal to zero and making $H(t, T) = \delta(T - t) = \delta\tau$ in equation (8.22). Hence, the bond price solution under the $A_{0r}(2)+$ model is given by equation (8.21), with $H(t, T) = \delta\tau$. The prices of bonds and interest rate derivatives under the fundamental $A_{0r}(2)$ model are identical to those under the time-homogeneous preference-free $A_{0r}(2)+$ model, except that the former model generally assumes a linear specification of the MPRs, and hence, the risk-neutral parameters estimated under these two models may be different.

The Ay Form: The Brigo and Mercurio [2001, 2006] Approach

Brigo and Mercurio [2001, 2006] give an alternative derivation to the Hull and White model using the Ay form given in Dai and Singleton [2000]. This model, denoted as the $A_{0y}(2)++$ model, is equivalent to both the $A_{0c}(2)++$ and $A_{0r}(2)++$ models.[1] The short rate under the $A_{0y}(2)++$ model is specified as follows:

$$r(t) = \delta(t) + Y_1(t) + Y_2(t), \quad Y_1(0) = 0 \text{ and } Y_2(0) = 0 \tag{8.34}$$

The risk-neutral stochastic processes of the state variables are given as follows:

$$dY_1(t) = -\tilde{k}_1 Y_1(t)\,dt + v_1\,d\tilde{W}_1, \quad Y_1(0) = 0$$
$$dY_2(t) = -\tilde{k}_2 Y_2(t)\,dt + v_2\,d\tilde{W}_2, \quad Y_2(0) = 0 \tag{8.35}$$

where the correlation between the two Wiener processes is given as ρ_{12}. Again, the market prices of risks are assumed to be of a general nonlinear form that can be defined in a similar fashion as in equation (8.11). By applying Ito's lemma to the bond price, taking risk-neutral expectation, and equating the change in bond price to riskless return, we get the PDE for the bond price as follows:

$$\frac{\partial P}{\partial t} - \frac{\partial P}{\partial Y_1}\tilde{k}_1 Y_1(t) - \frac{\partial P}{\partial Y_2}\tilde{k}_2 Y_2(t) + \frac{1}{2}\frac{\partial^2 P}{\partial Y_1^2}v_1^2 + \frac{1}{2}\frac{\partial^2 P}{\partial Y_2^2}v_2^2 + \frac{\partial^2 P}{\partial Y_1 \partial Y_2}v_1 v_2 \rho_{12}$$

$$= r(t)P(t, T) \tag{8.36}$$

Consider the following solution of the bond price:

$$P(t, \ T) = e^{A(\tau) - B_1(\tau)Y_1(t) - B_2(\tau)Y_2(t) - H(t, T)} \tag{8.37}$$

where

$$H(t, \ T) = \int_t^T \delta(v) \, dv \tag{8.38}$$

and $\tau = T - t$. Taking the partial derivatives of the bond price in equation (8.37), substituting them in equation (8.36), and using a change of variable $\tau = T - t$, we get the following three ODEs:

$$\frac{\partial A(\tau)}{\partial \tau} = \frac{1}{2} B_1^2(\tau) v_1^2 + \frac{1}{2} B_2^2(\tau) v_2^2 + B_1(\tau) B_2(\tau) v_1 v_2 \rho_{12}$$

$$\frac{\partial B_1(\tau)}{\partial \tau} = 1 - B_1(\tau) \tilde{k}_1 \tag{8.39}$$

$$\frac{\partial B_2(\tau)}{\partial \tau} = 1 - B_2(\tau) \tilde{k}_2$$

subject to $A(0) = B_1(0) = B_2(0) = 0$. The closed-form solutions for $A(\tau)$, $B_1(\tau)$, and $B_2(\tau)$ are given as follows:

$$A(\tau) = \frac{v_1^2}{2\tilde{k}_1^2} \left(\tau - 2B_1(\tau) + \frac{1}{2} B_1(2\tau) \right) + \frac{v_2^2}{2\tilde{k}_2^2} \left(\tau - 2B_2(\tau) + \frac{1}{2} B_2(2\tau) \right)$$

$$+ \rho_{12} \frac{v_1 v_2}{\tilde{k}_1 \tilde{k}_2} \left(\tau - B_1(\tau) - B_2(\tau) + \left(\frac{1 - e^{-(\tilde{k}_1 + \tilde{k}_2)\tau}}{\tilde{k}_1 + \tilde{k}_2} \right) \right) \tag{8.40}$$

$$B_1(\tau) = \frac{1 - e^{-\tilde{k}_1 \tau}}{\tilde{k}_1} \tag{8.41}$$

$$B_2(\tau) = \frac{1 - e^{-\tilde{k}_2 \tau}}{\tilde{k}_2} \tag{8.42}$$

The solution of $\delta(t)$ is obtained by taking the partial derivative of the logarithm of the time 0 bond price (given in equation (8.37)) with respect to bond maturity and then substituting the ODEs given in equation (8.39) to get:

$$\delta(t) = f(0, \ t) + \frac{1}{2} B_1^2(t) v_1^2 + \frac{1}{2} B_2^2(t) v_2^2 + B_1(t) B_2(t) v_1 v_2 \rho_{12} \tag{8.43}$$

where $f(0, t) = -\partial \ln P(0, t)/\partial t$, is the time 0 forward rate for term t and, by definition, $Y_1(0) = Y_2(0) = 0$. The solution to the term $H(t, T)$ can be given using equation (8.37) as follows:

$$
\begin{aligned}
H(t, T) &= \int_t^T \delta(v)\, dv = H(0, T) - H(0, t) \\
&= A(T) - A(t) - \ln P(0, T) + \ln P(0, t)
\end{aligned}
\tag{8.44}
$$

where $A(t)$ and $A(T)$ are given in equation (8.40), and $P(0, t)$ and $P(0, T)$ are initial zero-coupon bond prices.

The time-homogeneous preference-free $A_{0y}(2)+$ model can be obtained by making $\delta(t) = \delta$ a constant in equation (8.34), allowing $Y_1(0)$ and $Y_2(0)$ to be free parameters not equal to zero and making $H(t, T) = \delta(T - t) = \delta\tau$ in equation (8.38). The prices of bonds and interest rate derivatives under the fundamental $A_{0y}(2)$ model are identical to those under the time-homogeneous preference-free $A_{0y}(2)+$ model, except that the former model requires a linear specification of the MPRs, and hence, the risk-neutral parameters estimated under these two models may be different.

It can be shown that all three forms of the two-factor Gaussian models are equivalent. Since the $A_0(2)++$ model nests both the $A_0(2)+$ model and the $A_0(2)$ model for all three forms of the two-factor Gaussian models, we only show the equivalence relationships between the different forms for the $A_0(2)++$ model. Also, since different forms of $A_0(2)++$ models are used by practitioners, the following can be used to translate the parameters from one form to the other. We first show the relationship between the $A_{0c}(2)++$ and the $A_{0y}(2)++$ models, and then the relationship between the $A_{0r}(2)++$ and the $A_{0y}(2)++$ models.

Relationship between the $A_{0c}(2)++$ Model and the $A_{0y}(2)++$ Model

The $A_{0c}(2)++$ model can be obtained from the $A_{0y}(2)++$ model by setting the following parameter relations:

$$
\begin{aligned}
\tilde{\alpha}_{11} &= \tilde{k}_1 \\
\tilde{\alpha}_{22} &= \tilde{k}_2 \\
\tilde{\alpha}_{21} &= (\tilde{k}_2 - \tilde{k}_1)\left(\frac{\rho_{12}v_2}{v_1 + \rho_{12}v_2}\right) \\
\sigma_1 &= v_1 + \rho_{12}v_2 \\
\sigma_2 &= v_2\sqrt{1 - \rho_{12}^2}
\end{aligned}
\tag{8.45}
$$

The state variables of the $A_{0c}(2)++$ model can be given as linear functions of the state variables of the $A_{0y}(2)++$ model, as follows:

$$X_1(t) = \frac{(v_1 + \rho_{12}v_2)}{v_1} Y_1(t) \tag{8.46}$$

$$X_2(t) = Y_2(t) - \frac{\rho_{12}v_2}{v_1} Y_1(t) \tag{8.47}$$

Conversely, the $A_{0y}(2)++$ model can be obtained from the $A_{0c}(2)++$ model by setting the following parameter relations:

$$\tilde{k}_1 = \tilde{\alpha}_{11}$$

$$\tilde{k}_2 = \tilde{\alpha}_{22}$$

$$\rho_{12} = \frac{\tilde{\alpha}_{21}\sigma_1}{(\tilde{\alpha}_{22} - \tilde{\alpha}_{11})v_2} \tag{8.48}$$

$$v_1 = \left(1 - \frac{\tilde{\alpha}_{21}}{\tilde{\alpha}_{22} - \tilde{\alpha}_{11}}\right)\sigma_1$$

$$v_2 = \sqrt{\frac{(\tilde{\alpha}_{21}\sigma_1)^2 + (\tilde{\alpha}_{22} - \tilde{\alpha}_{11})^2\sigma_2^2}{(\tilde{\alpha}_{22} - \tilde{\alpha}_{11})^2}}$$

The state variables of the $A_{0y}(2)++$ model can be given as linear functions of the state variables of the $A_{0c}(2)++$ model, as follows:

$$Y_1(t) = \left(1 - \frac{\tilde{\alpha}_{21}}{\tilde{\alpha}_{22} - \tilde{\alpha}_{11}}\right) X_1(t) \tag{8.49}$$

$$Y_2(t) = X_2(t) + \left(\frac{\tilde{\alpha}_{21}}{\tilde{\alpha}_{22} - \tilde{\alpha}_{11}}\right) X_1(t) \tag{8.50}$$

Note that although the conditional correlation between the two state variables under the $A_{0y}(2)++$ model is nonzero, the conditional correlation between the two state variables under the $A_{0c}(2)++$ model is zero. This is similar to obtaining uncorrelated principal components from correlated variables by an orthogonal rotation. Equations (8.49) and (8.50) are obtained by applying an orthogonal rotation to equations (8.46) and (8.47), which give the two state variables of the $A_{0c}(2)++$ model that are conditionally uncorrelated. The parameter $\tilde{\alpha}_{21}$ contained in the drift of the X_2 process allows the drift to depend upon the current value of X_1, creating an unconditional correlation between X_1 and X_2, through the cross-dependency in the drift of X_2 process. The unconditional correlation parameter $\tilde{\alpha}_{21}$ of the $A_{0c}(2)++$ model is nonzero *if and only if* the conditional correlation parameter ρ_{12} of the $A_{0y}(2)++$ model is nonzero.

Relationship between the $A_{0r}(2)++$ Model and the $A_{0y}(2)++$ Model

The $A_{0r}(2)++$ model can be obtained from the $A_{0y}(2)++$ model by setting the following parameter relations:

$$\tilde{\alpha}_r = \tilde{k}_1$$

$$\tilde{\alpha}_u = \tilde{k}_2$$

$$\sigma_r = \sqrt{v_1^2 + v_2^2 + 2v_1 v_2 \rho_{12}} \qquad (8.51)$$

$$\sigma_u = v_2(\tilde{k}_1 - \tilde{k}_2)$$

$$\rho_{ru} = \frac{v_1 \rho_{12} + v_2}{\sqrt{v_1^2 + v_2^2 + 2v_1 v_2 \rho_{12}}}$$

The state variables of the $A_{0r}(2)++$ model can be given as linear functions of the state variables of the $A_{0y}(2)++$ model as follows:

$$r(t) = \delta(t) + Y(t) = \delta(t) + Y_1(t) + Y_2(t) \qquad (8.52)$$

$$u(t) = Y_2(t)(\tilde{k}_1 - \tilde{k}_2) \qquad (8.53)$$

where the function $\delta(t)$ is identical under these two models and Hull and White's $\theta(t)$ function is given as:

$$\theta(t) = \frac{\partial \delta(t)}{\partial t} + \tilde{k}_1 \delta(t) = \frac{\partial \delta(t)}{\partial t} + \tilde{\alpha}_r \delta(t) \qquad (8.54)$$

Conversely, the $A_{0y}(2)++$ model can be obtained from the $A_{0r}(2)++$ model by setting the following parameter relations:

$$\tilde{k}_1 = \tilde{\alpha}_r$$

$$\tilde{k}_2 = \tilde{\alpha}_u$$

$$v_1 = \sqrt{\sigma_r^2 + \frac{\sigma_u^2}{(\tilde{\alpha}_r - \tilde{\alpha}_u)^2} - \frac{2\sigma_r \sigma_u \rho_{ru}}{(\tilde{\alpha}_r - \tilde{\alpha}_u)}} \qquad (8.55)$$

$$v_2 = \frac{\sigma_u}{(\tilde{\alpha}_r - \tilde{\alpha}_u)}$$

$$\rho_{12} = \frac{\sigma_r \rho_{ru} - \dfrac{\sigma_u}{(\tilde{\alpha}_r - \tilde{\alpha}_u)}}{\sqrt{\sigma_r^2 + \dfrac{\sigma_u^2}{(\tilde{\alpha}_r - \tilde{\alpha}_u)^2} - \dfrac{2\sigma_r \sigma_u \rho_{ru}}{(\tilde{\alpha}_r - \tilde{\alpha}_u)}}}$$

The state variables of the $A_{0y}(2)++$ model can be given as linear functions of the state variables of the $A_{0r}(2)++$ model, as follows:

$$Y_1(t) = Y(t) - \frac{u(t)}{\tilde{\alpha}_r - \tilde{\alpha}_u} = r(t) - \delta(t) - \frac{u(t)}{\tilde{\alpha}_r - \tilde{\alpha}_u} \tag{8.56}$$

$$Y_2(t) = \frac{u(t)}{\tilde{\alpha}_r - \tilde{\alpha}_u} \tag{8.57}$$

and the term $\delta(t)$ is given as a function of Hull and White's $\theta(t)$ as follows:

$$\delta(t) = r(0)e^{-\tilde{\alpha}_r t} + \int_0^t \theta(v)e^{-\tilde{\alpha}_r(t-v)} \, dv \tag{8.58}$$

In the rest of this section, we focus only on the Ay form of the two-factor Gaussian model. The Ay form allows more efficient tree construction for numerical applications. Since the drift of each state variable depends only upon itself in equation (8.35) and since each drift mean-reverts to zero, a natural *truncation* applies to the tree of each state variable from both the positive side and the negative side. The truncation reduces the number of nodes and makes the trees more efficient under the Ay form. We demonstrate the tree construction for option pricing only using the Ay form.

Bond Price Process and Forward Rate Process

The risk-neutral bond price process and the risk-neutral forward rate process under the $A_{0y}(2)$, $A_{0y}(2)+$, and $A_{0y}(2)++$ models have the same form and are obtained using Ito's lemma as follows:

$$\frac{dP(t, T)}{P(t, T)} = r(t) \, dt - \sum_{i=1}^{i=2} B_i(T - t)v_i \, d\tilde{W}_i(t) \tag{8.59}$$

$$df(t, T) = \left(B_1(T - t)e^{-\tilde{k}_2(T-t)} + B_2(T - t)e^{-\tilde{k}_1(T-t)} \right) v_1 v_2 \rho_{12} \, dt$$
$$+ \left(\sum_{i=1}^{2} v_i^2 B_i(T - t)e^{-\tilde{k}_i(T-t)} \right) dt + \sum_{i=1}^{2} v_i e^{-\tilde{k}_i(T-t)} \, d\tilde{W}_i(t) \tag{8.60}$$

where the functions $B_1(T - t)$ and $B_2(T - t)$ are given in equations (8.41) and (8.42), respectively. The term structure of forward rate volatility can be given as:

$$\text{Vol}[df(t, T)] = \sqrt{v_1^2 e^{-2\tilde{k}_1(T-t)} + v_2^2 e^{-2\tilde{k}_2(T-t)} + 2v_1 v_2 \rho_{12} e^{-(\tilde{k}_1+\tilde{k}_2)(T-t)}} \tag{8.61}$$

The main advantage of the two-factor Gaussian models over the one-factor Gaussian models (i.e., the Vasicek model and the preference-free Vasicek models) is that the forward rate volatility curve can take more realistic humped shapes. A necessary (but not sufficient) condition to allow for humped shapes is that the correlation coefficient ρ_{12} in equation (8.61) is negative. The two-factor Gaussian model allows a much superior fit to the hump in the forward rate volatility curve with a negative value of ρ_{12}. A direct calibration of the $A_{0y}(2)++$ model to the prices of caps and swaptions produces correlation values ranging from -0.5 to -1. The correlation is closer to -0.5 using swaptions data and closer to -1 using the caps data.

Probability Density of the Short Rate

The risk-neutral mean and variance of the future short rate under the $A_{0y}(2)++$ model are given using equations (8.34), (8.35), and (8.43), as follows:

$$\tilde{E}_0[r(t)] = \delta(t) = f(0, \ t) + \frac{1}{2}B_1^2(t)v_1^2 + \frac{1}{2}B_2^2(t)v_2^2 + B_1(t)B_2(t)v_1v_2\rho_{12}$$

(8.62)

$$\tilde{V}_0[r(t)] = \frac{1}{2}B_1(2t)v_1^2 + \frac{1}{2}B_2(2t)v_2^2 + \frac{2v_1v_2\rho_{12}}{\tilde{k}_1 + \tilde{k}_2}(1 - e^{-(\tilde{k}_1+\tilde{k}_2)t})$$

where the functions $B_1(.)$ and $B_2(.)$ are defined in equations (8.41) and (8.42), respectively.

Though the variance remains the same, the formula for the risk-neutral mean of the short rate under the time-homogeneous models $A_{0y}(2)$ and $A_{0y}(2)+$ changes to the following:

$$\tilde{E}_0[r(t)] = \delta + Y_1(0)e^{-\tilde{k}_1 t} + Y_2(0)e^{-\tilde{k}_2 t}$$

(8.63)

The short rate becomes negative in the future with a positive probability. Given the mean reversion in both the state variables and the negative correlation between them, the probability of obtaining negative rates is small for realistic parameter values.[2] This probability is computed under the risk-neutral measure as follows:

$$P_0[r(t) < 0] = P_0\left[\frac{r(t) - \tilde{E}_0[r(t)]}{\sqrt{\tilde{V}_0[r(t)]}} < -\frac{\tilde{E}_0[r(t)]}{\sqrt{\tilde{V}_0[r(t)]}}\right] = \mathcal{N}\left[-\frac{\tilde{E}_0[r(t)]}{\sqrt{\tilde{V}_0[r(t)]}}\right]$$

(8.64)

where $\mathcal{N}(x)$ is the cumulative standard normal distribution evaluated at x. Since the empirically estimated risk-neutral parameters may be different under the fundamental $A_{0y}(2)$ model and the time-homogeneous preference-free $A_{0y}(2)+$ model, the probability of obtaining negative rates will also be different under these two models. And this probability is obviously different for the time-inhomogeneous preference-free $A_{0y}(2)++$ model under which the risk-neutral mean of the short rate is given by equation (8.62), and is determined by the shape of the initial forward rate curve.

The following section provides formulas for options on zero-coupon bonds. To avoid repetition, we do not provide solutions of futures on a zero-coupon bond and futures on a time deposit (such as Eurodollar and Euribor) here, as these solutions are nested in a more general solution provided for a multifactor preference-free affine term structure model given in Chapter 9.

Valuing Options

Chapter 2 presents a general framework for pricing options on zero-coupon bonds under all multifactor Gaussian models using the forward measure $\tilde{\mathcal{P}}^S$. Specifically, example 2.1 in Chapter 2 gives the time t price of a European call option maturing at time S with an exercise price K written on a \$1 face-value zero-coupon bond maturting at time T under all Gaussian models, as follows:

$$c(t) = P(t, T)\mathcal{N}(d_1) - KP(t, S)\mathcal{N}(d_2) \tag{8.65}$$

where $\mathcal{N}(x)$ is the cumulative standard normal distribution evaluated at x. The variables d_1 and d_2 are given as:

$$
\begin{aligned}
d_1 &= \frac{\ln([P(t, T)]/[P(t, S)K]) + V/2}{\sqrt{V}} \\
d_2 &= \frac{\ln([P(t, T)]/[P(t, S)K]) - V/2}{\sqrt{V}}
\end{aligned}
\tag{8.66}
$$

and V is given in equation (2.90) in Chapter 2. Since equation (2.90) in Chapter 2 assumes *uncorrelated* factors, V can be given using the canonical, or the Ac, form of the two-factor Gaussian model. By using the equivalence relationship between the stochastic bond price processes under the Ac form and the Ay form, V can be expressed under the Ay form as follows:

$$
V = \sum_{i=1}^{2} v_i^2 \int_t^S (B_i(T - u) - B_i(S - u))^2 \, du
$$

$$
+ 2v_1 v_2 \rho_{12} \int_t^S (B_1(T - u) - B_1(S - u)) (B_2(T - u) - B_2(S - u)) \, du
\tag{8.67}
$$

where $B_1(.)$ and $B_2(.)$ are given under the Ay form by equations (8.41) and (8.42), respectively. Integrating equation (8.67) and simplifying, we get:

$$V = \sum_{i=1}^{2} \left(\frac{v_i^2}{2} B_i^2(U) B_i(2s) \right) + 2v_1 v_2 \rho_{12} B_1(U) B_2(U) \left(\frac{1 - e^{-(\tilde{k}_1 + \tilde{k}_2)s}}{\tilde{k}_1 + \tilde{k}_2} \right) \quad (8.68)$$

where $U = T - S$ and $s = S - t$.

Using put-call parity, the value of a put option on a zero-coupon bond can be obtained as follows:

$$p(t) = KP(t, S)\big(1 - \mathcal{N}(d_2)\big) - P(t, T)\big(1 - \mathcal{N}(d_1)\big) \quad (8.69)$$

The previous option formulas apply under all three nested models $A_{0y}(2)$, $A_{0y}(2)+$, and $A_{0y}(2)++$. The option price formulas differ due to the different definitions of the bond price under the different nested models.

The initial bond price $P(0, T)$ is specified exogenously under the time-inhomogeneous preference-free $A_{0y}(2)++$ model. The five risk-neutral parameters $\tilde{k}_1$, $\tilde{k}_2$, v_1, v_2, and ρ_{12} under this model are obtained by calibrating the model to the cross section of prices of interest rate derivatives, such as caps and swaptions. To reduce the effect of time-inhomogeneity, this model is generally recalibrated daily, assuming $t = 0$.

The bond price $P(t, T)$ under the time-homogeneous preference-free $A_{0y}(2)+$ model is given by equation (8.37), assuming $\delta(t) = \delta$, a constant in equation (8.34), allowing $Y_1(t)$ and $Y_2(t)$ to be free parameters at $t = 0$ (i.e., $Y_1(0)$ and $Y_2(0)$ are not zero, as they are under the $A_{0y}(2)++$ model) and making $H(t, T) = \delta(T - t) = \delta\tau$ in equation (8.38). The model requires the estimation of six risk-neutral parameters: δ, $\tilde{k}_1$, $\tilde{k}_2$, v_1, v_2, and ρ_{12}. In addition, assuming the model is calibrated using the daily cross sections of prices on bonds and interest rate derivatives over K days, then two values of the state variables $Y_1(t)$ and $Y_2(t)$ are also required for each of the K days, giving a total of $6 + 2K$ number of parameters and state variable values to be estimated using nonlinear optimization.

The fundamental $A_{0y}(2)$ model is generally estimated using econometric techniques such as GMM, EMM, or maximum likelihood, giving estimates of both the risk-neutral parameters and the MPRs. This model does not generally use the price data on interest rate derivatives as an input and derives the parameter estimates based upon the time series behavior of yields under both the physical measure and the risk-neutral measure.

Two-Factor Gaussian Trees

The most efficient two-factor Gaussian trees are constructed using the Ay form of this model. This is because a natural truncation applies to the trees of both state variables, both from above and from below, using only the Ay form. After reaching the truncation points from above and below, the number of tree nodes remains the same moving forward on the tree. The short rate is given as the sum of a deterministic term and two state variables as follows:

$$r(t) = \delta(t) + Y_1(t) + Y_2(t) \tag{8.70}$$

where the risk-neutral processes of $Y_1(t)$ and $Y_2(t)$ are given by equation (8.35) for the $A_{0y}(2)++$ model, with $Y_1(0) = 0$, $Y_2(0) = 0$, and $r(0) = \delta(0)$. The risk-neutral processes under the time-homogeneous $A_{0y}(2)$ and $A_{0y}(2)+$ models are also given by equation (8.35), except that under these models, $\delta(t) = \delta$, a constant, and $Y_1(0)$ and $Y_2(0)$ are not constrained to equal zero.

The short rate tree under the time-inhomogeneous $A_{0y}(2)++$ model requires the solution of $\delta(t)$ at each node of the two-dimensional tree. As in the previous chapters, $\delta(t)$ can be solved using two methods. The first method solves $\delta(t)$ analytically using equation (8.43). However, since this solution is valid only in the continuous-time limit, it allows an exact match with the initial zero-coupon bond prices only when using a large number of steps on the tree. If an exact match is desired for an arbitrarily small number of steps, then $\delta(t)$ can be obtained numerically for $0 \leq t < T$ by defining a pseudo bond price $P^*(0, t)$, as follows:

$$P(0, t) = P^*(0, t)e^{-H(0,t)} = P^*(0, t)e^{-\int_0^t \delta(v)\,dv} \tag{8.71}$$

where $P(0, t)$ is the initially observed bond price and $P^*(0, t)$ is the pseudo bond price obtained by taking discounted risk-neutral expectation using $r^*(t) = Y_1(t) + Y_2(t)$ as the pseudo short rate. Given the values of $P(0, t)$ and $P^*(0, t)$ for different values of t, $\delta(t)$ can be obtained numerically as follows:

$$H(0, t) = \sum_{j=0}^{t/\Delta t - 1} \delta(j\Delta t)\Delta t = \ln P^*(0, t) - \ln P(0, t) \tag{8.72}$$

where $\Delta t = t/n$ and the integral in $H(0, t)$ is approximated as a discrete sum by dividing t into $t/\Delta t$ number of steps. The values of $\delta(j\Delta t)$ for $j = 0, 1, 2, \ldots, n - 1$ can be obtained iteratively by using successive values of t as $\Delta t, 2\Delta t, \ldots,$ and $n\Delta t$, such that an exact match is obtained with the initial bond price function $P(0, t)$. The values of $\delta(t)$ can be then added to the appropriate nodes on the n-step two-dimensional tree of $r^*(t) = Y_1(t) + Y_2(t)$ to obtain the corresponding tree for the short rate $r(t)$ (i.e., $r(t) = \delta(t) + r^*(t)$).

The trinomial trees for $Y_1(t)$ and $Y_2(t)$ processes are obtained as follows. The one period $Y_1(t)$ tree is shown in Figure 8.1.

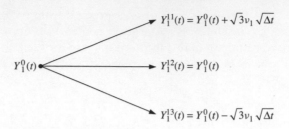

FIGURE 8.1 Trinomial Tree for the $Y_1(t)$ Process

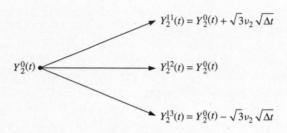

FIGURE 8.2 Trinomial Tree for the $Y_2(t)$ Process

Marginal probabilities for the $Y_1(t)$ process are computed as follows:

$$
\begin{aligned}
p_{y_1}^u &= \frac{1}{6} + \frac{1}{\sqrt{12}} \frac{(-\tilde{k}_1 Y_1(t))}{v_1} \sqrt{\Delta t} \\
p_{y_1}^d &= \frac{1}{6} - \frac{1}{\sqrt{12}} \frac{(-\tilde{k}_1 Y_1(t))}{v_1} \sqrt{\Delta t} \\
p_{y_1}^m &= 1 - p_{y_1}^u - p_{y_1}^d
\end{aligned}
\tag{8.73}
$$

Similarly, the $Y_2(t)$ process can also be modeled as a trinomial tree. A one-step $Y_2(t)$ tree is shown in Figure 8.2.

Marginal probabilities for the $Y_2(t)$ process are computed as follows:

$$
\begin{aligned}
p_{y_2}^u &= \frac{1}{6} + \frac{1}{\sqrt{12}} \frac{(-\tilde{k}_2 Y_2(t))}{v_2} \sqrt{\Delta t} \\
p_{y_2}^d &= \frac{1}{6} - \frac{1}{\sqrt{12}} \frac{(-\tilde{k}_2 Y_2(t))}{v_2} \sqrt{\Delta t} \\
p_{y_2}^m &= 1 - p_{y_2}^u - p_{y_2}^d
\end{aligned}
\tag{8.74}
$$

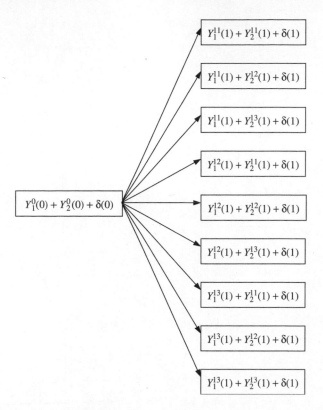

FIGURE 8.3 Two-Dimensional Short-Rate Tree

The nodes of the $Y_1(t)$ tree and the $Y_2(t)$ tree are then combined to generate the assumed correlation structure between the two processes. At each node, the short rate is obtained as $r(t) = \delta(t) + Y_1(t) + Y_2(t)$, where $\delta(t)$ is computed either using equation (8.43) or using equation (8.72), under the $A_{0y}(2)++$ model, and is assumed to be a constant under the $A_{0y}(2)$ and $A_{0y}(2)+$ models. The resulting short rate tree is shown in Figure 8.3.

The nine joint probabilities are computed using Hull's [2003] approach as follows:

Case 1: $\rho_{12} \geq 0$

$$p_1 = p_{y_1}^u \times p_{y_2}^u + 5e$$

$$p_2 = p_{y_1}^u \times p_{y_2}^m - 4e$$

$$p_3 = p_{y_1}^u \times p_{y_2}^d - e$$

$$p_4 = p_{y_1}^m \times p_{y_2}^u - 4e$$

$$p_5 = p_{y_1}^m \times p_{y_2}^m + 8e \qquad\qquad (8.75)$$

$$p_6 = p_{y_1}^m \times p_{y_2}^d - 4e$$

$$p_7 = p_{y_1}^d \times p_{y_2}^u - e$$

$$p_8 = p_{y_1}^d \times p_{y_2}^m - 4e$$

$$p_9 = p_{y_1}^d \times p_{y_2}^d + 5e$$

where $\quad e = \dfrac{\rho_{12}}{36}$

Case 2: $\rho_{12} < 0$

$$p_1 = p_{y_1}^u \times p_{y_2}^u - e$$

$$p_2 = p_{y_1}^u \times p_{y_2}^m - 4e$$

$$p_3 = p_{y_1}^u \times p_{y_2}^d + 5e$$

$$p_4 = p_{y_1}^m \times p_{y_2}^u - 4e$$

$$p_5 = p_{y_1}^m \times p_{y_2}^m + 8e \qquad\qquad (8.76)$$

$$p_6 = p_{y_1}^m \times p_{y_2}^d - 4e$$

$$p_7 = p_{y_1}^d \times p_{y_2}^u + 5e$$

$$p_8 = p_{y_1}^d \times p_{y_2}^m - 4e$$

$$p_9 = p_{y_1}^d \times p_{y_2}^d - e$$

where $\quad e = -\dfrac{\rho_{12}}{36}$

Example 8.1 demonstrates pricing a zero-coupon bond, using the afore mentioned tree-building procedure, with a two-period example.

Example 8.1   Consider a six-month zero-coupon bond with face value $F = \$100$. Let the current short rate equal 6 percent and the parameters under the time-inhomogeneous $A_{0y}(2)++$ model be given as follows: $\tilde{k}_1 = 0.5$; $v_1 = 0.2$; $\tilde{k}_2 = 0.5$; $v_2 = 0.2$; $\rho_{12} = -0.3$; and $T = 0.5$. For expositional purposes, consider a two-period tree for pricing this bond, such that $\Delta t = 0.5/2 = 0.25$. The underlying one-dimensional tree for the $Y_1(t)$ process is shown in Figure 8.4. A similar tree can be constructed for the $Y_2(t)$ process also.

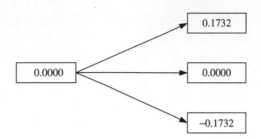

FIGURE 8.4 One-Dimensional Tree for the $Y_1(t)$ Process

In addition to the two-step trees for $Y_1(t)$ and $Y_2(t)$, we also require the values of $\delta(0)$ and $\delta(0.25)$. We solve $\delta(t)$ using the first method, given by the analytical solution in equation (8.43). To compute the value of $\delta(t)$ at each time step, we use the Nelson and Siegel [1987] model for the initially observable forward rate $f(0, t)$ defined as follows:

$$f(0,\ t) = a_1 + a_2 e^{-t/b} + a_3 \frac{t}{b} e^{-t/b}$$

with the parameters: $a_1 = 0.07$, $a_2 = -0.01$, $a_3 = 0.00087$, and $b = 1.98476$. The assumed forward rate is consistent with the assumption of 6 percent for the initial value of the short rate, since:

$$r(0) = f(0,0) = a_1 + a_2 = 0.07 - 0.01 = 0.06$$

Since, by definition, $\delta(0) = r(0)$, under the $A_{0y}(2)++$ model, we have:

$$\delta(0) = r(0) = 0.06$$

At time $t = 0.25$:

$$B_1(0.25) = \frac{1 - e^{-\tilde{k}_1 \tau}}{\tilde{k}_1} = \frac{1 - e^{-0.5 \times 0.25}}{0.5} = 0.235$$

$$B_2(0.25) = \frac{1 - e^{-\tilde{k}_2 \tau}}{\tilde{k}_2} = \frac{1 - e^{-0.5 \times 0.25}}{0.5} = 0.235$$

The value of the initially observable forward rate for term 0.25 years equals:

$$f(0,\ 0.25) = a_1 + a_2 e^{-t/b} + a_3 \frac{t}{b} e^{-t/b} = 0.07 - 0.01 \times e^{-0.25/1.98476}$$

$$+ 0.00087 \times \frac{0.25}{1.98476} \times e^{-0.25/1.98476} = 0.0613$$

Substituting the values from the previous two equations into equation (8.43), we get:

$$\delta(0.25) = f(0,\ t) + \frac{1}{2}B_1(t)^2 v_1^2 + \frac{1}{2}B_2(t)^2 v_2^2 + B_1(t)B_2(t)v_1 v_2 \rho_{12}$$

$$= 0.0613 + \frac{1}{2}(0.235^2).2^2 + \frac{1}{2}(0.235^2).2^2 + (0.235^2).2^2(-0.3)$$

$$= 0.0628$$

Combining the values of $Y_1(t)$, $Y_2(t)$, and $\delta(t)$ at each node, we compute the values of the short rate $r(t)$ at each node as shown in Figure 8.5.

The short rate values at each node are then used for discounting the appropriate bond values at the next time step as shown in Figure 8.6. For example, the bond value at time $t = 0$ is computed as follows. Marginal

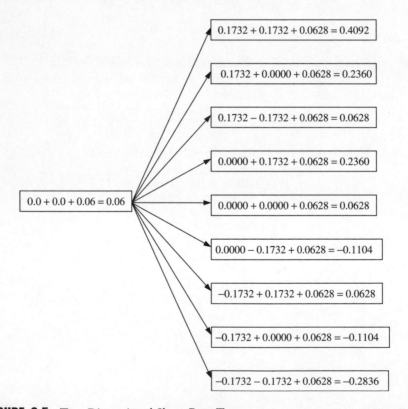

FIGURE 8.5 Two-Dimensional Short-Rate Tree

At each node:
Value = bond value

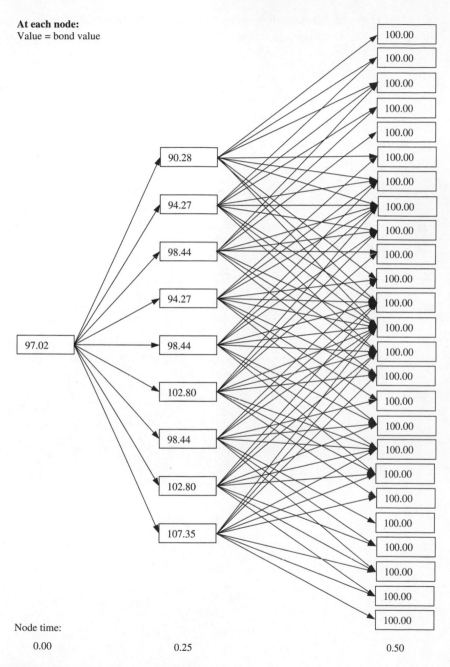

Node time:

    0.00   0.25   0.50

FIGURE 8.6 Two-Dimensional Bond Tree

trinomial probabilities for the $Y_1(t = 0)$ process are computed according to equation (8.73) as follows:

$$p^u_{y_1} = \frac{1}{6} + \frac{1}{\sqrt{12}} \times \frac{-0.5 \times 0.0}{0.2} \sqrt{0.25} = \frac{1}{6}$$

$$p^d_{y_1} = \frac{1}{6} - \frac{1}{\sqrt{12}} \times \frac{-0.5 \times 0.0}{0.2} \sqrt{0.25} = \frac{1}{6}$$

$$p^m_{y_1} = 1 - \frac{1}{6} - \frac{1}{6} = \frac{2}{3}$$

Marginal trinomial probabilities for the $Y_2(t = 0)$ process are computed according to equation (8.74) as follows:

$$p^u_{y_2} = \frac{1}{6} + \frac{1}{\sqrt{12}} \times \frac{-0.5 \times 0.0}{0.2} \sqrt{0.25} = \frac{1}{6}$$

$$p^d_{y_2} = \frac{1}{6} - \frac{1}{\sqrt{12}} \times \frac{-0.5 \times 0.0}{0.2} \sqrt{0.25} = \frac{1}{6}$$

$$p^m_{y_2} = 1 - \frac{1}{6} - \frac{1}{6} = \frac{2}{3}$$

Since $\rho_{12} < 0$, the joint probabilities for $t = 0$ are computed according to equation (8.76) as follows:

$$e = -\frac{\rho_{12}}{36} = -\frac{-0.3}{36} = 0.0083$$

$$p_1 = \frac{1}{6} \times \frac{1}{6} - 0.0083 = 0.0194$$

$$p_2 = \frac{1}{6} \times \frac{2}{3} - 4 \times 0.0083 = 0.0778$$

$$p_3 = \frac{1}{6} \times \frac{1}{6} + 5 \times 0.0083 = 0.0694$$

$$p_4 = \frac{2}{3} \times \frac{1}{6} - 4 \times 0.0083 = 0.0778$$

$$p_5 = \frac{2}{3} \times \frac{2}{3} + 8 \times 0.0083 = 0.5111$$

$$p_6 = \frac{2}{3} \times \frac{1}{6} - 4 \times 0.0083 = 0.0778$$

$$p_7 = \frac{1}{6} \times \frac{1}{6} + 5 \times 0.0083 = 0.0694$$

$$p_8 = \frac{1}{6} \times \frac{2}{3} - 4 \times 0.0083 = 0.0778$$

$$p_9 = \frac{1}{6} \times \frac{1}{6} - 0.0083 = 0.0194$$

Hence, the time 0 bond value is computed as follows:

$$P(0) = (90.28 \times 0.0194 + 94.27 \times 0.0778 + 98.44 \times 0.0694$$
$$+ 94.27 \times 0.0778 + 98.44 \times 0.5111 + 102.80 \times 0.0778$$
$$+ 98.44 \times 0.0694 + 102.80 \times 0.0778 + 107.35 \times 0.0194)/e^{0.06 \times 0.25}$$
$$= \$97.02$$

The bond price using the closed-form solution equals \$96.98. Using a 100-step two-dimensional tree, the time 0 bond price is also equal to \$96.98.

TWO-FACTOR HYBRID MODELS

The two-factor Gaussian models suffer from two limitations. First, they allow the occurrence of negative rates; second, they disallow conditional volatilities to depend upon the state variables. The two-factor square-root models can resolve both these limitations. However, the two-factor square-root models disallow a negative correlation between the state variables (due to admissibility conditions), which is necessary for capturing the conditional means of the yields. Between the two-factor Gaussian models and the two-factor square-root models are the two-factor hybrid models, which allow the conditional volatilities of the two state variables to be determined by only one state variable. The two-factor hybrid models allow a negative correlation between the state variables.

Similar to Gaussian models, we can identify three nested versions of the maximal two-factor hybrid models given: the fundamental model, the time-homogeneous preference-free model, and the time-inhomogeneous preference-free model, denoted as the $A_1(2)$ model, the $A_1(2)+$ model, and the $A_1(2)++$ model, respectively. These hybrid models can be expressed in three equivalent forms given as the Ac form, the Ay form, and the Ar form. Due to space constraints, we consider the two-factor hybrid models only in the canonical, or the Ac, form. More specifically, we consider the $A_{1c}(2)$ model, the $A_{1c}(2)+$ model, and the $A_{1c}(2)++$ model.

The $A_{1c}(2)$ Model   Consider the following short rate process:

$$r(t) = \delta + Y_1(t) + Y_2(t) \tag{8.77}$$

The risk-neutral stochastic processes for Y_1 and Y_2 under the fundamental $A_{1c}(2)$ model are given as follows:[3]

$$dY_1(t) = \tilde{\alpha}_{11}(\tilde{\theta}_1 - Y_1(t))\, dt + \sigma_1\sqrt{Y_1(t)}\, d\tilde{Z}_1(t)$$

$$dY_2(t) = \left(\tilde{\alpha}_{21}(\tilde{\theta}_1 - Y_1(t)) - \tilde{\alpha}_{22}Y_2(t)\right) dt + \sqrt{\beta_{20} + \beta_{21}Y_1(t)}\, d\tilde{Z}_2(t) \tag{8.78}$$

where the two Wiener processes are uncorrelated. The model in equation (8.78) requires the following sign restrictions on the risk-neutral parameters: $\tilde{\alpha}_{11}\tilde{\theta}_1 > 0, \sigma_1 > 0, \beta_{20} \geq 0$, and $\beta_{21} > 0$. A positive (negative) value for $\tilde{\alpha}_{11}$ is consistent with a stationary (explosive) risk-neutral process for the state variable Y_1.

The empirical estimates of the risk-neutral parameters under the fundamental pricing paradigm are tied to the empirical estimates of the physical parameters and the MPRs. The three types of fundamental ATSMs, known as the completely affine models, essentially affine models, and semiaffine models, are based upon different specifications of the functional forms of MPRs. The form of the MPRs under the completely affine $A_{1c}(2)$ model (see Dai and Singleton [2000]) is given by the following change of measure:

$$d\tilde{Z}_1(t) = dZ_1(t) + \frac{\gamma_{11}\sqrt{Y_1(t)}}{\sigma_1}\, dt$$

$$d\tilde{Z}_2(t) = dZ_2(t) + \gamma_{21}\sqrt{\beta_{20} + \beta_{21}Y_1(t)}\, dt \tag{8.79}$$

The form of the MPRs under the essentially affine $A_{1c}(2)$ model (see Duffee [2002], Dai and Singleton [2002]) is given by the following change of measure:

$$d\tilde{Z}_1(t) = dZ_1(t) + \frac{1}{\sigma_1}\left(\gamma_{11}\sqrt{Y_1(t)} + \frac{\gamma_{12}}{\sqrt{Y_1(t)}}\right) dt$$

$$d\tilde{Z}_2(t) = dZ_2(t) + \left(\gamma_{21}\sqrt{\beta_{20} + \beta_{21}Y_1(t)} + \gamma_{22}\frac{Y_2(t)}{\sqrt{\beta_{20} + \beta_{21}Y_1(t)}}\right) dt \tag{8.80}$$

And finally, the form of the MPRs under the semiaffine $A_{1c}(2)$ model (see Duarte [2004]) is given by the following change of measure:

$$d\tilde{Z}_1(t) = dZ_1(t) + \frac{1}{\sigma_1}\left(\gamma_{10} + \gamma_{11}\sqrt{Y_1(t)} + \frac{\gamma_{12}}{\sqrt{Y_1(t)}}\right) dt$$

$$d\tilde{Z}_2(t) = dZ_2(t) + \left(\gamma_{20} + \gamma_{21}\sqrt{\beta_{20} + \beta_{21}Y_1(t)} + \gamma_{22}\frac{Y_2(t)}{\sqrt{\beta_{20} + \beta_{21}Y_1(t)}}\right) dt \tag{8.81}$$

The semiaffine $A_{1c}(2)$ model nests the essentially affine $A_{1c}(2)$ model, which nests the completely affine $A_{1c}(2)$ model. As shown by Duffee [2002] and Duarte [2004], the extra parameters for measuring the MPRs under the essentially affine model and the semiaffine model are useful in improving the fit of the model, especially with the conditional means of the yields. By substituting equation (8.81) into equation (8.78), it can be seen that the semiaffine specification is affine under the risk-neutral measure but not under the physical measure. The Novikov condition of the Girsanov theorem under the essentially affine and the semiaffine models requires additional parameter restrictions to ensure that the state variable Y_1 does not reach zero with a positive probability under both the physical measure and the risk-neutral measure.[4]

By applying Ito's lemma to the bond price using equation (8.78), equating the change in bond price to riskless return, and then taking the risk-neutral expectation, we get the PDE for the bond price as follows:

$$
\frac{\partial P}{\partial t} + \frac{\partial P}{\partial Y_1}\tilde{\alpha}_{11}(\tilde{\theta}_1 - Y_1(t)) + \frac{\partial P}{\partial Y_2}\left(\tilde{\alpha}_{21}\left(\tilde{\theta}_1 - Y_1(t)\right) - \tilde{\alpha}_{22}Y_2(t)\right)
$$
$$
+ \frac{1}{2}\frac{\partial^2 P}{\partial Y_1^2}\sigma_1^2 Y_1(t) + \frac{1}{2}\frac{\partial^2 P}{\partial Y_2^2}(\beta_{20} + \beta_{21}Y_1(t)) = r(t)P(t,\ T)
$$

(8.82)

subject to the boundary condition $P(T,\ T) = 1$. Let the bond price solution be given as follows:

$$
P(t,\ T) = e^{A(\tau) - B_1(\tau)Y_1(t) - B_2(\tau)Y_2(t) - H(t,T)}
$$

(8.83)

where

$$
H(t,\ T) = \int_t^T \delta\, dv = \delta(T - t) = \delta\tau
$$

(8.84)

and $\tau = T - t$. Taking the partial derivatives of the bond price, substituting these into equation (8.82), and using a separation of variables gives the following three ODEs:

$$
\frac{\partial A(\tau)}{\partial \tau} = -\tilde{\alpha}_{11}\tilde{\theta}_1 B_1(\tau) - \tilde{\alpha}_{21}\tilde{\theta}_1 B_2(\tau) + \frac{1}{2}\beta_{20}B_2^2(\tau)
$$
$$
\frac{\partial B_1(\tau)}{\partial \tau} = 1 - \tilde{\alpha}_{11}B_1(\tau) - \tilde{\alpha}_{21}B_2(\tau) - \frac{1}{2}\sigma_1^2 B_1^2(\tau) - \frac{1}{2}\beta_{21}B_2^2(\tau)
$$
$$
\frac{\partial B_2(\tau)}{\partial \tau} = 1 - \tilde{\alpha}_{22}B_2(\tau)
$$

(8.85)

subject to the boundary condition $A(0) = B_1(0) = B_2(0) = 0$. The third ODE has an analytical solution, given as follows:

$$B_2(\tau) = \frac{1 - e^{-\tilde{\alpha}_{22}\tau}}{\tilde{\alpha}_{22}} \qquad (8.86)$$

Since an analytical solution of $B_1(\tau)$ does not exist, both $A(\tau)$ and $B_1(\tau)$ are solved numerically using finite difference methods by common software packages like Matlab.

The $A_{1c}(2)+$ Model and the $A_{1c}(2)++$ Model　　The solutions of the bond price and interest rate derivatives under the time-homogeneous preference-free $A_{1c}(2)+$ model are identical to those under the fundamental $A_{1c}(2)$ model, except that the risk-neutral parameters estimated under the two models may be different, since the latter model imposes restrictive functional forms on the MPRs. The solution of the bond price under the time-inhomogeneous preference-free $A_{1c}(2)++$ model can be obtained by following the same steps as under the fundamental $A_{1c}(2)$ model, except that the constant δ in equation (8.77) is replaced with a deterministic function $\delta(t)$, the time 0 value of the state variable $Y_2(0)$ is equated to zero, and $H(t, T)$ in equation (8.84) is replaced by the following:

$$H(t,\ T) = \int_t^T \delta(v)\, dv \qquad (8.87)$$

Following similar steps as under the case of two-factor Gaussian models in the previous section, the solutions of $\delta(t)$ and $H(t, T)$ can be given as follows:

$$\delta(t) = f(0,\ t) - Y_1(0) - B_1(t)\big(\tilde{\alpha}_{11}(\tilde{\theta}_1 - Y_1(0))\big) - B_2(t)\tilde{\alpha}_{21}(\tilde{\theta}_1 - Y_1(0))$$

$$+ \frac{1}{2}B_1^2(t)\sigma_1^2 Y_1(0) + \frac{1}{2}B_2^2(t)\big(\beta_{20} + \beta_{21}Y_1(0)\big) \qquad (8.88)$$

and

$$H(t,\ T) = \int_t^T \delta(v)\, dv = H(0,\ T) - H(0,\ t)$$

$$\qquad (8.89)$$

$$= A(T) - A(t) - Y_1(0)[B_1(T) - B_1(t)] - \ln P(0,\ T) + \ln P(0,\ t)$$

where $f(0,\ t) = -\partial \ln P(0,\ t)/\partial t$ is the time 0 forward rate for term t; $A(.)$ and $B_1(.)$ are solutions to the PDEs given in equation (8.85); the solution of $B_2(.)$ is given by equation (8.86); and $P(0,\ T)$ is the initial zero-coupon bond price.

Bond Price Process and Forward Rate Process

The risk-neutral bond price process and the risk-neutral forward rate process under the $A_{1c}(2)$, $A_{1c}(2)+$, and $A_{1c}(2)++$ models have the same form and are obtained using Ito's lemma as follows:

$$
\frac{dP(t,\ T)}{P(t,\ T)} = r(t)\,dt - \sigma_1\sqrt{Y_1(t)}B_1(T-t)\,d\tilde{Z}_1(t)
$$

$$
- \sqrt{\beta_{20} + \beta_{21}Y_1(t)}B_2(T-t)\,d\tilde{Z}_2(t) \tag{8.90}
$$

$$
df(t,\ T) = \sigma_1^2 Y_1(t)B_1(T-t)\frac{\partial B_1(T-t)}{\partial T}\,dt
$$

$$
+ \big(\beta_{20} + \beta_{21}Y_1(t)\big)B_2(T-t)\frac{\partial B_2(T-t)}{\partial T}\,dt \tag{8.91}
$$

$$
+ \sigma_1\sqrt{Y_1(t)}\frac{\partial B_1(T-t)}{\partial T}\,d\tilde{Z}_1(t)
$$

$$
+ \sqrt{\beta_{20} + \beta_{21}Y_1(t)}\frac{\partial B_2(T-t)}{\partial T}\,d\tilde{Z}_2(t)
$$

The conditional volatility of the forward rate process depends upon the current value of the state variable $Y_1(t)$. Substituting the partial derivatives $B_1(.)$ and $B_2(.)$ given by the ODEs in equation (8.85), the forward rate volatility function is given as follows:

$$
Vol[df(t,\ T)] = \sqrt{\begin{array}{l} \sigma_1^2 Y_1(t)\left(1 - \tilde{\alpha}_{11}B_1(T-t) - \tilde{\alpha}_{21}B_2(T-t)\right. \\[2mm] \left. -\frac{1}{2}\sigma_1^2 B_1^2(T-t) - \frac{1}{2}\beta_{21}B_2^2(T-t)\right)^2 \\[2mm] +\big(\beta_{20} + \beta_{21}Y_1(t)\big)\big(1 - \tilde{\alpha}_{22}B_2(T-t)\big)^2 \end{array}} \tag{8.92}
$$

The forward rate volatility depends upon six risk-neutral parameters and the current value of the state variable $Y_1(t)$. The shape of the forward rate volatility evolves stochastically with the changing value of $Y_1(t)$. A hump in the shape of the forward rate volatility can be allowed through the parameter $\tilde{\alpha}_{21}$, which measures the unconditional correlation between the state variables.

Valuing Futures

Futures on a Zero-Coupon Bond   The time t price of a futures contract expiring at time S written on a zero-coupon bond maturing at time T under the $A_{1c}(2)$, $A_{1c}(2)+$, and $A_{1c}(2)++$ models can be obtained in the same manner as in the previous chapters. Since the futures price $P_F(t, S, T)$ follows a martingale under the risk-neutral measure, the instantaneous change in the futures price equals zero. Using Ito's lemma to obtain the instantaneous change in the futures price and equating it to zero gives the following PDE:

$$\frac{\partial P_F}{\partial t} + \frac{\partial P_F}{\partial Y_1}\tilde{\alpha}_{11}\left(\tilde{\theta}_1 - Y_1(t)\right) + \frac{\partial P_F}{\partial Y_2}\left(\tilde{\alpha}_{21}\left(\tilde{\theta}_1 - Y_1(t)\right) - \tilde{\alpha}_{22}Y_2(t)\right)$$

$$+ \frac{1}{2}\frac{\partial^2 P_F}{\partial Y_1^2}\sigma_1^2 Y_1(t) + \frac{1}{2}\frac{\partial^2 P_F}{\partial Y_2^2}\left(\beta_{20} + \beta_{21}Y_1(t)\right) = 0 \tag{8.93}$$

subject to the boundary condition $P_F(S, S, T) = P(S, T)$. We assume that the solution to equation (8.93) has the following form:

$$P_F(t, S, T) = e^{A_F(s) - B_{1F}(s)Y_1(t) - B_{2F}(s)Y_2(t) - H(S,T)}, \quad s = S - t \tag{8.94}$$

subject to $A_F(0) = A(U)$, $B_{1F}(0) = B_1(U)$, $B_{2F}(0) = B_2(U)$, $U = T - S$ where $A(U)$ and $B_1(U)$ are the numerical solutions of the ODEs in equations (8.85), $B_2(U)$ is given by equation (8.86), $H(S, T) = \delta U$ using equation (8.84) under the $A_{1c}(2)$ and $A_{1c}(2)+$ models, and $H(S, T)$ is given by equation (8.89) under the $A_{1c}(2)++$ model.

Evaluating the partial derivatives of the futures price, using a change of variable $s = S - t$, and then substituting the partial derivatives back in equation (8.93), we get the following three ODEs:

$$\frac{\partial A_F(s)}{\partial s} = -\tilde{\alpha}_{11}\tilde{\theta}_1 B_{1F}(s) - \tilde{\alpha}_{21}\tilde{\theta}_1 B_{2F}(s) + \frac{1}{2}\beta_{20}B_{2F}^2(s)$$

$$\frac{\partial B_{1F}(s)}{\partial s} = -\tilde{\alpha}_{11}B_{1F}(s) - \tilde{\alpha}_{21}B_{2F}(s) - \frac{1}{2}\sigma_1^2 B_{1F}^2(s) - \frac{1}{2}\beta_{21}B_{2F}^2(s) \tag{8.95}$$

$$\frac{\partial B_{2F}(s)}{\partial s} = -\tilde{\alpha}_{22}B_{2F}(s)$$

where the boundary conditions are given in equation (8.94). While the ODEs of $A_F(s)$ and $B_{1F}(s)$ are solved numerically, the solution to $B_{2F}(s)$ is given as follows:

$$B_{2F}(s) = e^{-\tilde{\alpha}_{22}s}B_2(U) \tag{8.96}$$

where the solution of $B_2(U)$ is given in equation (8.86). The futures-forward price discount (FFPD) is given as:

$$FFPD = \frac{P_f(t, S, T) - P_F(t, S, T)}{P_f(t, S, T)} = 1 - P_F(t, S, T)\frac{P(t, S)}{P(t, T)}$$

$$= 1 - e^{(A_F(s) + A(s) - A(\tau)) - \sum_{i=1}^{2}(B_{iF}(s) + B_i(s) - B_i(\tau))Y_i(t)} \tag{8.97}$$

$$s = S - t \quad \text{and} \quad \tau = T - t$$

The FFPD is always between 0 and 1. In general, higher values of the speed of mean reversion coefficients $\tilde{\alpha}_{11}, \tilde{\alpha}_{21}$, and $\tilde{\alpha}_{22}$ lead to a lower FFPD, and higher values of β_{20} and $Y_1(t)$ lead to a higher FFPD. Though the FFPD has the same form under the $A_{1c}(2)$, $A_{1c}(2)+$, and $A_{1c}(2)++$ models, different estimates of risk-neutral parameters under these models will lead to different values of the FFPD.

Futures on a Time Deposit The price of a futures contract on a time deposit—such as Eurodollar and Euribor futures—can be obtained using equation (3.12) in Chapter 3:

$$P_F^{TD}(t, S, T) = \frac{100}{\hat{U}} \left(1 + \hat{U} - P_F^I(t, S, T) \right) \qquad (8.98)$$

where S is the futures expiration date, $U = T - S$ is the deposit time period calculated using the actual/actual day-count convention, $\hat{U}$ is the deposit time period calculated using actual/360 day-count convention, and $P_F^I(t, S, T)$ is the current price of a futures contract written on a hypothetical asset, which at the expiration date S is worth the inverse of a \$1 face-value zero-coupon bond maturing at time T. As shown in Chapter 3, the futures price, $P_F^I(t, S, T)$ is given by the following risk-neutral expectation:

$$P_F^I(t, S, T) = \tilde{E}_t \left(\frac{1}{P(S, T)} \right) \qquad (8.99)$$

The PDE followed by $P_F^I(t, S, T)$ is identical to the PDE followed by $P_F(t, S, T)$ in equation (8.93), except for the boundary condition given as $P_F^I(S, S, T) = 1/P(S, T)$. Using the same procedure as in previous chapters, the solution under the $A_{1c}(2)$, $A_{1c}(2)+$, and $A_{1c}(2)++$ models is given as:

$$P_F^I(t, S, T) = e^{a_F(s) - b_{1F}(s)Y_1(t) - b_{2F}(s)Y_2(t) + H(S,T)}, \quad s = S - t \qquad (8.100)$$

where $a_F(s)$ and $b_{1F}(s)$ are obtained as numerical solutions to the following ODEs:

$$\frac{\partial a_F(s)}{\partial s} = -\tilde{\alpha}_{11}\tilde{\theta}_1 b_{1F}(s) - \tilde{\alpha}_{21}\tilde{\theta}_1 b_{2F}(s) + \frac{1}{2}\beta_{20}b_{2F}^2(s)$$

$$\frac{\partial b_{1F}(s)}{\partial s} = -\tilde{\alpha}_{11}b_{1F}(s) - \tilde{\alpha}_{21}b_{2F}(s) - \frac{1}{2}\sigma_1^2 b_{1F}^2(s) - \frac{1}{2}\beta_{21}b_{2F}^2(s) \qquad (8.101)$$

subject to $a_F(0) = -A(U), b_{1F}(0) = -B_1(U), U = T - S$, and $A(U)$ and $B_1(U)$ are the numerical solutions of the ODEs in equations (8.85). The solution of b_{2F} is given as follows:

$$b_{2F}(s) = -e^{-\tilde{\alpha}_{22}s} B_2(U) \qquad (8.102)$$

where the solution of $B_2(U)$ is given in equation (8.86). The solution of $H(S, T)$ equals δU, using equation (8.84) under the $A_{1c}(2)$ and $A_{1c}(2)+$ models; and $H(S, T)$ is given by equation (8.89) under the $A_{1c}(2)++$ model.

The convexity bias, given as the difference between the futures rate and the forward rate on a time deposit, is defined in equation (3.17) in Chapter 3 as follows:

$$Convexity\ Bias = L_F(t, S, T) - L_f(t, S, T)$$

$$= \frac{1 + L_F(t, S, T)\hat{U}}{\hat{U}} \left(1 - \frac{P(t, S)}{P(t, T)P_F^I(t, S, T)}\right) \quad (8.103)$$

By substituting the appropriate formulas, we get the convexity bias, as follows:

$$Convexity\ Bias = L_F(t, S, T) - L_f(t, S, T)$$

$$= \frac{1 + L_F(t, S, T)\hat{U}}{\hat{U}} (1 - e^{A(s)-a_F(s)-A(\tau)-\sum_{i=1}^{2}\left(B_i(s)-b_{iF}(s)-B_i(\tau)\right)Y_i(t)}),$$

$$s = S - t, \quad and \quad \tau = T - t \quad (8.104)$$

The convexity bias is positive in general. Higher values of the speed of mean-reversion coefficients $\tilde{\alpha}_{11}$, $\tilde{\alpha}_{21}$, and $\tilde{\alpha}_{22}$ lead to a lower convexity bias, and higher values β_{20} and $Y_1(t)$ lead to a higher convexity bias. Though the convexity bias has the same form under the $A_{1c}(2)$, $A_{1c}(2)+$, and $A_{1c}(2)++$ models, different estimates of risk-neutral parameters under these models will lead to different values of the convexity bias.

Valuing Options

The solution for options under the $A_{1c}(2)$, $A_{1c}(2)+$, and $A_{1c}(2)++$ models can be obtained using the Fourier inversion method introduced in Chapter 5. The advantage of the Fourier inversion method is that it requires a *single* summation to solve the integrals for obtaining risk-neutral probabilities even under a multifactor model, while the traditional methods (such as Longstaff and Schwartz [1992]) require that the approximation be done using a multiple-order summation. The computation time difference between a single summation and a multiple-order summation grows nonlinearly and is quite significant even between a single summation and a double summation.

We use the four-step Fourier inversion method outlined in Chapter 5 for solving option prices. The prices of a European call option and a European put option, both written on a zero-coupon bond maturing at time T with a strike price of K and expiring at time S, are given as follows:

$$c(t) = P(t, T)\Pi_{1t} - KP(t, S)\Pi_{2t} \tag{8.105}$$

and

$$p(t) = KP(t, S)(1 - \Pi_{2t}) - P(t, T)(1 - \Pi_{1t}) \tag{8.106}$$

where

$$\Pi_{1t} = \int_{\ln K}^{\infty} f_{1t}(y)\,dy = \frac{1}{2} + \frac{1}{\pi}\int_0^{\infty} \text{Re}\left[\frac{e^{-i\omega \ln K} g_{1t}(\omega)}{i\omega}\right] d\omega \tag{8.107}$$

$$\Pi_{2t} = \int_{\ln K}^{\infty} f_{2t}(y)\,dy = \frac{1}{2} + \frac{1}{\pi}\int_0^{\infty} \text{Re}\left[\frac{e^{-i\omega \ln K} g_{2t}(\omega)}{i\omega}\right] d\omega \tag{8.108}$$

The characteristic functions $g_{1t}(\omega)$ and $g_{2t}(\omega)$ are given as follows:

$$g_{1t}(\omega) = \frac{e^{A_1^*(s) - B_{11}^*(s)Y_1(t) - B_{12}^*(s)Y_2(t) - H(S,T)(1+i\omega) - H(t,S)}}{P(t, T)}, \quad s = S - t \tag{8.109}$$

$$g_{2t}(\omega) = \frac{e^{A_2^*(s) - B_{21}^*(s)Y_1(t) - B_{22}^*(s)Y_2(t) - H(S,T)(i\omega) - H(t,S)}}{P(t, S)}, \quad s = S - t \tag{8.110}$$

The functions $A_1^*(s)$, $B_{11}^*(s)$, and $B_{12}^*(s)$ are given as solutions to the ODEs for $A(s)$, $B_1(s)$, and $B_2(s)$, respectively, given in equation (8.85), but with the following boundary conditions:

$$A_1^*(0) = A(U)(1 + i\omega)$$

$$B_{11}^*(0) = B_1(U)(1 + i\omega) \tag{8.111}$$

$$B_{12}^*(0) = B_2(U)(1 + i\omega)$$

where $U = T - S$. Similarly, the functions $A_2^*(s)$, $B_{21}^*(s)$, and $B_{22}^*(s)$ are given as solutions to the ODEs for $A(s)$, $B_1(s)$, and $B_2(s)$, respectively, given in equation (8.85), but with the following boundary conditions:

$$A_2^*(0) = A(U)(i\omega)$$

$$B_{21}^*(0) = B_1(U)(i\omega) \tag{8.112}$$

$$B_{22}^*(0) = B_2(U)(i\omega)$$

The functions $A(U)$ and $B_1(U)$ are solved numerically by solving the first two ODEs in equation (8.85), and the solution of function $B_2(U)$ is given in equation (8.86). The function $H(S, T) = \delta U$, given by equation (8.84) under the $A_{1c}(2)$ and $A_{1c}(2)+$ models, is given by equation (8.89) under the $A_{1c}(2)++$ model.

Since the initial bond price $P(0, T)$ is specified exogenously under the time-inhomogeneous preference-free $A_{1c}(2)++$ model, the seven risk-neutral parameters of this model, $\tilde{\alpha}_{11}, \tilde{\alpha}_{21}, \tilde{\alpha}_{22}, \tilde{\theta}_1, \beta_{20}, \beta_{21}, \sigma_1$, and the value of the first state variable $Y_1(0)$ are obtained by calibrating the model to the cross section of prices of interest rate derivatives, such as caps and swaptions, at time $t = 0$.

The bond price $P(t, T)$ under the time-homogeneous preference-free $A_{1c}(2)+$ model is given by equation (8.83), with both $Y_1(0)$ and $Y_2(0)$ as free parameters at time $t = 0$ (i.e., $Y_2(0)$ is not zero, as it is under the $A_{1c}(2)++$ model) and with $H(t, T) = \delta(T - t) = \delta\tau$ in equation (8.84). The model requires the estimation of eight risk-neutral parameters: $\delta, \tilde{\alpha}_{11}, \tilde{\alpha}_{21}, \tilde{\alpha}_{22}, \tilde{\theta}_1, \beta_{21}$, and σ_1. In addition, assuming the model is calibrated using the daily cross sections of prices on bonds and interest rate derivatives over K days, then two values of the state variables $Y_1(t)$ and $Y_2(t)$ are also required for each of the K days, giving a total of $8 + 2K$ number of parameters and state variable values to be estimated using nonlinear optimization.

The fundamental $A_{1c}(2)$ model is generally estimated using econometric techniques, such as GMM, EMM, or maximum likelihood, giving estimates of both the risk-neutral parameters and the MPRs. This model does not generally use the price data on interest rate derivatives as an input and derives the parameter estimates based upon the time-series behavior of yields under both the physical measure and the risk-neutral measure.

Two-Factor Stochastic Volatility Trees

Recently, Beliaeva and Nawalkha [2007] have derived recombining trees for stochastic volatility/jump-based equity option models of Heston [1993], Bakshi, Cao, and Chen [1997], Pan [2002], and Duffie, Pan, and Singleton [2000]. As a natural extension, these trees also apply to the stochastic volatility-based $A_{1c}(2)$, $A_{1c}(2)+$, and $A_{1c}(2)++$ models for pricing bonds and interest rate derivatives. The short rate under these models is given as the sum of a deterministic term and two state variables as follows:

$$r(t) = \delta(t) + Y_1(t) + Y_2(t) \tag{8.113}$$

where the risk-neutral processes of Y_1 and Y_2 are given by equation (8.78). The term $\delta(t) = \delta$, a constant, and $Y_1(0)$ and $Y_2(0)$ are not constrained to equal zero under the $A_{1c}(2)$ and $A_{1c}(2)+$ models. In contrast, the term $\delta(t)$ is deterministic, and $Y_2(0) = 0$ under the $A_{1c}(2)++$ model.

As under the two-factor Gaussian model, the term $\delta(t)$ can be solved using two methods under the $A_{1c}(2)++$ model. The first method solves

$\delta(t)$ analytically using equation (8.88). However, since this solution is valid only in the continuous-time limit, it allows an exact match with the initial zero-coupon bond prices only when using a large number of steps on the tree. If an exact match is desired for an arbitrarily small number of steps, then $\delta(t)$ can be obtained numerically using the technique demonstrated for two-factor Gaussian model in equations (8.71) and (8.72).

For expositional simplicity, we demonstrate how to build the stochastic volatility tree for the time-homogeneous preference-free $A_{1c}(2)+$ model. The risk-neutral processes of Y_1 and Y_2 are given by equation (8.78) under this model. This model requires estimates of eight risk-neutral parameters: $\delta, \tilde{\alpha}_{11}, \tilde{\alpha}_{21}, \tilde{\alpha}_{22}, \tilde{\theta}_1, \beta_{20}, \beta_{21}$, and σ_1, and time 0 values of the state variables $Y_1(0)$ and $Y_2(0)$.

We model two trinomial trees corresponding to the two state variable processes given in equation (8.78). The state variable $Y_1(t)$ has an identical form to the CIR model given in Chapter 6. Hence, the trinomial tree for $Y_1(t)$ is generated using the NB truncated-transform approach described in Chapter 6. This approach first obtains the tree for the X-transform and then using an inversion obtains the tree for $Y_1(t)$. The $X_1(t)$ tree allows constant volatility and is shown in Figure 8.7. The $X_1(t)$ tree generally allows multiple node jumps when the $Y_1(t)$ process comes close to zero. All of the details of the $X_1(t)$ tree, including the trinomial probabilities and the path of multiple-node jumps, can be obtained from Chapter 6.

The construction of a trinomial tree for the $Y_2(t)$ process is problematic for the following reasons. First, the results of Nelson and Ramaswamy (NR) [1990] are not applicable since the volatility of the $Y_2(t)$ process stochastically depends upon $Y_1(t)$. Second, under certain special cases,

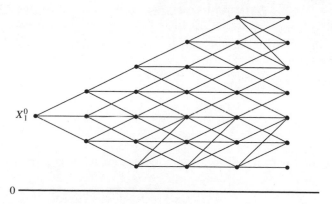

FIGURE 8.7 Trinomial Tree for the Transform $X_1(t)$

the volatility of the $Y_2(t)$ process approaches zero, while its drift remains very high, requiring multiple-node jumps away from zero. Finally, since volatility is stochastic, constructing recombining trees is difficult. We address these difficulties by constructing the following transform for the $Y_2(t)$ process:

$$X_2(t) = e^{\tilde{\alpha}_{22}t}\left(Y_2(t) - \frac{\tilde{\theta}_1\tilde{\alpha}_{21}}{\tilde{\alpha}_{22}}\right) \qquad (8.114)$$

The transform $X_2(t)$ should not be confused with the NR and NB transforms given in Chapter 6, as this transform *does not display a constant volatility*. In general, it is not possible to find a transform for $Y_2(t)$ that allows constant volatility, since the volatility of $Y_2(t)$ depends on another state variable $Y_1(t)$. The motivation of using the $X_2(t)$ transform can be understood by expressing it in the stochastic differential form and using Ito's lemma to give:

$$dX_2(t) = -\tilde{\alpha}_{21}e^{\tilde{\alpha}_{22}t}Y_1(t)\,dt + e^{\tilde{\alpha}_{22}t}\sqrt{\beta_{20} + \beta_{21}Y_1(t)}\,d\tilde{Z}_2(t) \qquad (8.115)$$

By virtue of the definition given in equation (8.114), the drift of the process in equation (8.115) does not contain any terms that are either constant or multiplied by $Y_2(t)$. The usefulness of this can be seen when $\beta_{20} = 0$. Under this case, one would require multiple-node jumps when $Y_1(t)$ approaches zero (and, as a result, the variance of the $X_2(t)$ process approaches zero) if the drift contains terms that are either constant or multiplied by $Y_2(t)$.

However, since the drift does not contain such terms (by virtue of the transform in equation (8.114)) and the drift also approaches zero when $Y_1(t)$ approaches zero, the matching of drift is not problematic and multiple-node jumps of the type required in Chapter 6 are not necessary.

However, since $Y_1(t)$ evolves stochastically, the variance of the $X_2(t)$ process is stochastic; and a new tree structure is required to capture the stochastically evolving variance of the $X_2(t)$ process. We now show how to model the trinomial tree for the $X_2(t)$ process. The starting value of the $X_2(t)$ process is given using equation (8.114) as follows:

$$X_2(0) = Y_2(0) - \frac{\tilde{\theta}_1\tilde{\alpha}_{21}}{\tilde{\alpha}_{22}} \qquad (8.116)$$

At time 0, the stochastic differential equation for $X_2(t)$ is given as follows:

$$dX_2(0) = -\tilde{\alpha}_{21}Y_1(0)\,dt + \sqrt{\beta_{20} + \beta_{21}Y_1(0)}\,d\tilde{Z}_2(0) \qquad (8.117)$$

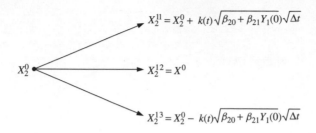

FIGURE 8.8 The Trinomial Tree for the $X_2(t)$ Process at Time 0

The trinomial tree at time 0, using equation (8.117), is shown in Figure 8.8.

Since the stochastic process for the $X_2(t)$ process in equation (8.115) does not follow constant volatility, the up node and the down node must be chosen to match the volatility at any given time t. We construct a grid with any two adjacent nodes separated by the same distance equal to $\sqrt{\beta_{20} + \beta_{21}Y_1(0)}\sqrt{\Delta t}$. Since the volatility at time t is given as $e^{\alpha_{22}t}\sqrt{\beta_{20} + \beta_{21}Y_1(t)}$ in equation (8.115), both the up jump and the down jump are allowed to move by multiple nodes. The number of nodes to move up and down is given by the variable $k(t)$, which is defined as the first integer value that is greater than or equal to the following ratio:

$$k(t) \geq \frac{e^{\tilde{\alpha}_{22}t}\sqrt{\beta_{20} + \beta_{21}Y_1(t)}}{\sqrt{\beta_{20} + \beta_{21}Y_1(0)}} \tag{8.118}$$

or

$$k(t) = CEILING\left(\frac{e^{\tilde{\alpha}_{22}t}\sqrt{\beta_{20} + \beta_{21}Y_1(t)}}{\sqrt{\beta_{20} + \beta_{21}Y_1(0)}}\right) \tag{8.119}$$

The *node span* is defined as the distance between the up node and the down node for the trinomial tree for the $X_2(t)$ process, as follows:

$$Node\ Span = 2k(t)\sqrt{\beta_{20} + \beta_{21}Y_1(0)}\sqrt{\Delta t} \tag{8.120}$$

A normal node span is obtained when $k(t)$ equals 1. When $k(t)$ is greater than 1, the node span can be a multiple of the normal node span. Restricting $k(t)$ to be an integer value ensures that the tree *recombines* at the future nodes. The definition of $k(t)$ ensures that the distance between the up node and the down node is sufficiently large for the middle probability to remain positive whenever $k(t)$ is greater than 1.

Figure 8.9 illustrates the tree construction of the $X_2(t)$ process by considering two cases $k(t) = 1$ and $k(t) = 2$ at time 1.

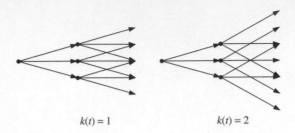

$$k(t) = 1 \qquad\qquad k(t) = 2$$

FIGURE 8.9 Node Span of $X_2(t)$ as a Function of $k(t)$

Note that even though the node span at time 1 when $k(t)$ equals 2 is twice the node span when $k(t)$ equals 1, the total number of nodes goes up only to seven from five, due to the recombining nature of the tree. Since the stochastic processes for $Y_1(t)$ and $X_2(t)$ follow a joint Markovian system given by equations (8.78) and (8.115), the tree for $X_2(t)$ must be obtained jointly with the tree for $Y_1(t)$. Example 8.2 illustrates the construction of the $X_2(t)$ tree.

Example 8.2 Assume that at time zero, $k(t)$ in equation (8.118) equals 1. Hence, the $X_2(t)$ tree has a normal node span at time 0. At time 1, $Y_1(t)$ can take three different values—Y_1^{11}, Y_1^{12}, and Y_1^{13}. Consider the case when $Y_1(t)$ takes its highest value, Y_1^{11}. Conditional on the occurrence of Y_1^{11}, assume that the ratio given on the right-hand side of equation (8.118) equals 1.5. Hence, $k(t)$ must be the first positive integer greater than 1.5, or $k(t)$ equals 2 at time 1 under this case.

The tree for $X_2(t)$ conditional on Y_1^{11} having occurred at time 1, is shown in Figure 8.10.

Next, suppose $Y_1(t)$ takes the middle node value Y_1^{12} at time 1. Assume that the ratio given on the right-hand side of equation (8.118) equals 1 under this case (e.g., assume $Y_1^{12} = Y_1^0$), which implies that $k(t)$ equals 1.

Conditional on Y_1^{12} having occurred at time 1, the tree for $X_2(t)$ is shown in Figure 8.11.

Note that under the case shown in Figure 8.11, the trinomial tree has a normal node span and only five nodes are needed, as opposed to seven nodes needed in the case shown in Figure 8.10.

Finally, suppose $Y_1(t)$ takes the bottom node value Y_1^{13} at time 1. Since this value will be lower than the middle node value Y_1^{12}, it follows that $k(t)$ will remain equal to 1 under this case also and that the nodes will be spaced normally as shown in Figure 8.11.

The time t probabilities of the up, middle, and down nodes of the $X_2(t)$ tree are obtained by matching the mean and variance of $dX_2(t)$ and requiring

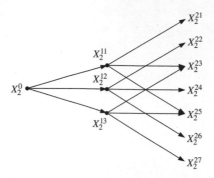

FIGURE 8.10 The Trinomial Tree for $X_2(t)$ Conditional on the Occurrence of Y_1^{11} at Time 1

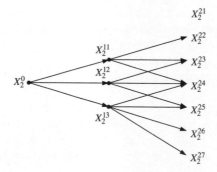

FIGURE 8.11 The Trinomial Tree for $X_2(t)$ Conditional on the Occurrence of Y_1^{12} at Time 1

that the three probabilities sum up to 1. Since this gives three equations in three unknowns, a unique solution exists and is given as follows:

$$p_2^u(t) = \frac{e^{2\tilde{\alpha}_{22}t}}{2(k(t))^2} \left(\frac{\beta_{20} + \beta_{21}Y_1(t)}{\beta_{20} + \beta_{21}Y_1(0)} \right) + \frac{1}{2k(t)} \frac{(-\tilde{\alpha}_{21}e^{\tilde{\alpha}_{22}t}Y_1(t))}{\sqrt{\beta_{20} + \beta_{21}Y_1(0)}} \sqrt{\Delta t}$$

$$p_2^d(t) = \frac{e^{2\tilde{\alpha}_{22}t}}{2(k(t))^2} \left(\frac{\beta_{20} + \beta_{21}Y_1(t)}{\beta_{20} + \beta_{21}Y_1(0)} \right) - \frac{1}{2k(t)} \frac{(-\tilde{\alpha}_{21}e^{\tilde{\alpha}_{22}t}Y_1(t))}{\sqrt{\beta_{20} + \beta_{21}Y_1(0)}} \sqrt{\Delta t} \quad (8.121)$$

$$p_2^m(t) = 1 - p_2^u(t) - p_2^d(t)$$

The joint probabilities of any state are obtained using the marginal probabilities of the $Y_1(t)$ and $X_2(t)$ processes. The marginal probabilities of the $X_2(t)$ process are given in equation (8.121). Since $Y_1(t)$ is a square root process, its marginal probabilities are obtained using the NB truncated transform given in Chapter 6. Even though the $Y_1(t)$ and $X_2(t)$ trees follow a joint Markovian system, they are conditionally independent, and hence, at any given time, the nine joint probabilities are obtained by simply multiplying the three probabilities of the $Y_1(t)$ tree with the three probabilities of the $X_2(t)$ tree. For example, Table 8.1 shows the nine joint probabilities conditional on the occurrence of Y_1^{11} and X_2^{11} at time 1.

The tree for the $Y_2(t)$ process is obtained by inverting equation (8.114) to get:

$$Y_2(t) = X_2(t)e^{-\tilde{\alpha}_{22}t} + \frac{\tilde{\theta}_1\tilde{\alpha}_{21}}{\tilde{\alpha}_{22}} \qquad (8.122)$$

Since the marginal probabilities of the $Y_2(t)$ tree are identical to those of the $X_2(t)$ tree, the joint probabilities of the $Y_1(t)$ and $Y_2(t)$ trees are identical to the joint probabilities of the $Y_1(t)$ and $X_2(t)$ trees, and are given in Table 8.1.

Since the $Y_1(t)$ tree has five nodes at time 2 and the $Y_2(t)$ tree has a maximum of seven nodes at time 2 (i.e., conditional on the occurrence of Y_1^{11} at time 1), the total number of values of the short rate at time 2 equals $7 \times 5 = 35$ on the two-dimensional tree. Similarly, since both trees have three nodes at time 1, the total number of values of the short rate at time 1 equals $3 \times 3 = 9$. The short rate tree grows at the order of N^3 using an N-step tree using the above-mentioned approach. This represents a significant improvement over using nonrecombining trees to model stochastic volatility, which would require 4^N number of nodes using an N-step tree. The two-dimensional stochastic volatility tree is demonstrated numerically in Example 8.3.

TABLE 8.1 Joint Probabilities Given as a Product of Marginal Probabilities, Conditional on the Occurrence of Y_1^{11} and X_2^{11} at Time 1

$p(Y_1^{21}$ and $X_2^{21}) = p_1^u(t) \times p_2^u(t) = p(Y_1^{21}) \times p(X_2^{21})$

$p(Y_1^{21}$ and $X_2^{23}) = p_1^u(t) \times p_2^m(t) = p(Y_1^{21}) \times p(X_2^{23})$

$p(Y_1^{21}$ and $X_2^{25}) = p_1^u(t) \times p_2^d(t) = p(Y_1^{21}) \times p(X_2^{25})$

$p(Y_1^{22}$ and $X_2^{21}) = p_1^m(t) \times p_2^u(t) = p(Y_1^{22}) \times p(X_2^{21})$

$p(Y_1^{22}$ and $X_2^{23}) = p_1^m(t) \times p_2^m(t) = p(Y_1^{22}) \times p(X_2^{23})$

$p(Y_1^{22}$ and $X_2^{25}) = p_1^m(t) \times p_2^d(t) = p(Y_1^{22}) \times p(X_2^{25})$

$p(Y_1^{23}$ and $X_2^{21}) = p_1^d(t) \times p_2^u(t) = p(Y_1^{23}) \times p(X_2^{21})$

$p(Y_1^{23}$ and $X_2^{23}) = p_1^d(t) \times p_2^m(t) = p(Y_1^{23}) \times p(X_2^{23})$

$p(Y_1^{23}$ and $X_2^{25}) = p_1^d(t) \times p_2^d(t) = p(Y_1^{23}) \times p(X_2^{25})$

Example 8.3 Consider a six-month zero-coupon bond with a face value $F = \$100$. Let the parameters under the time-homogeneous preference-free $A_{1c}(2)$ + model be given as: $\tilde{\alpha}_{11} = 0.5$; $\tilde{\theta}_1 = 0.02$; $\sigma_1 = 0.2$; $\tilde{\alpha}_{21} = 0.5$; $\tilde{\alpha}_{22} = 0.2$; $\beta_{20} = 0$; $\beta_{21} = 1.0$; and $T = 0.5$. The initial values of the state variable are $Y_1(0) = 0.02$, $Y_2(0) = 0.04$, and $\delta = 0$. These values give $r(0) = 0 + 0.02 + 0.04 = 0.06$. Consider the valuation of this bond using a two-step two-dimensional tree. The length of each time-step equals $\Delta t = 0.5/2 = 0.25$. The underlying one-dimensional trinomial tree for the $Y_1(t)$ process is shown in Figure 8.12.

The initial value for the $X_2(t)$ process is computed using equation (8.116) as follows:

$$X_2(0) = 0.04 - \frac{0.02 \times 0.5}{0.2} = -0.01$$

The span of the X_2 tree, $k(t)$, is determined according to equation (8.119). At time $t = 0, k(0) = 1$.

At time $t = 0.25$:

If $Y_1(t) = 0.045$, then:

$$k(t) = CEILING\left(\frac{e^{0.2 \times 0.25}\sqrt{0.045}}{\sqrt{0.02}}\right) = CEILING(1.58) = 2$$

If $Y_1(t) = 0.02$, then:

$$k(t) = CEILING\left(\frac{e^{0.2 \times 0.25}\sqrt{0.02}}{\sqrt{0.02}}\right) = CEILING(1.05) = 2$$

If $Y_1(t) = 0.005$, then:

$$k(t) = CEILING\left(\frac{e^{0.2 \times 0.25}\sqrt{0.005}}{\sqrt{0.02}}\right) = CEILING(0.53) = 1$$

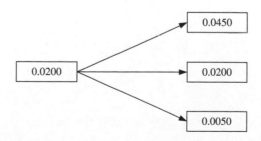

FIGURE 8.12 One-Dimensional Trinomial Tree for the $Y_1(t)$ Process

The one-dimensional tree for the $X_2(t)$ process is shown in Figure 8.13.

Using equation (8.122), the $Y_2(t)$ tree is inverted from the $X_2(t)$ tree, and is shown in Figure 8.14. Using the values of $Y_1(t)$ and $Y_2(t)$ at each node, the two-dimensional short rate tree is shown in Figure 8.15.

The short rate values at each node are used for discounting appropriate bond values at the next time step. For example, the bond value at time $t = 0$ is computed as follows.

The marginal trinomial probabilities for $Y_1(t = 0)$ are given as follows (for computational details refer to Chapter 6):

$$p_{y_1}^u = 0.1875$$

$$p_{y_1}^m = 0.5$$

$$p_{y_1}^d = 0.3125$$

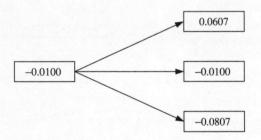

FIGURE 8.13 One-Dimensional Trinomial Tree for the $X_2(t)$ Process

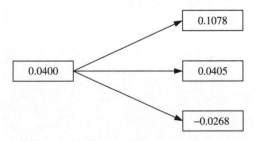

FIGURE 8.14 One-Dimensional Trinomial Tree for the $Y_2(t)$ Process

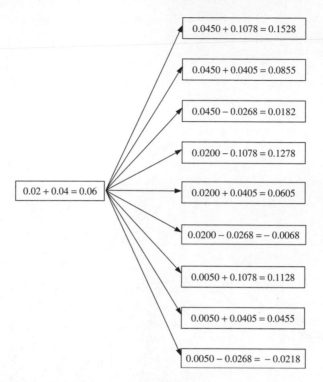

FIGURE 8.15 Two-Dimensional Short-Rate Tree

The marginal trinomial probabilities for the $Y_2(t = 0)$ process are computed according to equation (8.121) as follows:

$$p_2^u(t) = \frac{1}{2} + \frac{1}{2}\frac{(-0.5 \times 0.02)}{\sqrt{0.02}}\sqrt{0.25} = 0.4823$$

$$p_2^d(t) = \frac{1}{2} - \frac{1}{2}\frac{(-0.5 \times 0.02)}{\sqrt{0.02}}\sqrt{0.25} = 0.5177$$

$$p_2^m(t) = 1 - 0.4823 - 0.5177 = 0.0$$

The joint probabilities for $t = 0$ are computed as follows:

$$p_1 = 0.1875 \times 0.4823 = 0.0904$$

$$p_2 = 0.1875 \times 0.0 = 0.0$$

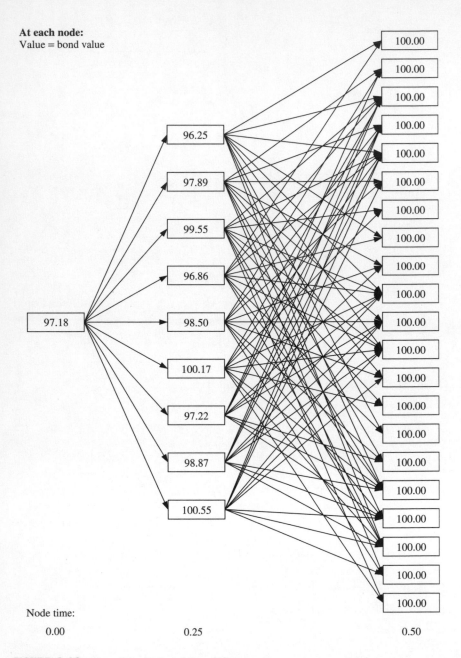

At each node:
Value = bond value

Node time:

0.00   0.25   0.50

FIGURE 8.16 Two-Dimensional Bond Tree

$$p_3 = 0.1875 \times 0.5177 = 0.0971$$

$$p_4 = 0.5 \times 0.4823 = 0.2412$$

$$p_5 = 0.5 \times 0.0 = 0.0$$

$$p_6 = 0.5 \times 0.5177 = 0.2588$$

$$p_7 = 0.3125 \times 0.4823 = 0.1507$$

$$p_8 = 0.3125 \times 0.0 = 0.0$$

$$p_9 = 0.3125 \times 0.5177 = 0.1618$$

The time 0 bond value is computed as follows:

$$
\begin{aligned}
P(0) = &(96.25 \times 0.0904 + 97.89 \times 0.0 + 99.55 \times 0.0971 \\
&+ 96.86 \times 0.2412 + 98.50 \times 0.0 + 100.17 \times 0.2588 \\
&+ 97.22 \times 0.1507 + 98.87 \times 0.0 + 100.55 \times 0.1618)/e^{0.06 \times 0.25} = \$97.10
\end{aligned}
$$

The time 0 bond price equals \$97.18, using a 100-step two-dimensional tree (see Figure 8.16). The bond price obtained by solving the ODEs in equation (8.85) also equals \$97.18 using the Matlab software.

TWO-FACTOR SQUARE-ROOT MODELS

Though two-factor square-root models disallow negative rates and allow state variable dependent volatilities, these models do not allow state variables to be correlated under the risk-neutral measure (without violating the admissibility conditions required for maintaining the affine structure of bond prices). Similar to Gaussian and hybrid models, the three nested two-factor square-root models can be given as the fundamental $A_2(2)$ model, the time-homogeneous preference-free $A_2(2)+$ model, and the time-inhomogeneous preference-free $A_2(2)++$ model. These nested models can be expressed in equivalent forms, given as the Ay form and the Ar form (since negative correlations are not allowed, state variables are assumed to be uncorrelated, which makes the canonical form and the Ay form converge).

The *Ay* Form

The $A_{2y}(2)$ Model   The short rate under the fundamental $A_{2y}(2)$ model is given as the sum of a constant and two state variables as follows:

$$r(t) = \delta + Y_1(t) + Y_2(t) \tag{8.123}$$

The stochastic processes of the state variables under the maximal $A_{2y}(2)$ specification are given under the risk-neutral measure, as follows:

$$dY_1(t) = \left(\tilde{\alpha}_{11}(\tilde{\theta}_1 - Y_1(t)) + \tilde{\alpha}_{12}(\tilde{\theta}_2 - Y_2(t))\right) dt + \sigma_1\sqrt{Y_1(t)}\, d\tilde{Z}_1(t)$$
$$dY_2(t) = \left(\tilde{\alpha}_{21}(\tilde{\theta}_1 - Y_1(t)) + \tilde{\alpha}_{22}(\tilde{\theta}_2 - Y_2(t))\right) dt + \sigma_2\sqrt{Y_2(t)}\, d\tilde{Z}_2(t)$$

$$(8.124)$$

where the two Wiener processes are uncorrelated. Dai and Singleton [2000] show that the unconditional correlation parameters $\tilde{\alpha}_{21}$ and $\tilde{\alpha}_{12}$ must be nonpositive for the state variable processes to be admissible in the affine class. Negative values of $\tilde{\alpha}_{21}$ and $\tilde{\alpha}_{12}$ imply that state variables are positively correlated, which is inconsistent with the observed time-series dynamics of yield changes. Hence, in the rest of this section, we only consider the special case of zero unconditional correlations (under the risk-neutral measure), under which the state variable processes simplify as follows:

$$dY_1(t) = \tilde{\alpha}_1(\tilde{\theta}_1 - Y_1(t))\, dt + \sigma_1\sqrt{Y_1(t)}\, d\tilde{Z}_1(t)$$
$$dY_2(t) = \tilde{\alpha}_2(\tilde{\theta}_2 - Y_2(t))\, dt + \sigma_2\sqrt{Y_2(t)}\, d\tilde{Z}_2(t)$$

$$(8.125)$$

where, for notational convenience, parameters $\tilde{\alpha}_{11}$ and $\tilde{\alpha}_{22}$ are redefined as $\tilde{\alpha}_1$ and $\tilde{\alpha}_2$, respectively. This model requires the following sign restrictions on the risk-neutral parameters: $\tilde{\alpha}_1\tilde{\theta}_1 > 0$, $\tilde{\alpha}_2\tilde{\theta}_2 > 0$, $\sigma_1 > 0$, and $\sigma_2 > 0$. A positive (negative) value for $\tilde{\alpha}_i$ is consistent with a stationary (explosive) risk-neutral process for the state variable Y_i for $i = 1$ and 2. The fundamental $A_{2y}(2)$ model is specified under completely affine form by Longstaff and Schwartz [1992], Chen and Scott [1992], and Dai and Singleton [2000]; under essentially affine form by Duffee [2002]; and under semiaffine form by Duarte [2004], using increasingly general specifications of MPRs. Using the most general specification of the MPRs given by Duarte [2004], the change of measure under the semiaffine form is given as follows:

$$d\tilde{Z}_1(t) = dZ_1(t) + \frac{1}{\sigma_1}\left(\gamma_{10} + \frac{\gamma_{11}}{\sqrt{Y_1(t)}} + \gamma_{12}\sqrt{Y_1(t)}\right) dt$$

$$(8.126)$$

$$d\tilde{Z}_2(t) = dZ_2(t) + \frac{1}{\sigma_2}\left(\gamma_{20} + \frac{\gamma_{21}}{\sqrt{Y_2(t)}} + \gamma_{22}\sqrt{Y_2(t)}\right) dt$$

The essentially affine form is obtained by setting the parameters γ_{10} and γ_{20} to zero. The completely affine form (see Chen and Scott [1992] and Dai and Singleton [2000]) is obtained by setting the parameters γ_{10}, γ_{20}, γ_{11}, and γ_{21} to zero. Since Y_1 and Y_2 also appear in the denominators in equation (8.126), the change of measure requires parameter restrictions to ensure that these state variables remain strictly positive under both the physical measure and the risk-neutral measure in order to satisfy the conditions of the Girsanov theorem for arbitrage-free pricing. For example, under the essentially affine form, the restrictions $2\tilde{\alpha}_1\tilde{\theta}_1 \geq \sigma_1^2$ and $2\tilde{\alpha}_2\tilde{\theta}_2 \geq \sigma_2^2$ ensure that the state variables remain strictly above zero under the risk-neutral measure. A similar restriction applies to the corresponding parameters of both state variables under the physical measure. Duarte [Appendix 4.1, 2004], gives general parameter restrictions required for arbitrage-free pricing under the semiaffine form.

Applying Ito's lemma to the bond price, equating the change in bond price to riskless return, and then taking risk-neutral expectation, we get the PDE for the bond price as follows:

$$
\frac{\partial P}{\partial t} + \frac{\partial P}{\partial Y_1}\tilde{\alpha}_1(\tilde{\theta}_1 - Y_1(t)) + \frac{\partial P}{\partial Y_2}\tilde{\alpha}_2(\tilde{\theta}_2 - Y_2(t)) + \frac{1}{2}\frac{\partial^2 P}{\partial Y_1^2}\sigma_1^2 Y_1(t)
$$
$$
+ \frac{1}{2}\frac{\partial^2 P}{\partial Y_2^2}\sigma_2^2 Y_2(t) = r(t)P(t,\ T) \tag{8.127}
$$

subject to the boundary condition $P(T,\ T) = 1$. Let the bond price solution be given as follows:

$$
P(t,\ T) = e^{A(\tau) - B_1(\tau)Y_1(t) - B_2(\tau)Y_2(t) - H(t,T)} \tag{8.128}
$$

where

$$
H(t,\ T) = \int_t^T \delta\, dv = \delta\tau \tag{8.129}
$$

and $\tau = T - t$. By taking the partial derivatives of the bond price and substituting these into equation (8.127), we get the following three ODEs:

$$
\frac{\partial A(\tau)}{\partial \tau} = -\tilde{\alpha}_1\tilde{\theta}_1 B_1(\tau) - \tilde{\alpha}_2\tilde{\theta}_2 B_2(\tau)
$$
$$
\frac{\partial B_1(\tau)}{\partial \tau} = 1 - \tilde{\alpha}_1 B_1(\tau) - \frac{1}{2}\sigma_1^2 B_1^2(\tau) \tag{8.130}
$$
$$
\frac{\partial B_2(\tau)}{\partial \tau} = 1 - \tilde{\alpha}_2 B_2(\tau) - \frac{1}{2}\sigma_2^2 B_2^2(\tau)
$$

subject to the boundary condition $A(0) = B_1(0) = B_2(0) = 0$. The solution is given as follows:

$$
A(\tau) = \sum_{i=1}^{2}\frac{2\tilde{\alpha}_i\tilde{\theta}_i}{\sigma_i^2}\ln\left[\frac{2\beta_i e^{\frac{1}{2}(\beta_i + \tilde{\alpha}_i)\tau}}{(\beta_i + \tilde{\alpha}_i)(e^{\beta_i\tau} - 1) + 2\beta_i}\right] \tag{8.131}
$$

$$B_i(\tau) = \frac{2(e^{\beta_i \tau} - 1)}{(\beta_i + \tilde{\alpha}_i)(e^{\beta_i \tau} - 1) + 2\beta_i}, \quad \text{for } i = 1 \text{ and } 2 \qquad (8.132)$$

where $\beta_i = \sqrt{\tilde{\alpha}_i^2 + 2\sigma_i^2}$.

The $A_{2y}(2)+$ and $A_{2y}(2)++$ Models The preference-free $A_{2y}(2)+$ and $A_{2y}(2)++$ models obtain the risk-neutral parameters directly from the cross sections of prices on bonds and interest rate derivatives, and hence, do not require restrictive assumptions on the functional forms of MPRs. Using general nonlinear MPRs, the change of measure can be given as follows:

$$d\tilde{Z}_i(t) = dZ_i(t) + \gamma_i(z, t)\, dt, \quad \text{for all } i = 1 \text{ and } 2 \qquad (8.133)$$

The functions $\gamma_i(z, t)$ can be nonlinear, and may depend upon multiple state variables. The change of measure also requires that these functions satisfy the parameter restrictions to ensure arbitrage-free pricing using the Girsanov theorem. We now consider a specific example of the functions $\gamma_i(z, t)$ that demonstrates the additional flexibility allowed by the preference-free paradigm.

Let the physical processes of the state variables be defined as follows:

$$dY_1(t) = \mu_1(t, Y_1(t), Y_2(t))\, dt + \sigma_1 \sqrt{Y_1(t)} dZ_1(t)$$
$$dY_2(t) = \mu_2(t, Y_1(t), Y_2(t))\, dt + \sigma_2 \sqrt{Y_2(t)} dZ_2(t) \qquad (8.134)$$

where the drift functions are defined as follows:

$$\mu_1(t, Y_1(t), Y_2(t)) = \begin{cases} \alpha_{11}(\theta_{11} - Y_1(t)) + \alpha_{12}(\theta_{12} - Y_2(t)), & \text{if } Y_1(t) > \varepsilon \\ \alpha_{11}(\theta_{11} - Y_1(t)), & \text{otherwise.} \end{cases}$$

$$(8.135)$$

$$\mu_2(t, Y_1(t), Y_2(t)) = \begin{cases} \alpha_{21}(\theta_{21} - Y_1(t)) + \alpha_{22}(\theta_{22} - Y_2(t)), & \text{if } Y_2(t) > \varepsilon \\ \alpha_{22}(\theta_{22} - Y_2(t)), & \text{otherwise.} \end{cases}$$

$$(8.136)$$

where constant ε is an arbitrarily defined finite value that is *strictly* greater than zero (e.g., $\varepsilon = 0.00001$). This drift specification assumes positive values for all physical parameters. Since the parameters α_{12} and α_{21} are positive, negative unconditional correlations are allowed between the state variables $Y_1(t)$ and $Y_2(t)$ under the physical measure, even though unconditional correlations are zero under the risk-neutral measure. The state variable processes are obviously not affine under the physical measure due to the "if" condition in equations (8.135) and (8.136). The nonlinearity in the drifts is essential for allowing negative physical correlations. However, the negative correlations are allowed only until the state variables $Y_1(t)$ and $Y_2(t)$ remain strictly above zero (with an arbitrary lower bound ε). As soon as the state variables hit the lower bound, the unconditional correlations become zero, thus preventing the state variables from becoming negative, which would invalidate the existence of square-root processes. The parameter restrictions that ensure that the state variables do not reach the zero boundary under the risk-neutral measure remain the same as under the fundamental $A_{2y}(2)$ model given earlier.

Due to the negative physical correlation between the state variables, the above-mentioned specification of drifts is consistent with a more realistic relationship between the expected returns of bonds and the slope of the term structure, breaking the tension between fitting conditional volatilities versus expected returns. Though the drift specifications are somewhat peculiar, they demonstrate that preference-free models can be consistent with more realistic expected return relations under the physical measure. Recall that all three forms of MPR specifications (i.e., under the completely affine, essentially affine, and semiaffine models) given earlier under the fundamental $A_{2y}(2)$ model require nonnegative correlation between the two state variables under both the physical measure and the risk-neutral measure, which prevents the breaking of tension between conditional volatilities and expected returns, using this model.

Comparing the stochastic processes of the state variables under the physical measure (see equation (8.134)) with the corresponding processes under the risk-neutral measure (see equation (8.125)), we can solve for functions $\gamma_i(z,\ t)$, related to the change of measure as follows:

$$\gamma_i(z,\ t) = \frac{\mu_i(t,\ Y_1(t),\ Y_2(t)) - \tilde{\alpha}_i(\tilde{\theta}_i - Y_i(t))}{\sigma_i\sqrt{Y_i(t)}}, \quad \text{for } i = 1 \text{ and } 2 \quad (8.137)$$

where $\mu_i(t,\ Y_1(t),\ Y_2(t))$ for $i = 1$ and 2 are defined in equations (8.135) and (8.136).

The solutions of the bond price and interest rate derivatives under the time-homogeneous preference-free $A_{2y}(2)+$ model are identical to those under the fundamental $A_{2y}(2)$ model, except that the risk-neutral parameters estimated under the two models may be different, since the latter model imposes restrictive functional forms on the MPRs.

The solution of the bond price under the time-inhomogeneous preference- free $A_{2y}(2)++$ model can be obtained by following the same steps as under the fundamental $A_{2y}(2)$ model, except that the constant δ in equation (8.123) is replaced with a deterministic function $\delta(t)$ and $H(t,\ T)$

in equation (8.129) is replaced by the following:

$$H(t, T) = \int_t^T \delta(v)\, dv \qquad (8.138)$$

Following similar steps as under the two-factor Gaussian and the two-factor hybrid models, the solutions of $\delta(t)$ and $H(t, T)$ can be given as follows:

$$\delta(t) = f(0, t) - \sum_{i=1}^{2}\left(Y_i(0) + \tilde{\alpha}_i B_i(t)(\tilde{\theta}_i - Y_i(0)) - \frac{1}{2}\sigma_i^2 B_i^2(t) Y_i(0)\right) \quad (8.139)$$

and

$$H(t, T) = H(0, T) - H(0, t) = A(T) - A(t) - \sum_{i=1}^{2}(Y_i(0)[B_i(T) - B_i(t)])$$

$$- \ln P(0, T) + \ln P(0, t) \qquad (8.140)$$

Bond Price Process and Forward Rate Process   The risk-neutral bond price process and the risk-neutral forward rate process under the $A_{2c}(2)$, $A_{2c}(2)+$, and $A_{2c}(2)++$ models have the same form and are obtained using Ito's lemma as follows:

$$\frac{dP(t, T)}{P(t, T)} = r(t)\, dt - \sum_{i=1}^{2} B_i(T - t)\sigma_i\sqrt{Y_i(t)}\, d\tilde{Z}_i(t) \qquad (8.141)$$

and

$$df(t, T) = \mu_f(t, T)\, dt + \sum_{i=1}^{2}\sqrt{Y_i(t)}\sigma_{f,i}(t, T)\, d\tilde{Z}_i(t) \qquad (8.142)$$

where

$$\mu_f(t, T) = \sum_{i=1}^{2} Y_i(t)\sigma_i^2 B_i(T - t)\left(1 - \tilde{\alpha}_i B_i(T - t) - \frac{1}{2}\sigma_i^2 B_i^2(T - t)\right)$$

$$\qquad (8.143)$$

$$\sigma_{f,i}(t, T) = \sigma_i\left(1 - \tilde{\alpha}_i B_i(T - t) - \frac{1}{2}\sigma_i^2 B_i^2(T - t)\right)$$

and $B_i(T - t)$ is defined in equation (8.132) for $i = 1$ and 2. The forward rate process is a two-factor generalization of the corresponding process under the one-factor CIR [1985] and preference-free CIR models.

The Ar Form

The Longstaff and Schwartz [1992] Model   The Longstaff and Schwartz (LS) [1992] model is nested in the maximal fundamental $A_2(2)$ model given in the Ar form. The LS model assumes that physical investment is performed by a single stochastic constant return-to-scale technology, which produces a single good that is either consumed or reinvested in production. The realized return on the investment under the physical measure is governed by the stochastic differential equation given as follows:

$$dQ(t)/Q(t) = (\mu S_1(t) + \theta S_2(t))\, dt + \sigma\sqrt{S_2(t)}\, dZ(t) \qquad (8.144)$$

where μ, θ, and σ are positive constants and $S_1(t)$ and $S_2(t)$ are the two state variables that determine the expected returns. The production uncertainty is related only to the second factor, $S_2(t)$. The state variables $S_1(t)$ and $S_2(t)$ follow square root processes under the physical measure, given as follows:

$$dS_1(t) = (a - bS_1(t))\, dt + c\sqrt{S_1(t)}\, dZ_1(t) \qquad (8.145)$$

$$dS_2(t) = (d - eS_2(t))\, dt + f\sqrt{S_2(t)}\, dZ_2(t) \qquad (8.146)$$

where $dZ_1(t) \times dZ(t) = 0$ and $dZ_1(t) \times dZ_2(t) = 0$. The condition $\theta > \sigma^2$ ensures nonnegativity of the short rate. Redefining $x_1(t) = S_1(t)/c^2$ and $x_2(t) = S_2(t)/f^2$ and applying Ito's lemma gives:

$$dx_1(t) = (\gamma - bx_1(t))\, dt + \sqrt{x_1(t)}\, dZ_1(t)$$
$$dx_2(t) = (\eta - ex_2(t))\, dt + \sqrt{x_2(t)}\, dZ_2(t) \qquad (8.147)$$

where $\gamma = a/c^2$ and $\eta = d/f^2$. Longstaff and Schwartz show that the short rate is given in the equilibrium as follows:

$$r(t) = \alpha x_1(t) + \beta x_2(t) \qquad (8.148)$$

where $\alpha = \mu c^2$ and $\beta = (\theta - \sigma^2)f^2$.

Using equation (8.147), the instantaneous variance of changes in the short rate can be derived as follows:

$$V(t) = \alpha^2 x_1(t) + \beta^2 x_2(t) \qquad (8.149)$$

The state variables $x_1(t)$ and $x_2(t)$ can be inverted and expressed as functions of the short rate and the variance of the changes in the short rate, as follows:

$$x_1(t) = \frac{\beta r(t) - V(t)}{\alpha(\beta - \alpha)}$$

$$x_2(t) = \frac{V(t) - \alpha r(t)}{\beta(\beta - \alpha)}$$

(8.150)

The MPR under the LS model is related only to the second state variable, since the production uncertainty is assumed to be caused by this variable. The change of measure consistent with the MPR specification under the LS model is given as follows:

$$d\tilde{Z}_1(t) = dZ_1(t)$$

$$d\tilde{Z}_2(t) = dZ_2(t) + \lambda\sqrt{x_2(t)}$$

(8.151)

Substituting equation (8.151) into equation (8.147), the state variable processes can be given under the risk-neutral measure as follows:

$$dx_1(t) = (\gamma - bx_1(t))\,dt + \sqrt{x_1(t)}\,d\tilde{Z}_1(t)$$

$$dx_2(t) = (\eta - \tilde{v}x_2(t))\,dt + \sqrt{x_2(t)}\,d\tilde{Z}_2(t)$$

(8.152)

where $\tilde{v} = e + \lambda$. By applying Ito's lemma to the bond price, equating the change in bond price to riskless return, and then taking risk-neutral expectation, we get the PDE for the bond price as follows:

$$\frac{\partial P}{\partial t} + \frac{\partial P}{\partial x_1}(\gamma - bx_1(t)) + \frac{\partial P}{\partial x_2}(\eta - \tilde{v}x_2(t)) + \frac{x_1(t)}{2}\frac{\partial^2 P}{\partial x_1^2} + \frac{x_2(t)}{2}\frac{\partial^2 P}{\partial x_2^2}$$

$$= r(t)P(t,\,T)$$

(8.153)

subject to the boundary condition $P(T,\,T) = 1$. Expressing $x_1(t)$ and $x_2(t)$ in terms of $r(t)$ and $V(t)$ using equations (8.148) and (8.149) and then using the standard procedure to solve for the bond price, the solution is given as follows:

$$P(t,\,T) = [A(\tau)]^{2\gamma} \times [B(\tau)]^{2\eta} \times e^{k\tau + C(\tau)r(t) + D(\tau)V(t)}$$

(8.154)

where

$$A(\tau) = \frac{2\phi}{(b + \phi)(e^{\phi\tau} - 1) + 2\phi}$$

$$B(\tau) = \frac{2\psi}{(\tilde{v} + \psi)(e^{\psi\tau} - 1) + 2\psi}$$

$$C(\tau) = \frac{\alpha\phi(e^{\psi\tau} - 1)B(\tau) - \beta\psi(e^{\phi\tau} - 1)A(\tau)}{\phi\psi(\beta - \alpha)}$$

$$D(\tau) = \frac{\psi(e^{\phi\tau} - 1)A(\tau) - \phi(e^{\psi\tau} - 1)B(\tau)}{\phi\psi(\beta - \alpha)}$$

and

$$\phi = \sqrt{2\alpha + b^2}$$

$$\psi = \sqrt{2\beta + \tilde{v}^2}$$

$$k = \gamma(b + \phi) + \eta(\tilde{v} + \psi)$$

The $A_{2r}(2)$, $A_{2r}(2)+$, and $A_{2r}(2)++$ Models The fundamental $A_{2r}(2)$ model is a generalization of the LS model, with the short rate given as follows:

$$r(t) = \delta + \alpha x_1(t) + \beta x_2(t) \tag{8.155}$$

where the risk-neutral processes of the state variables $x_1(t)$ and $x_2(t)$ are specified exogenously as follows:

$$\begin{aligned} dx_1(t) &= (\tilde{\gamma} - \tilde{b}x_1(t))\, dt + \sqrt{x_1(t)}\, d\tilde{Z}_1(t) \\ dx_2(t) &= (\tilde{\eta} - \tilde{v}x_2(t))\, dt + \sqrt{x_2(t)}\, d\tilde{Z}_2(t) \end{aligned} \tag{8.156}$$

The constant δ adds additional flexibility to the $A_{2r}(2)$ model over the LS model. Further, since the risk-neutral parameters $\tilde{\gamma}$, $\tilde{b}$, $\tilde{\eta}$, and $\tilde{v}$ are consistent with more general forms of MPRs (e.g., see Duffee [2002]), they are different from the corresponding risk-neutral parameters under the LS model. The bond price solution under the more general fundamental $A_{2r}(2)$ model is obtained as a simple extension of the solution under the LS model given in equation (8.154), as follows:

$$P(t, T) = [A(\tau)]^{2\gamma} \times [B(\tau)]^{2\eta} \times e^{k\tau + C(\tau)(r(t) - \delta) + D(\tau)V(t) - H(t,T)} \tag{8.157}$$

where

$$H(t, T) = \int_t^T \delta\, dv = \delta\tau \tag{8.158}$$

where the parameters $\tilde{\gamma}, \tilde{b}$, and $\tilde{\eta}$ replace the corresponding parameters without the tilde signs in equation (8.154). Assuming $\delta = 0$ and applying the restrictive form of MPR given by the change of measure in equation (8.151) results in the special case of the LS model.

The solutions of the bond price and interest rate derivatives under the time-homogeneous preference-free $A_{2r}(2)+$ model are identical to those under the fundamental $A_{2r}(2)$ model, except that the risk-neutral parameters estimated under the two models may be different since the latter model imposes restrictive linear functional forms on the MPRs. The solution of the bond price under the time-inhomogeneous preference-free $A_{2r}(2)++$ model can be obtained by following the same steps as under the $A_{2r}(2)+$ model, except that the constant δ in equation (8.155) is replaced with a deterministic function $\delta(t)$, and $H(t,\ T)$ in equation (8.158) is replaced by the following:

$$H(t,\ T) = \int_t^T \delta(v)\,dv \tag{8.159}$$

Following similar steps as under the other two-factor models, the solutions to the bond price $P(t,\ T), \delta(t)$, and $H(t,\ T)$ under the $A_{2r}(2)++$ model can be given as follows:

$$P(t,\ T) = [A(\tau)]^{2\gamma} \times [B(\tau)]^{2\eta} \times e^{k\tau + C(\tau)\left(r(t)-\delta(t)\right)+D(\tau)V(t)-H(t,T)} \tag{8.160}$$

where $A(\tau)$, $B(\tau)$, $C(\tau)$, and $D(\tau)$ are defined in equation (8.154) but with parameters $\tilde{\gamma}$, $\tilde{b}$, and $\tilde{\eta}$ replacing the corresponding parameters without the tilde signs, and with:

$$\delta(t) = f(0,\ t) + 2\gamma\frac{\partial \ln A(t)}{\partial t} + 2\eta\frac{\partial \ln B(t)}{\partial t} + k$$
$$+ \frac{\partial C(t)}{\partial t}(r(0) - \delta(0)) + \frac{\partial D(t)}{\partial t}V(0) \tag{8.161}$$

$$H(t,\ T) = H(0,\ T) - H(0,\ t) = 2\gamma \ln\left(\frac{A(T)}{A(t)}\right) + 2\eta \ln\left(\frac{B(T)}{B(t)}\right) + k(T - t)$$
$$+ (C(T) - C(t))(r(0) - \delta(0)) + (D(T) - D(t))V(0) \tag{8.162}$$
$$- \ln P(0,\ T) + \ln P(0,\ t)$$

Relationship between the Canonical Form and the *Ar* Form

The relationship between the *Ay* and the *Ar* forms of the two-factor square-root models can be given by noting the following relationship between the risk-neutral parameters:

$$\tilde{\alpha}_1 = \tilde{b} \qquad\qquad \tilde{b} = \tilde{\alpha}_1$$

$$\tilde{\alpha}_2 = \tilde{v} \qquad\qquad \tilde{v} = \tilde{\alpha}_2$$

$$\sigma_1 = \sqrt{\alpha} \qquad\qquad \alpha = \sigma_1^2$$

$$\sigma_2 = \sqrt{\beta} \qquad \text{or} \qquad \beta = \sigma_2^2 \qquad\qquad (8.163)$$

$$\tilde{\theta}_1 = \frac{\tilde{\gamma}\alpha}{\tilde{b}} \qquad\qquad \tilde{\gamma} = \frac{\tilde{\theta}_1\tilde{\alpha}_1}{\sigma_1^2}$$

$$\tilde{\theta}_2 = \frac{\tilde{\eta}\beta}{\tilde{v}} \qquad\qquad \tilde{\eta} = \frac{\tilde{\theta}_2\tilde{\alpha}_2}{\sigma_2^2}$$

The state variables under the Ay form are related to the state variables under the Ar form as follows:

$$Y_1(t) = \frac{\beta(r(t) - \delta(t)) - V(t)}{(\beta - \alpha)}$$

$$Y_2(t) = \frac{V(t) - \alpha(r(t) - \delta(t))}{(\beta - \alpha)} \qquad\qquad (8.164)$$

where the deterministic function $\delta(t)$ is identical under both forms.

To avoid repetition, we do not give analytical solutions for options and futures for the $A_2(2)$ model. These solutions are nested in the more general solutions provided for a multifactor affine model given in Chapter 9.

Two-Factor "Square-Root" Trees

The Ay form of the $A_2(2)$ model is more natural than the Ar form for tree construction, as it allows a direct generalization of the tree-building procedure for the CIR model outlined in Chapter 6. The short rate is given as the sum of a deterministic term and two state variables as follows:

$$r(t) = \delta(t) + Y_1(t) + Y_2(t) \qquad\qquad (8.165)$$

where the risk-neutral processes of $Y_1(t)$ and $Y_2(t)$ are given by equation (8.125) under the $A_{2y}(2)$, $A_{2y}(2)+$, and $A_{2y}(2)++$ models. The term $\delta(t)$ is a constant under the $A_{2y}(2)$ and $A_{2y}(2)+$ models and is deterministically changing under the $A_{2y}(2)++$ model.

The short rate tree under the $A_{2y}(2)++$ model requires the solution of $\delta(t)$ at each node of the two-dimensional tree. As under other two-factor models given earlier, $\delta(t)$ can be solved using two methods. The first method solves $\delta(t)$ analytically using equation (8.139). However, since this solution is valid only in the continuous-time limit, it allows an exact match with the initial zero-coupon bond prices only when using a large number of steps on the tree. If an exact match is desired for an arbitrarily small number of steps, then $\delta(t)$ can be obtained numerically using the technique demonstrated for two-factor Gaussian models in equations (8.71) and (8.72). The two-dimensional short rate tree is constructed by modeling two separate trinomial trees for $Y_1(t)$ and $Y_2(t)$. Since both $Y_1(t)$ and $Y_2(t)$ follow square-root processes, the implementation details of the trinomial trees follow directly from Chapter 6 and are not repeated here. The first step of the resulting short rate tree is shown in Figure 8.17.

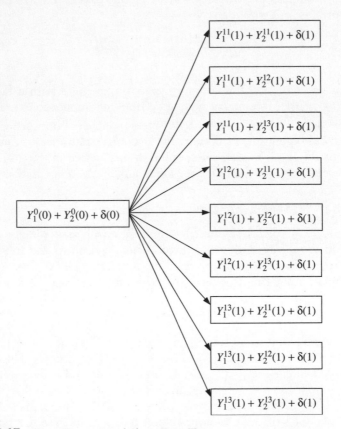

FIGURE 8.17 Two-Dimensional Short-Rate Tree

Since the state variables $Y_1(t)$ and $Y_2(t)$ are independent, the nine joint probabilities are computed by simply multiplying the marginal probabilities as follows:

$$p_1 = p_{y_1}^u \times p_{y_2}^u$$

$$p_2 = p_{y_1}^u \times p_{y_2}^m$$

$$p_3 = p_{y_1}^u \times p_{y_2}^d$$

$$p_4 = p_{y_1}^m \times p_{y_2}^u$$

$$p_5 = p_{y_1}^m \times p_{y_2}^m \qquad (8.166)$$

$$p_6 = p_{y_1}^m \times p_{y_2}^d$$

$$p_7 = p_{y_1}^d \times p_{y_2}^u$$

$$p_8 = p_{y_1}^d \times p_{y_2}^m$$

$$p_9 = p_{y_1}^d \times p_{y_2}^d$$

Example 8.4 Consider a six-month zero-coupon bond with a face value $F = \$100$. Let the parameters under the time-inhomogeneous preference-free $A_{2y}(2)++$ model be given as follows: $\tilde{\alpha}_1 = 0.5$; $\tilde{\theta}_1 = 0.02$; $\sigma_1 = 0.2$; $\tilde{\alpha}_2 = 0.5$; $\tilde{\theta}_2 = 0.04$; $\sigma_2 = 0.2$; and $T = 0.5$. The initial values of the state variable are $Y_1(0) = 0.02$, $Y_2(0) = 0.04$, and $\delta(0) = 0$. These values give $r(0) = 0 + 0.02 + 0.04 = 0.06$. Consider the valuation of this bond using a two-step, two-dimensional tree. The length of each time-step equals $\Delta t = 0.5/2 = 0.25$. The underlying one-dimensional trinomial tree for the $Y_1(t)$ process is shown in Figure 8.18. The underlying one-dimensional trinomial tree for the $Y_2(t)$ process is shown in Figure 8.19.

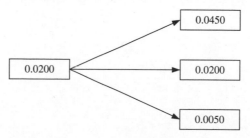

FIGURE 8.18 One-Dimensional Trinomial Tree for the $Y_1(t)$ Process

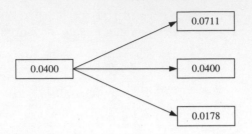

FIGURE 8.19 One-Dimensional Trinomial Tree for the $Y_2(t)$ Process

In addition to the two-step trees for $Y_1(t)$ and $Y_2(t)$, we also require the values of $\delta(0)$ and $\delta(0.25)$. We solve $\delta(t)$ using the first method, given by the analytical solution in equation (8.139). To compute the value of $\delta(t)$ at each time step, we use the Nelson and Siegel [1987] model for the initially observable forward rate $f(0, t)$ defined as follows:

$$f(0, t) = a_1 + a_2 e^{-t/b} + a_3 \frac{t}{b} e^{-t/b}$$

with the parameters: $a_1 = 0.07$, $a_2 = -0.01$, $a_3 = 0.00087$, and $b = 1.98476$.

The assumed forward rate is consistent with the assumption of 6 percent for the initial value of the short rate, since:

$$r(0) = f(0, 0) = a_1 + a_2 = 0.07 - 0.01 = 0.06$$

By assumption, $\delta(0) = 0$. The computation of $\delta(0.25)$ requires the following:

$$\beta_1 = \sqrt{\tilde{\alpha}_1^2 + 2\sigma_1^2} = \sqrt{0.5^2 + 2 \times 0.2^2} = 0.5745$$

$$\beta_2 = \sqrt{\tilde{\alpha}_2^2 + 2\sigma_2^2} = \sqrt{0.5^2 + 2 \times 0.2^2} = 0.5745$$

$$\begin{aligned}
B_1(0.25) &= \frac{2(e^{\beta_1\tau} - 1)}{(\beta_1 + \tilde{\alpha}_1)(e^{\beta_1\tau} - 1) + 2\beta_1} \\
&= \frac{2(e^{0.5745 \times 0.25} - 1)}{(0.5745 + 0.5)(e^{0.5745 \times 0.25} - 1) + 2 \times 0.5745} = 0.2349
\end{aligned}$$

$$\begin{aligned}
B_2(0.25) &= \frac{2(e^{\beta_2\tau} - 1)}{(\beta_2 + \tilde{\alpha}_2)(e^{\beta_2\tau} - 1) + 2\beta_2} \\
&= \frac{2(e^{0.5745 \times 0.25} - 1)}{(0.5745 + 0.5)(e^{0.5745 \times 0.25} - 1) + 2 \times 0.5745} = 0.2349
\end{aligned}$$

$$f(0, \ 0.25) = a_1 + a_2 e^{-t/b} + a_3 \frac{t}{b} e^{-t/b} = 0.07 - 0.01 \times e^{-0.25/1.98476}$$

$$+ \ 0.00087 \times \frac{0.25}{1.98476} \times e^{-0.25/1.98476} = 0.0613$$

Using the terms in the previous equation, $\delta(0.25)$ is computed using equation (8.139) as follows:

$$\delta(0.25) = f(0, 0.25) - Y_1(0) - \tilde{\alpha}_1 B_1(t)(\tilde{\theta}_1 - Y_1(0)) + \frac{1}{2} B_1^2(t) \sigma_1^2 Y_1(0)$$

$$- \ Y_2(0) - \tilde{\alpha}_2 B_2(t)(\tilde{\theta}_2 - Y_2(0)) + \frac{1}{2} B_2^2(t) \sigma_2^2 Y_2(0)$$

$$= 0.0613 - 0.02 - 0.5 \times 0.2349 \times (0.02 - 0.02) + \frac{1}{2}$$

$$\times \ 0.2349^2 \times 0.02^2 - 0.04 - 0.5 \times 0.2349$$

$$\times \ (0.04 - 0.04) + \frac{1}{2} \times 0.2349^2 \times 0.04^2 = 0.0013$$

Using the values of $Y_1(t)$, $Y_2(t)$, and $\delta(t)$ at time $t = 0$ and time $t = 0.25$, the two-dimensional short rate tree is shown in Figure 8.20.

The short rate values at each node are then used for discounting appropriate bond values as shown in Figure 8.21. For example, the bond value at time $t = 0$ is computed as follows. The marginal trinomial probabilities for the $Y_1(t = 0)$ process are given as follows (for computational details, refer to Chapter 6):

$$p_{y_1}^u = 0.1875$$

$$p_{y_1}^m = 0.5$$

$$p_{y_1}^d = 0.3125$$

The marginal trinomial probabilities for the $Y_2(t = 0)$ process are given as follows:

$$p_{y_2}^u = 0.2344$$

$$p_{y_2}^m = 0.4375$$

$$p_{y_2}^d = 0.3281$$

The joint probabilities for $t = 0$ are computed as follows:

$$p_1 = 0.1875 \times 0.2344 = 0.0440$$

$$p_2 = 0.1875 \times 0.4375 = 0.0820$$

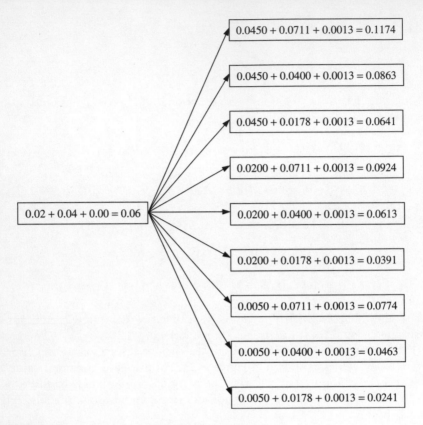

FIGURE 8.20 Two-Dimensional Short-Rate Tree

$$p_3 = 0.1875 \times 0.3281 = 0.0615$$

$$p_4 = 0.5 \times 0.2344 = 0.1172$$

$$p_5 = 0.5 \times 0.4375 = 0.2188$$

$$p_6 = 0.5 \times 0.3281 = 0.1641$$

$$p_7 = 0.3125 \times 0.2344 = 0.0732$$

$$p_8 = 0.3125 \times 0.4375 = 0.1367$$

$$p_9 = 0.3125 \times 0.3281 = 0.1025$$

At each node:
Value = bond value

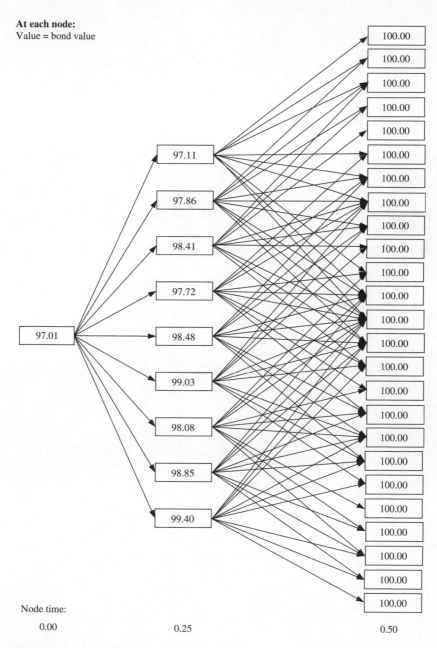

Node time:

0.00   0.25   0.50

FIGURE 8.21 Two-Dimensional Bond Tree

Finally, the bond value at time $t = 0$ is given as:

$$P(0) = (97.11 \times 0.0440 + 97.86 \times 0.0820 + 98.41 \times 0.0615$$
$$+ 97.72 \times 0.1172 + 98.48 \times 0.2188 + 99.03 \times 0.1641$$
$$+ 98.08 \times 0.0732 + 98.85 \times 0.1367 + 99.40 \times 0.1025)/e^{0.06 \times 0.25}$$
$$= \$97.01$$

The bond price using the closed-form solution is $96.98. Using a 100-step two-dimensional tree, the time 0 bond price is also equal to $96.98.

APPENDIX 8.1: HULL AND WHITE SOLUTION OF $\eta(t, T)$

Hull [2003, p. 592] gives the solution of the function $\eta(t, T)$ as follows:

$$\eta(t, T) = \frac{\sigma_r^2}{4\tilde{\alpha}_r}(1 - e^{-2\tilde{\alpha}_r t})B_2^2(\tau) - \rho_{ru}\sigma_r\sigma_u[B_1(t)B_2(t)B_2(\tau) + \lambda_4 - \lambda_2]$$

$$- \frac{1}{2}\sigma_u^2[B_1^2(t)B_2(\tau) + \lambda_6 - \lambda_5]$$

$$\lambda_1 = \frac{e^{-(\tilde{\alpha}_r + \tilde{\alpha}_u)T}(e^{(\tilde{\alpha}_r + \tilde{\alpha}_u)t} - 1)}{(\tilde{\alpha}_r + \tilde{\alpha}_u)(\tilde{\alpha}_r - \tilde{\alpha}_u)} - \frac{e^{-2\tilde{\alpha}_r T}(e^{2\tilde{\alpha}_r t} - 1)}{2\tilde{\alpha}_r(\tilde{\alpha}_r - \tilde{\alpha}_u)}$$

$$\lambda_2 = \frac{1}{\tilde{\alpha}_r\tilde{\alpha}_u}\left[\begin{array}{l} \lambda_1 + B_1(\tau) - B_1(T) + \frac{1}{2}B_2^2(\tau) - \frac{1}{2}B_2^2(T) \\ + \frac{t}{\tilde{\alpha}_r} - \frac{e^{-\tilde{\alpha}_r\tau} - e^{-\tilde{\alpha}_r T}}{\tilde{\alpha}_r^2} \end{array}\right] \qquad (8.167)$$

$$\lambda_3 = -\frac{e^{-(\tilde{\alpha}_r + \tilde{\alpha}_u)t} - 1}{(\tilde{\alpha}_r + \tilde{\alpha}_u)(\tilde{\alpha}_r - \tilde{\alpha}_u)} + \frac{e^{-2\tilde{\alpha}_r t} - 1}{2\tilde{\alpha}_r(\tilde{\alpha}_r - \tilde{\alpha}_u)}$$

$$\lambda_4 = \frac{1}{\tilde{\alpha}_r\tilde{\alpha}_u}\left[\lambda_3 - B_1(t) - \frac{1}{2}B_2^2(t) + \frac{t}{\tilde{\alpha}_r} + \frac{e^{-\tilde{\alpha}_r t} - 1}{\tilde{\alpha}_r^2}\right]$$

$$\lambda_5 = \frac{1}{\tilde{\alpha}_u}\left[\frac{1}{2}B_1^2(\tau) - \frac{1}{2}B_1^2(T) + \lambda_2\right]$$

$$\lambda_6 = \frac{1}{\tilde{\alpha}_u}\left[\lambda_4 - \frac{1}{2}B_1^2(t)\right]$$

Hull and White also show that the deterministic function $\theta(t)$ in equation (8.16) has the following solution:

$$\theta(t) = \tilde{\alpha}_r f(0, \ t) + \frac{\partial f(0, \ t)}{\partial t} + \tilde{\alpha}_r \phi(t) + \frac{\partial \phi(t)}{\partial t} \qquad (8.168)$$

where

$$\phi(t) = \frac{1}{2}\sigma_u^2 B_1^2(t) + \frac{1}{2}\sigma_r^2 B_2^2(t) + \rho_{ru}\sigma_r\sigma_u B_1(t)B_2(t) \qquad (8.169)$$

NOTES

1. Brigo and Mercurio [2001] denote this model as the G2++ model. Using the general framework presented in this book, we denote this model as the $A_{0y}(2)++$ model.
2. The probability could be high if the current short rate is close to zero. For example, the probability may be quite low if the short rate is higher than 5 percent but can be quite high if the current value of the short rate is 1 percent under realistic parameter values.
3. Dai and Singleton [2002] give the physical processes of the $A_{1c}(2)$ model in the reduced form, maximally flexible specification. But since we are interested in pricing under the risk-neutral measure, we give the risk-neutral processes under the reduced-form, maximally flexible specification of the $A_{1c}(2)$ model.
4. The restriction $2\tilde{\alpha}_{11}\tilde{\theta}_1 > \sigma^2$ applies under the risk-neutral measure. A similar restriction applies under the physical measure, too.

CHAPTER 9

Fundamental and Preference-Free Multifactor Affine Models

Contingent claims, such as equity options, mortgage prepayment options, and the various options embedded in corporate bonds, are frequently valued using only one or two *interest rate* factors. Since the valuation of these claims is more sensitive to noninterest rate factors, ignoring the errors caused by lumping many interest rate factors into one or two important factors does not lead to serious mispricing of these claims. The various one- and two-factor interest rate models can be combined with the non-interest factors to value such claims. Low-dimensional models are also computationally desirable for valuing contingent claims with American features.

However, a number of researchers, including Sidenius [2000], Longstaff, Santa-Clara, and Schwartz [2001], and Rebonato [2002], have discovered that the bond yields contain at least four and perhaps even a higher number of factors that are relevant for pricing interest rate derivatives. Rebonato and Cooper [1995] show that low-dimensional models cannot reproduce realistic correlation structures of changes in the interest rates, regardless of the type of model chosen. Sidenius [2000] analyzes the number of factors required for modeling different types of interest rate derivatives and finds that some exotic derivatives may need a large number of factors. In general, most econometric investigations by academics use at least three factors (see Dai and Singleton [2000, 2002] and Ahn, Dittmar, and Gallant [2002]), while calibrations of the LIBOR/String market models to interest rate derivatives by practitioners use a minimum of four to six factors.

One can consider at least three cases under which a large set of interest rate factors may be essential for derivative traders. In the first case, a trader may want to price exotic interest rate derivatives in addition to the

---

This chapter was coauthored with Iuliana Ismailescu.

plain vanilla interest rate options, such as caps and floors. Though low-dimensional models may fit the plain vanilla options well, more factors may be necessary to perform simultaneous calibration to the prices of exotic derivatives.[1] Second, even if a low-dimensional model fits a given class of interest rate derivatives, the trader may wish to know how to *cross-hedge* her exposure using other classes of derivatives. For example, hedging interest rate caps using swaptions will require more detailed information contained in the correlation structure of different factors. Finally, to make speculative or arbitrage trades based on *relative valuation*, one must understand how different factors affect different classes of interest rate derivatives.

This chapter considers four subfamilies of three-factor fundamental maximal affine term structure models (ATSMs), denoted as $A_0(3)$, $A_1(3)$, $A_2(3)$, and $A_3(3)$, and derives their preference-free extensions. The economically significant differences among the fundamental $A_M(3)$ models result from the trade-off between state-dependent conditional variances and the admissible structure of the correlation matrix for the state variables. At one end of this trade-off is the fundamental $A_0(3)$ model, which has most flexibility with regard to the signs and magnitudes of conditional and unconditional correlations among the state variables; but it assumes constant conditional variances. As a result, this model can explain expected return relations well (since expected returns depend upon correlations among state variables); but it cannot fit the conditional variances, as shown by Dai and Singleton [2002]. In the middle are the fundamental $A_1(3)$ and $A_2(3)$ models, which allow time-varying conditional variances to depend on, at most, one- and two-state variables, respectively, and allow unconstrained signs of some of the correlations. Finally, at the other end of the trade-off, is the fundamental $A_3(3)$ model, which does not allow negative correlations among the state variables but allows conditional variances to depend upon all three state variables. As a result, the fundamental $A_3(3)$ model is poor for explaining expected return relations, but it fits the conditional variances reasonably well.

It is difficult to resolve the trade-off between fitting correlations/expected returns *versus* conditional variances under the fundamental $A_M(3)$ models since these models generally assume affine forms of state variable processes under both the physical measure and the risk-neutral measure for the purpose of econometric estimation. In contrast, since the preference-free $A_M(3)+$ and $A_M(3)++$ models allow general nonlinear forms of market prices of risks (MPRs) with nonaffine physical processes, they are potentially consistent with a wider range of correlation structures/expected return relations, while maintaining the affine structure under the risk-neutral measure. For example, Chapter 8 gives an example of preference-free square-root models (i.e., the $A_2(2)+$ and $A_2(2)++$ models) that allow negative unconditional correlation between the two state variables under the physical measure, while allowing the correlation to be zero under the risk-neutral measure.

In addition to the maximal $A_M(3)$ models, this chapter derives *simple $A_M(N)$* models with N factors, under which M state variables follow square-root processes and $N - M$ state variables follow Gaussian processes. The simple $A_M(N)$ models are nested in the maximal $A_M(N)$ models. Similar to the maximal $A_M(N)$ models, the simple $A_M(N)$ models allow the Gaussian state variables to be correlated with each other, but unlike the maximal $A_M(N)$ models, the simple $A_M(N)$ models do not allow the Gaussian state variables to be correlated with the square-root state variables. We focus on simple $A_M(N)$ models for the following reasons.

First, the maximal $A_M(N)$ models with higher values of N (e.g., $N = 4$, 5, or 6) become very complex with an extremely large number of parameters. These models are not only infeasible for econometric estimation, but they are difficult to calibrate to real option data, due to overfitting and lack of analytical solutions/approximations for performing inversions.

Second, as noted by Rebonato and Cooper [1995], the failure of low-dimensional models in explaining the correlation structure of interest rate changes is *model independent*. These authors find that a high-dimensional model is necessary to capture the correlation patterns of changes in interest rates of different maturities. Our findings confirm that simple high-dimensional $A_M(N)$ models capture the correlation structure better than the maximal low-dimensional $A_M(N)$ models. Since simple high-dimensional $A_M(N)$ models allow analytical tractability with the use of the Fourier inversion method and the cumulant expansion method (both methods are covered in detail in this chapter), the solutions of caps and swaptions can be generated within seconds under these models (even with three to six factors).

Finally, even though Gaussian state variables must be uncorrelated with the square-root state variables, conditional and unconditional correlations are allowed among the Gaussian variables under the simple $A_M(N)$ models. Also, the preference-free extensions of the simple models, given as the $A_M(N)+$ and $A_M(N)++$ models, allow general nonlinear forms of MPRs and nonaffine physical processes, allowing physical correlations of any sign between the Gaussian and square-root variables and even among the square-root variables.

The simple $A_M(N)$, $A_M(N)+$, and $A_M(N)++$ models nest a variety of one-, two-, and three-factor ATSMs given in the literature (see Table 9.3). Since we derive solutions of futures (i.e., Eurodollar/Euribor futures and futures on zero-coupon bonds) and options (i.e., options on zero-coupon bonds or caplets using the Fourier inversion method and options on coupon bonds or swaptions using the cumulant expansion method) using the general framework of simple $A_M(N)$, $A_M(N)+$, and $A_M(N)++$ models, these solutions apply to all of the nested models given in Table 9.3. Since Chapter 8 did not provide solutions of futures and options under the $A_2(2)$, $A_2(2)+$, and $A_2(2)++$ models, these solutions can be now obtained using the general framework given in this chapter.

The reduced-form approach discovered by Jarrow and Turnbull [1995], Madan and Unal [1998], and Duffie and Singleton [1999] allows using the entire analytical apparatus of continuous-time term structure modeling for valuing credit derivatives. This approach requires exogenous modeling of the default intensity process, which together with assumptions about recovery and a given model for the short rate leads to analytical solutions to risky bond prices for wide classes of affine and quadratic term structure models. This chapter considers the simple $A_M(N)$, $A_M(N)+$, and $A_M(N)++$ models for valuing credit derivatives, deriving a general analytical solution for valuation of credit default swaps that not only nests the solutions of Longstaff, Mithal, and Neis (LMN) [2003] and Pan and Singleton [2005], but also generalizes these models to:

1. allow a higher number of factors,
2. make them consistent with the initial default-free zero-coupon bond prices, and
3. allow nonaffine physical processes consistent with general nonlinear MPRs using the preference-free extensions of the simple $A_M(N)$ models.

This chapter begins with the introduction to three-factor ATSMs. We consider the maximal models in the $A_1(3)$ and $A_2(3)$ subfamilies in the Ar form and derive preference-free extensions of these models. We do not consider the maximal models in the $A_0(3)$ and $A_3(3)$ subfamilies in the next section, as these models are nested in the simple $A_M(N)$ models given in the subsequent section.

THREE-FACTOR AFFINE TERM STRUCTURE MODELS

The $A_{1r}(3)$, $A_{1r}(3)+$, and $A_{1r}(3)++$ Models

Similar to the two-factor ATSMs, the fundamental $A_1(3)$ model and its preference-free extensions can also be given in three equivalent forms, given as the canonical form, the Ay form, and the Ar form. Due to space constraints, we only show these models in the Ar form. The Ar form has been used in the derivation of various models nested in the $A_1(3)$ subfamily, including the models of Balduzzi, Das, Foresi, and Sundaram (BDFS) [1996] and Dai and Singleton [2000].

The $A_{1r}(3)$ Model BDFS propose a three-factor model in which both the volatility of the short rate and the long-term mean of the short rate evolve stochastically over time. The $A_{1r}(3)_{BDFS}$ model can be specified directly under the risk-neutral measure as follows:

$$dv(t) = \tilde{\alpha}_v(\tilde{m}_v - v(t))\,dt + \eta\sqrt{v(t)}\,d\tilde{Z}_1(t)$$

$$d\theta(t) = \tilde{\alpha}_\theta(\tilde{m}_\theta - \theta(t))\,dt + \zeta\,d\tilde{Z}_2(t) \tag{9.1}$$

$$dr(t) = \tilde{\alpha}(\theta(t) - r(t))\,dt + \sigma_{rv}\eta\sqrt{v(t)}\,d\tilde{Z}_1(t) + \sqrt{v(t)}\,d\tilde{Z}_3(t)$$

where the first variable, $v(t)$, is a volatility factor; the second variable, $\theta(t)$, is the "central tendency" of the instantaneous short rate $r(t)$; and the three Wiener processes are independent. Though the $A_{1r}(3)_{BDFS}$ model allows the correlation between the short rate and its volatility to be nonzero, it restricts the correlation between the short rate and its long-term mean to be zero. Dai and Singleton (DS) [2000] generalize the $A_{1r}(3)_{BDFS}$ model to include two more parameters that allow correlation between the short rate and its long-term mean. The state variable processes under the generalized model, called the $A_{1r}(3)_{DS}$ model, can be specified directly under the risk-neutral measure as follows:

$$dv(t) = \tilde{\alpha}_v(\tilde{m}_v - v(t))\,dt + \eta\sqrt{v(t)}\,d\tilde{Z}_1(t)$$

$$d\theta(t) = \tilde{\alpha}_\theta(\tilde{m}_\theta - \theta(t))\,dt + \zeta\,d\tilde{Z}_2(t) + \sigma_{\theta r}\sqrt{v(t)}\,d\tilde{Z}_3(t) \tag{9.2}$$

$$dr(t) = \tilde{\alpha}(\theta(t) - r(t))\,dt + \sigma_{rv}\eta\sqrt{v(t)}\,d\tilde{Z}_1(t) + \sigma_{r\theta}\zeta\,d\tilde{Z}_2(t) + \sqrt{v(t)}\,d\tilde{Z}_3(t)$$

Dai and Singleton find that two additional parameters, $\sigma_{r\theta}$ and $\sigma_{\theta r}$ are statistically significant in capturing the time-series dynamics of bond yields. Dai and Singleton [2000] also propose the maximal model in the $A_{1r}(3)$ subfamily. The state variable processes under the $A_{1r}(3)_{MAX}$ model are specified under the risk-neutral measure as follows:[2]

$$dv(t) = \tilde{\alpha}_v(\tilde{m}_v - v(t))\,dt + \eta\sqrt{v(t)}\,d\tilde{Z}_1(t)$$

$$d\theta(t) = \tilde{\alpha}_\theta(\tilde{m}_\theta - \theta(t))\,dt + \sigma_{\theta v}\eta\sqrt{v(t)}\,d\tilde{Z}_1(t) + \sqrt{\zeta^2 + \beta_\theta v(t)}\,d\tilde{Z}_2(t)$$

$$\qquad + \sigma_{\theta r}\sqrt{\delta_r + v(t)}\,d\tilde{Z}_3(t) \tag{9.3}$$

$$dr(t) = \tilde{\alpha}_{rv}(\tilde{m}_v - v(t))\,dt + \tilde{\alpha}(\theta(t) - r(t))\,dt + \sigma_{rv}\eta\sqrt{v(t)}\,d\tilde{Z}_1(t)$$

$$\qquad + \sigma_{r\theta}\sqrt{\zeta^2 + \beta_\theta v(t)}\,d\tilde{Z}_2(t) + \sqrt{\delta_r + v(t)}\,d\tilde{Z}_3(t)$$

The $A_{1r}(3)_{MAX}$ model adds four new parameters, β_θ, $\sigma_{\theta v}$, $\tilde{\alpha}_{rv}$, and δ_r, to the $A_{1r}(3)_{DS}$ model, allowing additional flexibility in capturing the structure of correlations between the state variables. All three nested versions of the $A_{1r}(3)$ models, given as $A_{1r}(3)_{\text{BDFS}}$, $A_{1r}(3)_{\text{DS}}$, and $A_{1r}(3)_{\text{MAX}}$, are specified as fundamental models with completely affine form of MPRs. These models can be extended using the essentially affine and semiaffine specifications of MPRs given in Duffee [2002] and Duarte [2004], respectively. Since the functional forms of the more general MPR specifications are similar to those presented for two-factor models, we do not repeat the details here.

Using weekly time series of yields on six-month, two-year, and ten-year swap yields from 1987 to 1996, Dai and Singleton [2000] estimate the completely affine form of the three nested models given in this section using the simulated method of moments of Gallant and Tauchen [1996]. Table 9.1 gives the overall goodness-of-fit, chi-squared tests, which show that the $A_{1r}(3)_{\text{BDFS}}$ model is rejected, while the $A_{1r}(3)_{\text{DS}}$ model and the $A_{1r}(3)_{\text{MAX}}$ model cannot be rejected at conventional levels of significance. Though the $A_{1r}(3)_{\text{DS}}$ model significantly outperforms the $A_{1r}(3)_{\text{BDFS}}$ model with only two additional parameters, $\sigma_{\theta r}$ and $\sigma_{r\theta}$, it avoids overfitting by eliminating four parameters of the $A_{1r}(3)_{\text{MAX}}$ model without sacrificing the statistical performance of the latter. In a subsequent study, Dai and Singleton [2002] also estimate the canonical version of the $A_{1r}(3)$ model, allowing more general MPRs using the essentially affine form, and find further enhancement to the performance of the model.

By applying Ito's lemma to the bond price, equating the change in bond price to riskless return, and then taking risk-neutral expectation, we get the partial differential equation (PDE) for the bond price under the $A_{1r}(3)_{\text{Max}}$ model as follows:

$$
\frac{\partial P}{\partial t} + \frac{\partial P}{\partial v}\tilde{\alpha}_v(\tilde{m}_v - v(t)) + \frac{\partial P}{\partial \theta}\tilde{\alpha}_\theta(\tilde{m}_\theta - \theta(t))
$$

$$
+ \frac{\partial P}{\partial r}[\tilde{\alpha}_{rv}(\tilde{m}_v - v(t)) + \tilde{\alpha}(\theta(t) - r(t))] + \frac{1}{2}\frac{\partial^2 P}{\partial v^2}\eta^2 v(t)
$$

$$
+ \frac{1}{2}\frac{\partial^2 P}{\partial \theta^2}[\sigma_{\theta v}^2 \eta^2 v(t) + \zeta^2 + \beta_\theta v(t) + \sigma_{\theta r}^2(\delta_r + v(t))] \qquad (9.4)
$$

$$
+ \frac{1}{2}\frac{\partial^2 P}{\partial r^2}[\sigma_{rv}^2 \eta^2 v(t) + \sigma_{r\theta}^2(\zeta^2 + \beta_\theta v(t)) + \delta_r + v(t)] + \frac{\partial^2 P}{\partial v \partial \theta}\sigma_{\theta v}\eta^2 v(t)
$$

$$
+ \frac{\partial^2 P}{\partial v \partial r}\sigma_{rv}\eta^2 v(t) + \frac{\partial^2 P}{\partial \theta \partial r}[\sigma_{\theta v}\sigma_{rv}\eta^2 v(t) + \sigma_{r\theta}(\zeta^2 + \beta_\theta v(t)) + \sigma_{\theta r}(\delta_r + v(t))]
$$

$$
= r(t)P(t,T)
$$

TABLE 9.1 Overall Goodness-of-Fit, Chi-Square-Tests

	Model	χ^2	Df	p-value
$A_{1r}(3)_{\text{BDFS}}$	BDFS	84.212	25	0.000%
$A_{1r}(3)_{\text{DS}}$	BDFS $+\sigma_{\theta r}+\sigma_{r\theta}$	28.911	23	18.328%
$A_{1r}(3)_{\text{Max}}$	Maximal	28.901	19	6.756%

subject to $P(T,T)=1$. Consider the following affine solution to the bond price:

$$P(t,T)=e^{A(\tau)-B_1(\tau)v(t)-B_2(\tau)\theta(t)-B_3(\tau)r(t)} \tag{9.5}$$

where $\tau = T - t$. By taking the partial derivatives of the bond price, substituting these into equation (9.5), and using a separation of variables, we get the following four ordinary differential equations (ODEs):

$$\frac{\partial A(\tau)}{\partial \tau} = -B_1(\tau)\tilde{\alpha}_v\tilde{m}_v - B_2(\tau)\tilde{\alpha}_\theta\tilde{m}_\theta - B_3(\tau)\tilde{\alpha}_{rv}\tilde{m}_v + \frac{1}{2}B_2^2(\tau)[\sigma_{\theta r}^2\delta_r + \zeta^2]$$

$$+ \frac{1}{2}B_3^2(\tau)[\sigma_{r\theta}^2\zeta^2 + \delta_r] + B_2(\tau)B_3(\tau)[\sigma_{r\theta}\zeta^2 + \sigma_{\theta r}\delta_r]$$

$$\frac{\partial B_1(\tau)}{\partial \tau} = -B_1(\tau)\tilde{\alpha}_v - B_3(\tau)\tilde{\alpha}_{rv} - \frac{1}{2}B_1^2(\tau)\eta^2 - \frac{1}{2}B_2^2(\tau)[\beta_\theta + \sigma_{\theta v}^2\eta^2 + \sigma_{\theta r}^2]$$

$$- \frac{1}{2}B_3^2(\tau)[\sigma_{rv}^2\eta^2 + \sigma_{r\theta}^2\beta_\theta + 1] - B_1(\tau)B_2(\tau)\sigma_{\theta v}\eta^2 \tag{9.6}$$

$$- B_1(\tau)B_3(\tau)\sigma_{rv}\eta^2 - B_2(\tau)B_3(\tau)[\sigma_{\theta v}\sigma_{rv}\eta^2 + \sigma_{r\theta}\beta_\theta + \sigma_{\theta r}]$$

$$\frac{\partial B_2(\tau)}{\partial \tau} = -B_2(\tau)\tilde{\alpha}_\theta + B_3(\tau)\tilde{\alpha}$$

$$\frac{\partial B_3(\tau)}{\partial \tau} = 1 - B_3(\tau)\tilde{\alpha}$$

subject to the boundary condition $A(0)=B_1(0)=B_2(0)=B_3(0)=0$. The solutions to $B_2(.)$ and $B_3(.)$ are given as follows:

$$B_2(\tau) = \frac{1}{\tilde{\alpha}_\theta} - \frac{1}{\tilde{\alpha}_\theta - \tilde{\alpha}}e^{-\tilde{\alpha}\tau}$$

$$B_3(\tau) = \frac{1}{\tilde{\alpha}}(1 - e^{-\tilde{\alpha}\tau}) \tag{9.7}$$

The ODEs for $A(.)$ and $B_1(.)$ do not have analytical solutions; these must be solved using programming tools such as Matlab. The bond price solutions under the nested models $A_{1r}(3)_{\text{BDFS}}$ and $A_{1r}(3)_{\text{DS}}$ are obtained by setting the appropriate subsets of risk-neutral parameters to zero.

The $A_{1r}(3)+$ and $A_{1r}(3)++$ Models Similar to the two-factor models, the preference-free $A_{1r}(3)+$ and $A_{1r}(3)++$ models obtain the risk-neutral parameters directly from the cross sections of prices on bonds and interest rate derivatives and, hence, do not require restrictive assumptions on the functional forms of MPRs, which can be of general nonlinear form. Though the valuation formulas under the time-homogeneous preference-free $A_{1r}(3)+$ model are identical to those under the corresponding fundamental $A_{1r}(3)$ models (with potentially different empirical estimates of the risk-neutral parameters), these formulas must be adjusted for the time-inhomogeneous preference-free $A_{1r}(3)++$ models by redefining the short rate process as follows:

$$r(t) = \delta(t) + Y(t) \tag{9.8}$$

where $\delta(t)$ is a deterministic term and the risk-neutral process for the variable $Y(t)$ has the same form as the risk-neutral process for the short rate given earlier. For example, the risk-neutral process for the variable $Y(t)$ under the $A_{1r}(3)_{\text{MAX}}++$ model has the same form as the risk-neutral process for the short rate given in equation (9.3) under the $A_{1r}(3)_{\text{MAX}}$ model, and is given as follows:

$$
\begin{aligned}
dY(t) &= \tilde{\alpha}_{rv}(\tilde{m}_v - v(t))\,dt + \tilde{\alpha}(\theta(t) - Y(t))\,dt + \sigma_{rv}\eta\sqrt{v(t)}\,d\tilde{Z}_1(t) \\
&\quad + \sigma_{r\theta}\sqrt{\zeta^2 + \beta_\theta v(t)}\,d\tilde{Z}_2(t) + \sqrt{\delta_r + v(t)}\,d\tilde{Z}_3(t)
\end{aligned}
\tag{9.9}
$$

Similar adjustments apply to the $A_{1r}(3)_{\text{BDFS}}++$ and $A_{1r}(3)_{\text{DS}}++$ models using equations (9.1) and (9.2), respectively. The risk-neutral processes for the state variables $v(t)$ and $\theta(t)$ remain the same as under the corresponding fundamental models. Since conditional variances do not depend upon the state variables $\theta(t)$ and $Y(t)$, the initial time 0 values of these variables can be assumed to be zero (without loss of generality), or:

$$\theta(0) = 0 \text{ and } Y(0) = 0 \tag{9.10}$$

Following the approach outlined earlier for two-factor models, the solution of the bond price $P(t, T)$ under the $A_{1r}(3)_{\text{MAX}}++$ model is given as follows:

$$P(t, T) = e^{A(\tau) - B_1(\tau)v(t) - B_2(\tau)\theta(t) - B_3(\tau)(r(t) - \delta(t)) - H(t,T)} \tag{9.11}$$

where $A(\tau)$, $B_1(\tau)$, $B_2(\tau)$, and $B_3(\tau)$ are as defined earlier under the fundamental $A_{1r}(3)_{\text{MAX}}$ model. The solutions of $\delta(t)$ and $H(t, T)$ are given as follows:

$$\delta(t) = f(0, t) + \frac{\partial A(t)}{\partial t} - \frac{\partial B_1(t)}{\partial t} v(0) \tag{9.12}$$

and

$$H(t, T) = H(0, T) - H(0, t)$$

$$= A(T) - A(t) - \big(B_1(T) - B_1(t)\big)v(0) - \ln P(0, T) + \ln P(0, t) \quad (9.13)$$

where the partial derivatives of $A(t)$ and $B_1(t)$ are defined by the ODEs in equation (9.6). Since the $A_{1r}(3)_{\text{BDFS}}{+}{+}$ and $A_{1r}(3)_{\text{DS}}{+}{+}$ models are nested in the $A_{1r}(3)_{\text{MAX}}{+}{+}$ model, the bond price solution under these models can be obtained with the appropriate parameter restrictions given earlier.

The $A_{2r}(3)$, $A_{2r}(3)+$, and $A_{2r}(3)++$ Models

The $A_{2r}(3)$ Model   Similar to BDFS, Chen [1996] proposes a three-factor model in which both the volatility and the central tendency of the short rate evolve stochastically over time. While the central tendency follows a Gaussian process under the BDFS model, Chen assumes this factor to follow a square-root process. Since the conditional variances of the three state variables are determined by two state variables and since the Chen model is specified in the Ar form, we denote this model as $A_{2r}(3)_{\text{CHEN}}$. Chen allows unconditional correlation between the short rate and the central tendency variable but disallows all other correlations. The state variables under the $A_{2r}(3)_{\text{CHEN}}$ model are given under the risk-neutral measure as follows:

$$dv(t) = \tilde{\alpha}_v(\tilde{m}_v - v(t))\,dt + \eta\sqrt{v(t)}\,d\tilde{Z}_1(t)$$

$$d\theta(t) = \tilde{\alpha}_\theta(\tilde{m}_\theta - \theta(t))\,dt + \zeta\sqrt{\theta(t)}\,d\tilde{Z}_2(t) \qquad (9.14)$$

$$dr(t) = \tilde{\alpha}(\theta(t) - r(t))\,dt + \sqrt{v(t)}\,d\tilde{Z}_3(t)$$

where all three Wiener processes are independently distributed. Dai and Singleton [2000] generalize the $A_{2r}(3)_{\text{CHEN}}$ model to include three more parameters that allow unconditional and conditional correlations between the short rate and the volatility variable, and unconditional correlation between the central tendency variable and the volatility variable. The state variable processes under the generalized model, denoted as the $A_{2r}(3)_{\text{DS}}$ model, can be specified directly under the risk-neutral measure as follows:

$$dv(t) = \tilde{\alpha}_v(\tilde{m}_v - v(t))\,dt + \eta\sqrt{v(t)}\,d\tilde{Z}_1(t)$$

$$d\theta(t) = \tilde{\alpha}_\theta(\tilde{m}_\theta - \theta(t))\,dt + \tilde{\alpha}_{\theta v}(\tilde{m}_v - v(t))\,dt + \zeta\sqrt{\theta(t)}\,d\tilde{Z}_2(t)$$

$$dr(t) = \tilde{\alpha}_{rv}(\tilde{m}_v - v(t))\,dt + \tilde{\alpha}(\theta(t) - r(t))\,dt + \sigma_{rv}\eta\sqrt{v(t)}\,d\tilde{Z}_1(t) \qquad (9.15)$$

$$\qquad + \sqrt{v(t)}\,d\tilde{Z}_3(t)$$

Dai and Singleton find that three additional parameters, $\tilde{\alpha}_{\theta v}$, $\tilde{\alpha}_{rv}$, and σ_{rv}, are statistically significant in capturing the time-series dynamics of bond yields. Dai and Singleton also propose the maximal model in the $A_{2r}(3)$ subfamily. The state-variable processes under the $A_{2r}(3)_{\mathrm{MAX}}$ model are specified under the risk-neutral measure as follows:[3]

$$
\begin{aligned}
dv(t) &= \tilde{\alpha}_v(\tilde{m}_v - v(t))\,dt + \tilde{\alpha}_{v\theta}(\tilde{m}_\theta - \theta(t))\,dt + \eta\sqrt{v(t)}\,d\tilde{Z}_1(t) \\
d\theta(t) &= \tilde{\alpha}_\theta(\tilde{m}_\theta - \theta(t))\,dt + \tilde{\alpha}_{\theta v}(\tilde{m}_v - v(t))\,dt + \zeta\sqrt{\theta(t)}\,d\tilde{Z}_2(t) \\
dr(t) &= \tilde{\alpha}_{rv}(\tilde{m}_v - v(t))\,dt - \tilde{\alpha}_{r\theta}(\tilde{m}_\theta - \theta(t))\,dt + \tilde{\alpha}(\tilde{m}_r - r(t))\,dt \\
&\quad + \sigma_{rv}\eta\sqrt{v(t)}\,d\tilde{Z}_1(t) + \sigma_{r\theta}\zeta\sqrt{\theta(t)}\,d\tilde{Z}_2(t) + \sqrt{\delta_r + \beta_\theta\theta(t) + v(t)}\,d\tilde{Z}_3(t)
\end{aligned}
\tag{9.16}
$$

The $A_{2r}(3)_{\mathrm{DS}}$ model can be obtained as a special case of the $A_{2r}(3)_{\mathrm{MAX}}$ model by equating the parameters β_θ, $\tilde{\alpha}_{v\theta}$, $\sigma_{r\theta}$, and δ_r to zero and restricting $\tilde{\alpha} = \tilde{\alpha}_{r\theta}$ and $\tilde{m}_\theta = \tilde{m}_r$. In addition, the $A_{2r}(3)_{\mathrm{CHEN}}$ model can be obtained as a special case of the $A_{2r}(3)_{\mathrm{DS}}$ model by equating the parameters $\tilde{\alpha}_{\theta v}$, $\tilde{\alpha}_{rv}$, and σ_{rv} to zero. Though all three nested versions of the $A_{2r}(3)$ models were originally derived in the completely affine form, they can be easily extended to the essentially affine form and semiaffine form using the MPR specifications in Duffee [2002] and Duarte [2004], respectively.

Table 9.2 gives the overall goodness-of-fit, chi-squared tests of Dai and Singleton [2000], which show that the $A_{2r}(3)_{\mathrm{CHEN}}$ model is rejected, while the $A_{2r}(3)_{\mathrm{DS}}$ and $A_{2r}(3)_{\mathrm{MAX}}$ models cannot be rejected at conventional levels of significance. Though the $A_{2r}(3)_{\mathrm{DS}}$ model significantly outperforms the $A_{2r}(3)_{\mathrm{CHEN}}$ model with only three additional parameters, $\tilde{\alpha}_{\theta v}$, $\tilde{\alpha}_{rv}$, and σ_{rv}, it avoids overfitting by eliminating six additional parameters of the $A_{2r}(3)_{\mathrm{MAX}}$ model without sacrificing the statistical performance of the latter.

By applying Ito's lemma to the bond price, equating the change in bond price to riskless return, and then taking the risk-neutral expectation, we get the PDE for the bond price under the $A_{2r}(3)_{\mathrm{MAX}}$ model as follows:

$$
\frac{\partial P}{\partial t} + \frac{\partial P}{\partial v}[\tilde{\alpha}_v(\tilde{m}_v - v(t)) + \tilde{\alpha}_{v\theta}(\tilde{m}_\theta - \theta(t))]
$$

TABLE 9.2 Overall Goodness-of-Fit, Chi-Squared Tests

	Model	χ^2	df	p value
$A_{2r}(3)_{\mathrm{CHEN}}$	Chen	84.212	26	0.000%
$A_{2r}(3)_{\mathrm{DS}}$	Chen $+\tilde{\alpha}_{\theta v} + \tilde{\alpha}_{rv} + \sigma_{rv}$	28.911	24	52.387%
$A_{2r}(3)_{\mathrm{MAX}}$	Maximal	28.901	18	56.479%

$$+ \frac{\partial P}{\partial \theta}[\tilde{\alpha}_\theta(\tilde{m}_\theta - \theta(t)) + \tilde{\alpha}_{\theta v}(\tilde{m}_v - v(t))]$$

$$+ \frac{\partial P}{\partial r}[\tilde{\alpha}_{rv}(\tilde{m}_v - v(t)) - \tilde{\alpha}_{r\theta}(\tilde{m}_\theta - \theta(t)) + \tilde{\alpha}(\tilde{m}_r - r(t))] + \frac{1}{2}\frac{\partial^2 P}{\partial v^2}\eta^2 v(t)$$

$$+ \frac{1}{2}\frac{\partial^2 P}{\partial \theta^2}\zeta^2\theta(t) + \frac{1}{2}\frac{\partial^2 P}{\partial r^2}[\sigma_{rv}^2\eta^2 v(t) + \sigma_{r\theta}^2\zeta^2\theta(t) + \delta_r + \beta_\theta\theta(t) + v(t)] \quad (9.17)$$

$$+ \frac{\partial^2 P}{\partial v\partial r}\sigma_{rv}\eta^2 v(t) + \frac{\partial^2 P}{\partial\theta\partial r}\sigma_{r\theta}\zeta^2\theta(t) = r(t)P(t, T)$$

subject to $P(T, T) = 1$. Consider the following affine solution to the bond price:

$$P(t, T) = e^{A(\tau) - B_1(\tau)v(t) - B_2(\tau)\theta(t) - B_3(\tau)r(t)} \quad (9.18)$$

where $\tau = T - t$. By taking the partial derivatives of the bond price, substituting these into equation (9.18), and using a separation of variables, we get the following four ODEs:

$$\frac{\partial A(\tau)}{\partial \tau} = -B_1(\tau)[\tilde{\alpha}_v\tilde{m}_v + \tilde{\alpha}_{v\theta}\tilde{m}_\theta] - B_2(\tau)[\tilde{\alpha}_\theta\tilde{m}_\theta + \tilde{\alpha}_{\theta v}\tilde{m}_v]$$

$$- B_3(\tau)[\tilde{\alpha}_{rv}\tilde{m}_v - \tilde{\alpha}_{r\theta}\tilde{m}_\theta + \tilde{\alpha}\tilde{m}_r] + \frac{1}{2}B_3^2(\tau)\delta_r$$

$$\frac{\partial B_1(\tau)}{\partial \tau} = -B_1(\tau)\tilde{\alpha}_v - B_2(\tau)\tilde{\alpha}_{\theta v} - B_3(\tau)\tilde{\alpha}_{rv} - \frac{1}{2}B_1^2(\tau)\eta^2 - \frac{1}{2}B_3^2(\tau)[\sigma_{rv}^2\eta^2 + 1]$$

$$- B_1(\tau)B_3(\tau)\sigma_{rv}\eta^2 \quad (9.19)$$

$$\frac{\partial B_2(\tau)}{\partial \tau} = -B_1(\tau)\tilde{\alpha}_{v\theta} - B_2(\tau)\tilde{\alpha}_\theta - B_3(\tau)\tilde{\alpha}_{r\theta} - \frac{1}{2}B_2^2(\tau)\zeta^2$$

$$- \frac{1}{2}B_3^2(\tau)[\sigma_{r\theta}^2\zeta^2 + \beta_\theta] - B_2(\tau)B_3(\tau)\sigma_{r\theta}\zeta^2$$

$$\frac{\partial B_3(\tau)}{\partial \tau} = 1 - B_3(\tau)\tilde{\alpha}$$

subject to the boundary condition $A(0) = B_1(0) = B_2(0) = B_3(0) = 0$. The solution to $B_3(.)$ is given as follows:

$$B_3(\tau) = \frac{1}{\tilde{\alpha}}(1 - e^{-\tilde{\alpha}\tau}) \quad (9.20)$$

The ODEs for $A(.)$, $B_1(.)$, and $B_2(.)$ do not have analytical solutions; these must be solved using programming tools such as Matlab. The bond price solutions under the nested models $A_{2r}(3)_{\text{CHEN}}$ and $A_{2r}(3)_{\text{DS}}$ are obtained by setting the appropriate parameter restrictions given earlier.

The $A_{2r}(3)+$ and $A_{2r}(3)++$ Models Though the valuation formulas under the time-homogeneous preference-free $A_{2r}(3)+$ models are identical to those under the corresponding fundamental $A_{2r}(3)$ models (with potentially different empirical estimates of the risk-neutral parameters), these formulas must be adjusted for the time-inhomogeneous preference-free $A_{2r}(3)++$ models by redefining the short rate process as follows:

$$r(t) = \delta(t) + Y(t) \tag{9.21}$$

where $\delta(t)$ is a deterministic term and the risk-neutral process for the variable $Y(t)$ has the same form as the risk-neutral process for the short rate under the $A_{2r}(3)$ models. For example, the risk-neutral process for the variable $Y(t)$ under the $A_{2r}(3)_{\text{MAX}}++$ model has the same form as the risk-neutral process for the short rate given in equation (9.16) under the $A_{2r}(3)_{\text{MAX}}$ model and is given as follows:

$$dY(t) = \tilde{\alpha}_{rv}(\tilde{m}_v - v(t)) \, dt - \tilde{\alpha}_{r\theta}(\tilde{m}_\theta - \theta(t)) \, dt + \tilde{\alpha}(\tilde{m}_r - Y(t)) \, dt$$

$$+ \sigma_{rv}\eta\sqrt{v(t)} \, d\tilde{Z}_1(t) + \sigma_{r\theta}\zeta\sqrt{\theta(t)} \, d\tilde{Z}_2(t) + \sqrt{\delta_r + \beta_\theta\theta(t) + v(t)} \, d\tilde{Z}_3(t) \tag{9.22}$$

Similar adjustments apply to the $A_{2r}(3)_{\text{CHEN}}++$ and $A_{2r}(3)_{\text{DS}}++$ models using equations (9.14) and (9.15), respectively. The risk-neutral processes for the state variables $v(t)$ and $\theta(t)$ remain the same as under the corresponding fundamental models. Since conditional variances do not depend upon the state variable $Y(t)$, the initial time 0 value of $Y(t)$ can be assumed to be zero (without loss of generality), or:

$$Y(0) = 0 \tag{9.23}$$

Following the approach outlined earlier for two-factor models, the solution of the bond price $P(t, T)$, under the $A_{2r}(3)_{\text{MAX}}++$ model is given as follows:

$$P(t, T) = e^{A(\tau) - B_1(\tau)v(t) - B_2(\tau)\theta(t) - B_3(\tau)(r(t) - \delta(t)) - H(t,T)} \tag{9.24}$$

where $A(\tau)$, $B_1(\tau)$, $B_2(\tau)$, and $B_3(\tau)$ are as defined earlier under the fundamental $A_{2r}(3)_{\text{MAX}}$ model. The solutions of $\delta(t)$ and $H(t, T)$ are given as follows:

$$\delta(t) = f(0, t) + \frac{\partial A(t)}{\partial t} - \frac{\partial B_1(t)}{\partial t}v(0) - \frac{\partial B_2(t)}{\partial t}\theta(0) \tag{9.25}$$

and

$$H(t, T) = H(0, T) - H(0, t) = A(T) - A(t) - \big(B_1(T) - B_1(t)\big)v(0)$$
$$- \big(B_2(T) - B_2(t)\big)\theta(0) - \ln P(0, T) + \ln P(0, t) \tag{9.26}$$

where the partial derivatives of $A(t)$, $B_1(t)$, and $B_2(t)$ are defined by the ODEs in equation (9.19). Since the $A_{2r}(3)_{\text{CHEN}}++$ and $A_{2r}(3)_{\text{DS}}++$ models are nested in the $A_{2r}(3)_{\text{MAX}}++$ model, the bond price solution under these models can be obtained using the appropriate parameter restrictions given earlier.

The solutions to futures and options under the $A_{1r}(3)$, $A_{1r}(3)+$, $A_{1r}(3)++$, $A_{2r}(3)$, $A_{2r}(3)+$, and $A_{2r}(3)++$ models previously given can be obtained using the same approach followed under the two-factor hybrid model given in equations (8.93) to (8.113) in Chapter 8.

SIMPLE MULTIFACTOR AFFINE MODELS WITH ANALYTICAL SOLUTIONS

The maximal $A_0(3)$ and $A_3(3)$ subfamilies of three-factor models were not considered in the previous section, since these models are nested in the *simple $A_M(N)$* models given in this section. The simple $A_M(N)$ models require that the $N - M$ correlated Gaussian processes be orthogonal to the M square-root processes. Though the maximal $A_M(N)$ subfamilies of models are theoretically more appealing than the simple $A_M(N)$ models, we focus on the latter for three reasons. First, the simple $A_M(N)$ models allow easy closed-form solutions and fast computation of the prices of bonds and interest rate derivatives. Second, by allowing a large number of factors, the simple $A_M(N)$ models can capture realistic correlation structures and shapes of volatility functions, while not increasing the computational burden proportionately. Finally, preference-free extensions of the simple $A_M(N)$ models allow arbitrary forms of MPRs, and hence allow flexibility in capturing the expected bond returns and expected yields under the physical measure.

The Simple $A_M(N)$ Models

The simple $A_M(N)$ models are specified with $N - M$ number of correlated Gaussian processes that are uncorrelated with M number of square-root processes. The $N - M$ Gaussian state variables are given under the risk-neutral measure, as follows:

$$dY_i(t) = -\tilde{k}_i Y_i(t)\, dt + v_i\, d\tilde{W}_i(t), \quad \text{for all } i = 1, 2, \ldots, N - M \qquad (9.27)$$

where $d\tilde{W}_i(t)\, d\tilde{W}_j(t) = \rho_{ij}\, dt$ for all $i\ j = 1, 2, \ldots, N - M$. By definition, $\rho_{ij} = \rho_{ji}$, and $\rho_{ii} = 1$. The M square-root state variables are given under the risk-neutral measure as follows:

$$dX_m(t) = \tilde{\alpha}_m(\tilde{\theta}_m - X_m(t))\,dt + \sigma_m\sqrt{X_m(t)}\,d\tilde{Z}_m(t),$$
$$\text{for } m = 1, 2, \ldots, M \tag{9.28}$$

where $d\tilde{Z}_m(t)$ are independent Wiener processes for all $m = 1, 2, \ldots, M$, $d\tilde{W}_i(t)\,d\tilde{Z}_m(t) = 0$ for all $i = 1, 2, \ldots, N - M$ and $m = 1, 2, \ldots, M$. The short rate is defined as the sum of all N state variables plus a constant as follows:

$$r(t) = \delta + \sum_{m=1}^{M} X_m(t) + \sum_{i=1}^{N-M} Y_i(t) \tag{9.29}$$

Since the simple $A_M(N)$ models are fundamental models, they require specific functional forms of MPRs, which can be given using the completely affine, essentially affine, or semiaffine specifications using the frameworks of Dai and Singleton [2000], Duffee [2002], and Duarte [2004], respectively.

By applying Ito's lemma to the bond price, taking the risk-neutral expectation, and equating the change in bond price to riskless return, we get the PDE for the bond price as follows:

$$\frac{\partial P}{\partial t} + \sum_{m=1}^{M} \frac{\partial P}{\partial X_m}\left(\tilde{\alpha}_m(\tilde{\theta}_m - X_m(t))\right) + \frac{1}{2}\sum_{m=1}^{M} \frac{\partial^2 P}{\partial X_m^2}\sigma_m^2 X_m(t)$$
$$- \sum_{i=1}^{N-M} \frac{\partial P}{\partial Y_i}\tilde{k}_i Y_i(t) + \frac{1}{2}\sum_{i=1}^{N-M}\sum_{j=1}^{N-M} \frac{\partial^2 P}{\partial Y_i \partial Y_j}v_i v_j \rho_{ij} = r(t)P(t,T) \tag{9.30}$$

subject to the boundary condition $P(T, T) = 1$. Consider the following solution of the bond price:

$$P(t, T) = e^{A(\tau) - \sum_{m=1}^{M} B_m(\tau)X_m(t) - \sum_{i=1}^{N-M} C_i(\tau)Y_i(t) - H(t,T)} \tag{9.31}$$

where

$$H(t, T) = \int_t^T \delta\,dv = \delta\tau \tag{9.32}$$

and $\tau = T - t$. Taking the partial derivatives of the bond price in equation (9.31), substituting them in equation (9.30), and using a change of variable $\tau = T - t$, we get the following $N + 1$ ODEs:

$$\frac{\partial A(\tau)}{\partial \tau} = -\sum_{m=1}^{M} \tilde{\alpha}_m\tilde{\theta}_m B_m(\tau) + \frac{1}{2}\sum_{i=1}^{N-M}\sum_{j=1}^{N-M} C_i(\tau)C_j(\tau)v_i v_j \rho_{ij}$$

$$\frac{\partial B_m(\tau)}{\partial \tau} = 1 - \tilde{\alpha}_m B_m(\tau) - \frac{1}{2}\sigma_m^2 B_m^2(\tau), \quad \text{for } m = 1, 2, \ldots, M$$

$$\frac{\partial C_i(\tau)}{\partial \tau} = 1 - \tilde{k}_i C_i(\tau), \quad \text{for } i = 1, 2, \ldots, N - M \tag{9.33}$$

subject to $A(0) = B_m(0) = C_i(0) = 0$, for all i and m. The closed-form solutions for $A(\tau)$, $B_m(\tau)$, and $C_i(\tau)$ are given as follows:

$$A(\tau) = \sum_{m=1}^{M} \frac{2\tilde{\alpha}_m \tilde{\theta}_m}{\sigma_m^2} \ln \left[\frac{2\beta_m e^{\frac{1}{2}(\beta_m + \tilde{\alpha}_m)\tau}}{(\beta_m + \tilde{\alpha}_m)(e^{\beta_m \tau} - 1) + 2\beta_m} \right]$$

$$+ \frac{1}{2}\sum_{i=1}^{N-M}\sum_{j=1}^{N-M} \frac{\nu_i \nu_j \rho_{ij}}{\tilde{k}_i \tilde{k}_j} \left(\tau - C_i(\tau) - C_j(\tau) + \left(\frac{1 - e^{-(\tilde{k}_i + \tilde{k}_j)\tau}}{\tilde{k}_i + \tilde{k}_j} \right) \right) \tag{9.34}$$

$$B_m(\tau) = \frac{2(e^{\beta_m \tau} - 1)}{(\beta_m + \tilde{\alpha}_m)(e^{\beta_m \tau} - 1) + 2\beta_m}, \quad \text{for } m = 1, 2, \ldots, M \tag{9.35}$$

$$C_i(\tau) = \frac{1 - e^{-\tilde{k}_i \tau}}{\tilde{k}_i}, \quad \text{for } i = 1, 2, \ldots, N - M \tag{9.36}$$

where $\quad \beta_m = \sqrt{\tilde{\alpha}_m^2 + 2\sigma_m^2}$.

The Simple $A_M(N)+$ and $A_M(N)++$ Models

Since the simple fundamental $A_M(N)$ models restrict the correlations between the Gaussian processes and square-root processes, allowing general nonlinear MPRs using the simple preference-free $A_M(N)+$ and $A_M(N)++$ models is especially useful. Assuming that a sufficient number of factors are used under the simple preference-free $A_M(N)+$ and $A_M(N)++$ models in order to match the second moments of bond returns or yield changes, then allowing general nonlinear MPRs given as functions of *all* state variables may allow matching of the first moments, too. The real test of how well the simple preference-free $A_M(N)+$ and $A_M(N)++$ models perform is a function of how well these models can explain the cross-sections of prices of bonds and interest rate derivatives and how effective the hedging performance of these models is.

Using a high number of factors under the simple preference-free $A_M(N)+$ and $A_M(N)++$ models does not imply a proportionately high computational burden, since bond prices are given in closed form and since efficient analytical approximations can be used for solving the prices of interest rate derivatives. In contrast, the numerical approximations of bond prices and interest rate derivatives are much slower under the maximal $A_M(N)$ models and their preference-free extensions, even with a small number of factors.

Using general nonlinear MPRs, the change of measure can be given as follows:

$$
\begin{aligned}
d\tilde{Z}_m(t) &= dZ_m(t) + \gamma_{Xm}(z,t)\,dt, \quad \text{for all } m = 1,2,\ldots,M \\
d\tilde{W}_i(t) &= dW_i(t) + \gamma_{Yi}(z,t)\,dt, \quad \text{for all } i = 1,2,\ldots,N-M
\end{aligned}
\tag{9.37}
$$

The functions $\gamma_{Xm}(z,t)$ and $\gamma_{Yi}(z,t)$ can be general and nonlinear and may even include other state variables in addition to the N state variables X_m and Y_i for all $m = 1,2,\ldots,M$ and $i = 1,2,\ldots,N-M$. The change of measure requires that these functions are bounded, such that the Novikov condition of the Girsanov theorem is satisfied.

The solutions of the bond price and interest rate derivatives under the simple time-homogeneous preference-free $A_M(N)+$ models are identical to those under the corresponding simple fundamental $A_M(N)$ models, except that the risk-neutral parameters estimated under these models may be different, since the latter models impose restrictive functional forms on the MPRs.

Since conditional variances do not depend upon the state variables $Y_i(t)$ and since the exact fit with the initial bond price function at time 0 is guaranteed by construction under the simple $A_M(N)++$ models, the initial time 0 values of $Y(t)$ can be assumed to be zero (without loss of generality) under these models, or:

$$
Y_i(0) = 0, \quad \text{for all } i = 1,2,\ldots,N-M
\tag{9.38}
$$

The solution of the bond price under the simple time-inhomogeneous preference-free $A_M(N)++$ models can be obtained by following the same steps as under the corresponding simple fundamental $A_M(N)$ models, except that the constant δ in equation (9.29) and $H(t,T)$ in equation (9.32) are replaced with $\delta(t)$ and $H(t,T)$, defined as follows:

$$
\delta(t) = f(0,t) - \sum_{m=1}^{M} \left(X_m(0) + \tilde{\alpha}_m B_m(t)(\tilde{\theta}_m - X_m(0)) - \frac{1}{2}B_m^2(t)\sigma_m^2 X_m(0) \right)
$$

$$
+ \frac{1}{2}\sum_{i=1}^{N-M}\sum_{j=1}^{N-M} C_i(t)C_j(t)v_i v_j \rho_{ij}
\tag{9.39}
$$

where $f(0, t) = -\partial \ln P(0, t)/\partial t$ is the time 0 forward rate for term t. The solution to the term $H(t, T)$ can be given using equation (9.31) as follows:

$$H(t, T) = \int_t^T \delta(v)\, dv = H(0, T) - H(0, t)$$

$$= A(T) - A(t) - \sum_{m=1}^M X_m(0)[B_m(T) - B_m(t)] - \ln P(0, T) + \ln P(0, t)$$

$$(9.40)$$

where $P(0, t)$ and $P(0, T)$ are initial zero-coupon bond prices.

The Nested ATSMs

The simple $A_M(N)$ models and the simple $A_M(N)++$ models nest many well-known ATSMs given in the literature, which are given with appropriate parameter restrictions in Table 9.3.

The multiple-factor ATSMs nested in the simple $A_M(N)$ and $A_M(N)++$ models have the $N - M$ Gaussian processes specified in the Ay form and the M square-root processes specified in the canonical/Ay form. Since *time-homogeneous* preference-free models have been introduced for the first time in this book, models nested in $A_M(N)+$ models don't exist in the current literature. The time-homogeneity property of the $A_M(N)+$ models makes them appealing theoretically, while independence from the specifications of MPRs makes them appealing to practitioners for the valuing and hedging of interest rate derivatives.

Since Chapter 8 did not derive analytical solutions of interest rate derivatives for some of the nested two-factor ATSMs given in Table 9.3, these solutions can be obtained as special cases of the solutions derived for the simple $A_M(N)$, $A_M(N)+$, and $A_M(N)++$ models in the following sections.

Valuing Futures

Futures on a Zero-Coupon Bond   The time t price of a futures contract expiring at time S written on a zero-coupon bond maturing at time T can be obtained as follows: We know that the futures price is a martingale under the risk-neutral measure, or:

$$P_F(t, S, T) = \tilde{E}_t(P(S, T)) \tag{9.41}$$

Using Ito's lemma to solve the differential of the futures price and equating the risk-neutral expectation to zero, we get the PDE for the futures price, as follows:

$$
\frac{\partial P_F}{\partial t} + \sum_{m=1}^{M} \frac{\partial P_F}{\partial X_m} \left(\tilde{\alpha}_m (\tilde{\theta}_m - X_m(t)) \right) + \frac{1}{2} \sum_{m=1}^{M} \frac{\partial^2 P_F}{\partial X_m^2} \sigma_m^2 X_m(t)
$$

$$
- \sum_{i=1}^{N-M} \frac{\partial P_F}{\partial Y_i} \tilde{k}_i Y_i(t) + \frac{1}{2} \sum_{i=1}^{N-M} \sum_{j=1}^{N-M} \frac{\partial^2 P_F}{\partial Y_i \partial Y_j} \nu_i \nu_j \rho_{ij} = 0
$$

(9.42)

TABLE 9.3   The ATSMs Nested in the Simple $A_M(N)$ and $A_M(N)++$ Models

Model Name	Nested Model	Values of M and N	Parameter Restrictions
Merton [1973]	$A_0(1)$	$M = 0, N = 1$	$\tilde{k}_1 = 0$
Ho and Lee [1986]	$A_0(1)++$	$M = 0, N = 1$	$\tilde{k}_1 = 0$
Vasicek [1977]	$A_0(1)$	$M = 0, N = 1$	None
Extended Vasicek (Hull and White [1993])	$A_0(1)++$	$M = 0, N = 1$	None
CIR [1985]	$A_1(1)$	$M = 1, N = 1$	$\delta = 0$
Duffie and Kan [1996]	$A_1(1)$	$M = 1, N = 1$	None
CIR++ (Brigo and Mercurio [2001])	$A_1(1)++$	$M = 1, N = 1$	None
Dai and Singleton [2000]	$A_0(2)$	$M = 0, N = 2$	None
Hull and White [1996]	$A_0(2)++$	$M = 0, N = 2$	None
Longstaff and Schwartz [1992], and Chen and Scott [1992]	$A_2(2)$	$M = 2, N = 2$	$\delta = 0^*$
Dai and Singleton [2000]	$A_2(2)$	$M = 2, N = 2$	None*
CIR2++ (Brigo and Mercurio [2001])	$A_2(2)++$	$M = 2, N = 2$	None*
Dai and Singleton [2000, 2002]	$A_0(3)$	$M = 0, N = 3$	None
Preference-free extension of Dai and Singleton [2000, 2002]	$A_0(3)++$	$M = 0, N = 3$	None
Jagannathan, Kaplin, and Sun [2003]	$A_3(3)$	$M = 3, N = 3$	None*
Preference-free extension of Jagannathan, Kaplin, and Sun [2003]	$A_3(3)++$	$M = 3, N = 3$	None*

*These models assume zero unconditional correlations between the state variables, consistent with the framework of *simple* $A_N(N)$ and $A_N(N)++$ models. Though the empirical data requires negative correlations between the state variables, the admissibility requirement for these models disallows negative unconditional correlations under the risk-neutral measure. Hence, for all practical purposes, only zero unconditional correlations can be allowed under the risk-neutral measure for these models.

subject to the boundary condition $P_F(S, S, T) = P(S, T)$. We assume that the solution to equation (9.42) has the following form:

$$P_F(t, S, T) = e^{A_F(s) - \sum_{m=1}^{M} B_{mF}(s)X_m(t) - \sum_{i=1}^{N-M} C_{iF}(s)Y_i(t) - H(S,T)}, \quad s = S - t \quad (9.43)$$

subject to $A_F(0) = A(U)$, $B_{mF}(0) = B_m(U)$, $C_{iF}(0) = C_i(U)$, and $U = T - S$. The terms $A(U), B_m(U)$, and $C_i(U)$ are given by equations (9.34), (9.35), and (9.36), respectively.

Evaluating the partial derivatives of the futures price and substituting these back into equation (9.42) after using a change of variable $s = S - t$, we get the following $N + 1$ ODEs:

$$\frac{\partial A_F(s)}{\partial s} = -\sum_{m=1}^{M} \tilde{\alpha}_m \tilde{\theta}_m B_{mF}(s) + \frac{1}{2}\sum_{i=1}^{N-M}\sum_{j=1}^{N-M} C_{iF}(s)C_{jF}(s)v_i v_j \rho_{ij}$$

$$\frac{\partial B_{mF}(s)}{\partial s} = -\tilde{\alpha}_m B_{mF}(s) - \frac{1}{2}\sigma_m^2 B_{mF}^2(s), \quad \text{for } m = 1, 2, \ldots, M \quad (9.44)$$

$$\frac{\partial C_{iF}(s)}{\partial s} = -\tilde{k}_i C_{iF}(s), \quad \text{for } i = 1, 2, \ldots, N - M$$

where the boundary conditions are as defined in equation (9.43). The solutions are given as follows:

$$A_F(s) = A(U) - \sum_{m=1}^{M} \frac{2\tilde{\alpha}_m \tilde{\theta}_m}{\sigma_m^2} \ln\left|\frac{\sigma_m^2 B_m(U)\left(e^{-\tilde{\alpha}_m s} - 1\right) - 2\tilde{\alpha}_m}{2\tilde{\alpha}_m}\right|$$

$$+ \frac{1}{2}\sum_{i=1}^{N-M}\sum_{j=1}^{N-M} v_i v_j \rho_{ij} C_i(U)C_j(U)\left(\frac{1 - e^{-\left(\tilde{k}_i + \tilde{k}_j\right)s}}{\tilde{k}_i + \tilde{k}_j}\right) \quad (9.45)$$

$$B_{mF}(s) = \frac{-2\tilde{\alpha}_m B_m(U)e^{-\tilde{\alpha}_m s}}{\sigma_m^2 B_m(U)\left(e^{-\tilde{\alpha}_m s} - 1\right) - 2\tilde{\alpha}_m}, \quad \text{for } m = 1, 2, \ldots, M \quad (9.46)$$

$$C_{iF}(s) = e^{-\tilde{k}_i s} C_i(U), \quad \text{for } i = 1, 2, \ldots, N - M \quad (9.47)$$

The term $H(S, T)$ in equation (9.43) is equal to $\delta(T - S) = \delta U$ under the $A_M(N)$ and $A_M(N)+$ models and is given by equation (9.40) under the $A_M(N)++$ models.

The futures-forward price discount (FFPD): is given as,

$$FFPD = \frac{P_f(t, S, T) - P_F(t, S, T)}{P_f(t, S, T)} = 1 - P_F(t, S, T)\frac{P(t, S)}{P(t, T)}$$

$$= 1 - e^{(A_F(s) + A(s) - A(\tau)) - \sum_{m=1}^{M} (B_{mF}(s) + B_m(s) - B_m(\tau)) X_m(t)}$$

$$s = S - t \text{ and } \tau = T - t \tag{9.48}$$

Futures on a Time Deposit The price of a futures contract on a time deposit—such as Eurodollar and Euribor futures—can be obtained using equation (3.12) in Chapter 3:

$$P_F^{TD}(t, S, T) = \frac{100}{\hat{U}} \left(1 + \hat{U} - P_F^I(t, S, T) \right) \tag{9.49}$$

where S is the futures expiration date, $U = T - S$ is the deposit time period calculated using the actual/actual day-count convention, $\hat{U}$ is the deposit time period calculated using the actual/360 day-count convention, and $P_F^I(t, S, T)$ is the current price of a futures contract written on a hypothetical asset, which at the expiration date S is worth the inverse of a \$1 face-value zero-coupon bond maturing at time T. As shown in Chapter 3, the futures price, $P_F^I(t, S, T)$, is given by the following risk-neutral expectation:

$$P_F^I(t, S, T) = \tilde{E}_t \left(\frac{1}{P(S, T)} \right) \tag{9.50}$$

We assume that the solution to equation (9.50) has the following form:

$$P_F^I(t, S, T) = e^{a_F(s) - \sum_{m=1}^{M} b_{mF}(s) X_m(t) - \sum_{i=1}^{N-M} c_{iF}(s) Y_i(t) + H(S, T)}, \quad s = S - t \tag{9.51}$$

Using the same logic as in earlier chapters, the solutions of $a_F(s)$, $b_{mF}(s)$, and $c_{iF}(s)$ immediately follow from equations (9.45), (9.46), and (9.47), respectively, by switching the signs of the constants $A(U)$, $B_m(U)$, and $C_i(U)$ and are given as follows:

$$a_F(s) = -A(U) - \sum_{m=1}^{M} \frac{2\tilde{\alpha}_m \tilde{\theta}_m}{\sigma_m^2} \ln \left| \frac{\sigma_m^2 B_m(U)(1 - e^{-\tilde{\alpha}_m s}) - 2\tilde{\alpha}_m}{2\tilde{\alpha}_m} \right|$$

$$+ \frac{1}{2} \sum_{i=1}^{N-M} \sum_{j=1}^{N-M} v_i v_j \rho_{ij} C_i(U) C_j(U) \left(\frac{1 - e^{-(\tilde{k}_i + \tilde{k}_j) s}}{\tilde{k}_i + \tilde{k}_j} \right) \tag{9.52}$$

$$b_{mF}(s) = \frac{2\tilde{\alpha}_m B_m(U) e^{-\tilde{\alpha}_m s}}{\sigma_m^2 B_m(U)(1 - e^{-\tilde{\alpha}_m s}) - 2\tilde{\alpha}_m}, \quad \text{for } m = 1, 2, \ldots, M \tag{9.53}$$

$$c_{iF}(s) = -e^{-\tilde{k}_i s} C_i(U), \quad \text{for } i = 1, 2, \ldots, N - M \tag{9.54}$$

The term $H(S, T)$ in equation (9.51) is equal to $\delta(T - S) = \delta U$ under the $A_M(N)$ and $A_M(N)+$ models and is given by equation (9.40) under the $A_M(N)++$ models.

The convexity bias, given as the difference between the futures rate and the forward rate on a time deposit, is defined in equation (3.17) in Chapter 3 as follows:

$$
\begin{aligned}
Convexity\ \ Bias &= L_F(t, S, T) - L_f(t, S, T) \\
&= \frac{1 + L_F(t, S, T)\hat{U}}{\hat{U}} \left(1 - \frac{P(t, S)}{P(t, T)P_F^I(t, S, T)}\right)
\end{aligned}
$$
(9.55)

By substituting the appropriate formulas, the convexity bias is given as:

$$
\begin{aligned}
Convexity\ \ Bias &= L_F(t, S, T) - L_f(t, S, T) \\
&= \frac{1 + L_F(t, S, T)\hat{U}}{\hat{U}} \\
&\quad \times \left(1 - e^{A(s) - a_F(s) - A(\tau) - \sum_{m=1}^{M}\left(B_m(s) - b_{mF}(s) - B_m(\tau)\right)X_m(t)}\right)
\end{aligned}
$$
(9.56)

Valuing Options on Zero-Coupon Bonds or Caplets: The Fourier Inversion Method

A significant advantage of the Fourier inversion method for solving option prices is that it requires only a *single* summation to solve the integrals for obtaining risk-neutral probabilities even under a multifactor model, while the traditional methods (such as Longstaff and Schwartz [1992]) require the approximation to be done using a multiple-order summation under a multifactor model. The computation time difference between a single summation and a multiple-order summation grows nonlinearly and is quite significant even between a single summation and a double summation. The advantage of the Fourier inversion method is especially relevant in the context of the simple $A_M(N)$, $A_M(N)+$, and $A_M(N)++$ models with a large number of factors.

We use the four-step Fourier inversion method outlined in Chapter 5 (see equations (5.114) through (5.168)) for solving option prices. The prices of a European call option and a European put option, both written on a zero-coupon bond maturing at time T, with a strike price of K, and expiring at time S, are given as follows:

$$
c(t) = P(t, T)\Pi_{1t} - KP(t, S)\Pi_{2t}
$$
(9.57)

and

$$p(t) = KP(t, S)(1 - \Pi_{2t}) - P(t, T)(1 - \Pi_{1t}) \tag{9.58}$$

where

$$\Pi_{1t} = \int_{\ln K}^{\infty} f_{1t}(y)\, dy = \frac{1}{2} + \frac{1}{\pi} \int_0^{\infty} \text{Re}\left[\frac{e^{-i\omega \ln K} g_{1t}(\omega)}{i\omega} \right] d\omega \tag{9.59}$$

$$\Pi_{2t} = \int_{\ln K}^{\infty} f_{2t}(y)\, dy = \frac{1}{2} + \frac{1}{\pi} \int_0^{\infty} \text{Re}\left[\frac{e^{-i\omega \ln K} g_{2t}(\omega)}{i\omega} \right] d\omega \tag{9.60}$$

Following the general approach given in Chapter 5, the characteristic functions $g_{1t}(\omega)$ and $g_{2t}(\omega)$ are obtained as follows:

$$g_{1t}(\omega) = \frac{e^{A_1^*(s) - \sum_{m=1}^M B_{1m}^*(s)X_m(t) - \sum_{i=1}^{N-M} C_{1i}^*(s)Y_i(t) - H(S,T)(1+i\omega) - H(t,S)}}{P(t,T)}, \quad s = S - t \tag{9.61}$$

$$g_{2t}(\omega) = \frac{e^{A_2^*(s) - \sum_{m=1}^M B_{2m}^*(s)X_m(t) - \sum_{i=1}^{N-M} C_{2i}^*(s)Y_i(t) - H(S,T)(i\omega) - H(t,S)}}{P(t,S)}, \quad s = S - t \tag{9.62}$$

where the functions $A_1^*(s)$, $B_{1m}^*(s)$, and $C_{1i}^*(s)$ in equation (9.61) are given as solutions to the ODEs for $A(s)$, $B_m(s)$, and $C_i(s)$, respectively, given in equation (9.33), but with the following boundary conditions:

$$A_1^*(0) = a_1 = A(U)(1 + i\omega)$$

$$B_{1m}^*(0) = b_{1m} = B_m(U)(1 + i\omega), \quad \text{for } m = 1, 2, \ldots, M \tag{9.63}$$

$$C_{1i}^*(0) = c_{1i} = C_i(U)(1 + i\omega), \quad \text{for } i = 1, 2, \ldots, N - M$$

where $U = T - S$. The solutions are given as follows:

$$A_1^*(s) = a_1 + \frac{1}{2} \sum_{i=1}^{N-M} \sum_{j=1}^{N-M} \frac{\nu_i \nu_j \rho_{ij}}{\tilde{k}_i \tilde{k}_j} \left(s - q_i C_i(s) - q_j C_j(s) + q_i q_j \left(\frac{1 - e^{-(\tilde{k}_i + \tilde{k}_j)s}}{\tilde{k}_i + \tilde{k}_j} \right) \right)$$

$$- 2 \sum_{m=1}^M \frac{\tilde{\alpha}_m \tilde{\theta}_m}{\sigma_m^2} \left(\beta_{3m} s + \ln\left(\frac{1 - \beta_{4m} e^{\beta_{1m}s}}{1 - \beta_{4m}} \right) \right) \tag{9.64}$$

$$B_{1m}^*(s) = \frac{2}{\sigma_m^2} \left(\frac{\beta_{2m} \beta_{4m} e^{\beta_{1m}s} - \beta_{3m}}{\beta_{4m} e^{\beta_{1m}s} - 1} \right), \quad \text{for } m = 1, 2, \ldots, M \tag{9.65}$$

$$C_{1i}^*(s) = \frac{1 - q_i e^{-\tilde{k}_i s}}{\tilde{k}_i}, \quad \text{for } i = 1, 2, \ldots, N - M \tag{9.66}$$

where

$$q_i = 1 - \tilde{k}_i c_{1i}, \quad \text{for } i = 1, 2, \ldots, N - M \tag{9.67}$$

and

$$\beta_{1m} = \sqrt{\tilde{\alpha}_m^2 + 2\sigma_m^2}, \qquad \beta_{2m} = \frac{-\tilde{\alpha}_m + \beta_{1m}}{2}, \qquad \beta_{3m} = \frac{-\tilde{\alpha}_m - \beta_{1m}}{2},$$

$$\beta_{4m} = \frac{-\tilde{\alpha}_m - \beta_{1m} - b_{1m}\sigma_m^2}{-\tilde{\alpha}_m + \beta_{1m} - b_{1m}\sigma_m^2}, \qquad \text{for } m = 1, 2, \ldots, M \tag{9.68}$$

Similarly, the functions $A_2^*(s)$, $B_{2m}^*(s)$, and $C_{2i}^*(s)$ in equation (9.62) are given as solutions to the ODEs for $A(s)$, $B_m(s)$, and $C_i(s)$, respectively, given in equation (9.33) but with the following boundary conditions:

$$A_2^*(0) = a_2 = A(U)(i\omega)$$

$$B_{2m}^*(0) = b_{2m} = B_m(U)(i\omega), \quad \text{for } m = 1, 2, \ldots, M \tag{9.69}$$

$$C_{2i}^*(0) = c_{2i} = C_i(U)(i\omega), \quad \text{for } i = 1, 2, \ldots, N - M$$

The solutions of $A_2^*(s)$, $B_{2m}^*(s)$, and $C_{2i}^*(s)$ are identical to the solutions of $A_1^*(s)$, $B_{1m}^*(s)$, and $C_{1i}^*(s)$ given in equations (9.64), (9.65), and (9.66), respectively, except that a_1 is replaced by a_2 in equation (9.64), c_{1i} is replaced by c_{2i} in equation (9.67), and b_{1m} is replaced by b_{2m} in equation (9.68).

Once the characteristic functions have been obtained, step 4 in Chapter 5 (see equation (5.149)) demonstrates how to approximate the integrals in equations (9.59) and (9.60) numerically by using a truncated discrete summation.

The solution of the option price under the $A_M(N)$ and $A_M(N)+$ models is different from its solution under the $A_M(N)++$ model. The term $H(t, T)$ equals $\delta \times (T - t)$ under the $A_M(N)$ and $A_M(N)+$ models and is given by equation (9.40) under the $A_M(N)++$ model.

Valuing Options on Coupon Bonds or Swaptions: The Cumulant Expansion Approximation

The Fourier inversion method provides closed-form solutions for zero-coupon bond options or caplets under affine term structure models. However, this method cannot be used to solve options on coupon bonds or swaptions under *multifactor* affine models.[4] Collin-Dufresne and Goldstein [2001b] propose a fast and accurate cumulant expansion approximation for pricing options on coupon bonds or swaptions. This approach exploits the fact that the moments of a coupon bond also have affine closed-form solutions. Using these moments to uniquely identify the cumulants of the distribution of the coupon bond, the probability distribution of the coupon bond's future price at the option expiration date is obtained using an Edgeworth expansion technique. This approach is very fast as no numerical integrations are performed. In our simulations, we find that this approach is also significantly faster than the Fourier inversion approach given in the previous section, and hence, can be used to price options on zero-coupon bonds or caplets, as well.

The following steps show how to solve for the price of an option on a coupon bond or a swaption using the cumulant expansion approach.

Step 1: Probability Transformations for the Valuation of an Option on a Coupon Bond   Consider a European call option on a coupon bond with an expiration date S and exercise price K. The coupon bond has n cash flows maturing after the option expiration date S, given as CF_i at time $T_i > S$, for $i = 1, 2, \ldots, n$. The price of the bond at the expiration date S is given as:

$$P_c(S) = \sum_{i=1}^{n} CF_i P(S, T_i) \qquad (9.70)$$

The price of the option at time t $(t \leq S)$ depends on the risk-neutral probability of the option ending in the money at time S and can be mathematically represented as follows:

$$
\begin{aligned}
c(t) &= \tilde{E}_t \left[e^{-\int_t^S r(u)\,du} \max(P_c(S) - K, 0) \right] \\
&= \tilde{E}_t \left[e^{-\int_t^S r(u)\,du} (P_c(S) 1_{P_c(S)>K} - K 1_{P_c(S)>K}) \right]
\end{aligned}
\qquad (9.71)
$$

where $1_{P_c(S)>K}$ is an indicator function that equals 1 if the bond ends up in the money and equals 0 otherwise. Using equation (9.70) and the law of iterated expectations, we get:

$$c(t) = \sum_{i=1}^{n} CF_i \tilde{E}_t \left[e^{-\int_t^{T_i} r(u)\,du} 1_{P_c(S)>K} \right] - K \tilde{E}_t \left[e^{-\int_t^S r(u)\,du} 1_{P_c(S)>K} \right] \qquad (9.72)$$

Using a change of measure, the expectations in equation (9.72) can be calculated under different forward measures instead of the risk-neutral measure, as follows:

$$c(t) = \sum_{i=1}^{n} CF_i P(t, T_i) \tilde{E}_t \left[\frac{e^{-\int_t^{T_i} r(u)\,du}}{P(t, T_i)} 1_{P_c(S)>K} \right] - K P(t, S) \tilde{E}_t \left[\frac{e^{-\int_t^S r(u)\,du}}{P(t, S)} 1_{P_c(S)>K} \right]$$

$$= \sum_{i=1}^{n} CF_i P(t, T_i) E_t^{T_i}[1_{P_c(S)>K}] - K P(t, S) E_t^S[1_{P_c(S)>K}] \qquad (9.73)$$

Define the probability of the option being in the money under the forward probability measure W as follows:

$$\Pi_t^W(P_c(S) > K) = E_t^W[1_{P_c(S)>K}] \tag{9.74}$$

The call option can be given using the probability measures $\Pi_t^W(P_c(S) > K)$ for $W = S, T_1, T_2, \ldots, T_n$ as follows:

$$c(t) = \sum_{i=1}^n CF_i P(t, T_i) \Pi_t^{T_i}(P_c(S) > K) - KP(t, S)\Pi_t^S(P_c(S) > K) \tag{9.75}$$

Using put-call parity, the price of the put option is given as follows:

$$p(t) = KP(t, S)[1 - \Pi_t^S(P_c(S) > K)] - \sum_{i=1}^n CF_i P(t, T_i)[1 - \Pi_t^{T_i}(P_c(S) > K)]$$

$$\tag{9.76}$$

For many option problems, the analytical solution of the probabilities does not exist, even though the characteristic functions associated with these probabilities have analytical solutions. Hence, the probabilities are obtained by solving the characteristic function and then using Fourier inversion to invert the probabilities from the characteristic functions. Unfortunately, this approach cannot be applied in the current context because even the characteristic functions associated with the probabilities $\Pi_t^W(P_c(S) > K)$ do not have analytical solutions.

However, the characteristic functions can be approximated by using a finite set of cumulants. The cumulants are defined as the coefficients of a Taylor series expansion of the logarithm of the characteristic function. Since a one-to-one relationship exists between the cumulants and the moments associated with a given probability distribution, and since the moments of the coupon bond price can be solved in closed form under affine models, the cumulants can be obtained using these moments.[5] The probability distribution of the coupon bond price is then obtained from the cumulants using an Edgeworth expansion.[6] Since no numerical integrations are performed, this approach is very fast in computing options prices and can be used to price options on both coupon bonds and zero-coupon bonds.

Step 2. Obtaining the Probability Distribution from the Cumulants For expositional simplicity, we first explain the relationships among the cumulants, the characteristic function, and the probability distribution function, but without using explicit notation for a specific probability measure (such as forward measure or risk-neutral measure), which is added later.

Let $f_t(y = P_c(S))$ be the time t probability density function of the coupon bond price $P_c(S)$. Then the probability distribution function can be given as:

$$\Pi_t(P_c(S) > K) = \int_K^\infty f_t(y)\,dy \tag{9.77}$$

The characteristic function corresponding to a given probability density $f_t(y)$ of the coupon bond price $P_c(S)$ is defined as follows:[7]

$$g_t(\omega) = E_t[e^{i\omega y}] = \int_{-\infty}^\infty e^{i\omega y} f_t(y)\,dy \tag{9.78}$$

where i is the imaginary number given as the square root of -1.

The probability density $f_t(y)$ can be obtained using the inverse Fourier transform as follows:

$$f_t(y) = \frac{1}{2\pi} \int_{-\infty}^\infty e^{-i\omega y} g_t(\omega)\,d\omega \tag{9.79}$$

The cumulants of $P_c(S)$ under the given probability measure are defined as the coefficients of the Taylor expansion of the logarithm of the characteristic function:

$$\ln(g_t(\omega)) = \sum_{j=1}^\infty c_j \frac{(i\omega)^j}{j!} \tag{9.80}$$

Using the result in equation (9.80), equation (9.79) can be alternatively expressed as follows:

$$\begin{aligned}
f_t(y) &= \frac{1}{2\pi} \int_{-\infty}^\infty e^{-i\omega y} e^{\ln(g_t(\omega))}\,d\omega \\
&= \frac{1}{2\pi} \int_{-\infty}^\infty e^{-i\omega y} e^{\sum_{j=1}^\infty c_j (i\omega)^j / j!}\,d\omega
\end{aligned} \tag{9.81}$$

Removing the first two cumulants from the summation, we obtain:

$$f_t(y) = \frac{1}{2\pi} \int_{-\infty}^\infty e^{-i\omega(y - c_1) - 0.5\,\omega^2 c_2} e^\Lambda\,d\omega \tag{9.82}$$

where

$$\Lambda = \sum_{j=3}^\infty c_j \frac{(i\omega)^j}{j!} \tag{9.83}$$

The solution of the probability density $f_t(y)$ given in (9.82) is exact, as it uses an infinite number of cumulants. Since the relative importance of higher-order cumulants diminishes, we approximate e^Λ by retaining only a finite number of terms, including the powers of ω up to a specific order Q. Since the summation for Λ starts from 3, as shown in equation (9.83), it implies that the Taylor series expansion of e^Λ is of the order $Int(Q/3)$:

$$e^\Lambda \approx \sum_{q=0}^{Int(Q/3)} \frac{\Lambda^q}{q!} \tag{9.84}$$

The choice of Q depends on the trade-off between accuracy and computational cost. Collin-Dufresne and Goldstein [2001b] demonstrate high accuracy with $Q = 7$, using examples of a three-factor Gaussian model and a two-factor CIR (Cox, Ingersoll and Ross) model.

To illustrate the expansion, consider $Q = 7$, which implies that the series expansion of e^Λ includes the powers of Λ of order less than or equal to 2, or:

$$e^\Lambda \approx 1 + \Lambda + \frac{\Lambda^2}{2!} \tag{9.85}$$

Substituting equation (9.83) in (9.85), we get:

$$e^\Lambda \approx 1 + \sum_{j=3}^{\infty} c_j \frac{(i\omega)^j}{j!} + \frac{1}{2}\left(\sum_{j=3}^{\infty} c_j \frac{(i\omega)^j}{j!}\right)^2 \tag{9.86}$$

Retaining only the terms with powers of ω of the order less than or equal to $Q = 7$, we obtain:

$$\begin{aligned}
e^\Lambda \approx 1 &+ \frac{(i\omega)^3}{3!}c_3 + \frac{(i\omega)^4}{4!}c_4 + \frac{(i\omega)^5}{5!}c_5 + \frac{(i\omega)^6}{6!}c_6 \\
&+ \frac{(i\omega)^7}{7!}c_7 + \frac{1}{2}\frac{(i\omega)^6}{(3!)^2}c_3^2 + \frac{(i\omega)^7}{4!3!}c_3 c_4
\end{aligned} \tag{9.87}$$

Collecting the terms with the same powers of ω, equation (9.87) simplifies to give:[8]

$$\begin{aligned}
e^\Lambda \approx 1\omega^0 &+ 0\omega^1 + 0\omega^2 - \frac{c_3}{3!}i\omega^3 + \frac{c_4}{4!}\omega^4 \\
&+ \frac{c_5}{5!}i\omega^5 - \left(\frac{c_6}{6!} + \frac{1}{2}\frac{c_3^2}{(3!)^2}\right)\omega^6 - \left(\frac{c_7}{7!} + \frac{c_3 c_4}{3!4!}\right)i\omega^7 \\
&= \sum_{q=0}^{7} \phi_q \omega^q
\end{aligned} \tag{9.88}$$

In general, for order Q, we have:[9]

$$e^{\Lambda} \approx \sum_{q=0}^{Q} \phi_q \omega^q \tag{9.89}$$

Substituting the approximation in equation (9.82), the probability density $f_t(y)$ can be approximated as follows:

$$f_t(y) \approx \sum_{q=0}^{Q} \phi_q \frac{1}{2\pi} \int_{-\infty}^{\infty} \omega^q e^{-i\omega(y-c_1)-0.5\omega^2 c_2} \, d\omega \tag{9.90}$$

The expression on the right-hand side of equation (9.90) can be further simplified by noting that:

$$\frac{1}{2\pi} \int_{-\infty}^{\infty} \omega^q e^{-i\omega(y-c_1)-0.5\omega^2 c_2} \, d\omega = \left. \frac{\partial^q}{\partial \beta^q} \left[\frac{1}{2\pi} \int_{-\infty}^{\infty} e^{\beta\omega-0.5\omega^2 c_2} \, d\omega \right] \right|_{\beta=-i(y-c_1)}$$

$$= \left. \frac{1}{\sqrt{2\pi c_2}} \frac{\partial^q}{\partial \beta^q} \left[e^{\beta^2/(2c_2)} \right] \right|_{\beta=-i(y-c_1)} \tag{9.91}$$

$$= \frac{1}{\sqrt{2\pi c_2}} e^{-(y-c_1)^2/(2c_2)} \left(\sum_{j=0}^{Q} a_j^q (y-c_1)^j \right)$$

where a_j^q for $j = 0, 1, \ldots, Q$ and $q = 0, 1, \ldots, Q$ define a new set of coefficients.[10]

Substituting equation (9.91) into equation (9.90), the probability density can be approximated as follows:

$$f_t(y) \approx \frac{1}{\sqrt{2\pi c_2}} e^{-(y-c_1)^2/(2c_2)} \left(\sum_{j=0}^{Q} \kappa_j^Q (y-c_1)^j \right) \tag{9.92}$$

where[11]

$$\kappa_j^Q = \sum_{q=0}^{Q} \phi_q a_j^q \tag{9.93}$$

Substituting equation (9.92) into equation (9.77), the probability distribution function, which gives the probability of the option ending up in the money, is given as follows:

$$\Pi_t(P_c(S) > K) = \int_K^{\infty} f_t(y) \, dy \approx \sum_{j=0}^{Q} \kappa_j^Q \lambda_j \tag{9.94}$$

where, by using a change of variable $z = (y - c_1)/\sqrt{c_2}$, the terms λ_j are defined as follows:

$$\lambda_j = \frac{1}{\sqrt{2\pi}} c_2^{j/2} \int_{(K-c_1)/\sqrt{c_2}}^{\infty} z^j e^{-z^2/2} \, dz \qquad (9.95)$$

To compute the probability of the option being in the money, we only need to specify an appropriate value for Q and calculate the sets of coefficients κ_j^Q and λ_j with $j = 0, 1, \ldots, Q$. Obtaining κ_j^Q requires computing the coefficients ϕ_q and a_j^q with $q = 0, 1, \ldots, Q$ and $j = 0, 1, \ldots, Q$ as shown in equation (9.93). According to (9.89), (9.91), and (9.95), these coefficients depend on the cumulants of the distribution of the bond price at the expiration date. The cumulants, in turn, have a one-to-one relationship with the moments of the coupon bond price. The next step gives the solutions of κ_j^Q and λ_j for $Q = 7$ as functions of the cumulants and shows how to obtain the cumulants from the moments. And in step 4, we demonstrate how to obtain the moments of the coupon bond price under the simple $A_M(N)$, $A_M(N)+$, and $A_M(N)++$ models. Though the moments, the cumulants, and the coefficients κ_j^Q and λ_j must be computed for each of the $n + 1$ forward measures corresponding to the expiration time S and the n payment times $T_1, T_2, \ldots, T_n$, we suppress the dependence on the specific measures for expositional simplicity. In step 4, we generalize the notation to allow the dependence on the specific forward measures.

Step 3. Relationship between Moments and Cumulants, and Solutions of κ_j^Q and λ_j as Functions of Cumulants   The well-known relationship between cumulants and moments of a probability distribution is given as follows:

$$c_j = \mu_j - \sum_{i=1}^{j-1} \binom{j-1}{i} c_{j-i} \mu_i \qquad (9.96)$$

Using equation (9.96), the cumulants of order less than or equal to 7 can be obtained from the moments of the probability distribution, as follows:

$c_1 = \mu_1$

$c_2 = \mu_2 - \mu_1^2$

$c_3 = \mu_3 - 3\mu_1\mu_2 + 2\mu_1^3$

$c_4 = \mu_4 - 4\mu_1\mu_3 - 3\mu_2^2 + 12\mu_1^2\mu_2 - 6\mu_1^4$

$c_5 = \mu_5 - 5\mu_1\mu_4 - 10\mu_2\mu_3 + 20\mu_1^2\mu_3 + 30\mu_1\mu_2^2 - 60\mu_1^3\mu_2 + 24\mu_1^5$

$$c_6 = \mu_6 - 6\mu_1\mu_5 - 15\mu_2\mu_4 + 30\mu_1^2\mu_4 - 10\mu_3^2 + 120\mu_1\mu_2\mu_3 - 120\mu_1^3\mu_3$$
$$+ 30\mu_2^3 - 270\mu_1^2\mu_2^2 + 360\mu_1^4\mu_2 - 120\mu_1^6$$

$$c_7 = \mu_7 - 7\mu_1\mu_6 - 21\mu_2\mu_5 - 35\mu_3\mu_4 + 140\mu_1\mu_3^2 - 630\mu_1\mu_2^3$$
$$+ 210\mu_1\mu_2\mu_4 - 1260\mu_1^2\mu_2\mu_3 + 42\mu_1^2\mu_5 + 2520\mu_1^3\mu_2^2 - 210\mu_1^3\mu_4$$
$$+ 210\mu_2^2\mu_3 + 840\mu_1^4\mu_3 - 2520\mu_1^5\mu_2 + 720\mu_1^7 \tag{9.97}$$

Step 4 shows how to obtain the moments of the probability distributions under specific forward measures associated with the coupon bond price. The cumulants obtained in equation (9.97) can be used to compute the sets of coefficients κ_j^Q and λ_j with $j = 0, 1, \ldots, Q$. The formulas for these coefficients are obtained according to the procedure described earlier and are given for $Q = 7$ as follows:

$$\kappa_0^7 = 1 + \frac{3c_4}{4!c_2^2} - \frac{15}{c_2^3}\left(\frac{c_6}{6!} + \frac{c_3^2}{2(3!)^2}\right)$$

$$\kappa_1^7 = -\frac{3c_3}{3!c_2^2} + \frac{15c_5}{5!c_2^3} - \frac{105}{c_2^4}\left(\frac{c_7}{7!} + \frac{c_3c_4}{3!4!}\right)$$

$$\kappa_2^7 = -\frac{6c_4}{4!c_2^3} + \frac{45}{c_2^4}\left(\frac{c_6}{6!} + \frac{c_3^2}{2(3!)^2}\right)$$

$$\kappa_3^7 = \frac{c_3}{3!c_2^3} - \frac{10c_5}{5!c_2^4} + \frac{105}{c_2^5}\left(\frac{c_7}{7!} + \frac{c_3c_4}{3!4!}\right)$$

$$\kappa_4^7 = \frac{c_4}{4!c_2^4} - \frac{15}{c_2^5}\left(\frac{c_6}{6!} + \frac{c_3^2}{2(3!)^2}\right) \tag{9.98}$$

$$\kappa_5^7 = \frac{c_5}{5!c_2^5} - \frac{21}{c_2^6}\left(\frac{c_7}{7!} + \frac{c_3c_4}{3!4!}\right)$$

$$\kappa_6^7 = \frac{1}{c_2^6}\left(\frac{c_6}{6!} + \frac{c_3^2}{2(3!)^2}\right)$$

$$\kappa_7^7 = \frac{1}{c_2^7}\left(\frac{c_7}{7!} + \frac{c_3c_4}{3!4!}\right)$$

and

$$\lambda_0 = D$$
$$\lambda_1 = c_2\, d$$
$$\lambda_2 = c_2 D + c_2(K - c_1)\, d$$

$$\lambda_3 = \left(c_2(K - c_1)^2 + 2c_2^2\right) d$$

$$\lambda_4 = 3c_2^2 D + \left(c_2(K - c_1)^3 + 3c_2^2(K - c_1)\right) d$$

$$\lambda_5 = \left(c_2(K - c_1)^4 + 4c_2^2(K - c_1)^2 + 8c_2^3\right) d \qquad (9.99)$$

$$\lambda_6 = 15c_2^3 D + \left(c_2(K - c_1)^5 + 5c_2^2(K - c_1)^3 + 15c_2^3(K - c_1)\right) d$$

$$\lambda_7 = \left(c_2(K - c_1)^6 + 6c_2^2(K - c_1)^4 + 24c_2^3(K - c_1)^2 + 48c_2^4\right) d$$

where

$$D = \mathcal{N}\left[\frac{c_1 - K}{\sqrt{c_2}}\right]$$

$$d = \frac{1}{\sqrt{2\pi c_2}} e^{-\frac{(K - c_1)^2}{2c_2}} \qquad (9.100)$$

and $\mathcal{N}(.)$ gives the cumulative normal distribution function.

Step 4: Solving the Moments of Coupon Bond Price under the Simple $A_M(N)$, $A_M(N)+$ and $A_M(N)++$ Models   As shown in equation (9.75), the price of the option on a coupon bond or a swaption requires the solutions of the following probabilities:

$$\Pi_t^W(P_c(S) > K) \qquad (9.101)$$

under the forward measures associated with $n + 1$ different maturities, given as $W = S, T_1, T_2, \ldots, T_n$. By generalizing the notation for specific forward measures, the probability obtained in equation (9.94) in step 2 can be expressed as follows:

$$\Pi_t^W(P_c(S) > K) = \int_K^\infty f_t^W(y)\, dy \approx \sum_{j=0}^{Q} \kappa_j^{Q,W} \lambda_j^W \qquad (9.102)$$

The moments of the coupon bond price under a given forward measure are defined as follows:

$$\mu_h^W = E_t^W[P_c(S)^h], \quad \text{for } h = 1, 2, \ldots, Q \qquad (9.103)$$

The relationships given in step 2 and step 3 can be made specific to the appropriate forward measure by using the notation μ_h^W instead of μ_h, in equations (9.96) and (9.97) for $h = 1, 2, \ldots, 7$. This allows us to obtain the cumulants under the appropriate forward measure, and the coefficients on the right-hand side of equation (9.102) can be obtained from the cumulants specific to the given forward measure using equations (9.98) and (9.100). Hence, by obtaining the moments under the appropriate forward measure, the probabilities in equation (9.102) can be solved. The rest of the discussion in this step demonstrates how to solve the moments of the coupon bond price μ_h^W corresponding to the given forward measure under the simple $A_M(N)$, $A_M(N)+$, and $A_M(N)++$ models.

The computation of the moments in equation (9.103) requires solving the expectation of different powers of the coupon bond price. Expressing the coupon bond price as the sum of zero-coupon bond prices and raising the coupon bond price to the integer power h gives the moments as follows:

$$\mu_h^W = E_t^W(P_c(S)^h) = E_t^W\left((CF_1 P(S, T_1) + CF_2 P(S, T_2) + \cdots + CF_n P(S, T_n))^h\right)$$

$$= \sum_{l_1, l_2, \ldots, l_h = 1}^{n} E_t^W\left[(CF_{l_1} CF_{l_2} \ldots CF_{l_h})\left(P(S, T_{l_1}) P(S, T_{l_2}) \ldots P(S, T_{l_h})\right)\right]$$

$$(9.104)$$

To solve for the moments of the coupon bond price under the simple $A_M(N)$, $A_M(N)+$, and $A_M(N)++$ models, consider the time S solution of the zero-coupon bond price given in equation (9.31) as follows:

$$P(S, T) = e^{A(U) - \sum_{m=1}^{M} B_m(U) X_m(S) - \sum_{i=1}^{N-M} C_i(U) Y_i(S) - H(S, T)} \tag{9.105}$$

where $U = T - S$ and $A(U)$ where $B_m(U)$, and $C_i(U)$ are as defined in equations (9.34), (9.35), and (9.36), respectively. The term $H(S, T) = \delta U$ under the simple $A_M(N)$ and $A_M(N)+$ models and is given by equation (9.40) under the $A_M(N)++$ model. The initial values of the Gaussian state variables $Y_i(0)$ are equal to zero under the $A_M(N)++$ model.

The hth moment of the distribution of the future coupon bond price under the forward measure associated with maturity W for $W = S, T_1, T_2, \ldots, T_n$ is given using the zero-coupon bond price formula in equation (9.105), as follows:

$$\mu_h^W = E_t^W[P_c(S)^h]$$

$$= \sum_{l_1, l_2, \ldots, l_h = 1}^{n} (CF_{l_1} CF_{l_2} \ldots CF_{l_h}) \exp\left(-\sum_{k=1}^{h} H(S, T_{l_k})\right)$$

$$\times M_h^W(t; l_1, l_2, \ldots, l_h) \tag{9.106}$$

$$= \sum_{l_1=1}^{n} \sum_{l_2=1}^{n} \cdots \sum_{l_h=1}^{n} (CF_{l_1} CF_{l_2} \cdots CF_{l_h}) \exp\left(-\sum_{k=1}^{h} H(S, T_{l_k})\right)$$

$$\times M_h^W(t; l_1, l_2, \ldots, l_h)$$

where

$$M_h^W(t; l_1, l_2, \ldots, l_h) = E_t^W\left(e^{\left(F_A - \sum_{m=1}^{M} F_{Bm} X_m(S) - \sum_{i=1}^{N-M} F_{Ci} Y_i(S)\right)}\right) \tag{9.107}$$

and

$$F_A = \sum_{k=1}^{h} A(U_{l_k})$$

$$F_{Bm} = \sum_{k=1}^{h} B_m(U_{l_k}), \quad \text{for } m = 1, 2, \ldots, M$$

$$F_{Ci} = \sum_{k=1}^{h} C_i(U_{l_k}), \quad \text{for } i = 1, 2, \ldots, N - M \tag{9.108}$$

$$U_{l_k} = T_{l_k} - S$$

By using a change of measure, the expectation in equation (9.107) can be evaluated using the risk-neutral measure, as follows:

$$M_h^W(t; l_1, l_2, \ldots, l_h)$$

$$= \frac{1}{P(t, W)} \tilde{E}_t\left(e^{-\int_t^W r(v)\, dv} e^{\left(F_A - \sum_{m=1}^{M} F_{Bm} X_m(S) - \sum_{i=1}^{N-M} F_{Ci} Y_i(S)\right)}\right)$$

$$= \frac{1}{P(t, W)} \tilde{E}_t\left(e^{-\int_t^S r(v)\, dv} e^{\left(F_A - \sum_{m=1}^{M} F_{Bm} X_m(S) - \sum_{i=1}^{N-M} F_{Ci} Y_i(S)\right)}\right.$$

$$\left. \times \tilde{E}_S\left(e^{-\int_S^W r(v)\, dv}\right)\right) \tag{9.109}$$

$$= \frac{1}{P(t, W)} \tilde{E}_t\left(e^{-\int_t^S r(v)\, dv} e^{\left(F_A - \sum_{m=1}^{M} F_{Bm} X_m(S) - \sum_{i=1}^{N-M} F_{Ci} Y_i(S)\right)} P(S, W)\right)$$

$$= \frac{e^{-H(S, W)}}{P(t, W)} \tilde{E}_t\left(e^{-\int_t^S r(v)\, dv} e^{\left(G_A - \sum_{m=1}^{M} G_{Bm} X_m(S) - \sum_{i=1}^{N-M} G_{Ci} Y_i(S)\right)}\right)$$

where

$$
\begin{aligned}
G_A &= F_A + A(W - S) \\
G_{Bm} &= F_{Bm} + B_m(W - S), \quad \text{for } m = 1, 2, \ldots, M \\
G_{Ci} &= F_{Ci} + C_i(W - S), \quad \text{for } i = 1, 2, \ldots, N - M
\end{aligned}
\tag{9.110}
$$

where solutions of $A(W - S)$, $B_m(W - S)$, and $C_i(W - S)$ are defined in equations (9.34), (9.35), and (9.36), respectively. Using the Feynman-Kac theorem in Chapter 2, the solution of the expectation given in the last equation of (9.109) can be shown to follow the same PDE as followed by the bond price under the simple $A_M(N)$, $A_M(N)+$, and $A_M(N)++$ models, but with a different boundary condition. Hence, following the usual procedure to solve a PDE using Riccati equations, the solution of $M_h^W(t; l_1, l_2, \ldots, l_h)$ is given as follows:

$$
M_h^W(t; l_1, l_2, \ldots, l_h) = \frac{e^{-H(t, W)} e^{\left(A_G^*(s) - \sum_{m=1}^{M} B_{Gm}^*(s) X_m(t) - \sum_{i=1}^{N-M} C_{Gi}^*(s) Y_i(t)\right)}}{P(t, W)}
\tag{9.111}
$$

where $s = S - t$ and solutions of $A_G^*(s)$, $B_{Gm}^*(s)$, and $C_{Gi}^*(s)$ are identical to the solutions of $A_1^*(s)$, $B_{1m}^*(s)$, and $C_{1i}^*(s)$, respectively, obtained in equations (9.64) through (9.68) in the previous section with:

$$
\begin{aligned}
a_1 &= G_A \\
b_{1m} &= G_{Bm}, \quad \text{for } m = 1, 2, \ldots, M \\
c_{1i} &= G_{Ci}, \quad \text{for } i = 1, 2, \ldots, N - M
\end{aligned}
\tag{9.112}
$$

Though the solutions in equations (9.64) through (9.68) were derived for pricing options on zero-coupon bonds using the Fourier inversion method, these solutions also solve the moments of a coupon bond price, which allows the pricing of coupon bond options using the cumulant approximation method.

By substituting the solution of $M_h^W(t; l_1, l_2, \ldots, l_h)$ from equation (9.111) into equation (9.106), the hth moment of the distribution of the future coupon bond price under the forward measure associated with maturity W, for $W = S, T_1, T_2, \ldots, T_n$, can be obtained in closed form. In general, the solution of the hth moment μ_h^W in equation (9.106) requires summing up n^h number of terms, using an h-order summation. Since many of the summation terms differ only in the order of the indices $l_1, l_2, \ldots, l_h$ and have identical values for the expressions inside the summation, it is possible to achieve significant savings in computation time if repeated summing up of the same terms can be avoided. This is especially important when the number of cash flows n and the order of the moment h are both high. Example 9.1 shows how to reduce the number of terms in the summation.

Example 9.1 Consider the third moment (i.e., $h = 3$) of a coupon bond with two cash flows (i.e., $n = 2$), as follows:

$$\mu_3^W = E_t^W(P_c(S)^3) = E_t^W([CF_1 P(S, T_1) + CF_2 P(S, T_2)]^3)$$

$$= \sum_{l_1, l_2, l_3 = 1}^{2} E_t^W([CF_{l_1} CF_{l_2} CF_{l_3}][P(S, T_{l_1})P(S, T_{l_2})P(S, T_{l_3})]) \qquad (9.113)$$

$$= \sum_{l_1=1}^{2} \sum_{l_2=1}^{2} \sum_{l_3=1}^{2} E_t^W([CF_{l_1} CF_{l_2} CF_{l_3}][P(S, T_{l_1})P(S, T_{l_2})P(S, T_{l_3})])$$

The above summation has $2 \times 2 \times 2 = 2^3 = 8$ expectation terms. In general, the summation given in equation (9.104) has n^h expectation terms. Since many of the expectations are identical, with just different ordering of terms inside the expectation operators, combining these terms can make the computation run significantly faster. For example, the eight expectation terms can be reduced to four terms, given as follows:

$$\mu_3^W = E_t^W(P_c(S)^3) = E_t^W([CF_1 P(S, T_1) + CF_2 P(S, T_2)]^3)$$

$$= CF_1^3 E_t^W[P(S, T_1)^3]$$

$$+ 3CF_1^2 CF_2 E_t^W[P(S, T_1)^2 P(S, T_2)] \qquad (9.114)$$

$$+ 3CF_1 CF_2^2 E_t^W[P(S, T_1)P(S, T_2)^2]$$

$$+ CF_2^3 E_t^W[P(S, T_2)^3]$$

In equation (9.113), the eight possible orderings of the summation indices $l_1, l_2,$ and l_3, with $n = 2$, are given as: $(1, 1, 1)$, $(1, 1, 2)$, $(1, 2, 1)$, $(2, 1, 1)$, $(1, 2, 2)$, $(2, 1, 2)$, $(2, 2, 1)$, and $(2, 2, 2)$. By rearranging the eight sets of orderings in ascending order, we get: $(1, 1, 1)$, $(1, 1, 2)$, $(1, 1, 2)$, $(1, 1, 2)$, $(1, 2, 2)$, $(1, 2, 2)$, $(1, 2, 2)$, and $(2, 2, 2)$. The first ordering leads to the term $CF_1^3 E_t^W [P(S, T_1)^3]$. The next three orderings lead to the term $CF_1^2 CF_2 E_t^W[P(S, T_1)^2 P(S, T_2)]$. The next three orderings lead to the term $CF_1 CF_2^2 E_t^W[P(S, T_1) P(S, T_2)^2]$. Finally, the last ordering leads to the term $CF_2^3 E_t^W[P(S, T_2)^3]$, giving the four different expressions in equation (9.114).

In general, the n^h number of expectation terms in equations (9.104) and (9.106) can be reduced to $(n + h - 1)!/[(n - 1)!h!]$ number of terms. In this example, we get $(2 + 3 - 1)!/[(2 - 1)!(3!)]$, or four, terms by combining the same terms out of the original eight terms. The savings by reducing the expectation terms from n^h to $(n + h - 1)!/[(n - 1)!h!]$ can be significant. For example, if $n = 10$ and $h = 5$, then the number of terms reduces from 100,000 to 2,002.

Though the four-step method shown here is mathematically involved, *it does not use a single numerical integral*. Hence, this method is extremely fast in computing the price of a coupon bond option or a swaption, generally solving these in a fraction of a second. The computation proceeds in the reverse direction, with step 4 obtaining the moments of the coupon bond price using equations (9.106) and (9.111), followed by step 3 obtaining the cumulants from the moments using equation (9.97) and the coefficients κ_j^Q and λ_j from the cumulants using equations (9.98) and (9.100), followed by step 2 obtaining the probabilities of the option ending in the money from the coefficients κ_j^Q and λ_j using equation (9.94), and finally step 1 obtaining option prices from the probabilities of the option ending in the money using equations (9.75) and (9.76). All computations are done under $n + 1$ different forward measures for solving the price of an option on a coupon bond with n payments.

CALIBRATION TO INTEREST RATE CAPS DATA

This section evaluates the ability of *simple* preference-free double-plus affine models to price interest rate caps. The data used in our calibration consists of end-of-day prices and Black's implied volatilities of U.S. dollar interest rate caps and swap rates for the period beginning June 1, 2006, until June 30, 2006. Our results, based on the one month of daily data, are quite similar to the results contained in Nawalkha, Beliaeva, and Soto [2007a], which are based on a larger sample period. We consider caps with ten different maturities, ranging from one to ten years, with four strikes of 3, 4, 5, and 6 percent, and quarterly tenors. Since forward LIBOR rates are within the range of 3 to 6 percent in the sample period, our data includes in-the-money (ITM), at-the-money (ATM), and out-of-the-money (OTM) caps. The cap payments are made "in arrears." So, for example, a one-year cap on three-month LIBOR with a strike of 5 percent represents a portfolio of three caplets with quarterly payment dates that occur three months after the caplets expire: at the end of six months, nine months, and one year, respectively. We consider *difference caps* defined as the difference between caps of adjacent maturities with the same strike price for performing daily calibrations. The use of difference caps instead of caps ensures that the information related to caplets comprising the caps is not used repetitively in the optimization process.

TABLE 9.4 Descriptive Statistics of Difference Cap Prices

					Maturity (years)					
	1	2	3	4	5	6	7	8	9	10
Strike Price					Mean					
3%	–	223.67	216.09	212.17	207.70	203.07	196.95	190.29	183.15	175.58
4%	–	134.18	136.83	140.43	142.21	141.97	140.00	136.74	133.03	128.21
5%	–	56.04	68.66	77.90	84.25	88.95	90.32	90.70	89.79	87.98
6%	–	13.48	26.65	37.08	44.26	50.71	53.50	55.26	56.06	55.97
					Standard Deviation					
3%	–	11.55	9.97	8.43	7.13	6.04	5.29	4.71	4.16	3.56
4%	–	11.11	9.04	7.45	6.33	5.15	4.53	4.14	3.71	3.40
5%	–	8.79	7.62	6.36	5.16	4.67	4.09	3.81	3.36	2.92
6%	–	3.26	3.56	3.31	3.30	2.87	2.60	2.46	2.10	1.77

Table 9.4 reports the means and the standard deviations of the difference cap prices during the sample period. The prices are shown in basis points, or cents per $100 face value of the cap. Figure 9.1 plots the Black's implied volatilities of difference caps across strike rate and maturity averaged over the sample period. The graph reveals the existence of a hump around three to five years in the curve of Black's implied volatilities of difference caps for each strike rate. There is also a volatility skew for difference caps for all maturities (difference caps with lower strikes have higher Black implied volatilities) that is more pronounced in shorter contracts.

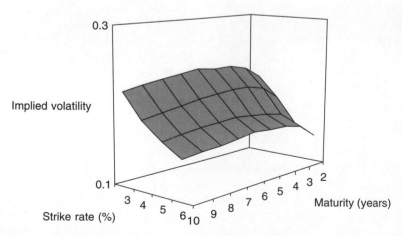

FIGURE 9.1 Average Black Implied Volatilities of Difference Caps

We consider six simple affine models for daily calibration to caps data given as follows:

1. The $A_1(1)++$ model
2. The $A_1^1(1)++$ model
3. The $A_3(3)++$ model
4. The $A_3^3(3)++$ model
5. The $A_0(2)++$ model
6. The $A_0(3)++$ model

The superscript m in the notation $A_M^m(N)++$ represents the number of explosive risk-neutral processes out of M square-root processes (such that $m \leq M \leq N$). Though a few other models were also considered, the six models given here are most illustrative of the main results. The first model is the well-known preference-free double-plus model corresponding to the CIR model (also denoted as the CIR++ model by Brigo and Mercurio [2001], introduced in Chapter 7 of this book) with a stationary risk-neutral process. The second model is the preference-free double-plus model corresponding to the CIR model, but with an explosive risk-neutral process. Recall from Chapter 7 that an explosive risk-neutral square-root process can not only be consistent with a stationary physical process, but it also does not violate the arbitrage-free pricing conditions given by Dybvig, Ingersoll, and Ross [1996] and can arise with a sufficiently high market price of interest rate risk. The third model is the preference-free double-plus model corresponding to the fundamental three-factor CIR model of Jagannathan, Kaplin, and Sun (JKS) [2003]. The fourth model is similar to the third model, except that each of the three square-root processes is explosive under the risk-neutral measure. We also considered $A_3^1(3)++$ and $A_3^2(3)++$ models with one and two explosive risk-neutral processes, respectively, out of the three square-root processes, but their performance was worse than the $A_3^3(3)++$ model. The fifth model is the famous two-factor model of Hull and White [1994b], also known as the G2++ model (see Brigo and Mercurio [2001]). And finally, the sixth model is the three-factor version of the Hull and White model.

The parameters of the models are obtained daily by minimizing the sum of squared percentage pricing errors (SSE), where percentage errors = (market price − model price)/market. Table 9.5 reports the estimated parameter values for each model averaged over the sample period.

The summary performance of the six models is illustrated in Figure 9.2, which gives the root mean square pricing error (RMSE) for each model over the sample period. In general, two-factor and three-factor Gaussian models (i.e., models 5 and 6) outperform the square-root models. Among the

TABLE 9.5 Estimated Parameter Values Averaged Over the Sample Period

	Process 1				Process 2				Process 3			
	Speed	Mean	Volatility	X(0)	Speed	Mean	Volatility	X(0)	Speed	Mean	Volatility	X(0)
Model 1	0.1351	0.1004	0.0336	0.0963	–	–	–	–	–	–	–	–
Model 2	-0.0178	-0.0331	0.0413	0.0378	–	–	–	–	–	–	–	–
Model 3	0.0012	0.0088	0.0393	0.0084	0.0008	0.0133	0.0329	0.0143	0.0000	0.0372	0.0358	0.0374
Model 4	-0.0692	-0.0087	0.0374	0.0087	-0.0012	-0.0448	0.0344	0.0450	-0.0463	-0.0044	0.0015	0.0043

	Process 1		Process 2		Process 3		Correlation		
	Speed	Volatility	Speed	Volatility	Speed	Volatility	2/1	3/1	3/2
Model 5	0.0062	0.0101	0.7512	0.0054	–	–	-0.7563	–	–
Model 6	0.0008	0.0100	0.5051	0.0052	0.3024	0.0053	0.0002	-0.4980	-0.5090

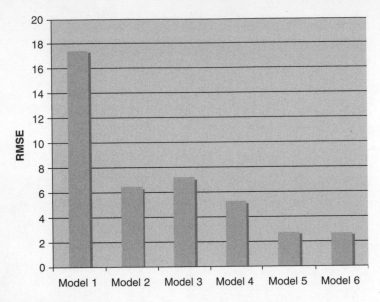

FIGURE 9.2   Root Mean Square Pricing Errors in Pooled Data

square-root models, the explosive models outperform the stationary models, and the three-factor explosive model (i.e., model 4) outperforms the one-factor explosive model (i.e., model 2). Though it is possible that these results are specific to the sample period used, they reveal the importance of considering explosive risk-neutral processes in calibration of square-root models to caps data.

Table 9.6 provides more insight on the patterns of errors across strikes and maturities for the six models considered. This table gives average percentage pricing errors over the sample period for different strikes and maturities. Though the magnitudes of average percentage pricing errors are generally lower than the RMSEs (because errors of opposite signs cancel out), the differences in the magnitudes were very small; and, hence, we report only the former, which is more informative about the direction of mispricing.[12]

The negative errors in Table 9.6 imply that market prices are lower than the model prices, or that the model overprices the difference caps, while positive errors imply the opposite, or that the model underprices the difference caps. The pattern of errors shows that the stationary one-factor square-root model (i.e., model 1) and the stationary three-factor square-root model (i.e., model 3) significantly overprice the short-maturity high-strike difference caps and underprice the long-maturity high-strike difference caps. The magnitudes of errors are lower for difference caps with

TABLE 9.6 Average Percentage Pricing Errors

Model	Strike (%)	Maturity (years)								
		2	3	4	5	6	7	8	9	10
Model 1	3	−0.05	0.45	1.41	2.35	3.62	4.50	5.36	6.14	6.78
	4	−0.59	2.17	4.81	7.11	8.98	10.42	11.54	12.72	13.42
	5	−11.02	0.29	6.69	11.40	15.75	18.02	20.25	21.96	23.35
	6	−47.12	−2.75	12.06	19.08	26.08	28.79	31.32	33.50	35.24
Model 2	3	0.01	0.61	1.76	2.79	3.58	3.74	3.67	3.34	2.71
	4	1.03	4.05	5.48	5.06	4.50	3.29	1.59	−0.13	−2.51
	5	−1.39	6.02	6.73	3.13	2.72	0.23	−2.13	−4.97	−8.12
	6	−16.92	7.62	13.15	11.83	12.69	9.45	6.51	3.55	0.38
Model 3	3	0.01	0.53	1.36	2.15	3.07	3.43	3.69	3.84	3.82
	4	0.36	2.83	4.55	5.17	5.03	4.81	4.26	3.81	2.84
	5	−5.67	2.10	5.29	5.41	5.37	4.62	4.06	3.09	1.89
	6	−29.52	−0.28	7.60	8.55	10.70	9.43	8.51	7.60	6.51
Model 4	3	0.04	0.62	1.44	2.32	3.22	2.90	2.52	1.86	0.75
	4	0.82	3.45	4.99	5.70	5.06	3.48	1.77	0.01	−2.54
	5	−2.43	4.48	6.61	5.68	4.16	1.93	−0.20	−2.91	−6.01
	6	−17.02	5.65	10.36	7.67	7.08	4.70	1.64	−1.69	−5.18
Model 5	3	0.04	0.38	0.68	0.69	0.89	0.66	0.41	0.07	−0.39
	4	0.54	2.11	2.53	2.49	2.09	1.38	0.44	−0.29	−1.48
	5	−2.18	1.75	1.90	1.59	1.89	0.48	−0.53	−1.80	−3.23
	6	−5.54	5.42	5.62	3.22	3.81	0.64	−1.77	−3.95	−6.24
Model 6	3	−0.49	0.26	0.68	0.79	1.09	0.89	0.63	0.26	−0.27
	4	−1.43	1.68	2.52	2.80	2.53	1.87	0.89	0.06	−1.26
	5	0.59	0.48	1.87	2.33	2.79	1.44	0.30	−1.18	−2.86
	6	−3.26	2.15	5.61	4.64	5.42	2.33	−0.37	−2.92	−5.64

lower strike prices under both of these models. Though these two models are *preference-free double-plus* models, the large magnitudes of pricing errors are consistent with the poor performance of the fundamental square-root models corresponding to these two models (see JKS [2003] for the empirical performance of the fundamental square-root models).

The magnitudes of pricing errors of the explosive one-factor square-root model (i.e., model 2) and the explosive three-factor square-root model (i.e., model 4) are significantly lower than those of the corresponding stationary models (i.e., model 1 and model 3, respectively), with the three-factor model outperforming the one-factor model. Finally, the two-factor and the three-factor Gaussian models (i.e., models 5 and 6, respectively) have the lowest magnitudes of pricing errors with similar performance. Though there is some evidence of higher magnitudes of errors for higher strikes, overall the volatility skew is much smaller under the Gaussian models than under the square-root models. The good pricing performance of the Gaussian models is also confirmed by an overall RMSE of only about 2 percent for these models illustrated earlier in Figure 9.2.

The results of models 5 and 6 (with RMSEs of a little above 2 percent) and model 4 (with RMSE of a little above 5 percent) indicate that the pricing using two- and three-factor affine models is comparable to that of using the LIBOR market model (LMM) with time-homogeneous volatilities.[13] Though some versions of the LMM can be fitted perfectly to interest rate cap prices (see Rebonato [2002] and Chapter 12 of this book), doing this requires using *time-inhomogeneous* forward rate volatilities. As argued in Chapter 3 (last section) and Chapter 12 of this book, the use of time-inhomogeneous volatilities leads to *smoothing* (defined as the use of arbitrary time-dependent variables to fit prices, while ignoring important economic relationships). Though some degree of smoothing is present even in preference-free double-plus affine models and all HJM (Heath, Jarrow, and Morton) models, this problem is much more serious when volatilities evolve in a time-inhomogeneous manner.

Overall, our results are consistent with previous research on the calibration of affine models to interest rate cap prices. We find that multifactor square-root models with stationary processes cannot fit cap prices (consistent with the results of JKS [2003]); but two- and three-factor Gaussian models do well in fitting cap prices, including the volatility skew. Surprisingly, however, we find that single- and multifactor square-root models with *explosive* risk-neutral processes perform significantly better than the corresponding models with stationary risk-neutral processes over the sample period considered. Though the results using the explosive square root models are still not as good as those using the Gaussian models, more research is needed to evaluate these models vis-à-vis stationary square-root models.

An investigation of the stability of parameters revealed that the coefficients of variation (defined as the ratios of the standard deviations of the parameters to their means over the sample period) for virtually all parameters were less than 0.2 under most of the models, implying that the parameters were quite stable over the sample period. The only exception was model 3, which uses three stationary square-root processes. This model had highly unstable speeds of mean reversions corresponding to all three factors. Interestingly, model 4, with three explosive square-root processes, had stable parameters, including stable speeds of mean reversion.

In our ongoing research (see Nawalkha, Beliaeva, and Soto [2007a]), we find that preference-free double-plus multifactor affine models can be made to fit the volatility skew (or the smile) better by extending these models with stochastic volatility and exponential jumps. A basic outline of these extensions is given in Appendix 9.2. Given the analytical tractability of the *preference-free double-plus* affine models, which utilize fast computational methods (such as the Fourier inversion method for pricing interest rate caps, the cumulant expansion method for pricing swaptions, and trees for pricing American options) more research is needed to assess the usefulness of these models for pricing interest rate derivatives.

UNSPANNED STOCHASTIC VOLATILITY

Many researchers have recently investigated the joint dynamics of bond prices and plain vanilla derivatives such as caps and swaptions. Using a principal component analysis, Collin-Dufresne and Goldstein (CDG) [2002] and Heidari and Wu [2003] discovered factors that affect the implied volatilities of caps and swaptions without affecting bond prices. The caps and swaptions cannot be replicated using any number of bonds, and hence, are not spanned by the underlying bonds. Similar difficulty in explaining the joint dynamics of bond prices and plain vanilla derivatives is found by Longstaff, Santa-Clara, and Schwartz [2002] and Li and Zhao [2006] in the context of LIBOR/string models and quadratic models, respectively. These papers contradict the predictions of the standard term structure theories, under which bonds must span all fixed income derivatives. CDG label this feature "unspanned stochastic volatility" (USV). In subsequent papers, Casassus, Collin-Dufresne, and Goldstein (CCDG) [2005] and Collin-Dufresne, Goldstein, and Jones (CDGJ) [2004] give two-, three-, and four-factor fundamental ATSMs that allow the USV feature, such that bonds are spanned by lesser number of factors than are fixed income derivatives. The empirical work of Han [2004], Jarrow, Li, and Zhao [2004], and Rebonato [2002] also supports the existence of USV, but in the context of a time-inhomogeneous preference-free paradigm.

CDGJ give another motivation for USV based upon the joint role played by interest rate volatilities in explaining the cross section of bond prices and time series of bond returns. CDGJ demonstrate that traditional affine models, such as the $A_1(3)$ model, generates a time series for the volatility state variable that is strongly negatively correlated with a generalized autoregressive conditional heteroscedasticity (GARCH) estimate of the volatility process. Apparently, the volatility state variable fits the cross section of bond prices at the expense of the time series of the true volatility process. CDGJ then investigate the fundamental $A_1(3)$ and $A_1(4)$ affine models that exhibit USV and find that only the $A_1(4)$ USV model can generate both realistic volatility estimates and a good cross-sectional fit with bond prices.

However, other recent econometric investigations have questioned the existence of USV in the context of affine short rate models. Thompson

[2004], using a new class of specification tests, detects problems with the unrestricted affine model at the short end of the yield curve. In contrast to CDGJ, he demonstrates that the USV restriction is rejected. Fan, Gupta, and Ritchken (FGR) [2003] find that methodological problems lead to the appearance of USV, while Bikbov and Chernov [2005] find that measurement errors create the appearance of USV in the original study of CDG [2002]. FGR question CDG's methodology of using linear regressions of straddle returns on swap rates for assessing whether underlying bonds can span fixed income derivatives. Using swaption straddles, they show low explanatory power of the regressions of straddle returns on the swap rate changes. However, FGR postulate that the low R^2 values in the linear regression should be *expected*, due to the highly convex payoff structure of straddles, which are nonlinear functions of yields. Further, despite low explanatory power of the regressions, FGR find that the returns on delta and gamma hedged bond portfolios can hedge 80 percent of the returns on swaption straddles. The findings of FGR suggest that USV factors are not relevant, at least in the pricing and hedging of swaptions, and raise concern about the linear regression approach of CDG for assessing the presence of USV.

Bikbov and Chernov [2005] consider affine term structure models with three volatility specifications: constant volatility, stochastic volatility, and USV. They use prices of Eurodollar futures and options and conduct a comprehensive statistical and economic analysis. They find that swaps data and futures data cannot distinguish between constant volatility, stochastic volatility, and USV models. However, based on options data, the stochastic volatility models outperform both the Gaussian models and the USV models; and the pricing errors from stochastic volatility models are smaller than those from the USV models by up to six times. Most important, Bikbov and Chernov discover that the weak linear relationship between option-implied volatility and yields found by CDG [2002] can be easily explained by small measurement errors that can be attributed to the market microstructure features. Based on the results of Bikbov and Chernov, and the results in Figure 9.2 and Table 9.6, our ongoing research considers the $A_1(3)$-EJ++ model (see Appendix 9.2), which allows stochastic volatility and jumps and nests the $A_0(2)$++ model of Hull and White [1994b].

Unlike the case of affine term structure models, in which stochastic volatility is different from USV, the forward rate models (e.g., HJM models, LIBOR market models, etc.) lead to stochastic volatility, which is, by construction, not spanned by the underlying bond prices. Hence, stochastic volatility is equivalent to USV under the forward rate models. To distinguish stochastic volatility specifications under the affine models from those under the forward rate models, we refer to the stochastic volatility specifications under the latter as USV specifications. Various USV-based forward rate models have been derived in fixed income literature (e.g., see Rebonato [2002], Andersen and Brotherton-Ratcliffe [2005], Han [2004], Jarrow, Li, and Zhao (JLZ) [2007], and the HJM-based USV models given in CDG [2002]). Since these models belong to the time-inhomogeneous preference-free paradigm, they already fit the initial bond prices. These models cannot be estimated econometrically, as they do not impose any restriction on the cross section of bond prices. The risk-neutral parameters of the forward rate–based USV models are generally inverted from the cross section of fixed income derivative prices.

Though the idea of USV term structure modeling has merit in the context of forward rate models, its success in explaining the joint dynamics of bonds and fixed-income derivatives has be to yet confirmed properly under this paradigm. For example, JLZ find that multifactor USV models can explain the implied volatility surface of caps quite well, while Han finds that both caps and swaptions can be priced consistently using the USV models. However, neither JLZ nor Han demonstrate the hedging effectiveness of their USV models using the method of FGR. Hence, whether the good pricing performance of these models is due to simply using more parameters or more USV factors is not clear. More research is needed to assess whether forward rate models, which display USV naturally, can outperform the stochastic volatility models in the affine family (such as the $A_1(3)$-EJ + + model given in Appendix 9.2, and the stochastic volatility models in Bikbov and Chernov [2005]), in terms of *hedging effectiveness* by constructing delta- and gamma-netural bond portfolios to hedge returns on caps and swaptions straddles (as in FGR[2003]). An interesting area for future research is the empirical investigation of single-plus and double-plus extensions of the original USV affine models of CDG [2002]. Since the critique of Bikbov and Chernov [2005] applies only to the fundamental USV affine models, the preference-free extensions of these models, such as the double-plus USV affine models of Casassus, Collin-Dufresne, and Goldstein [2005] may be good alternatives to the traditional USV affine models.

MULTIFACTOR ATSMs FOR PRICING CREDIT DERIVATIVES

The past decade has witnessed an explosive growth in the notional amounts of credit derivatives instruments, especially credit default swaps (CDS). The reduced-form approach is the preferred choice for valuing not only credit default swaps but also many other types of credit derivatives, including spread options, total return swaps, credit sensitive notes, collateralized debt obligations, and the like. As explained in Chapter 3, the reduced-form approach makes available the entire analytical apparatus of continuous-time term structure modeling for valuing credit derivatives. This approach requires exogenous modeling of the default intensity process, which together with assumptions about recovery and a given model for the short rate leads to analytical solutions to risky bond prices for wide classes of affine and quadratic term structure models. Though this is the subject matter of book three in the trilogy, this chapter demonstrates how the fundamental and preference-free ATSMs presented in this book are naturally suited for valuing credit derivatives using the reduced-form approach.

We demonstrate the power of the reduced-form approach by using the *simple* $A_M(N)$, $A_M(N)+$, and $A_M(N)++$ models derived earlier in this chapter. This approach is, however, quite general and can be used with all maximal ATSMs. The credit default swaps models of LMN and Pan and Singleton [2005] assume one-factor square-root processes for both the short rate and the default intensity and are nested as the $A_2(2)$ model using our simple ATSM framework.

We illustrate the reduced-form models using both the "recovery of market value" assumption and the "recovery of face value" assumption, described in Chapter 3. The risky zero-coupon bond prices are assumed to be driven by interest and credit risks only; and so these prices may be different from those implied by the risky coupon bond prices of corporate bonds, which may be exposed to tax-related and liquidity factors.

Simple Reduced-Form ATSMs under the RMV Assumption

Consider the *risky* short rate $R(t)$ defined in equation (3.106) in Chapter 3 as follows:

$$R(t) = r(t) + s(t) \qquad (9.115)$$

where $r(t)$ is the default-free short rate and $s(t)$ is the spread over the short rate due to the risk of default. The short spread equals the *mean loss rate* under the RMV assumption as shown in equation (3.104) in Chapter 3:

$$s(t) = \tilde{\lambda}(t)\tilde{L}_M \qquad (9.116)$$

where $\tilde{\lambda}(t)$ is the risk-neutral default intensity, which means that $\tilde{\lambda}(t)\,dt$ is the risk-neutral probability of default over the interval t to $t + dt$, given no default has occurred until time t, and $\tilde{L}_M$ is the risk-neutral loss rate in the event of default. Under the RMV assumption, the price of a \$1 face-value risky zero-coupon bond is given as follows (see equation (3.107) in Chapter 3):

$$D(t, T) = \tilde{E}_t \left(\frac{1}{e^{\int_t^T (r(v)+s(v))\,dv}} \right) = \tilde{E}_t \left(\frac{1}{e^{\int_t^T R(v)\,dv}} \right) \qquad (9.117)$$

The value of the risky zero-coupon bond that defaults at time t is given as a fraction $(1 - \tilde{L}_M)$ of its value just before default, or equal to $(1 - \tilde{L}_M)D(t, T)$.

The Simple $A_M(N)$ Model under the RMV Assumption We assume N state variables composed of M variables X_m (for $m = 1, 2, \ldots, M$), which follow square-root processes, and $N - M$ variables Y_i (for $i = 1, 2, \ldots, N - M$), which follow Gaussian processes. Though the Gaussian processes are correlated among themselves, they are uncorrelated with the square-root processes. The short rate and the short spread are defined as follows:

$$r(t) = \delta_r + \sum_{m=1}^{M} a_m X_m(t) + \sum_{i=1}^{N-M} c_i Y_i(t) \tag{9.118}$$

$$s(t) = \delta_s + \sum_{m=1}^{M} b_m X_m(t) + \sum_{i=1}^{N-M} d_i Y_i(t) \tag{9.119}$$

where δ_r, δ_s, a_m, b_m, c_i, and d_i (for all $m = 1, 2, \ldots, M$, and all $i = 1, 2, \ldots, N - M$) are constants greater than or equal to zero.

The M square-root state variables are given under the risk-neutral measure as follows:

$$dX_m(t) = \tilde{\alpha}_m(\tilde{\theta}_m - X_m(t)) \, dt + \sigma_m \sqrt{X_m(t)} \, d\tilde{Z}_m(t),$$
$$\text{for } m = 1, 2, \ldots, M \tag{9.120}$$

where $d\tilde{Z}_m(t)$ are independent Wiener processes for all $m = 1, 2, \ldots, M$. The $N - M$ Gaussian state variables are given under the risk-neutral measure as follows:

$$dY_i(t) = -\tilde{k}_i Y_i(t) \, dt + v_i \, d\tilde{W}_i(t), \quad \text{for all } i = 1, 2, \ldots, N - M \tag{9.121}$$

where $d\tilde{W}_i(t) \, d\tilde{W}_j(t) = \rho_{ij} \, dt$, for all $i, j = 1, 2, \ldots, N - M$, and where $d\tilde{W}_i(t) \, d\tilde{Z}_m(t) = 0$, for all $i = 1, 2, \ldots, N - M$, and $m = 1, 2, \ldots, M$. By definition, $\rho_{ij} = \rho_{ji}$ and $\rho_{ii} = 1$.

The default-free bond price $P(t, T)$ is obtained in the same manner as under the simple $A_M(N)$ models given in the previous section, with a slight modification to account for the constants a_m and c_i in the definition of the short rate in equation (9.118). The solution is given as follows:

$$P(t, T) = e^{A(\tau) - \sum_{m=1}^{M} a_m(B_m(\tau)X_m(t)) - \sum_{i=1}^{N-M} c_i(C_i(\tau)Y_i(t)) - H(t,T)} \tag{9.122}$$

where

$$H(t, T) = \int_t^T \delta_r \, dv = \delta_r \tau \tag{9.123}$$

$$A(\tau) = \sum_{m=1}^{M} \frac{2\tilde{\alpha}_m \tilde{\theta}_m}{\sigma_m^2} \ln \left[\frac{2\beta_m e^{\frac{1}{2}(\beta_m + \tilde{\alpha}_m)\tau}}{(\beta_m + \tilde{\alpha}_m)(e^{\beta_m \tau} - 1) + 2\beta_m} \right]$$

$$+ \frac{1}{2} \sum_{i=1}^{N-M} \sum_{j=1}^{N-M} \frac{c_i c_j v_i v_j \rho_{ij}}{\tilde{k}_i \tilde{k}_j} \left(\tau - C_i(\tau) - C_j(\tau) + \left(\frac{1 - e^{-(\tilde{k}_i + \tilde{k}_j)\tau}}{\tilde{k}_i + \tilde{k}_j} \right) \right) \tag{9.124}$$

$$B_m(\tau) = \frac{2(e^{\beta_m \tau} - 1)}{(\beta_m + \tilde{\alpha}_m)(e^{\beta_m \tau} - 1) + 2\beta_m}, \quad \text{for } m = 1, 2, \ldots, M \tag{9.125}$$

$$C_i(\tau) = \frac{1 - e^{-\tilde{k}_i \tau}}{\tilde{k}_i}, \quad \text{for } i = 1, 2, \ldots, N - M \tag{9.126}$$

and

$$\beta_m = \sqrt{\tilde{\alpha}_m^2 + 2 a_m \sigma_m^2}$$

The solution given in equation (9.122) is similar to the solution of bond price given in equation (9.31), except for the new parameters a_m and c_i contained in equation (9.16). To obtain the solution of the risky zero-coupon bond price $D(t, T)$, the risky short rate can be given by adding equations (9.118) and (9.119) as follows:

$$R(t) = r(t) + s(t)$$

$$= \delta_R + \sum_{m=1}^{M} (a_m + b_m) X_m(t) + \sum_{i=1}^{N-M} (c_i + d_i) Y_i(t) \tag{9.127}$$

where $\delta_R = \delta_r + \delta_s$. The risky bond price $D(t, T)$ is obtained as a discounted expectation using the risky short rate $R(t)$ in equation (9.117) in the same manner that the default-free bond price $P(t, T)$ is obtained using the short rate $r(t)$. Hence, by comparing the definition of the risky short rate $R(t)$ in equation (9.127) with the definition of the short rate $r(t)$ in equation (9.118), the solution of the risky zero-coupon bond can be given as follows:

$$D(t, T) = e^{\overline{A}(\tau) - \sum_{m=1}^{M} (a_m + b_m)\overline{B}_m(\tau) X_m(t) - \sum_{i=1}^{N-M} (c_i + d_i)\overline{C}_i(\tau) Y_i(t) - \overline{H}(t, T)} \tag{9.128}$$

where the solutions of $D(t, T), \overline{H}(t, T), \overline{A}(\tau), \overline{B}_m(\tau)$, and $\overline{C}_i(\tau)$ are identical to the corresponding solutions of $P(t, T), H(t, T), A(\tau), B_m(\tau)$, and $C_i(\tau)$, given in equations (9.122), (9.123), (9.124), (9.125), and (9.126), respectively, except that:

1. a_m is replaced with $(a_m + b_m)$, for all $m = 1, 2, \ldots, M$,
2. c_i is replaced with $(c_i + d_i)$, for all $i = 1, 2, \ldots, N - M$, and
3. δ_r is replaced with $\delta_R = \delta_r + \delta_s$.

The risky zero-coupon bond price is obtained by a *simple inspection* of the terms of the corresponding solution of the default-free bond price given in equation (9.122), demonstrating the power of the reduced-form approach.

Since value-additivity holds under the reduced-form approach (in contrast to the structural approach of Merton [1974]), the price of a risky coupon bond can be obtained as follows: Consider a risky coupon bond with coupons C occurring at time T_i $(i = 1, 2, \ldots, n)$ and face value F occurring at time T_n. This bond can be valued using equation (9.128) as follows:

$$D_{Coup}(t) = \sum_{i=1}^{n} C \times D(t, T_i) + F \times D(t, T_n) \qquad (9.129)$$

In general, since the simple $A_M(N)$ model allows $N - M$ Gaussian processes with arbitrary correlations among themselves, this model can potentially allow negative correlation between the short rate and the short spread. A potential criticism of this approach is that it allows the possibility of a negative short rate and a negative short spread. The possibility of a negative short spread implies that *the risk-neutral default intensity may become negative*, leading to riskless arbitrage. However, if the probabilities of the occurrence of a negative short rate and a negative short spread can be kept sufficiently small, then this theoretical limitation may not be very limiting for most practical applications. For example, relatively larger positive values of the speeds of mean-reversion coefficients $\tilde{k}_i$, lower values of the volatility coefficients v_i, and negative correlations among Gaussian processes may allow capturing realistic correlations between the default-free and risky term structures of interest rates without seriously violating the riskless arbitrage condition. Since the simple $A_M(N)$ models are frequently used for modeling the default-free interest rates (see Table 9.3), the reduced-form extension given here allows using all the nested multifactor models given under this framework for valuing risky bonds. The simple $A_M(N)$ models also nest the models of LMN and Pan and Singleton, which assume one-factor square-root processes for both the short rate and the default intensity. However, these models are obtained using the recovery of face value (RFV) assumption, which is considered later in this chapter.

The Simple $A_M(N)+$ and $A_M(N)++$ Models under the RMV Assumption Being a fundamental model, the simple $A_M(N)$ model requires the estimates of the physical parameters together with MPRs to obtain the empirical estimates of the risk-neutral parameters. The MPRs can be given using completely affine, essentially affine, and semiaffine specifications as under the default-free term structure models. Duffie and Singleton [1999] give a detailed discussion of estimating the physical and the risk-neutral parameters under affine specifications. This section gives the preference-free simple $A_M(N)+$ and $A_M(N)++$ reduced-form models that obtain the estimates of the risk-neutral parameters directly by using the cross sections of prices of default-free bonds, risky bonds, and credit derivatives, such as credit default swaps. The preference-free simple $A_M(N)+$ and $A_M(N)++$ models are consistent with general non linear MPRs, which do not have to be explicitly estimated. The analytical solutions of the prices of risky bonds and credit derivatives under the simple time-homogeneous preference-free $A_M(N)+$ models are identical to the corresponding solutions under the fundamental $A_M(N)$ models, except that the estimates of the risk-neutral parameters may be different under the two approaches, as the latter models impose restrictive forms on the MPRs.

Since conditional variances do not depend upon the state variables $Y_i(t)$ and since the exact fit with the default-free and risky initial bond prices at time 0 are guaranteed by construction under the simple time-inhomogeneous preference-free $A_M(N)++$ models, the time 0 values of $Y(t)$ can be assumed to be zero (without loss of generality) under these models, or:

$$Y_i(0) = 0, \quad \text{for all } i = 1, 2, \ldots, N - M \tag{9.130}$$

We assume that initial zero-coupon bond prices of default-free bonds and risky bonds are given exogenously as $P(0, T)$ and $D(0, T)$, respectively. The default-free bond price under the simple $A_M(N)++$ models given in equation (9.122) can be calibrated to the initially given bond price $P(0, T)$ by replacing the constant δ_r in equation (9.118) with $\delta_r(t)$ and by replacing $H(t, T)$ in equation (9.123) with its new definition, as follows:

$$\delta_r(t) = f(0, t) - \sum_{m=1}^{M} a_m \left(X_m(0) + \tilde{\alpha}_m B_m(t)(\tilde{\theta}_m - X_m(0)) - \frac{1}{2} a_m \sigma_m^2 B_m^2(t) X_m(0) \right)$$

$$+ \frac{1}{2} \sum_{i=1}^{N-M} \sum_{j=1}^{N-M} c_i c_j v_i v_j \rho_{ij} C_i(t) C_j(t) \tag{9.131}$$

and

$$H(t, T) = \int_t^T \delta_r(v) \, dv = H(0, T) - H(0, t)$$

$$= A(T) - A(t) - \sum_{m=1}^M a_m X_m(0)[B_m(T) - B_m(t)] \qquad (9.132)$$

$$- \ln P(0, T) + \ln P(0, t)$$

where $f(0, t) = -\partial \ln P(0, t)/\partial t$ is the time 0 instantaneous forward rate for term t, and the solutions of $A(.)$, $B_m(.)$, and $C_i(.)$ are given in equations (9.124), (9.125), and (9.126), respectively.

The risky bond price under the simple $A_M(N)++$ models given in equation (9.128) can be calibrated to the initially given risky bond price $D(0, T)$ by replacing the constant δ_R in equation (9.127) with $\delta_R(t)$ and by replacing $\overline{H}(t, T)$ in equation (9.128) with its new definition, as follows:

$$\delta_R(t) = f_D(0, t) + \frac{1}{2} \sum_{i=1}^{N-M} \sum_{j=1}^{N-M} (c_i + d_i)(c_j + d_j) v_i v_j \rho_{ij} \overline{C}_i(t) \overline{C}_j(t)$$

$$- \sum_{m=1}^M (a_m + b_m) \left(X_m(0) + \tilde{\alpha}_m \overline{B}_m(t)(\tilde{\theta}_m - X_m(0)) \right. \qquad (9.133)$$

$$\left. - \frac{1}{2}(a_m + b_m)\sigma_m^2 \overline{B}_m^2(t) X_m(0) \right)$$

and

$$\overline{H}(t, T) = \int_t^T \delta_R(v) \, dv = \overline{H}(0, T) - \overline{H}(0, t)$$

$$= \overline{A}(T) - \overline{A}(t) - \sum_{m=1}^M (a_m + b_m) X_m(0)[\overline{B}_m(T) - \overline{B}_m(t)] \qquad (9.134)$$

$$- \ln D(0, T) + \ln D(0, t)$$

where $f_D(0, t) = -\partial \ln D(0, t)/\partial t$ is the time 0 instantaneous risky forward rate for term t.

Duffie and Singleton [1999] show how to generalize their reduced-form approach to the HJM [1992] forward rate models. The main advantage of the HJM forward rate models is that they allow exact calibration to both the initial default-free bond prices and initial risky bond prices. However, the HJM forward rate models are typically non-Markovian and do not allow closed-form solutions. In contrast, the simple $A_M(N)++$ models given in this section are Markovian and allow closed-form solutions for risky bond prices. Also, given the existence of analytical solutions under the simple $A_M(N)++$ models, even Monte Carlo simulations can be run faster under these models to value some classes of credit derivatives. Finally, for credit derivatives with American features, low-dimensional simple $A_M(N)++$ models allow construction of efficient trees, similar to those demonstrated for two-factor models earlier in this chapter.

Example 9.2 The specifications allowed under the $A_M(N)$, $A_M(N)+$, and $A_M(N)++$ models can be demonstrated by a simple example. Consider the following specification of the short rate process and the short spread process under the simple $A_3(5)+$ model:

$$r(t) = \delta_r + X_1(t) + Y_1(t) + Y_2(t) \tag{9.135}$$

$$s(t) = \delta_R - \delta_r + X_2(t) + Y_3(t) \tag{9.136}$$

This example is nested in the $A_M(N)+$ models, with $N = 5$, $M = 3$, $a_1 = 1$, $a_2 = 0$, $b_1 = 0$, $b_2 = 1$, $c_1 = 1$, $c_2 = 1$, $c_3 = 0$, $d_1 = 0$, $d_2 = 0$, and $d_3 = 1$. The five-factor time-homogeneous preference-free ATSM given in equations (9.135) and (9.136) assumes that the short rate is driven by three factors (consisting of one square-root and two Gaussian factors) and the short spread is driven by two factors (one square-root and one Gaussian factor). The square-root factors X_m are uncorrelated with each other and with the Gaussian factors Y_i. The three Gaussian factors may have negative correlations in order to allow a humped volatility curve for default-free forward rates, and matching of the correlation between the short rate and the spread. To ensure that this model has reasonable properties, the estimates of risk-neutral parameters must imply very small probabilities of obtaining a negative short rate and a negative short spread.

The risk-neutral parameters can be obtained using nonlinear optimization under the simple $A_M(N)+$ model, using K days of cross-sectional data on default-free bond prices, risky bond prices, and credit derivatives. Potentially, one could also use the prices of interest rate derivatives, such as caps and swaptions (since formulas for options have been derived under the simple $A_M(N)$, $A_M(N)+$, and $A_M(N)++$ models in the previous section) in addition to credit derivatives, if consistency is desired among the pricing of these securities by a trading firm. Replacing δ_r with $\delta_r(t)$ defined in equation (9.131) and replacing δ_R with $\delta_R(t)$ defined in equation (9.133) gives the simple $A_M(N)++$ model corresponding to the simple $A_N(M)+$ model. The simple $A_M(N)++$ model can be used if exact calibration is desired with initial default-free bond prices and initial risky bond prices.

Pricing Credit Options under the RMV Assumption Due to their analytical tractability, the reduced-form ATSMs are used frequently for valuing credit derivatives. This section considers the valuation of credit spread options under the RMV assumption, while the next section considers the valuation of credit default swaps under the RFV assumption. We consider an American credit spread put option expiring at time S written on a risky bond maturing at time T. The option gives a right to sell the risky bond at a spread K_t over the default-free yield at any time until the expiration date S, where the spread K_t may be constant or change deterministically with time. Let $D(S, y_D(S))$ be the time S price of the *nondefaulted* risky bond with $y_D(S)$ representing the risky bond's yield at time S. Similarly, let $P(S, y_P(S))$ define the price of an equivalent default-free bond, with $y_P(S)$ representing the default-free bond's yield at time S. The terminal payoff of the credit spread put option at time S, assuming default has not occurred, is given as:

$$Max[D(S, y_P(S) + K_S) - D(S, y_D(S)), 0] \tag{9.137}$$

The terminal payoff is positive if $y_D(S) > y_P(S) + K_S$, since a bond is inversely related to its own yield. The nonlinearity of payoff does not allow it to be discounted using the risky short rate $R(t)$. Yet, it is not very uncommon in the literature to discount the option payoff over a small interval Δt, using the risky short rate as follows:

$$P_{CSP}^d(S - \Delta t) = \frac{\tilde{E}_{S-\Delta t}(Max[D(S, y_P(S) + K_S) - D(S, y_D(S)), 0])}{e^{R(S-\Delta t)\Delta t}} \tag{9.138}$$

where $P_{CSP}^d(S - \Delta t)$ is the discounted value of the option at time $S - \Delta t$. Though this discounting valuation method is similar to how risky bonds are valued under the RMV assumption, it is incorrect to apply this method to value options *whose payoffs are nonlinear functions of risky bond prices* (see Duffie and Singleton [1999]). The valuation of credit options requires separating the combined effect of risk-neutral loss rate and risk-neutral default intensity, which appear as one term in equation (9.116) and are a part of the risky short rate $R(S - \Delta t)$ in equation (9.138). The theoretically correct discounted value of the option is given as follows:

$$
\begin{aligned}
P_{CSP}^d&(S - \Delta t) \\
&= \frac{\tilde{E}_{S-\Delta t}(Max[D(S, y_P(S) + K_S) - D(S, y_D(S)), 0])}{e^{r(S-\Delta t)\Delta t}}(1 - \tilde{\lambda}(S - \Delta t)\Delta t) \\
&\quad + \frac{\tilde{E}_{S-\Delta t}(Max[D(S, y_P(S) + K_S) - (1 - \tilde{L}_M)D(S, y_D(S)), 0])}{e^{r(S-\Delta t)\Delta t}} \\
&\quad \times (\tilde{\lambda}(S - \Delta t)\Delta t)
\end{aligned}
\tag{9.139}
$$

Equation (9.139) considers the option payoff separately when the bond defaults versus when the bond does not default. The risk-neutral expected value of the option payoff is computed by taking a probability-weighted average of the payoffs, *discounted by the default-free short rate.* Under the RMV assumption, the defaulted bond price is always given as the $(1 - \tilde{L}_M)$ fraction of the nondefaulted bond price. Hence, the effects of the risk-neutral loss rate $\tilde{L}_M$ and the risk-neutral default intensity $\tilde{\lambda}(S - \Delta t)$ are captured separately in equation (9.139), and not as a combined product through the definition of the risky short rate as in the case of valuing risky bonds in equation (9.117). Since option payoffs are nonlinear in bond prices, equations (9.138) and (9.139) do not give the same discounted value for the option price. For example, if $y_D(S) = y_P(S) + K_S$, then the discounted value of the option in equation (9.138) is zero but it is positive using equation (9.139). Since the option is valuable in the event of default $(\tilde{L}_M < 1)$, considering the option values separately for the default and no-default cases gives a positive option value. In general, the price of an out-of-the-money credit spread put would increase if $\tilde{L}_M$ is increased and $\tilde{\lambda}(S - \Delta t)$ is decreased, even though such a change does not affect the underlying risky bond value under the RMV assumption if the product $\tilde{L}_M \tilde{\lambda}$ $(S - \Delta t)$ remains constant.[14]

Due to the American feature, the discounted value of the credit spread put option will be compared to its intrinsic value at time $S - \Delta t$ given as follows:

$$
P^i_{CSP}(S - \Delta t) =
\begin{cases}
Max[D(S - \Delta t, y_P(S - \Delta t) + K_{S-\Delta t}) \\
-D(S - \Delta t, y_D(S - \Delta t)), 0] \\
\text{when no default occurs} \\
\text{and} \\
Max[D(S - \Delta t, y_P(S - \Delta t) + K_{S-\Delta t}) \\
-(1 - \tilde{L}_M)D(S - \Delta t, y_D(S - \Delta t)), 0] \\
\text{when default occurs}
\end{cases}
\tag{9.140}
$$

The price of the credit spread put option at time $S - \Delta t$ is given as the maximum of its discounted value by equation (9.139) and its intrinsic value given by equation (9.140) as follows:

$$
P_{CSP}(S - \Delta t) = Max(P^i_{CSP}(S - \Delta t), P^d_{CSP}(S - \Delta t))
\tag{9.141}
$$

Hence, the option price would depend on whether the underlying risky bond experiences default at time $S - \Delta t$. The intrinsic value is more likely to exceed the discounted value in case of a default and less likely to do so when there is no default. The discounting process discussed here is used recursively to price the credit spread put option at times $S - 2\Delta t$ and $S - 3\Delta t$ until reaching time zero.

Pricing American credit spread put options using the simple ATSMs with many factors is generally difficult since no analytical solutions exist. However, for two- to three-factor ATSMs, trees such as those demonstrated under the two-factor ATSMs can be used. For example, trees under the simple $A_0(2)$, $A_1(2)$, and $A_2(2)$ reduced-form models and their preference-free extensions can be constructed with slight modifications to these trees for default-free short rate, shown earlier in this chapter. As a specific case, consider the simple $A_2(2)+$ reduced-form model with $a_1 = 1$, $a_2 = 0$, $b_1 = 0$, $b_2 = 1$, which gives the following definitions to the short rate and the short spread:

$$
\begin{aligned}
r(t) &= \delta_r + X_1(t) \\
s(t) &= \delta_s + X_2(t) = \delta_R - \delta_r + X_2(t)
\end{aligned}
\tag{9.142}
$$

where $\delta_R = \delta_r + \delta_s$. Assuming that the risk-neutral loss rate $\tilde{L}_M$ is constant, the risk-neutral default intensity can be given using equation (9.116) as follows:

$$
\tilde{\lambda}(t) = \frac{1}{\tilde{L}_M} s(t) = \frac{1}{\tilde{L}_M}(\delta_R - \delta_r + X_2(t))
\tag{9.143}
$$

Using the square-root processes for $X_1(t)$ and $X_2(t)$, a two-factor tree can be generated as under the $A_2(2)$ model given in canonical/Ay form in Chapter 8. Using this tree, the values of $r(t)$, $s(t)$, and $\tilde{\lambda}(t)$ can be obtained at all nodes using equations (9.142) and (9.143). The price of the American credit spread put option can be obtained using a backward recursion to get the discounted risk-neutral expectation by appropriate specifications of the terminal boundary values and the intrinsic payoff values at all node combinations of the two-factor tree, as specified in equations (9.139), (9.140), and (9.141).

The valuation of a European credit spread put may not be necessarily simpler than the valuation of an American credit spread put. The chief difficulty here is the nature of assumptions to be made in case of a default occurrence before the option expiration date. If the bond continues to trade after the default event, then one must know the post-default risk-neutral distributional properties of the bond return, as the distribution is no longer determined by the process for the default intensity. The situation is simpler if contractually the European credit spread option expires at the date of default, in which case the previous method can still be used without evaluating an early exercise feature when the bond does not default and evaluating the optimality of exercise in the event of default.

The two-factor affine model with two square-root processes has an inherent limitation of restricting the instantaneous correlation between the two state variables to zero in order to maintain the affine structure. By sacrificing the affine property, this limitation can be overcome by constructing two-factor trees with a negative correlation between the square-root processes. Such a model would allow the short spread to be negatively correlated with the short rate, consistent with the empirical data. Since the nonaffine specification does not allow an analytical solution, the delta functions $\delta_R(t)$ and $\delta_r(t)$ required to fit the model to initial risky and default-free bond prices are solved using an iterative method shown in Chapter 8. The correlation between the two trees can be modeled in the same manner as shown for the $A_{0y}(2)$ model earlier in this chapter.

This numerical method is not limited to valuing credit spread options. For example, risky bonds with embedded options, such as callable and putable bonds, can be handled in the same manner by simply specifying the terminal and intrinsic payoffs under default and no-default cases. In book three of the trilogy, we demonstrate how to price other credit derivatives under the RMV assumption.

Simple Reduced-Form ATSMs under the RFV Assumption

Credit default swaps are priced more naturally under the RFV assumption, as shown by LMN and Pan and Singleton. The main difference between the RMV assumption and the RFV assumption is that under the former, the risky bond's defaulted value at any given time equals $(1 - \tilde{L}_M)$ fraction of its nondefaulted value before the default, while under the latter, the risky bond's value upon default equals $(1 - \tilde{L}_F)$ fraction of the face value of the bond. This section demonstrates how to price risky bonds and credit default swaps under the RFV assumption using the simple $A_M(N)$ and $A_M(N)+$ reduced-form models.

The Simple $A_M(N)$ Models for Pricing Risky Bonds under the RFV Assumption
Consider a risky coupon bond with coupons C occurring at time T_i ($i = 1, 2, \ldots, n$), and face value F occurring at time T_n. This bond can be valued as the risk-neutral expectation of the sum of two sets of cash flows:

1. the cash flows if the bond never defaults, and
2. the cash flows if the bond defaults.

As shown in Chapter 3, the time t risk-neutral probability of survival of the bond until time T is given as follows:

$$Survival\ Probability = e^{-\int_t^T \tilde{\lambda}(v)\,dv} \qquad (9.144)$$

where $\tilde{\lambda}(t)$ is the risk-neutral default intensity. The first set of cash flows can be valued by computing risk-neutral expectations of the cash flows using the survival probability as follows:

$$\tilde{E}_t \left(\sum_{i=1}^{n} \left(e^{-\int_t^{T_i} \tilde{\lambda}(v)\,dv} \frac{C}{e^{\int_t^{T_i} r(v)\,dv}} \right) + e^{-\int_t^{T_n} \tilde{\lambda}(v)\,dv} \frac{F}{e^{\int_t^{T_n} r(v)\,dv}} \right) \qquad (9.145)$$

To value the second set of cash flows, we use the RFV assumption that a bondholder recovers a fraction $1 - \tilde{L}_F$ of the face value of the bond at the *default time u*. However, computing this requires the time t risk-neutral probability density of default time, which is the time t probability that default will occur in the infinitesimal interval u to $u + du$, where $u \in [t, T_n]$. This density must equal the time t risk-neutral probability of survival until time u multiplied by the time u probability of default in the next instantaneous interval du. Hence, this density is given as follows:

$$Probability\ Density\ of\ Default\ Time = \left(e^{-\int_t^u \tilde{\lambda}(v)\,dv} \right) \tilde{\lambda}(u)\,du \qquad (9.146)$$

Note that this probability density is a random variable at time t. The discounted risk-neutral expectation of the second set of cash flows (or the recovery cash flow in the event of default) can be given as follows:

$$\tilde{E}_t \left(\int_t^{T_n} \left(\frac{F(1 - \tilde{L}_F)e^{-\int_t^u \tilde{\lambda}(v)\,dv}\tilde{\lambda}(u)}{e^{\int_t^u r(v)\,dv}} \right) du \right)$$
$$= F(1 - \tilde{L}_F)\tilde{E}_t \left(\int_t^{T_n} \tilde{\lambda}(u)e^{-\int_t^u (r(v)+\tilde{\lambda}(v))\,dv}\,du \right) \qquad (9.147)$$

Adding the risk-neutral expected values of the two sets of cash flows in equations (9.145) and (9.147) and simplifying, we get the price of the risky coupon bond as follows:

$$D_{Coup}(t) = \tilde{E}_t \left(\sum_{i=1}^{n} Ce^{-\int_t^{T_i} (r(v)+\tilde{\lambda}(v))\,dv} + Fe^{-\int_t^{T_n} (r(v)+\tilde{\lambda}(v))\,dv} \right)$$
$$+ F(1 - \tilde{L}_F)\tilde{E}_t \left(\int_t^{T_n} \tilde{\lambda}(u)e^{-\int_t^u (r(v)+\tilde{\lambda}(v))\,dv}\,du \right) \qquad (9.148)$$

Equation (9.148) can be rewritten as follows:

$$D_{Coup}(t) = \sum_{i=1}^{n} C \times D_F(t,T_i) + F \times D_F(t,T_n) + F(1 - \tilde{L}_F) \int_t^{T_n} G(t,u)\, du$$

(9.149)

where

$$D_F(t,T) = \tilde{E}_t \left(e^{-\int_t^T (r(v)+\tilde{\lambda}(v))\, dv} \right)$$

$$G(t,T) = \tilde{E}_t \left(\tilde{\lambda}(T) e^{-\int_t^T (r(v)+\tilde{\lambda}(v))\, dv} \right)$$

(9.150)

LMN obtain a formula for a \$1 face-value coupon bond under the RFV assumption with a continuously paid annualized coupon rate c. Using LMN's continuous-coupon framework with a \$1 face value, the formula in equation (9.149) simplifies to:

$$D_{Coup}(t) = c \int_t^{T_n} D_F(t,u)\, du + D_F(t,T_n) + (1 - \tilde{L}_F) \int_t^{T_n} G(t,u)\, du \quad (9.151)$$

The valuation of coupon bonds under the RFV assumption requires computing the risk-neutral expectations to solve $D_F(t,T)$ and $G(t,T)$. The numerical integrals given in equations (9.149) and (9.151) can be evaluated easily with analytical solutions of $D_F(t,T)$ and $G(t,T)$. The solutions of $D_F(t,T)$ and $G(t,T)$ are given in the following two steps.

Step 1: Solution of $D_F(t, T)$ Let the short rate and the risk-neutral default intensity be defined under the simple $A_M(N)$ model using the RFV assumption, as follows:

$$r(t) = \delta_r + \sum_{m=1}^{M} a_m X_m(t) + \sum_{i=1}^{N-M} c_i Y_i(t)$$

(9.152)

$$\tilde{\lambda}(t) = \delta_\lambda + \sum_{m=1}^{M} b_m X_m(t) + \sum_{i=1}^{N-M} d_i Y_i(t)$$

(9.153)

where variables X_m (for $m = 1, 2, \ldots, M$) follow square-root processes and variables Y_i (for $i = 1, 2, \ldots, N - M$) follow Gaussian processes. Though the Gaussian processes are correlated among themselves, they are uncorrelated with the square-root processes. The risk-neutral stochastic processes of X_m and Y_i are defined as in equations (9.120) and (9.121).

A simple mathematical trick allows obtaining the solution of $D_F(t,T)$ from the solution of the risky zero-coupon bond price $D(t,T)$ under the RMV assumption given earlier. Assuming that the risk-neutral loss rate $\tilde{L}_M$ is 100 percent, or 1, under the RMV assumption and that $\delta_\lambda = \delta_s$ implies that $s(t)$ defined in equation (9.119) is identical to $\tilde{\lambda}(t)$ defined in equation (9.153). Under these assumptions, $D_F(t, T)$ given in equation (9.150) is identical to the definition of $D(t, T)$ in equation (9.117). Hence, the solution of $D_F(t, T)$ is given by $D(t, T)$ in equation (9.128), with $\delta_\lambda = \delta_s$.

Step 2: Solution of G(t,T)   The solution of $G(t, T)$ is based upon the results in Duffie, Pan, and Singleton [2000] and Chacko and Das [2002]. Under mild regularity conditions, the solution of $G(t, T)$ in equation (9.150) can be alternatively expressed as follows:

$$G(t, T) = \tilde{E}_t \left(\tilde{\lambda}(T) e^{-\int_t^T (r(v) + \tilde{\lambda}(v)) dv} \right) = \frac{\partial}{\partial \phi} \left(\eta(t, T, \phi) \right)_{\phi=0} \qquad (9.154)$$

where

$$\eta(t, T, \phi) = \tilde{E}_t \left(e^{-\int_t^T (r(v) + \tilde{\lambda}(v)) dv} e^{\phi \tilde{\lambda}(T)} \right) \qquad (9.155)$$

The expectation in equation (9.155) is solved in Appendix 9.1 at the end of this chapter and is given as follows:

$$\eta(t, T, \phi) = e^{A^\dagger(\tau) - \sum_{m=1}^{M} (a_m + b_m) B_m^\dagger(\tau) X_m(t) - \sum_{i=1}^{N-M} (c_i + d_i) C_i^\dagger(\tau) Y_i(t) - H^\dagger(t, T)} \qquad (9.156)$$

where

$$H^\dagger(t, T) = \int_t^T (\delta_r + \delta_\lambda) \, dv = (\delta_r + \delta_\lambda) \tau \qquad (9.157)$$

$$A^\dagger(\tau) = \phi \delta_\lambda + \frac{1}{2} \sum_{i=1}^{N-M} \sum_{j=1}^{N-M} \frac{(c_i + d_i)(c_j + d_j) v_i v_j \rho_{ij}}{\tilde{k}_i \tilde{k}_j} \left(\begin{array}{c} \tau - q_i C_i^\dagger(\tau) - q_j C_j^\dagger(\tau) \\ + q_i q_j \left(\dfrac{1 - e^{-(\tilde{k}_i + \tilde{k}_j)\tau}}{\tilde{k}_i + \tilde{k}_j} \right) \end{array} \right)$$

$$\qquad - 2 \sum_{m=1}^{M} \frac{\tilde{\alpha}_m \tilde{\theta}_m}{\sigma_m^2} \left(\beta_{3m} \tau + \ln \left(\frac{1 - \beta_{4m} e^{\beta_{1m}\tau}}{1 - \beta_{4m}} \right) \right) \qquad (9.158)$$

$$B_m^\dagger(\tau) = \frac{2}{(a_m + b_m)\sigma_m^2} \left(\frac{\beta_{2m} \beta_{4m} e^{\beta_{1m}\tau} - \beta_{3m}}{\beta_{4m} e^{\beta_{1m}\tau} - 1} \right), \quad \text{for } m = 1, 2, \ldots, M \qquad (9.159)$$

$$C_i^\dagger(\tau) = \frac{1 - q_i e^{-\tilde{k}_i \tau}}{\tilde{k}_i}, \qquad \text{for } i = 1, 2, \ldots, N - M \tag{9.160}$$

$$q_i = 1 + \phi \tilde{k}_i \frac{d_i}{c_i + d_i}, \qquad \text{for } i = 1, 2, \ldots, N - M \tag{9.161}$$

and

$$\beta_{1m} = \sqrt{\tilde{\alpha}_m^2 + 2(a_m + b_m)\sigma_m^2}, \qquad \beta_{2m} = \frac{-\tilde{\alpha}_m + \beta_{1m}}{2}, \qquad \beta_{3m} = \frac{-\tilde{\alpha}_m - \beta_{1m}}{2},$$

$$\text{and} \quad \beta_{4m} = \frac{-\tilde{\alpha}_m - \beta_{1m} + \phi b_m \sigma_m^2}{-\tilde{\alpha}_m + \beta_{1m} + \phi b_m \sigma_m^2}, \qquad \text{for } m = 1, 2, \ldots, M \tag{9.162}$$

Though the formula for $\eta(t, T, \phi)$ given in equation (9.156) looks formidable, it uses basic algebra and can be programmed easily. The solution of $G(t, T)$ in equation (9.154) can be numerically evaluated as follows:

$$G(t, T) = \frac{\partial}{\partial \phi}(\eta(t, T, \phi))_{\phi=0} = \lim_{h \to 0} \left(\frac{\eta(t, T, h) - \eta(t, T, 0)}{h} \right) \tag{9.163}$$

Hence, solving $\eta(t, T, \phi)$ twice with $\phi = h$ and $\phi = 0$ for a very small value of h (e.g., $h = 0.000001$) gives the solution of $G(t, T)$ in equation (9.163).

The formula for risky coupon bond price given in equations (9.149) and (9.150) generalizes the $A_2(2)$ models of Pan and Singleton and LMN, respectively, to the entire class of simple $A_M(N)$ models, using the RFV assumption. The $A_2(2)$ models by these authors have three potential limitations. First, the default-free interest rates (and the default intensity) are driven by a *single* square-root process. As shown by Dai and Singleton [2000] and Jagannathan, Kaplin, and Sun [2003], at least three factors are needed to explain the behavior of swap rates. In fact, it is virtually impossible to fit the shape of the default-free term structure using only one factor. Second, the default intensity process may be influenced by more than one factor, even though one dominant factor may explain most of the variation (see Pan and Singleton). Finally, some correlation between default-free rates and default intensity may be required, even though LMN do not find this to be relevant in their preliminary investigation. The simple $A_M(N)$ models offer a variety of alternatives to deal with these limitations in a multifactor setting without sacrificing the analytical tractability of the models of LMN and Pan and Singleton that are essential for practical applications.

The Simple $A_M(N)$ Models for Pricing Credit Default Swaps under the RFV Assumption Much of the rapid growth in the global credit derivatives market, from a notional amount of only $180 billion in 1997 to more than $3.5 trillion in 2003 to more than $20 trillion by the end of 2006, has come from the single-name credit default swaps (CDS, hereafter) based on risky corporate bonds and sovereign debt. The CDS is not only one of the most successful financial innovations of the past decade but it has also spawned a second generation of derivatives that use it as the valuation benchmark. In general, there is a well-defined relationship between the CDS spreads and the bond yield spreads. Researchers using the swap rates as the benchmark for risk-free rates have shown CDS spreads to be priced consistently with the corresponding bond yield spreads (see Blanco, Brennan, and Marsh [2003], Houweling and Vorst [2005], and Hull, Predescu, and White [2003]). Though Longstaff, Mithal, and Neis (LMN) [2003] find that the risky yield curve implied by the CDS spreads is generally *lower* than the risky yield curve implied by risky coupon bond prices, the results of LMN seem to be driven by using Treasury rates instead of swap rates for computing the bond yield spreads. Due to various reasons such as lower tax rates and institutional demand for U.S. Treasuries, the Treasury rates are typically lower than the swap rates. Blanco, Brennan, and Marsh [2003] and Hull, Predescu, and White [2003] also find that the CDS market leads the bond market and that most of the price discovery occurs first in the CDS market.

Consider a single-name credit default swap that requires the protection buyer to pay p $(p = n/(T_n - t))$ number of premiums each year until the bond defaults for a maximum number of n periods over $T_n - t$ years. Let the time t value of the annualized CDS premium (or spread) be given as $CDS(t)$ for every \$1 of the face value of the bond. The premium leg of the credit default swap makes payments only in those states in which the underlying bond does not default. Hence, the present value of the premium leg is given by the following risk-neutral expectation:

Present Value of Premium Leg

$$= \tilde{E}_t \left(\sum_{i=1}^{n} (CDS(t)/p)e^{-\int_t^{t+i/p} (r(v)+\tilde{\lambda}(v))\, dv} \right) \qquad (9.164)$$

The protection seller must pay the difference between the face value of the bond and the market value of the bond when the bond defaults. This loss is exogenously specified as $\tilde{L}_F$ fraction of the face value of the bond under the RFV assumption. Using the probability density of default time given in equation (9.146), the present value of the protection leg for every \$1 of face value of the bond is given by the following risk-neutral expectation:

Present Value of Protection Leg

$$= \tilde{L}_F \tilde{E}_t \left(\int_t^{T_n} \tilde{\lambda}(u) e^{-\int_t^u (r(v) + \tilde{\lambda}(v)) \, dv} \, du \right) \tag{9.165}$$

Equating the present value of the premium leg to the present value of the protection leg solves the CDS spread as follows:

$$CDS(t) = \frac{p \tilde{L}_F \tilde{E}_t \left(\int_t^{T_n} \tilde{\lambda}(u) e^{-\int_t^u (r(v) + \tilde{\lambda}(v)) \, dv} \, du \right)}{\tilde{E}_t \left(\sum_{i=1}^{n} e^{-\int_t^{t+i/p} (r(v) + \tilde{\lambda}(v)) \, dv} \right)} \tag{9.166}$$

Using the definitions of $D_F(t, T)$ and $G(t, T)$ in equation (9.150), the CDS spread can be given as follows:

$$CDS(t) = \frac{p \tilde{L}_F \int_t^{T_n} G(t, u) \, du}{\sum_{i=1}^{n} D_F(t, t + i/p)} \tag{9.167}$$

Substituting the solutions of $D_F(t, T)$ and $G(t, T)$ obtained in step 1 and step 2 of the previous section, equation (9.167) gives an analytical solution to the CDS spread under the large class of simple $A_M(N)$ models.

Pan and Singleton use formula (9.167) to price the CDS on sovereign debt issues of Mexico, Turkey, and Russia. Their two-factor square-root model is nested within the simple $A_M(N)$ models, with $M = 2, N = 2, a_1 = 1$, $a_2 = 0$, $b_1 = 0$, and $b_2 = 1$. Pan and Singleton find the RFV assumption very useful, as it allows identification of the implied risk-neutral loss rate $\tilde{L}_F$ separately from the risk-neutral default intensity $\tilde{\lambda}(t)$. Recall that under the RMV assumption, a separate identification of these variables is not possible, as they both always appear as a product that defines the short spread $s(t)$ in equation (9.116). Pan and Singleton find that, based upon the historical experience of sovereign defaults, the value of physical loss rate L_F is close to 0.75 and that the risk-neutral loss rate $\tilde{L}_F$ implied from CDS spreads is only 0.25, implying a significant risk premium associated with the loss rate. Pan and Singleton also find that although the risk-neutral default intensity $\tilde{\lambda}(t)$ follows a stationary process under the physical measure, it generally follows an explosive process (i.e., negative speed of mean reversion) under the risk-neutral measure, implying another significant size risk premium related to the risk-neutral default intensity.

LMN [2003] specify their model using a continuously paid CDS premium (or spread). Under continuous payment specification, the present value of the premium leg in equation (9.164) becomes:

Present Value of Premium Leg

$$= \tilde{E}_t \left(\int_t^{T_n} CDS(t) e^{-\int_t^u \left(r(v) + \tilde{\lambda}(v) \right) dv} \, du \right) \tag{9.168}$$

and the annualized CDS spread in equation (9.167) becomes:

$$CDS(t) = \frac{\tilde{L}_F \tilde{E}_t \left(\int_t^{T_n} \tilde{\lambda}(u) e^{-\int_t^u \left(r(v) + \tilde{\lambda}(v) \right) dv} \, du \right)}{\tilde{E}_t \left(\int_t^{T_n} e^{-\int_t^u \left(r(v) + \tilde{\lambda}(v) \right) dv} \, du \right)}$$

$$= \frac{\tilde{L}_F \int_t^{T_n} G(t, u) \, du}{\int_t^{T_n} D_F(t, u) \, du} \tag{9.169}$$

where the analytical solutions of $D_F(t, T)$ and $G(t, T)$ are given in step 1 and step 2, respectively, in the previous section.

The Simple $A_M(N)+$ Models for Pricing Risky Bonds and Credit Default Swaps under the RFV Assumption   The formulas of corporate bond prices and CDS spreads under the simple time-homogeneous preference-free $A_M(N)+$ models are identical to the corresponding formulas under the simple fundamental $A_M(N)$ models given in the previous section, except that the empirical estimates of the risk-neutral parameters may be different under these models since the latter models impose restrictive forms on MPRs. The LMN model is nested in the simple time-homogeneous preference-free $A_M(N)+$ models (with $M = 2$, $N = 2$, $a_1 = 1$, $a_2 = 0$, $b_1 = 0$, $b_2 = 1$), as the risk-neutral parameters under this model are implied directly from the cross sections of CDS spreads and default-free bond prices, without requiring the estimation of MPRs (which may be of general nonlinear forms). On the other hand, the Pan and Singleton square-root model is nested in the simple fundamental $A_M(N)$ models (with $M = 2$, $N = 2$, $a_1 = 1$, $a_2 = 0$, $b_1 = 0$, $b_2 = 1$), as both the risk-neutral parameters and the physical parameters are jointly estimated using an essentially affine form of MPRs related to the risk-neutral default intensity process under this model.

The simple *time-inhomogeneous* preference-free $A_M(N)++$ models cannot be obtained under the RFV assumption since the risk-neutral loss rate $\tilde{L}_F$ is valid only under a specific coupon size and specific maturity. The initial prices of risky *zero-coupon* bonds cannot be inverted from the initial prices of risky coupon bonds, which may have a different value of $\tilde{L}_F$ for different sizes of coupons and maturities. The time-inhomogeneous $A_M(N)++$ models may not be required, however, if increasing the number of factors allows good fitting with the prices of default-free bonds, risky bonds, and credit default swaps using the time-homogeneous $A_M(N)+$ models.

APPENDIX 9.1: THE SOLUTION OF $\eta(t, T, \phi)$ FOR CDS PRICING USING SIMPLE $A_M(N)$ MODELS UNDER THE RFV ASSUMPTION

By substituting equations (9.152) and (9.153), equation (9.155) can be rewritten as follows:

$$
\begin{aligned}
&\eta(t, T, \phi) \\
&= \tilde{E}_t \left(\begin{aligned} &\exp\left(-\int_t^T \left((\delta_r + \delta_\lambda) + \sum_{m=1}^{M}(a_m + b_m)X_m(v) + \sum_{i=1}^{N-M}(c_i + d_i)Y_i(v)\right)dv\right) \\ &\times \exp\left(\phi\left(\delta_\lambda + \sum_{m=1}^{M} b_m X_m(T) + \sum_{i=1}^{N-M} d_i Y_i(T)\right)\right) \end{aligned} \right)
\end{aligned}
$$

$$(9.170)$$

Using the Feynman-Kac theorem given in Chapter 2, the PDE corresponding to the risk-neutral expectation in equation (9.170) is given as follows:

$$
\begin{aligned}
&\frac{\partial \eta}{\partial t} + \sum_{m=1}^{M} \frac{\partial \eta}{\partial X_m}(\tilde{\alpha}_m(\tilde{\theta}_m - X_m(t))) + \frac{1}{2}\sum_{m=1}^{M} \frac{\partial^2 \eta}{\partial X_m^2}\sigma_m^2 X_m(t) \\
&- \sum_{i=1}^{N-M} \frac{\partial \eta}{\partial Y_i}\tilde{k}_i Y_i(t) + \frac{1}{2}\sum_{i=1}^{N-M}\sum_{j=1}^{N-M} \frac{\partial^2 \eta}{\partial Y_i \partial Y_j}v_i v_j \rho_{ij} \\
&= \left((\delta_r + \delta_\lambda) + \sum_{m=1}^{M}(a_m + b_m)X_m(t) + \sum_{i=1}^{N-M}(c_i + d_i)Y_i(t)\right)\eta(t, T, \phi)
\end{aligned}
$$

$$(9.171)$$

subject to the boundary condition:

$$
\eta(T, T, \phi) = \exp\left(\phi\left(\delta_\lambda + \sum_{m=1}^{M} b_m X_m(T) + \sum_{i=1}^{N-M} d_i Y_i(T)\right)\right) \tag{9.172}
$$

Consider the following solution for $\eta(t, T, \phi)$:

$$
\eta(t, T, \phi) = e^{A^\dagger(\tau) - \sum_{m=1}^{M}(a_m + b_m)B_m^\dagger(\tau)X_m(t) - \sum_{i=1}^{N-M}(c_i + d_i)C_i^\dagger(\tau)Y_i(t) - H^\dagger(t,T)} \tag{9.173}
$$

where

$$H^\dagger(t, T) = \int_t^T (\delta_r + \delta_\lambda) \, dv = (\delta_r + \delta_\lambda)\tau \qquad (9.174)$$

subject to the following boundary conditions

$$A^\dagger(0) = \phi\delta_\lambda$$

$$B_m^\dagger(0) = \frac{-\phi b_m}{a_m + b_m}, \quad \text{for all } m = 1, 2, \ldots, M \qquad (9.175)$$

$$C_i^\dagger(0) = \frac{-\phi d_i}{c_i + d_i}, \quad \text{for all } i = 1, 2, \ldots, N - M$$

and $\tau = T - t$. Taking the partial derivatives of $\eta(t, T, \phi)$ in equation (9.173), substituting these in equation (9.171), and using a change of variable $\tau = T - t$, we get the following $N + 1$ ODEs:

$$\frac{\partial A^\dagger(\tau)}{\partial \tau} = -\sum_{m=1}^M \tilde{\alpha}_m \tilde{\theta}_m (a_m + b_m) B_m^\dagger(\tau)$$

$$+ \frac{1}{2} \sum_{i=1}^{N-M} \sum_{j=1}^{N-M} C_i^\dagger(\tau) C_j^\dagger(\tau)(c_i + d_i)(c_j + d_j)v_i v_j \rho_{ij} \qquad (9.176)$$

$$\frac{\partial B_m^\dagger(\tau)}{\partial \tau} = 1 - \tilde{\alpha}_m B_m^\dagger(\tau) - \frac{1}{2}(a_m + b_m)\sigma_m^2 (B_m^\dagger(\tau))^2, \quad \text{for } m = 1, 2, \ldots, M$$

$$\frac{\partial C_i^\dagger(\tau)}{\partial \tau} = 1 - \tilde{k}_i C_i^\dagger(\tau), \text{for } i = 1, 2, \ldots, N - M$$

subject to the boundary conditions given in equation (9.175). The solutions of $A^\dagger(\tau)$, $B_m^\dagger(\tau)$, and $C_i^\dagger(\tau)$ are given in equations (9.158), (9.159), and (9.160), respectively.

APPENDIX 9.2: STOCHASTIC VOLATILITY JUMP-BASED MIXED-SIGN $A_N(N)$-*EJ*++ MODEL AND $A_1(3)$-*EJ*++ MODEL

This appendix gives two extensions of affine models considered in Nawalkha Beliaeva, and Soto (NBS) [2007a], which allow stochastic volatility and jumps. The first model extends multifactor CIR models to allow both positive and negative exponential jumps. The second model extends multifactor

Gaussian models to allow stochastic volatility and positive and negative exponential jumps.

The Mixed-Sign $A_N(N)$-EJ++ Model

Let $A_N(N)$-EJ++ denote the preference-free double-plus affine model with N square-root processes, each of which is extended with an exponential jump. The mixed-sign $A_N(N)$-EJ++ model defines the short rate as follows:

$$r(t) = \delta(t) + I_1 Y_1(t) + I_2 Y_2(t) + \cdots + I_N Y_N(t) \tag{9.177}$$

where $I_1, I_2, \ldots, I_N$ are sign variables that can take values of either 1 or -1 and where $\delta(t)$ is the deterministic term that allows calibration to the initial zero-coupon bond prices. Each of the state variables $Y_m(t)$ follows a square-root process extended with an exponential jump, given under the risk-neutral measure as follows:

$$dY_m(t) = \tilde{\alpha}_m(\tilde{\theta}_m - Y_m(t))\,dt + \sigma_m \sqrt{Y_m(t)}\,d\tilde{Z}_m(t) + J_m\,dN(\tilde{\lambda}_m) \tag{9.178}$$

where the Wiener processes $\tilde{Z}_m(t)$, jump-size variables J_m, and the Poisson processes $N(\tilde{\lambda}_m)$ are all independently distributed for all $m = 1, 2, \ldots, N$. The jump-size variables J_m are exponentially distributed with positive means $1/\eta_m$, and the risk-neutral intensities of the Poisson processes are given as $\tilde{\lambda}_m$ for $m = 1, 2, \ldots, N$.

The mixed-sign $A_N(N)$-EJ++ model is similar to the multifactor CIR model in that conditional volatilities are state variable dependent. However, unlike the multifactor CIR model, the mixed-sign $A_N(N)$-EJ++ model allows state variables to have both positive and negative signs in the definition of the short rate (using the sign variables $I_1, I_2, \ldots, I_N$ in equation (9.177)) and allows jumps in the short rate in both positive and negative directions. Negative jumps cannot be modeled using the traditional multifactor CIR model extended with exponential jumps.

The state variables, which enter with a negative sign in equation (9.177), allow the possibility of a negative short rate in the future. However, similar to the multifactor Gaussian models, the probability of reaching a negative short rate may be low with realistic values of the parameters. For example, assume $r(t) = \delta(t) + Y_1(t) - Y_2(t)$, with stationary risk-neutral processes for both state variables. Assuming (1) $\delta(0)$ has a high positive value; (2) the initial value of $Y_1(0)$ is greater than the initial value of $Y_2(0)$; (3) the risk-neutral long-term mean of $Y_1(t)$ is high and that of $Y_2(t)$ is low; and (4) the risk-neutral intensity and the jump size associated with the state variable $Y_2(t)$ are not very high; then the probability of negative short rate would be low. The analytical solutions of the bond price and quasi-analytical solutions of caps and swaptions prices can be derived under the multifactor generalization of the corresponding solutions under the exponential jump-extended CIR++ model given in Chapter 6, with a slight modification to allow for mixed signs. NBS [2007a] investigate the probability density of the short rate and the empirical performance of the mixed-sign $A_N(N)$-EJ++ models with two and three state variables (i.e., $N = 2$ and 3).

The $A_1(3)$-*EJ*++ Model

The excellent performance of the $A_0(2)$++ model (i.e., the Hull and White [1994b] two-factor model) for pricing interest rate caps (see the performance of model 5 in Figure 9.2 and in Table 9.6) implies that any generalization of this model should at least contain this model as a nested model. The standard method to generalize the $A_0(2)$++ model is to consider models in the affine subfamily $A_0(N)$++ with higher values of N (e.g., $N = 3$, 4). However, the performance of model 6 in both Figure 9.2 and Table 9.6 shows that the $A_0(3)$++ model does not lead to significant improvement in the pricing performance over the $A_0(2)$++ model.

Since there is some evidence of volatility skew in Table 9.6, NBS [2007a] consider a generalization of the $A_0(2)$++ model that is nested in the $A_1(3)$ subfamily to allow stochastic volatility and that is extended to allow jumps. Specifically, NBS propose the $A_1(3)$-EJ++ model under which the short rate is defined as:

$$r(t) = \delta(t) + Y(t) \tag{9.179}$$

where $\delta(t)$ is the deterministic term that allows calibration to the initial zero-coupon bond prices. The state variable processes are given under the risk-neutral measure as follows:

$$dv(t) = \tilde{\alpha}_v(\tilde{m}_v - v(t))\, dt + \eta\sqrt{v(t)}\, d\tilde{Z}_1(t)$$

$$d\theta(t) = -\tilde{\alpha}_\theta\theta(t)\, dt + \zeta\, d\tilde{Z}_2(t) + \sigma_{\theta r}\sqrt{\delta_r + v(t)}\, d\tilde{Z}_3(t) \tag{9.180}$$

$$dY(t) = \tilde{\alpha}(\theta(t) - Y(t))\, dt + \sigma_{rv}\eta\sqrt{v(t)}\, d\tilde{Z}_1(t) + \sigma_{r\theta}\zeta\, d\tilde{Z}_2(t) + \sqrt{\delta_r + v(t)}\, d\tilde{Z}_3(t)$$
$$+ J_u\, dN(\tilde{\lambda}_u) - J_d\, dN(\tilde{\lambda}_d)$$

where the jump-size variables J_u and J_d are distributed exponentially with means $1/\eta_u$ and $1/\eta_d$, respectively, and the Poisson processes $N(\tilde{\lambda}_u)$ and $N(\tilde{\lambda}_d)$ have risk-neutral intensities given as $\tilde{\lambda}_u$ and $\tilde{\lambda}_d$, respectively. All of the Wiener processes, the jump-size variables, and the Poisson processes are distributed independently of each other.

Since the $A_1(3)$-EJ++ model is a *double-plus* model that fits the initially observed bond prices and since conditional volatilities do not depend on the state variables $Y(t)$ and $\theta(t)$, the initial values of these variables can be assumed to be zero without any loss in generality, or:

$$Y(0) = \theta(0) = 0 \qquad (9.181)$$

The reader may note that the $A_1(3)$-EJ++ model is an extended double-plus version of the preferred $A_1(3)_{DS}$ model of Dai and Singleton [2000] (given in equation (9.2)), with an additional parameter δ_r and with two added Poisson components for modeling positive and negative jumps in the short rate. The additional parameter δ_r is required for the $A_0(2)$++ model to be nested in the $A_1(3)$-EJ++ model. Though Dai and Singleton [2000] do not find this parameter to be important, their econometric analysis is based upon the behavior of yield changes and not on the valuation of interest rate derivatives. Since we require the generalization of the $A_0(2)$++ model with stochastic volatility and jumps to at least nest the $A_0(2)$++ model (given the excellent performance of the $A_0(2)$++ model shown in Figure 9.2 and Table 9.6), the additional parameter δ_r is essential for the $A_1(3)$-EJ++ model. The $A_0(2)$++ model is obtained as a special case of the $A_1(3)$-EJ++ model (in the form given in equations (8.17) and (8.19) in Chapter 8), by rescaling of the second state variable as $u(t) = \tilde{\alpha}\theta(t)$, assuming $v(t) = 0$ and removing the jump components. Note that other stochastic volatility-based three-factor models in the literature, such as the $A_1(3)_{BDFS}$ model given in equation (9.1), the $A_2(3)_{CHEN}$ model given in equation (9.14), and the $A_2(3)_{MAX}$ model given in equation (9.16), do not nest the $A_0(2)$++ model. NBS [2007a] derive a fast algorithm to solve the bond price and option prices under the $A_1(3)$-EJ++ model and investigate the effectiveness of this model for capturing the volatility skew.

NOTES

1. A variety of exotic interest rate options came into existence in the 1990s, including autocaps, captions, knock-out caps, ratchet caps, path-dependent options such as range Asian options, trigger swaps, look-back options, Bermudan swaptions, and callable inverse floaters.
2. Dai and Singleton [2000] use the maximal form to specify the processes under the physical measure. We use this form to specify the processes under the risk-neutral measure. With general specifications of MPRs, such as those under the semi-affine form, the physical processes may not have the same form as in Dai and Singleton [2000]. Since our purpose is to value interest rate derivatives, we specify the maximal form under the risk-neutral measure.

3. Dai and Singleton [2000] use the maximal form to specify the processes under the physical measure. We use this form to specify the processes under the risk-neutral measure. The definition of $\alpha_{r\theta}$ is slightly different than that given in Dai and Singleton [2000, equation. 28, p. 1953].

4. Chapter 3 shows a caplet (or floorlet) to be equivalent to an option on a zero-coupon bond and a swaption to be equivalent to an option on a coupon bond. Since Jamshidian's [1989] trick of pricing a European coupon bond option as a portfolio of European zero-coupon bond options applies only under single-factor term structure models, the Fourier inversion method cannot be applied to price European options on coupon bonds or European swaptions in a multifactor setting.

5. See http://mathworld.wolfram.com/Cumulant.html, and http://www.answers.com/cumulants

6. See http://www.answers.com/topic/edgeworth-series

7. For expositional simplicity, we have omitted the dependence of the probability density function on the forward measure. However, it is important to emphasize that the probability density function, the characteristic function, and the cumulants depend on the forward measure. As can be seen from equation (9.75), to end up in the money, the computation of the probability of the bond price will have to be carried out for the $n+1$ forward measures. We will come back to this point later.

8. Considering the trade-off between accuracy and computational burden introduced by the higher-order cumulants c_6 and c_7, Collin-Dufresne and Goldstein set these cumulants to zero. As they clarify, this does not means that Q is set to 5. In fact, equation (9.88) shows that under this assumption, terms involving ω^6 and ω^7 still remain.

9. Note that the coefficients ϕ_q only depend on Q as long as terms are added or removed from the Taylor expansion of e^Λ in equation (9.84).

10. Note that different values of Q will decrease or increase the number of coefficients, but they do not alter their values.

11. We use the superscript Q to indicate that the value of the coefficient γ depends on Q.

12. Average percentage pricing errors are not informative if we pool all the errors from different strikes and maturities together. Then positive errors from a given strike/maturity category cancel out with the negative errors from another strike/maturity category. However, the pricing errors for a specific strike/maturity category remain of the same sign over different days in the sample period; and, hence, these are quite close to the corresponding root mean squared errors. Jarrow, Li, and Zhao [2007] also report average percentage pricing errors when using different strike/maturity categories as in Table 9.6.

13. See Chapter 12 for a detailed description of the LIBOR market model.

14. See Duffie and Singleton [1999].

CHAPTER 10

Fundamental and Preference-Free Quadratic Models

The market prices of risks (MPRs) simultaneously determine both the conditional mean returns and the cross-sectional volatility shape/correlation patterns of interest rate changes under the fundamental affine term structure models (ATSMs). However, econometric studies using time-series data on as few as two or three zero-coupon yields demonstrate a tension between fitting conditional mean returns and conditional volatilities. For example, though the $A_3(3)$ model fits conditional volatilities well, it fits conditional means poorly; whereas the $A_0(3)$ model fits conditional means well but fits conditional volatilities poorly (see Dai and Singleton [2002]).

The usefulness of a given term structure model for pricing interest rate derivatives is not determined by how well it explains conditional mean returns on bonds but by how well it captures the *volatility information* that comprises:

1. cross-sectional volatility shape/correlation patterns of the changes in rates of different maturities, and
2. conditional volatilities of interest rate changes.

Since preference-free ATSMs are based on the principle of *relative valuation*, these models can value interest rate derivatives using a preference-free framework that allows these models to use only the volatility information and to ignore the conditional mean returns on bonds. The tension between fitting conditional mean returns and conditional volatilities can be circumvented by the preference-free ATSMs by allowing general nonlinear specifications of MPRs. These MPRs do not have to be empirically estimated for valuing interest rate derivatives since the volatility information can be

---

This chapter was coauthored with Iuliana Ismailescu.

directly obtained from prices of bonds and/or plain vanilla derivatives, such as caps and swaptions.

In a series of papers, Beaglehole and Tenney [1991, 1992], Constantinidies [1992], Karoui, Myneni, and Viswanathan [1992], Ahn [1998], Leippold and Wu [2002], Ahn, Dittmar, and Gallant (ADG) [2002], Chen, Filipovic, and Poor [2003], and others have developed the quadratic term structure models (QTSMs), in which the short rate is given as a quadratic function of the underlying state variables. These models represent an important recent innovation in the area of dynamic term structure modeling. Due to their richer structure, the fundamental QTSMs fit the time-series and cross-sectional behavior of interest rates better than the fundamental ATSMs do. Unlike the fundamental ATSMs, which require a trade-off between fitting conditional means versus conditional volatilities, quadratic models can provide a better fit to both by allowing negative as well as positive correlations between the state variables. As shown by ADG [2002] and Brandt and Chapman [2005], this advantage allows QTSMs to outperform ATSMs in explaining the yield dynamics in the U.S. Treasury market.

Though fundamental QTSMs outperform fundamental ATSMs, this advantage may not be so crucial for pricing interest rate derivatives using the preference-free QTSMs. Since conditional means are irrelevant under the preference-free paradigm, more empirical work is needed to assess whether the preference-free QTSMs are better or worse than the preference-free ATSMs for pricing interest rate derivatives. Some preliminary evidence on this issue is provided in this chapter.

This chapter introduces single and multifactor QTSMs, in which the state variables follow Gaussian processes. Unlike the affine models, in which an N-factor affine model can belong to $N + 1$ nonnested subfamilies of maximal models, an N-factor quadratic model always leads to a single maximal model that nests all other N-factor quadratic models. We consider both the fundamental and the preference-free QTSMs and show how to calibrate the preference-free N-factor QTSM to the prices of bonds, caps, and swaptions. We also provide basic formulas of pricing credit derivatives, such as credit default swaps, using the preference-free N-factor QTSM.

SINGLE-FACTOR QUADRATIC TERM STRUCTURE MODEL

The state variable under the fundamental single-factor QTSM ($Q(1)$, hereafter) follows an Ornstein-Uhlenbeck process under the physical measure given as follows:

$$dY(t) = (\mu + \xi Y(t))\, dt + \sigma\, dZ(t) \tag{10.1}$$

The state variable reverts to its long-term mean of $-\mu/\xi$ at the speed of mean reversion equal to $-\xi$. Let the Wiener process under the risk-neutral measure be given as follows:

$$d\tilde{Z}(t) = dZ(t) + \frac{\gamma_0 + \gamma_1 Y(t)}{\sigma} \, dt \qquad (10.2)$$

Substituting the process in equation (10.2) into equation (10.1), the risk-neutral process followed by the state variable is given as follows:

$$dY(t) = (\tilde{\mu} + \tilde{\xi} Y(t)) \, dt + \sigma \, d\tilde{Z}(t) \qquad (10.3)$$

where

$$\tilde{\mu} = \mu - \gamma_0$$
$$\tilde{\xi} = \xi - \gamma_1 \qquad (10.4)$$

The Novikov condition of the Girsanov theorem, which permits the change of measure in equation (10.2), is satisfied by assuming that the state variable volatility σ is greater than zero.

Unlike affine models, under which the short rate is always a linear function of state variables, quadratic models allow the short rate to be a squared function of state variables. Consider the following specification of the short rate for the $Q(1)$ model:

$$r(t) = \delta + Y^2(t) \qquad (10.5)$$

Since by definition $Y^2(t)$ must be nonnegative, the minimum value that the short rate can attain equals the constant δ. To prevent the occurrence of negative rates, δ is generally assumed to be nonnegative.

Unlike the single-factor affine models, the short rate does not have a one-to-one relationship with the underlying state variable under the $Q(1)$ model. Due to the quadratic relationship, both states, $Y(t) = \sqrt{r(t) - \delta} > 0$ and $Y(t) = -\sqrt{r(t) - \delta} < 0$, give the same value of the short rate under the $Q(1)$ model. We define the state in which $Y(t)$ is greater than zero as the "positive state" and the state in which $Y(t)$ is less than zero as the "negative state." The bond price, duration, and convexity are different under the positive state and the negative state, *even if the short rate value is the same under both states* under the $Q(1)$ model. If the state variable $Y(t)$ follows a stationary risk-neutral process with a positive long-term mean, then both duration and convexity remain positive under the positive state but may be either positive or negative under the negative state. A negative duration implies that the bond price may increase (decrease) when the short rate increases (decreases), even though economic uncertainty is captured by only one factor. Such rich behavior in interest rate movements is possible only with two or more factors under the affine class of models.

Further insight on the $Q(1)$ model can be gained by considering the stochastic process followed by the short rate. Using Ito's lemma on equation (10.5), the short rate process is given under the risk-neutral measure as follows:

$$dr(t) = (\sigma^2 + 2\,\tilde{\mu}\,Y(t) + 2\tilde{\xi}\,Y^2(t))\,dt + 2\sigma Y(t)\,d\tilde{Z}(t) \qquad (10.6)$$

The volatility of the short rate is directly proportional to the magnitude of the state variable. The conditional correlation between the short rate process and the state variable process equals 1 in the positive state (i.e., when the state variable $Y(t) > 0$) and -1 in the negative state (i.e., when the state variable $Y(t) < 0$). The drift of the short rate process is a quadratic function of the state variable. When the state variable $Y(t)$ becomes zero, the volatility of the short rate equals zero. Interestingly, a zero volatility of the short rate does not imply a zero volatility of the bond return, and hence, when $Y(t) = 0$, the traditional duration measure—defined with respect to short rate changes—explodes to infinity under the quadratic model.

Equation (10.6) can also be expressed in terms of the short rate, as follows:

$$dr(t) = \begin{cases} (\sigma^2 + 2\,\tilde{\mu}\,\sqrt{r(t) - \delta} + 2\tilde{\xi}(r(t) - \delta))\,dt + 2\sigma\sqrt{r(t) - \delta}\,d\tilde{Z}(t), \\ \qquad\qquad\qquad\qquad\qquad\qquad\qquad\qquad \text{if } Y(t) \geq 0 \\ (\sigma^2 - 2\,\tilde{\mu}\,\sqrt{r(t) - \delta} + 2\tilde{\xi}(r(t) - \delta))\,dt - 2\sigma\sqrt{r(t) - \delta}\,d\tilde{Z}(t), \\ \qquad\qquad\qquad\qquad\qquad\qquad\qquad\qquad \text{if } Y(t) < 0 \end{cases} \qquad (10.7)$$

Assuming that $Y(t)$ follows a stationary risk-neutral process with a positive risk-neutral long-term mean in equation (10.3) implies the following parameter restrictions: $\tilde{\xi} < 0$ and $\tilde{\mu} > 0$. Hence, the drift of the short rate process is higher under the positive state under these restrictions. The lower drift in the negative state makes the state variable quickly reach zero and become positive again, while the higher drift in the positive state makes it more difficult for the state variable to reach zero. For realistic parameter values, the probability of $Y(t)$ being in the positive state is generally significantly higher than it being in the negative state.

Expressing the bond price as a function of $Y(t)$ and t, using Ito's lemma, and taking the risk-neutral expectation of the change in the bond price, the PDE for the bond price is given as follows:

$$\frac{\partial P}{\partial Y}(\tilde{\mu} + \tilde{\xi}Y(t)) + \frac{1}{2}\sigma^2\frac{\partial^2 P}{\partial Y^2} - \frac{\partial P}{\partial \tau} - (\delta + Y^2(t))P(t,T) = 0 \qquad (10.8)$$

subject to the boundary conditions $P(T, T) = 1$ and $\tau = T - t$. Assume that the solution to equation (10.8) has the following form:

$$P(t, T) = e^{A(\tau) + B(\tau)Y(t) + C(\tau)Y^2(t) - H(t,T)} \tag{10.9}$$

subject to $A(0) = B(0) = C(0) = 0$. The function $H(t, T)$ is defined as follows:

$$H(t, T) = \int_t^T \delta \, dv = \delta \tau \tag{10.10}$$

Evaluating the partial derivatives of the bond price with respect to $Y(t)$ and τ gives:

$$\frac{\partial P}{\partial Y} = P(t, T)(B(\tau) + 2Y(t)C(\tau))$$

$$\frac{\partial^2 P}{\partial Y^2} = P(t, T)((B(\tau) + 2Y(t)C(\tau))^2 + 2C(\tau)) \tag{10.11}$$

$$\frac{\partial P}{\partial \tau} = P(t, T)\left(\frac{\partial A(\tau)}{\partial \tau} + \frac{\partial B(\tau)}{\partial \tau}Y(t) + \frac{\partial C(\tau)}{\partial \tau}Y^2(t) - \delta\right)$$

Substituting the partial derivatives from equation (10.11) in equation (10.8) and then using a separation of variables gives the following three ODEs:

$$\frac{\partial A(\tau)}{\partial \tau} = \tilde{\mu}B(\tau) + \frac{1}{2}\sigma^2 B^2(\tau) + \sigma^2 C(\tau)$$

$$\frac{\partial B(\tau)}{\partial \tau} = \tilde{\xi}B(\tau) + 2\sigma^2 B(\tau)C(\tau) + 2\tilde{\mu}C(\tau) \tag{10.12}$$

$$\frac{\partial C(\tau)}{\partial \tau} = 2\tilde{\xi}C(\tau) + 2\sigma^2 C^2(\tau) - 1$$

subject to $A(0) = B(0) = C(0) = 0$. The third equation in (10.12) is the well-known Riccati equation, and the technique to solve this equation was outlined in Chapter 6. The first and second equation are first-order linear ODEs that can be solved by substituting the solution of $C(\tau)$ (obtained by solving the third equation) into the second equation to solve $B(\tau)$ and then substituting the solutions of $B(\tau)$ and $C(\tau)$ in the first equation to solve $A(\tau)$. The solutions are given as follows:

$$A(\tau) = \left[-\left(\frac{\tilde{\mu}}{\beta}\right)^2 \tau\right] + \left[\frac{\tilde{\mu}^2(e^{\beta\tau} - 1)[(-2\tilde{\xi} + \beta)(e^{\beta\tau} - 1) + 2\beta]}{\beta^3[(\beta - \tilde{\xi})(e^{2\beta\tau} - 1) + 2\beta]}\right]$$

$$+ \frac{1}{2}\ln\left[\frac{2\beta e^{(\beta - \tilde{\xi})\tau}}{(\beta - \tilde{\xi})(e^{2\beta\tau} - 1) + 2\beta}\right]$$

$$B(\tau) = -\frac{2\,\tilde{\mu}(e^{\beta\tau} - 1)^2}{\beta[(\beta - \tilde{\xi})(e^{2\beta\tau} - 1) + 2\beta]} \tag{10.13}$$

$$C(\tau) = -\frac{e^{2\beta\tau} - 1}{(\beta - \tilde{\xi})(e^{2\beta\tau} - 1) + 2\beta}$$

$$\beta = \sqrt{\tilde{\xi}^2 + 2\sigma^2}$$

The risk-neutral stochastic bond price process can be obtained using Ito's lemma on equation (10.9), as follows:

$$\frac{dP(t, T)}{P(t, T)} = r(t)\,dt + \sigma\big(B(T - t) + 2Y(t)C(T - t)\big)\,d\tilde{Z}(t) \tag{10.14}$$

Duration and Convexity

Under the $Q(1)$ model, the signs and the magnitudes of duration and convexity measures depend upon the state of nature and can be given by considering three cases as follows:

Case 1: Positive state, or $Y(t) = \sqrt{r(t) - \delta} > 0$ Under this case, the bond price in equation (10.9) simplifies to:

$$P(t, T) = e^{A(\tau) + B(\tau)\sqrt{r(t) - \delta} + C(\tau)(r(t) - \delta)} \tag{10.15}$$

By taking the partial derivative of the bond price with respect to the short rate, bond duration is defined as follows:

$$
\begin{aligned}
Duration &= -\frac{\partial P(t, T)/\partial r(t)}{P(t, T)} = -\frac{B(\tau) + 2C(\tau)\sqrt{r(t) - \delta}}{2\sqrt{r(t) - \delta}} \\
&= -\frac{B(\tau) + 2Y(t)C(\tau)}{2Y(t)}
\end{aligned} \tag{10.16}
$$

By taking the second-order partial derivative of the bond price with respect to the short rate, bond convexity is defined as follows:

$$
\begin{aligned}
Convexity &= \frac{\partial^2 P(t, T)/\partial r(t)^2}{P(t, T)} = \frac{\big(B(\tau) + 2C(\tau)\sqrt{r(t) - \delta}\big)^2}{4(r(t) - \delta)} - \frac{B(\tau)}{4(\sqrt{r(t) - \delta})^3} \\
&= \frac{\big(B(\tau) + 2Y(t)C(\tau)\big)^2}{4Y^2(t)} - \frac{B(\tau)}{4Y^3(t)}
\end{aligned} \tag{10.17}
$$

Both bond duration and convexity are positive under a stationary risk-neutral process for the state variable. As an example, consider the following parameter values. Let $\delta = 0$ and $r(t) = 6.25\% = 0.0625$. This implies that $Y(t) = \sqrt{r(t)} = 0.25$. Also assume that the state variable reverts to its risk-neutral long-term mean, equal to its current value of 0.25, at the risk-neutral mean-reversion speed of 0.5. Since, by definition, the risk-neutral mean-reversion speed equals $-\tilde{\xi}$ and the risk-neutral long-term mean equals $-\tilde{\mu}/\tilde{\xi}$, the parameter $\tilde{\xi}$ equals -0.5, and the parameter $\tilde{\mu}$ equals 0.125. Finally, since the short rate volatility is defined as $2\sigma Y(t)$ (see equation (10.6)), assuming $\sigma = 0.04$ gives the short rate volatility as $2 \times 0.04 \times 0.25 = 0.02$, or 2 percent per year. For these parameter values, the state variable $Y(t)$ follows a risk-neutral stationary process with a positive mean equal to 0.25. Since both $B(\tau)$ and $C(\tau)$ are negative, this implies that both duration and convexity are positive when $Y(t) > 0$. For these parameter values, the duration and convexity of a five-year zero-coupon bond equal 1.827 and 10.034, respectively.

Case 2: Negative state, or $Y(t) = -\sqrt{r(t) - \delta} < 0$ Generally, the probability of $Y(t)$ remaining positive is higher when the initial value of the state variable $Y(0)$ is positive and the risk-neutral long-term mean $-\tilde{\mu}/\tilde{\xi}$ and the risk-neutral speed of mean reversion $-\tilde{\xi}$ are both positive. Though $Y(t)$ generally remains positive under the $Q(1)$ model, it may become negative with a small but economically significant probability. The bond price given in equation (10.9) can be rewritten in the negative state as follows:

$$P(t, T) = e^{A(\tau) - B(\tau)\sqrt{r(t) - \delta} + C(\tau)(r(t) - \delta)} \tag{10.18}$$

The bond duration and convexity in the negative state become:

$$Duration = -\frac{\partial P(t, T)/\partial r(t)}{P(t, T)} = \frac{B(\tau) - 2C(\tau)\sqrt{r(t) - \delta}}{2\sqrt{r(t) - \delta}} \tag{10.19}$$

$$= -\frac{B(\tau) + 2Y(t)C(\tau)}{2Y(t)}$$

$$Convexity = \frac{\partial^2 P(t, T)/\partial r(t)^2}{P(t, T)} = \frac{(B(\tau) - 2C(\tau)\sqrt{r(t) - \delta})^2}{4(r(t) - \delta)} + \frac{B(\tau)}{4(\sqrt{r(t) - \delta})^3}$$

$$= \frac{(B(\tau) + 2Y(t)C(\tau))^2}{4Y^2(t)} - \frac{B(\tau)}{4Y^3(t)} \tag{10.20}$$

Note that the bond price, duration, and convexity formulas appear different under the positive state and the negative state, when these are expressed as functions of the short rate $r(t)$. However, when these formulas are expressed as functions of the state variable $Y(t)$, their definitions are identical under both states. This happens because states of nature are not uniquely captured by the short rate values under the $Q(1)$ model, and a given value of the short rate is consistent with both a positive and a negative value of the state variable.

Though the negative state occurs less frequently (using realistic parameter values), when it does occur, the duration and convexity measures switch signs and become negative near the origin.

Figure 10.1 shows the relationship between the bond price and the short rate for two zero-coupon bonds maturing at 5 years and 10 years, respectively. The lower region of each parabola represents the positive state (i.e., $Y(t) > 0$), and the upper region represents the negative state (i.e., $Y(t) < 0$). Since each value of the short rate corresponds to two states, two bond prices exist for each value of the short rate, with the bond price in the negative state always higher than the bond price in the positive state. Though the bond price behavior in the positive state is consistent with conventional wisdom (declining exponentially with the short rate), the behavior in the negative state seems counterintuitive, since the bond price increases initially along the upper region of the parabola. In fact, duration switches from positive infinity to negative infinity as the state variable $Y(t)$ switches from an infinitesimally small positive value to an infinitesimally small negative value at the origin. As the variable $Y(t)$ becomes more negative, the short

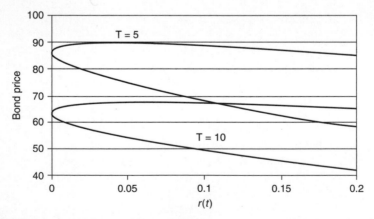

FIGURE 10.1   Five- and Ten-Year Bond Prices versus $r(t)$, with Default Parameters $\delta = 0$, $\tilde{\xi} = -0.5$, $\tilde{\mu} = 0.125$, and $\sigma = 0.04$

rate increases and the bond price increases initially as shown by the upper region of the parabola. Since the slope of the price curve is positive, it implies *negative* duration values in this region. As the short rate increases further with $Y(t)$ becoming more negative, duration increases, reaches zero, and then becomes positive again. The value of duration is identical under both states when the short rate becomes infinite.

The behavior of the bond price in the negative state is a unique characteristic of quadratic models. It implies scenarios in which the short rate and a few other shorter maturity forward rates may increase, with a simultaneous decrease in the longer maturity forward rates, such that the overall effect increases the bond price, even as the short rate increases. Hence, twists in the yield curve can happen with even one factor under the quadratic class of models.

To obtain further insight into the bond price behavior in the negative states, consider a τ-maturity zero-coupon bond. The volatility of this bond equals zero when the state variable takes the following value:

$$Y(t) = -\frac{B(\tau)}{2C(\tau)} \tag{10.21}$$

Since zero volatility implies zero duration, the value of the state variable shown in equation 10.21 gives the point in Figure 10.1 at which the bond price curve flattens out in the upper region of the parabola. Note that for different negative values of the state variable, bonds of different maturities will have zero volatility and zero duration. Also, for a given increase in the short rate caused by the state variable becoming *more* negative, shorter maturity bonds will decrease in value, while longer maturity bonds may increase in value.

Under realistic parameter values, the state variable $Y(t)$ becomes positive quickly after becoming negative, due to the mean reversion of the state variable to its positive risk-neutral mean. Hence, the unusual behavior caused by the negative states does not last for long, which is consistent with casual empiricism, as twists in the yield curve are not very frequent.

Similar to duration, even convexity switches from positive infinity to negative infinity as the state variable $Y(t)$ switches from an infinitesimally positive value to an infinitesimally negative value at the origin. As the variable $Y(t)$ becomes more negative, the short rate increases and the bond price increases initially as shown by the upper region of the parabola in Figure 10.1. Since the curvature of the price curve is negative, it implies *negative* convexity values in this region. As the short rate increases further with $Y(t)$ becoming more negative, convexity increases, reaches zero, and then becomes positive again. The value of convexity is identical under both states when the short rate reaches infinity (positive convexity under negative states cannot be seen in Figure 10.1, however, since it occurs at higher values of the short rate).

Case 3: Zero State, or $Y(t) = 0$ As can be seen from Figure 10.1, both duration and convexity switch from positive infinity to negative infinity as the state variable $Y(t)$ switches from an infinitesimally small positive value to an infinitesimally small negative value at the origin. The risk measures duration and convexity are undefined when the state variable is *exactly* equal to zero. However, the bond price process remains well defined and can be given as follows by substituting $Y(t) = 0$ in equation (10.14):

$$\frac{dP(t, T)}{P(t, T)} = r(t)\, dt + \sigma B(T - t)\, d\tilde{Z}(t) \qquad (10.22)$$

The bond return is well behaved with a deterministic volatility, which has a limiting asymptotic value. Interestingly, under this case, the forward rate volatility must always have a humped shape. The forward rate volatility converges to zero as the maturity term converges to zero (since short rate volatility is zero), rises to a maximal value, and then falls to zero as maturity becomes infinite (since bond volatility has a limiting asymptotic value). The next section investigates humped forward rate volatility curves in more detail. In fact, it is shown that not only is the forward rate volatility humped under this case but it is also humped when the state variable $Y(t)$ takes positive values that are significantly smaller than the risk-neutral mean, $-\tilde{\mu}/\tilde{\xi}$. Hence, if the physical long-term mean of the state variable is significantly smaller than its risk-neutral long-term mean, then humped forward rate volatilities would be observed frequently in the empirical data.

PREFERENCE-FREE SINGLE-FACTOR QUADRATIC MODEL

As mentioned earlier, the preference-free models allow arbitrary nonlinear specifications of MPRs, allowing them to match the volatility characteristics that are important for pricing interest rate derivatives, yet without imposing strong restrictions on conditional mean returns under the physical measure. However, the volatility characteristics may be hard to capture, simply due to the restrictive nature of the assumed model. For example, the preference-free single-factor affine models, such as the Vasicek+ and Vasicek++ models and the preference-free CIR+ and CIR++ models, imply exponentially declining shapes of the forward rate volatility function under a *stationary* risk-neutral process for the short rate, precluding the humped shape observed in the empirical data. As shown in Chapter 7, a humped-shaped forward rate volatility function can be allowed by CIR+ and CIR++ models only by assuming an *explosive* risk-neutral process for the short rate.

This section derives preference-free extensions of the single-factor quadratic term structure model that allows humped shape for the forward rate volatilities, even under a stationary risk-neutral process for the short rate. Like the case of affine models, we use the notation with a single plus sign, or $Q(1)+$, to denote the time-homogeneous preference-free $Q(1)$ model and with two plus signs, or $Q(1)++$, to denote the time-inhomogeneous preference-free $Q(1)$ model. Though both the $Q(1)+$ and $Q(1)++$ models allow general, nonlinear specifications of MPRs, the $Q(1)+$ model allows a time-homogeneous short rate process, while the $Q(1)++$ model makes the short rate process time-inhomogeneous in order to exactly fit the initial zero-coupon bond prices. The $Q(1)++$ model nests the $Q(1)+$ model, which in turn nests the fundamental $Q(1)$ model.

Preference-free $Q(1)+$ and $Q(1)++$ models can be obtained by exogenous specifications of the stochastic bond price processes and of specific bond price solutions at time 0, using the method outlined in Chapter 4 and Chapter 7 for affine models. This technique allows obtaining the stochastic process for the short rate directly under the risk-neutral measure, circumventing the requirement of modeling the market prices of risks. This approach is also equivalent to specifying the short rate process directly under the risk-neutral measure.

The short rate under the preference-free single-factor QTSM is given as a quadratic function of the state variable, as follows:

$$r(t) = \delta(t) + Y^2(t) \tag{10.23}$$

where $\delta(t)$ is a function of time under the $Q(1)++$ model and $\delta(t) = \delta$, a constant under the $Q(1)+$ model. The risk-neutral stochastic process of the state variable is given as follows:

$$dY(t) = (\tilde{\mu} + \tilde{\xi} Y(t))\, dt + \sigma\, d\tilde{Z}(t) \tag{10.24}$$

Though the solutions of bond price and interest rate derivatives under the $Q(1)+$ model are identical to the corresponding solutions under the fundamental $Q(1)$ model, the similarity is only in form, since the risk-neutral parameters estimated under the $Q(1)+$ model are generally different from the corresponding parameters estimated under the fundamental $Q(1)$ model, due to the restrictive MPRs assumed by the latter model.

The solution of the bond price under the $Q(1)++$ model is obtained by following the same steps as under the $Q(1)$ model, except that $H(t, T)$ in equation (10.10) must be replaced by the following:

$$H(t, T) = \int_t^T \delta(v)\, dv \qquad (10.25)$$

To calibrate the bond price solution in equation (10.9) to the initially observable bond price function $P(0, T)$, consider the log of bond price evaluated at time 0 as follows:

$$\ln P(0, T) = A(T) + B(T)Y(0) + C(T)Y^2(0) - H(0, T) \qquad (10.26)$$

Differentiating equation (10.26) with respect to T, then replacing T with t, and simplifying, we get:

$$\delta(t) = \frac{\partial A(t)}{\partial t} + Y(0)\frac{\partial B(t)}{\partial t} + Y^2(0)\frac{\partial C(t)}{\partial t} - \frac{\partial \ln P(0, t)}{\partial t} \qquad (10.27)$$

Substituting the ODEs given in equation (10.12), we get:

$$\begin{aligned}
\delta(t) = {} & f(0, t) + B(t)(\tilde{\mu} + \tilde{\xi} Y(0)) + C(t)(\sigma^2 + 2\tilde{\mu} Y(0) + 2\tilde{\xi} Y^2(0)) \\
& + B^2(t)(\sigma^2/2) + 2C(t)^2(\sigma^2 Y^2(0)) \qquad (10.28) \\
& + 2B(t)C(t)Y(0)\sigma^2 - Y^2(0)
\end{aligned}$$

Using equation (10.26), the solution to $H(t, T)$ can be obtained as follows:

$$\begin{aligned}
H(t, T) = \int_t^T \delta(v)\, dv & = H(0, T) - H(0, t) \\
& = A(T) - A(t) + Y(0)\big(B(T) - B(t)\big) + Y(0)^2\big(C(T) - C(t)\big) \quad (10.29) \\
& \quad - \ln P(0, T) + \ln P(0, t)
\end{aligned}$$

The formula for the bond price under the $Q(1)++$ model is the same as under the $Q(1)$ model in equation (10.9), except that $H(t, T)$ in equation (10.10) is replaced by equation (10.29).

Since an exact fit with the initial zero-coupon bond prices is always ensured by the deterministic term $\delta(t)$ under the $Q(1)++$ model, the risk-neutral parameters $\tilde{\mu}, \tilde{\xi}$, and σ and the initial value of the state variable $Y(0)$ are obtained by calibrating the model to the cross-sectional data on the prices of interest rate derivatives, such as caps and swaptions. In contrast, the corresponding parameters for the time-homogeneous $Q(1)+$ model are obtained by simultaneously fitting the cross-sectional data on the prices of zero-coupon bonds as well as the prices of interest rate derivatives, such as caps and swaptions. Though neither preference-free model estimates the physical parameters or the MPRs, both models are consistent with general nonlinear specifications of MPRs.

Forward Rate Volatility

The risk-neutral forward rate process under the fundamental and the preference-free $Q(1)$ models is given as follows:

$$df(t, T) = \mu_f(t, T)\, dt + \big(\sigma_{f1}(t, T) + \sigma_{f2}(t, T)Y(t)\big)\, d\tilde{Z}(t) \qquad (10.30)$$

where

$$\sigma_{f1}(t, T) = -\sigma \frac{\partial B(T - t)}{\partial T}, \quad \sigma_{f2}(t, T) = -2\sigma \frac{\partial C(T - t)}{\partial T}, \text{ and}$$

$$\mu_f(t, T) = \sigma^2 \big(B(T - t) + 2Y(t)C(T - t)\big) \left(\frac{\partial B(T - t)}{\partial T} + 2Y(t)\frac{\partial C(T - t)}{\partial T} \right)$$

Substituting the ODEs for the functions $B(.)$ and $C(.)$ from equation (10.12), the deterministic components of the forward rate volatility, $\sigma_{f1}(t, T)$ and $\sigma_{f2}(t, T)$, are given as follows:

$$\sigma_{f1}(t, T) = -\sigma\big(\tilde{\xi}B(T - t) + 2\sigma^2 B(T - t)C(T - t) + 2\,\tilde{\mu}C(T - t)\big) \quad (10.31)$$

$$\sigma_{f2}(t, T) = -2\sigma\big(2\tilde{\xi}C(T - t) + 2\sigma^2 C^2(T - t) - 1\big) \qquad (10.32)$$

Both $\sigma_{f1}(t, T)$ and $\sigma_{f2}(t, T)$ are functions of the maturity term $T - t$ and the risk-neutral parameters $\tilde{\mu}$, $\tilde{\xi}$, and σ. Under a stationary risk-neutral process with a positive long-term mean (i.e., $\tilde{\mu} > 0$ and $\tilde{\xi} < 0$), both $\sigma_{f1}(t, T)$ and $\sigma_{f2}(t, T)$ are positive-valued functions. The function $\sigma_{f1}(t, T)$ equals zero both when $t = T$ and when $T = \infty$, and hence, the shape of this function is always humped. In contrast, the function $\sigma_{f2}(t, T)$ is always exponentially declining. This function is similar to the cross-sectional volatility of the forward rates under the Cox, Ingersoll, and Ross [1985] model with a suitable parameterization.

The forward rate volatility $\sigma_{f1}(t, T) + \sigma_{f2}(t, T)Y(t)$ has many empirically desirable features. When the value of $Y(t)$ is low, the humped shape of the function $\sigma_{f1}(t, T)$ dominates the exponentially declining shape of the function $\sigma_{f2}(t, T)$, leading to an overall humped shape for the forward rate volatility function. The magnitude and the position of the hump is determined by the stochastic evolution of the state variable $Y(t)$.

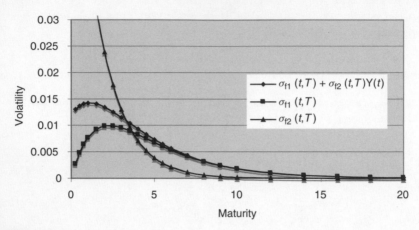

FIGURE 10.2 The Deterministic Functions $\sigma_{f1}(t, T)$ and $\sigma_{f2}(t, T)$ and the Forward Rate Volatility Function $\sigma_{f1}(t, T) + \sigma_{f2}(t, T) Y(t)$

Figure 10.2 demonstrates the typical shapes of the humped function $\sigma_{f1}(t, T)$, the exponentially declining function $\sigma_{f2}(t, T)$, and the forward rate volatility function $\sigma_{f1}(t, T) + \sigma_{f2}(t, T)Y(t)$. These functions are plotted using the parameters $Y(0) = 0.15$, $\tilde{\xi} = -0.3$, $\tilde{\mu} = 0.15$, and $\sigma = 0.04$.

The flexible specification of the forward rate volatility function under the $Q(1)$ models contrasts with other single-factor models, such as Vasicek [1977] and Cox, Ingersoll, and Ross (CIR) [1985], which allow only an exponentially declining shape for the volatility function. Though the fundamental CIR model and preference-free CIR models (see Chapters 6 and 7) can allow a humped shape for the forward rate volatility function, they can do so only with an *explosive* risk-neutral short rate process. In contrast, the forward rate volatility function for the $Q(1)$ models can have a humped shape even when the state variable $Y(t)$ follows a stationary risk-neutral process.

Since the preference-free $Q(1)$ models are more flexible than the fundamental $Q(1)$ model, the risk-neutral parameters under these models lead to a variety of volatility shapes, including humps. The initial value of the state variable $Y(0)$ plays a useful role in calibration of the preference-free $Q(1)$ models to a given set of derivative prices, such as caps and swaptions. In general, lower values of $Y(0)$ allow the forward rate volatility shape to be humped. If the physical long-term mean of the state variable is lower than the risk-neutral long-term mean, then the observed $Y(0)$ will generally be lower than its risk-neutral mean, allowing for a humped forward rate volatility curve.

Model Implementation Using Trees

Since the state variable follows a Gaussian process under the $Q(1)$, $Q(1)+$, that and $Q(1)++$ models, the tree-building procedure is a straightforward extension of the Gaussian trees given in Chapter 4. Recall that the risk-neutral process of the state variable is given as:

$$dY(t) = (\tilde{\mu} + \tilde{\xi}Y(t))\,dt + \sigma\,d\tilde{Z}(t) \tag{10.33}$$

Figure 10.3 shows the trinomial tree for the $Y(t)$ process.

The trinomial probabilities are given as follows:

$$p_u = \frac{1}{6} + \frac{1}{6}\frac{\tilde{\mu} + \tilde{\xi}Y(t)}{\sigma}\sqrt{3\Delta t}$$

$$p_m = \frac{2}{3} \tag{10.34}$$

$$p_d = \frac{1}{6} - \frac{1}{6}\frac{\tilde{\mu} + \tilde{\xi}Y(t)}{\sigma}\sqrt{3\Delta t}$$

Once the tree for the $Y(t)$ process is constructed, the value of the short rate at each node is computed according to equation (10.23), with $\delta(t)$ defined by equation (10.28) under the $Q(1)++$ model and $\delta(t) = \delta$, a constant, under the $Q(1)$ and $Q(1)+$ models. The value of any interest rate contingent claim can be obtained by taking the discounting risk-neutral expectations of the terminal values.

Example 10.1 Consider the valuation of a zero-coupon bond that pays \$100 $(F = 100)$ at the end of six months $(T = 0.5)$. Assume that the risk-neutral parameters of the $Y(t)$ process are given as: $Y(0) = 0.25$, $\tilde{\xi} = -0.5$, $\tilde{\mu} = 0.125$, and $\sigma = 4\%$. The term $\delta(t)$ under the $Q(1)++$ model can

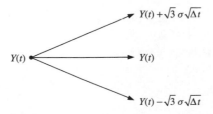

FIGURE 10.3 Trinomial Tree for the $Y(t)$ Process

be solved using two methods. The first method uses the analytical formula of $\delta(t)$ given in equation (10.28). However, since this formula holds only in the continuous-time limit, the bond price obtained using this formula may not match the initial bond price *exactly* using a finite number of steps on the tree, and hence, a large number of steps may be needed. The second method allows a fewer number of steps by solving $\delta(t)$ iteratively (using the short rate in equation (10.23)) at every step to match the initial bond price (see Chapters 4 and 7 for application of this method under the Vasicek++ and CIR++ models, respectively).

For expositional simplicity, assume that $\delta(t) = 0$ and $r(0) = 0 + (Y(0))^2 = 0.0625 = 6.25\%$. The resulting trinomial tree is illustrated in Figure 10.4. Each node consists of three rows. The number in the top row gives the discounted value of the bond price at that node. The number in the middle row gives the value of the state variable $Y(t)$ at that node. And finally, the number in the bottom row gives the value of the short rate $r(t)$ at that node.

For demonstration of valuation using the tree, consider the node N_{22}. At this node, $Y(t = 0.25) = 0.2745$. The value of the short rate at this node equals:

$$r(0.25) = Y(0.25)^2 = 0.2745^2 = 0.0754$$

The trinomial probabilities are computed using equation (10.34) as follows:

$$p_u = \frac{1}{6} + \frac{1}{6} \times \frac{0.125 - 0.5 \times 0.2745}{0.04}\sqrt{3 \times 0.125} = 0.1354$$

$$p_m = 0.6667$$

$$p_d = \frac{1}{6} - \frac{1}{6} \times \frac{0.125 - 0.5 \times 0.2745}{0.04}\sqrt{3 \times 0.125} = 0.1979$$

The bond price at node N_{22} is given as:

$$P_{22} = \frac{98.89 \times 0.1354 + 99.06 \times 0.6667 + 99.22 \times 0.1979}{e^{0.0754 \times 0.125}} = 98.14$$

The values for the rest of the nodes are computed in a similar manner. The bond price at time 0 equals \$96.91. Using a 100-step tree and the closed-form solution also gives the same value for the bond price.

Extension to Jumps

Backus, Foresi, and Wu [1997], Das [2002], Das and Foresi [1996], Johannes [2004], and Piazzesi [1998, 2005] find that jumps caused by market crashes,

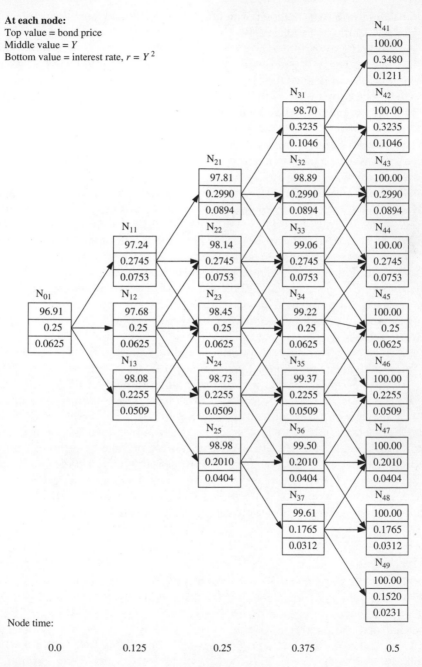

FIGURE 10.4 Trinomial Tree for the Quadratic Model

interventions by the Federal Reserve, economic surprises, shocks in the foreign exchange markets, and other rare events play a significant role in explaining the dynamics of interest rate changes. Jump models assume that the size of the jump is a random variable with some probability distribution, which is independent of the length of the time interval over which the jump occurs. The probability of the jump is assumed to be directly proportional to the length of the time interval.

A limitation of the jump-extended Vasicek model given in Chapter 5 is that both the diffusion component and the jump component can lead to the occurrence of a negative short rate with a positive probability. In general, researchers have found it difficult to allow the short rate to experience positive and negative jumps and to simultaneously ensure the nonnegativity of the short rate. For example, Ahn and Thompson [1988] extend the Cox, Ingersoll, and Ross [1985] model by adding a constant-size negative jump. However, to prevent the short rate from becoming negative, Ahn and Thompson impose a highly restrictive upper bound on the size of the jump. As another example, the exponential jump-extended square-root model of Duffie, Pan, and Singleton [2000] allows *only positive jumps*. The only known extension of the CIR model that allows both positive and negative jumps and still disallows negative interest rates without additional restrictions is given by Nawalkha and Beliaeva [2007b], who add a *lognormal jump component* to the CIR model. This allows both positive and negative jumps, while keeping interest rates nonnegative (see Chapter 6).

Unlike ATSMs, in which adding jumps and simultaneously guaranteeing nonnegative interest rates is generally difficult, adding a jump component to the state variable does not lead to negative interest rates under the QTSMs. This is because the short rate is given as a squared function of the state variable(s) under the QTSMs. A significant advantage of adding a jump component to the fundamental and the preference-free $Q(1)$ models is that it allows using the entire numerical apparatus of the jump-extended Vasicek trees given in Chapter 5. To see this, let the state variable $Y(t)$ follow a jump-diffusion process under the risk-neutral measure given as follows:

$$dY(t) = (\tilde{\mu} + \tilde{\xi} Y(t)) \, dt + \sigma \, dZ(t) + J dN(\tilde{\lambda}) \qquad (10.35)$$

where J is the size of the jump assumed to follow a Gaussian distribution and $N(\tilde{\lambda})$ is the Poisson process with the risk-neutral intensity given as $\tilde{\lambda}$. With a slight change of notation for the drift term, equation (10.35) is identical to the equation for the short rate process in Chapter 5 (see equation 5.11), and thus, the tree for the $Y(t)$ process can be obtained by following the steps defined in Chapter 5 in equations (5.25) through (5.33). Once the jump-diffusion tree for the $Y(t)$ process has been obtained, the tree for the short rate process can be obtained by using the relationship $r(t) = \delta(t) + Y^2(t)$ for the $Q(1)++$ model and $\delta(t) = \delta$, a constant, for the $Q(1)$ and $Q(1)+$ models. Since a closed-form solution does not exist for the bond price under the jump-extended $Q(1)++$ model, an analytical solution cannot be derived for $\delta(t)$ and this term must be solved using an iterative process that matches the model zero-coupon bond price to the initially observed zero-coupon bond price, using bonds maturing at each step of the tree. Once the term $\delta(t)$ is obtained, contingent claims can be valued by taking discounted risk-neutral expectations of the terminal values of the claims.

FUNDAMENTAL MULTIFACTOR QTSMs

Consider the stochastic processes of state variables under the N-factor QTSM given in the canonical form under the physical measure as follows:

$$dY_i(t) = \left(\mu_i + \sum_{j=1}^{i} \xi_{ij} Y_j(t) \right) dt + \sigma_i dZ_i(t), \quad \text{for all } i = 1, 2, \ldots, N \quad (10.36)$$

where the Wiener processes are assumed to be independently distributed. The nonzero values of the risk-neutral parameters ξ_{ij}, for $i > j$, allow the state variables to be (unconditionally) correlated, even though the Wiener processes are independently distributed.

The short rate is given as a quadratic function of the state variables, which under an econometrically identifiable maximal specification is given as follows:

$$r(t) = \delta + \sum_{i=1}^{N} \sum_{j=1}^{N} Y_i(t) Y_j(t) \psi_{ij} \quad (10.37)$$

where $\psi_{ij} = \psi_{ji}$ are constants for all $i, j = 1, 2, \ldots, N$ and where $\psi_{ii} = 1$ for all $i = 1, 2, \ldots, N$.

Though ADG derive the change of measure by specifying an affine diffusion process for the stochastic discount factor, we directly specify the change of measure, which is consistent with AD 6's stochastic discount factor. Using this specification, the Wiener processes under the risk-neutral measure are related to the Wiener processes under the physical measure, as follows:

$$d\tilde{Z}_i(t) = dZ_i(t) + \frac{\gamma_{i0} + \sum_{j=1}^{i} \gamma_{ij} Y_j(t)}{\sigma_i} dt, \quad \text{for all } i = 1, 2, \ldots, N \quad (10.38)$$

By substituting equation (10.38) into equation (10.36), the stochastic processes of state variables under the risk-neutral measure are given as follows:

$$dY_i(t) = \left(\tilde{\mu}_i + \sum_{j=1}^{i} \tilde{\xi}_{ij} Y_j(t) \right) dt + \sigma_i \, d\tilde{Z}_i(t), \quad \text{for all } i = 1, 2, \ldots, N$$

$$(10.39)$$

where

$$\tilde{\mu}_i = \mu_i - \gamma_{i0}, \text{ for all } i = 1, 2, \ldots, N$$

$$\tilde{\xi}_{ij} = \xi_{ij} - \gamma_{ij}, \text{ for all } i, j = 1, 2, \ldots, N, \text{ such that } i \geq j$$

$$(10.40)$$

The fundamental N-factor QTSMs can be classified in four nested subfamilies given as $Q_1(N)$, $Q_2(N)$, $Q_3(N)$, and $Q_4(N)$, with $Q_1(N)$ nesting $Q_2(N)$, $Q_2(N)$ nesting $Q_3(N)$, and finally, $Q_3(N)$ nesting $Q_4(N)$. The parameter restrictions and the total number of parameters to be estimated under these subfamilies are given as follows:

1. *The $Q_1(N)$ Model: Maximally flexible model.* For the maximally flexible N-factor QTSM, the physical state variable processes, the short rate, the MPRs, and the risk-neutral state variable processes are defined by equations (10.36), (10.37), (10.38), and (10.39), respectively. The model requires the estimation of the following parameters: $N(N-1)/2$ number of parameters ψ_{ij} (since $\psi_{ij} = \psi_{ji}$ for all $i, j = 1, 2, \ldots, N$, and $\psi_{ii} = 1$, for all $i = 1, 2, \ldots, N$); N number of parameters μ_i (for $i = 1, 2, \ldots, N$); $N(N+1)/2$ number of parameters ξ_{ij} (for $i, j = 1, 2, \ldots, N$, and $i \geq j$); N number of parameters σ_i (for $i = 1, 2, \ldots, N$); $N(N+1)/2$ number of parameters γ_{ij} (for $i, j = 1, 2, \ldots, N$, and $i \geq j$); N number of parameters γ_{i0} (for $i = 1, 2, \ldots, N$), and the parameter δ. Hence, the econometric estimation of $Q_1(N)$ model requires $N(N-1)/2 + N + N(N+1)/2 + N + N(N+1)/2 + N + 1 = (N+1)^2 + N(N+3)/2$ number of parameters.

2. *The $Q_2(N)$ Model: Orthogonal state variables and interactions.* This model requires zero unconditional correlations between the state variables under both the physical measure and the risk-neutral measure. Hence, the $N(N-1)/2$ number of parameters $\tilde{\xi}_{ij}$ (for $i, j = 1, 2, \ldots, N$, and $i > j$) are set to zero, which ensures zero unconditional correlations under the risk-neutral measure. Further, to ensure zero unconditional correlations under the physical measure requires that an additional set of $N(N-1)/2$ parameters γ_{ij} (for $i, j = 1, 2, \ldots, N$, and $i > j$) are also set to zero. Hence, the parameters under this model are

$N(N-1)$ less than the parameters under the $Q_1(N)$ model, or equal to $(N+1)^2 + N(N+3)/2 - N(N-1) = (N+1)^2 - N(N-5)/2$.

3. *The $Q_3(N)$ Model: Orthogonal state variables and no interactions.* This model not only requires zero unconditional correlations between the state variables under both the physical and the risk-neutral measures, but also disallows interactions of the state variables in determining the short rate in equation (10.37). Hence, another set of $N(N-1)/2$ parameters $\psi_{ij} = \psi_{ji}$ (for $i, j = 1, 2, \ldots, N$, and $i \neq j$) are set to zero. Since by definition $\psi_{ii} = 1$, for all $i = 1, 2, \ldots, N$, in equation (10.37) disallowing the interactions simplifies the definition of the short rate as follows: $r(t) = \delta + Y_1^2(t) + Y_2^2(t) + \cdots + Y_N^2(t)$. The total number of parameters under this model is $N(N-1)/2$ less than the parameters under the $Q_2(N)$ model, or equal to $(N+1)^2 - N(N-5)/2 - N(N-1)/2 = (N+1)^2 - N(N-3)$.

4. *The $Q_4(N)$ Model: The SAINTS model.* The squared-autoregressive-independent-variable nominal term structure (SAINTS) model of Constantinidies [1992] is nested in the $Q_3(N)$ model since this model is based upon orthogonal state variables and no interactions. The SAINTS model imposes additional restrictions on the MPRs such that these are not free parameters but are endogenously determined by the physical parameters of the state variable processes. Specifically, the set of $2N$ parameters γ_{ii} and γ_{i0} (for $i = 1, 2, \ldots, N$), are determined endogenously and are given as follows by ADG:

$$\gamma_{i0} = -\mu_i \left(\frac{\xi_{ii} - \sqrt{\xi_{ii}^2 - 2\sigma_i^2}}{\sqrt{\xi_{ii}^2 - 2\sigma_i^2}} \right) \quad \text{and } \gamma_{ii} = -\xi_{ii}(\sqrt{\xi_{ii}^2 - 2\sigma_i^2}), \tag{10.41}$$

$$\text{for all } i = 1, 2, \ldots, N$$

The total number of parameters under the SAINTS model is $2N$ less than the number of parameters under the $Q_3(N)$ model, or equal to $(N+1)^2 - N(N-3) - 2N = (N+1)^2 - N(N-1)$.

We now derive a solution of the bond price under the $Q_1(N)$ model (i.e., the maximal N-factor QTSM). Bond price solutions under the other nested models, $Q_2(N)$, $Q_3(N)$, and $Q_4(N)$ can be obtained as special cases of the solution of the $Q_1(N)$ model by applying the parameter restrictions given in this section. Expressing the bond price as a function of $t, Y_1(t), Y_2(t), \ldots, Y_N(t)$, using Ito's lemma, and taking risk-neutral expectation of the change in the bond price, the PDE for the bond price is given as follows:

$$\frac{\partial P}{\partial t} + \sum_{i=1}^{N} \frac{\partial P}{\partial Y_i} \left[\tilde{\mu}_i + \sum_{j=1}^{i} \tilde{\xi}_{ij} Y_j(t) \right] + \frac{1}{2} \sum_{i=1}^{N} \frac{\partial^2 P}{\partial Y_i^2} \sigma_i^2 - r(t)P(t,T) = 0 \quad (10.42)$$

subject to the boundary condition $P(T, T) = 1$. We propose the following solution to the bond price with a change of variable $\tau = T - t$:

$$P(t, T) = e^{A(\tau) + \sum_{i=1}^{N} B_i(\tau) Y_i(t) + \sum_{i=1}^{N} \sum_{j=1}^{N} C_{ij}(\tau) Y_i(t) Y_j(t) - H(t,T)} \tag{10.43}$$

subject to $A(0) = B_i(0) = C_{ij}(0) = 0$ for all $i, j = 1, 2, \ldots, N$ and $H(t, T)$ defined as follows:

$$H(t, T) = \int_t^T \delta \, dv = \delta(T - t) = \delta \tau \tag{10.44}$$

Evaluating the partial derivatives of the bond price with respect to t, $Y_1(t)$, $Y_2(t)$, $\ldots$, $Y_N(t)$, substituting these back into equation (10.42), and using a separation of variables, we get the following system of ODEs:

$$\frac{\partial A(\tau)}{\partial \tau} = \sum_{i=1}^{N} \tilde{\mu}_i B_i(\tau) + \frac{1}{2} \sum_{i=1}^{N} \sigma_i^2 B_i^2(\tau) + \sum_{i=1}^{N} \sigma_i^2 C_{ii}(\tau)$$

$$\frac{\partial B_i(\tau)}{\partial \tau} = \sum_{j=i}^{N} \tilde{\xi}_{ji} B_j(\tau) + 2 \sum_{j=1}^{N} \sigma_j^2 B_j(\tau) C_{ij}(\tau) + 2 \sum_{j=1}^{N} \tilde{\mu}_j C_{ij}(\tau) \tag{10.45}$$

$$\frac{\partial C_{ij}(\tau)}{\partial \tau} = \sum_{k=i}^{N} \tilde{\xi}_{ki} C_{jk}(\tau) + \sum_{k=j}^{N} \tilde{\xi}_{kj} C_{ik}(\tau) + 2 \sum_{k=1}^{N} \sigma_k^2 C_{ik}(\tau) C_{jk}(\tau) - \psi_{ij}$$

subject to $A(0) = B_i(0) = C_{ij}(0) = 0$ for all $i, j = 1, 2, \ldots, N$. Since $\psi_{ij} = \psi_{ji}$ for all $i, j = 1, 2, \ldots N$, it can be shown that $C_{ij}(\tau) = C_{ji}(\tau)$ for all $i, j = 1, 2, \ldots, N$. Hence, the solution to this system requires solving one ODE for $A(\tau)$, N ODEs for $B_i(\tau)$, and $N(N + 1)/2$ ODEs for $C_{ij}(\tau)$, giving a total of $(N + 1)(N + 2)/2$ ODEs to be solved. In general, these ODEs are solved using numerical methods (e.g., with programming languages such as Matlab) under the maximal QTSM.

The risk-neutral stochastic bond price process can be obtained by applying Ito's lemma to equation (10.43) and is given as follows:

$$\frac{dP(t, T)}{P(t, T)} = r(t) \, dt + \sum_{i=1}^{N} \sigma_i \left(B_i(T - t) + 2 \sum_{j=1}^{N} C_{ij}(T - t) Y_j(t) \right) d\tilde{Z}_i(t) \tag{10.46}$$

where $\tau = T - t$ and the equality $C_{ij}(T - t) = C_{ji}(T - t)$ for all $i, j = 1, 2, \ldots,$ N is applied to obtain equation (10.46).

Bond Price Formulas under $Q_3(N)$ and $Q_4(N)$ Models

Though analytical solutions do not exist for $Q_1(N)$ and $Q_2(N)$ models, they do exist for the nested $Q_3(N)$ and $Q_4(N)$ models. The $Q_3(N)$ model assumes orthogonal state variables and does not allow interactions between the state variables. Hence, for this model, $N(N-1)/2$ number of parameters $\tilde{\xi}_{ij}$ (for $i,j = 1, 2, \ldots, N$, and $i > j$) and $N(N-1)/2$ number of parameters $\psi_{ij} = \psi_{ji}$ (for $i,j = 1, 2, \ldots, N$, and $i \neq j$) are set to zero. With these parameter restrictions, the terms $C_{ij}(\tau)$ for $i \neq j$ are not needed in the proposed bond price solution in equation (10.43). Applying these restrictions, the bond price and the system of ODEs given in equations (10.43) and (10.45) simplify under the $Q_3(N)$ model as follows:

$$P(t, T) = e^{A(\tau) + \sum_{i=1}^{N} B_i(\tau) Y_i(t) + \sum_{i=1}^{N} C_i(\tau) Y_i^2(t) - H(t,T)} \tag{10.47}$$

and

$$\frac{\partial A(\tau)}{\partial \tau} = \sum_{i=1}^{N} \tilde{\mu}_i B_i(\tau) + \frac{1}{2} \sum_{i=1}^{N} \sigma_i^2 B_i^2(\tau) + \sum_{i=1}^{N} \sigma_i^2 C_i(\tau)$$

$$\frac{\partial B_i(\tau)}{\partial \tau} = \tilde{\xi}_{ii} B_i(\tau) + 2\, \tilde{\mu}_i C_i(\tau) + 2\sigma_i^2 B_i(\tau) C_i(\tau) \tag{10.48}$$

$$\frac{\partial C_i(\tau)}{\partial \tau} = 2\tilde{\xi}_{ii} C_i(\tau) + 2\sigma_i^2 C_i^2(\tau) - 1$$

where, for notational convenience, the terms $C_{ii}(\tau)$ are now represented as $C_i(\tau)$ for all $i = 1, 2, \ldots, N$. Equation (10.48) represents a system of $2N + 1$ ODEs. The last equation in (10.48) is the well-known Riccati equation with constant coefficients, which has a standard solution given in Chapter 6. The linear first-order ODEs in the first two equations in (10.48) are solved easily using the analytical solution of $C_i(\tau)$. The solutions are generalizations of the single-factor solution in equation (10.13), and are given as follows:

$$A(\tau) = \sum_{i=1}^{N} A_i(\tau)$$

$$A_i(\tau) = \left[-\left(\frac{\tilde{\mu}_i}{\beta_i}\right)^2 \tau \right] + \left[\frac{\tilde{\mu}_i^2 (e^{\beta_i \tau} - 1)[(-2\tilde{\xi}_{ii} + \beta_i)(e^{\beta_i \tau} - 1) + 2\beta_i]}{\beta_i^3 [(\beta_i - \tilde{\xi}_{ii})(e^{2\beta_i \tau} - 1) + 2\beta_i]} \right]$$

$$+ \frac{1}{2} \ln \left[\frac{2\beta_i e^{(\beta_i - \tilde{\xi}_{ii})\tau}}{(\beta_i - \tilde{\xi}_{ii})(e^{2\beta_i \tau} - 1) + 2\beta_i} \right]$$

$$B_i(\tau) = -\frac{2\,\tilde{\mu}_i(e^{\beta_i\tau} - 1)^2}{\beta_i[(\beta_i - \tilde{\xi}_{ii})(e^{2\beta_i\tau} - 1) + 2\beta_i]}$$

$$C_i(\tau) = -\frac{e^{2\beta_i\tau} - 1}{(\beta_i - \tilde{\xi}_{ii})(e^{2\beta_i\tau} - 1) + 2\beta_i} \qquad (10.49)$$

$$\beta_i = \sqrt{\tilde{\xi}_{ii}^2 + 2\sigma_i^2}$$

The solution in equation (10.49) also applies to the $Q_4(N)$ model (i.e., the SAINTS model) with the risk-neutral parameters defined in equation (10.40) and the restrictions on the MPRs given by equation (10.41). The risk-neutral stochastic bond price process under the nested $Q_3(N)$ and $Q_4(N)$ models has a simpler form and is given as follows:

$$\frac{dP(t,T)}{P(t,T)} = r(t)\,dt + \sum_{i=1}^{N} \sigma_i\big(B_i(T-t) + 2C_i(T-t)Y_i(t)\big)\,d\tilde{Z}_i(t) \qquad (10.50)$$

where $\tau = T - t$.

PARAMETER ESTIMATES

The unobserved state variables under the QTSMs do not have a one-to-one correspondence with the observed yields. For example, even under the single-factor case, the movements in the short rate or the zero-coupon yield of any given maturity do not uniquely identify the dynamics of the unobserved state variable due to the assumed quadratic relationship. Under the multifactor case, this is a more serious issue since multiple states can correspond to the same values of zero-coupon yields, and hence, yields cannot be inverted to uniquely identify the factors. Further, since the continuous-time model is estimated using discrete time-series data, this leads to a discretization bias (see Ait-Sahalia [1996a, 1996b]). Recent econometric advances allow addressing both these issues using the simulated method of moments techniques. ADG [2002] employ a specific version of this technique known as the efficient method of moments (EMM) and developed by Gallant and Tauchen [1996, 1989] to estimate the parameters of the three-factor QTSMs.[1]

Table 10.1 gives the parameter estimates and goodness-of-fit tests for the nested versions of the three-factor QTSMs, given as $Q_1(3)$, $Q_2(3)$, $Q_3(3)$, and $Q_4(3)$. The $Q_4(3)$, or the SAINTS, model of Constantinidies [1992] is the most restrictive model among the four models. This model imposes strong overidentifying restrictions on the market prices of risks and is rejected with

TABLE 10.1 EMM Estimates of the Parameters for Fundamental Three-Factor QTSMs

	Estimate (Standard Error)			
	$Q_1(3)$	$Q_2(3)$	$Q_3(3)$	$Q_4(3)$
δ	0.0338 (0.0053)	0.0180(0.0059)	0.0176 (0.0062)	0.0373 (0.0524)
ψ_{12}	−0.5847(0.2926)	0.0393(0.0541)		
ψ_{13}	−0.3866(0.3586)	0.0409(0.1301)		
ψ_{23}	0.9101(0.0731)	−0.0555(0.0250)		
μ_1	0.0608(0.1019)	0.0214(0.2088)	0.0436(0.1087)	0.0547(0.0084)
μ_2	0.0007(0.0000)	0.0006(0.0000)	0.0007(0.0001)	0.2937(0.2549)
μ_3	0.1343(0.1453)	0.2055(0.1550)	0.0299(0.0641)	0.0625(0.0725)
ξ_{11}	−1.7318(0.2629)	−1.6815(0.1850)	−1.5412(0.2879)	−0.4030(0.0005)
ξ_{21}	0.0043(0.0131)			
ξ_{31}	2.7202(1.1386)			
ξ_{22}	−0.0037(0.0006)	−0.0003(0.0000)	−0.0003(0.0000)	−0.1690(0.0378)
ξ_{32}	−1.1898(0.2570)			
ξ_{33}	−0.3411(0.0521)	−2.7772(0.3115)	−2.8718(0.2408)	−3.9839(0.5243)
$\sigma_1{}^2$	1.5143×10^{-4}(1.2167)	0.0147(0.0037)	0.0173(0.0037)	0.0805(0.0001)
$\sigma_2{}^2$	1.1543×10^{-4}(0.0472)	0.0008(0.0001)	0.0009(0.0001)	0.0023(0.0019)
$\sigma_3{}^2$	1.5916×10^{-4}(0.1132)	0.4980(0.0420)	0.4924(0.0428)	1.1673(0.1273)
μ_1	−0.0416(0.0762)	0.0428(0.2345)	−0.0665(0.1063)	−0.4784(0.0000)
μ_2	0.0317(0.0301)	−0.1338(0.0217)	−0.1197(0.0187)	0.2668(0.0000)
μ_3	0.2534(0.1451)	0.0851(0.0341)	0.1398(0.0144)	0.0573(0.0000)
ξ_{11}	−1.8465(2.1800)	1.7873(0.0996)	1.6130(0.1828)	−0.0375(0.0000)
ξ_{21}	0.0226(0.5891)			
ξ_{31}	−2.4858(1.8197)			
ξ_{22}	−0.2782(0.0413)	0.0328(0.0074)	0.0358(0.0056)	−0.1548(0.0000)
ξ_{32}	−1.2022(0.1988)			−3.6792(0.0000)
ξ_{33}	−0.2459(0.0215)	0.6323(0.0806)	0.6474(0.0450)	
χ^2	51.297	114.504	122.599	508.120
df	17	23	26	32
Z	5.882	13.491	13.396	59.515

a large z statistic of 59.515. The $Q_3(3)$ model removes the restrictions on the market prices of risks leading to a substantial improvement in model performance, but the model is still rejected with a z statistic of 13.396. Though the $Q_3(3)$ model is nested in the $Q_2(3)$ model, the z statistic of the latter model is slightly *higher*, equal to 13.491. Though both these models assume orthogonal state variables, the additional flexibility of allowing interdependencies among state variables in determining the short rate by the $Q_2(3)$ model is more than offset by reduced degrees of freedom under this model. Hence, allowing interdependencies is not a statistically important feature of the QTSMs. Given that the $Q_3(3)$ model allows analytical solutions for the bond price and also leads to computationally fast quasi-analytical solutions of interest rate derivatives using either the Fourier inversion method or the cumulant expansion method (these are derived later in this chapter), this model should be preferred to the more flexible $Q_2(3)$ model.

The $Q_1(3)$ model outperforms all other nested models with a z statistic of 5.882. The additional flexibility achieved by allowing unconditional correlations under the $Q_1(3)$ model leads to a substantial improvement in its performance. Though all three-factor QTSMs are rejected at conventional significance levels, the z statistics of $Q_1(3)$, $Q_2(3)$, and $Q_3(3)$ models are significantly lower than those of the preferred three-factor ATSMs of Dai and Singleton [2000]. Even the $Q_3(3)$ model, which assumes orthogonal state variables and no interdependencies, performs significantly better than the preferred three-factor affine models of Dai and Singleton [2000], which allow correlated state variables.

Brandt and Chapman [2005], using "economic moments" of the height, slope, and curvature factors constructed from six-month, two-year, and ten-year yields, apply a simulated method of moments estimator (see Lee and Ingram [1991] and Duffie and Singleton [1993]) and compare the performance of various three-factor affine and quadratic models. They find that $Q_1(3)$ model cannot be rejected by the specification tests, while the three-factor ATSMs are rejected. Other studies show mixed performance of the QTSMs. Sufana [2003] develops a discrete-time version of the three-factor quadratic model, but finds that this model is rejected by the EMM specification test. Leippold and Wu [2003], using a generalized method of moments estimator, find that an unrestricted two-factor quadratic model can explain the basic characteristics of the first two moments of yields and returns. Overall, the preliminary evidence by ADG and Brandt and Chapman points to the superiority of the QTSMs over ATSMs in explaining the U.S. yield curve dynamics.

PREFERENCE-FREE MULTIFACTOR QTSMs

Though fundamental QTSMs outperform fundamental ATSMs based upon the time-series behavior of yields, no direct comparisons between these two classes of models have been made for pricing interest rate derivatives, such as caps and swaptions. Some studies have analyzed specific models in isolation and considered whether these models can jointly price bonds and interest rate derivatives. For example, Jagannathan, Kaplin, and Sun (JKS) [2003] show that the fundamental three-factor CIR model (or the $A_3(3)$ model) leads to large errors in valuing caps and swaptions, even though this model fits very well to swap rates. JKS suggest that the inability of the fundamental $A_3(3)$ model to price caps and swaptions may be due to the restrictive nature of stochastic volatility assumed by this model and that nonaffine models with more general forms of stochastic volatility may be necessary for more accurate pricing of these claims.

Even if the JKS conjecture is correct, a significant portion of the mispricing of interest rate derivatives may be resolved by simply using the preference-free models corresponding to the fundamental models. As demonstrated in Chapter 9, the preference-free explosive $A_3(3)++$ model can price interest rate caps better than the fundamental $A_3(3)$ model of JKS. The superior performance of the $A_3(3)++$ model can be understood as follows. The MPRs under the fundamental $A_3(3)$ model determine both the conditional means of the returns and the volatility shape/correlation patterns of the forward rate changes. The MPRs under the fundamental $A_3(3)$ model, if specified incorrectly for estimating the conditional means, will lead to errors in pricing caps and swaptions, since these MPRs also determine the volatility shape/correlation patterns of forward rate changes through the risk-neutral parameters.

Further, the pricing errors in the JKS model are high because of the basic tension in fitting bond prices versus implied volatilities of option prices. This tension is avoided by the $A_3(3)++$ model by allowing a time-inhomogeneous short rate, which ensures that this model fits the bond prices exactly, such that the risk-neutral parameters are used to fit only the option prices. A time-inhomogeneous short rate is also assumed by virtually all models in the fixed income literature that lead to low errors in pricing interest rate options.

In general, this insight applies to QTSMs also. This section derives preference-free N-factor QTSMs corresponding to the first three fundamental N-factor QTSMs given earlier. We consider both time-homogeneous preference-free QTSMs and time-inhomogeneous preference-free QTSMs. Extending the earlier notation, the three nested time-homogeneous preference-free QTSMs are denoted as $Q_1(N)+$, $Q_2(N)+$, and $Q_3(N)+$, and the three corresponding time-inhomogeneous preference-free QTSMs are denoted as $Q_1(N)++$, $Q_2(N)++$, and $Q_3(N)++$. Separate preference-free QTSMs cannot be identified corresponding to the $Q_4(N)$ model (i.e., the SAINTS model of Constantinidies [1992]), since MPRs are endogenous functions of physical parameters under the $Q_4(N)$ model, and eliminating this endogenous relationship by allowing general nonlinear MPRs basically reduces the $Q_4(N)++$ model to $Q_3(N)++$ model.

Preference-free QTSMs can be obtained by exogenous specifications of the stochastic bond price processes and specific bond price solutions at time 0, using the method outlined in Chapter 4 and Chapter 7 for affine models. This technique allows obtaining the stochastic process for the short rate directly under the risk-neutral measure, circumventing the requirement of modeling the market prices of risks. This approach is also equivalent to specifying the short rate process directly under the risk-neutral measure.

Hence, the preference-free QTSMs are modeled with an exogenous specification of the risk-neutral stochastic process of the state variables given as follows:

$$dY_i(t) = \left(\tilde{\mu}_i + \sum_{j=1}^{i} \tilde{\xi}_{ij} Y_j(t) \right) dt + \sigma_i \, d\tilde{Z}_i(t), \text{ for all } i = 1, 2, \ldots, N \quad (10.51)$$

The short rate is given as a quadratic function of the state variables, which under the maximal specification is given as follows:

$$r(t) = \delta(t) + \sum_{i=1}^{N} \sum_{j=1}^{N} Y_i(t) Y_j(t) \psi_{ij} \quad (10.52)$$

where $\psi_{ij} = \psi_{ji}$ are constants for all $i, j = 1, 2, \ldots, N$ and $\psi_{ii} = 1$ for all $i = 1, 2, \ldots, N$. The term $\delta\ (t)$ is a function of time under the time-inhomogeneous preference-free models (i.e., $Q_1(N)++$, $Q_2(N)++$, and $Q_3(N)++$ models), which allow an exact fitting with initial zero-coupon bond prices and $\delta(t) = \delta$, a constant, under the time-homogeneous preference-free models (i.e., $Q_1(N)+$, $Q_2(N)+$, and $Q_3(N)+$ models).

Though the risk-neutral processes of the state variables in equation (10.51) are identical to the corresponding processes under the fundamental QTSMs in equation (10.39), the MPRs under the preference-free QTSMs are of a general, nonlinear form, defined using the change of measure as follows:

$$d\tilde{Z}_i(t) = dZ_i(t) + \gamma_i(z, t) \, dt, \quad \text{for all } i = 1, 2, \ldots, N \quad (10.53)$$

This change of measure requires that all of the N functions $\gamma_i(z, t)$ are bounded such that the Novikov condition of the Girsanov theorem is satisfied. The physical processes for the state variables can be obtained by substituting equation (10.53) into equation (10.51) as follows:

$$dY_i(t) = \left(\tilde{\mu}_i + \sum_{j=1}^{i} \tilde{\xi}_{ij} Y_j(t) + \sigma_i \gamma_i(z, t) \right) dt + \sigma_i dZ_i(t) \quad (10.54)$$

for all $i = 1, 2, \ldots, N$. The state variable processes may be nonaffine, and the drifts may include other state variables in addition to the N state variables. Hence, the restrictions on state-variable processes that distinguish the different nested preference-free QTSMs apply only to the risk-neutral parameters, and not to the physical parameters. This is useful since it allows a similar level of flexibility in defining the physical processes of the nested N-factor preference-free QTSMs. For example, unconditional correlations may exist for each of the nested N-factor preference-free QTSMs under the physical measure.

The risk-neutral processes for the state variables given in equation (10.51) and the quadratic specification of the short rate given in (10.52) are sufficient to derive the solutions of bond price and interest rate derivatives under the preference-free QTSMs. The solutions of the bond price under the preference-free $Q_M(N)+$ models are identical to the solutions of the bond price under the fundamental $Q_M(N)$ models (for $M = 1, 2$, and 3) and are given by equation (10.43). Of course, the similarity is only in form, estimates of the risk-neutral parameters under the $Q_M(N)+$ models can be different from the corresponding estimates under the $Q_M(N)$ models, given that the functional forms of MPRs and the physical processes are restricted under the latter but not under the former.

The parameter restrictions and the total number of parameters and state variable values that can be obtained by nonlinear optimization under the nested time-homogeneous preference-free QTSMs are given as follows:

1. *The $Q_1(N)+$ Model: Maximally flexible time-homogeneous preference-free model.* For this model, the risk-neutral state variable processes and the short rate are defined by equations (10.51) and (10.52), respectively. The model requires the estimation of the following parameters: $N(N - 1)/2$ number of parameters ψ_{ij} (since $\psi_{ij} = \psi_{ji}$ for all $i, j = 1, 2, \ldots, N$, and $\psi_{ii} = 1$, for all $i = 1, 2, \ldots, N$); N number of parameters $\tilde{\mu}_i$ (for $i = 1, 2, \ldots, N$); $N(N + 1)/2$ number of parameters $\tilde{\xi}_{ij}$ (for $i, j = 1, 2, \ldots, N$ and $i \geq j$); N number of parameters σ_i (for $i = 1, 2, \ldots, N$); and the parameter $\delta(t) = \delta$. Hence, the estimation of the $Q_1(N)+$ model requires $N(N - 1)/2 + N + N(N + 1)/2 + N + 1 = (N + 1)^2$ number of parameters. In addition, if the model is calibrated using the daily cross sections of prices on bonds and interest rate derivatives over K days, then N values of the state variables $Y_1(t)$, $Y_2(t)$, $\ldots$, $Y_N(t)$ are also required for each of the K days, giving a grand total of $(N + 1)^2 + NK$ number of parameters and state variable values to be estimated using nonlinear optimization.

2. *The $Q_2(N)+$ Model: Time-homogeneous preference-free model with orthogonal state variables and interactions.* This model requires zero unconditional correlations between the state variables under the risk-neutral measure. Hence, the $N(N - 1)/2$ number of parameters $\tilde{\xi}_{ij}$ (for $i, j = 1, 2, \ldots, N$ and $i > j$) are set to zero. As mentioned earlier, unconditional correlations may be nonzero under the physical measure

under the $Q_2(N)+$ model. The parameters and state variable values for calibrating using the daily cross sections of prices on bonds and interest rate derivatives over K days are $N(N-1)/2$ less than those under the $Q_1(N)+$ model, or equal to $(N+1)^2 + NK - N(N-1)/2$.

3. *The $Q_3(N)+$ Model: Time-homogeneous preference-free model with orthogonal state variables and no interactions.* This model not only requires zero unconditional correlations between the state variables under the risk-neutral measure but also disallows interactions of the state variables in determining the short rate in equation (10.52). Hence, another set of $N(N-1)/2$ parameters $\psi_{ij} = \psi_{ji}$ (for $i, j = 1, 2, \ldots, N$ and $i \neq j$) are set to zero. The total number of parameters and state-variable values for calibrating using the daily cross sections of prices on bonds and interest rate derivatives over K days are $N(N-1)/2$ less than those under the $Q_2(N)+$ model, or equal to $(N+1)^2 + NK - N(N-1)$.

The solutions of the bond price under the time-inhomogeneous preference-free $Q_M(N)++$ models are slightly different than those under the $Q_M(N)+$ and $Q_M(N)$ models and can be obtained by following the same steps as under the $Q_M(N)$ models, except that $H(t, T)$ in equation (10.44) must be replaced by the following:

$$H(t, T) = \int_t^T \delta(v)\, dv \qquad (10.55)$$

Consider the initially observable zero-coupon bond price function given as $P(0, T)$. To calibrate the bond price solution in equation (10.43) to the initial bond price function $P(0, T)$, consider the log of bond price evaluated at time 0 as follows:

$$\ln P(0, T) = A(T) + \sum_{i=1}^N B_i(T) Y_i(0) + \sum_{i=1}^N \sum_{j=1}^N C_{ij}(T) Y_i(0) Y_j(0) - H(0, T) \qquad (10.56)$$

Differentiating equation (10.56) with respect to T, then replacing T with t, and simplifying, we get:

$$\delta(t) = \frac{\partial A(t)}{\partial t} + \sum_{i=1}^N Y_i(0) \frac{\partial B_i(t)}{\partial t} + \sum_{i=1}^N \sum_{j=1}^N Y_i(0) Y_j(0) \frac{\partial C_{ij}(t)}{\partial t} - \frac{\partial \ln P(0, t)}{\partial t} \qquad (10.57)$$

Since the functions $A(t)$, $B_i(t)$, and $C_{ij}(t)$ are time-homogeneous, we can use the ODEs given in equation (10.45) to evaluate the partial derivatives in equation (10.57) and simplify to give:

$$\delta(t) = f(0,t) + \sum_{i=1}^{N} \tilde{\mu}_i B_i(t) + \sum_{i=1}^{N} \sigma_i^2 (B_i^2(t)/2 + C_{ii}(t))$$

$$+ \sum_{i=1}^{N} Y_i(0) \left(\sum_{j=i}^{N} \tilde{\xi}_{ji} B_j(t) + 2 \sum_{j=1}^{N} \sigma_j^2 B_j(t) C_{ij}(t) + 2 \sum_{j=1}^{N} \tilde{\mu}_j C_{ij}(t) \right)$$

$$+ \sum_{i=1}^{N} \sum_{j=1}^{N} Y_i(0) Y_j(0) \tag{10.58}$$

$$\times \left(\sum_{k=i}^{N} \tilde{\xi}_{ki} C_{jk}(t) + \sum_{k=j}^{N} \tilde{\xi}_{kj} C_{ik}(t) + 2 \sum_{k=1}^{N} \sigma_k^2 C_{ik}(t) C_{jk}(t) - \psi_{ij} \right)$$

The function $H(t, T)$ can be expressed as follows:

$$H(t, T) = \int_t^T \delta(v) \, dv = \int_0^T \delta(v) \, dv - \int_0^t \delta(v) \, dv = H(0, T) - H(0, t) \tag{10.59}$$

Using equation (10.56), the solution to $H(t, T)$ is given as:

$$H(t, T) = A(T) - A(t) + \sum_{i=1}^{N} Y_i(0)(B_i(T) - B_i(t))$$

$$+ \sum_{i=1}^{N} \sum_{j=1}^{N} Y_i(0) Y_j(0)(C_{ij}(T) - C_{ij}(t)) \tag{10.60}$$

$$- \ln P(0, T) + \ln P(0, t)$$

The bond price under the $Q_M(N)++$ models remains the same as in equation (10.43), except that $H(t, T)$ in equation (10.44) is replaced by its new definition in equation (10.60).

Each of the three time-homogeneous preference-free models $Q_1(N)+$, $Q_2(N)+$, and $Q_3(N)+$ given earlier has a time-inhomogeneous preference-free model corresponding to it, which follows the same parameter restrictions as the time-homogeneous model (under the risk-neutral measure), except that it is calibrated *exactly* to the initial forward rate curve $f(0, t)$, using the definitions of the terms $\delta(t)$ and $H(t, T)$ given in equations (10.58) and (10.60), respectively. Since $f(0, t)$ is given, the parameter $\delta(0) = \delta$ can be computed by substituting the values of $f(0, 0) = r(0)$ and the initial values of $Y_1(0), Y_2(0), \ldots, Y_N(0)$ in equation (10.52). Hence, calibrating the $Q_1(N)++$, $Q_2(N)++$, and $Q_3(N)++$ models using the daily cross sections of prices on bonds and interest rate derivatives over K days (with day 0 as the initial day) requires one less parameter than required by the $Q_1(N)+$, $Q_2(N)+$, and $Q_3(N)+$ models, respectively. This makes the total number of parameters and state-variable values to be estimated using nonlinear optimization equal to $(N + 1)^2 + NK - 1$ under the $Q_1(N)++$ model, $(N + 1)^2 + NK - N(N - 1)/2 - 1$ under the $Q_2(N)++$ model, and $(N + 1)^2 + NK - N(N - 1) - 1$ under the $Q_3(N)++$ model. Due to the time-inhomogeneity problem, these models are typically estimated using only one day of cross-sectional price data, or $K = 1$, though the general framework given here allows using more than one day of cross-sectional price data.

Finally, since the $Q_3(N)++$ model allows an analytical solution, the terms $\delta(t)$ and $H(t, T)$ under this model can be simplified by setting the terms $\tilde{\xi}_{ij}$, $\psi_{ij} = \psi_{ji}$, and $C_{ij}(T - t)$ to zero, for all $i \neq j$, in equations (10.58) and (10.60) to give:

$$\delta(t) = f(0, t) + \sum_{i=1}^{N} \tilde{\mu}_i B_i(t) + \sum_{i=1}^{N} \sigma_i^2 \left(B_i^2(t)/2 + C_i(t) \right)$$

$$+ \sum_{i=1}^{N} Y_i(0) \left(\tilde{\xi}_{ii} B_i(t) + 2\sigma_i^2 B_i(t) C_i(t) + 2\tilde{\mu}_i C_i(t) \right) \quad (10.61)$$

$$+ \sum_{i=1}^{N} Y_i^2(0) \left(2\tilde{\xi}_{ii} C_i(t) + 2\sigma_i^2 C_i^2(t) - 1 \right)$$

and

$$H(t, T) = A(T) - A(t) + \sum_{i=1}^{N} Y_i(0) \left(B_i(T) - B_i(t) \right) + \sum_{i=1}^{N} Y_i^2(0) \left(C_i(T) - C_i(t) \right)$$

$$- \ln P(0, T) + \ln P(0, t) \quad (10.62)$$

where, for notational convenience, the terms $C_{ii}(.)$ are now represented as $C_i(.)$, for all $i = 1, 2, \ldots, N$, and the analytical formulas for $A(.)$, $B_i(.)$, and $C_i(.)$ are given in equation (10.49).

Forward Rate Volatility and Correlation Matrix

The risk-neutral forward rate process has an identical form under the fundamental and preference-free QTSMs and is given under the maximal N-factor QTSMs as follows:

$$df(t, T) = \mu_f(t, T)\,dt + \sum_{i=1}^{N}\left(\sigma_{f1,i}(t, T) + \sum_{j=1}^{N}\sigma_{f2,i,j}(t, T)Y_j(t)\right)d\tilde{Z}_i(t)$$

$$(10.63)$$

where

$$\sigma_{f1,i}(t, T) = -\sigma_i\frac{\partial B_i(T - t)}{\partial T}, \quad \sigma_{f2,i,j}(t, T) = -2\sigma_i\frac{\partial C_{ij}(T - t)}{\partial T}, \text{and}$$

$$\mu_f(t, T) = \sum_{i=1}^{N}\sigma_i^2\left(B_i(T - t) + 2\sum_{j=1}^{N}Y_j(t)C_{ij}(T - t)\right)$$

$$\times\left(\frac{\partial B_i(T - t)}{\partial T} + 2\sum_{j=1}^{N}Y_j(t)\frac{\partial C_{ij}(T - t)}{\partial T}\right)$$

Substituting the ODEs for the functions $B_i(.)$ and $C_{ij}(.)$ from equation (10.45), the deterministic components of the forward rate volatility, $\sigma_{f1,i}(t, T)$ and $\sigma_{f2,i,j}(t, T)$, are given as follows:

$$\sigma_{f1,i}(t, T)$$

$$= -\sigma\left(\sum_{j=i}^{N}\tilde{\xi}_{ji}B_j(T - t) + 2\sum_{j=1}^{N}\sigma_j^2 B_j(T - t)C_{ij}(\tau) + 2\sum_{j=1}^{N}\tilde{\mu}_j C_{ij}(T - t)\right)$$

$$(10.64)$$

and

$$\sigma_{f2,i,j}(t, T) = -2\sigma_i\left(\sum_{k=i}^{N}\tilde{\xi}_{ki}C_{jk}(T - t) + \sum_{k=j}^{N}\tilde{\xi}_{kj}C_{ik}(T - t)\right.$$

$$\left. + 2\sum_{k=1}^{N}\sigma_k^2 C_{ik}(T - t)C_{jk}(T - t) - \psi_{ij}\right)$$

$$(10.65)$$

The forward rate volatility under the maximal N-factor QTSMs allows stochastically varying cross-sectional shapes, including time-varying humps, that evolve with the changing values of the state variables. The instantaneous correlation between the changes in forward rates of maturities T_1 and T_2 can be given as follows:

$$\rho(t, T_1, T_2) = \frac{\sum_{i=1}^{N}\left(\sigma_{f1,i}(t, T_1) + \sum_{j=1}^{N}\sigma_{f2,i,j}(t, T_1)Y_j(t)\right)}{\sqrt{\sum_{i=1}^{N}\left(\sigma_{f1,i}(t, T_2) + \sum_{j=1}^{N}\sigma_{f2,i,j}(t, T_2)Y_j(t)\right)}} \quad (10.66)$$

$$\sqrt{\sum_{i=1}^{N}\left(\sigma_{f1,i}(t, T_1) + \sum_{j=1}^{N}\sigma_{f2,i,j}(t, T_1)Y_j(t)\right)^2}$$

$$\times \sqrt{\sum_{i=1}^{N}\left(\sigma_{f1,i}(t, T_2) + \sum_{j=1}^{N}\sigma_{f2,i,j}(t, T_2)Y_j(t)\right)^2}$$

The risk-neutral forward rate process has the same functional form under the $Q_3(N)$, $Q_3(N)+$, and $Q_3(N)++$ models and can be obtained as a special case of equation (10.63) by setting the terms $\tilde{\xi}_{ij}$, $\psi_{ij} = \psi_{ji}$, $C_{ij}(T-t)$, and $\partial C_{ij}(T-t)/\partial T$ to zero for all $i \neq j$, as follows:

$$df(t, T) = \mu_f(t, T)\,dt + \sum_{i=1}^{N}(\sigma_{f1,i}(t, T) + \sigma_{f2,i}(t, T)Y_i(t))\,d\tilde{Z}_i(t) \quad (10.67)$$

where

$$\sigma_{f1,i}(t, T) = -\sigma_i\frac{\partial B_i(T-t)}{\partial T}, \quad \sigma_{f2,i}(t, T) = -2\sigma_i\frac{\partial C_i(T-t)}{\partial T}, \text{ and}$$

$$\mu_f(t, T) = \sum_{i=1}^{N}\sigma_i^2\big(B_i(T-t) + 2Y_i(t)C_i(T-t)\big)$$

$$\times \left(\frac{\partial B_i(T-t)}{\partial T} + 2Y_i(t)\frac{\partial C_i(T-t)}{\partial T}\right)$$

where, for notational simplicity, $C_{ii}(T-t)$ is replaced by $C_i(T-t)$, and $\partial C_{ii}(T-t)/\partial T$ is replaced by $\partial C_i(T-t)/\partial T$.

Substituting the ODEs for the functions $B_i(.)$ and $C_i(.)$ from equation (10.48), the deterministic components of the forward rate volatility, $\sigma_{f1,i}(t, T)$ and $\sigma_{f2,i}(t, T)$, are given as follows:

$$\sigma_{f1,i}(t, T) = -\sigma\big(\tilde{\xi}_{ii}B_i(T-t) + 2\sigma_i^2 B_i(T-t)C_i(T-t) + 2\tilde{\mu}_i C_i(T-t)\big)$$
$$(10.68)$$

and

$$\sigma_{f2,i}(t,T) = -2\sigma_i\big(2\tilde{\xi}_{ii}C_i(T-t) + 2\sigma_i^2 C_i^2(T-t) - 1\big) \qquad (10.69)$$

Since $B_i(.)$ and $C_i(.)$ are given in closed form in equation (10.49), the forward rate volatility is also given in closed form.

To get more insight on the forward rate volatility specification given in equation (10.67), we digress from the QTSM framework, and consider the general N-factor Heath, Jarrow, and Morton (HJM) [1992] forward rate process given as follows:

$$df(t,T) = \mu_f(t,T)\,dt + \sum_{i=1}^{N} \sigma_{i,HJM}(t,T,z)\,d\tilde{Z}_i(t) \qquad (10.70)$$

It is well known that if sufficient flexibility is allowed in the shapes of the HJM forward rate volatility functions $\sigma_{i,HJM}(t,T,z)$, then assuming uncorrelated Brownian motions does not prevent the modeling of realistic correlations between forward rate changes. In fact, any correlated factor model can be converted into an uncorrelated factor model by factor rotations giving orthogonal principal components. However, for such factor rotations to preserve the correlation structure of the forward rate changes, *a sufficient degree of flexibility and nonlinearity* in the shapes of the volatility functions $\sigma_{i,HJM}(t,T,z)$ must be allowed.

The shapes of forward rate volatility functions corresponding to the state variables under the $Q_3(N)$ models (i.e., N-factor orthogonal Gaussian-quadratic models with no interactions) have a much higher degree of flexibility than the corresponding shapes of the forward rate volatility functions under the multifactor CIR models, as each of the volatility functions in equation (10.67) can depend upon three risk-neutral parameters and the current value of the corresponding state variable. The volatility functions can be exponentially declining as well as hump-shaped, even if the corresponding state variables follow stationary risk-neutral processes. The flexibility in the shape of the forward rate volatility functions can be seen in Figure 10.2 for the single-factor case. This implies that the risk-neutral parameters of the $Q_3(N)$ models can capture more realistic forward rate volatility shapes and correlation structures, *even though state variables are orthogonal under these models.*

The instantaneous correlation between the changes in forward rates of maturities T_1 and T_2 under the $Q_3(N)$ models can be obtained as a special case of equation (10.66), and is given as follows:

$$
\rho(t, T_1, T_2) = \frac{\displaystyle\sum_{i=1}^{N}\left(\sigma_{f1,i}(t, T_1) + \sigma_{f2,i}(t, T_1)Y_i(t)\right) \times \left(\sigma_{f1,i}(t, T_2) + \sigma_{f2,i}(t, T_2)Y_i(t)\right)}{\sqrt{\displaystyle\sum_{i=1}^{N}\left(\sigma_{f1,i}(t, T_1) + \sigma_{f2,i}(t, T_1)Y_i(t)\right)^2} \times \sqrt{\displaystyle\sum_{i=1}^{N}\left(\sigma_{f1,i}(t, T_2) + \sigma_{f2,i}(t, T_2)Y_i(t)\right)^2}}
\tag{10.71}
$$

where $\sigma_{f1,i}(t, T)$ and $\sigma_{f2,i}(t, T)$ are defined in equations (10.68) and (10.69), respectively.

The rest of this chapter focuses on the valuation of interest rate derivatives, such as futures and options, and on the valuation of credit derivatives, such as credit default swaps, using the multifactor QTSMs.

VALUING FUTURES

Futures on a Zero-Coupon Bond   We first derive the time t price of a futures contract expiring at time S, written on a zero-coupon bond maturing at time T under the maximal $Q_1(N)$, $Q_1(N)+$, and $Q_1(N)++$ models. The solutions under the $Q_3(N)$, $Q_3(N)+$, and $Q_3(N)++$ models are obtained as special cases. We know that futures price is a martingale under the risk-neutral measure, or:

$$
P_F(t, S, T) = \tilde{E}_t(P(S, T))
\tag{10.72}
$$

Applying Ito's lemma to get the differential of futures price and equating the differential to zero using the martingale relationship given in equation (10.72), the partial differential equation of the futures price is obtained as follows:

$$
\frac{\partial P_F}{\partial t} + \sum_{i=1}^{N} \frac{\partial P_F}{\partial Y_i}\left[\tilde{\mu}_i + \sum_{j=1}^{i} \tilde{\xi}_{ij} Y_j(t)\right] + \frac{1}{2}\sum_{i=1}^{N}\frac{\partial^2 P_F}{\partial Y_i^2}\sigma_i^2 = 0
\tag{10.73}
$$

subject to the boundary condition $P_F(S, S, T) = P(S, T)$. Consider the following proposed solution to the futures price:

$$
P_F(t, S, T) = e^{A_F(s) + \sum_{i=1}^{N} B_{iF}(s)Y_i(t) + \sum_{i=1}^{N}\sum_{j=1}^{N} C_{ijF}(s)Y_i(t)Y_j(t) - H(S,T)}, \qquad = S - t
\tag{10.74}
$$

subject to the boundary conditions $A_F(0) = A(U)$, $B_{iF}(0) = B_i(U)$, and $C_{ijF}(0) = C_{ij}(U)$, where $U = T - S$ and $A(.)$, $B_i(.)$, and $C_{ij}(.)$ are defined in equation (10.43) and solved by the system of ODEs in equation (10.45). Taking the partial derivatives of the futures price, substituting them in equation (10.73), and then using a separation of variables gives the following ODEs:

$$\frac{\partial A_F(s)}{\partial s} = \sum_{i=1}^{N} \tilde{\mu}_i B_{iF}(s) + \frac{1}{2} \sum_{i=1}^{N} \sigma_i^2 B_{iF}^2(s) + \sum_{i=1}^{N} \sigma_i^2 C_{iiF}(s)$$

$$\frac{\partial B_{iF}(s)}{\partial s} = \sum_{j=i}^{N} \tilde{\xi}_{ji} B_{jF}(s) + 2 \sum_{j=1}^{N} \sigma_j^2 B_{jF}(s) C_{ijF}(s) + 2 \sum_{j=1}^{N} \tilde{\mu}_j C_{ijF}(s) \qquad (10.75)$$

$$\frac{\partial C_{ijF}(s)}{\partial s} = \sum_{k=i}^{N} \tilde{\xi}_{ki} C_{jkF}(s) + \sum_{k=j}^{N} \tilde{\xi}_{kj} C_{ikF}(s) + 2 \sum_{k=1}^{N} \sigma_k^2 C_{ikF}(s) C_{jkF}(s)$$

subject to the boundary conditions given in the previous paragraph. In general, since $C_{ij}(U) = C_{ji}(U)$ for all $i, j = 1, 2, \ldots, N$, and using symmetry in equation (10.75), $C_{ijF}(s) = C_{jiF}(s)$ for all $i, j = 1, 2, \ldots, N$. Hence, the solution to the above system requires solving one ODE for $A_F(s)$, N ODEs for $B_{iF}(s)$, and $N(N + 1)/2$ ODEs for $C_{ijF}(s)$, giving a total of $(N + 1)(N + 2)/2$ ODEs to be solved. In general, these ODEs are solved using numerical methods (e.g., with programming languages such as Matlab) under the $Q_1(N)$, $Q_1(N)+$, and $Q_1(N)++$ models. The time-homogeneous $Q_1(N)$ and $Q_1(N)+$ models require $H(S, T) = \delta(T - S) = \delta U$, while the time-inhomogeneous $Q_1(N)++$ model requires $H(S, T)$ be given by equation (10.60).

Next, consider the special case of $Q_3(N)$, $Q_3(N)+$, and $Q_3(N)++$ models, which allow analytical formulas for the price of the futures on a zero-coupon bond. Applying the parameter restrictions given earlier, the futures price and the system of ODEs given in equations (10.74) and (10.75), respectively, simplify under the $Q_3(N)$, $Q_3(N)+$, and $Q_3(N)++$ models as follows:

$$P_F(t, S, T) = e^{A_F(s) + \sum_{i=1}^{N} B_{iF}(s) Y_i(t) + \sum_{i=1}^{N} C_{iF}(s) Y_i^2(t) - H(S,T)}, \qquad s = S - t \qquad (10.76)$$

and

$$\frac{\partial A_F(s)}{\partial s} = \sum_{i=1}^{N} \tilde{\mu}_i B_{iF}(s) + \frac{1}{2} \sum_{i=1}^{N} \sigma_i^2 B_{iF}^2(s) + \sum_{i=1}^{N} \sigma_i^2 C_{iF}(s)$$

$$\frac{\partial B_{iF}(s)}{\partial s} = \tilde{\xi}_{ii} B_{iF}(s) + 2\,\tilde{\mu}_i C_{iF}(s) + 2\sigma_i^2 B_{iF}(s) C_{iF}(s) \tag{10.77}$$

$$\frac{\partial C_{iF}(s)}{\partial s} = 2\tilde{\xi}_{ii} C_{iF}(s) + 2\sigma_i^2 C_{iF}^2(s)$$

where, for notational convenience, the terms $C_{iiF}(s)$ are now represented as $C_{iF}(s)$ for all $i = 1, 2, \ldots, N$. Equation (10.77) represents a system of $2N + 1$ ODEs, subject to the boundary conditions $A_F(0) = A(U)$, $B_{iF}(0) = B_i(U)$, and $C_{iF}(0) = C_i(U)$ where, $U = T - S$ and analytical solutions of $A(U)$, $B_i(U)$, and $C_i(U)$ are given in equation (10.49). The solutions of the ODEs are given as follows:

$$A_F(s) = \int_0^s \sum_{i=1}^N \left(\tilde{\mu}_i B_{iF}(v) + \frac{1}{2}\sigma_i^2 B_{iF}^2(v) + \sigma_i^2 C_{iF}(v) \right) dv + A(U)$$

$$B_{iF}(s) = -e^{s\tilde{\xi}_{ii}} \left(\frac{\tilde{\xi}_{ii} B_i(U) + 2C_i(U)\,\tilde{\mu}_i (e^{s\tilde{\xi}_{ii}} - 1)}{\sigma_i^2 C_i(U)(e^{2s\tilde{\xi}_{ii}} - 1) - \tilde{\xi}_{ii}} \right) \tag{10.78}$$

$$C_{iF}(s) = -\frac{2\tilde{\xi}_{ii} C_i(U) e^{2s\tilde{\xi}_{ii}}}{2\sigma_i^2 C_i(U)(e^{2s\tilde{\xi}_{ii}} - 1) - 2\tilde{\xi}_{ii}}$$

Though the solutions of $B_{iF}(s)$ and $C_{iF}(s)$ are given in closed form, the term $A_F(s)$ is evaluated using a numerical integral for expositional simplicity. The time-homogeneous $Q_3(N)$ and $Q_3(N)+$ models require that $H(S, T) = \delta(T - S) = \delta U$, while the time-inhomogeneous $Q_3(N)++$ model requires that $H(S, T)$ be given by equation (10.62).

Futures on a Time Deposit The price of a futures contract on a time deposit—such as Eurodollar and Euribor futures—can be obtained using equation (3.12) in Chapter 3:

$$P_F^{TD}(t, S, T) = \frac{100}{\hat{U}} (1 + \hat{U} - P_F^I(t, S, T)) \tag{10.79}$$

where S is the futures expiration date, $U = T - S$ is the deposit time period calculated using the actual/actual day-count convention, $\hat{U}$ is the deposit time period calculated using actual/360 day-count convention, and $P_F^I(t, S, T)$ is the current price of a futures contract written on a hypothetical asset, which at the expiration date S is worth the inverse of a \$1 face-value zero-coupon bond maturing at time T. As shown in Chapter 3, the futures price, $P_F^I(t, S, T)$, is given by the following risk-neutral expectation:

$$P_F^I(t, S, T) = \tilde{E}_t \left(\frac{1}{P(S, T)} \right) \tag{10.80}$$

Using Ito's lemma to solve the differential of the futures price and equating the risk-neutral expectation to zero, we get the PDE for the futures price, as follows:

$$\frac{\partial P_F^I}{\partial t} + \sum_{i=1}^{N} \frac{\partial P_F^I}{\partial Y_i} \left[\tilde{\mu}_i + \sum_{j=1}^{i} \tilde{\xi}_{ij} Y_j(t) \right] + \frac{1}{2} \sum_{i=1}^{N} \frac{\partial^2 P_F^I}{\partial Y_i^2} \sigma_i^2 = 0 \tag{10.81}$$

subject to the boundary condition $P_F^I(S, S, T) = 1/P(S, T)$. Consider the following proposed solution to the futures price:

$$P_F^I(t, S, T) = e^{a_F(s) + \sum_{i=1}^{N} b_{iF}(s) Y_i(t) + \sum_{i=1}^{N} \sum_{j=1}^{N} c_{ijF}(s) Y_i(t) Y_j(t) + H(S, T)}, \qquad s = S - t \tag{10.82}$$

subject to the boundary conditions $a_F(0) = -A(U)$, $b_{iF}(0) = -B_i(U)$, and $c_{ijF}(0) = -C_{ij}(U)$, where $U = T - S$ and $A(.)$, $B_i(.)$, and $C_{ij}(.)$ are defined in equation (10.43) and solved by the system of ODEs in equation (10.45). Taking the partial derivatives of the futures price, substituting them in equation (10.81), and then using a separation of variables gives the following ODEs:

$$\frac{\partial a_F(s)}{\partial s} = \sum_{i=1}^{N} \tilde{\mu}_i b_{iF}(s) + \frac{1}{2} \sum_{i=1}^{N} \sigma_i^2 b_{iF}^2(s) + \sum_{i=1}^{N} \sigma_i^2 c_{iiF}(s)$$

$$\frac{\partial b_{iF}(s)}{\partial s} = \sum_{j=i}^{N} \tilde{\xi}_{ji} b_{jF}(s) + 2 \sum_{j=1}^{N} \sigma_j^2 b_{jF}(s) c_{ijF}(s) + 2 \sum_{j=1}^{N} \tilde{\mu}_j c_{ijF}(s) \tag{10.83}$$

$$\frac{\partial c_{ijF}(s)}{\partial s} = \sum_{k=i}^{N} \tilde{\xi}_{ki} c_{jkF}(s) + \sum_{k=j}^{N} \tilde{\xi}_{kj} c_{ikF}(s) + 2 \sum_{k=1}^{N} \sigma_k^2 c_{ikF}(s) c_{jkF}(s)$$

subject to the boundary conditions given in the previous paragraph. In general, since $C_{ij}(U) = C_{ji}(U)$ for all $i, j = 1, 2, \ldots, N$ and using symmetry in equation (10.83), $c_{ijF}(s) = c_{jiF}(s)$ for all $i, j = 1, 2, \ldots, N$. Hence, the solution to this system requires solving one ODE for $a_F(s)$, N ODEs for $b_{iF}(s)$, and $N(N + 1)/2$ ODEs for $c_{ijF}(s)$, giving a total of $(N + 1)(N + 2)/2$ ODEs to be solved. The futures price $P_F^I(t, S, T)$ under the $Q_1(N)$, $Q_1(N)+$, and $Q_1(N)++$ models differs in the way $H(S, T)$ is defined in equation (10.82).

The time-homogeneous $Q_1(N)$ and $Q_1(N)+$ models require $H(S, T) = \delta$ $(T - S) = \delta U$, while the time-inhomogeneous $Q_1(N)++$ model requires $H(S, T)$ be given by equation (10.60). The price of the futures on a time deposit $P_F^{TD}(t, S, T)$ can be obtained by substituting the solution of $P_F^I(t, S, T)$ in equation (10.79).

Next, consider the special case of $Q_3(N)$, $Q_3(N)+$, and $Q_3(N)++$ models, which allow analytical formulas for $P_F^{TD}(t, S, T)$, the price of the futures on a time deposit. Applying the parameter restrictions given earlier, the futures price $P_F^I(t, S, T)$ and the system of ODEs given in equations (10.82) and (10.83), respectively, simplify under the $Q_3(N)$, $Q_3(N)+$, and $Q_3(N)++$ models as follows:

$$P_F^I(t, S, T) = e^{a_F(s) + \sum_{i=1}^{N} b_{iF}(s) Y_i(t) + \sum_{i=1}^{N} c_{iF}(s) Y_i^2(t) + H(S, T)}, \qquad s = S - t \qquad (10.84)$$

and

$$\frac{\partial a_F(s)}{\partial s} = \sum_{i=1}^{N} \tilde{\mu}_i b_{iF}(s) + \frac{1}{2} \sum_{i=1}^{N} \sigma_i^2 b_{iF}^2(s) + \sum_{i=1}^{N} \sigma_i^2 c_{iF}(s)$$

$$\frac{\partial b_{iF}(s)}{\partial s} = \tilde{\xi}_{ii} b_{iF}(s) + 2\,\tilde{\mu}_i c_{iF}(s) + 2\sigma_i^2 b_{iF}(s) c_{iF}(s) \qquad (10.85)$$

$$\frac{\partial c_{iF}(s)}{\partial s} = 2\tilde{\xi}_{ii} c_{iF}(s) + 2\sigma_i^2 c_{iF}^2(s)$$

subject to $a_F(0) = -A(U)$, $b_{iF}(0) = -B_i(U)$, and $c_{iF}(0) = -C_i(U)$, where, for notational convenience, the terms $c_{iiF}(s)$ are now represented as $c_{iF}(s)$ for all $i = 1, 2, \ldots, N$.

Note that the solution form in equation (10.84) is identical to the solution form in equation (10.76) and that the ODEs in equation (10.85) are identical to the ODEs in equation (10.77), except that $H(S, T)$ and the constants in the boundary conditions are of opposite signs. Hence, the solutions of $a_F(s)$, $b_{iF}(s)$, and $c_{iF}(s)$ immediately follow from equation (10.78) by switching the signs of the constants $A(U)$, $B_i(U)$, and $C_i(U)$ and are given as follows:

$$a_F(s) = \int_0^s \sum_{i=1}^{N} \left(\tilde{\mu}_i b_{iF}(v) + \frac{1}{2} \sigma_i^2 b_{iF}^2(v) + \sigma_i^2 c_{iF}(v) \right) dv - A(U)$$

$$b_{iF}(s) = -e^{s\tilde{\xi}_{ii}} \left(\frac{\tilde{\xi}_{ii} B_i(U) + 2C_i(U) \tilde{\mu}_i (e^{s\tilde{\xi}_{ii}} - 1)}{\sigma_i^2 C_i(U)(e^{2s\tilde{\xi}_{ii}} - 1) + \tilde{\xi}_{ii}} \right) \qquad (10.86)$$

$$c_{iF}(s) = -\frac{2\tilde{\xi}_{ii} C_i(U) e^{2s\tilde{\xi}_{ii}}}{2\sigma_i^2 C_i(U)(e^{2s\tilde{\xi}_{ii}} - 1) + 2\tilde{\xi}_{ii}}$$

where analytical solutions of $A(U)$, $B_i(U)$, and $C_i(U)$ are given in equation (10.49). The time-homogeneous $Q_3(N)$ and $Q_3(N)+$ models require that $H(S, T) = \delta(T - S) = \delta U$, while the time-inhomogeneous $Q_3(N)++$ model requires $H(S, T)$ be given by equation (10.62). The price of the futures on a time deposit $P_F^{TD}(t, S, T)$ is obtained by substituting the solution of $P_F^I(t, S, T)$ in equation (10.79).

The convexity bias, given as the difference between the futures rate and the forward rate on a time deposit, is defined in equation (3.17) in Chapter 3 as follows:

$$Convexity\ Bias = L_F(t, S, T) - L_f(t, S, T)$$

$$= \frac{1 + L_F(t, S, T)\hat{U}}{\hat{U}}\left(1 - \frac{P(t, S)}{P(t, T)P_F^I(t, S, T)}\right) \qquad (10.87)$$

By substituting the appropriate formulas, the convexity bias under the $Q_1(N)$, $Q_1(N)+$, and $Q_1(N)++$ models is given as follows:

Convexity Bias

$$= L_F(t, S, T) - L_f(t, S, T)$$

$$= \frac{1 + L_F(t, S, T)\hat{U}}{\hat{U}} \qquad (10.88)$$

$$\times (1 - e^{[A(s)-a_F(s)-A(\tau)]+\sum_{i=1}^{N}[B_i(s)-b_{iF}(s)-B_i(\tau)]Y_i(t)+\sum_{i=1}^{N}\sum_{j=1}^{N}[C_{ij}(s)-c_{ijF}(s)-C_{ij}(\tau)]Y_i(t)Y_j(t)}),$$

$$s = S - t \text{ and } \tau = T - t$$

where $A(.)$, $B_i(.)$, and $C_{ij}(.)$ are solved using the system of ODEs in equation (10.45) and where $a_F(.)$, $b_{iF}(.)$, and $c_{ijF}(.)$ are solved using the system of ODEs in equation (10.83).

An analytical solution to the convexity bias is given under the $Q_3(N)$, $Q_3(N)+$, and $Q_3(N)++$ models, as follows:

Convexity Bias

$$= L_F(t, S, T) - L_f(t, S, T)$$

$$= \frac{1 + L_F(t, S, T)\hat{U}}{\hat{U}} \qquad (10.89)$$

$$\times (1 - e^{[A(s)-a_F(s)-A(\tau)]+\sum_{i=1}^{N}[B_i(s)-b_{iF}(s)-B_i(\tau)]Y_i(t)+\sum_{i=1}^{N}[C_i(s)-c_{iF}(s)-C_i(\tau)]Y_i^2(t)}),$$

$$s = S - t \text{ and } \tau = T - t$$

where the solutions of $A(.)$, $B_i(.)$, and $C_i(.)$ are given by equation (10.49) and the solutions of $a_F(.)$, $b_{iF}(.)$, and $c_{iF}(.)$ are given by equation (10.86).

Valuing Options on Zero-Coupon Bonds or Caplets: The Fourier Inversion Method

This section extends the Fourier inversion method (introduced by Heston [1993] and generalized by Duffie, Pan, and Singleton [2000], Bakshi and Madan [2000], and Chacko and Das [2002]) to quadratic models for pricing interest rate derivatives. This method requires only a *single* summation to solve the integrals for obtaining risk-neutral probabilities even under a multifactor model, while the traditional methods, such as Longstaff and Schwartz [1992], require a multiple-order summation to obtain the risk-neutral probabilities under a multifactor model. The computation time difference between a single summation and a multiple-order summation grows nonlinearly and is quite significant even between a single summation and a double summation.

We use the four-step Fourier inversion method outlined in Chapter 5 (see equations (5.114) through (5.168)) for solving option prices. As shown in Chapter 5, the prices of a European call option (c) and a European put option (p), both written on a zero-coupon bond maturing at time T with a strike price of K and expiring at time S, are given as follows:

$$c(t) = P(t, T)\Pi_{1t} - KP(t, S)\Pi_{2t} \tag{10.90}$$

$$p(t) = KP(t, S)(1 - \Pi_{2t}) - P(t, T)(1 - \Pi_{1t}) \tag{10.91}$$

where

$$\Pi_{1t} = \int_{\ln K}^{\infty} f_{1t}(y)\, dy = \frac{1}{2} + \frac{1}{\pi} \int_0^{\infty} \mathrm{Re}\left[\frac{e^{-i\omega \ln K} g_{1t}(\omega)}{i\omega}\right] d\omega \tag{10.92}$$

$$\Pi_{2t} = \int_{\ln K}^{\infty} f_{2t}(y)\, dy = \frac{1}{2} + \frac{1}{\pi} \int_0^{\infty} \mathrm{Re}\left[\frac{e^{-i\omega \ln K} g_{2t}(\omega)}{i\omega}\right] d\omega \tag{10.93}$$

and where $y = \ln P(S, T)$, $f_{1t}(y)$, and $f_{2t}(y)$ are the *forward* probability densities defined in equations (6.124) and (6.125), respectively, and the functions $g_{1t}(\omega)$ and $g_{2t}(\omega)$ are the characteristic functions corresponding to these probability densities. As in Heston, equations (10.92) and (10.93) obtain the forward probabilities Π_{1t} and Π_{2t} by solving the Fourier inverses of the characteristic functions $g_{1t}(\omega)$ and $g_{2t}(\omega)$. The solutions of the characteristic functions $g_{1t}(\omega)$ and $g_{2t}(\omega)$ under the $Q_1(N)$, $Q_1(N)+$, and $Q_1(N)++$

models can be obtained by following the steps outlined in Chapter 5, as follows:

$$g_{1t}(\omega) = \frac{e^{A_1^*(s)+\sum_{i=1}^N B_{1i}^*(s)Y_i(t)+\sum_{i=1}^N \sum_{j=1}^N C_{1ij}^*(s)Y_i(t)Y_j(t)-H(S,T)(1+i\omega)-H(t,S)}}{P(t,T)}, \quad s = S - t$$

(10.94)

$$g_{2t}(\omega) = \frac{e^{A_2^*(s)+\sum_{i=1}^N B_{2i}^*(s)Y_i(t)+\sum_{i=1}^N \sum_{j=1}^N C_{2ij}^*(s)Y_i(t)Y_j(t)-H(S,T)(i\omega)-H(t,S)}}{P(t,S)}, \quad s = S - t$$

(10.95)

where functions $A_1^*(s)$, $B_{1i}^*(s)$, and $C_{1ij}^*(s)$ in equation (10.94) follow the same ODEs as $A(s)$, $B_i(s)$, and $C_{ij}(s)$, respectively, given in equation (10.45), but with the following boundary conditions:

$$A_1^*(0) = a_1 = A(U)(1 + i\omega)$$
$$B_{1i}^*(0) = b_{1i} = B_i(U)(1 + i\omega), \quad \text{for } i = 1, 2, \ldots, N \qquad (10.96)$$
$$C_{1ij}^*(0) = c_{1ij} = C_{ij}(U)(1 + i\omega), \quad \text{for } i,j = 1, 2, \ldots, N$$

where $U = T - S$. Similarly, functions $A_2^*(s)$, $B_{2i}^*(s)$, and $C_{2ij}^*(s)$ in equation (10.95) follow the same ODEs as $A(s)$, $B_i(s)$, and $C_{ij}(s)$, respectively, given in equation (10.45), but with the following boundary conditions:

$$A_2^*(0) = a_2 = A(U)(i\omega)$$
$$B_{2i}^*(0) = b_{2i} = B_i(U)(i\omega), \quad \text{for } i = 1, 2, \ldots, N \qquad (10.97)$$
$$C_{2ij}^*(0) = c_{2ij} = C_{ij}(U)(i\omega), \quad \text{for } i,j = 1, 2, \ldots, N$$

The solutions of $A_2^*(s)$, $B_{2i}^*(s)$, and $C_{2ij}^*(s)$ do not have to be obtained by solving ODEs, since these solutions can be obtained directly from the solutions to the ODEs for $A_1^*(s)$, $B_{1i}^*(s)$, and $C_{1ij}^*(s)$, respectively, by replacing a_1 with a_2, b_{1i} with b_{2i}, and c_{1ij} with c_{2ij}, for all $i, j = 1, 2, \ldots, N$ (these constants are defined in equations (10.96) and (10.97)). In general, the ODEs for $A_1^*(s)$, $B_{1i}^*(s)$, and $C_{1ij}^*(s)$ must be solved repeatedly to obtain the values of the characteristic functions $g_{1t}(\omega)$ and $g_{2t}(\omega)$ for a discrete range of values of ω to approximate the numerical integrals in equations (10.92) and (10.93). The option pricing solution given in equations (10.90) and (10.91) applies to both the time-homogeneous $Q_1(N)$ and $Q_1(N)+$ models and the time-inhomogeneous $Q_1(N)++$ model. For the $Q_1(N)$ and $Q_1(N)+$ models, $H(t, T) = \delta \times (T - t)$, while for the $Q_1(N)++$ model, $H(t, T)$ is given by equation (10.60).

These solutions of European options on zero-coupon bonds apply to all quadratic models nested in the maximal $Q_1(N)$, $Q_1(N)+$, and $Q_1(N)++$ models under the appropriate parameter restrictions given earlier. The computational time can be further reduced for the special case of $Q_3(N)$, $Q_3(N)+$, and $Q_3(N)++$ models, which allow analytical solutions of the characteristic functions, given as follows:

$$g_{1t}(\omega) = \frac{e^{A_1^*(s) + \sum_{i=1}^N B_{1i}^*(s)Y_i(t) + \sum_{i=1}^N C_{1i}^*(s)Y_i^2(t) - H(S,T)(1+i\omega) - H(t,S)}}{P(t,T)}, \quad s = S - t \quad (10.98)$$

$$g_{2t}(\omega) = \frac{e^{A_2^*(s) + \sum_{i=1}^N B_{2i}^*(s)Y_i(t) + \sum_{i=1}^N C_{2i}^*(s)Y_i^2(t) - H(S,T)(i\omega) - H(t,S)}}{P(t,S)}, \quad s = S - t \quad (10.99)$$

where functions $A_1^*(s)$, $B_{1i}^*(s)$, and $C_{1i}^*(s)$ in equation (10.98) follow the same ODEs as $A(s)$, $B_i(s)$, and $C_i(s)$, respectively, given in equation (10.48), but with the following boundary conditions:

$$A_1^*(0) = a_1 = A(U)(1 + i\omega)$$

$$B_{1i}^*(0) = b_{1i} = B_i(U)(1 + i\omega), \quad \text{for } i = 1, 2, \ldots, N \quad (10.100)$$

$$C_{1i}^*(0) = c_{1i} = C_i(U)(1 + i\omega), \quad \text{for } i = 1, 2, \ldots, N$$

The analytical solutions of $A_1^*(s)$, $B_{1i}^*(s)$, and $C_{1i}^*(s)$ are given as follows:

$$A_1^*(s) = a_1 + \int_0^s \left(\sum_{i=1}^N \tilde{\mu}_i B_{1i}^*(v) + \frac{1}{2} \sum_{i=1}^N \sigma_i^2 (B_{1i}^*(v))^2 + \sum_{i=1}^N \sigma_i^2 C_{1i}^*(v) \right) dv$$

$$B_{1i}^*(s) = \frac{\tilde{\mu}_i}{\beta_i \sigma_i^2} \left(\frac{(e^{\beta_i s} - 1)((\tilde{\xi}_{ii} + \beta_i)\theta_i e^{\beta_i s} - (\tilde{\xi}_{ii} - \beta_i))}{1 - \theta_i e^{2\beta_i s}} \right) + \frac{b_{1i}(1 - \theta_i)e^{\beta_i s}}{1 - \theta_i e^{2\beta_i s}}$$

$$C_{1i}^*(s) = \frac{1}{2\sigma_i^2} \left(\frac{(\tilde{\xi}_{ii} + \beta_i)\theta_i e^{2\beta_i s} - (\tilde{\xi}_{ii} - \beta_i)}{1 - \theta_i e^{2\beta_i s}} \right) \quad (10.101)$$

where

$$\beta_i = \sqrt{\tilde{\xi}_{ii}^2 + 2\sigma_i^2}$$

$$\theta_i = \frac{\tilde{\xi}_{ii} - \beta_i + 2c_{1i}\sigma_i^2}{\tilde{\xi}_{ii} + \beta_i + 2c_{1i}\sigma_i^2} \quad (10.102)$$

For expositional simplicity, the term $A_1^*(s)$ is evaluated using a numerical integral. The functions $A_2^*(s)$, $B_{2i}^*(s)$, and $C_{2i}^*(s)$ in equation (10.99) follow the same ODEs as $A(s)$, $B_i(s)$, and $C_i(s)$, respectively, given in equation (10.48), but with the following boundary conditions:

$$A_2^*(0) = a_2 = A(U)(i\omega)$$

$$B_{2i}^*(0) = b_{2i} = B_i(U)(i\omega), \quad \text{for } i = 1, 2, \ldots, N \qquad (10.103)$$

$$C_{2i}^*(0) = c_{2i} = C_i(U)(i\omega), \quad \text{for } i = 1, 2, \ldots, N$$

The solutions of $A_2^*(s)$, $B_{2i}^*(s)$, and $C_{2ij}^*(s)$ can be obtained directly from the solutions of $A_1^*(s)$, $B_{1i}^*(s)$, and $C_{1ij}^*(s)$, respectively, given in equation (10.101) by replacing a_1 with a_2, b_{1i} with b_{2i}, and c_{1i} with c_{2i}, for all $i = 1, 2, \ldots, N$ (these constants are defined in equations (10.100) and (10.103)). Since the characteristic functions $g_{1t}(\omega)$ and $g_{2t}(\omega)$ are solved analytically, these allow a very fast approximation to the numerical integrals in equations (10.92) and (10.93). The option pricing solution under this special case applies to both the time-homogeneous $Q_3(N)$ and $Q_3(N)+$ models and the time-inhomogeneous $Q_3(N)++$ model. For the $Q_3(N)$ and $Q_3(N)+$ models, $H(t, T) = \delta \times (T - t)$, while for the $Q_3(N)++$ model, $H(t, T)$ is given by equation (10.62).

Valuing Options on Coupon Bonds or Swaptions: The Cumulant Expansion Approximation

Chapter 9 described a four-step cumulant expansion approach for pricing options on coupon bonds or swaptions under the simple ATSMs. Since steps 1 to 3 (see equations (9.70) through (9.104)) of this approach are model independent, only equations (9.105) through (9.112) of step 4 have to be modified to compute the moments of the coupon bond price under QTSMs. Substituting these moments in steps 1 to 3 in equations (9.70) through (9.104) gives the solutions of options on coupon bonds or swaptions under QTSMs instead of under simple ATSMs.

Let the coupon bond underlying the option contract have n cash flows that mature after the option expiration date S at times $T_i > S$ for $i = 1, 2, \ldots, n$. The price of the bond at the expiration date S is given as:

$$P_c(S) = \sum_{i=1}^{n} CF_i P(S, T_i) \qquad (10.104)$$

The hth moment of the distribution of the future coupon bond price under the forward measure associated with maturity W, for $W = S, T_1, T_2, \ldots, T_n$, is given using the zero-coupon bond price formula under the maximal $Q_1(N)$, $Q_1(N)+$, and $Q_1(N)++$ models given in equation (10.43) as follows:

$$
\begin{aligned}
\mu_b^W &= E_t^W[P_c(S)^b] \\
&= \sum_{l_1,l_2,\ldots,l_b=1}^{n} (CF_{l_1} CF_{l_2} \ldots CF_{l_b}) \exp\left(-\sum_{k=1}^{b} H(S, T_{l_k})\right) M_b^W(t; l_1, l_2, \ldots, l_b) \\
&= \sum_{l_1=1}^{n}\sum_{l_2=1}^{n}\cdots\sum_{l_b=1}^{n}(CF_{l_1} CF_{l_2} \ldots CF_{l_b}) \exp\left(-\sum_{k=1}^{b} H(S, T_{l_k})\right) \\
&\quad \times M_b^W(t; l_1, l_2, \ldots, l_b)
\end{aligned} \tag{10.105}
$$

where

$$
M_b^W(t; l_1, l_2, \ldots, l_b) = E_t^W\left(e^{\left(F_A + \sum_{i=1}^{N} F_{Bi} Y_i(S) + \sum_{i=1}^{N}\sum_{j=1}^{N} F_{Cij} Y_i(S) Y_j(S)\right)}\right) \tag{10.106}
$$

and

$$
\begin{aligned}
F_A &= \sum_{k=1}^{b} A(U_{l_k}) \\
F_{Bi} &= \sum_{k=1}^{b} B_i(U_{l_k}), \quad \text{for } i = 1, 2, \ldots, N \\
F_{Cij} &= \sum_{k=1}^{b} C_{ij}(U_{l_k}), \quad \text{for } i, j = 1, 2, \ldots, N \\
U_{l_k} &= T_{l_k} - S
\end{aligned} \tag{10.107}
$$

The terms $A(U)$, $B_i(U)$, and $C_{ij}(U)$ are solved numerically using the ODEs given in equation (10.45). By using a change of measure, the expectation in equation (10.106) can be evaluated using the risk-neutral measure as follows:

$$
\begin{aligned}
&M_b^W(t; l_1, l_2, \ldots, l_b) \\
&= \frac{1}{P(t, W)} \tilde{E}_t\left(e^{-\int_t^W r(v)dv} e^{\left(F_A + \sum_{i=1}^{N} F_{Bi} Y_i(S) + \sum_{i=1}^{N}\sum_{j=1}^{N} F_{Cij} Y_i(S) Y_j(S)\right)}\right) \\
&= \frac{1}{P(t, W)} \tilde{E}_t\left(e^{-\int_t^S r(v)dv} e^{\left(F_A + \sum_{i=1}^{N} F_{Bi} Y_i(S) + \sum_{i=1}^{N}\sum_{j=1}^{N} F_{Cij} Y_i(S) Y_j(S)\right)} \tilde{E}_S\left(e^{-\int_S^W r(v)dv}\right)\right) \\
&= \frac{1}{P(t, W)} \tilde{E}_t\left(e^{-\int_t^S r(v)dv} e^{\left(F_A + \sum_{i=1}^{N} F_{Bi} Y_i(S) + \sum_{i=1}^{N}\sum_{j=1}^{N} F_{Cij} Y_i(S) Y_j(S)\right)} P(S, W)\right) \\
&= \frac{e^{-H(S,W)}}{P(t, W)} \tilde{E}_t\left(e^{-\int_t^S r(v)dv} e^{\left(G_A + \sum_{i=1}^{N} G_{Bi} Y_i(S) + \sum_{i=1}^{N}\sum_{j=1}^{N} G_{Cij} Y_i(S) Y_j(S)\right)}\right)
\end{aligned} \tag{10.108}
$$

where

$$G_A = F_A + A(W - S)$$

$$G_{Bi} = F_{Bi} + B_i(W - S), \quad \text{for } i = 1, 2, \ldots, N \qquad (10.109)$$

$$G_{Cij} = F_{Cij} + C_{ij}(W - S), \quad \text{for } i, j = 1, 2, \ldots, N$$

where $A(W - S)$, $B_i(W - S)$, and $C_{ij}(W - S)$ are obtained numerically using the ODEs given in equation (10.45). Using the Feynman-Kac theorem in Chapter 2, the solution of the expectation given in equation (10.108) can be shown to follow the same PDE as followed by the bond price under the $Q_1(N)+$ and $Q_1(N)++$ models, but with a different boundary condition. Hence, following the usual procedure to solve a PDE using Riccati equations, the solution of $M_h^W(t; l_1, l_2, \ldots, l_h)$ is given as follows:

$$M_h^W(t; l_1, l_2, \ldots, l_h) = \frac{e^{-H(t, W)} e^{\left(A_G^*(s) + \sum_{i=1}^N B_{Gi}^*(s) Y_i(t) + \sum_{i=1}^N \sum_{j=1}^N C_{Gij}^*(s) Y_i(t) Y_j(t)\right)}}{P(t, W)}$$

$$(10.110)$$

where $s = S - t$ and the functions $A_G^*(s)$, $B_{Gi}^*(s)$, and $C_{Gij}^*(s)$ follow the same ODEs as $A(s)$, $B_i(s)$, and $C_{ij}(s)$, respectively, given in equation (10.45), but with the following boundary conditions:

$$A_G^*(0) = G_A$$

$$B_{Gi}^*(0) = G_{Bi}, \quad \text{for } i = 1, 2, \ldots, N \qquad (10.111)$$

$$C_{Gij}^*(0) = G_{Cij}, \quad \text{for } i, j = 1, 2, \ldots, N$$

In general, the ODEs of $A_G^*(s)$, $B_{Gi}^*(s)$, and $C_{Gij}^*(s)$ must be solved using numerical methods using programming languages such as Matlab. The solution of moments μ_h^W given in equation (10.105) applies to both the time-homogeneous $Q_1(N)$ and $Q_1(N)+$ models and the time-inhomogeneous $Q_1(N)++$ model. For the $Q_1(N)$ and $Q_1(N)+$ models, $H(t, T) = \delta \times (T - t)$, while for the $Q_1(N)++$ model, $H(t, T)$ is given by equation (10.60).

The moments of the price of a coupon bond have analytical solutions under the special case of $Q_3(N)+$ and $Q_3(N)++$ models. Under these models, the solution of $M_h^W(t; l_1, l_2, \ldots, l_h)$ in equation (10.106) is modified as follows:

$$M_h^W(t; l_1, l_2, \ldots, l_h) = E_t^W \left(e^{\left(F_A + \sum_{i=1}^N F_{Bi} Y_i(S) + \sum_{i=1}^N F_{Ci} Y_i^2(S)\right)}\right) \qquad (10.112)$$

where

$$F_A = \sum_{k=1}^{b} A(U_{l_k})$$

$$F_{Bi} = \sum_{k=1}^{b} B_i(U_{l_k}), \quad \text{for } i = 1, 2, \ldots, N$$

$$F_{Ci} = \sum_{k=1}^{b} C_i(U_{l_k}), \quad \text{for } i = 1, 2, \ldots, N$$

$$U_{l_k} = T_{l_k} - S$$

(10.113)

The analytical solutions of the terms $A(U)$, $B_i(U)$, and $C_i(U)$ in equation (10.113) are given in equation (10.49). By using a change of measure, the expectation in equation (10.112) can be evaluated using the same method as in equation (10.108), as follows:

$$M_b^W(t; l_1, l_2, \ldots, l_b) = \frac{1}{P(t, W)} \tilde{E}_t \left(e^{-\int_t^W r(v)dv} e^{\left(F_A + \sum_{i=1}^N F_{Bi} Y_i(S) + \sum_{i=1}^N F_{Ci} Y_i^2(S) \right)} \right)$$

$$= \frac{e^{-H(S,W)}}{P(t, W)} \tilde{E}_t \left(e^{-\int_t^S r(v)dv} e^{\left(G_A + \sum_{i=1}^N G_{Bi} Y_i(S) + \sum_{i=1}^N G_{Ci} Y_i^2(S) \right)} \right)$$

(10.114)

where

$$G_A = F_A + A(W - S)$$

$$G_{Bi} = F_{Bi} + B_i(W - S), \quad \text{for } i = 1, 2, \ldots, N$$

$$G_{Ci} = F_{Ci} + C_i(W - S), \quad \text{for } i = 1, 2, \ldots, N$$

(10.115)

where $A(W - S)$, $B_i(W - S)$, and $C_i(W - S)$ are given in equation (10.49). Using the Feynman-Kac theorem in Chapter 2, the solution of the expectation given in equation (10.114) can be shown to follow the same PDE as followed by the bond price under the $Q_3(N)+$ and $Q_3(N)++$ models, but with a different boundary condition. Hence, following the usual procedure to solve a PDE using Riccati equations, the solution of $M_b^W(t; l_1, l_2, \ldots, l_b)$ is given as follows:

$$M_b^W(t; l_1, l_2, \ldots, l_b) = \frac{e^{-H(t,W)} e^{\left(A_G^*(s) + \sum_{i=1}^N B_{Gi}^*(s) Y_i(t) + \sum_{i=1}^N C_{Gi}^*(s) Y_i^2(t) \right)}}{P(t, W)}$$

(10.116)

where $s = S - t$ and the solutions of $A_G^*(s)$, $B_{Gi}^*(s)$, and $C_{Gi}^*(s)$ are identical to the solutions of $A_1^*(s)$, $B_{1i}^*(s)$, and $C_{1i}^*(s)$, respectively, obtained in equation (10.101) in the previous section with:

$$a_1 = G_A$$
$$b_{1i} = G_{Bi}, \quad \text{for } i = 1, 2, \ldots, N \qquad (10.117)$$
$$c_{1i} = G_{Ci}, \quad \text{for } i = 1, 2, \ldots, N$$

Though the solutions in equation (10.101) were derived for pricing options on zero-coupon bonds using the Fourier inversion method, these solutions also solve the moments of a coupon bond price, which allows the pricing of options on coupon bonds using the cumulant approximation method under the $Q_3(N)$, $Q_3(N)+$, and $Q_3(N)++$ models. The solution of moments μ_h^W given in equation (10.105) applies to both the time-homogeneous $Q_3(N)$ and $Q_3(N)+$ models and the time-inhomogeneous $Q_3(N)++$ model. For the $Q_3(N)$ and $Q_3(N)+$ models, $H(t, T) = \delta \times (T - t)$, while for the $Q_3(N)++$ model, $H(t, T)$ is given by equation (10.62).

By substituting the solution of $M_h^W(t; l_1, l_2, \ldots, l_h)$ from equation (10.116) into equation (10.105), the hth moment of the distribution of the future coupon bond price under the forward measure associated with maturity W, for $W = S, T_1, T_2, \ldots, T_n$, can be obtained in closed form. In general, the solution of the hth moment μ_h^W in equation (10.105) requires summing up n^h number of terms using an h-order summation. However, as shown in Chapter 9 (see example 9.1), many of the summation terms differ only in the order of the indices $l_1, l_2, \ldots, l_h$ and have identical values for the expressions inside the summation, and so it is possible to achieve significant savings in computation time by avoiding repeated summing up of the same terms. The discussion on how to price options on coupon bonds or swaptions using the moments of the price of a coupon bond is given in Chapter 9 and is not repeated here.

CALIBRATION TO INTEREST RATE CAPS DATA

This section evaluates the ability of the preference-free $Q_3(N)++$ models to price interest rate caps. Though these models assume orthogonal state variables with no interdependencies, they are analytically tractable with closed-form solutions for the bond price and quasi-analytical solutions for the prices of interest rate caps. A direct comparison of the $Q_3(N)++$ models with square-root $A_N(N)++$ models is useful since both classes of models assume orthogonal state variables and use the same number of risk-neutral parameters. However, $Q_3(N)++$ models allow a richer variety of term structure movements, including yield twists and humped forward rate volatility shapes, even with a single factor that follows a stationary risk-neutral process. The $A_N(N)++$ models can allow humped forward rate volatility shapes only by using explosive risk-neutral processes as shown in Chapters 7 and 9.

The data used in our calibration consists of end-of-day prices and Black's implied volatilities of U.S. dollar interest rate caps and the swap rates for the period beginning June 1, 2006, until June 30, 2006. This is the same data that was used in Chapter 9 to estimate the simple $A_M(N)++$ models. We consider caps with ten different maturities, ranging from 1 to 10 years, with four strikes of 3, 4, 5, and 6 percent and quarterly tenors. Since forward LIBOR rates are within the range of 3 to 6 percent in the sample period, our data includes in-the-money (ITM), at-the-money (ATM), and out-of-the-money (OTM) caps. As in Chapter 9, we consider *difference caps* defined as the difference between caps of adjacent maturities with the same strike price for performing daily calibrations. The use of difference caps instead of caps ensures that the information related to caplets comprising the caps is not used repetitively in the optimization process.

Table 9.4 reports the means and standard deviations of the difference cap prices during the sample period. The prices are shown in basis points, or cents per \$100 face value of the cap. Figure 9.1 plots the Black's implied volatilities of difference caps across strike rate and maturity averaged over the sample period.

We consider three quadratic models with one, two, and three factors given as follows:

1. The $Q_3(1)++$ model
2. The $Q_3(2)++$ model
3. The $Q_3(3)++$ model

The parameters of the models are obtained daily by minimizing the sum of squared percentage pricing errors (SSE), where percentage errors are defined as (Market price − Model price)/Market. Table 10.2 reports the estimated parameter values for each model averaged over the sample period.

The summary performance of the three models is illustrated in Figure 10.5, which gives the root mean square pricing error (RMSE) for each model over the sample period. It is illustrative to compare the performance of the $Q_3(N)++$ models with the square-root $A_N(N)++$ models given in Chapter 9, as both classes of models assume orthogonal state variables and use the same number of risk-neutral parameters. Comparing the RMSEs in Figure 10.5 with those in Figure 9.2, it can be seen that the $Q_3(1)++$

TABLE 10.2 Estimated Risk-Neutral Parameter Values and Initial State Variable Values Averaged over the Sample Period

	Process 1				Process 2				Process 3			
	μ	ξ	σ	$Y(0)$	μ	ξ	σ	$Y(0)$	μ	ξ	σ	$Y(0)$
$Q_3(1)$++	0.0021	−0.0007	0.0193	0.2191	—	—	—	—	—	—	—	—
$Q_3(2)$++	0.0060	−0.0032	0.0164	0.1821	0.0005	−0.0028	0.0191	0.1429	—	—	—	—
$Q_3(3)$++	0.0003	−0.0001	0.0315	0.0267	0.0095	−0.0290	0.0158	0.1310	0.0043	−0.0047	0.0190	0.1644

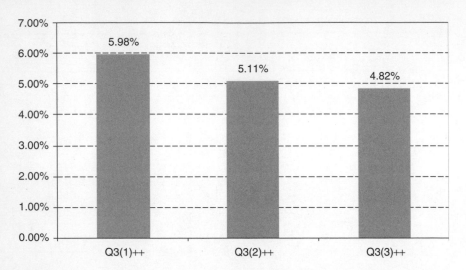

FIGURE 10.5 Root Mean Square Pricing Errors in Pooled Data

model significantly outperforms the $A_1(1)++$ model with a stationary risk-neutral process (i.e., Model 1 in Figure 9.2) and marginally outperforms the $A_1(1)++$ model with an explosive risk-neutral process (i.e., Model 2 in Figure 9.2). Similar comparisons for other models show that the $Q_3(2)++$ and $Q_3(3)++$ models significantly outperform the stationary $A_3(3)++$ model but perform similarly as the explosive $A_3(3)++$ model. However, the $A_0(2)++$ and $A_0(3)++$ models (i.e., the Gaussian models) outperform the $Q_3(2)++$ and $Q_3(3)++$ models.

Table 10.3 provides more insight on the patterns of errors across strikes and maturities for the three models considered. This table gives average percentage pricing errors over the sample period for different strikes and maturities. Though the magnitudes of average percentage pricing errors are generally lower than the RMSEs (because errors of opposite signs cancel out), the differences in the magnitudes were very small, and hence, we report only the former, which is more informative about the direction of mispricing. The errors for the quadratic models in Table 10.3 are similar to the errors of the explosive square-root models in Table 9.6, with the same number of factors. For example, the errors of the $Q_3(1)++$ model are similar to the errors of the explosive $A_1(1)++$ model (i.e., Model 2 in Table 9.6), and errors of the $Q_3(3)++$ model are similar to the errors of the explosive $A_3(3)++$ model (i.e., Model 4 in Table 9.6).

TABLE 10.3 Average Percentage Pricing Errors

Model	Strike (%)	Maturity (years)								
		2	3	4	5	6	7	8	9	10
$Q_3(1)++$	3	0.01	0.57	1.45	2.34	3.06	3.23	3.26	3.10	2.73
	4	0.62	3.20	4.81	4.55	4.37	3.67	2.60	1.60	0.05
	5	−4.20	3.16	5.73	3.07	3.56	2.04	0.72	−1.00	−2.95
	6	−25.39	1.62	8.33	7.15	8.99	6.59	4.55	2.52	0.29
$Q_3(2)++$	3	0.03	0.58	1.37	2.01	2.61	2.56	2.35	1.95	1.33
	4	0.76	3.30	4.75	4.71	4.12	3.27	2.06	0.94	−0.71
	5	−2.87	3.90	5.93	4.51	3.88	2.17	0.70	−1.16	−3.23
	6	−19.44	3.87	8.78	7.35	7.71	4.47	1.66	−1.13	−4.11
$Q_3(3)++$	3	0.01	0.52	1.32	1.63	1.64	0.98	0.10	−0.97	−2.22
	4	0.99	3.68	4.66	3.22	2.15	0.58	−1.31	−3.03	−5.23
	5	−0.74	5.54	5.96	2.40	1.98	−0.32	−2.26	−4.50	−6.86
	6	−13.59	6.35	9.83	8.32	8.73	5.18	2.16	−0.70	−3.67

The overall RMSEs of 6 percent for the $Q_3(1)++$ model and about 5 percent for the $Q_3(2)++$ and $Q_3(3)++$ models in Figure 10.5 are significantly lower than the RMSEs of the *fundamental* quadratic models reported by Li and Zhao [2006] using the caps price data over the three-year period 2000–2002. Li and Zhao use the extended Kalman filter to estimate the model parameters and extract the latent state variables of three nested three-factor fundamental quadratic models given as $Q_1(3)$, $Q_2(3)$, and $Q_3(3)$. Though all three models allow three factors, the $Q_1(3)$ model allows correlations and interdependencies between the state variables, the $Q_2(3)$ model allows interdependencies but disallows nonzero correlations, and the $Q_3(3)$ model disallows both interdependencies and nonzero correlations. The RMSE of approximately 5 percent for the time-inhomogeneous preference-free $Q_3(3)++$ model in Figure 10.5 is significantly lower than the average RMSEs of 44 percent, 31 percent, and 15 percent for the fundamental $Q_3(3)$, $Q_2(3)$, and $Q_1(3)$ models, respectively (computed by averaging the RMSEs in each of the Panels A, B, and C of Table 5 in Li and Zhao [2006]). The high RMSEs for the fundamental quadratic models are not simply due to the volatility skew, since the average RMSEs using even the ATM difference caps are 26 percent, 25 percent, and 11 percent for the fundamental $Q_3(3)$, $Q_2(3)$, and $Q_1(3)$ models, respectively.[2]

The significant difference between the performance of preference-free $Q_3(N)++$ models in Figure 10.5 and that of the fundamental three-factor quadratic models given in Li and Zhao [2006] could be due to using data over different time periods. However, two main reasons for such high differences in the RMSEs between the preference-free quadratic models in Figure 10.5 and the fundamental quadratic models in Li and Zhao are given as follows:

1. The preference-free models do not assume specific functional forms for the market prices of risks (MPRs), and hence, are consistent with arbitrary nonlinear specifications of MPRs. On the other hand, the fundamental models in Li and Zhao [2006] assume linear specifications of MPRs.
2. Similar to other studies on fundamental models (see Jagannathan, Kaplin, and Sun [2003]), the pricing errors are high because of the basic tension in fitting bond prices versus implied volatilities of option prices. This tension is avoided by the $Q_3(N)++$ models by allowing a time-inhomogeneous short rate, which ensures that these models fit the bond prices exactly, such that the risk-neutral parameters are used to fit only the option prices. A time-inhomogeneous short rate is also assumed by virtually all models in the fixed income literature that lead to low RMSEs in pricing interest rate options (e.g., the $A_0(2)++$ model of Hull and White [1994b] and various versions of the LIBOR market model (LMM), including the stochastic volatility–based LMMs of Joshi and Rebonato [2003] and Jarrow, Li, and Zhao [2007]). Though theoretically unappealing, the robustness of time-inhomogeneous models can be checked by testing their out-of-sample hedging effectiveness, in addition to their pricing performance.

Though it is possible that low RMSEs of the preference-free $Q_3(N)++$ models result from daily calibrations that allow the parameters to change every day, our investigation revealed that the coefficients of variation (i.e., the ratio of the standard deviation of a parameter to its mean) are less than 0.3 for virtually all parameters. The only exception is the parameter $\tilde{\mu}_i$ associated with one of the state variables in the three-factor $Q_3(3)++$ model, which has a coefficient of variation equal to 0.9. Since all of the parameters of the $Q_3(2)++$ model are quite stable, this model may be preferred over the $Q_3(3)++$ model, especially since the RMSEs of the two models are very similar (see Figure 10.5).

As a final comment, note that significant improvement in RMSEs and percentage pricing errors may occur by considering time-inhomogeneous preference-free quadratic models that allow interdependencies and correlations between the state variables. Though we focused on the $Q_3(N)++$ models due to their analytical tractability, the $Q_2(N)++$ and $Q_1(N)++$ models may improve the fit with difference cap prices, especially those corresponding to the higher strikes as shown in Table 10.3. This is especially relevant since the parameters given in Table 10.2 cannot produce a realistic level of decorrelation between forward rate changes.

MULTIFACTOR QTSMs FOR VALUING CREDIT DERIVATIVES

An interesting observation regarding QTSMs is that even the fundamental $Q_3(3)$ model, which assumes orthogonal state variables and disallows interdependencies in the definition of the short rate, outperforms the fundamental maximal three-factor ATSMs in explaining the dynamics of bond yields (see Ahn, Dittmar, and Gallant [2002]). Further, since the quadratic feature allows more diversity in the nonlinear shapes of the volatility functions corresponding to different state variables, the $Q_3(3)$ model may allow realistic correlations between forward rate changes, despite the fact that the state variables are orthogonal to each other under this model.

Since QTSMs disallow nonnegative values for the state variables, they are naturally suited for modeling the short rate and the default intensity for pricing credit derivatives using the reduced-form approach. This section focuses on the $Q_3(N)$ models and their preference-free extensions (i.e., the $Q_3(N)+$ and $Q_3(N)++$ models) for pricing risky bonds and credit derivatives using the reduced-form approach. The general methodology presented here can be easily extended to models in the $Q_1(N)$ and $Q_2(N)$ subfamilies and their preference-free extensions.

We illustrate the $Q_3(N)$ models and their preference-free extensions using both the "recovery of market value" (RMV) assumption and the "recovery of face value" (RFV) assumption, described in Chapter 3. The risky zero-coupon bond prices are assumed to be driven by interest and credit risks only; so these prices may be different from those implied by the risky coupon bond prices of corporate bonds, which may be exposed to tax-related and liquidity factors.

Reduced-Form $Q_3(N)$, $Q_3(N)+$, and $Q_3(N)++$ Models under the RMV Assumption

Consider the *risky* short rate $R(t)$ defined in Chapter 3 as follows:

$$R(t) = r(t) + s(t) \qquad (10.118)$$

where $r(t)$ is the default-free short rate and $s(t)$ is the spread over the short rate due to the risk of default. The short spread equals the *mean loss rate* under the RMV assumption as shown in equation (3.104) in Chapter 3:

$$s(t) = \tilde{\lambda}(t)\tilde{L}_M \tag{10.119}$$

where $\tilde{\lambda}(t)$ is the risk-neutral default intensity, which means that $\tilde{\lambda}(t)dt$ is the risk-neutral probability of default over the interval t to $t + dt$, given that no default has occurred until time t, and where $\tilde{L}_M$ is the risk-neutral loss rate in the event of default. The price of a \$1 face-value risky zero-coupon bond under the RMV assumption is given as follows (see equation (3.107) in Chapter 3):

$$D(t,T) = \tilde{E}_t \left(\frac{1}{e^{\int_t^T (r(v)+s(v))dv}} \right) = \tilde{E}_t \left(\frac{1}{e^{\int_t^T R(v)dv}} \right) \tag{10.120}$$

The value of the risky zero-coupon bond that defaults at time t is given as a fraction $(1 - \tilde{L}_M)$ of its value just before default, or equal to $(1 - \tilde{L}_M)D(t,T)$.

The Fundamental $Q_3(N)$ Model under the RMV Assumption   The fundamental $Q_3(N)$ model assumes orthogonal state variables and does not allow interactions between the state variables. Hence, the parameters $\tilde{\xi}_{ij}$ (for $i,j = 1,2,\ldots,N$ and $i > j$) and $\psi_{ij} = \psi_{ji}$ (for $i,j = 1,2,\ldots,N$ and $i \neq j$) are set to zero in equations (10.39) and (10.37), respectively. The short rate and the short spread are defined as follows:

$$r(t) = \delta_r + \sum_{i=1}^N a_i Y_i^2(t) \tag{10.121}$$

$$s(t) = \delta_s + \sum_{i=1}^N b_i Y_i^2(t) \tag{10.122}$$

where δ_r, δ_s, a_i, and b_i (for all $i = 1,2,\ldots,N$) are constants greater than or equal to zero. The stochastic processes of the state variables are given under the risk-neutral measure as follows:

$$dY_i(t) = \left(\tilde{\mu}_i + \tilde{\xi}_{ii} Y_i(t) \right) dt + \sigma_i \, d\tilde{Z}_i(t), \quad \text{for all } i = 1,2,\ldots,N \tag{10.123}$$

where $d\tilde{Z}_i(t)$ are independent Wiener processes for all $i = 1,2,\ldots,N$.

The default-free bond price $P(t,T)$ is obtained in the same manner as under the fundamental $Q_3(N)$ model given earlier, with a slight modification to account for the constants a_i in the definition of the short rate in equation (10.121). The solution is given as follows:

$$P(t, T) = e^{A(\tau) + \sum_{i=1}^{N} \sqrt{a_i}(B_i(\tau) Y_i(t)) + \sum_{i=1}^{N} a_i(C_i(\tau) Y_i^2(t)) - H(t,T)} \tag{10.124}$$

where

$$A(\tau) = \sum_{i=1}^{N} A_i(\tau)$$

$$A_i(\tau) = \left[-a_i \left(\frac{\tilde{\mu}_i}{\beta_i} \right)^2 \tau \right] + \left[\frac{a_i \tilde{\mu}_i^2 (e^{\beta_i \tau} - 1)[(-2\tilde{\xi}_{ii} + \beta_i)(e^{\beta_i \tau} - 1) + 2\beta_i]}{\beta_i^3 [(\beta_i - \tilde{\xi}_{ii})(e^{2\beta_i \tau} - 1) + 2\beta_i]} \right] \tag{10.125}$$

$$+ \frac{1}{2} \ln \left[\frac{2\beta_i e^{(\beta_i - \tilde{\xi}_{ii})\tau}}{(\beta_i - \tilde{\xi}_{ii})(e^{2\beta_i \tau} - 1) + 2\beta_i} \right]$$

$$B_i(\tau) = -\frac{2\sqrt{a_i} \tilde{\mu}_i (e^{\beta_i \tau} - 1)^2}{\beta_i [(\beta_i - \tilde{\xi}_{ii})(e^{2\beta_i \tau} - 1) + 2\beta_i]} \tag{10.126}$$

$$C_i(\tau) = -\frac{e^{2\beta_i \tau} - 1}{(\beta_i - \tilde{\xi}_{ii})(e^{2\beta_i \tau} - 1) + 2\beta_i} \tag{10.127}$$

$$H(t, T) = \int_t^T \delta_r \, dv = \delta_r (T - t) = \delta_r \tau \tag{10.128}$$

$$\beta_i = \sqrt{\tilde{\xi}_{ii}^2 + 2a_i \sigma_i^2}$$

The solution in equation (10.124) is similar to the solution of the bond price given in equation (10.47), except for the parameter a_i, contained in equation (10.124).

The risky short rate is given as a sum of the short rate and the short spread (given in equations (10.121) and (10.122), respectively) as follows:

$$R(t) = r(t) + s(t) = \delta_R + \sum_{i=1}^{N} (a_i + b_i) Y_i^2(t) \tag{10.129}$$

where $\delta_R = \delta_r + \delta_s$. The risky bond price $D(t, T)$ is obtained as a discounted expectation using the *risky* short rate $R(t)$ in equation (10.120) in the same manner as the default-free bond price $P(t, T)$ is obtained using the short rate $r(t)$. Hence, by comparing the definition of the risky short rate $R(t)$ in equation (10.129) with that of the short rate $r(t)$ in equation (10.121), the solution of the risky zero-coupon bond can be given as follows:

$$D(t, T) = e^{\overline{A}(\tau) + \sum_{i=1}^{N} \sqrt{a_i + b_i}(\overline{B}_i(\tau) Y_i(t)) + \sum_{i=1}^{N}(a_i + b_i)(\overline{C}_i(\tau) Y_i^2(t)) - \overline{H}(t, T)} \qquad (10.130)$$

where the solutions of $D(t, T)$, $\overline{A}(\tau)$, $\overline{B}_i(\tau)$, $\overline{C}_i(\tau)$, and $\overline{H}(t, T)$ are identical to the corresponding solutions of $P(t, T)$, $A(\tau)$, $B_i(\tau)$, $C_i(\tau)$, and $H(t, T)$ given in equations (10.124), (10.125), (10.126), (10.127), and (10.128), respectively, except that:

1. a_i is replaced with $(a_i + b_i)$, for all $i = 1, 2, \ldots, N$, and
2. δ_r is replaced with $\delta_R = \delta_r + \delta_s$.

Since value-additivity holds under the reduced-form approach (in contrast to the structural approach of Merton [1974]), the price of a risky-coupon bond can be obtained as follows. Consider a risky coupon bond with coupons C occurring at time T_i $(i = 1, 2, \ldots, n)$ and face value F occurring at time T_n. This bond can be valued using equation (10.130) as follows:

$$D_{Coup}(t) = \sum_{i=1}^{n} C \times D(t, T_i) + F \times D(t, T_n) \qquad (10.131)$$

The $Q_3(N)+$ and $Q_3(N)++$ Models under the RMV Assumption   The preference-free simple $Q_3(N)+$ and $Q_3(N)++$ models obtain the estimates of the risk-neutral parameters directly by using the cross sections of prices of default-free bonds, risky bonds, and credit derivatives (such as credit default swaps). The analytical solutions of the prices of risky bonds and credit derivatives under the simple time-homogeneous preference-free $Q_3(N)+$ models are identical to the corresponding solutions under the fundamental $Q_3(N)$ models, except that the estimates of the risk-neutral parameters may be different under the two approaches, as the latter models impose restrictive forms on the MPRs.

The time-inhomogeneous preference-free $Q_3(N)++$ models assume that initial zero-coupon bond prices of default-free bonds and risky bonds are given exogenously as $P(0, T)$ and $D(0, T)$, respectively. The default-free bond price given in equation (10.124) can be calibrated to the initially given bond price $P(0, T)$ by replacing the constant δ_r in equation (10.121) with $\delta_r(t)$ and by replacing $H(t, T)$ in equation (10.128) with its new definition, as follows:

$$\delta_r(t) = f(0, t) + \sum_{i=1}^{N} \sqrt{a_i}\, \tilde{\mu}_i B_i(t) + \sum_{i=1}^{N} a_i \sigma_i^2 \left(B_i^2(t)/2 + C_i(t)\right)$$

$$+ \sum_{i=1}^{N} \sqrt{a_i} Y_i(0)\left(\tilde{\xi}_{ii} B_i(t) + 2a_i\sigma_i^2 B_i(t)C_i(t) + 2\sqrt{a_i}\,\tilde{\mu}_i C_i(t)\right) \quad (10.132)$$

$$+ \sum_{i=1}^{N} a_i Y_i^2(0)\left(2\tilde{\xi}_{ii} C_i(t) + 2a_i\sigma_i^2 C_i^2(t) - 1\right)$$

and

$$H(t, T) = A(T) - A(t) + \sum_{i=1}^{N} \sqrt{a_i} Y_i(0)\left(B_i(T) - B_i(t)\right)$$

$$+ \sum_{i=1}^{N} a_i Y_i^2(0)\left(C_i(T) - C_i(t)\right) - \ln P(0, T) + \ln P(0, t) \quad (10.133)$$

where $f(0, t) = -\partial \ln P(0, t)/\partial t$ is the time 0 instantaneous forward rate for term t and where the solutions of $A(.)$, $B_i(.)$, and $C_i(.)$ are given in equations (10.125), (10.126), and (10.127), respectively.

The risky bond price under the $Q_3(N)++$ models given in equation (10.130) can be calibrated to the initially given risky bond price $D(0, T)$ by replacing the constant δ_R in equation (10.129) with $\delta_R(t)$ and by replacing $\overline{H}(t, T)$ in equation (10.130) with its new definition, as follows:

$$\delta_R(t) = f_D(0, t) + \sum_{i=1}^{N} \sqrt{a_i + b_i}\, \tilde{\mu}_i \overline{B}_i(t) + \sum_{i=1}^{N} (a_i + b_i)\sigma_i^2 \left(\overline{B}_i^2(t)/2 + \overline{C}_i(t)\right)$$

$$+ \sum_{i=1}^{N} \sqrt{a_i + b_i}\, Y_i(0)\left(\tilde{\xi}_{ii} \overline{B}_i(t) + 2(a_i + b_i)\sigma_i^2 \overline{B}_i(t)\overline{C}_i(t)\right.$$

$$\left. + 2\sqrt{a_i + b_i}\, \tilde{\mu}_i \overline{C}_i(t)\right) \quad (10.134)$$

$$+ \sum_{i=1}^{N} (a_i + b_i) Y_i^2(0)\left(2\tilde{\xi}_{ii} \overline{C}_i(t) + 2(a_i + b_i)\sigma_i^2 \overline{C}_i^2(t) - 1\right)$$

and

$$\overline{H}(t,T) = \overline{A}(T) - \overline{A}(t) + \sum_{i=1}^{N} \sqrt{a_i + b_i} Y_i(0)\big(\overline{B}_i(T) - \overline{B}_i(t)\big)$$

$$+ \sum_{i=1}^{N} (a_i + b_i) Y_i^2(0)\big(\overline{C}_i(T) - \overline{C}_i(t)\big) - \ln D(0,T) + \ln D(0,t)$$

$$(10.135)$$

where $f_D(0,t) = -\partial \ln D(0,t)/\partial t$ is the time 0 instantaneous risky forward rate for term t.

The time-inhomogeneous preference-free $Q_3(N)++$ models have obvious advantages over the HJM [1992] forward rate models. The $Q_3(N)++$ models are Markovian and allow closed-form solutions for risky bond prices. Also, given the existence of analytical solutions under the $Q_3(N)++$ models, Monte Carlo simulations can run much faster under these models to value certain classes of credit derivatives. Finally, for credit derivatives with American features, low-dimensional $Q_3(N)++$ models allow construction of efficient trees, similar to those demonstrated for two-factor Gaussian models in Chapter 9.

Example 10.2 The specifications allowed under the $Q_3(N)$, $Q_3(N)+$, and $Q_3(N)++$ models can be demonstrated by a simple example. Consider the following specification of the short rate process and the short spread process under the $Q_3(5)+$ model:

$$r(t) = \delta_r + Y_1(t) + Y_2(t) + Y_3(t) \qquad (10.136)$$

$$s(t) = \delta_R - \delta_r + Y_4(t) + Y_5(t) \qquad (10.137)$$

This $Q_3(5)+$ model assumes $a_1 = 1, a_2 = 1, a_3 = 1, a_4 = 0, a_5 = 0, b_1 = 0,$ $b_2 = 0, b_3 = 0, b_4 = 1,$ and $b_5 = 1$. The $Q_3(5)+$ model allows the short rate to be given as a sum of three state variables, similar to how the short rate is defined under the fundamental $Q_3(3)$ model of Ahn, Dittmar, and Gallant [2002]. As these authors show, the fundamental $Q_3(3)$ performs better than the maximal three-factor affine models, even though it assumes orthogonal state variables. Hence, the preference-free $Q_3(5)+$ model may also fit well the dynamics of the default-free interest rates using three orthogonal state variables, especially since it allows MPRs to be of general nonlinear form. The short spread may be captured well by using two more state variables. Though this model uses five state variables, the analytical solutions of risky bond prices can be computed quickly using the formulas given in equations (10.130) through (10.135). Replacing δ_r with $\delta_r(t)$ as defined in equation (10.132) and replacing δ_R with $\delta_R(t)$ as defined in equation (10.134) gives the $Q_3(5)++$ model corresponding to the $Q_3(5)+$ model. The $Q_3(5)++$ model can be used if exact calibration is desired with the initial default-free bond prices and initial risky bond prices.

Reduced-Form $Q_3(N)$ and $Q_3(N)+$ Models under the RFV Assumption

As mentioned in Chapter 3, the main difference between the RMV assumption and the RFV assumption is that under the former, the risky bond's defaulted value at any given time equals $(1 - \tilde{L}_M)$ fraction of its nondefaulted value just before default, while under the latter, the risky bond's value upon default equals $(1 - \tilde{L}_F)$ fraction of the face value of the bond. This section demonstrates how to price risky bonds and credit default swaps under the RFV assumption using the $Q_3(N)$ and $Q_3(N)+$ models.

Consider a risky coupon bond with coupons C occurring at time T_i $(i = 1, 2, \ldots, n)$ and face value F occurring at time T_n. The price of the risky coupon bond is derived in Chapter 9 under the RFV assumption, as follows:

$$
\begin{aligned}
D_{Coup}(t) = \tilde{E}_t \left(\sum_{i=1}^{n} \frac{C}{e^{\int_t^{T_i}(r(v)+\tilde{\lambda}(v))\,dv}} + \frac{F}{e^{\int_t^{T_n}(r(v)+\tilde{\lambda}(v))\,dv}} \right) \\
+ F(1 - \tilde{L}_F)\tilde{E}_t \left(\int_t^{T_n} \tilde{\lambda}(u)e^{-\int_t^u(r(v)+\tilde{\lambda}(v))\,dv}\,du \right)
\end{aligned}
\tag{10.138}
$$

Equation (10.138) can be rewritten as follows:

$$
D_{Coup}(t) = \sum_{i=1}^{n} C \times D_F(t, T_i) + F \times D_F(t, T_n) + F(1 - \tilde{L}_F) \int_t^{T_n} G(t, u)\,du
\tag{10.139}
$$

where

$$
\begin{aligned}
D_F(t, T) &= \tilde{E}_t \left(e^{-\int_t^T (r(v)+\tilde{\lambda}(v))dv} \right) \\
G(t, T) &= \tilde{E}_t \left(\tilde{\lambda}(T)e^{-\int_t^T (r(v)+\tilde{\lambda}(v))dv} \right)
\end{aligned}
\tag{10.140}
$$

The valuation of coupon bonds under the RFV assumption requires computing the risk-neutral expectations to solve $D_F(t, T)$ and $G(t, T)$. The numerical integral given in equation (10.139) can be evaluated easily with an analytical solution of $G(t, T)$. The solutions of $D_F(t, T)$ and $G(t, T)$ are given in the following two steps.

Step 1: Solution of $D_F(t, T)$ Let the short rate and the risk-neutral default intensity be defined under the $Q_3(N)$ model using the RFV assumption, as follows:

$$r(t) = \delta_r + \sum_{i=1}^{N} a_i Y_i^2(t) \qquad (10.141)$$

$$\tilde{\lambda}(t) = \delta_\lambda + \sum_{i=1}^{N} b_i Y_i^2(t) \qquad (10.142)$$

where the risk-neutral stochastic processes of Y_i are defined in the same manner as under the RMV framework in equation (10.123).

A simple mathematical trick allows obtaining the solution of $D_F(t, T)$ from the solution of the risky zero-coupon bond price $D(t, T)$ under the RMV assumption given earlier. Assume that the risk-neutral loss rate $\tilde{L}_M$ is 100 percent, or equal to 1, under the RMV assumption and that $\delta_\lambda = \delta_s$ implies that $s(t)$ defined in equation (10.122) is identical to $\tilde{\lambda}(t)$ defined in equation (10.142). Under these assumptions, $D_F(t, T)$ given in equation (10.140) is identical to the definition of $D(t, T)$ in equation (10.120). Hence, the solution of $D_F(t, T)$ is given by $D(t, T)$ in equation (10.130), with $\delta_\lambda = \delta_s$.

Step 2: Solution of $G(t, T)$ Under mild regularity conditions, the solution of $G(t, T)$ in equation (10.140) can be alternatively expressed as follows:

$$G(t, T) = \tilde{E}_t \left(\tilde{\lambda}(T) e^{-\int_t^T (r(v) + \tilde{\lambda}(v)) dv} \right) = \frac{\partial}{\partial \phi} (\eta(t, T, \phi))_{\phi=0} \qquad (10.143)$$

where

$$\eta(t, T, \phi) = \tilde{E}_t \left(e^{-\int_t^T (r(v) + \tilde{\lambda}(v)) dv} e^{\phi \tilde{\lambda}(T)} \right) \qquad (10.144)$$

The expectation shown in equation (10.144) is solved in Appendix 10.1 and is given as follows:

$$\eta(t, T, \phi) = e^{A^\dagger(\tau) + \sum_{i=1}^{N} \sqrt{a_i + b_i}(B_i^\dagger(\tau) Y_i(t)) + \sum_{i=1}^{N} (a_i + b_i)(C_i^\dagger(\tau) Y_i^2(t)) - H^\dagger(t, T)} \qquad (10.145)$$

where

$$H^\dagger(t, T) = \int_t^T (\delta_r + \delta_\lambda) \, dv = (\delta_r + \delta_\lambda)\tau \qquad (10.146)$$

subject to the boundary conditions:

$$A^\dagger(0) = \phi\delta_\lambda$$

$$B_i^\dagger(0) = 0, \quad \text{for } i = 1, 2, \ldots, N \tag{10.147}$$

$$C_i^\dagger(0) = \frac{\phi b_i}{a_i + b_i}, \quad \text{for } i = 1, 2, \ldots, N$$

The solutions are given as follows:

$$A^\dagger(\tau) = \phi\delta_\lambda + \int_0^\tau \left(\sum_{i=1}^N \tilde{\mu}_i \sqrt{a_i + b_i} B_i^\dagger(v) \right.$$

$$\left. + \frac{1}{2} \sum_{i=1}^N \sigma_i^2(a_i + b_i)\left((B_i^\dagger(v))^2 + 2C_i^\dagger(v)\right) \right) dv \tag{10.148}$$

$$B_i^\dagger(\tau) = \frac{\tilde{\mu}_i}{\beta_i\sigma_i^2\sqrt{a_i + b_i}} \left(\frac{(e^{\beta_i\tau} - 1)((\tilde{\xi}_{ii} + \beta_i)\theta_i e^{\beta_i\tau} - (\tilde{\xi}_{ii} - \beta_i))}{1 - \theta_i e^{2\beta_i\tau}} \right),$$

$$\text{for } i = 1, 2, \ldots, N \tag{10.149}$$

$$C_i^\dagger(\tau) = \frac{1}{2\sigma_i^2(a_i + b_i)} \left(\frac{(\tilde{\xi}_{ii} + \beta_i)\theta_i e^{2\beta_i\tau} - (\tilde{\xi}_{ii} - \beta_i)}{1 - \theta_i e^{2\beta_i\tau}} \right), \quad \text{for } i = 1, 2, \ldots, N$$

$$\tag{10.150}$$

where

$$\beta_i = \sqrt{\tilde{\xi}_{ii}^2 + 2\sigma_i^2(a_i + b_i)}$$

$$\theta_i = \frac{\tilde{\xi}_{ii} - \beta_i + 2\phi b_i\sigma_i^2}{\tilde{\xi}_{ii} + \beta_i + 2\phi b_i\sigma_i^2} \tag{10.151}$$

For expositional simplicity, the term $A^\dagger(\tau)$ is evaluated using a numerical integral.

The solution of $G(t, T)$ in equation (10.143) can be numerically evaluated as follows:

$$G(t, T) = \frac{\partial}{\partial\phi}(\eta(t, T, \phi))_{\phi=0} = \lim_{h\to 0} \left(\frac{\eta(t, T, h) - \eta(t, T, 0)}{h} \right) \tag{10.152}$$

Hence, solving $\eta(t, T, \phi)$ twice with $\phi = h$ and $\phi = 0$ for a very small value of h (e.g., $h = 0.000001$) gives the solution of $G(t, T)$ in equation (10.152).

Pricing Credit Default Swaps under the RFV Assumption   Consider a single-name credit default swap that requires the protection-buyer to pay p $(p = n/(T_n - t))$ number of premiums each year until the bond defaults, for a maximum number of n periods over $T_n - t$ years. Let the time t value of an annualized credit default swap spread (or premium) be given as $CDS(t)$ for every \$1 of the face value of the bond. The premium leg of the credit default swap makes payments only in those states in which the underlying bond does not default. Hence, the present value of the premium leg is given by the following risk-neutral expectation:

$$Present\ Value\ of\ Premium\ Leg = \tilde{E}_t \left(\sum_{i=1}^{n} \frac{CDS(t)/p}{e^{\int_t^{t+i/p} (r(v)+\tilde{\lambda}(v))\,dv}} \right) \quad (10.153)$$

The protection-seller must pay the difference between the face value of the bond and the market value of the bond when the bond defaults. This loss is exogenously specified as $\tilde{L}_F$ fraction of the face value of the bond under the RFV assumption. As shown in Chapter 9, the present value of the protection leg for every \$1 of face value of the bond is given by the following risk-neutral expectation:

$$Present\ Value\ of\ Protection\ Leg = \tilde{L}_F \tilde{E}_t \left(\int_t^{T_n} \tilde{\lambda}(u) e^{-\int_t^u (r(v)+\tilde{\lambda}(v))\,dv}\,du \right)$$
$$(10.154)$$

By equating the present value of the premium leg to the present value of the protection leg solves the credit default swap spread as follows:

$$CDS(t) = \frac{p\tilde{L}_F \tilde{E}_t \left(\int_t^{T_n} \tilde{\lambda}(u) e^{-\int_t^u (r(v)+\tilde{\lambda}(v))\,dv}\,du \right)}{\tilde{E}_t \left(\sum_{i=1}^{n} e^{-\int_t^{t+i/p} (r(v)+\tilde{\lambda}(v))\,dv} \right)} \quad (10.155)$$

Using the definitions of $D_F(t, T)$ and $G(t, T)$ in equation (10.140), the credit default swap spread can be given as follows:

$$CDS(t) = \frac{p\tilde{L}_F \int_t^{T_n} G(t, u)\,du}{\sum_{i=1}^{n} D_F(t, t + i/p)} \quad (10.156)$$

Substituting into equation (10.156) the solutions of $D_F(t, T)$ and $G(t, T)$ obtained in step 1 and step 2 of the previous section gives an analytical solution to the credit default swap spread under the $Q_3(N)$ models.

The analytical solutions of the price of a risky bond and the credit default swap spread under the time-homogeneous preference-free $Q_3(N)+$ model are identical to the corresponding solutions under the fundamental $Q_3(N)$ model given in equations (10.139) and (10.156), respectively, except that the estimates of the risk-neutral parameters may be different under the two approaches, as the latter model imposes restrictive functional forms on the MPRs. The preference-free $Q_3(N)+$ model obtains the estimates of the risk-neutral parameters directly by using the cross sections of prices of default-free bonds, risky bonds, and/or credit default swaps.

The time-inhomogeneous preference-free $Q_3(N)++$ model cannot be obtained under the RFV assumption since the risk-neutral loss rate $\tilde{L}_F$ is valid only under a specific coupon size and specific maturity. The initial prices of risky *zero-coupon* bonds cannot be inverted from the initial prices of risky coupon bonds, which may have a different value of $\tilde{L}_F$ for different sizes of coupons and maturities. The time-inhomogeneous $Q_3(N)++$ model may not be required, however, if increasing the number of factors allows good fitting with the prices of default-free bonds, risky bonds, and credit default swaps using the time-homogeneous $Q_3(N)+$ model.

APPENDIX 10.1 THE SOLUTION OF $\eta(t, T, \phi)$ FOR CDS PRICING USING THE $Q_3(N)$ MODEL UNDER THE RFV ASSUMPTION

By substituting equations (10.141) and (10.142), equation (10.144) can be rewritten as follows:

$$
\eta(t, T, \phi) = \tilde{E}_t \left(\exp\left(-\int_t^T \left((\delta_r + \delta_\lambda) + \sum_{i=1}^N (a_i + b_i) Y_i^2(v) \right) dv \right) \right.
$$

$$
\left. \times \exp\left(\phi \left(\delta_\lambda + \sum_{i=1}^N b_i Y_i^2(T) \right) \right) \right) \tag{10.157}
$$

Using the Feynman-Kac theorem given in Chapter 2, the PDE corresponding to the risk-neutral expectation shown in equation (10.157) is given as follows:

$$
\frac{\partial \eta}{\partial t} + \sum_{i=1}^N \frac{\partial \eta}{\partial Y_i} [\tilde{\mu}_i + \tilde{\xi}_{ii} Y_i(t)] + \frac{1}{2} \sum_{i=1}^N \frac{\partial^2 \eta}{\partial Y_i^2} \sigma_i^2
$$

$$
= \left((\delta_r + \delta_\lambda) + \sum_{i=1}^N (a_i + b_i) Y_i^2(t) \right) \eta(t, T, \phi) \tag{10.158}
$$

subject to the boundary condition:

$$\eta(T, T, \phi) = \exp\left(\phi\left(\delta_\lambda + \sum_{i=1}^{N} b_i Y_i^2(T)\right)\right) \tag{10.159}$$

Consider the following solution for $\eta(t, T, \phi)$:

$$\eta(t, T, \phi) = e^{A^\dagger(\tau) + \sum_{i=1}^{N} \sqrt{a_i + b_i}\left(B_i^\dagger(\tau) Y_i(t)\right) + \sum_{i=1}^{N} (a_i + b_i)\left(C_i^\dagger(\tau) Y_i^2(t)\right) - H^\dagger(t, T)} \tag{10.160}$$

where

$$H^\dagger(t, T) = \int_t^T (\delta_r + \delta_\lambda)\, dv = (\delta_r + \delta_\lambda)\tau \tag{10.161}$$

and $\tau = T - t$, subject to the following boundary conditions:

$$\begin{aligned}
A^\dagger(0) &= \phi\delta_\lambda \\
B_i^\dagger(0) &= 0, \quad \text{for } i = 1, 2, \dots, N \\
C_i^\dagger(0) &= \frac{\phi b_i}{a_i + b_i}, \quad \text{for } i = 1, 2, \dots, N
\end{aligned} \tag{10.162}$$

Taking the partial derivatives of $\eta(t, T, \phi)$ in equation (10.160), substituting these in equation (10.158), and using a change of variable $\tau = T - t$, we get the following $2N + 1$ ODEs:

$$\frac{\partial A^\dagger(\tau)}{\partial \tau} = \sum_{i=1}^{N} \tilde{\mu}_i \sqrt{a_i + b_i} B_i^\dagger(\tau) + \frac{1}{2}\sum_{i=1}^{N} \sigma_i^2 (a_i + b_i)(B_i^\dagger(\tau))^2$$

$$+ \sum_{i=1}^{N} \sigma_i^2 (a_i + b_i) C_i^\dagger(\tau) \tag{10.163}$$

$$\frac{\partial B_i^\dagger(\tau)}{\partial \tau} = \tilde{\xi}_{ii} B_i^\dagger(\tau) + 2\tilde{\mu}_i \sqrt{a_i + b_i} C_i^\dagger(\tau) + 2\sigma_i^2 (a_i + b_i) B_i^\dagger(\tau) C_i^\dagger(\tau)$$

$$\frac{\partial C_i^\dagger(\tau)}{\partial \tau} = 2\tilde{\xi}_{ii} C_i^\dagger(\tau) + 2\sigma_i^2 (a_i + b_i)(C_i^\dagger(\tau))^2 - 1$$

subject to the boundary conditions given in equation (10.162). The solution of $A^\dagger(\tau)$, $B_i^\dagger(\tau)$, and $C_i^\dagger(\tau)$ are given in equations (10.148), (10.149), and 10.150, respectively.

NOTES

1. This method uses the seminonparametric (SNP) conditional density estimator of Gallant and Tauchen [1989] as the candidate auxiliary model.
2. Calculated by averaging the RMSEs for ATM difference caps in each of the Panels A, B, and C of Table 5 in Li and Zhao [2006].

CHAPTER 11

The HJM Forward Rate Model

Unlike affine and quadratic models, which first originated as fundamental models and were subsequently generalized as preference-free models, the forward rate models of Heath, Jarrow, and Morton (HJM) [1992], the LIBOR market model (LMM),[1] and the String model[2] are preference-free by construction. Since these models exogenously specify the forward rate process, which uniquely determines the risk-neutral short rate process without requiring the specification of market prices of risks, preferences do not enter into the valuation process.

The forward rate models typically assume historical forward rate volatilities and an initially observed set of forward rates (or an observed set of bond prices from which the forward rates are derived) as *model inputs*. Since these models do not generally impose restrictions on the functional forms of term structures of historical volatilities and time 0 forward rates, they imply a time-inhomogeneous short rate process.[3]

The preference-free HJM forward rate model is not a "model" in the traditional sense. The HJM framework basically imposes the no-arbitrage "forward rate drift restriction" consistent with a finite-factor volatility structure for the forward rate processes. In a sense, all preference-free finite-factor term structure models are HJM models, such that every preference-free model introduced from Chapter 4 through Chapter 10 can be classified as an HJM model using the forward rate processes implied by these affine and quadratic models. For example, Vasicek+ and CIR+ models can be alternatively conceptualized as single-plus HJM models with *specific* functional forms for both the forward rate volatility function and an initial forward rate function, which lead to a time-homogeneous risk-neutral short rate process. Similarly, Vasicek++ and CIR++ models can be conceptualized as double-plus HJM models, which do not impose any restrictions on the functional form of the initially observed forward rates but allow only *specific* functional forms for the forward rate volatility function. But such classification of existing preference-free term structure models as "HJM models" serves little purpose, especially when many of these models have been derived

---

This chapter was coauthored with Lixiong Guo and Jun Zhang.

independently by other researchers (e.g., the Vasicek++ and Vasicek+++ models of Hull and White [1990], and the CIR++ model suggested by CIR [1985] and developed fully by Dybvig [1988], Scott [1995], and Brigo and Mercurio [2001]). In contrast to the HJM framework, the LMM imposes deterministic volatilities on the lognormal forward rate processes and so represents a specific term structure model.

Since most commonly used models in the HJM class are double-plus models, we do not use two plus symbols to denote these models and simply refer to them as HJM models. By allowing *time-inhomogeneous* forward rate volatilities, triple-plus HJM models can also be derived. Similar to HJM models, even string models may be double-plus or triple-plus, depending on whether or not these models allow time-homogeneous forward rate volatility functions. However, unless the correlation function underlying the string model reduces to give a finite-factor representation, single-plus string models cannot be generally obtained.

The general double-plus and triple-plus HJM/LMM/string models allow more flexibility in modeling of the term structure dynamics. However, this added flexibility also comes at a cost of making the short rate process non-Markovian. A non-Markovian short rate process not only sacrifices much of the analytical tractability of the affine and quadratic models, but it also makes it difficult to value derivatives with American features.

The state dependent forward rate processes under the HJM model typically require a nonrecombining tree for the numerical valuation of interest rate derivatives. The traditional *imperative* programming requires forward induction to generate the terminal values of a given derivative security, followed by a backward induction for valuation of the security. Due to the non-Markovian nature of the short rate under the HJM model, the entire short rate tree must be stored in memory for performing the backward induction. Since nonrecombining trees grow exponentially, this can put huge requirements on the allocation of memory.

Das [1998] demonstrates that the special structure of a nonrecombining tree allows the use of the *recursive* programming technique for valuing interest rate derivatives. In our simulations, we find recursive programming to be not only faster than imperative programming, but significantly more efficient with memory allocation.

THE HJM FORWARD RATE MODEL

HJM consider a continuous trading economy with a fixed trading interval. Let $f(t, T)$ be the time t instantaneous forward rate for the term $T \geq t$ and $P(t, T)$ be the time t price of a zero-coupon bond that pays \$1 at time T, where both t and T belong to the fixed trading interval. Recall the following relationship between the zero-coupon bond price and the forward rates:

$$f(t, T) = -\frac{\partial \ln P(t, T)}{\partial T} \tag{11.1}$$

$$P(t, T) = \exp\left(-\int_t^T f(t, s)\, ds\right) \tag{11.2}$$

The HJM model specifies the forward rate process using the following stochastic differential equation under the physical measure:

$$df(t, T) = \alpha(t, T, \omega)\, dt + \sum_{i=1}^n \sigma_i(t, T, \omega)\, dZ_i(t) \tag{11.3}$$

where dZ_is are n independent Brownian motions. The forward rate volatilities can depend upon the entire history of forward rates until time t through the term ω. The forward rate process is very general and, under appropriate restrictions, nests virtually all finite-dimensional term structure models. In this sense, the forward rate process in equation (11.3) *does not constitute a specific model*, since all models, including the affine short rate models (e.g., Vasicek and CIR), the nonaffine constant-elasticity-of variance (CEV) short rate models (e.g., Courtadon [1982]), the preference-free affine and quadratic models, the LIBOR market models, and so forth, are special cases of the HJM forward rate process.

Integrating equation (11.3) stochastically over time, we get:

$$f(t, T) = f(0, T) + \int_0^t \alpha(v, T)\, dv + \sum_{i=1}^n \int_0^t \sigma_i(v, T)\, dZ_i(v) \tag{11.4}$$

where $f(0, T)$ is the initial forward rate observed at time 0. For notational convenience, we have suppressed the term ω in equation (11.4), even though the volatility functions and the drift function may depend upon the current and past values of the state variables.

As T tends to t, equation (11.4) gives the short rate in the integral form as follows:

$$r(t) = f(t, t) = f(0, t) + \int_0^t \alpha(v, t)\, dv + \sum_{i=1}^n \int_0^t \sigma_i(v, t) dZ_i(v) \tag{11.5}$$

Using rule 2 given in equation (1.33) in Chapter 1, the stochastic differential equation of the short rate can be given as follows:

$$dr(t) = \left[\frac{\partial f(0, t)}{\partial t} + \alpha(t, t) + \int_0^t \frac{\partial \alpha(v, t)}{\partial t}\, dv + \sum_{i=1}^n \int_0^t \frac{\partial \sigma_i(v, t)}{\partial t}\, dZ_i(v)\right] dt$$
$$+ \sum_{i=1}^n \sigma_i(t, t)\, dZ_i(t) \tag{11.6}$$

For arbitrary functional forms of the volatility functions $\sigma_i(t, T)$, the short rate process in equation (11.6) is non-Markovian. A non-Markovian short rate process not only has limited analytical tractability for deriving closed-form solutions of interest rate derivatives but also does not allow recombining trees for valuing American options. Caverhill [1994], Hull and White [1993], Ritchken and Sankarasubramanian [1995], and Inui and Kijima [1998] have investigated special cases under which this short rate process becomes Markovian and allows a recombining tree.

The stochastic dynamics of the zero-coupon bonds can be obtained by taking the logarithm of both sides of equation (11.2) as follows:

$$\ln P(t, T) = -\int_t^T f(t, s)\, ds \tag{11.7}$$

where $f(t, s)$ is given in the stochastic integral specified in equation (11.4). Substituting equation (11.4) in equation (11.7) gives:

$$\ln P(t, T) = -\int_t^T f(0, s)\, ds - \int_t^T \left[\int_0^t \alpha(v, s)\, dv\right] ds$$
$$- \sum_{i=1}^n \int_t^T \left[\int_0^t \sigma_i(v, s)\, dZ_i(v)\right] ds \tag{11.8}$$

The first term on the right-hand side equals $\ln P(0, T)$. Evaluating the double integrals in the next two terms using the regularity conditions given in the appendix of Heath, Jarrow, and Morton [1992] gives the solution of equation (11.8) as follows:

$$\ln P(t, T) = \ln P(0, T) + \int_0^t \left[r(v) + b(v, T)\right] dv - \frac{1}{2} \sum_{i=1}^n \int_0^t a_i^2(v, T)\, dv$$

$$+ \sum_{i=1}^n \int_0^t a_i(v, T)\, dZ_i(v) \tag{11.9}$$

where

$$a_i(t, T) = -\int_t^T \sigma_i(t, s)\, ds \tag{11.10}$$

$$b(t, T) = -\int_t^T \alpha(t, s)\, ds + \frac{1}{2} \sum_{i=1}^n a_i^2(t, T) \tag{11.11}$$

Using Ito's lemma, the stochastic bond price process is given as follows:

$$\frac{dP(t, T)}{P(t, T)} = [r(t) + b(t, T)]\, dt + \sum_{i=1}^n a_i(t, T)\, dZ_i(t) \tag{11.12}$$

Though the stochastic bond price process in equation (11.12) is consistent with the forward rate process given in equation (11.3), it does not ensure the absence of arbitrage between bonds of different maturities. To rule out arbitrage opportunities requires the existence of an equivalent risk-neutral measure, under which discounted bond prices are martingales (see Chapter 2). Let the n Wiener processes under the risk-neutral measure be given as follows:

$$d\tilde{Z}_i(t) = dZ_i(t) + \gamma_i(t)\,dt \tag{11.13}$$

where $\gamma_i(t)$ is the market price for risk associated with the Brownian motion $Z_i(t)$ for all $i = 1, 2, \ldots, n$. Substituting the Wiener processes in equation (11.13) into equation (11.3) gives the bond price process under the risk-neutral measure as follows:

$$\frac{dP(t,T)}{P(t,T)} = [r(t) + \tilde{b}(t,T)]\,dt + \sum_{i=1}^{n} a_i(t,T)\,d\tilde{Z}_i(t) \tag{11.14}$$

where

$$\tilde{b}(t,T) = -\int_t^T \alpha(t,s)\,ds + \frac{1}{2}\sum_{i=1}^{n} a_i^2(t,T) - \sum_{i=1}^{n} a_i(t,T)\gamma_i(t) \tag{11.15}$$

The term $\tilde{b}(t,T)$ defines the excess bond return under the risk-neutral measure. Since by definition the excess bond return is zero under the risk-neutral measure, we have:

$$\int_t^T \alpha(t,s)\,ds = \frac{1}{2}\sum_{i=1}^{n} a_i^2(t,T) - \sum_{i=1}^{n} a_i(t,T)\gamma_i(t) \tag{11.16}$$

Substituting equation (11.10), equation (11.16) can be rewritten as follows:

$$\int_t^T \alpha(t,s)\,ds = \frac{1}{2}\sum_{i=1}^{n} \left(-\int_t^T \sigma_i(t,s)\,ds \right)^2 + \sum_{i=1}^{n} -\gamma_i(t)\left(-\int_t^T \sigma_i(t,s)\,ds \right) \tag{11.17}$$

Differentiating with respect to T gives the forward rate drift as follows:

$$\alpha(t,T) = \sum_{i=1}^{n} \sigma_i(t,T)\left(\int_t^T \sigma_i(t,s)\,ds + \gamma_i(t) \right) \tag{11.18}$$

Though the physical drift of the forward rate process contains the market prices of risk, these can be eliminated from the risk-neutral drift such that valuation is preference-free under the HJM model. This can be seen by substituting equations (11.13) and (11.18) into equation (11.3), which gives:

$$df(t,T) = \tilde{\alpha}(t,T)\,dt + \sum_{i=1}^{n}\sigma_i(t,T)\,d\tilde{Z}_i(t) \qquad (11.19)$$

where

$$\tilde{\alpha}(t,T) = \sum_{i=1}^{n}\sigma_i(t,T)\left(\int_{t}^{T}\sigma_i(t,s)\,ds\right) \qquad (11.20)$$

The volatility functions completely determine the risk-neutral drift of the forward rate process. In general, the knowledge of the time 0 forward rates and the n volatility functions are sufficient for valuation under the HJM model.

The short rate process can be obtained under the risk-neutral measure by substituting equations (11.13) and (11.18) into equation (11.5), which gives:

$$r(t) = f(t,t) = f(0,t) + \int_{0}^{t}\tilde{\alpha}(v,t)\,dv + \sum_{i=1}^{n}\int_{0}^{t}\sigma_i(v,t)\,d\tilde{Z}_i(v) \qquad (11.21)$$

where the risk-neutral drift function $\tilde{\alpha}(t,T)$ is defined in equation (11.20). Just like the forward rate process, the stochastic evolution of $r(t)$ does not require the market prices of risk under the risk-neutral measure.

The time t value of a contingent claim with a payoff $c(T)$ at time T is given as follows:

$$c(t) = \tilde{E}_t\left(\frac{c(T)}{e^{\int_{t}^{T}r(v)\,dv}}\right) \qquad (11.22)$$

NUMERICAL IMPLEMENTATION USING NONRECOMBINING TREES

Obtaining closed-form solutions is generally difficult under the HJM models, except for the simple Gaussian cases considered in Chapter 4. Since the volatility functions are specified exogenously, these often lead to a non-Markovian short rate process requiring the construction of path-dependent nonrecombining trees. Under a nonrecombining tree, an upward move followed by a downward move does not result in the same forward rate as a downward move followed by an upward move. Therefore, the number of nodes after N time steps equals 2^N for a binomial tree and 3^N for a trinomial tree.

Since a large amount of computational time and memory are required for valuation using HJM trees (for example, after 20 time steps there are more than 1 million nodes on the tree), we describe another technique called "recursive programming" that substantially eases the burden of time and memory costs.[4] Implementation by the recursive method has several distinct advantages. First, the code is parsimonious. Second, the model uses less memory than the standard implementation. Third, the computational time is reduced significantly in our simulations. Also, due to the nonrecombining nature of the tree, the path-dependent features of many exotic options are easily handled. In the following section, we illustrate the construction of one-factor and two-factor nonrecombining trees, followed by the description of the recursive programming technique.

A One-Factor Nonrecombining Binomial Tree

The risk-neutral forward rate process under the one-factor HJM model is given as follows:

$$df(t, T) = \tilde{\alpha}(t, T) \, dt + \sigma(t, T) \, d\tilde{Z}(t) \tag{11.23}$$

where the forward rate drift is given as follows:

$$\tilde{\alpha}(t, T) = \sigma(t, T) \int_t^T \sigma(t, s) \, ds \tag{11.24}$$

To understand the construction of a nonrecombining tree, first consider the evolution of only three forward rates $f(0, 0)$, $f(0, 1)$, and $f(0, 2)$ over two periods, from time 0 to 1 and from time 1 to 2, as shown in Figure 11.1.

At time 0, the initial forward rate curve is represented by the vector of forward rates given as:

$$\begin{bmatrix} f(0,0) \\ f(0,1) \\ f(0,2) \end{bmatrix} \tag{11.25}$$

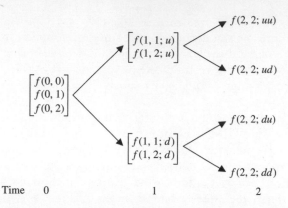

FIGURE 11.1 The Evolution of a One-Factor Forward Rate Curve

With probability 0.5, the forward rate curve shifts up to:

$$\begin{bmatrix} f(1,1;u) \\ f(1,2;u) \end{bmatrix} \tag{11.26}$$

For clarity, the notation for the forward rate is augmented to include the state "u." The forward rate vector has one less element in equation (11.26) since the rate for time 0 no longer exists at time 1. Similarly, with probability 0.5, the forward rate curve in expression (11.25) shifts down to:

$$\begin{bmatrix} f(1,1;d) \\ f(1,2;d) \end{bmatrix} \tag{11.27}$$

At each of the two nodes at time 1, the forward rate can again either go "up" or "down" in the next period. Therefore, the four possible states at time 2 are denoted as "uu," "ud," "du," and "dd," respectively. Since the forward rate evolution is path-dependent, the tree does not recombine.

We now consider finer partitions of time and the evolution of the entire forward rate curve over time. Consider discrete points in time over the trading interval 0 to $\hat{T}$, given as $0, h, 2h, \dots, \hat{T}$. Let the forward rates at time t be given as $f(t, t), f(t, t+h), f(t, t+2h), \dots, f(t, \hat{T})$. The change in the forward rate $f(t, T)$ (where $0 \leq t < T \leq \hat{T}$) over a small interval h can be given as follows:

$$f(t+h, T) - f(t, T) = \tilde{\alpha}_d(t, T)h + \sigma(t, T)X\sqrt{h} \tag{11.28}$$

where $\sigma(t, T)$ is defined in equation (11.23). The random variable X is binomially distributed with realizations of 1 and -1 with equal probabilities.

$p_u = 1/2$

$p_d = 1/2$

FIGURE 11.2   Forward Rate Evolution at Each Node of the Tree

Hence, the tree has only two outcomes of equal probabilities at any given node, as shown in Figure 11.2.

The discrete-time approximation of the change in forward rate in equation (11.28) requires estimates of both $\tilde{\alpha}_d(t, T)$ and $\sigma(t, T)$. Though $\sigma(t, T)$ can be obtained directly from historical estimates, the formula for $\tilde{\alpha}_d$ (t, T) is no longer given by $\tilde{\alpha}(t, T)$ in equation (11.24). Instead, the formula for $\tilde{\alpha}_d$ (t, T) is derived by ruling out arbitrage opportunities in *discrete time* using a noninfinitesimal value of h. The following derives a formula for $\tilde{\alpha}_d(t, T)$, which converges to $\tilde{\alpha}(t, T)$ when h becomes infinitesimally small in the continuous-time limit.

In the discretized economy, define the time t value of the money market account as follows:

$$B(t) = \exp\left[\sum_{i=0}^{\frac{t}{h}-1} r(ih)h\right] \qquad (11.29)$$

Define the time t price of a T-maturity zero-coupon bond as follows:

$$P(t, T) = \exp\left[-\sum_{i=\frac{t}{h}}^{\frac{T}{h}-1} f(t, ih)h\right] \qquad (11.30)$$

As shown in Chapter 2, all bond prices discounted by the money market account are martingales under the risk neutral measure, or:

$$\frac{P(t, T)}{B(t)} = \tilde{E}_t\left(\frac{P(t + h, T)}{B(t + h)}\right) \qquad (11.31)$$

Equation (11.31) can be rewritten as follows:

$$\tilde{E}_t\left(\frac{P(t + h, T)}{P(t, T)} \times \frac{B(t)}{B(t + h)}\right) = 1 \qquad (11.32)$$

where

$$\frac{P(t+h,T)}{P(t,T)} = \exp\left[-\sum_{i=\frac{t}{h}+1}^{\frac{T}{h}-1} f(t+h,ih)h\right] \exp\left[\sum_{i=\frac{t}{h}}^{\frac{T}{h}-1} f(t,ih)h\right]$$

$$= \exp\left[\left\{-\sum_{i=\frac{t}{h}+1}^{\frac{T}{h}-1} (f(t+h,ih)-f(t,ih))h\right\} + f(t,t)h\right] \quad (11.33)$$

and

$$\frac{B(t+h)}{B(t)} = \exp\left[\sum_{i=0}^{\frac{t}{h}} r(ih)h\right] \exp\left[-\sum_{i=0}^{\frac{t}{h}-1} r(ih)h\right]$$

$$= \exp[r(t)h] \quad (11.34)$$

$$= \exp[f(t,t)h]$$

Substituting equations (11.33) and (11.34) into equation (11.32), we get

$$\tilde{E}_t\left[\exp\left(-\sum_{i=\frac{t}{h}+1}^{\frac{T}{h}-1} [f(t+h,ih)-f(t,ih)]h\right)\right] = 1 \quad (11.35)$$

Substituting equation (11.28) into equation (11.35) gives:

$$\tilde{E}_t\left[\exp\left(-\sum_{i=\frac{t}{h}+1}^{\frac{T}{h}-1} [\tilde{\alpha}_d(t,ih)h + \sigma(t,ih)X\sqrt{h}]h\right)\right] = 1 \quad (11.36)$$

Further simplification gives:

$$\sum_{i=\frac{t}{h}+1}^{\frac{T}{h}-1} \tilde{\alpha}_d(t,ih) = \frac{1}{h^2}\ln\left\{\tilde{E}_t\left[\exp\left(-\sum_{i=\frac{t}{h}+1}^{\frac{T}{h}-1} \sigma(t,ih)Xh^{1.5}\right)\right]\right\}$$

$$= \frac{1}{h^2}\ln\left\{\frac{1}{2}\left[\exp\left(-\sum_{i=\frac{t}{h}+1}^{\frac{T}{h}-1} \sigma(t,ih)h^{1.5}\right) + \exp\left(\sum_{i=\frac{t}{h}+1}^{\frac{T}{h}-1} \sigma(t,ih)h^{1.5}\right)\right]\right\}$$

$$(11.37)$$

Equation (11.37) is a recursive equation defining the risk-neutral drift term $\tilde{\alpha}_d(t, ih)$. By taking differences of the successive sums in this series, the drift over all maturities given as $\tilde{\alpha}_d(t, t + h)$, $\tilde{\alpha}_d(t, t + 2h)$, ..., $\tilde{\alpha}_d(t, T - h)$ can be obtained at time t. The drift terms converge to their continuous-time limit given in equation (11.24) as h becomes infinitesimally small.

The forward rate tree is constructed using equation (11.28) in the same manner as demonstrated earlier in equations (11.25) to (11.27) and in Figure 11.1. The time t bond price is obtained by using a discrete summation of time t forward rates as shown in equation (11.30). Pricing of contingent claims such as options follows a similar procedure of discounting the cash flows from the expiration date using the short rate process. An advantage of using equation (11.30) is that the forward rate tree does not have to grow until the maturity of the underlying bond in order to price an option written on the bond. For example, to price a six-month option written on a 30-year zero-coupon bond requires the forward rate tree for only six months, not 30 years as is required under the short rate models of Vasicek and CIR.

Example 11.1 Consider a European call option on the four-period zero-coupon bond with an exercise price $K = 0.84$ and an expiration date $S = 2$. The prices of zero-coupon bonds are given by the following vector:

$$\begin{bmatrix} P(0,1) \\ P(0,2) \\ P(0,3) \\ P(0,4) \end{bmatrix} = \begin{bmatrix} 0.9418 \\ 0.8781 \\ 0.8106 \\ 0.7408 \end{bmatrix} \tag{11.38}$$

The historical volatility matrix is given by:

$$\begin{pmatrix} \sigma(0,1) & \sigma(0,2) & \sigma(0,3) \\ 0 & \sigma(1,2) & \sigma(1,3) \\ 0 & 0 & \sigma(2,3) \end{pmatrix} = \begin{pmatrix} 0.020 & 0.015 & 0.011 \\ 0 & 0.018 & 0.012 \\ 0 & 0 & 0.020 \end{pmatrix} \tag{11.39}$$

To demonstrate the generality of the approach, we allow time-inhomogeneous volatilities, such that $\sigma(0, 1) \neq \sigma(1, 2)$ and $\sigma(0, 2) \neq \sigma(1, 3)$. However, for most applications, volatilities are assumed to be time-homogeneous.

Step 1: Determine the forward rates. Using equation (11.30), we have:

$$P(0,1) = \exp[-f(0,0)h]$$

$$P(0,2) = \exp[-(f(0,0) + f(0,1))h]$$

$$P(0,3) = \exp[-(f(0,0) + f(0,1) + f(0,2))h]$$

$$P(0,4) = \exp[-(f(0,0) + f(0,1) + f(0,2) + f(0,3))h]$$

For expositional simplicity, we assume $h = 1$. Solving the preceding four equations iteratively, we get:

$$f(0,0) = -\ln P(0,1) = -\ln(0.9418) = 0.06$$

$$f(0,1) = -\ln P(0,2) - f(0,0) = -\ln(0.8781) - 0.06 = 0.07$$

$$f(0,2) = -\ln P(0,3) - f(0,0) - f(0,1) = -\ln(0.8106) - 0.06 - 0.07$$
$$= 0.08$$

$$f(0,3) = -\ln P(0,4) - f(0,0) - f(0,1) - f(0,2)$$
$$= -\ln(0.7408) - 0.06 - 0.07 - 0.08 = 0.09$$

Hence, the initial forward rate curve is given by:

$$\begin{bmatrix} f(0,0) \\ f(0,1) \\ f(0,2) \\ f(0,3) \end{bmatrix} = \begin{bmatrix} 0.06 \\ 0.07 \\ 0.08 \\ 0.09 \end{bmatrix} \tag{11.40}$$

Step 2: Construction of the forward rate tree. The forward rate tree can be constructed using the initial forward rates in step 1 and the equation for the discrete change in forward rates given by (11.28). Figure 11.3 shows the forward rate tree for the first step from time 0 to time 1.

Obtaining the forward rates at time 1 requires the forward rate drifts $\tilde{\alpha}_d(0,1), \tilde{\alpha}_d(0,2)$, and $\tilde{\alpha}_d(0,3)$, which are calculated using equation (11.37):

$$\tilde{\alpha}_d(0,1) = \ln\left(0.5[\exp(-\sigma(0,1)) + \exp(\sigma(0,1))]\right)$$
$$= \ln\left(0.5[\exp(-0.02) + \exp(0.02)]\right) = 0.0002 \tag{11.41}$$

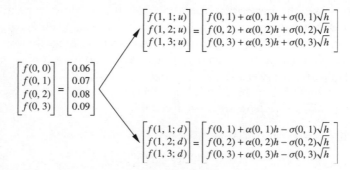

FIGURE 11.3   Evolution of the Tree from Time 0 to Time 1 (where $h = 1$)

Since

$$\sum_{i=1}^{2} \tilde{\alpha}_d(0, i) = \ln \left\{ 0.5 \left[\exp\left(-\sum_{i=1}^{2} \sigma(0, i)\right) + \exp\left(\sum_{i=1}^{2} \sigma(0, i)\right) \right] \right\}$$

$$= \ln\left(0.5[\exp(-0.02 - 0.015) + \exp(0.02 + 0.015)]\right) \quad (11.42)$$

$$= 0.000612$$

we have:

$$\tilde{\alpha}_d(0, 2) = 0.000612 - 0.0002 = 0.000412 \quad\quad (11.43)$$

Similarly, since

$$\sum_{i=1}^{3} \tilde{\alpha}_d(0, i) = \ln \left\{ 0.5 \left[\exp\left(-\sum_{i=1}^{3} \sigma(0, i)\right) + \exp\left(\sum_{i=1}^{3} \sigma(0, i)\right) \right] \right\}$$

$$= \ln\left(0.5 \left[\begin{matrix} \exp(-0.02 - 0.015 - 0.011) \\ + \exp(0.02 + 0.015 + 0.011) \end{matrix} \right]\right) \quad (11.44)$$

$$= 0.00106$$

we have:

$$\alpha(0, 3) = 0.001057 - 0.000612 = 0.000445 \quad\quad (11.45)$$

The three forward rates in the up state can be calculated as follows:

$$f(1, 1; u) = 0.07 + 0.0002 + 0.02 = 0.0902 \quad\quad (11.46)$$

$$f(1, 2; u) = 0.08 + 0.000412 + 0.015 = 0.0954 \quad\quad (11.47)$$

$$f(1, 3; u) = 0.09 + 0.000445 + 0.011 = 0.1014 \quad\quad (11.48)$$

The three forward rates in the down state are calculated in the same manner, and the results are summarized in Figure 11.4.

   The tree has two nodes at time 1 as shown in Figure 11.4. From each of these nodes, two separate nodes are generated at time 2, leading to a total of four nodes at time 2. From the up node at time 1, the tree is expanded to time 2 as shown in Figure 11.5.

   The computation of the time 2 forward rates requires solving the drifts $\tilde{\alpha}_d(1, 2)$ and $\tilde{\alpha}_d(1, 3)$. These are solved as follows:

$$\tilde{\alpha}_d(1, 2) = \ln\left(0.5[\exp(-\sigma(1, 2)) + \exp(\sigma(1, 2))]\right)$$

$$= \ln\left(0.5[\exp(-0.018) + \exp(0.018)]\right) \quad\quad (11.49)$$

$$= 0.00016$$

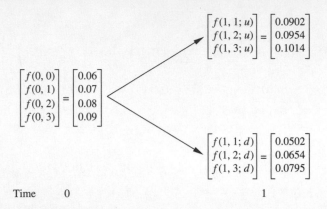

Time   0   1

FIGURE 11.4 The One-Period Forward Rate Tree

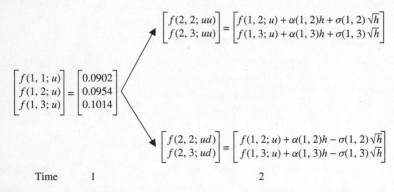

Time   1   2

FIGURE 11.5 Evolution of the Tree from Time 1 to Time 2, Starting from the Up State at Time 1

Since

$$\sum_{i=2}^{3} \tilde{\alpha}_d(1,i) = \ln\left(0.5\left[\exp\left(-\sum_{i=2}^{3}\sigma(1,i)\right) + \exp\left(\sum_{i=2}^{3}\sigma(1,i)\right)\right]\right) \quad (11.50)$$

$$= \ln\left(0.5[\exp(-0.018 - 0.012) + \exp(0.018 + 0.012)]\right)$$

$$\approx 0.00045$$

we have:

$$\tilde{\alpha}_d(1,3) = 0.00045 - 0.00016 = 0.00029 \quad (11.51)$$

The forward rates in the *uu* state at time 2 can be calculated as follows:

$$f(2, 2; uu) = 0.0954 + 0.00016 + 0.018 = 0.1136 \qquad (11.52)$$

$$f(2, 3; uu) = 0.1014 + 0.00029 + 0.012 = 0.1137 \qquad (11.53)$$

Similarly, the forward rates $f(2, 2)$ and $f(2, 3)$ can be calculated in the three other states at time 2, corresponding to the *ud, du*, and *dd* nodes. These are shown in Figure 11.6.

Step 3: Compute the bond price at the option expiration date. Since the option matures at time 2, we need the bond prices at all four nodes at time 2. Using equation (11.30), the bond price at time 2 in state *uu* is given as follows:

$$\begin{aligned} P(2, 4; uu) &= \exp(-f(2, 2; uu) - f(2, 3; uu)) \\ &= \exp(-0.1136 - 0.1137) = 0.7967 \end{aligned} \qquad (11.54)$$

Similarly, the bond prices in states *ud, du*, and *dd* at time 2 can be computed and are shown at the terminal nodes in Figure 11.7.

Step 4: Compute the option price by taking the discounted expectation under the risk-neutral measure. The value of a European call option on the four-period zero-coupon bond with an exercise price $K = 0.84$ and an expiration date $S = 2$ is computed by taking the discounted expectation of its terminal value under the risk-neutral measure. Figure 11.7 illustrates the computation of the value of a call option. The risk-neutral probabilities of up and down movements are 0.5 at each node, and the short rate required for discounting is given as $r(t) = f(t, t)$. The European call option price equals 0.0127.

The nonrecombining tree can be used not only for pricing European options but also for a variety of Asian options with path-dependent features and American options with early exercise features by modifying the payoffs and boundary conditions appropriately.

A Two-Factor Nonrecombining Trinomial Tree

Consider a two-factor discrete-time forward rate process given as follows:

$$f(t + h, T) = f(t, T) + \tilde{\alpha}_d(t, T)h + \sigma_1(t, T)X_1\sqrt{h} + \sigma_2(t, T)X_2\sqrt{h} \qquad (11.55)$$

where $\tilde{\alpha}_d(t, T)$ is the drift and $\sigma_1(t, T)$ and $\sigma_2(t, T)$ are the volatility coefficients of the two factors. Both the drift and the volatility coefficients

Parameters:
Time step, $h = 1$
Probability of going up, $p_u = 0.5$
Probability of going down, $p_d = 0.5$

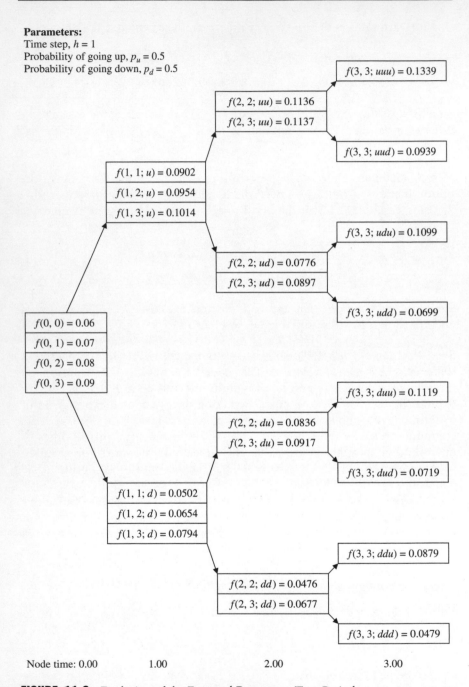

$f(3, 3; uuu) = 0.1339$

$f(2, 2; uu) = 0.1136$
$f(2, 3; uu) = 0.1137$

$f(3, 3; uud) = 0.0939$

$f(1, 1; u) = 0.0902$
$f(1, 2; u) = 0.0954$
$f(1, 3; u) = 0.1014$

$f(3, 3; udu) = 0.1099$

$f(2, 2; ud) = 0.0776$
$f(2, 3; ud) = 0.0897$

$f(3, 3; udd) = 0.0699$

$f(0, 0) = 0.06$
$f(0, 1) = 0.07$
$f(0, 2) = 0.08$
$f(0, 3) = 0.09$

$f(3, 3; duu) = 0.1119$

$f(2, 2; du) = 0.0836$
$f(2, 3; du) = 0.0917$

$f(3, 3; dud) = 0.0719$

$f(1, 1; d) = 0.0502$
$f(1, 2; d) = 0.0654$
$f(1, 3; d) = 0.0794$

$f(3, 3; ddu) = 0.0879$

$f(2, 2; dd) = 0.0476$
$f(2, 3; dd) = 0.0677$

$f(3, 3; ddd) = 0.0479$

Node time: 0.00   1.00   2.00   3.00

FIGURE 11.6 Evolution of the Forward Rates over Two Periods

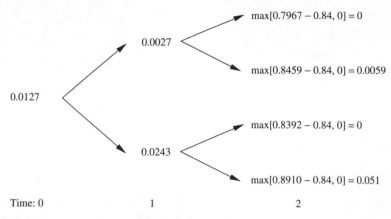

FIGURE 11.7 Valuation of a European Call Option on the Four-Period Zero-Coupon Bond with Exercise Date 2 and Exercise Price $K = 0.84$

can depend on the history of forward rates up to and including time t. The variables X_1 and X_2 are independently distributed binomial variables, taking the values of $+1$ and -1 with equal probability. The two-factor HJM models are generally approximated using a multinomial nonrecombining tree with four branches from each nonterminal node, where each branch corresponds to one of the four combinations resulting from two outcomes of X_1 and two outcomes of X_2. Hence, a nonrecombining tree for a two-factor HJM model requires 4^N nodes at the last step of an N-step tree (e.g., see Heath, Jarrow, and Morton [1990] and Amin and Bodurtha [1995]). With ten steps, this leads to a 1,048,576 number of nodes at the last step. In this section, we show how to reduce the number of nodes to the order 3^N by using a nonrecombining *trinomial* tree to approximate the two-factor HJM model. The trinomial tree requires only 59,049 nodes with ten steps in the tree.

In order to generate the trinomial tree, the forward rate process in equation (11.55) can be approximated as follows:

$$f(t+h, T) = \begin{cases} f(t, T) + \tilde{\alpha}_d(t, T)h + \sigma_1(t, T)\sqrt{h} & \textit{with probability } \frac{1}{2} \\[2mm] f(t, T) + \tilde{\alpha}_d(t, T)h - \sigma_1(t, T)\sqrt{h} + \sqrt{2}\sigma_2(t, T)\sqrt{h} \\ \hspace{4cm} \textit{with probability } \frac{1}{4} \\[2mm] f(t, T) + \tilde{\alpha}_d(t, T)h - \sigma_1(t, T)\sqrt{h} - \sqrt{2}\sigma_2(t, T)\sqrt{h} \\ \hspace{4cm} \textit{with probability } \frac{1}{4} \end{cases}$$

(11.56)

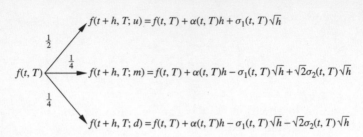

FIGURE 11.8 Evolution of the Forward Rate in the Discretized Two-Factor HJM Model Using a Trinomial Tree

The mean, variance, and covariance of the changes in forward rates using equation (11.55) converge to the corresponding moments obtained using equation (11.56) as h becomes infinitesimally small. The evolution of the forward rate process given in equation (11.56) is shown in Figure 11.8.

The forward rate process in equation (11.56) can be rewritten as follows:

$$f(t + h, T) = f(t, T) + \tilde{\alpha}_d(t, T)h + X(t, T)\sqrt{h} \qquad (11.57)$$

where $X(t, T)$ is a random variable satisfying

$$X(t, T) = \begin{cases} \sigma_1(t, T) & \text{with probability } \frac{1}{2} \\ -\sigma_1(t, T) + \sqrt{2}\sigma_2(t, T) & \text{with probability } \frac{1}{4} \\ -\sigma_1(t, T) - \sqrt{2}\sigma_2(t, T) & \text{with probability } \frac{1}{4} \end{cases} \qquad (11.58)$$

The drift $\tilde{\alpha}_d(t, T)$ can be obtained using absence of arbitrage as it is in the one-factor case. As shown earlier, absence of arbitrage implies the following restriction given in equation (11.35):

$$\tilde{E}_t \left[\exp\left(-\sum_{i=\frac{t}{h}+1}^{\frac{T}{h}-1} [f(t + h, ih) - f(t, ih)]h \right) \right] = 1 \qquad (11.59)$$

Substituting equation (11.57) in equation (11.59) gives:

$$\tilde{E}_t \left[\exp\left(-\sum_{i=\frac{t}{h}+1}^{\frac{T}{h}-1} [\tilde{\alpha}_d(t, ih)h + X(t, ih)\sqrt{h}]h \right) \right] = 1 \qquad (11.60)$$

Simplifying equation (11.60) gives:

$$\sum_{i=\frac{t}{h}+1}^{\frac{T}{h}-1} \tilde{\alpha}_d(t, ih) = \frac{1}{h^2} \ln \left\{ \tilde{E}_t \left[\exp \left(-\sum_{i=\frac{t}{h}+1}^{\frac{T}{h}-1} X(t, ih) h^{1.5} \right) \right] \right\} \quad (11.61)$$

The expectation in equation (11.61) can be computed by substituting the variable $X(t, T)$ given in equation (11.58). Computing this expectation simplifies equation (11.61) as follows:

$$\sum_{i=\frac{t}{h}+1}^{\frac{T}{h}-1} \tilde{\alpha}_d(t, ih) = \frac{1}{h^2} \ln \left\{ \begin{array}{l} \dfrac{1}{2} \exp \left(-\displaystyle\sum_{i=\frac{t}{h}+1}^{\frac{T}{h}-1} \sigma_1(t, ih) h^{1.5} \right) \\[2em] +\dfrac{1}{4} \exp \left(\displaystyle\sum_{i=\frac{t}{h}+1}^{\frac{T}{h}-1} (\sigma_1(t, ih) - \sqrt{2}\sigma_2(t, ih)) h^{1.5} \right) \\[2em] +\dfrac{1}{4} \exp \left(\displaystyle\sum_{i=\frac{t}{h}+1}^{\frac{T}{h}-1} (\sigma_1(t, ih) + \sqrt{2}\sigma_2(t, ih)) h^{1.5} \right) \end{array} \right\}$$

$$(11.62)$$

Equation (11.62) defines the risk-neutral drifts using a recursive relationship. By taking differences of the successive sums in this series, the drift over all maturities given as $\tilde{\alpha}_d(t, t + h), \tilde{\alpha}_d(t, t + 2h), \ldots, \tilde{\alpha}_d(t, T - h)$ can be obtained at time t. Once all the arbitrage-free drifts are determined, the nonrecombining trinomial tree can be generated as shown in Figure 11.8. Bonds and options are valued using discounted risk-neutral expectations, similar to the case of the one-factor model.

Recursive Programming

In this section, we introduce the recursive implementation of the HJM models. This method of programming is significantly more efficient than imperative programming for memory allocation, due to the path-dependent nature of the nonrecombining tree. A function under the recursive method calls itself either directly or indirectly. For example, consider a function $s(n)$ that returns the sum of the first n positive integers. Then a recursive function $s(n) = s(n - 1) + n$ is solved by calling itself for a smaller value of n until the case of $n = 1$ is reached. For $n = 1, s(1)$ is defined to equal 1. Since $s(1)$ equals 1 by definition and is not obtained through a recursive call, it is called the *base case*. Figure 11.9 shows a straightforward implementation of the function $s(n)$ written in pseudocode.

```
1:     function s(n)
2:        if n = 1
3:              s(n) = 1;
4:         else
5:              s(n) = s(n - 1) + n;
6:        end if;
7:     end function;
```

FIGURE 11.9   A Recursive Program

As an example, consider how a call to $s(3)$ is evaluated. When the call to $s(3)$ is made, the test at line 2 fails. The program then executes line 5, which calculates $s(3)$ in terms of $s(2)$. A call to $s(2)$ is made and the calculation of $s(3)$ is temporarily suspended, waiting for the value of $s(2)$ to return. When $s(2)$ is called, the test in line 2 still fails because $n = 2$. The program again executes line 5, which calculates $s(2)$ in terms of $s(1)$. A call to $s(1)$ is made and the calculation of $s(2)$ is temporarily suspended. Since now $n = 1$, the call to $s(1)$ returns 1. At this point, $s(2)$ is computed by adding $s(1) = 1$ and 2 to give 3. Finally, $s(3)$ is computed by adding $s(2) = 3$ and 3 to give 6.

An improperly written recursive function fails to work because either there is no base case or, even if there is a base case, the recursive calls do not move toward the base case. In this example, the base case exists, and the recursive function $s(n)$ moves toward the base case. Therefore, the two fundamental rules of recursion are given as follows:

1. *Base case:* Always have at least one case that can be solved without using recursion.
2. *Make progress:* Any recursive call must make progress toward the base case.

The difference between recursive programming and imperative programming can be summarized as follows:

1. Both methods execute the same block of code repeatedly. The imperative method executes the same code using a loop, while the recursive method executes the same code by a function that calls itself.
2. The imperative method has a terminal condition that stops the loop from repeating the execution of the same code, while the recursive method has a base case, which results in the termination of the recursive calls.
3. The current state is updated as the loop progresses under imperative programming, while the current state is changed by updating the parameters using recursive programming.

Recursive programming naturally applies to a nonrecombining tree but not to a recombining tree. Since the general HJM models require a non-recombining tree, the valuation of derivatives under these models can be performed using recursive programming. Figure 11.10 illustrates the recursive pseudocode for pricing an option on a zero-coupon bond, with the initial forward rate vector and volatility matrix given by equations (11.40)

```
1:      function result = opt(t,f,sig);
2:          h = 1;
3:          k = 0.80;
4:          T = 2;
5:          n = length(f);
6:      if n == 1
7:          p = exp(-f(1)*h)*1;
8:          if t == T
9:              result = max(0,p - k);
10:         else
11:             result = p;
12:         end
13:     end
14:     if n > 1
15:         m = length(f)-1;
16:         fu = f(2:m + 1);
17:         fd = f(2:m + 1);
18:         if t+1 == 1
19:             sigma = sig;
20:         else
21:             sigma = sig(:, 2:m + 1);
22:         end
23:         alpha = zeros(1, m);
24:         for j = 1:m
25:             if j == 1
26:                 sumsig = exp(sigma(t+1,j)*h*sqrt(h));
27:                 alpha(j) = log(0.5*((1/sumsig) + sumsig))/(h^2);
28:             end
29:             if j > 1
30:                 sumsig = exp(-sum(sigma(t+1,1:j))*h*sqrt(h));
31:                 alpha(j) = log(0.5*((1/sumsig)+sumsig))/
                                 (h^2)-sum(alpha(1:j-1));
32:             end
33:         end
34:         fu = fu + alpha * h + sigma(t+1,:) * sqrt(h);
35:         fd = fd + alpha * h- sigma(t+1,:) * sqrt(h);
36:         p = exp(-f(1)*h)*0.5*(opt(t+1,fu, sigma)+
                 opt(t+1,fd,sigma) );
37:         if t == T
38:             result = max(0,p - k);
39:         else
40:             result = p;
41:         end
42:     end
```

FIGURE 11.10 Pseudocode to Solve the Price of a Call Option under the HJM Model

and (11.39), respectively. When pricing a zero-coupon bond, the base case is the value of the bond at its maturity; when pricing a call option on a zero-coupon bond, the base case is the value of the option at the option expiration date.

In Figure 11.10, lines 2 through 4 define the step size h, exercise price k, and exercise date T. The inputs to the function $opt(\cdot)$ are current time t, current forward rate vector f, and current volatility matrix sig. Lines 6 through 13 give the code for the base case, while lines 14 through 41 give the code for the recursive case. The base case is easy to understand, but the recursive case requires some explanation. Lines 16 through 22 give the current forward rate vector and volatility matrix for calculating the forward rate vectors for the next period and for making the recursive calls. Lines 23 through 33 calculate the risk-neutral forward rate drift vector. Lines 34 and 35 calculate the forward rate vectors for the next period. Finally, the recursive call to function $opt(\cdot)$ is made in line 36. The option's payoff at the exercise date is calculated in lines 8 through 12 and lines 37 through 41, respectively.

A RECOMBINING TREE FOR THE PROPORTIONAL VOLATILITY HJM MODEL

A nonrecombining tree requires significant computational time to price long-dated options, even though recursive programming alleviates the memory allocation problem. Hence, a recombining tree is always preferable to a nonrecombining tree when pricing long-dated options. Though recombining trees exist for Markovian HJM models, such as the constant volatility model or the exponentially decaying volatility model, such trees do not exist for non-Markovian models, such as the proportional volatility HJM model.

This section demonstrates the application of a recombining tree for the proportional volatility HJM model. In a recent study, Gupta and Subrahmanyam [2005] examined alternative one-factor and two-factor models based on the accuracy of their out-of-sample price prediction and their ability to hedge caps and floors. These authors found the proportional volatility HJM forward rate model to outperform the other competing one-factor models in pricing accuracy using out-of-sample tests. The estimated parameters of the proportional volatility model were also more stable than those for corresponding two-parameter models, indicating that this model led to more robust estimation. Further, the one-factor LIBOR market model also provided accurate pricing results, but outperformed the proportional volatility model only in tests, which were not strictly out-of-sample. In terms of hedging effectiveness, the two-factor models outperformed the one-factor models.

A Markovian construction of the proportional volatility forward rate model allows it to be used for pricing European options with *recombining* trees, not only as a single-factor model but also as part of a two-factor model in which the forward rates are given as affine functions of two state variables, one of which displays proportional volatility. We show that under the *forward measure*, the state variables under the proportional volatility HJM model can be transformed from an infinite number of forward rates to a single variable given as the forward price of a zero-coupon bond. Further, we show how to construct a recombining tree for the forward price in order to value a European option on a zero-coupon bond under the forward measure. To our knowledge, this is the first demonstration of using a recombining tree for valuation under the proportional volatility HJM model. The simulations demonstrate that option values obtained by using a recombining tree for the forward price converge to the corresponding values obtained by using a nonrecombining tree for the forward rate.

Forward Price Dynamics under the Forward Measure

Consider the following form of the risk-neutral HJM forward rate process. For all $0 \le t < T \le \hat{T} < \infty$:

$$f(t, T) = f(0, T) + \int_0^t \tilde{\alpha}(v, T) \, dv + \int_0^t \sigma(v, T) \, d\tilde{Z}(s) \qquad (11.63)$$

where the volatility function may depend upon $f(t, T)$.

The stochastic bond price process consistent with the forward rate process in equation (11.63) is given as follows:

$$\frac{dP(t, T)}{P(t, T)} = r(t) \, dt + a(t, T) \, d\tilde{Z}(t) \qquad (11.64)$$

where

$$a(t, T) = -\int_t^T \sigma(t, s) \, ds \qquad (11.65)$$

Let $P_f(t) = P(t, T)/P(t, S)$ define the time S forward price of the bond maturing at time T. The stochastic process for the forward price can be given as follows:

$$\frac{dP_f(t)}{P_f(t)} = \mu_f(t, S, T) \, dt + a_f(t, S, T) \, d\tilde{Z}(t) \qquad (11.66)$$

where

$$a_f(t, S, T) = a(t, T) - a(t, S) \tag{11.67}$$

and

$$\mu_f(t, S, T) = a^2(t, S) - a(t, S)a(t, T) \tag{11.68}$$

To remove the drift from the forward price process, consider the S-forward measure defined by the following transformation:

$$
\begin{aligned}
d\tilde{Z}^S(t) &= d\tilde{Z}(t) + \frac{\mu_f(t, S, T)}{a_f(t, S, T)}\, dt = d\tilde{Z}(t) + \frac{a^2(t, S) - a(t, S)a(t, T)}{a(t, T) - a(t, S)} \\
&= d\tilde{Z}(t) - a(t, S)
\end{aligned}
\tag{11.69}
$$

Since $a_f(t, S, T)$ is always nonzero for the proportional volatility processes that we consider next, the Novikov condition of the Girsanov theorem is satisfied (see Chapter 2). Substituting equation (11.69) into equation (11.66), we get:

$$\frac{dP_f(t)}{P_f(t)} = a_f(t, S, T)\, d\tilde{Z}^S(t) \tag{11.70}$$

In general, the *forward* return volatility function $a_f(t, S, T)$ depends on forward rates; and since forward rates are non-Markovian under HJM models with respect to a *finite* number of state variables, recombining trees cannot be constructed. However, for the proportional volatility HJM model that follows, the forward return volatility function $a_f(t, S, T)$ depends only upon $P_f(t)$ and not on the infinite number of forward rates. Hence, the forward price process becomes Markovian, and the options on zero-coupon bonds can be priced under the forward measure using a recombining tree.

The time 0 price of a European call option expiring at time S and written on a zero-coupon bond maturing at time T can be given using the S-forward measure by the following expectation:

$$c(0) = P(0, S)\, \tilde{E}_0^S\, [Max(P_f(S) - K, 0)] \tag{11.71}$$

where K is the strike price. The price of a put option is defined in a similar manner as follows:

$$p(0) = P(0, S)\, \tilde{E}_0^S\, [Max(K - P_f(S), 0)] \tag{11.72}$$

A Markovian Forward Price Process under the Proportional Volatility Model

The forward rate volatility under the proportional volatility HJM [1992] model is given as follows:

$$\sigma(t, T) = \sigma\, Max[f(t, T), \lambda] \qquad (11.73)$$

The forward rate volatility is proportional to the level of forward rate if the forward rate is less than a positive constant $\lambda < \infty$ and is constant if the forward rate exceeds λ. The bounded volatility in equation (11.73) is necessary to prevent the forward rates from exploding to infinity in finite time and to ensure that the change of measure is arbitrage-free in equation (11.69). However, Amin and Morton [1994] and Amin and Bodurtha [1995] find that ignoring the upper bound λ has an insignificant effect for valuing options under realistic parameter values. Hence, for the purpose of model implementation, the bounded volatility assumption can be relaxed and the forward rate volatility can be given as follows:

$$\sigma(t, T) = \sigma f(t, T) \qquad (11.74)$$

Substituting equation (11.74) into equation (11.65) gives:

$$a(t, T) \equiv -\int_t^T \sigma f(t, s)\, ds = \sigma \ln P(t, T) \qquad (11.75)$$

Substituting equation (11.75) into equation (11.67) gives the forward return volatility as follows:

$$
\begin{aligned}
a_f(t, S, T) &= a(t, T) - a(t, S) = \sigma \ln P(t, T) - \sigma \ln P(t, S) \\
&= \sigma \ln \big(P(t, T)/P(t, S) \big) \qquad (11.76) \\
&= \sigma \ln P_f(t)
\end{aligned}
$$

Hence, the forward price process in equation (11.70) becomes:

$$dP_f(t) = \sigma P_f(t) \ln P_f(t)\, d\tilde{Z}^S(t) \qquad (11.77)$$

Note that the only state variable that the preceding process depends upon is the forward price $P_f(t)$. The forward price process begins at time 0, as $P_f(0) = P(0, T)/P(0, S)$, and then it evolves as a *Markovian process* under the *S*-forward measure.[5]

A Recombining Tree for the Proportional Volatility Model Using the Nelson and Ramaswamy Transform

A recombining tree can be generated for the proportional volatility model given in the Markovian form in equation (11.77). Since the volatility of $dP_f(t)$ is not constant, the Nelson and Ramaswamy [1990] transform is used to construct the recombining tree. Though the proportional volatility model given in equation (11.73) requires the bounded volatility restriction, we ignore this restriction for two reasons. First, we can arbitrarily set the value of λ to be very large, such that the forward rates on the recombining tree never reach this value. Second, as shown by Amin and Morton [1994] and Amin and Bodurtha [1995], the effect of ignoring the bounded volatility restriction is quite insignificant for the practical implementation of the proportional volatility model.

Chapter 6 introduced the Nelson and Ramaswamy [1990] transform in the context of the CIR model. Since volatility of $dP_f(t) = \sigma P_f(t) \ln P_f(t)$ (see equation (11.77)), the X-transform for the $P_f(t)$ process can be identified as follows:

$$X(t) = \int^{P_f(t)} \frac{dU}{\sigma U \ln U} = \frac{\ln(|\ln P_f(t)|)}{\sigma} \qquad (11.78)$$

Since the forward rates can never reach zero under the proportional volatility HJM model, $P_f(t) = P(t, T)/P(t, S)$ is strictly less than 1, implying $\ln P_f(t) < 0$. Hence, the transform in equation (11.78) can be rewritten as follows:

$$X(t) = \int^{P_f(t)} \frac{dU}{\sigma U \ln U} = \frac{\ln(-\ln P_f(t))}{\sigma} \qquad (11.79)$$

Using Ito's lemma, the stochastic process for $X(t)$ is given as:

$$dX(t) = \mu_X(t)dt + d\tilde{Z}^S(t) \qquad (11.80)$$

Hence, the stochastic process for $X(t)$ has constant volatility equal to 1. The evolution of the $X(t)$ process begins at $X(0) = \ln(-\ln P_f(0))/\sigma$, and the up and down movements over any future time interval t to $t + h$ are shown in Figure 11.11.

Since the X-process has constant volatility, the tree for this process grows in a recombining fashion. The up and down probabilities are obtained by matching the zero drift of the forward price process given in equation (11.77). To get these probabilities, the inverse transform is used

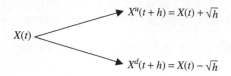

FIGURE 11.11 The X-Process Tree

to obtain the forward prices on the nodes of the recombining tree using equation (11.79) as follows:

$$P_f(t) = \exp\left(-\exp(\sigma X(t))\right) \qquad (11.81)$$

$$P_f^u(t+h) = \exp\left(-\exp(\sigma X^u(t+h))\right) \qquad (11.82)$$

$$P_f^d(t+h) = \exp\left(-\exp(\sigma X^d(t+h))\right) \qquad (11.83)$$

The up probability is computed as follows:

$$\frac{P_f(t) - P_f^d(t+h)}{P_f^u(t+h) - P_f^d(t+h)} \qquad (11.84)$$

And the down probability is computed as follows:

$$\frac{P_f^u(t+h) - P_f(t)}{P_f^u(t+h) - P_f^d(t+h)} \qquad (11.85)$$

We perform numerical simulations for pricing European call and put options assuming that the term structure of forward rates evolves according to the proportional volatility model. The asset underlying the option contracts is a ten-year zero-coupon bond with face value of \$100, and the initial forward rate curve is assumed to be flat at 6 percent. We consider short-term options with one-year expiry and long-term options with five-year expiry.

For each option expiry date, three strike prices are considered: at-the-money, 10 percent in-the-money, and 10 percent out-of-the-money. The moneyness is defined in terms of the strike prices relative to the forward price of the underlying bond. For example, for a European call maturing in five years, written on a ten-year maturity zero-coupon bond with \$100 face value, the at-the-money strike price equals \$74.08, which is the five-year forward price of the bond; the in-the-money strike price equals \$81.49, which is 110 percent of \$74.08; and the out-of-the-money strike price

TABLE 11.1 European Call Option Prices for the Proportional Volatility HJM Model (in dollars)

Strike price K ($)	Option maturity τ years	Volatility coefficient σ	Recombining			Nonrecombining		
			50	100	200	10	15	20
58.2748	1	0.1	1.1758	1.1787	1.1802	1.1596	1.2012	1.1719
			0.33%	0.58%	0.70%	−1.06%	2.50%	0.00%
58.2748	1	0.3	3.5121	3.5209	3.5253	3.4990	3.5815	3.5249
			−0.36%	−0.11%	0.01%	−0.73%	1.61%	0.00%
58.2748	1	0.5	5.8030	5.8175	5.8247	5.8232	5.8951	5.8512
			−0.83%	−0.58%	−0.45%	−0.48%	0.75%	0.00%
64.1023	1	0.1	0.0269	0.0277	0.0278	0.0190	0.0247	0.0262
			2.43%	5.50%	5.85%	−27.48%	−5.99%	0.00%
64.1023	1	0.3	1.3166	1.3122	1.3132	1.2814	1.3490	1.3280
			−0.86%	−1.19%	−1.11%	−3.51%	1.58%	0.00%
64.1023	1	0.5	3.2654	3.2379	3.2486	3.3667	3.1804	3.3022
			−1.12%	−1.95%	−1.62%	1.95%	−3.69%	0.00%
52.4473	1	0.1	5.5333	5.5331	5.5339	5.5289	5.5256	5.5277
			0.10%	0.10%	0.11%	0.02%	−0.04%	0.00%
52.4473	1	0.3	7.0389	7.0387	7.0460	6.9644	7.0651	7.0754
			−0.52%	−0.52%	−0.42%	−1.57%	−0.15%	0.00%
52.4473	1	0.5	9.2034	9.1954	9.1975	9.2723	9.2501	9.1270
			0.84%	0.75%	0.77%	1.59%	1.35%	0.00%
74.0818	5	0.1	1.4581	1.4617	1.4636	1.4488	1.4882	1.4604
			−0.16%	0.09%	0.22%	−0.79%	1.91%	0.00%
74.0818	5	0.3	4.2956	4.3063	4.3117	4.3419	4.3403	4.3454
			−1.15%	−0.90%	−0.78%	−0.08%	−0.12%	0.00%
74.0818	5	0.5	6.9040	6.9211	6.9296	6.9965	6.8856	6.9691
			−0.93%	−0.69%	−0.57%	0.39%	−1.20%	0.00%
81.4900	5	0.1	0.0542	0.0567	0.0562	0.0581	0.0568	0.0567
			−4.38%	0.03%	−0.88%	2.43%	0.14%	0.00%
81.4900	5	0.3	1.6256	1.6407	1.6379	1.7134	1.6703	1.6279
			−0.14%	0.78%	0.61%	5.25%	2.60%	0.00%
81.4900	5	0.5	3.7118	3.7145	3.7130	3.6743	3.7631	3.7052
			0.18%	0.25%	0.21%	−0.84%	1.56%	0.00%
66.6736	5	0.1	5.6546	5.6548	5.6551	5.6436	5.6472	5.6455
			0.16%	0.17%	0.17%	−0.03%	0.03%	0.00%
66.6736	5	0.3	8.0324	8.0185	8.0150	7.9602	8.0639	8.0180
			0.18%	0.01%	−0.04%	−0.72%	0.57%	0.00%
66.6736	5	0.5	10.6977	10.7332	10.7189	10.7246	10.7247	10.6689
			0.27%	0.60%	0.47%	0.52%	0.52%	0.00%

The underlying bond is a ten-year zero-coupon bond with face value of $100.
The initial forward rate curve is flat at 6 percent.
The boundary K is set at 10,000.
The value printed below each option price is the difference (in percentage) from the price obtained from the corresponding 20-step nonrecombining tree.

TABLE 11.2 European Put Option Prices for the Proportional Volatility HJM Model (in dollars)

Strike price K ($)	Option maturity τ years	Volatility coefficient σ	Recombining			Nonrecombining		
			50	100	200	10	15	20
58.2748	1	0.1	1.1758	1.1787	1.1802	1.1596	1.2012	1.1719
			0.33%	0.58%	0.70%	−1.06%	2.50%	0.00%
58.2748	1	0.3	3.5121	3.5209	3.5253	3.4990	3.5815	3.5249
			−0.36%	−0.11%	0.01%	−0.73%	1.61%	0.00%
58.2748	1	0.5	5.8030	5.8175	5.8247	5.8232	5.8951	5.8512
			−0.83%	−0.58%	−0.45%	−0.48%	0.75%	0.00%
64.1023	1	0.1	5.5150	5.5158	5.5159	5.5071	5.5128	5.5144
			0.01%	0.03%	0.03%	−0.13%	−0.03%	0.00%
64.1023	1	0.3	6.8047	6.8004	6.8013	6.7695	6.8371	6.8161
			−0.17%	−0.23%	−0.22%	−0.68%	0.31%	0.00%
64.1023	1	0.5	8.7535	8.7260	8.7367	8.8548	8.6685	8.7903
			−0.42%	−0.73%	−0.61%	0.73%	−1.39%	0.00%
52.4473	1	0.1	0.0452	0.0450	0.0458	0.0407	0.0375	0.0396
			14.12%	13.55%	15.60%	2.91%	−5.30%	0.00%
52.4473	1	0.3	1.5507	1.5506	1.5579	1.4763	1.5770	1.5873
			−2.30%	−2.31%	−1.85%	−6.99%	−0.65%	0.00%
52.4473	1	0.5	3.7153	3.7073	3.7094	3.7842	3.7620	3.6389
			2.10%	1.88%	1.94%	3.99%	3.38%	0.00%
74.0818	5	0.1	1.4581	1.4617	1.4636	1.4488	1.4882	1.4604
			−0.16%	0.09%	0.22%	−0.79%	1.91%	0.00%
74.0818	5	0.3	4.2956	4.3063	4.3117	4.3419	4.3403	4.3454
			−1.15%	−0.90%	−0.78%	−0.08%	−0.12%	0.00%
74.0818	5	0.5	6.9040	6.9211	6.9296	6.9965	6.8856	6.9691
			−0.93%	−0.69%	−0.57%	0.39%	−1.20%	0.00%
81.4900	5	0.1	5.5423	5.5448	5.5443	5.5462	5.5449	5.5448
			−0.04%	0.00%	−0.01%	0.02%	0.00%	0.00%
81.4900	5	0.3	7.1137	7.1288	7.1260	7.2015	7.1585	7.1160
			−0.03%	0.18%	0.14%	1.20%	0.60%	0.00%
81.4900	5	0.5	9.1999	9.2026	9.2011	9.1624	9.2512	9.1933
			0.07%	0.10%	0.08%	−0.34%	0.63%	0.00%
66.6736	5	0.1	0.1665	0.1667	0.1669	0.1554	0.1591	0.1574
			5.78%	5.92%	6.09%	−1.22%	1.12%	0.00%
66.6736	5	0.3	2.5443	2.5303	2.5269	2.4721	2.5757	2.5299
			0.57%	0.02%	−0.12%	−2.28%	1.81%	0.00%
66.6736	5	0.5	5.2096	5.2451	5.2308	5.2365	5.2365	5.1808
			0.56%	1.24%	0.97%	1.07%	1.08%	0.00%

The underlying bond is a ten-year zero-coupon bond with face value of $100.
The initial forward rate curve is flat at 6 percent.
The boundary K is set at 10,000.
The value printed below each option price is the difference (in percentage) from the price obtained from the corresponding 20-step nonrecombining tree.

equals $66.67, which is 90 percent of $74.08. Finally, for each set of option maturity and strike price, the volatility coefficient σ varies from 0.1 to 0.5.

The call and put prices are reported in Table 11.1 and Table 11.2, respectively. The options are valued using recombining trees for the forward price with 50, 100, and 200 steps. The option prices converge very quickly, and the prices from the 50-step trees are very close to those from the 200-step trees. To validate the results, we also calculate the option prices using 10-, 15-, and 20-step nonrecombining trees for the one-year and five-year options using the recursive programming method introduced earlier. The nonrecombining trees are constructed as shown earlier in this chapter and satisfy the forward rate drift restriction in the HJM model. It can be seen that the option prices computed by using the 20-step nonrecombining trees for the forward rates converge to the corresponding option prices computed using the 200-step recombining trees for the forward price. However, the computation is significantly faster using the recombining tree. In general, the CPU time needed for computing the option price using the 200-step recombining tree is less by a factor of 10 to 50 times than that needed by using the 20-step nonrecombining tree.

Table 11.3 reports numerical simulations for pricing caps and floors under the proportional volatility HJM model. We use the formulas for caps and floors derived in Chapter 3, which express these interest rate options as portfolios of options on zero-coupon bonds. We consider five-year cap (or floor) agreements with interest-rate-resetting intervals of six months and a notional value of $1,000. The value of a cap (or a floor) agreement is the sum of the prices of nine put (or call) options that mature at time 0.5 year, 1 year, 1.5 years, ... , 4.5 years, where these options are written on zero-coupon bonds maturing at time 1 year, 1.5 years, 2 years, ... , 5 years, respectively. The initial forward rate curve is again assumed to be flat at 6 percent. The results are simulated for three different cap rates equal to 7 percent, 8 percent, and 9 percent and three different floor rates equal to 3 percent, 4 percent, and 5 percent. The volatility coefficient σ varies from 0.1 to 0.5.

Table 11.3 reports the cap and the floor prices obtained by using 50-, 100-, and 200-step recombining trees. The computation time is reasonably short, and the prices converge quickly. In contrast, using a nonrecombining tree for pricing a five-year cap is virtually impossible. This is because even using 8 steps per year implies about 36 steps over 4.5 years, leading to more than a billion nodes. Using separate trees for individual caplets allows the use of the nonrecombining tree with fewer nodes per period for caplets expiring at longer horizons. However, even this method requires significant cost for computing the prices of *all* caplets based on 15- to 20-step trees.[6]

TABLE 11.3 Recombining Trees to Price Caps and Floors for the Proportional Volatility HJM Model (prices are in dollars)

Volatility coefficient σ	Cap rate	5-year cap Recombining (steps)			Floor rate	5-year floor Recombining (steps)		
		50	100	200		50	100	200
0.1	7%	3.9949	3.9907	3.9870	3%	0.0005	0.0006	0.0007
0.2	7%	15.8393	15.8075	15.7992	3%	0.3950	0.4007	0.4040
0.3	7%	29.1834	29.2038	29.1959	3%	2.5833	2.6011	2.6014
0.4	7%	42.9097	42.7932	42.8221	3%	6.5988	6.6225	6.6240
0.5	7%	56.4708	56.2823	56.2419	3%	11.8732	11.8612	11.8548
0.1	8%	0.9581	0.9638	0.9617	4%	0.0914	0.0936	0.0949
0.2	8%	8.7537	8.7477	8.7374	4%	2.7420	2.7405	2.7438
0.3	8%	20.5233	20.4916	20.4607	4%	8.7082	8.6989	8.6932
0.4	8%	33.6433	33.5997	33.5765	4%	16.3442	16.3729	16.3597
0.5	8%	46.9821	47.1127	47.0353	4%	24.8446	24.7704	24.7767
0.1	9%	0.2219	0.2227	0.2263	5%	1.7947	1.7936	1.7949
0.2	9%	4.9685	4.9633	4.9673	5%	10.0363	10.0293	10.0238
0.3	9%	14.7154	14.6724	14.6878	5%	20.5264	20.5152	20.5004
0.4	9%	26.8234	26.7958	26.7857	5%	31.5107	31.5638	31.5328
0.5	9%	39.9949	39.8518	39.8791	5%	42.6379	42.5737	42.6225

The caps and floors are all five-year agreements with price reset every six months.
The notional value is $1,000.
The initial forward rate curve is flat at 6 percent.
The boundary K is set at 10,000.

Though recombining trees can be constructed to price European options under the proportional-volatility HJM model, this technique cannot be applied to price options under other non-Markovian HJM models. In general, most HJM models that are not subsets of the preference-free affine and quadratic classes (given in Chapters 4 though 10) do not allow Markovian short rate processes. One exception is the one-factor, two-state variable Markovian forward rate process of Li, Ritchken, and Sankarasubramanian (LRS) [1995]. We do not consider this model for the simple reason that a variety of HJM–type multiple-factor preference-free affine and quadratic models have been given in this book in Chapters 4 though 10. Since these Markovian models have a richer structure for the state variable dynamics and do not require more state variables than factors, these models are computationally less demanding, and their performance is generally superior to the LRS model.

NOTES

1. Chapter 12 introduces this model.
2. The String models were developed in a series of papers by Kennedy [1994, 1997], Goldstein [2000], and Santa-Clara and Sornette [2001].
3. Though time-inhomogeneous double-plus and triple-plus models exist corresponding to every time-homogeneous single-plus model, a time-homogeneous single-plus model does not exist corresponding to every time-inhomogeneous double-plus and triple-plus model (see Chapter 3 for the taxonomy of single-plus, double-plus, and triple-plus term structure models).
4. Though recursive programming is a standard technique for solving problems in the fields of engineering and computer science, this technique was introduced in finance by Das in 1998.
5. See Nawalkha and Zhang [2004].
6. The simulations in C programming language take more than two days on a Pentium-4 computer with 500 MB RAM.

CHAPTER 12

The LIBOR Market Model

T he origins of the LIBOR market model can be traced to the practically motivated applications of Black's [1976] option formula for pricing derivatives in the LIBOR-based interest rate derivatives market. By using the LIBOR rate as the underlying asset and the current forward rate as the expectation of the future LIBOR rate, and assuming constant volatility, the Black formula immediately gives prices for European options written on the future LIBOR rate. Initially, the theoretical underpinnings of this approach seemed dubious. How could the LIBOR rate be considered a traded asset? How could the risk-neutral expectation of LIBOR rate be the current forward rate? And how could one assume constant volatility? All three assumptions seemed to be theoretically unjustified.

Yet, as practitioners were to be pleasantly surprised, the heuristic Black formulas became precursors to a whole new theoretical apparatus for pricing interest rate derivatives, which came to be known as the *LIBOR Market Model* (LMM). The main insight behind the development of the LMM is that the discretely compounded LIBOR rate can be represented as a portfolio of two zero-coupon bonds, and hence, it is a *traded asset*. By the virtue of being a traded asset, the method of martingale valuation could be used for pricing options based on the LIBOR rate. Since the expectation of the LIBOR rate can be shown to be the current forward rate under the chosen "forward measure," the Black-type formulas are justified for pricing options. Further, since the Black implied volatilities can be given as different constants for different option expiration dates, these are consistent with a time-dependent volatility function for the term structure of volatilities of forward rate changes. Thus, the practically motivated applications of Black's [1976] option formula for pricing caps and swaptions turned out to have full theoretical justification. Further, since Black formulas were already in use by practitioners, the LMM became the industry benchmark model for pricing interest rate derivatives.

The LMM was discovered by Brace, Gatarek, and Musiela [1997] and was initially referred to as the BGM model by practitioners. However,

---

This chapter was coauthored with Lixiong Guo.

Miltersen, Sandmann, and Sondermann [1997] discovered this model independently, and Jamshidian [1997] also contributed significantly to its initial development. To reflect the contribution of multiple authors, many practitioners, including Rebonato [2002], renamed this model the LIBOR market model.

This chapter gives a basic description of the LMM, arguably the most widely used preference-free term structure model for pricing fixed income derivatives. The wide adoption of this model has resulted from three main features:

1. Simple Black-type formulas for caps and swaptions
2. Perfect calibration with the prices of plain vanilla interest rate derivatives, such as at-the-money caps or swaptions
3. A natural interpretation of forward rate volatilities using observable Black-implied volatilities

Using the classification outlined throughout this book, the LMM is *a triple-plus* model, or a preference-free time-inhomogeneous model that takes initial bond prices (or initial forward rates) as given and allows time-inhomogeneous forward rate volatilities in order to calibrate exactly to cap or swaption prices. Though a double-plus version of the LMM can be derived, both Rebonato [2002] and Brigo and Mercurio [2001] recommend triple-plus versions of this model. Though the LMM has become the industry benchmark, its triple-plus features raise concerns about its performance. In a brief survey of the literature, we found that much research on this model focuses solely on how well this model "fits" and not on how well it performs in hedging derivative exposures.

The two commonly used versions of the LMM are the lognormal forward LIBOR model (LFM) for pricing caps and the lognormal forward swap model (LSM) for pricing swaptions. The LFM assumes that the discrete forward LIBOR rate follows a lognormal distribution under its own numeraire, while the LSM assumes that the discrete forward swap rate follows a lognormal distribution under the swap numeraire. Though the two assumptions are theoretically inconsistent, they lead to small discrepancies in calibrations using realistic parameterizations. This chapter also derives a joint framework by deriving the LFM using a *single* numeraire, which leads to exact formulas for pricing caps and approximate formulas for pricing swaptions. A variety of specifications of instantaneous volatilities and correlations are considered for the LFM with a single numeraire, consistent with the double-plus and the triple-plus versions of this model.

Beginning in the mid-1990s, a smile (or smirk) appeared in the pricing of caplets using the LFM, resulting in a monotonically decreasing Black implied volatility as a function of the strike rate of the caplets. The smile in the interest rate derivative market didn't seem to be related to a sudden increase in risk aversion or "crashophobia" as it was in the equity options market.[1] A more likely explanation of the appearance of the smile was the realization among traders that the lognormal forward rate distribution did not capture the forward rate dynamics properly. Two models that resolve this type of misspecification of the LFM are:

1. Models that use a general CEV process for capturing the forward rate dynamics
2. Models with a displaced diffusion for the forward rate process

This chapter gives analytical solutions to caplets under both extensions of the LFM. However, both the CEV and the displaced-diffusion extensions of the LFM can only allow monotonically decreasing smiles. Since 1998, the caplet smile has taken more complex shapes, decreasing first for a wide range of strikes, and then increasing over a short range of strikes, resembling the "hockey-stick shape." Joshi and Rebonato [2003] and others have derived unspanned stochastic volatility (USV) extensions of the CEV and displaced-diffusion–based LFMs. The use of the CEV and/or the displaced-diffusion processes explains the decreasing portion of the smile, and the use of USV explains the increasing portion of the smile. The chapter gives a basic outline of the Joshi and Rebonato [2003] model and shows how to price caps and swaptions using their model.

Finally, this chapter also describes the Jarrow, Li, and Zhao (JLZ) [2007] extension of the LFM, which uses an alternative approach for explaining the hockey-stick shaped smile using a framework that allows both unspanned stochastic volatility and jumps. The original JLZ model is a triple-plus model, as it requires time-inhomogeneous volatilities due to the time-inhomogeneous risk-premiums related to the market prices of volatility and jump risks. A double-plus extension of the JLZ model is presented that allows time-homogeneous volatilities by using time-homogeneous risk premiums related to the market prices of volatility and jump risks.

THE LOGNORMAL FORWARD LIBOR MODEL (LFM)

Consider the relationship between the discrete LIBOR rate $L(T_i, T_{i+1})$ for the term $U_i = T_{i+1} - T_i$ and the zero-coupon bond price $P(T_i, T_{i+1})$, given as follows:

$$1 + L(T_i, T_{i+1})\hat{U}_i = \frac{1}{P(T_i, T_{i+1})} \tag{12.1}$$

where $t \leq T_0 < T_1 < T_2 < \cdots < T_n$ is the timeline and $\hat{U}_i$ is the accrual factor for the period T_i to T_{i+1}, calculated using actual/360 day-count basis.

The time t discrete forward rate for the term $U_i = T_{i+1} - T_i$ is related to the price ratio of two zero-coupon bonds maturing at times T_i and T_{i+1} as follows:

$$1 + f(t, T_i, T_{i+1})\hat{U}_i = \frac{P(t, T_i)}{P(t, T_{i+1})} \tag{12.2}$$

The forward rate converges to the future LIBOR rate at time T_i, or:

$$f(T_i, T_i, T_{i+1}) = L(T_i, T_{i+1}) \tag{12.3}$$

Equation (12.2) can be rewritten as follows:

$$f(t, T_i, T_{i+1})P(t, T_{i+1}) = \frac{1}{\hat{U}_i}\left(P(t, T_i) - P(t, T_{i+1})\right) \tag{12.4}$$

The expression $f(t, T_i, T_{i+1})P(t, T_{i+1})$ is equal to a constant times the difference between zero-coupon bond prices maturing at dates T_i and T_{i+1}. Hence, the expression $f(t, T_i, T_{i+1})P(t, T_{i+1})$ gives the price of a *traded asset*. Now consider a non-dividend-paying, positive-valued numeraire asset with a price $x(t)$. From Chapter 2, we know that under absence of arbitrage, an equivalent martingale measure exists corresponding to the asset $x(t)$ such that the ratio of the price of any traded asset to the price of the asset $x(t)$ is a martingale under this measure. Hence, the process:

$$y(t) = \frac{f(t, T_i, T_{i+1})P(t, T_{i+1})}{x(t)} \tag{12.5}$$

must have a zero drift under an equivalent martingale measure corresponding to the numeraire asset $x(t)$. If $x(t) = P(t, T_{i+1})$, then $f(t, T_i, T_{i+1}) = [f(t, T_i, T_{i+1})P(t, T_{i+1})]/P(t, T_{i+1})$ is a martingale under the equivalent measure defined with respect to the numeraire $P(t, T_{i+1})$. The equivalent measure with respect to the numeraire $P(t, T_{i+1})$ is also called the *forward measure* defined with respect to the maturity T_{i+1}. Since $f(t, T_i, T_{i+1})$ is a martingale under this forward measure, the stochastic process of $f(t, T_i, T_{i+1})$ has zero drift under this measure. The LFM specifies the following zero-drift stochastic process for $f(t, T_i, T_{i+1})$ under this forward measure:

$$\frac{df(t, T_i, T_{i+1})}{f(t, T_i, T_{i+1})} = \sigma_i(t)\,dZ_i(t) \tag{12.6}$$

where $dZ_i(t)$ is a Wiener process under the forward measure $\tilde{\mathcal{P}}^i$ defined with respect to the numeraire asset $P(t, T_{i+1})$ and where $\sigma_i(t)$ measures the volatility of the forward rate process. The volatility can depend upon time and various types of time-dependent volatility functions that are considered later in this chapter. Using Ito's lemma, the stochastic process of the logarithm of the forward rate is given as follows:

$$d \ln f(t, T_i, T_{i+1}) = \frac{-\sigma_i^2(t)}{2} dt + \sigma_i(t) \, dZ_i(t) \qquad (12.7)$$

The stochastic integral of equation (12.7) can be given as follows. For all $0 \le t \le T_i$,

$$\ln f(t, T_i, T_{i+1}) = \ln f(0, T_i, T_{i+1}) - \int_0^t \frac{\sigma_i^2(v)}{2} \, dv + \int_0^t \sigma_i(v) \, dZ_i(v) \qquad (12.8)$$

Since the volatility function $\sigma_i(t)$ is deterministic, the logarithm of forward rates is normally distributed, implying that the forward rate is lognormally distributed. For $t = T_i$, equation (12.8) implies that the future LIBOR rate $L(T_i, T_{i+1}) = f(T_i, T_i, T_{i+1})$ is also lognormally distributed. This explains why this model is called the lognormal forward LIBOR model. Though each forward rate is lognormally distributed under its own forward measure, it is not lognormally distributed under any arbitrary forward measure. The implications of this observation are addressed later in this chapter.

The lognormal forward rate process provides a theoretical justification for the widely used Black formula for caplets. To see this, consider the Black formula for pricing caplets given in Chapter 3. The payoff of the ith caplet at time T_{i+1} is defined as follows:

$$\text{Caplet Payoff at } T_{i+1} = F \times \hat{U}_i \times Max[L(T_i, T_{i+1}) - K_i, 0] \qquad (12.9)$$

where F is the notional value of the caplet and K_i is the caplet strike rate. Even though the payment is made at time T_{i+1}, the amount to be paid is known with certainty at time T_i; and, hence, the option expires at time T_i. The Black formula for the time t price of the ith caplet is given as follows:

$$P_{Caplet_i}(t) = F \times \hat{U}_i \times P(t, T_{i+1})\{f(t, T_i, T_{i+1})\mathcal{N}(d_{1,i}) - K_i\mathcal{N}(d_{2,i})\} \qquad (12.10)$$

where

$$d_{1,i} = \frac{\ln(f(t, T_i, T_{i+1})/K_i) + \vartheta_i^2(T_i - t)/2}{\vartheta_i\sqrt{T_i - t}}$$

$$d_{2,i} = \frac{\ln(f(t, T_i, T_{i+1})/K_i) - \vartheta_i^2(T_i - t)/2}{\vartheta_i\sqrt{T_i - t}}$$

where ϑ_i is the Black implied volatility of the caplet, assumed to be a constant. Though the formula in equation (12.10) was initially developed using heuristic arguments based upon Black's [1976] option formula, the forward rate process given in equation (12.6) provides a theoretical justification for using this formula. To see this, note that the forward rate $f(t, T_i, T_{i+1})$ follows a martingale under the forward measure (see equation (12.6)), and hence, the time t price of the caplet can be obtained by solving the expectation of the caplet payoff given by equation (12.9) as follows:

$$P_{Caplet_i}(t) = F \times \hat{U}_i \times P(t, T_{i+1}) \times E_t^i(Max[L(T_i, T_{i+1}) - K_i, 0]) \qquad (12.11)$$

where the expectation is taken under the forward measure associated with the numeraire $P(t, T_{i+1})$. It can be easily verified that solving the expectation in equation (12.11) gives the same caplet price defined in equation (12.10) but with the following definition of the Black implied volatility:

$$\vartheta_i = \sqrt{\frac{1}{T_i - t} \int_t^{T_i} \sigma_i^2(u) \, du} \qquad (12.12)$$

Hence, the widely used Black caplet price formula is theoretically valid under the LFM. The attractive feature about equation (12.12) is that it provides traders with a simple and intuitive definition of Black implied volatility, given as the square root of the average variance of the percentage changes in the forward rate over the period t to T_i (also called the "root mean square volatility" of forward rates).

Multifactor LFM under a Single Numeraire

Since individual caplets comprising the cap can be priced using different numeraires, the lognormal assumption can be maintained for different forward rates (see equation (12.6)) for pricing caps. However, swaptions and coupon bond options represent *options on portfolios* (and not portfolios of options, like caps), and hence, the joint stochastic evolution of different forward rates must be modeled for pricing these instruments. Modeling the joint evolution of forward rates requires that all forward rate processes be measured under a single forward measure corresponding to a single numeraire asset. As we show in the following discussion, using a single forward measure allows only a specific forward rate (corresponding to this measure) to be distributed lognormally. All other forward rates are not distributed lognormally and do not have known densities. Hence, swaptions must be priced either by using Monte Carlo simulations or by using approximate analytical solutions under the multifactor LFM.

To allow for a single numeraire, redefine the forward rate process given in equation (12.6) under the forward measure $\tilde{P}^k$ with a nonzero drift as follows:

$$\frac{df(t, T_i, T_{i+1})}{f(t, T_i, T_{i+1})} = \mu_i^k(t)\, dt + \sigma_i(t) dZ_i^k(t) \tag{12.13}$$

Equation (12.13) defines Wiener processes $dZ_i^k(t)$ corresponding to the stochastic processes of different forward rates $f(t, T_i, T_{i+1})$ for $i = 0, 1, \ldots,$ $n-1$ under a single numeraire asset $P(t, T_{k+1})$. The generalized notation in equation (12.13) also redefines the Wiener process $dZ_i(t)$ corresponding to the stochastic process of the ith forward rate in equation (12.6) as $dZ_i^i(t)$. The relationship between $dZ_i^k(t)$ and $dZ_i^i(t)$ is given as:

$$dZ_i^k(t) = dZ_i^i(t) - \left(\mu_i^k(t)/\sigma_i(t)\right) dt \tag{12.14}$$

In general, any zero-coupon bond of maturity T_{k+1} can serve as the numeraire. However, in order have the numeraire "alive" for pricing derivatives with all maturities, the zero-coupon bond with the longest maturity date T_n can be chosen.

Though the drift of the ith forward rate process $f(t, T_i, T_{i+1})$ is zero under its own numeraire $P(t, T_{i+1})$, it is nonzero under the numeraire $P(t, T_{k+1})$ with $i \neq k$. Mathematically, this can be stated as:

$$\mu_i^k(t) \neq 0, \quad \text{for } i \neq k$$
$$\mu_i^k(t) = \mu_i^i(t) = 0, \quad \text{for } i = k \tag{12.15}$$

The solution for $\mu_i^k(t)$ when $i \neq k$ can be obtained as follows. Let the numeraire asset in equation (12.5) be given as $x(t) = P(t, T_{k+1})$. Then, in absence of arbitrage, an equivalent measure must exist under which the $y(t)$ process in equation (12.5) is a martingale, or:

$$E^k(dy(t)) = 0 \tag{12.16}$$

where

$$y(t) = \frac{f(t, T_i, T_{i+1})P(t, T_{i+1})}{P(t, T_{k+1})} \tag{12.17}$$

Equation (12.17) can be simplified under three different cases as follows:

1. For $i > k$:

$$y(t) = f(t, T_i, T_{i+1}) \times \frac{P(t, T_{k+2})}{P(t, T_{k+1})} \times \frac{P(t, T_{k+3})}{P(t, T_{k+2})} \times \cdots \times \frac{P(t, T_{i+1})}{P(t, T_i)}$$

$$= \frac{f(t, T_i, T_{i+1})}{\prod\limits_{j=k+1}^{i} \left(1 + f(t, T_j, T_{j+1})\hat{U}_j\right)} \tag{12.18}$$

2. For $i < k$:

$$y(t) = f(t, T_i, T_{i+1}) \times \frac{P(t, T_{i+1})}{P(t, T_{i+2})} \times \frac{P(t, T_{i+2})}{P(t, T_{i+3})} \times \cdots \times \frac{P(t, T_k)}{P(t, T_{k+1})}$$

$$= f(t, T_i, T_{i+1}) \prod\limits_{j=i+1}^{k} \left(1 + f(t, T_j, T_{j+1})\hat{U}_j\right) \tag{12.19}$$

3. For $i = k$:

$$y(t) = f(t, T_i, T_{i+1}) \tag{12.20}$$

Using Ito's lemma on the three previous equations to get the stochastic differential of $y(t)$, substituting equations (12.6) and (12.14) (under the generalized notation $dZ_i(t) = dZ_i^i(t)$), and then equating the expectation of $dy(t)$ to zero using equation (12.16) gives the solutions of the drift terms under the three different cases as follows:

$$\mu_i^k(t) = \sigma_i(t) \sum_{j=k+1}^{i} \frac{\sigma_j(t)\rho_{ij}(t)f(t, T_j, T_{j+1})\hat{U}_j}{(1 + f(t, T_j, T_{j+1})\hat{U}_j)}, \quad \text{for } i > k$$

$$\mu_i^k(t) = -\sigma_i(t) \sum_{j=i+1}^{k} \frac{\sigma_j(t)\rho_{ij}(t)f(t, T_j, T_{j+1})\hat{U}_j}{(1 + f(t, T_j, T_{j+1})\hat{U}_j)}, \quad \text{for } i < k \tag{12.21}$$

$$\mu_i^k(t) = \mu_i^i(t) = 0, \quad \text{for } i = k$$

where $\rho_{ij}(t)$ gives the correlation between the changes in the ith and jth forward rate defined as follows:[2]

$$\rho_{ij}(t)\, dt = dZ_i(t)dZ_j(t) \tag{12.22}$$

Since the quantity $f(t, T_j, T_{j+1})\hat{U}_j/(1 + f(t, T_j, T_{j+1})\hat{U}_j)$ is always between 0 and 1 and since $\sigma_i(t)$ and $\rho_{ij}(t)$ are bounded, the drifts in equation (12.21) remain bounded. Hence, the change of measure in equation (12.14) satisfies the Novikov condition of the Girsanov theorem (see Chapter 2), and all interest rate derivatives can be priced in an arbitrage-free manner using the numeraire $P(t, T_{k+1})$.

However, the drifts under the single numeraire are no longer deterministic and depend upon the current values of the forward rates. This implies that the LFM does not have lognormally distributed forward rates under a single numeraire, even though each forward rate is lognormally distributed under its own numeraire. The drift specification in equation (12.21) also makes the forward rate process non-Markovian. Further, since this drift specification does not allow a known distribution function for the forward rates, analytical solutions cannot be obtained for interest rate derivatives that require modeling of the joint evolution of multiple forward rate processes under a single numeraire (e.g., swaptions and many exotic interest rate derivatives, except plain vanilla caps). In the absence of analytical solutions, these derivatives may be solved using Monte Carlo simulations.

Though the Monte Carlo method can handle many other interest rate derivative products, it is difficult to apply to credit derivative products, many of which have embedded American options (for example, even standard credit instruments such as credit spread options, callable bonds, and convertible bonds have embedded options with American features). In contrast, analytical solutions or very fast approximations exist for most interest rate derivative products including caps, swaptions, and path-dependent derivatives under the preference-free affine and quadratic models given in Chapters 8, 9, and 10. More importantly, unlike the LFM, the preference-free affine and quadratic models can be easily extended for valuing credit derivatives with American type options using the reduced-form approach, providing an integrated modeling platform for the valuation of interest rate derivatives and credit derivatives. The applications of the preference-free affine and quadratic models to credit derivatives are considered in the third book of the trilogy on the fixed income valuation course, *Credit Risk Modeling*.

THE LOGNORMAL FORWARD SWAP MODEL (LSM)

Analogous to how the LFM can price caps using Black's cap formula, the lognormal forward swap model (LSM) (see Jamshidian [1997]) can price swaptions using Black's swaption formula. Together, the LFM and the LSM provide a strong mathematical foundation for the widespread use of Black formulas for pricing caps and swaptions, respectively. Until the discovery of these two models, the use of Black formulas was based on heuristic arguments for using Black-type option formulas for pricing caps and swaptions. This section derives the LSM, which provides a theoretical justification for Black's swaption pricing formula. The next section shows how Black's swaption formula may be used even under the LFM by applying the approximations given by Rebonato [1998, 2002] and Hull and White [1999].

Recall that the fixed leg and the floating leg of an interest rate swap are defined in Chapter 3 as follows: The time line for the fixed-leg payments is given as $S_1 < S_2 < \cdots < S_N$ and for the floating-leg payments is given as $T_1 < T_2 < \cdots < T_n$, where $S_N = T_n$. The current time is t, and the first reset date is $S_0 = T_0$, where $S_0 < S_1$ and $T_0 < T_1$. The general notation allows the number of fixed payments N to be different from the number of floating payments n. Let $s_j = S_{j+1} - S_j$ define the length of time between S_j and S_{j+1}. The payment from the fixed leg of an \$$F$ notional value swap at time S_{j+1} is given as follows:

$$Fixed\text{-}Leg\ Payment = F \times K \times \hat{s}_j \qquad (12.23)$$

where $\hat{s}_j$ is the accrual factor corresponding to the period $s_j = S_{j+1} - S_j$ and K is the interest rate applicable to the fixed leg. Typically, the accrual factors $\hat{s}_j$ for the fixed leg of the swap are based on a 30/360 day-count basis, and hence, are of constant size, even though the actual lengths of the corresponding periods s_j are not the same.

The payment from the floating leg of the swap at time T_{i+1} is given as:

$$Floating\text{-}Leg\ Payment = F \times \hat{U}_i \times L(T_i, T_{i+1}) \qquad (12.24)$$

where $U_i = T_{i+1} - T_i$ and $\hat{U}_i$ is the corresponding accrual factor, generally calculated using actual/360 day-count basis and $L(T_i, T_{i+1})$ is the discrete LIBOR rate observed at time T_i.

The payoffs of a payer swaption and a receiver swaption at the expiration date $S_0 = T_0$ are given in the numeraire economy in equations (3.73) and (3.74) in Chapter 3 (the reader may wish to quickly review the section on swaptions in Chapter 3), as follows:

$$\frac{P_{Payer\ Swaption}(S_0)}{A(S_0)} = F \times Max(f^s(S_0) - K, 0) \qquad (12.25)$$

and

$$\frac{P_{Receiver\ Swaption}(S_0)}{A(S_0)} = F \times Max(K - f^s(S_0), 0) \qquad (12.26)$$

The expressions in equations (12.25) and (12.26) give the swaption payoffs measured in the units of the numeraire asset price $A(S_0)$, which is defined in equation (3.69) in Chapter 3 as follows:

$$A(S_0) = \sum_{j=0}^{N-1} \hat{s}_j P(S_0, S_{j+1}) \tag{12.27}$$

and $f^s(S_0)$ is the going swap rate at time S_0, defined in equation (3.68) in Chapter 3 as that value of fixed rate K, which makes the present values of fixed payments equal to the present values of floating payments, as follows:

$$f^s(S_0) = \frac{1 - P(S_0, S_N)}{A(S_0)} \tag{12.28}$$

From the martingale pricing results in Chapter 2, we know that in absence of arbitrage, an equivalent measure must exist under which all asset prices measured in the units of a given numeraire asset price are martingales. Hence, the time t expectation of the payer swap payoff measured in the units of the numeraire asset price $A(t)$ is given as:

$$\frac{P_{Payer\ Swaption}(t)}{A(t)} = E_t^A \left(\frac{P_{Payer\ Swaption}(S_0)}{A(S_0)} \right) \tag{12.29}$$

where E_t^A is the time t expectation taken under the equivalent measure $\tilde{\mathcal{P}}^A$ corresponding to the numeraire asset price $A(t)$. This measure is called the *forward swap measure*. Substituting equation (12.29) into equation (12.25) and rearranging the terms, we get:

$$P_{Payer\ Swaption}(t) = A(t) \times F \times E_t^A \big(Max(f^s(S_0) - K, 0) \big) \tag{12.30}$$

Computation of expectation (12.30) requires the knowledge of the distribution of the swap rate $f^s(S_0)$. From equation (12.28), it can be seen that the expression $f^s(S_0)A(S_0) = 1 - P(S_0, S_N)$ is a traded portfolio. The time t value of this traded portfolio equals $f^s(t)A(t) = P(t, S_0) - P(t, S_N)$, where $f^s(t)$ is the forward swap rate. Since any traded portfolio measured in the units of the numeraire asset price $A(t)$ must be a martingale under the forward swap measure, the forward swap rate $f^s(t) = (P(t, S_0) - P(t, S_N))/A(t)$ is also a martingale and is given as follows:

$$f^s(t) = E_t^A(f^s(S_0)) \tag{12.31}$$

Equations (12.30) and (12.31) are derived using absence of arbitrage only and thus hold under all term structure models, including both the LFM and the LSM. What distinguishes the LSM from the LFM for pricing swaptions is the assumption regarding the stochastic process of the forward swap rate $f^s(t)$.

The LSM specifies the following stochastic process for $f^s(t)$ under the forward swap measure:

$$\frac{df^s(t)}{f^s(t)} = \sigma_s(t)dZ^A(t) \tag{12.32}$$

where $\sigma_s(t)$ is a deterministic function of time. The zero-drift assumption for this process is necessary to ensure that the martingale condition in equation (12.31) is satisfied. Using Ito's lemma, the stochastic process of $\ln f^s(t)$ is given as follows:

$$d\ln f^s(t) = -\frac{1}{2}\sigma_s^2(t)\,dt + \sigma_s(t)dZ^A(t) \tag{12.33}$$

Taking the stochastic integral of equation (12.33), we get:

$$\ln f^s(S_0) = \ln f^s(t) - \frac{1}{2}\int_t^{S_0} \sigma_s^2(u)\,du + \int_t^{S_0} \sigma_s(u)dZ^A(u) \tag{12.34}$$

Since $\sigma_s(t)$ is a deterministic function of time, $\ln f^s(S_0)$ is normally distributed with time t mean and variance given as follows:

$$E_t^A(\ln f^s(S_0)) = \ln f^s(t) - \frac{1}{2}\int_t^{S_0} \sigma_s^2(u)\,du \tag{12.35}$$

$$V_t^A(\ln f^s(S_0)) = \int_t^{S_0} \sigma_s^2(u)\,du \tag{12.36}$$

Hence, $f^s(S_0)$ is lognormally distributed; and the expectation in equation (12.30) can be easily calculated, leading to Black's formula for the payer swaption given in Chapter 3 as follows:

$$P_{Payer\ Swaption}(t) = A(t) \times F \times \{f^s(t)\mathcal{N}(d_1) - K\mathcal{N}(d_2)\} \tag{12.37}$$

where

$$d_1 = \frac{\ln(f^s(t)/K) + \vartheta_{s,LSM}^2(S_0 - t)/2}{\vartheta_{s,LSM}\sqrt{S_0 - t}}$$

$$d_2 = \frac{\ln(f^s(t)/K) - \vartheta_{s,LSM}^2(S_0 - t)/2}{\vartheta_{s,LSM}\sqrt{S_0 - t}}$$

and where the Black implied volatility $\vartheta_{s,LSM}$ is given as follows:

$$\vartheta_{s,LSM} = \sqrt{\left(\int_t^{S_0} \sigma_s^2(u)\, du\right)/(S_0 - t)} \qquad (12.38)$$

Following similar steps, the price of a receiver swaption can be given as follows:

$$P_{Receiver\ Swaption}(t) = A(t) \times F \times \{K\mathcal{N}(-d_2) - f^s(t)\mathcal{N}(-d_1)\} \qquad (12.39)$$

It can be seen that the main link between the LSM and Black's swaption formula is through the definition of Black implied volatility $\vartheta_{s,LSM}$ in equation (12.38). The Black implied volatility is given as given as the square root of the average variance of the percentage changes in the forward swap rate over the period t to S_0. Since the swap rate volatility is deterministic, the numerical integral in equation (12.38) can be easily computed, allowing swaptions to be priced efficiently.

A JOINT FRAMEWORK FOR USING BLACK'S FORMULAS FOR PRICING CAPS AND SWAPTIONS

Since caps and swaptions constitute virtually all of the market of plain vanilla interest rate options, it is important to investigate the theoretical consistency between the LFM and the LSM. The two models are not compatible since the LFM assumes that each discrete forward rate is distributed lognormally under its own measure, while the LSM assumes that the forward swap rate is distributed lognormally under its own measure. However, since swap rates can be shown to be portfolios of forward rates, forward rates and swap rates cannot both be distributed lognormally. This theoretical incompatibility does not invalidate the simultaneous use of Black's formulas for pricing caps and swaptions. Researchers have found that the theoretical inconsistency between the LFM and the LSM does not translate into significant empirical discrepancy between these two models.

However, one still needs to select a single framework, either the LFM or the LSM, if both caps and swaptions must be priced simultaneously with one set of internally consistent assumptions. Researchers agree that using the LFM is a better choice than using the LSM, both from a theoretical perspective and for computational reasons. Swap rates are easier to express in terms of forward rates than vice versa, and numeraire changes such as those given by equation (12.21) are much easier under the LFM than under the LSM.

Though the LSM provides a theoretical basis for the widely used Black's swaption formula, Black's formula also holds as an *approximate* solution for pricing a swaption under the multifactor LFM with a single numeraire. This approximation is not only easy to compute but also quite accurate, as shown by Hull and White [1999] and Rebonato [2002]. Since most exotic interest rate products are priced off the price curves of caps and swaptions, having a single framework for pricing these vanilla products is quite useful.

The Relationship between the Forward Swap Rate and Discrete Forward Rates

The dynamics of the forward swap rate can be obtained endogenously from the dynamics of the discrete forward rates under the LFM. Equation (3.70) in Chapter 3 defines the forward swap rate as follows:

$$f^s(t) = \frac{P(t, S_0) - P(t, S_N)}{A(t)} \tag{12.40}$$

where

$$A(t) = \sum_{j=0}^{N-1} \hat{s}_j P(t, S_{j+1}) \tag{12.41}$$

Since the tenors and the corresponding accrual factors used for defining the discrete forward rates in the cap market may be different from the tenors and corresponding accrual factors used for defining the forward swap rate in the swaptions market, we express equation (12.40) as follows:

$$f^s(t) = \frac{P(t, S_0) - P(t, S_N)}{A(t)} = \frac{P(t, T_0) - P(t, T_n)}{A(t)}$$

$$= \frac{\displaystyle\sum_{i=0}^{n-1} \hat{U}_i P(t, T_{i+1}) f(t, T_i, T_{i+1})}{\displaystyle\sum_{j=0}^{N-1} \hat{s}_j P(t, S_{j+1})} \tag{12.42}$$

where $S_0 = T_0$ and $S_N = T_n$. The tenors $U_i = T_{i+1} - T_i$ and the corresponding accrual factor $\hat{U}_i$ (typically computed using actual/360 day-count convention) used for caps may be different from the tenors $s_j = S_{j+1} - S_j$ and the corresponding accrual factors $\hat{s}_j$ (typically computed using 30/360 day-count convention) used for making fixed payments on the swaps underlying the swaptions. Hence, the total number of discrete forward rates n may be different from the total number of fixed swap payments N (on the swap underlying the swaption). The general notation allows expressing the forward swap rate used in the swaption market as a function of the n number of discrete forward rates used in the cap market. If the tenors and accrual factors are assumed to be the same in the caps and swaptions markets, then equation (12.42) simplifies to:

$$f^s(t) = \frac{P(t, S_0) - P(t, S_N)}{A(t)} = \frac{\sum_{i=0}^{n-1} \tau_i P(t, T_{i+1}) f(t, T_i, T_{i+1})}{\sum_{i=0}^{n-1} \tau_i P(t, T_{i+1})} \qquad (12.43)$$

Many authors use equation (12.43) to define the forward swap rate, where it is implicitly assumed that $\tau_i = U_i = \hat{U}_i = \hat{s}_i = s_i$ and $n = N$. The generalized notation in equation (12.42) not only allows the tenors in the caps and swaptions market to be of different length (e.g., quarterly versus semi-annual), but also allows the corresponding accrual factors to be based on different day-count conventions (e.g., actual/360 versus 30/360).

Equation (12.42) can be rewritten as follows:

$$f^s(t) = \sum_{i=0}^{n-1} w_i(t) f(t, T_i, T_{i+1}) \qquad (12.44)$$

where the weights $w_i(t)$ are given as follows:

$$w_i(t) = \frac{\hat{U}_i P(t, T_{i+1})}{\sum_{j=0}^{N-1} \hat{s}_j P(t, S_{j+1})} \qquad (12.45)$$

for $i = 0, 1, 2, \ldots, n-1$. Hence, the forward swap rate can be considered a portfolio of discrete forward rates used in the cap market.

Approximating the Black Implied Volatility of a Swaption under the LFM

The relationship between the forward swap rate and the discrete forward rates given in equation (12.44) results in stochastic swap rate volatility under the LFM. However, under certain approximations, the stochastic swap rate volatility can be converted into a deterministic volatility, allowing the use of Black's swaption formula under the LFM also. Consider the LFM with a single numeraire as outlined in equations (12.13) through (12.22). Applying Ito's lemma on equation (12.44) gives:

$$df^s(t) = m(t)\, dt + \sum_{i=0}^{n-1} \hat{w}_i(t)\, df(t, T_i, T_{i+1}) \qquad (12.46)$$

where

$$\hat{w}_i(t) = \left(w_i(t) + \sum_{j=0}^{n-1} f(t, T_j, T_{j+1}) \frac{\partial w_j(t)}{\partial f(t, T_i, T_{i+1})} \right) \tag{12.47}$$

and where $m(t)$ contains the second-order terms obtained from applying Ito's lemma. Substituting equation (12.13) into equation (12.46) gives:

$$df^s(t) = m(t)\, dt + \left(\sum_{i=0}^{n-1} \hat{w}_i(t) f(t, T_i, T_{i+1}) \mu_i^k(t) \right) dt$$

$$+ \sum_{i=0}^{n-1} \hat{w}_i(t) f(t, T_i, T_{i+1}) \sigma_i(t) dZ_i^k(t) \tag{12.48}$$

where $dZ_i^k(t)$ (for $i = 0, 1, 2, \ldots, n-1$) is the Wiener process under the forward measure $\tilde{\mathcal{P}}^k$ associated with the numeraire asset $P(t, T_{k+1})$. Though the forward swap rate is not a martingale under the measure $\tilde{\mathcal{P}}^k$ (for any value of k), it is a martingale under the forward swap measure $\tilde{\mathcal{P}}^A$ as shown earlier in equation (12.31). By using a change of measure on equation (12.48), the stochastic process for the forward swap rate can be given as follows:

$$df^s(t) = \sum_{i=0}^{n-1} \hat{w}_i(t) f(t, T_i, T_{i+1}) \sigma_i(t) dZ_i^A(t) \tag{12.49}$$

The change of measure obviously does not alter the volatilities and correlations between the forward rates but does make the drift zero since the forward swap rate is a martingale under the forward swap measure. Since the drifts are finite and the volatilities are strictly above zero in equation (12.48), the Novikov condition of the Girsanov theorem will be satisfied, allowing the change of measure under absence of arbitrage. Dividing both sides of equation (12.49) by $f^s(t)$, we get:

$$\frac{df^s(t)}{f^s(t)} = \sum_{i=0}^{n-1} x_i(t) \sigma_i(t) dZ_i^A(t) \tag{12.50}$$

where

$$x_i(t) = \frac{\hat{w}_i(t) f(t, T_i, T_{i+1})}{f^s(t)} \tag{12.51}$$

By combining the n Wiener processes into a single Wiener process, the stochastic process for the forward swap rate in equation (12.50) can be expressed as follows:

$$\frac{df^s(t)}{f^s(t)} = \sigma_{s,LFM}(t)dZ^A_{LFM}(t) \tag{12.52}$$

where

$$\sigma_{s,LFM}(t) = \sqrt{\sum_{i=0}^{n-1}\sum_{j=0}^{n-1} x_i(t)x_j(t)\sigma_i(t)\sigma_j(t)\rho_{ij}} \tag{12.53}$$

and where the Wiener process $dZ^A_{LFM}(t)$ is defined as follows:

$$dZ^A_{LFM}(t) = \frac{\sum_{i=0}^{n-1} x_i(t)\sigma_i(t)dZ^A_i(t)}{\sigma_{s,LFM}(t)} \tag{12.54}$$

A number of researchers, including Hull and White [1999], Brigo and Mercurio [2001], and Rebonato [2002], have shown that the variables $x_i(t)$ tend be quite stable, and hence, approximating them at their time 0 values $x_i(0)$ leads to a good approximation of swap rate volatility under the LFM given as follows:

$$\sigma_{s,LFM}(t) = \sqrt{\sum_{i=0}^{n-1}\sum_{j=0}^{n-1} x_i(0)x_j(0)\sigma_i(t)\sigma_j(t)\rho_{ij}} \tag{12.55}$$

The main difference between the LSM and the LFM for valuing swaptions is how these two models define the stochastic process of the forward swap rate. Under the LSM, the forward swap rate process is exogenously specified with deterministic volatility in equation (12.32), while under the LFM, this process is endogenously derived (from the stochastic processes of the discrete forward rates) and has stochastic volatility. However, by approximating the swap rate volatility under the LFM as a deterministic function using equation (12.55), Black's swaption formula can be used under the LFM also. The time 0 Black implied volatility of a swaption under the LFM using the approximation given in equation (12.55) can be obtained by simply replacing the forward swap rate volatility $\sigma_s(t)$ in equation (12.38) by $\sigma_{s,LFM}(t)$, as follows:

$$
\vartheta_{s,LFM} \approx \sqrt{\left(\int_0^{S_0} \sigma_{s,LFM}^2(u)\, du \right) / S_0}
$$

$$
= \sqrt{\left(\sum_{i=0}^{n-1} \sum_{j=0}^{n-1} x_i(0) x_j(0) \int_0^{S_0} \sigma_i(u) \sigma_j(u) \rho_{ij}\, du \right) / S_0} \tag{12.56}
$$

Since $x_i(0)$ are functions of $\hat{w}_i(0)$ (for all $i = 0, 1, 2, \ldots, n-1$), which in turn depend upon the partial derivatives of the weights with respect to the forward rates (see equation (12.47)), the solutions to these partial derivatives are required to solve $x_i(0)$. These partial derivatives can be computed numerically by assuming that the initial zero-coupon bond price function is generated by the n discrete initial forward rates. Of course, since the general framework shown here allows tenors in the swaption market to be different from the tenors in the cap market (see equation (12.45)), the initial zero-coupon bond price function for the full maturity spectrum would have to be first obtained as a function of the n initial forward rates. Depending on the length of the tenors, zero-coupon bond prices of certain maturities would have to be obtained by interpolation of other zero-coupon bond prices. However, once the entire zero-coupon bond price function is specified as a function of only the n discrete forward rates, the partial derivatives in equation (12.47) can be easily obtained numerically.

Various authors, including Jaeckel and Rebonato [2001], Brigo and Mercurio [2001], and Rebonato [2002], have tested the approximation of the LFM given in equation (12.56) against the true model using Monte Carlo simulations and have concluded that the approximation error is relatively small for pricing swaptions. Rebonato [1998] also suggests a slightly less accurate but a simpler approximation that assumes that partial derivatives of the weights with respect to the forward rates are zero in equation (12.47).[3] For nearly flat term structures, Rebonato's original approximation is sufficiently accurate but for significantly nonflat shapes, such as steeply rising, falling, or humped, the partial derivatives in equation (12.47) must be utilized to get better accuracy (see Jaeckel and Rebonato [2001]).

SPECIFYING VOLATILITIES AND CORRELATIONS

Forward Rate Volatilities: Some General Results

It is clear from the foregoing discussion that the Black implied volatilities given in equations (12.12) and (12.56) are what really matter for pricing caps and swaptions, respectively, under the joint framework of the LFM. Since initial forward rates are not under the control of the financial modeler, the only part of the Black implied volatilities that can be optimally chosen by the modeler are the expressions $\int_0^{T_i} \sigma_i^2(u)du$ (for pricing a caplet expiring at time T_i) and $\int_0^{S_0} \sigma_i(u)\sigma_j(u)\rho_{ij}(t)du$ (for pricing a swaption expiring at time S_0), for all $i, j = 0, 1, 2, \ldots, n-1$.

Unfortunately, there are almost infinite ways to calibrate the forward rate volatilities $\sigma_i(t)$ and the correlation function $\rho_{ij}(t)$, which lead to the same values for the expressions $\int_0^{T_i} \sigma_i^2(u)du$ and $\int_0^{S_0} \sigma_i(u)\sigma_j(u)\rho_{ij}(t)du$, using a set of cap and swaption prices with different expiration dates. In the discussion to follow, we define the term *smoothing* to imply fitting financial models to a set of observed prices without an underlying economic rationale. The concept of "smoothing" is different from "overfitting" in that the former implies fitting without an economic rationale, while the latter implies fitting based upon some economic rationale but using more parameters than needed to obtain a good fit. Smoothing may overlook some important relationships that could potentially be modeled endogenously, while overfitting fits to the noise present in the data. In other words, smoothing allows the modeler to ignore some important economic relationships by making ad hoc adjustments to fit the model to observed prices (thus, failing to deal with the misspecification error caused by some hidden variables), while overfitting allows the modeler to invent economic relationships that don't exist but are artifacts of the noise present in the observed prices.

A simple example of smoothing uses the Black and Scholes model for pricing call options of different strikes and using different volatilities corresponding to different strikes to fit the "smile." If the dynamics of the smile are not modeled based on some economic fundamentals, then a trader may not know why and how the option smile changes over time. The option smile obviously represents some systematic economic factor(s), but incorporating these factor(s) into the option prices is beyond the scope of the Black and Scholes model. Perhaps a stochastic volatility/jump model is needed to fit the smile. Yet, if traders continue to use the Black and Scholes model to price options by adjusting the implied volatilities across different strikes to fit the smile, then they are smoothing. Smoothing basically allows the option trader to price an option of a given strike, given the observed prices of options with strikes surrounding the given strike.

It would be wise to be aware of the dangers of smoothing and overfitting while considering various specifications of the forward rate volatility functions. For example, choosing a time-inhomogeneous forward rate volatility function that does not have an underlying economic rationale but that fits caps and swaption prices would imply economically implausible behavior of the future forward rate movements. The short rate models of Black, Derman, and Toy [1991] and Black and Karasinski [1991] and the Vasicek+++ model of Hull and White [1993] (see Chapter 4) imply strange evolution of future volatilities of the forward rates, even though they fit the current structure of forward rate volatilities. Before we discuss some examples of the specific functional forms of the volatility functions under the LFM, we demonstrate that it is virtually impossible for the LFM to allow a time-homogeneous volatility function if the Black implied term structure of volatilities of caplets is significantly humped, which is very often the case.

Using the time 0 definition of Black implied volatilities in equation (12.12) and rearranging terms, we get:

$$\vartheta_i^2 T_i = \int_0^{T_i} \sigma_i^2(u)\, du \tag{12.57}$$

Taking the partial derivative of the left-hand side of equation (12.57), we get:

$$\frac{\partial(\vartheta_i^2 T_i)}{\partial T_i} = 2\vartheta_i \frac{\partial \vartheta_i}{\partial T_i} T_i + \vartheta_i^2 \tag{12.58}$$

From equation (12.58), it follows that:

IF

$$\frac{\partial \vartheta_i}{\partial T_i} < -\frac{\vartheta_i}{2T_i} \tag{12.59}$$

THEN

$$\frac{\partial(\vartheta_i^2 T_i)}{\partial T_i} < 0 \tag{12.60}$$

It is well known that the Black implied volatility function ϑ_i is humped under normal market conditions, and hence, for a range of maturities (generally, somewhere after 1.5 and 2.5 years), the partial derivative $\partial \vartheta_i / \partial T_i$ is less than zero. Very often this partial derivative is significantly negative, such that the condition in equation (12.59) is satisfied and hence, the inequality in equation (12.60) holds.

Now, assume that the forward rate volatility is time-homogeneous, such that:

$$\sigma_i(t) = h(T_i - t) \tag{12.61}$$

The time-homogeneity assumption implies that:

$$\vartheta_i^2 T_i = \int_0^{T_i} \sigma_i^2(u)\, du = \int_0^{T_i} h^2(T_i - u)\, du = \int_{dT_i}^{T_i + dT_i} h^2(T_i + dT_i - u)\, du$$
$$(12.62)$$

for any infinitesimally small dT_i. Taking the partial derivative of equation (12.62) with respect to T_i, we get:

$$\frac{\partial(\vartheta_i^2 T_i)}{\partial T_i} = \lim_{dT_i \to 0} \frac{\left(\int_0^{T_i + dT_i} h^2(T_i + dT_i - u)\, du - \int_0^{T_i} h^2(T_i - u)\, du \right)}{dT_i} \quad (12.63)$$

Substituting the last equality from equation (12.62) into equation (12.63), we get:

$$\frac{\partial(\vartheta_i^2 T_i)}{\partial T_i} = \lim_{dT_i \to 0} \frac{\left(\int_0^{T_i + dT_i} h^2(T_i + dT_i - u)\, du - \int_{dT_i}^{T_i + dT_i} h^2(T_i + dT_i - u)\, du \right)}{dT_i}$$

$$= \lim_{dT_i \to 0} h^2(T_i + dT_i) \quad (12.64)$$

$$= h^2(T_i)$$

Since the square of any function h has to be positive, the partial derivative of $\vartheta_i^2 T_i$ with respect to T_i can never be negative. Hence, the expression $\vartheta_i^2 T_i$ is a strictly increasing function of T_i under the LFM with a time-homogeneous forward rate volatility function. As noted earlier, the *observed* term structure of Black implied volatilities is generally humped; often the hump is significant enough that the inequality given in equation (12.59) holds, making the partial derivative of $\vartheta_i^2 T_i$ with respect to T_i negative. Thus, the LFM with a time-homogeneous forward rate volatility function is frequently inconsistent with the observed implied volatilities of caps.

Unlike the LFM, the preference-free affine and quadratic models given in Chapters 8 through 10 can allow negative values for the partial derivative of $\vartheta_i^2 T_i$ with respect to T_i, using time-homogeneous forward rate volatility functions. This is because the preference-free affine and quadratic models allow stochastic forward rate volatilities, under which the Black implied volatilities are not expressed as integrals of "deterministic" volatilities. Hence, the main implication of the inequalities given in equations (12.59) and (12.60) does not apply to these models.

Forward Rate Volatilities: Specific Functional Forms

Consider the following six forward rate volatility functions for the LFM:[4]

1. $\sigma_i(t) = g(t)$

2. $\sigma_i(t) = k(T_i)$

3. $\sigma_i(t) = g(t)k(T_i)$

4. $\sigma_i(t) = h(T_i - t)k(T_i)$

5. $\sigma_i(t) = h(T_i - t)g(t)$

6. $\sigma_i(t) = h(T_i - t)g(t)k(T_i)$

$$(12.65)$$

where $h, g,$ and k are deterministic functions ($h, g,$ and k do not represent the same functions in the different equations given in (12.65)). Both economic reasoning and econometric estimation using historical data would require that the deterministic forward rate volatilities remain time-homogeneous. However, all specifications given in this section allow some degree of time-inhomogeneous behavior since these functions allow the forward rate volatilities to either display pure time dependence (e.g., through the function $g(t)$) or pure maturity dependence (e.g., through the function $k(T_i)$). Using the classification scheme in this book, the LFM consistent with the specifications of volatilities in equation (12.65) is a *triple-plus* model. The only special case of these volatility functions, which are time homogeneous and hence, allow a double-plus LFM, is given as $\sigma_i(t) = h(T_i - t)$. This can be obtained as a special case of functions 4, 5, and 6 given in equation (12.65) by assuming that functions g and k are constants equal to 1. The typical applications of the LFM are not based upon a time-homogeneous volatility specification, as often no functional form exists for the forward rate volatilities, which is consistent with the observed Black implied market volatilities (since $\vartheta_i^2 T_i$ is not always an increasing function of T_i).

Rebonato [2002] proposes a three-step calibration method that minimizes the effects of time-inhomogeneous forward rate volatilities by capturing as much of the volatility as possible in a time-homogeneous fashion. To see how this method works, assume that the Black implied market volatilities $\vartheta_{i,Market}$ of caplets have been already obtained by an inversion from a cross section of interest rate cap prices for $i = 0, 1, 2, \ldots, n-1$. Now consider a forward rate volatility function given as $\sigma_i(t) = h(T_i - t)g(t)k(T_i)$, where $h(T_i - t)$ is the time-homogeneous component, $g(t)$ is the time-dependent component, and $k(T_i)$ is the maturity-specific component.

Step 1   The time-homogeneous component of the forward rate volatility is defined as follows:

$$h(T_i - t) = [a + b(T_i - t)] \exp[-c(T_i - t)] + d \qquad (12.66)$$

where $a + d > 0, d > 0$, and $c > 0$. This form is flexible enough to allow varied shapes, including monotonically declining and humped with different sizes and locations of humps. As t approaches T_i, the volatility of the shortest maturity forward rate $f(t, T_i, T_{i+1})$ converges to $a + d > 0$. On the other hand, the time-homogeneous volatility of the infinite maturity forward rate converges to the asymptotic value $d > 0$. By taking the first and second derivatives of the volatility function in equation (12.66), it is easy to show that a hump will be present if $b > 0$, with a maximum value occurring at term $T_i - t = 1/c - a/b$. The time-homogeneous component of the forward rate volatility function is fitted to the Black implied market volatilities of caplets by minimizing the following sum at time $t = 0$:

$$\underset{a,b,c,d}{Min} \sum_{i=0}^{n-1} \varepsilon_i^2 \qquad (12.67)$$

where

$$\varepsilon_i^2 = \left(\vartheta_{i,Market}^2 T_i - \int_0^{T_i} h^2(T_i - u) \, du \right)^2 \qquad (12.68)$$

This optimization gives the values of parameters a, b, c, and d, which allows much of the forward rate volatility to be captured by the time-homogeneous component. As mentioned earlier, the LFM cannot explain the pricing of caps using time-homogeneous volatility alone, since $\vartheta_{i,Market}^2 T_i$ is not always increasing with T_i. The next two steps capture the nonhomogeneous component of the forward rate volatility function $\sigma_i(t)$. Since the forward rate volatility is defined as $\sigma_i(t) = h(T_i - t)g(t)k(T_i)$, the nonhomogeneous volatility can be captured either by the function $g(t)$, which allows the volatilities of all forward rates to change as pure function of time, and/or by the function $k(T_i)$, which allows the volatilities of different forward rates to change by different magnitudes.

Both functions $g(t)$ and $k(T_i)$ suffer from the problem of smoothing (the concept of smoothing was introduced in an earlier chapter and defined in a previous section of this chapter, and it is different from overfitting), as these functions are used mainly to make Black's caplet formula fit the observed prices without a strong underlying economic rationale. Rebonato [2002] justifies the function $g(t)$, as some future event(s) may be expected to increase or decrease the volatilities of all forward rates in the future in some predictable manner (e.g., scheduled meeting of the central bank's board members at a future date that is known today, etc.). However, this justification is questionable, as it assumes that the forward rate volatilities will be impacted by an identical factor $g(t)$, regardless of the length of the term $T_i - t$. For example, using this justification implies that the volatility of the infinite-maturity forward rate is affected by an event scheduled one month from now by the same factor as is the volatility of the six-month forward rate.

Moreover, a quick glance at the adjustment of the forward rate volatility by the function $g(t)$ in Rebonato [2002, Figure 8.15, p. 240] reveals that the maximum adjustment occurs at around six years. For this specific case considered by Rebonato (which, of course, does not represent a general finding), it is unclear what economic rationale would make the function $g(t)$ have its highest impact at around six years and not at around six months or two years. Traders obviously have little knowledge about elections scheduled or board meetings planned after six years and are more concerned about the events in the window of the next one to two years.

In short, the main point of this discussion is that the function $g(t)$ represents a smoothing variable that allows improvising the fit between the Black implied market volatilities and the Black implied model volatilities for the LFM.[5] The use of time-dependent volatilities as smoothing variables can be traced to the models of Black, Derman, and Toy [1990], Black and Karasinski [1991], and Hull and White [1990], and initially practitioners used $g(t)$ as the only component for $\sigma_i(t)$, without requiring a time-homogeneous component $h(T_i - t)$. Rebonato [2002], recognizing the arbitrariness of this approach, recommends the three-step process that puts most of the burden of capturing the forward rate volatility on the time-homogeneous component $h(T_i - t)$.

The second step of the optimization process recommended by Rebonato [2002] is given as follows:

Step 2 Minimize the following sum at time $t = 0$:

$$\underset{\alpha_m}{Min} \sum_{i=0}^{n-1} \varepsilon_i^2 \qquad (12.69)$$

where

$$\varepsilon_i^2 = \left(\vartheta_{i,Market}^2 T_i - \int_0^{T_i} h^2(T_i - u) g^2(u)\, du \right)^2 \qquad (12.70)$$

and where α_m $(m = 1, 2, \ldots)$ are the parameters that define the function $g(t)$ and the function $h(T_i - t)$ has already been estimated in step 1. Since for standard applications, the dates T_j and T_{j+1} are quite close (e.g., three months apart), the function $g(t)$ can be approximated as a piecewise continuous function, which simplifies equation (12.70) by dividing the integral on the right-hand side of this equation into $i + 1$ additive components and by bringing function $g(t)$ out of the integral, as follows:

$$\varepsilon_i^2 = \left(\vartheta_{i,Market}^2 T_i - \sum_{j=0}^{i} g^2(T_j) \int_{T_{j-1}}^{T_j} h^2(T_i - u)\, du \right)^2 \tag{12.71}$$

where the time line is given as $0, T_0, T_1, T_2, \ldots T_i, \ldots T_{n-1}$ (and, hence, $T_{-1} = 0$). The optimization requires a parametric form for the function $g(t)$, which is defined as follows:

$$g(t) = \left(\sum_{m=1}^{3} \alpha_m \sin\left(\frac{t\pi m}{T_{n-1}} + \alpha_{m+1} \right) \right) \exp(-\alpha_7 t) \tag{12.72}$$

where T_{n-1} is the expiration date of the longest maturity caplet used for normalizing the sine wave function. The functional form shown in equation (12.72) gives a linear combination of three sine waves of increasing frequency, which are multiplied by a decaying exponential term. As shown by Rebonato [2002], this functional form is very flexible in fitting a variety of shapes and converges to zero asymptotically.

Step 3   The Black implied market volatilities cannot be generally recovered fully by the LFM using the first two steps. To fully recover these volatilities, a maturity-specific function $k(T_i)$ is defined as follows:

$$k(T_i) = \sqrt{\frac{\vartheta_{i,Market}^2 T_i}{\displaystyle\sum_{j=0}^{i} g^2(T_j) \int_{T_{j-1}}^{T_j} h^2(T_i - u)\, du}} \tag{12.73}$$

where both functions $h(T_i - t)$ and $g(t)$ have already been estimated in step 1 and step 2, respectively. The definition given previously ensures that Black implied market volatilities are exactly matched by the forward rate volatility function under the LFM.

Though little economic justification exists for using the function $k(T_i)$, except that it allows obtaining a perfect fit with Black implied volatilities, this function is treated as an essential part of the LFM. To understand the implications of using the function $k(T_i)$, first consider the case where the forward rate volatility $\sigma_i(t) = k(T_i)$, such that both $g(t)$ and $h(T_i - t)$ equal 1. For this case, the volatility of a given forward rate does not change at all with the passage of time, such that a ten-year forward rate has the same volatility after nine years, when it becomes a one-year forward rate. Also, the volatilities of different forward rates with the *same* residual maturities (at different points in time) have different volatilities.

Of course, the three-step procedure outlined here minimizes the effect of such economically undesirable implications of using the function $k(T_i)$. Since $\sigma_i(t) = h(T_i - t) \, g(t) \, k(T_i)$, most of the forward rate volatility is explained away by functions $h(T_i - t)$ and $g(t)$ in the first two steps. The function $k(T_i)$ is generally "close to unity" when it is estimated using the third step (see equation (12.73)), as shown by Rebonato [2002]. However, what is defined as close to unity is left unspecified in statistical and economic terms by Rebonato. For example, if $k(T_i)$ is close to unity, it may reflect only trading noise, and so it should be ignored. But since $k(T_i)$ is considered significant enough in economic terms to be included as an essential part of the three-step procedure for calibrating the LFM, it obviously serves as a smoothing variable that captures the effects of some systematic factor(s).

For more insight, consider the values of function $k(T_i)$ given in Rebonato [2002, Figure 8.18, p. 242]. From this figure it can be seen that $k(1) = 1.03$ and $k(3) = 0.96$ (approximately) at time 0. After two years, $k(3)$ is still 0.96 (since $k(T_i)$ does not change with the passage of time), but now impacts the volatility of the one-year forward rate observed at time 2. Hence, at time 0, the volatility of the one-year forward rate is increased by a factor of 1.03, and at time 2, the volatility of the one-year forward rate is decreased by a factor of 0.96. The difference in how the volatility of the one-year forward rate is impacted by the function $k(T_i)$ from time 0 to time 2 changes by a factor of $0.96/1.03 = 0.93$, or by approximately 7 percent.[6]

Instantaneous Correlations and Terminal Correlations

Consider the pricing of caps using the preference-free models (e.g., LFM, HJM, and other preference-free affine and quadratic models) in two different economic scenarios, A and B, in which all variables (such as the level of interest rates, volatility of interest rates, and so on) are the same, except that the correlations between the interest rate changes are significantly higher in scenario A. Now consider the following question: Under which economic scenario are interest rate caps valued higher?

A casual reading of the term structure literature provides two seemingly contradictory answers to this question. Using the LFM framework, correlations do not matter for the pricing of caps, and hence, caps are priced exactly the same in either economic scenario, regardless of the sign and the magnitudes of the correlations. In contrast, using the HJM or preference-free affine/quadratic models, increasing the average correlation between different interest rate changes, while keeping all other variables the same, *decreases* the prices of caps significantly.

As with all paradoxes, the resolution to the seemingly contradictory answers requires understanding the question more deeply. The LFM uses the percentage changes in discrete forward rates to measure correlations and volatilities, while the HJM and affine/quadratic models use the changes in instantaneous forward rates to measure correlations and volatilities. This distinction plays a crucial role in answering the interest rate cap valuation question. Since instantaneous forward rates are the building blocks of discrete forward rates, we consider this question using the correlations between the instantaneous forward rate changes.

Since an interest rate cap is a portfolio of caplets, we analyze the pricing of a caplet, which can be considered an option on a zero-coupon bond with a unique feature—the expiration date of the option is always very close to the maturity date of the bond underlying the option (generally only three months apart). The volatility that matters for pricing a caplet is not the volatility of the return on the underlying zero-coupon bond, but the volatility of the return on this bond measured in the units of the zero-coupon bond that serves as the numeraire. Since the underlying bond and the numeraire bond have very close maturities, a higher correlation under economic scenario A decreases the volatility of the return on the underlying bond measured in the units of the numeraire bond. The reduced volatility decreases the price of the caplet. Since a cap is a portfolio of caplets, an overall increase in the average correlation between instantaneous forward rate changes in scenario A reduces the prices of caplets, thereby reducing the price of the cap.

Now consider how an LFM modeler would view the same effects in scenario A versus scenario B. The LFM modeler observes the volatilities of the percentage changes in the *discrete* forward rates. Since discrete forward rates are represented using the ratio of two bond prices with very close maturities (see equation (12.2)), the volatility of the percentage of change in discrete forward rates crucially depends upon the correlation between the instantaneous returns of these two bonds, which in turn depends upon the correlations between changes in the instantaneous forward rates. A general increase in these correlations will decrease the volatility of the return on the bond price ratio, and hence, reduce the volatility of the percentage of change in discrete forward rates. Since the correlations between the instantaneous forward rate changes are high in scenario A, and assuming that the volatilities of the instantaneous forward rate changes remain the same in both scenarios, the LFM modeler would notice that the volatilities of the percentage changes in the discrete forward rates are lower under scenario A than under scenario B.

In other words, the size of the correlations between the changes in instantaneous forward rates is endogenously related to the size of the volatilities of the percentage changes in discrete forward rates. Hence, the LFM modeler observes lower volatilities of the percentage changes in discrete forward rates in scenario A and higher volatilities of the percentage changes in discrete forward rates in scenario B, while the volatilities of instantaneous forward rate changes remain the same under both scenarios. Therefore, caps would have lower prices in scenario A, even for the LFM modeler, but the modeler would claim the reason to be lower forward rate volatilities, and not higher correlations.

Hence, the question, "What would happen to cap prices if correlations increase while volatilities remain the same?" is not a well-posed question without specifying whether one is using discrete forward rates or instantaneous forward rates to measure correlations and volatilities. In general, a rise in the correlations happens simultaneously with a fall in the volatilities of the discrete forward rate changes under the LFM, when the correlations between the instantaneous forward rate changes increase but the volatilities of the instantaneous forward rate changes remain the same.

This explains why a modeler using the HJM or affine/quadratic models would claim that increases in correlations decrease cap prices, while an LFM modeler would claim that correlations have no effect on cap prices. Regardless of their reasoning, both modelers agree on the valuation of caps, as they both observe lower cap prices in scenario A and higher cap prices in scenario B. Yet their claims about the effects of correlations on cap prices may sound paradoxical if one is not careful about specifying which forward rates—discrete or instantaneous—are being used to measure correlations.[7]

A similar observation applies to the valuation of swaptions. It is well known that a swaption can be considered an option on a coupon bond. What matters for pricing a swaption is the volatility of the return of the price of the coupon bond measured in the units of the price of the zero-coupon bond maturing at the swaption expiration date (which serves as the numeraire asset for valuation). Let this volatility be $\sigma_s(t)$. Under the HJM and affine/quadratic models, an increase in the average correlation between instantaneous forward rate changes without any change in the volatilities has two offsetting effects on $\sigma_s(t)$. Since the coupon bond is a portfolio of zero-coupon bonds, $\sigma_s(t)$ increases with an increase in average correlation. We call this effect the "portfolio effect." However, since $\sigma_s(t)$ is measured with the zero-coupon bond serving as the numeraire, an increase in the average correlation reduces $\sigma_s(t)$. We call this effect the "numeraire effect." As shown by Collin-Dufresne and Goldstein [2001], these two offsetting effects cancel each other out, such that for a realistically wide range of correlations, the changes in correlations do not affect $\sigma_s(t)$ significantly, and hence, the valuation of swaptions is relatively immune to changes in the average correlation.

Now let's consider how an LFM modeler would view these effects. Under the LFM, what matters for pricing a swaption is the volatility of the changes in the *swap rate* given as a portfolio of discrete forward rates. Also, the discrete forward rates are proportional to the ratio of two bond prices with close maturities. Hence, both the portfolio effect and the numeraire effect resulting from an increase in the average correlation between instantaneous forward rate changes apply under the LFM also, but in a slightly different manner. The numeraire effect reduces the volatility of the percentage changes in each discrete forward rate, hence reducing the volatility of the percentage changes in the swap rate (given as the portfolio of discrete forward rates). In contrast, due to the portfolio effect, an increase in correlation increases the volatility of the percentage changes in the swap rate, since the swap rate is a portfolio of discrete forward rates. Again, these two effects cancel each other out, making swaptions insensitive to an increase in the size of the average correlation between instantaneous forward rate changes.

Note, however, that Brigo and Mercurio [2001] and Rebonato [2002] find that an increase in the average correlation increases the valuation of swaptions. Again, this apparent inconsistency can be resolved by noting that the average correlation mentioned in the previous paragraph is between the changes in instantaneous forward rates, while the average correlation modeled by Brigo and Mercurio [2001] and Rebonato [2002] is between the percentage changes in discrete forward rates. The increase in the former correlation, while keeping the volatilities of the changes in instantaneous forward rates constant, allows the portfolio effect to be offset by the numeraire effect. The increase in the latter correlation, while keeping the volatilities of the percentage changes in discrete forward rates constant, leads to only the portfolio effect.

In summary, comparing the correlation and volatility dynamics of instantaneous forward rate changes with those of the discrete forward rate changes is like comparing apples and oranges. Our discussion resolves some of the misconceptions that exist regarding the effects of changes in correlations on the valuations of caps and swaptions. We now give analytical formulas for approximating the instantaneous and terminal correlations between discrete forward rate changes that apply under the LFM.

Full-Rank Instantaneous Correlations

The instantaneous correlations between the changes in discrete forward rates can be modeled with either as many factors as the number of forward rates or with fewer factors than the forward rates. In general, modeling as many factors as the forward rates does not create any problem for valuing plain vanilla instruments, such as caps and European swaptions, using the LFM. However, computational considerations require using a lower number of factors than for the forward rates for the more exotic interest rate derivatives with path-dependent and American features. As shown by Rebonato [1999a, 1999d, 2002] and Rebonato and Cooper [1995], the low-dimensional models with two or three factors cannot typically recover the exogenously specified correlations with rapid decorrelation between the changes in forward rates of shorter maturities.

The first part of this section gives two approaches to obtain a correlation matrix using all of the forward rate changes. The second part gives two approaches to approximate a full-rank correlation matrix with a reduced-rank correlation matrix.

Let the instantaneous correlation between the percentage of change in the forward rates $f(t, T_i, T_{i+1})$ and $f(t, T_j, T_{j+1})$ be given as $\rho_{ij}(t)$. A desirable instantaneous correlation structure should have the following properties: For all i and j equal to $0, 1, 2, \ldots, n - 1$:

1. $\rho_{ii}(t) = 1$
2. $\rho_{ij}(t) = \rho_{ji}(t)$
3. $-1 \leq \rho_{ij}(t) \leq 1$
4. The correlation matrix is positive semidefinite (or all eigenvalues are nonnegative).
5. $\rho_{ij}(t) = g(T_i - t, T_j - t)$
6. $\lim_{T_j \to \infty} \rho_{ij}(t) = \rho_\infty > 0$
7. $\rho_{j,j+k}(t) > \rho_{i,i+k}(t)$ for $j > i$ and $k > 0$

The first four properties are mathematical properties of any well-defined correlation matrix. The last three properties are based on economic considerations regarding the LFM. The fifth property requires that the correlations be time-homogeneous functions and depend only on the residual maturities $T_i - t$ and $T_j - t$. The sixth property requires that the asymptotic correlation defined as the correlation between the percentage changes of any forward rate and that of the infinite maturity forward rate is positive. The intuition behind this observation is based upon using long-maturity forward rates (e.g., ten to twenty years) as a proxy for the infinite maturity forward rate. Economic arguments based on the possibility of riskless arbitrage (see Dybvig, Ingersoll, and Ross [1996]) require that the infinite-maturity forward rate be constant, and hence, that the asymptotic correlation must be zero. On the other hand, typical applications of the LFM assume that the asymptotic correlation is positive. We don't take a strong theoretical position on this issue for the exposition of the LFM. The seventh property requires that the correlations between the percentage changes in forward rates with the same difference in maturities should be higher for longer-maturity forward rates. In other words, the correlation between the percentage changes in the 15-year and the 16-year maturity forward rates should be higher than the correlation between the percentage changes in the one-year and the two-year maturity forward rates.

Now consider the following three functional forms (see Rebonato [1999d]):

1. $\rho_{ij}(t) = \exp\left(-\beta(|(T_i - t) - (T_j - t)|)\right) = \exp\left(-\beta|T_i - T_j|\right)$ (12.74)

2. $\rho_{ij}(t) = \rho_\infty + (1 - \rho_\infty)\exp\left(-\beta|T_i - T_j|\right)$ (12.75)

3. $\rho_{ij}(t) = \rho_\infty + (1 - \rho_\infty)\exp\left(-\beta(|(T_i - t)^\lambda - (T_j - t)^\lambda|)\right)$ (12.76)

where the parameters β, ρ_∞, and λ are nonnegative. The first three mathematical properties given earlier are satisfied by all of the three correlation functions given in equations (12.74), (12.75), and (12.76). The fourth property requiring the correlation matrix to be positive-definite is satisfied only by the first two correlation functions. For the third correlation function, this property holds only for a certain range of parameter values, and therefore, it must be ensured by confirming the nonnegativity of eigenvalues. This leads to computational difficulties for inversion of the parameters β, ρ_∞, and λ, since not all parameter combinations obtained by calibration to the Black implied market volatilities can guarantee a positive-definite correlation matrix. The fifth property related to time-homogeneity is satisfied by all of the three correlation functions. The sixth property is satisfied by the second and the third correlation function, but not by the first one, under which the asymptotic correlation is zero. And finally, the seventh property related to the size of decorrelation is satisfied only by the third correlation function. In general, although the third functional form is flexible enough to generate realistic instantaneous correlation structures, it does not guarantee that the correlation matrix remains positive semidefinite.

Table 12.1 displays a sample correlation matrix between ten forward rates, $f(t, T_0, T_1), f(t, T_1, T_2), \ldots, f(t, T_9, T_{10})$, with parameters $\rho_\infty = 0.613$ and $\beta = 0.1$, using the second function given in equation (12.75), and assuming that $T_0 - t = T_{i+1} - T_i = 1$ year for all $i = 0, 1, 2, \ldots, 9$. An empirically desirable correlation matrix should have the top row with correlations decreasing at a decreasing rate (i.e., a positive convexity pattern), the

TABLE 12.1 Correlations among Ten Forward Rates Generated Using the Function in Equation (12.75), with $\rho_\infty = 0.613$ and $\beta = 0.1$

	0	1	2	3	4	5	6	7	8	9
0	1.000	0.963	0.930	0.900	0.872	0.848	0.825	0.805	0.787	0.770
1	0.963	1.000	0.963	0.930	0.900	0.872	0.848	0.825	0.805	0.787
2	0.930	0.963	1.000	0.963	0.930	0.900	0.872	0.848	0.825	0.805
3	0.900	0.930	0.963	1.000	0.963	0.930	0.900	0.872	0.848	0.825
4	0.872	0.900	0.930	0.963	1.000	0.963	0.930	0.900	0.872	0.848
5	0.848	0.872	0.900	0.930	0.963	1.000	0.963	0.930	0.900	0.872
6	0.825	0.848	0.872	0.900	0.930	0.963	1.000	0.963	0.930	0.900
7	0.805	0.825	0.848	0.872	0.900	0.930	0.963	1.000	0.963	0.930
8	0.787	0.805	0.825	0.848	0.872	0.900	0.930	0.963	1.000	0.963
9	0.770	0.787	0.805	0.825	0.848	0.872	0.900	0.930	0.963	1.000

bottom row with correlations increasing at a decreasing rate (i.e., a negative convexity pattern), and intermediate rows allowing a smooth switch from the positive convexity pattern to the negative convexity pattern.

It can be seen from the top row of the correlation matrix that the *rate* of decorrelation of the first forward rate $f(t, T_0, T_1)$ with other forward rates decreases with maturity. For example, the decorrelation between $f(t, T_1, T_2)$ and $f(t, T_2, T_3)$ equals 0.033, which is less than the decorrelation between $f(t, T_0, T_1)$ and $f(t, T_1, T_2)$ equal to 0.037. Since the correlation decreases at a decreasing rate, this leads to the desirable *positive* convexity in the decorrelation pattern for the top row of the correlation matrix.

The bottom row of the correlation matrix in Table 12.1 shows that the rate of decorrelation of the last forward rate $f(t, T_9, T_{10})$ with other forward rates *increases* with maturity. Thus, the correlation increases at an increasing rate for the bottom row. This positive convexity pattern is, however, undesirable for the longer-maturity forward rates, as both economic intuition and empirically observed correlations suggest that the rate of decorrelation of the longer-maturity forward rates with other forward rates should decrease with maturity. This limitation can be resolved by using the third function given in equation (12.76) with values of $\lambda > 0$, significantly lower than 1. However, since the third function does not always guarantee a positive semidefinite correlation matrix, it is difficult to use this function for performing calibrations.

Schoenmakers and Coffey [2000, 2003] derive an alternative set of parametric functional forms for the correlation function that allow a switch from positive convexity to negative convexity in the decorrelation pattern when going from the top row to the bottom row of the correlation matrix. They begin with a finite sequence of positive real numbers given as follows:

$$1 = a_0 < a_1 < a_2 < \cdots < a_{n-1} \tag{12.77}$$

such that

$$\frac{a_0}{a_1} < \frac{a_1}{a_2} < \cdots < \frac{a_{n-2}}{a_{n-1}} \tag{12.78}$$

The correlations between the percentage changes in discrete forward rates are defined as follows:

$$\rho_{i,j}(t) = \frac{a_i}{a_j}, \text{ where } i \leq j \quad \text{for all } i, j = 0, 1, 2, \ldots, n-1 \tag{12.79}$$

Equation (12.79) only defines the upper triangle of the correlation matrix, including the diagonal elements. The elements in the lower triangle of the correlation matrix, excluding the diagonal elements, are defined as:

$$\rho_{i,j}(t) = \rho_{j,i}(t), \quad \text{where } i > j$$
$$\text{for all } j = 0, 1, 2, \dots, n-2 \text{ and } i = 1, 2, \dots, n-1 \tag{12.80}$$

using the second property of a correlation matrix given earlier. The framework shown here allows the correlations between the percentage changes in forward rates with the same difference in maturities to be higher for longer-maturity forward rates, or $\rho_{j,j+k}(t) > \rho_{i,i+k}(t)$ for $j > i$ and $k > 0$ (see property 7). In general, these correlations satisfy all seven properties given earlier using n number of parameters $a_0, a_1, a_2, \dots, a_{n-1}$.

Schoenmakers and Coffey [2000] demonstrate that this representation of the correlation matrix can always be characterized in terms of a finite sequence of nonnegative numbers $\Delta_1, \Delta_2, \dots, \Delta_{n-1}$, as follows:

$$\rho_{i,j}(t) = \exp\left(-\sum_{k=i+1}^{j}(k-i)\Delta_K + \sum_{k=j+1}^{n-1}(j-i)\Delta_k\right) \quad \text{for all } i < j \tag{12.81}$$

where $i = 0, 1, 2, \dots, n-2$, and $j = 1, 2, \dots, n-1$, and

$$\rho_{i,i}(t) = 1, \quad \text{for all } i = 0, 1, 2, \dots, n-1 \tag{12.82}$$

This representation is neither parametric nor nonparametric. It is not parametric since the number of parameters is of the order $O(n)$, and it increases linearly with the number of forward rates. The representation is also not purely nonparametric since that would require $O(n^2)$ number of parameters. Hence, Schoenmakers and Coffey [2000] call this representation *semiparametric*.

However, by putting additional restrictions on the sequence of nonnegative numbers $\Delta_1, \Delta_2, \dots, \Delta_{n-1}$, simple parametric forms of correlation functions can be derived as special cases of the semiparametric correlation matrix. As the first case, consider two parameters given as: $\alpha = \Delta_1 = \Delta_2 = \cdots = \Delta_{n-2} \geq 0$ and $\beta = \Delta_{n-1}$. Substituting these values and analytically solving the two summations in equation (12.81) gives a two-parameter correlation function as follows:

$$\rho_{i,j}(t) = \exp\left(-|i-j|\left(\beta + \alpha\left(n-1-\frac{i+j+1}{2}\right)\right)\right) \tag{12.83}$$

for $i, j = 0, 1, 2, \dots, n-1$.

Let the asymptotic correlation defined as the correlation between the percentage of change in the first forward rate $f(t, T_0, T_1)$ and the last forward rate $f(t, T_{n-1}, T_n)$ be given as $\rho_{0,n-1}(t) = \rho_\infty$. Then by redefining the two parameters in equation (12.83), it can be expressed as follows:

$$\rho_{i,j} = \exp\left(-\frac{|i-j|}{n-1}\left(-\ln \rho_\infty + \eta\left(\frac{n-i-j-1}{n-2}\right)\right)\right) \qquad (12.84)$$

where

$$\eta = \frac{\alpha(n-1)(n-2)}{2} \qquad (12.85)$$

and

$$-\ln \rho_\infty = \eta + \beta(n-1) \qquad (12.86)$$

Substituting $i = 0$ and $j = n - 1$, it is easy to verify that the asymptotic correlation $\rho_{0,n-1}(t)$ equals ρ_∞ in equation (12.84). The correlation function defined in equation (12.84) displays stability, in that a small perturbation of the observed correlation matrix leads to only small changes in the parameters ρ_∞ and η. Interestingly, even though this correlation function only uses two parameters, it satisfies all seven properties of a good correlation function noted earlier; and, hence, it is generally preferred over the classical functional forms given by Rebonato [1999d] (see equations (12.74) through (12.76)).

Table 12.2 displays the correlation matrix between ten forward rates, $f(t, T_0, T_1), f(t, T_1, T_2), \ldots, f(t, T_9, T_{10})$ with parameters $\rho_\infty = 0.77$, $\eta = 0.1$, and $n = 10$, where it is implicitly assumed that $T_{i+1} - T_i$ is a constant for all $i = 0, 1, 2, \ldots, 9$. It can be seen that the correlation matrix captures the decorrelation pattern mentioned earlier quite well, as the top row of the correlation matrix exhibits positive convexity (i.e., correlations decrease at a decreasing rate), while the bottom row exhibits negative convexity (i.e., correlations increase at a decreasing rate). This contrasts with the correlation matrix in Table 12.1, in which both the top row and the bottom row exhibit positive convexity.

To further refine the convexity pattern related to the speed of decorrelation between the forward rate changes, Schoenmakers and Coffey [2003] propose a higher order three-parameter correlation function. They define the parameters as follows: $\alpha_1 = \Delta_1$, $\alpha_2 = \Delta_{n-2}$, $\beta = \Delta_{n-1}$, and for all $i = 1, 2, \ldots, n - 2$:

$$\Delta_i = \alpha_1 \frac{n-2-i}{n-3} + \alpha_2 \frac{i-1}{n-3} \qquad (12.87)$$

TABLE 12.2 Correlations among Ten Forward Rates Generated Using the Function in Equation (12.84), with $\rho_\infty = 0.77$, $\eta = 0.1$, and $n = 10$

	0	1	2	3	4	5	6	7	8	9
0	1.000	0.961	0.925	0.894	0.866	0.841	0.819	0.800	0.784	0.770
1	0.961	1.000	0.963	0.931	0.901	0.876	0.853	0.833	0.816	0.802
2	0.925	0.963	1.000	0.966	0.936	0.909	0.885	0.865	0.847	0.832
3	0.894	0.931	0.966	1.000	0.969	0.941	0.917	0.895	0.877	0.861
4	0.866	0.901	0.936	0.969	1.000	0.971	0.946	0.924	0.905	0.889
5	0.841	0.876	0.909	0.941	0.971	1.000	0.974	0.951	0.932	0.915
6	0.819	0.853	0.885	0.917	0.946	0.974	1.000	0.977	0.957	0.940
7	0.800	0.833	0.865	0.895	0.924	0.951	0.977	1.000	0.980	0.962
8	0.784	0.816	0.847	0.877	0.905	0.932	0.957	0.980	1.000	0.982
9	0.770	0.802	0.832	0.861	0.889	0.915	0.940	0.962	0.982	1.000

Unlike the previous case, the sequence of nonnegative numbers $\Delta_1, \Delta_2, \ldots,$ Δ_{n-2} are not equal but change in a linear fashion. Substituting the values given in the previous paragraph and those given in equation (12.87) into equation (12.81) and analytically solving the summations gives a three-parameter correlation function. This correlation function can be reparameterized with a change of variables, such that it can be expressed as a function of the asymptotic correlation $\rho_{0,n-1}(t) = \rho_\infty$ and two other redefined parameters. By calibrating to realistic correlation structures, Schoenmakers and Coffey [2003] find that one of the redefined parameters is almost always close to zero, and hence, they remove this parameter. The resulting two-parameter correlation function is given after some involved but basic algebra, as follows:

$$\rho_{i,j} = \exp\left(-\frac{|i-j|}{n-1}\left(-\ln\rho_\infty + \eta\left(\frac{i^2 + j^2 + ij - 3(n-2)(i+j)}{-3(n-1) + 2(n-1)^2}\right)\right)\right)$$

(12.88)

Substituting $i = 0$ and $j = n - 1$, one can verify that the asymptotic correlation $\rho_{0,n-1}(t)$ equals ρ_∞ in equation (12.88). Though equation (12.88) and equation (12.84) seem somewhat different than the corresponding equations given by Schoenmakers and Coffey [2003], this is only due to the differences in the notation used.[8]

Table 12.3 displays the sample correlation matrix between ten forward rates with the same parameters used in Table 12.2 (i.e., $\rho_\infty = 0.77$, $\eta = 0.1$, and $n = 10$). As in Table 12.2, the sign of convexity switches from positive to negative when going from the top row to the bottom row of the correlation matrix. However, the speed of decorrelation is faster at the shorter end and slower at the longer end in Table 12.3. This speed can be controlled by changing the parameters ρ_∞ and η.

Reduced-Rank Correlation Structures

The correlation functions in the previous section assume that the number of forward rates equals the number of factors, an assumption that works well for pricing plain vanilla instruments such as caps and European swaptions. However, for pricing more complex instruments that require Monte Carlo simulations, using fewer factors than the forward rates is often desirable for computational purposes.

Let ρ be the $n \times n$ correlation matrix with elements ρ_{ij} for $i, j = 0, 1, 2, \ldots, n-1$. Since ρ is a positive-definite symmetric matrix, it can be

TABLE 12.3 Correlations among Ten Forward Rates Generated Using the Function in Equation (12.88), with $\rho_\infty = 0.77$, $\eta = 0.1$, and $n = 10$

	0	1	2	3	4	5	6	7	8	9
0	1.000	0.950	0.910	0.878	0.852	0.831	0.814	0.798	0.784	0.770
1	0.950	1.000	0.958	0.924	0.897	0.875	0.856	0.840	0.825	0.811
2	0.910	0.958	1.000	0.965	0.936	0.913	0.894	0.877	0.861	0.846
3	0.878	0.924	0.965	1.000	0.971	0.947	0.926	0.909	0.893	0.877
4	0.852	0.897	0.936	0.971	1.000	0.975	0.954	0.936	0.920	0.903
5	0.831	0.875	0.913	0.947	0.975	1.000	0.979	0.960	0.943	0.926
6	0.814	0.856	0.894	0.926	0.954	0.979	1.000	0.981	0.964	0.947
7	0.798	0.840	0.877	0.909	0.936	0.960	0.981	1.000	0.982	0.965
8	0.784	0.825	0.861	0.893	0.920	0.943	0.964	0.982	1.000	0.982
9	0.770	0.811	0.846	0.877	0.903	0.926	0.947	0.965	0.982	1.000

expressed as follows:

$$\rho = AEA' \tag{12.89}$$

where A is an orthogonal $n \times n$ matrix such that $AA' = A'A = I_n$, the transpose of A is A', and I_n is an $n \times n$ identity matrix. The matrix E is a diagonal matrix, which contains the n positive eigenvalues of ρ. The matrix ρ can be expressed as follows:

$$\rho = A\sqrt{E}\sqrt{E}A' = BB' \tag{12.90}$$

where $B = A\sqrt{E}$ and $\sqrt{E}$ is a diagonal matrix with elements given as square roots of the elements of the diagonal matrix E.

The correlation matrix ρ of rank n can be approximated by a correlation matrix of a reduced rank m $(m < n)$ as follows:

$$\hat{\rho} = \hat{B}\hat{B}' \tag{12.91}$$

where $\hat{B}$ is an $n \times m$ matrix of rank m. This implicitly reduces the number of factors under the LFM from n to m. Using our notation, the rows of matrix $\hat{B}$ are indexed as $i = 0, 1, 2, \ldots, n-1$, and the columns of matrix $\hat{B}$ are indexed as $j = 0, 1, 2, \ldots, m-1$. The element $\hat{\rho}_{ij}$ of the matrix $\hat{\rho}$ approximates the correlation between the percentage changes in the forward rates $f(t, T_i, T_{i+1})$ and $f(t, T_j, T_{j+1})$ for $i, j = 0, 1, 2, \ldots, n-1$. Rebonato [1999a] suggests the following parametric form for the elements $\hat{b}_{ij}$ of the matrix $\hat{B}$, which guarantees that $\hat{\rho}$ satisfies the requirements of being a rank m correlation matrix:

$$\hat{b}_{i,0} = \cos\theta_{i,0}$$

$$\hat{b}_{i,j} = \cos\theta_{i,j} \prod_{k=0}^{j-1} \sin\theta_{i,k}, \quad \text{for } j = 1, 2, \ldots, m-2 \tag{12.92}$$

$$\hat{b}_{i,m-1} = \prod_{k=0}^{j-1} \sin\theta_{i,k}, \quad j = m-1$$

for $i = 0, 1, 2, \ldots, n-1$.

To understand the intuition regarding these trigonometric functions, consider the following two cases, in which the actual correlation matrix is approximated using rank 2 and rank 3 correlation matrices.

Case 1: Rank 2 Correlations To obtain a rank 2 correlation matrix, assume $m = 2$, such that $\hat{B}$ becomes an $n \times 2$ matrix with elements of the two columns given as follows:

$$\hat{b}_{i,0} = \cos\theta_{i,0} \quad \text{and} \quad \hat{b}_{i,1} = \sin\theta_{i,0} \tag{12.93}$$

for $i = 0, 1, 2, \ldots, n-1$. Using equation (12.91), the elements of the rank 2 correlation matrix $\hat{\rho}$ are given as follows:

$$\begin{aligned}\hat{\rho}_{ij} &= \hat{b}_{i0}\hat{b}_{j0} + \hat{b}_{i1}\hat{b}_{j1} \\ &= \cos\theta_{i,0}\cos\theta_{j,0} + \sin\theta_{i,0}\sin\theta_{j,0} \\ &= \cos(\theta_{i,0} - \theta_{j,0}) = \cos(\theta_{j,0} - \theta_{i,0}) \end{aligned} \tag{12.94}$$

for $i, j = 0, 1, 2, \ldots, n-1$. Hence, the correlation matrix requires estimating n parameters, given as $\theta_{i,0}$ for $i = 0, 1, 2, \ldots, n-1$.

Case 2: Rank 3 Correlations To obtain a rank 3 correlation matrix, assume $m = 3$, such that $\hat{B}$ becomes an $n \times 3$ matrix with elements of the three columns given as follows:

$$\hat{b}_{i,0} = \cos\theta_{i,0}, \quad \hat{b}_{i,1} = \cos\theta_{i,1}\sin\theta_{i,0}, \quad \text{and} \quad \hat{b}_{i,2} = \sin\theta_{i,0}\sin\theta_{i,1} \tag{12.95}$$

for $i = 0, 1, 2, \ldots, n-1$. Using equation (12.91), the elements of the rank 3 correlation matrix $\hat{\rho}$ are given as follows:

$$\begin{aligned}\hat{\rho}_{ij} =& \hat{b}_{i0}\hat{b}_{j0} + \hat{b}_{i1}\hat{b}_{j1} + \hat{b}_{i2}\hat{b}_{j2} \\ =& \cos\theta_{i,0}\cos\theta_{j,0} + \cos\theta_{i,1}\sin\theta_{i,0}\cos\theta_{j,1}\sin\theta_{j,0} \\ & + \sin\theta_{i,0}\sin\theta_{i,1}\sin\theta_{j,0}\sin\theta_{j,1} \\ =& \cos\theta_{i,0}\cos\theta_{j,0} + \sin\theta_{i,0}\sin\theta_{j,0}(\cos\theta_{i,1}\cos\theta_{j,1} + \sin\theta_{i,1}\sin\theta_{j,1}) \\ =& \cos\theta_{i,0}\cos\theta_{j,0} + \sin\theta_{i,0}\sin\theta_{j,0}\cos(\theta_{i,1} - \theta_{j,1}) \end{aligned} \tag{12.96}$$

for $i, j = 0, 1, 2, \ldots, n-1$. Hence, the correlation matrix requires estimating $2n$ parameters, given as $\theta_{i,0}$ and $\theta_{i,1}$ for $i = 0, 1, 2, \ldots, n-1$.

In general, it can be shown that a rank m correlation matrix allows $n(m-1)$ number of free parameters. For example, using 20 different forward rates gives 20 free parameters under a rank 2 correlation matrix and 40 free parameters under a rank 3 correlation matrix. Various approaches can be used to minimize the number of correlation parameters. For example, as suggested by Brigo [2002], a subparameterization can be given as follows:

$$\theta_{i,0} = k_0(i) \quad \text{and} \quad \theta_{i,1} = k_1(i) \tag{12.97}$$

where $k_0(i)$ and $k_1(i)$ can be defined as exponential functions of T_i (similar to the one given by equation (12.66)) requiring only three or four parameters.

Terminal Correlations

Since the Black implied volatilities given in equations (12.12) and (12.56) are really what matters for pricing caps and swaptions, the expressions $\int_0^{T_i} \sigma_i^2(u)du$ and $\int_0^{S_0} \sigma_i(u)\sigma_j(u)\rho_{ij}(t)du$ are the main determinants of the joint pricing of caps and swaptions. There are many approaches one could use to calibrate the volatilities $\sigma_i(t)$ and the correlations $\rho_{ij}(t)$ to the prices of caps and swaptions.

For example, one could obtain $\sigma_i(t)$ from the Black implied market volatilities of caplets using the three-step process as shown earlier in this section. Once volatilities have been obtained from cap prices, correlations can be obtained in the next stage by calibration to swaption prices. The correlations $\rho_{ij}(t)$ can be approximated by $\hat{\rho}_{ij}$ (see equations (12.91) and (12.92)) derived from a lower-rank correlation matrix. The calibration of $\hat{\rho}_{ij}$ to swaption prices would optimally select the parameters $\theta_{i,j}$ defined in equation (12.92). However, this approach generally yields unrealistically low correlations, which implies that the forward rate volatilities in the swaptions market are significantly lower than those in the cap market. Low correlations simply compensate for using higher volatilities from the cap market to allow a good fit to the swaption prices.

EXPLAINING THE SMILE: THE FIRST APPROACH

Beginning in the mid-1990s, a smile (or smirk) appeared in the pricing of caplets, resulting in a monotonically decreasing Black implied volatility as a function of the strike rate of the caplets. The smile in the interest rate derivative market didn't seem to be related to a sudden increase in risk aversion or "crashophobia," as it was in the equity options market.[9] Furthermore, unless the downward jumps in the interest rates had become more likely to occur after the mid-1990s or if the investors' risk aversion against a sudden drop in interest rates had increased significantly, the caplet smile didn't seem to be driven by jump-induced risk-aversion/distributional effects. A more likely explanation of the appearance of the smile was the realization among traders that the lognormal forward rate distribution did not capture the forward rate dynamics properly. The lognormal distribution implies a strong dependence of the forward rate volatility on its level. For example, under the lognormal distribution, a given forward rate is twice as volatile when it is at 6 percent versus when it is at 3 percent. Though interest rate volatilities do increase with the level of the rates, the increase is not so strong as to be *proportional* to their level. Hence, a more likely explanation of the appearance of the caplet smile beginning in the mid-1990s is that traders replaced the LFM with better models that correct the misspecification of this model. Of course, this view is not shared by all researchers. For example, Jarrow, Li, and Zhao [2007] use a model with unspanned stochastic volatility and jumps to explain the caplet smile.[10] Two models that resolve this type of misspecification of the LFM are:

1. Models that use a general constant-elasticity-of-variance (CEV) process for capturing the forward rate dynamics
2. Models with a displaced diffusion for the forward rate process

In the following section, we give analytical solutions to caplets under both extensions of the LFM. Before giving these solutions, we would like to make two related observations. First, as shown by Marris [1999], with suitable parameterizations, an almost perfect correspondence exists between the solutions of caplets using the CEV approach and the displaced-diffusion approach over a range of strikes. Since the displaced-diffusion approach is significantly easier to use analytically, this approach can be used as a numerical approximation of the CEV approach even if the trader believed the CEV approach to be true. Second, the two extensions mentioned in this section are not the only approaches to fit the caplet smile. As shown by Glasserman and Kou [2000], the caplet smile can be also fitted using a jump-diffusion model with time-dependent jump intensity and jump-size distribution parameters. However, the time-dependent jump approach of Glasserman and Kou introduces a highly time-inhomogeneous caplet smile, such that future caplet smiles can be markedly different from the current caplet smile.

The CEV Extension of the LFM

The CEV extension of the LFM by Andersen and Andreasen [2000] specifies the following zero-drift stochastic process for $f(t, T_i, T_{i+1})$ under the forward measure $\tilde{\mathcal{P}}^i$ defined with respect to the numeraire asset $P(t, T_{i+1})$:

$$df(t, T_i, T_{i+1}) = \sigma_i(t)f(t, T_i, T_{i+1})^\beta dZ_i(t), \quad 0 < \beta < 1 \qquad (12.98)$$

where $dZ_i(t)$ is a Wiener process under the forward measure $\tilde{\mathcal{P}}^i$ and $\sigma_i(t)$ measures the volatility of the forward rate process. The values of $\beta = 0$ and $\beta = 1$ correspond to the cases of Gaussian and lognormal forward rate dynamics, respectively. For the values of $0 < \beta < 0.5$, equation (12.98) has a unique solution if $f(t, T_i, T_{i+1}) = 0$ is assumed to be the absorbing barrier. The analytical solution of the probability density of $f(T, T_i, T_{i+1})$, conditional on $f(t, T_i, T_{i+1})$, is given as follows:[11]

$$p(x) = 2(1 - \beta)k^{1/(2-2\beta)}(uw^{1-4\beta})^{1/(4-4\beta)}e^{-(u+w)}I_{1/(2-2\beta)}(2\sqrt{uw}) \quad (12.99)$$

where

$$k = \frac{1}{2v_T^2(T-t)(1-\beta)^2}$$

$$u = k(f(t, T_i, T_{i+1}))^{2(1-\beta)}$$

$$w = kx^{2(1-\beta)}$$

I_q is the modified Bessel function of the first kind of order q

$$v_T = \sqrt{\frac{1}{T-t}\int_t^T \sigma_i^2(u)du}$$

The knowledge of the conditional probability density given in equation (12.99) is useful in pricing exotic options using Monte Carlo simulations. The analytical formula of a caplet can be obtained by using the following formula given in equation (12.11):

$$P_{Caplet_i}(t) = F \times \hat{U}_i \times P(t, T_{i+1}) \times E_t^i(max[L(T_i, T_{i+1}) - K_i, 0]) \quad (12.100)$$

where, by definition, $L(T_i, T_{i+1}) = f(T_i, T_i, T_{i+1})$. Using the conditional density given in equation (12.99), the expectation in equation (12.100) can be solved to give:

$$P_{Caplet_i}(t) = F \times \hat{U}_i \times P(t, T_{i+1})$$

$$\times \left\{ \begin{array}{l} f(t, T_i, T_{i+1})\left(1 - \chi^2\left(2K_i^{1-\beta}; \frac{1}{1-\beta} + 2, 2u\right)\right) \\ -K_i\chi^2\left(2u; \frac{1}{1-\beta}, 2kK_i^{1-\beta}\right) \end{array} \right\} \quad (12.101)$$

where $\chi^2(x; a, b)$ is the cumulative distribution of the noncentral chi-squared distribution with a degrees of freedom and a parameter of noncentrality equal to b computed at point x. The formula in equation (12.101) implies a monotonically decreasing Black implied volatility as a function of the strike rate of the caplets. The smile becomes steeper with decreasing values of β.

Hence, by appropriately choosing the parameter β, the CEV forward rate process can be calibrated to fit the caplet smile.

Recall that one of the appealing features of the LFM is that it allows a perfect fit with the at-the-money caplets using the three-step method outlined by Rebonato [2002]. Unfortunately, in the presence of a caplet smile, a perfect fit with the caplets of all maturities and all strikes cannot be obtained. Hence, one must choose the β value that minimizes the deviations of the model caplet prices from the actual caplet prices.

Displaced-Diffusion Extension of the LFM

As mentioned earlier, with suitable parameterizations, an almost perfect correspondence exists between the solutions of caplets using the CEV approach and the displaced-diffusion approach over a range of strikes. Hence, the displaced-diffusion model can be used as a numerical approximation to the caplet prices even when the trader believes the CEV approach to be true. Using the displaced-diffusion framework, the forward rates are defined as follows:

$$f(t, T_i, T_{i+1}) = \delta + Y_i(t) \tag{12.102}$$

where the stochastic process of the state variable $Y_i(t)$ is given as follows:

$$\frac{dY_i(t)}{Y_i(t)} = \sigma_{yi}(t)\, dZ_i(t) \tag{12.103}$$

Using Ito's lemma, the stochastic process of the forward rate is given as follows:

$$df(t, T_i, T_{i+1}) = \sigma_{yi}(t)\big(f(t, T_i, T_{i+1}) - \delta\big)\, dZ_i(t) \tag{12.104}$$

Taking the stochastic integral of equation (12.103) and then substituting equation (12.102), the forward rate at time T (such that $t \le T < T_i < T_{i+1}$) can be represented as follows:

$$f(T, T_i, T_{i+1}) = \delta + \big(f(t, T_i, T_{i+1}) - \delta\big)e^{-(1/2)\int_t^T \sigma_{yi}^2(v)\,dv + \int_t^T \sigma_{yi}(v)\,dZ_i(v)} \tag{12.105}$$

Hence, the forward rates follow a shifted lognormal distribution. To solve for caplet prices, note that substituting $f(T_i, T_i, T_{i+1}) = L(T_i, T_{i+1}) = \delta + Y_i(T_i)$ in the caplet valuation formula in equation (12.100) gives:

$$
\begin{aligned}
P_{Caplet_i}(t) &= F \times \hat{U}_i \times P(t, T_{i+1}) \times E_t^i(max[\delta + Y_i(T_i) - K_i, 0]) \\
&= F \times \hat{U}_i \times P(t, T_{i+1}) \times E_t^i(max[Y_i(T_i) - K_{yi}, 0])
\end{aligned}
\tag{12.106}
$$

where

$$K_{yi} = K_i - \delta \qquad (12.107)$$

Since $Y_i(T_i)$ is lognormally distributed, the expectation in equation (12.106) has the same form of solution as under the LFM and can be obtained by a simple inspection of equations (12.10) and (12.12). Hence, the caplet price is given as follows:

$$P_{Caplet_i}(t) = \text{Black}_{Caplet_i}\big(f(t, T_i, T_{i+1}) - \delta, K_i - \delta, T_i - t, \vartheta_{yi}\big) \qquad (12.108)$$

$$= F \times \hat{U}_i \times P(t, T_{i+1})\{(f(t, T_i, T_{i+1}) - \delta)\mathcal{N}(d_{1,i}) - (K_i - \delta)\mathcal{N}(d_{2,i})\}$$

where

$$d_{1,i} = \frac{\ln\big((f(t, T_i, T_{i+1}) - \delta)/(K_i - \delta)\big) + \vartheta_{yi}^2(T_i - t)/2}{\vartheta_{yi}\sqrt{T_i - t}}$$

$$d_{2,i} = \frac{\ln\big((f(t, T_i, T_{i+1}) - \delta)/(K_i - \delta)\big) - \vartheta_{yi}^2(T_i - t)/2}{\vartheta_{yi}\sqrt{T_i - t}}$$

and where ϑ_{yi} is defined as:

$$\vartheta_{yi} = \sqrt{\frac{1}{T_i - t}\int_t^{T_i} \sigma_{yi}^2(u)\, du} \qquad (12.109)$$

The caplet formula in equation (12.108) is identical to the corresponding formula under the LFM given in equation (12.10), except for the term δ, which allows for fitting the caplet smile. In general, negative values of δ allow fitting a monotonically decreasing caplet smile.

A potential criticism of the displaced-diffusion model is that negative values of δ allow for the occurrence of negative forward rates. However, for the range of values of δ required for fitting the caplet smile, the probability of occurrence of negative rates is extremely low. Hence, for most practical purposes, the displaced-diffusion model works well in capturing the caplet smile. Further, since a direct one-to-one correspondence exists between the displaced-diffusion model and the CEV extension of the LFM (see Marris [1999]), the formula in equation (12.108) can be also used as an analytical approximation of the latter model, with a suitable parameterization.

In order to allow maximum generality that allows pricing of swaptions also, we model the forward rates using a single numeraire under the displaced-diffusion model. Similar to the single numeraire-based LFM (see equations (12.13) and (12.21)), the joint dynamics of forward rates under the displaced-diffusion model are given by transforming equations (12.103) and (12.104) using a change of measure, as follows:

$$\frac{dY_i(t)}{Y_i(t)} = \mu_{yi}^k(t)\, dt + \sigma_{yi}(t) dZ_i^k(t) \tag{12.110}$$

and

$$df(t, T_i, T_{i+1}) = \big(f(t, T_i, T_{i+1}) - \delta\big)\big(\mu_{yi}^k(t)\, dt + \sigma_{yi}(t) dZ_i^k(t)\big) \tag{12.111}$$

where

$$\mu_i^k(t) = \sigma_{yi}(t) \sum_{j=k+1}^{i} \frac{\sigma_{yj}(t)\rho_{ij}\big(f(t, T_j, T_{j+1}) - \delta\big)\hat{U}_j}{(1 + f(t, T_j, T_{j+1})\hat{U}_j)}, \quad \text{for } i > k$$

$$\mu_i^k(t) = -\sigma_{yi}(t) \sum_{j=i+1}^{k} \frac{\sigma_{yj}(t)\rho_{ij}\big(f(t, T_j, T_{j+1}) - \delta\big)\hat{U}_j}{(1 + f(t, T_j, T_{j+1})\hat{U}_j)}, \quad \text{for } i < k \tag{12.112}$$

$$\mu_i^k(t) = \mu_i^i(t) = 0, \quad \text{for } i = k$$

Since individual caplets comprising the cap can be priced using different numeraires, the lognormal assumption can be maintained for different forward rates (see equations (12.103) and (12.104)) for pricing caps. However, swaptions and coupon bond options represent *options on portfolios* (and not portfolios of options, like caps), and hence, the joint stochastic evolution of different forward rates must be modeled for pricing these instruments. Modeling the joint evolution of forward rates requires that all forward rate processes be measured under a single forward measure; these are given by equations (12.111) and (12.112), respectively.

The price of a swaption under the displaced diffusion model can be computed numerically by the freezing drift technique introduced earlier. The time 0 price of a payer swaption can be given as a generalization of equation (12.37), as follows:

$$P_{PayerSwaption}(0) = \text{Black}_{PayerSwaption}\big(f^s(0) - \delta, K - \delta, S_0, \vartheta_{ys}\big)$$

$$\tag{12.113}$$

$$= A(0) \times F \times \{(f^s(0) - \delta)\mathcal{N}(d_1) - (K - \delta)\mathcal{N}(d_2)\}$$

where

$$d_1 = \frac{\ln\left((f^s(0) - \delta)/(K - \delta)\right) + \vartheta_{ys}^2 S_0/2}{\vartheta_{ys}\sqrt{S_0}}$$

$$d_2 = \frac{\ln\left((f^s(0) - \delta)/(K - \delta)\right) - \vartheta_{ys}^2 S_0/2}{\vartheta_{ys}\sqrt{S_0}}$$

and

$$\vartheta_{ys} = \sqrt{\left(\sum_{i=0}^{n-1}\sum_{j=0}^{n-1} x_i(0)x_j(0)\rho_{ij} \int_0^{S_0} \sigma_{yi}(u)\sigma_{yj}(u)\,du\right)/S_0} \quad (12.114)$$

where $x_i(0)$ is given as a generalization of its earlier definition in equation (12.51), as follows:

$$x_i(0) = \hat{w}_i(0) \times \left(\frac{f(0, T_i, T_{i+1}) - \delta}{f^s(0) - \delta}\right) \quad (12.115)$$

with $\hat{w}_i(0)$ defined by equation (12.47). Similarly, the time 0 price of a receiver swaption is given as follows:

$$P_{ReceiverSwaption}(0) = A(0) \times F \times \{(K - \delta)\mathcal{N}(-d_2) - (f^s(0) - \delta)\mathcal{N}(-d_1)\}$$

$$(12.116)$$

UNSPANNED STOCHASTIC VOLATILITY JUMP MODELS

Both the CEV and displaced-diffusion extensions of the LFM can only allow monotonically decreasing smiles. However, since 1998, the caplet smile has taken more complex shapes, decreasing first for a wide range of strikes and then increasing over a short range of strikes, resembling the "hockey-stick shape." Collin-Dufresne and Goldstein (CDG) [2002] and Heidari and Wu [2003] find that the risk factors driving the caps and swaptions markets are not spanned by the risk factors that explain the LIBOR or swap rates. CDG call this feature *unspanned stochastic volatility* (USV). Unlike the traditional affine models, which require strong parameter restrictions to generate USV, the forward rate models, such as the HJM models or the LFM, can easily allow USV. A number of USV models have been proposed in the literature to explain the hockey-stick shaped smile, including Andersen and Brotherton-Ratcliffe [2001], Wu and Zhang [2002], Piterbarg [2003], Hagan, Kumar, Lesniewski, and Woodward [2002], and Joshi and Rebonato [2003]. The use of CEV processes and/or the displaced-diffusion processes explains the decreasing portion of the smile, and the use of USV explains the increasing portion of the smile.

Jarrow, Li, and Zhao (JLZ) [2007] use an alternative approach for explaining the hockey-stick shaped smile that does not use either the CEV processes or the displaced-diffusion processes. They note that a *symmetric* smile can be produced by a USV extension of the LFM. In order to generate the asymmetric hockey-stick shaped smile, JLZ add a Poisson component that generates significantly negative jumps in the forward rates. In the following section, we summarize the two different approaches of Joshi and Rebonato [2003] and JLZ for capturing the asymmetric smile in the cap market.

Joshi and Rebonato [2003] Model

The state variable processes, forward rate processes, and the drift restrictions under the displaced-diffusion USV model of Joshi and Rebonato [2003] are identical to those given in equations (12.110), (12.111), and (12.112), respectively, except that the volatility functions $\sigma_{yi}(t)$ are stochastic and are specified as follows:

$$\sigma_{yi}(t) = h(T_i - t) = [a(t) + b(t)(T_i - t)] \exp[-c(t)(T_i - t)] + d(t) \quad (12.117)$$

where the stochastic processes of $a(t)$, $b(t)$, $c(t)$, and $d(t)$ are given as:

$$
\begin{aligned}
da(t) &= \alpha_a(m_a - a(t))\,dt + \sigma_a dZ_a(t) \\
db(t) &= \alpha_b(m_b - b(t))\,dt + \sigma_b dZ_b(t) \\
d\ln c(t) &= \alpha_c(m_c - \ln c(t))\,dt + \sigma_c dZ_c(t) \\
d\ln d(t) &= \alpha_d(m_d - \ln d(t))\,dt + \sigma_d dZ_d(t)
\end{aligned}
\quad (12.118)
$$

The Wiener processes in equation (12.118) are assumed to be independent of each other and independent of the Wiener processes of the forward rates given in equation (12.111).

The price of a caplet under the Joshi and Rebonato model can be computed numerically using the Hull and White [1987] method. Given the independence between the forward rates and their volatility processes, the caplet price can be given as follows:

$$P_{Caplet_i}(t) = \int_0^\infty \text{Black}_{Caplet_i}\big(f(t, T_i, T_{i+1}) - \delta, K_i - \delta, T_i - t, v\big)p_i(v)\,dv$$

$$(12.119)$$

where the Black caplet price in the integrand in equation (12.119), is defined in equation (12.108) and where $p_i(v)$ is the density of the root mean square volatility:

$$\sqrt{\frac{1}{T_i - t} \int_t^{T_i} \sigma_{yi}^2(u)\, du}$$
(12.120)

with $\sigma_{yi}(t)$ defined in equation (12.117). Since $\sigma_{yi}(t)$ is stochastic, the density $p_i(v)$ must be simulated using the Monte Carlo method.

The price of a swaption under the Joshi and Rebonato model can be computed numerically by the freezing drift technique introduced earlier and by applying the Hull and White [1987] method. Given the independence between the forward rates and their volatility processes, the time 0 price of a payer swaption can be given as follows:

$$P_{PayerSwaption}(0) = \int_0^\infty \text{Black}_{PayerSwaption}\big(f^s(0) - \delta, K - \delta, S_0, v\big) p(v)\, dv$$
(12.121)

where the Black payer swaption price in the integrand in equation (12.121) is defined in equation (12.113) $p(v)$ is the density of the root mean square volatility:

$$\sqrt{\left(\sum_{i=0}^{n-1} \sum_{j=0}^{n-1} x_i(0) x_j(0) \rho_{ij} \int_0^{S_0} \sigma_{yi}(u) \sigma_{yj}(u)\, du \right) \Big/ S_0}$$
(12.122)

and $x_i(0)$ is defined in equation (12.115). Since $\sigma_{yi}(t)$ is stochastic, the density $p(v)$ must be simulated using the Monte Carlo method. The time 0 price of a receiver swaption can be given in a similar manner.

Jarrow, Li, and Zhao [2007] Model

Jarrow, Li, and Zhao (JLZ) extend the LFM to allow both USV and jumps. Typical USV models can only generate symmetric-shaped smiles. Joshi and Rebonato [2003] generate an asymmetric smile by combining the USV feature with either a CEV process or a displaced-diffusion process for the LIBOR rates. JLZ use jumps instead of the CEV or displaced-diffusion processes for explaining the asymmetric smile.

JLZ assume that instantaneous change in the forward rate $f(t, T_i, T_{i+1})$ is given by the following stochastic process under the forward measure associated with the numeraire asset $P(t, T_{i+1})$:

$$\frac{df(t, T_i, T_{i+1})}{f(t, T_i, T_{i+1})} = -\beta^i \lambda \, dt + \sum_{m=1}^{M} \sigma_m(T_i - t)\sqrt{v_m(t)}dZ_m^i(t) + (e^{J^i} - 1)\, dN(\lambda)$$

$$(12.123)$$

for all $i = 0, 1, 2, \ldots, n - 1$. The forward rate process follows a mixed jump-diffusion process with M *independent* Wiener processes and one Poisson process distributed independently of the Wiener processes. The diffusion volatility of the mth factor ($m = 1, 2, \ldots, M$) has a deterministic time-dependent component $\sigma_m(T_i - t)$, which is a piecewise constant function defined as follows:

$$\sigma_m(T_i - t) = \sigma_{mk}, \text{ such that } T_j \leq t < T_{j+1}$$

$$\text{for all } k = i - j - 1, \ j = -1, 0, 1, 2, \ldots, i - 1, \text{ and } i = 0, 1, 2, \ldots, n - 1$$

$$(12.124)$$

where the time line is defined with points $0 = T_{-1}, T_0, T_1, \ldots, T_{n-1}, T_n$. Hence, the volatility function $\sigma_m(T_i - t)$ is specified as a piecewise constant function with $i + 1$ number of constants given as $\sigma_{m0}, \sigma_{m1}, \sigma_{m2}, \ldots, \sigma_{mi}$. JLZ show how the M deterministic volatility functions $\sigma_m(T_i - t)$ (for $m = 1, 2, \ldots, M$) can be estimated using the M eigenvectors associated with the historical covariance matrix of changes in *constant-maturity* discrete forward rates. To show this, JLZ assume that the instantaneous covariance matrix of the changes in forward LIBOR rates shares the same eigenvectors as the historical covariance matrix.

JLZ assume that the stochastic component $v_m(t)$ (for $m = 1, 2, \ldots, M$) of the diffusion volatilities can be represented as the first M eigenvalues associated with the instantaneous covariance matrix of discrete forward LIBOR rates. The stochastic processes of $v_m(t)$ under the forward measure associated with the numeraire asset $P(t, T_{i+1})$ are given as follows:

$$dv_m(t) = \alpha_m^i(\theta_m^i - v_m(t))\, dt + \xi_m\sqrt{v_m(t)}dW_m^i(t) \qquad (12.125)$$

for all $m = 1, 2, \ldots, M$. The stochastic volatilities follow square-root processes similar to the process of the short rate under the CIR [1985] model. The M Wiener processes in equation (12.125) are independent of each other and independent of the Wiener processes and the Poisson process related to the forward rates given in equation (12.123).

The variable J^i is related to the jump size, which is normally distributed with mean μ_J^i and variance σ_J^2 under the forward measure. The variable $N(\lambda)$ is a Poisson process with intensity λ, such that over an infinitesimally small interval dt, the change $dN(\lambda)$ equals 1 with probability λdt and zero with probability $(1 - \lambda dt)$. The parameter β^i is defined as follows:

$$\beta^i = E^i(e^{J^i} - 1) = \exp\left(\mu^i_J + \frac{1}{2}\sigma^2_J\right) - 1 \qquad (12.126)$$

where the expectation is taken under the forward measure associated with the numeraire asset $P(t, T_{i+1})$.

By construction, the expectation of the change in forward rate in equation (12.123) equals zero, since the forward rate $f(t, T_i, T_{i+1})$ is a martingale under the forward measure. The parameters α^i_m and θ^i_m related to USV and the parameter μ^i_J related to jumps are different from the corresponding parameters under the physical measure, due to the existence of market prices of volatility risk and jump risk, respectively. Though estimates of physical parameters are not required to calibrate the JLZ model to the caps data, the specification of the term structure of risk premiums related to USV and jumps is required for different forward measures associated with numeraire assets of different maturities (i.e., $P(t, T_{i+1})$ for $i = 0, 1, 2, \ldots, n - 1$).

By assuming the one-year forward LIBOR rate as the benchmark rate, JLZ assume the one-year-based USV and jump parameters as the reference parameters given as follows:

$$\alpha^1_m = \alpha_m$$
$$\theta^1_m = \theta_m \qquad (12.127)$$
$$\mu^1_J = \mu_J$$

The USV and jump parameters of other forward rates under their respective forward measures are given as follows:

$$\alpha^i_m = \alpha_m - \xi_m c_{mv}(T_i - 1)$$
$$\theta^i_m = \frac{\alpha_m \theta_m}{\alpha^i_m} \qquad (12.128)$$
$$\mu^i_J = \mu_J + c_J(T_i - 1)$$

for $m = 1, 2, \ldots, M$ and $i = 0, 1, \ldots, n - 1$. The parameters $c_{1v}, c_{2v}, \ldots, c_{Mv}$ and c_J allow the JLZ model to capture the term structure of risk premiums related to USV and jumps, respectively. The term structure of risk premiums is assumed to be linearly related to maturity.

Due to its affine structure, the JLZ model can be used to price options on zero-coupon bonds and caplets using the Fourier inversion method introduced in Chapter 5. This method solves the probabilities of the option ending in the money under the appropriate forward measures and then calculates the option price using these probabilities. JLZ use the Levy inversion formula, based upon the results in Duffie, Pan, and Singleton (DPS) [2000]. This approach is outlined in the following two steps:

Step 1   Let Y_t be a vector given as $[\ln f(t, T_i, T_{i+1}), v_1(t), v_2(t), \ldots, v_M(t)]$. Consider the following expectation under the forward measure associated with the numeraire $P(t, T_{i+1})$:

$$E_t^i\big(\exp[u\ln(f(T_i, T_i, T_{i+1}))]\big) = \psi(u, Y_t, t, T_i) \tag{12.129}$$

Following Duffie, Pan, and Singleton [2000], define:

$$G_{j,k}^i(y; Y_t, T_i) = E_t^i\big(\exp[j\ln f(T_i, T_i, T_{i+1})]1_{\{k\ln(f(T_i,T_i,T_{i+1}))\leq y\}}\big) \tag{12.130}$$

and its Fourier transform

$$
\begin{aligned}
H_{j,k}^i(v; Y_t, T_i) &= E_t^i\big(\exp[(j + ivk)\ln f(T_i, T_i, T_{i+1})]\big) \\
&= \psi(j + ivk, Y_t, t, T_i)
\end{aligned}
\tag{12.131}
$$

where $i = \sqrt{-1}$.

Using the Levy's inversion formula:

$$G_{j,k}^i(y; Y_t, T_i) = \frac{\psi(j, Y_t, t, T_i)}{2} - \frac{1}{\pi}\int_0^\infty \frac{\text{Im}[\psi(j + ivk, Y_t, t, T_i)\exp(-ivy)]}{v}\, dv \tag{12.132}$$

The time 0 price of a caplet is defined in equation (12.11) as follows:

$$P_{Caplet_i}(0) = F \times \hat{U}_i \times P(0, T_{i+1}) \times E_0^i\big(max[L(T_i, T_{i+1}) - K_i, 0]\big) \tag{12.133}$$

where $L(T_i, T_{i+1}) = f(T_i, T_i, T_{i+1})$. The expectation in equation (12.133) can be given using the Levy inversion formula as follows:

$$
\begin{aligned}
E_0^i\big(max[L(T_i, T_{i+1}) - K_i, 0]\big) &= G_{1,-1}^i(-\ln K_i; Y_0, T_i) \\
&\quad - K_i G_{0,-1}^i(-\ln K_i; Y_0, T_i)
\end{aligned}
\tag{12.134}
$$

Step 2   Computing the expectation in equation (12.134) requires solving $\psi(u, Y_t, t, T_i)$ in order to apply the Levy inversion formula (see equation (12.132)) to obtain $G_{1,-1}^i(.)$ and $G_{0,-1}^i(.)$. Since $f(t, T_i, T_{i+1})$ follows a Markovian process, the expectation in equation (12.129) can be represented as a function of the parameter u, the state vector Y_t, t, and T_i. Assume the following solution form for this expectation:

$$\psi(u, Y_t, t, T_i) = \exp\left(A^i(\tau_i) + u\ln(f(t, T_i, T_{i+1})) + \sum_{m=1}^{M} B_m^i(\tau_i)v_m(t)\right)$$

(12.135)

where $\tau_i = T_i - t$. Using the law of iterated expectation, the expectation of the differential of $\psi(u, Y_t, t, T_i)$ equals zero, or:

$$E_t^i(d\psi(u, Y_t, t, T_i)) = E_t^i\left(E_{t+dt}^i(\exp[u\ln(f(T_i, T_i, T_{i+1}))])\right.$$
$$\left. - E_t^i(\exp[u\ln(f(T_i, T_i, T_{i+1}))])\right) = 0$$

(12.136)

By applying Ito's lemma and then using $E_t^i(d\psi(u, Y_t, t, T_i)) = 0$ gives the partial differential equation (PDE) for $\psi(u, Y_t, t, T_i)$. Taking the appropriate partial derivatives using equation (12.135), substituting these in the PDE of $\psi(u, Y_t, t, T_i)$, and using a separation of variables gives the following $M+1$ ordinary differential equations (ODEs):

$$\frac{\partial B_m^i(\tau_i)}{\partial \tau_i} = -\alpha_m^i B_m^i(\tau_i) + \frac{1}{2}(B_m^i(\tau_i))^2\xi_m^2 + \frac{1}{2}(u^2 - u)\sigma_m(\tau_i)$$

(12.137)

for $m = 1, 2, \ldots, M$, and

$$\frac{\partial A^i(\tau_i)}{\partial \tau_i} = \sum_{m=1}^{M} \alpha_m^i \theta_m^i B_m^i(\tau_i) + \lambda_J[\phi(u) - \phi(1)u]$$

(12.138)

where

$$\phi(x) = \exp\left(\mu_j^i x + \frac{1}{2}\sigma_j^2 x^2\right) - 1$$

(12.139)

The solution to the M Riccati equations in equation (12.137) are not straightforward because the functions $\sigma_m(\tau_i) = \sigma_m(T_i - t)$ are piecewise constants, defined in equation (12.124). Let the time line until T_i be given as $0 = T_{-1}, T_0, T_1, \ldots, T_i$. The time 0 solution of $B_m^i(T_i)$ (which is alternatively expressed as $B_m^i(T_i - T_{-1})$) is obtained iteratively, as follows:

$$B_m^i(s_{k+1}) = b_k - \frac{(b_k + d_k)(b_k - B_m^i(s_k))}{(d_k + B_m^i(s_k))\exp(-q_k\delta_k) + (b_k - B_m^i(s_k))}$$

(12.140)

where, for $k = 0, 1, 2, \ldots, i$,

$$s_k = T_i - T_{i-k} \tag{12.141}$$

$$\delta_k = s_{k+1} - s_k = T_{i-k} - T_{i-(k+1)} \tag{12.142}$$

and where the parameters b_k, d_k, p_k, and q_k are defined as follows:

$$b_k = \frac{p_k}{q_k - \alpha_m^i}, \quad d_k = \frac{p_k}{q_k + \alpha_m^i}, \quad p_k = (u - u^2)\sigma_{mk}^2 \tag{12.143}$$

and

$$q_k = \sqrt{(\alpha_m^i)^2 + p_k \xi_m^2} \tag{12.144}$$

The time 0 solution of $A^i(T_i)$ (which is alternatively expressed as $A^i(T_i - T_{-1})$) is also obtained iteratively as follows:

$$A^i(s_{k+1}) = A^i(s_k) + \lambda_J \delta_k [\phi(u) - \phi(1)u]$$

$$- \sum_{m=1}^{M} \left(\alpha_m^i \theta_m^i \left[d_k \delta_k + \frac{2}{\xi_m^2} \ln \left(\frac{(d_k + B_m^i(s_k)) \exp(-q_k \delta_k)}{+(b_k - B_m^i(s_k))} \right) \right] \right) \tag{12.145}$$

The solutions in equations (12.140) and (12.145) are obtained iteratively by starting at $k = 0$, with the boundary conditions $A^i(s_0) = A^i(0) = 0$ and $B_m^i(s_0) = B_m^i(0) = 0$ and by then solving them with successively higher values of $k = 1, 2, \ldots, i$ to get $B_m^i(T_i)$ and $A^i(T_i)$, respectively.

An Extension of the JLZ Model

A potential limitation of the JLZ model is that the term structure of risk premiums related to volatility and jump risks are *time-inhomogeneous*, leading to time-inhomogeneous volatilities, which makes this model a *triple-plus* model using the classification scheme in this book. This can be seen from the definition of the two USV parameters, α_m^i and θ_m^i, and the jump parameter, μ_j^i, given in equation (12.128). These parameters are functions of the maturity date, and not the time to maturity of the forward rate $f(t, T_i, T_{i+1})$. This introduces time-inhomogeneity of volatilities in the JLZ model.

Nawalkha, Beliaeva, and Soto (NBS) [2007b] extend the JLZ model by allowing the USV and jump parameters to be piecewise constant functions of the time to maturity of the forward rate under the respective forward measure. Using piecewise constant functions allows analytical solutions for the Riccati equations associated with the Fourier transform of the forward rate, and yet allows a time-homogeneous specification of the risk premiums consistent with time-homogeneous volatilities.

To see this, recall that the time line until T_i is given as $0 = T_{-1}$, T_0, $T_1, \ldots, T_i$. NBS redefine the USV and jump parameters given in equation (12.128) as follows:

For all t, such that $T_j \leq t < T_{j+1}$:

$$\alpha_{m,k} = \alpha_m - \xi_m c_{m\upsilon}(T_k - 1)$$

$$\theta_{m,k} = \frac{\alpha_m \theta_m}{\alpha_{m,k}} \qquad\qquad (12.146)$$

$$\mu_{Jk} = \mu_J + c_J(T_k - 1)$$

for all $k = i - j - 1$, $j = -1, 0, 1, 2, \ldots, i - 1$, and $i = 0, 1, 2, \ldots, n - 1$ Substituting $\alpha_m^i = \alpha_{m,k}$, $\theta_m^i = \theta_{m,k}$, and $\mu_J^i = \mu_{Jk}$ in equations (12.143), (12.144), and (12.145) transforms the solution under the JLZ model to the solution under the NBS extension, which gives a *double-plus* version of the JLZ model consistent with time-homogeneous volatilities. Other steps for obtaining the analytical solutions of caps remain the same under both models.

Empirical Performance of the JLZ [2007] Model

JLZ study the relative pricing of interest rate caps with different strikes, using daily cap prices from August 1, 2000, until September 23, 2003. Unlike previous studies that primarily focused on at-the-money (ATM) caps, JLZ study cap prices with different strikes and document volatility smiles in the cap market. In order to use nonoverlapping information, JLZ use *difference caps*, which are defined as the differences between the prices of caps with the same strike but adjacent maturities. JLZ examine and compare the performance of six models: USV1, USV2, and USV3 (defined as the unspanned stochastic volatility (USV) models with one, two, and three principle components that drive the forward rate curve) and USVJ1, USVJ2, and USVJ3 (defined as unspanned stochastic volatility jump (USVJ) models that allow jumps in LIBOR rates in each of the corresponding USV models). Both the USV models and the USVJ models are consistent with *unspanned stochastic volatility*, since only option prices, and not the zero-coupon bond prices, are spanned by the stochastic volatility under the JLZ framework.[12]

The models estimation is based on three principal components extracted from historical LIBOR forward rates between June 1997 and July 2000. The first principal component is interpreted as the "level" factor—it represents a parallel shift of the forward rate curve. The second principal component is interpreted as the "slope" as it twists the forward rate curve by moving the short end of the curve in opposite directions from the long end. The third principal component is interpreted as the "curvature" and it increases the curvature of the curve by moving the short and the long ends of the curve in one direction and the middle part of the curve in another direction. The first factor explains 77.78 percent of the variation of LIBOR rates up to ten years, the second factor explains 14.35 percent of the variation, and the third factor explains 7.85 percent of the variation.

Table 12.4 lists parameter estimates for the USV models. The most volatile USV is associated with the level factor, followed by the curvature factor and then by the slope factor. This can be seen from the fact that the long-run mean and volatility of volatility coefficients of the "level" factor are much larger compared to the other two factors. The table also reports significantly negative volatility risk-premium estimates for each of the three models. This suggests that for LIBOR rates with longer maturity, the stochastic volatility factors under the forward measure are less volatile, with low long-run mean and fast speed of mean reversion.

Table 12.5 reports average pricing errors of difference caps with different moneyness and maturities for the three USV models. The USV1 model tends to underprice the short-term difference caps and overprice the long-term ATM difference caps. It also tends to underprice the in-the-money (ITM) differences caps and overprice the out-of-the-money (OTM) difference caps. This means that the USV1 model does not generate enough skewness in the implied volatilities to be consistent with the data. The USV2 model has some improvement over the USV1 model for the short-term ATM difference caps and the mid term slightly OTM difference caps. However, the USV2 model performance gets worse for the deepest ITM difference caps. The USV3 model shows improvement over both the USV1 and the USV2 models for pricing most long-term ITM, mid-term OTM, and short-term ATM difference caps; but it has larger average pricing errors for the mid-term ITM difference caps. The underpricing of the ITM difference caps and the overpricing of the OTM difference caps is still significant even under the USV3 model.

Overall, the USV models with more factors tend to perform better than the models with fewer factors. However, even the most sophisticated USV

TABLE 12.4 Parameter Estimates of Unspanned Stochastic Volatility Models

This table reports parameter estimates of the one-, two-, and three-factor unspanned stochastic volatility models. The estimates are based on the first stage generalized method of moments estimates with an identity weighting matrix. The objective functions are the rescaled objective function of the first GMM and equal to the root mean squared error of each model.

Parameter	USV1		USV2		USV3	
	Estimate	Std. Error	Estimate	Std. Error	Estimate	Std. Error
α_1	0.0179	0.0144	0.0091	0.0111	0.0067	0.0148
α_2			0.1387	0.0050	0.0052	0.0022
α_3					0.0072	0.0104
θ_1	1.3727	1.1077	1.7100	2.0704	2.1448	4.7567
θ_2			0.0097	0.0006	0.0344	0.0142
θ_3					0.1305	0.1895
xi_1	1.0803	0.0105	0.8992	0.0068	0.8489	0.0098
xi_2			0.0285	0.0050	0.0117	0.0065
xi_3					0.1365	0.0059
c_{1v}	−0.0022	0.0000	−0.0031	0.0000	−0.0015	0.0000
c_{2v}			−0.0057	0.0010	−0.0007	0.0001
c_{3v}					−0.0095	0.0003
Objective function	0.0834		0.0758		0.0692	

TABLE 12.5 Average Percentage Pricing Errors of Unspanned Stochastic Volatility Models

This table reports average pricing errors of difference caps with different moneyness and maturity of three unspanned stochastic volatility models. Average percentage pricing errors are defined as the difference between market price and model price divided by market price.

Panel A. Average percentage pricing errors of USV1

Moneyness	1.5yr	2yr	2.5yr	3yr	3.5yr	4yr	4.5yr	5yr	6yr	7yr	8yr	9yr	10yr
0.7	—	—	—	—	0.034	0.0258	0.0122	0.0339	0.0361	0.0503	0.0344	0.0297	0.0402
0.8	—	—	0.0434	0.0412	0.0323	0.018	0.0106	0.0332	0.0322	0.0468	0.0299	0.0244	0.0325
0.9	—	0.1092	0.0534	0.0433	0.0315	0.01	0.0003	0.0208	0.0186	0.0348	0.0101	0.0062	0.0158
1.0	0.0293	0.1217	0.0575	0.0378	0.0227	−0.0081	−0.0259	−0.0073	−0.0079	0.0088	−0.0114	−0.0192	−0.0062
1.1	−0.1187	0.0604	−0.0029	−0.0229	−0.034	−0.0712	−0.0815	−0.0562	—	—	—	—	—

Panel B. Average percentage pricing errors of USV2

Moneyness	1.5yr	2yr	2.5yr	3yr	3.5yr	4yr	4.5yr	5yr	6yr	7yr	8yr	9yr	10yr
0.7	—	—	—	—	0.0482	0.0425	0.0304	0.0524	0.0544	0.0663	0.0456	0.0304	0.0378
0.8	—	—	0.0509	0.051	0.0443	0.032	0.0258	0.0486	0.0472	0.0586	0.0344	0.0138	0.0202
0.9	—	0.1059	0.0498	0.0421	0.0333	0.0145	0.0069	0.0284	0.0265	0.0392	0.0054	−0.0184	−0.008
1.0	−0.0002	0.0985	0.0369	0.0231	0.0134	−0.0123	−0.0261	−0.005	−0.0042	0.008	−0.024	−0.0572	−0.0403
1.1	−0.1056	0.0584	−0.0085	−0.026	−0.0326	−0.0653	−0.0721	−0.0454	—	—	—	—	—

Panel C. Average percentage pricing errors of USV3

Moneyness	1.5yr	2yr	2.5yr	3yr	3.5yr	4yr	4.5yr	5yr	6yr	7yr	8yr	9yr	10yr
0.7	—	—	—	—	0.0489	0.0437	0.0308	0.0494	0.0431	0.0466	0.031	0.03	0.028
0.8	—	—	0.044	0.0476	0.0462	0.0378	0.0322	0.0506	0.0367	0.0365	0.0226	0.0249	0.0139
0.9	—	0.0917	0.0367	0.0379	0.0398	0.0288	0.0226	0.0377	0.0178	0.0145	−0.0026	0.0068	−0.0109
1.0	−0.0126	0.0782	0.0198	0.0194	0.0252	0.0105	−0.0012	0.011	−0.0129	−0.0221	−0.0299	−0.0192	−0.0432
1.1	−0.1184	0.0314	−0.0323	−0.0336	−0.0212	−0.0397	−0.0438	−0.0292	—	—	—	—	—

model fails to capture the volatility smile in the caps market completely. The problem with the USV models is that they can only generate a symmetric volatility smile, whereas the smile or skew observed in the actual caps data is asymmetric. The smile in the caps markets is very similar to the pattern of the smile observed in index options markets—the ITM calls tend to be overpriced and the OTM calls tend to be underpriced relative to the Black model. The smile in the caps markets could be due to a market expectation of declining LIBOR rates. To capture the smile effect, JLZ extend their three USV models with jumps.

Table 12.6 shows parameter estimates for one-, two- and three-factor USVJ models. The three stochastic volatility factors of the USVJ models resemble the corresponding factors of the USV models. The most volatile factor is the level factor followed by the curvature factor and then the slope factor. Compared to the USV models, the USVJ models tend to be less volatile. This follows from the observation that compared to the USV models, the USVJ models have faster mean reversion, lower long-run mean, and smaller volatility of volatility. Estimates of the volatility risk premium are negative, which is indicative of the fact that under the forward measure, the volatility of LIBOR rates with longer maturities have a lower long-run mean and a faster speed of mean reversion. JLZ also find that the volatility of the level factor steadily increases over the sample period, whereas the volatility of the other two factors is relatively stable.

JLZ find significant evidence of large negative jumps in the LIBOR rates under the forward measure, which implies that the market expects significant decline in the LIBOR rates over the sample period. Compared to the estimates from index options reported by Pan [2002], JLZ find lower estimates of the jump intensity and much higher estimates of the jump size. However, JLZ do not report any negative moves in the LIBOR rates under the physical measure. This discrepancy in jump sizes under the physical measure and the forward measure is similar to the one observed in index options markets (e.g., Pan [2002]) and could be explained by a large jump risk premium.

Table 12.7 reports the average pricing errors for the three USVJ models. In general, the USVJ models do a better job at capturing the volatility smile than the USV models do. For example, although the USVJ1 still underprices the short-term and overprices the long-term ATM difference caps, the degree of mispricing is much smaller compared to that of the USV1 model. The same is true for the degree of mispricing observed for the deeper ITM caps, especially with longer maturities. Therefore, the addition of

TABLE 12.6 Parameter Estimates of Unspanned Stochastic Volatility Jump Models

This table reports parameter estimates of the one-, two-, and three-factor unspanned stochastic volatility jumps models. The estimates are based on the first stage generalized method of moments estimates with an identity weighting matrix. The objective functions are the rescaled objective function of the first GMM and are equal to the root mean squared error of each model.

Parameter	USVJ1		USVJ2		USVJ3	
	Estimate	Std. Error	Estimate	Std. Error	Estimate	Std. Error
α_1	0.1377	0.0085	0.0062	0.0057	0.0069	0.0079
α_2			0.0050	0.0001	0.0032	0.0000
α_3					0.0049	0.0073
θ_1	0.1312	0.0084	0.7929	0.7369	0.9626	1.1126
θ_2			0.3410	0.0030	0.2051	0.0021
θ_3					0.2628	0.3973
ξ_1	0.8233	0.0057	0.7772	0.0036	0.6967	0.0049
ξ_2			0.0061	0.0104	0.0091	0.0042
ξ_3					0.1517	0.0035
c_{1v}	−0.0041	0.0000	−0.0049	0.0000	−0.0024	0.0000
c_{2v}			−0.0270	0.0464	−0.0007	0.0006
c_{3v}					−0.0103	0.0002
λ	0.0134	0.0001	0.0159	0.0001	0.0132	0.0001
μ_J	−3.8736	0.0038	−3.8517	0.0036	−3.8433	0.0063
c_J	0.2632	0.0012	0.3253	0.0010	0.2473	0.0017
σ_J	0.0001	3.2862	0.0003	0.8723	0.0032	0.1621
Objective function	0.0748		0.0670		0.0622	

TABLE 12.7 Average Percentage Pricing Errors of Unspanned Stochastic Volatility Jump Models

This table reports average pricing errors of difference caps with different moneyness and maturity of three stochastic volatility jump models. Average percentage pricing errors are defined as the difference between market price and model price divided by market price.

Panel A. Average percentage pricing errors of USVJ1

Moneyness	1.5yr	2yr	2.5yr	3yr	3.5yr	4yr	4.5yr	5yr	6yr	7yr	8yr	9yr	10yr
0.7	–	–	–	–	0.0164	0.0073	−0.0092	0.01	0.0102	0.0209	−0.0001	−0.0061	0.0077
0.8	–	–	0.014	0.0167	0.0116	−0.0014	−0.0091	0.0111	0.007	0.0207	−0.0009	−0.0076	0.0053
0.9	–	0.0682	0.0146	0.0132	0.0112	−0.0035	−0.0103	0.0104	0.0038	0.0204	−0.0062	−0.0114	−0.0042
1.0	−0.009	0.0839	0.0233	0.016	0.0158	−0.0004	−0.0105	0.0105	0.0062	0.0194	0.0013	−0.0083	0.0094
1.1	−0.098	−0.0625	−0.0038	−0.0144	−0.0086	−0.0255	−0.0199	0.0094	–	–	–	–	–

Panel B. Average percentage pricing errors of USVJ2

Moneyness	1.5yr	2yr	2.5yr	3yr	3.5yr	4yr	4.5yr	5yr	6yr	7yr	8yr	9yr	10yr
0.7	–	–	–	–	0.0243	0.0148	−0.0008	0.0188	0.0175	0.0279	0.0116	0.0106	0.0256
0.8	–	–	0.0232	0.0271	0.0211	0.0062	−0.0035	0.0172	0.0137	0.0255	0.0081	0.0061	0.0139
0.9	–	0.0698	0.019	0.0205	0.0172	−0.0012	−0.0119	0.0068	0.0039	0.0198	−0.0041	−0.0047	−0.002
1.0	−0.0375	0.0668	0.013	0.0131	0.015	−0.0058	−0.0214	−0.0047	−0.0054	0.0127	−0.0058	−0.0112	−0.0128
1.1	−0.089	0.0612	−0.0048	−0.0094	0.0003	−0.0215	−0.0273	−0.0076	–	–	–	–	–

Panel C. Average percentage pricing errors of USVJ3

Moneyness	1.5yr	2yr	2.5yr	3yr	3.5yr	4yr	4.5yr	5yr	6yr	7yr	8yr	9yr	10yr
0.7	–	–	–	–	0.0261	0.0176	0.0008	0.017	0.0085	0.0167	0.0008	−0.0049	−0.0021
0.8	–	–	0.0222	0.0249	0.0223	0.0115	0.0027	0.0185	0.0016	0.0131	0.004	−0.0008	−0.0063
0.9	–	0.0713	0.014	0.0155	0.0182	0.0073	−0.0002	0.0129	−0.0108	0.0072	0.0044	0.0048	−0.0092
1.0	−0.0204	0.0657	0.005	0.0054	0.0142	0.0033	−0.0068	0.0047	−0.0232	−0.001	0.019	0.0206	−0.0058
1.1	−0.0688	0.0528	−0.02	−0.0242	−0.0085	−0.0199	−0.0182	−0.0028	–	–	–	–	–

negative jumps to the USV1 model results in significant improvement in the model performance. Switching from the USVJ1 to the USVJ2 model further reduces underpricing in deep ITM caps, especially with longer maturities. Additionally, the USVJ3 model performs better than the USVJ2 model. Average pricing errors for the USVJ3 model are less than 1 percent, which means that the model captures the smile effect in caps data pretty well.

Overall, JLZ find that a model with three principal components driving the forward rate curve, with stochastic volatility for each component and large negative jumps, captures the smile effect in the caps markets well. Three factors are necessary to capture the variations in levels of LIBOR rates; the volatility of each component is necessary to capture the time-varying volatility of the LIBOR rates; and finally, large negative jumps are necessary to capture the smile effect. However, despite the overall good performance of the USVJ3 model, JLZ find that the USVJ model has large pricing errors for the first 20 weeks of the data sample. They explain it by a possible structural change in the data-generating process. It seems that the caps prices have the expectation of large negative jumps built into them only after these first 20 weeks. Similarly, index options prices have the expectation of large negative jumps built into them after the 1987 market crash. However, during that time period, there was not any single event that would cause caps prices to change so dramatically. JLZ leave this question open to further investigation.

The work of Joshi and Rebonato [2003] and others,[13] which uses USV models with CEV and/or displaced-diffusion forward rate processes, and the work of JLZ, which uses USV models extended with jumps, present two alternative perspectives on the existence of the caplet smile. According to the former models, the LFM is misspecified such that lognormal forward rate distribution does not capture the forward rate dynamics properly. The lognormal distribution implies a strong dependence of the forward rate volatility on its level. Though interest rate volatilities do increase with the level of the rates, the increase is not so strong as to be *proportional* to their level. Hence, according to the former models, a more likely explanation of the appearance of the caplet smile beginning in the mid-1990s is that the LFM was replaced by traders with the CEV or displaced-diffusion extensions of the LFM. Further extending these models by adding USV factors allows these models to capture the hockey-stick shaped smile.

In contrast, according to the JLZ model, the USV extension of the LFM can be modeled to generate symmetric hockey-stick shaped smiles, while the asymmetric hockey-stick shaped smile can be generated by using downward jumps in forward rates under the forward measures, instead of under the CEV or displaced-diffusion forward rate processes.

NOTES

1. The smile first appeared in the equity options market after the equity market crash of 1987. The shape of the smile became more pronounced a few years after the crash, which made the implied volatilities of out-of-the-money put options significantly higher than the implied volatilities of at-the-money put options. Increases in the aversion to risk of another equity market crash or a reassessment of the probabilities around the tail of the stock return distribution (caused by sudden downward jumps in returns in 1987) were likely explanations of the smile in the equity options market.

2. Since the correlation does not depend on the specific numeraire being used, the Wiener processes in equation (12.21) are written without the superscripts.

3. Also see Brace, Dun, and Barton [1998].

4. See Rebonato [2002].

5. One may argue instead that the function $g(t)$ is *overfitting* the LFM, as it is capturing the noise element in the valuation of caps. We believe smoothing is a better explanation than overfitting in the present case, as the LFM most likely suffers from a *misspecification bias*, which disallows it from fitting the observed Black implied market volatilities using a time-homogeneous volatility function.

6. This is the best-case scenario, since it minimizes the deviations of $k(T_i)$ from unity by combining step 1 and step 2 into a single step by jointly optimizing for the parameters of functions $h(T_i - t)$ and $g(t)$. Rebonato [2002, Section 8.5.5, pp. 240-42] recommends this approach as an alternative to the three-step procedure, by matching both a current term structure of volatility and a future term structure of volatility. This approach obviously puts more burden on the function $g(t)$ to fit both the current volatilities and the future volatilities. However, note that the fit is guaranteed at only two points in time: the current time and a *chosen* point of time in the future. Rebonato does not investigate whether the volatilities will behave in some weird fashion at other points in time in the future.

7. As an example, consider the case when correlations between instantaneous forward rate changes are close to one in scenario A and close to zero in scenario B. Then the corresponding correlations between percentage changes in the discrete forward rates will also be close to one in scenario A and close to zero in scenario B. Though the volatilities of instantaneous forward rate changes are the same under both scenarios (by assumption), the volatilities of the percentage changes in the discrete forward rates will be significantly lower under scenario A. Hence, the modeler using HJM or preference-free affine models would claim that caps are priced significantly lower in scenario A because of much higher correlations, while the LFM modeler would claim that caps are priced significantly lower under scenario A because of much lower volatilities. The LFM modeler may erroneously assume that correlations do not matter for pricing caps, without realizing that the very reason for having lower

volatilities of the percentage changes in discrete forward rates in scenario A is linked with having higher correlations between the changes in instantaneous forward rates in scenario A.

8. Throughout this book, the time line is given as $t, T_0, T_1, \ldots, T_n$, where T_0 is either the first reset date of a cap or the swaption expiration date. The correlation function $\rho_{i,j}(t)$ is defined as the correlation between the forward rates $f(t, T_i, T_{i+1})$ and $f(t, T_j, T_{j+1})$, where i and j are defined over the range $0, 1, 2, \ldots, n - 1$. Many authors, including Schoenmakers and Coffey [2000, 2003], do not use T_0 in the time line, which explains why the formulas in equations (12.84) and (12.88) seem slightly different from those in the original paper by these authors.

9. The smile first appeared in the equity options market after the equity market crash of 1987. The shape of the smile became more pronounced a few years after the crash, which made the implied volatilities of out-of-the-money put options significantly higher than the implied volatilities of at-the-money put options. Increases in the aversion to risk of another equity market crash or a reassessment of the probabilities around the tail of the stock return distribution (caused by sudden downward jumps in returns in 1987) were likely explanations of the smile in the equity options market.

10. The Jarrow, Li, and Zhao [2007] model is described in the next section.

11. See Brigo and Mercurio [2001].

12. For notational simplicity, JLZ refer to these models as stochastic volatility models, but we refer to them as unspanned stochastic volatility models in order to distinguish them from the stochastic volatility models in the affine and quadratic classes.

13. See Andersen and Brotherton-Ratcliffe [2001]; Wu and Zhang [2002]; Piterbarg [2003]; and Hagan, Kumar, Lesniewski, and Woodward [2002].

References

Acharya, Viral V., and Jennifer N. Carpenter, 2002, "Corporate Bond Valuation and Hedging with Stochastic Interest Rates and Endogenous Bankruptcy," *Review of Financial Studies*, 15(5), 1355–1383.

Ahn, Dong-Hyun, 1998, "Generalized Squared-Autoregressive-Independent-Variable Term Structure Model," Working paper, University of North Carolina.

Ahn, Dong-Hyun, Robert F. Dittmar, and A. Ronald Gallant, 2002, "Quadratic Term Structure Models: Theory and Evidence," *The Review of Financial Studies*, 15(1), 243–288.

Ahn, Dong-Hyun, and Bin Gao, 1999, "A Parametric Nonlinear Model of Term Structure Dynamics," *Review of Financial Studies*, 12(4), 721–762.

Ahn, Chang Mo, and Howard E. Thompson, 1988, "Jump-Diffusion Processes and the Term Structure of Interest Rates," *The Journal of Finance*, 43(1), 155–174.

Aït-Sahalia, Yacine, 1996a, "Nonparametric Pricing of Interest Rate Derivative Securities," *Econometrica*, 6(4), 527–560.

Aït-Sahlia, Yacine, 1996b, "Testing Continuous-Time Models of the Spot Rate," *The Review of Financial Studies*, 9(2), 385–426.

Amin, Kaushik I., 1993, "Jump Diffusion Option Valuation in Discrete Time," *The Journal of Finance*, 48(5), 1833–1863.

Amin, Kaushik I., and James N. Bodurtha Jr., 1995, "Discrete-Time Valuation of American Options with Stochastic Interest Rates," *Review of Financial Studies*, 8(1), 193–234.

Amin, Kaushik I., and Andrew J. Morton, 1994, "Implied Volatility Functions in Arbitrage-Free Term Structure Models," *Journal of Financial Economics*, 35(2), 141–180.

Andersen, Leif B.G., and Jesper Andreasen, 2000, "Volatility Skews and Extensions of the LIBOR Market Model," *Applied Mathematical Finance*, 7(1), 1–32.

Andersen, Leif B.G., and Rupert Brotherton-Ratcliffe, 2005, "Extended LIBOR Market Models with Stochastic Volatility," *Journal of Computational Finance*, 9(1), 1–40.

Arrow, Kenneth, J., 1964, "The Role of Securities in the Optimal Allocation of Risk-Bearing," *The Review of Economic Studies*, 31(2), 91–96.

Back, Kerry, and Stanley R. Pliska, 1991, "On the Fundamental Theorem of Asset Pricing with an Infinite State Space," *Journal of Mathematical Economics*, 20(1), 1–18.

Backus, David K., Silverio Foresi, and Liuren Wu, 1997, "Macroeconomic Foundations of Higher Order Moments in Bond Yields," Working paper, New York University.

Bailey, David H., and Paul N. Swarztrauber, 1991, "The Fractional Fourier Transform and Applications," *SIAM Review*, 33(3), 389–404.

Bailey, David H., and Paul N. Swarztrauber, 1994, "A Fast Method for the Numerical Evaluation of Continuous Fourier and Laplace Transforms," *SIAM Journal of Scientific Computing*, 15(5), 1105–1110.

Bakshi, Gurdip, Charles Cao, and Zhiwu Chen, 1997, "Empirical Performance of Alternative Option Pricing Models," *The Journal of Finance*, 52(5), 2003–2049.

Bakshi, Gurdip, and Dilip Madan, 2000, "Spanning and Derivative-Security Valuation," *Journal of Financial Economics*, 55(2), 205–238.

Balduzzi, Pierluigi, Sanjiv R. Das, Silverio Foresi, and Rangarajan Sundaram, 1996, "A Simple Approach to Three-Factor Affine Term Structure Models," *Journal of Fixed Income*, 6(4), 43–53.

Bali, Turan G., Liuren Wu, 2006, "A Comprehensive Analysis of the Short-Term Interest Rate Dynamics," *Journal of Banking and Finance*, 30, 1269–1290.

Ball, Clifford A., and Walter N. Torous, 1983, "Bond Price Dynamics and Options," *Journal of Financial and Quantitative Analysis*, 18 (December), 517–531.

Ball, Clifford A., and Walter N. Torous, 1995, Regime Shifts in Short-Term Riskless Interest Rates, Working paper #15-95, Anderson School of Management, University of California at Los Angeles.

Baz, Jamil, and Sanjiv R. Das, 1996, "Analytical Approximations of the Term Structure for Jump-Diffusion Processes: A Numerical Analysis," *Journal of Fixed Income*, 78–86.

Beaglehole, David R., and Mark S. Tenney, 1991, "General Solutions of Some Interest Rate-Contingent Claim Pricing Equations," *Journal of Fixed Income*, 1(2), 69–83.

Beaglehole, David R., and Mark S. Tenney, 1992, "Corrections and Additions to 'A Nonlinear Equilibrium Model of the Term Structure of Interest Rates'," *Journal of Financial Economics*, 32(3), 345–353.

Beliaeva, Natalia A., and Sanjay K. Nawalkha, 2006, "Pricing American Interest Rate Options under the Jump-Extended Vasicek Model," Working paper, Suffolk University, Boston.

Beliaeva, Natalia A., and Sanjay K. Nawalkha, 2007a, "A Two-Dimensional Transform for Lattice Construction under Stochastic-Volatility-Jump Models," Working Paper, University of Massachusetts, Amherst.

Beliaeva, Natalia A., and Sanjay K. Nawalkha, 2007b, "Simple Formulas for Pricing CDS spreads and yield spreads under multifactor affine and quadratic term structure models," Working paper, University of Massachusetts, Amherst.

Bikbov, Ruslan, and Mikhail Chernov, 2004, "Term Structure and Volatility: Lessons from the Eurodollar Markets," Working paper, Columbia Business School.

Bikbov, Ruslan, and Mikhail Chernov, 2005, "Term Structure and Volatility: Lessons from the Eurodollar Futures and Options," Working paper, Columbia Business School.

Black, Fischer, 1976, "The Pricing of Commodity Contracts," *Journal of Financial Economics*, 3(1), 167–179.

Black, Fischer, Emanuel Derman, and William Toy, 1990, "A One-Factor Model of Interest Rates and its Application to Treasury Bond Options," *Financial Analysts Journal*, 46, 33–39.

Black, Fischer, and Piotr Karasinski, 1991, "Bond and Option Pricing When Short Rates are Lognormal," *Financial Analysts Journal*, 47(4), 52–59.

Black, Fischer, and Myron Scholes, 1973, "The Pricing of Options and Corporate Liabilities," *Journal of Political Economy*, 81(3), 637–655.

Blanco, Roberto, Simon Brennan, and Ian W. Marsh, 2005, "An Empirical Analysis of the Dynamic Relation between Investment-Grade Bonds and Credit Default Swaps," *Journal of Finance*, 60(5), 2255–2281.

Bliss, Robert, and David Smith, 1998, "The Elasticity of Interest Rate Volatility," *Journal of Risk*, 1(1), 21–46.

Boudoukh, Jacob, and Matthew Richardson, 1999, "A Multifactor, Nonlinear, Continuous Time Model of Interest Rate Volatility," NBER Working paper 7213.

Brace, Alan, Tim Dun, Geo Barton, 1998, "Towards a Central Interest Rate Model," ICBI Global Derivatives Conference, Paris.

Brace, Alan, Dariusz Gatarek, Marek Musiela, 1997, "The Market Model of Interest Rate Dynamics," *Mathematical Finance*, 7(2), 127–155.

Brandt, Michael, and David A. Chapman, 2005, "Comparing Multifactor Models of the Term Structure," Working Paper, Boston College.

Breeden, Douglas T., 1979, "An Intertemporal Asset Pricing Model with Stochastic Consumption and Investment Opportunities," *Journal of Financial Economics*, 7(3), 265–296.

Brennan, Michael J., and Eduardo S. Schwartz, 1980, "Analyzing Convertible Bonds," *The Journal of Financial and Quantitative Analysis*, 15(4), 907–929.

Brigo, Damiano, 2002, "A Note on Correlation and Rank Reduction." Working paper, www.damianobrigo.it.

Brigo, Damiano, and Fabio Mercurio, 2001, *Interest Rate Models: Theory and Practice*, Springer Finance.

Brigo, Damiano, and Fabio Mercurio, 2006, *Interest Rate Models—Theory and Practice: With Smile Inflation, and Credit*, Springer Finance, Second Edition.

Campbell, John Y., Andrew W. Lo, and A. Craig MacKinlay, 1997, *The Econometrics of Financial Markets*, Princeton University Press.

Campbell, John Y., and Robert J. Shiller, 1991, "Yield Spreads and Interest Rate Movements: A Bird's Eye View," *Review of Economic Studies*, 58, 495–514.

Carr, Peter, and Dilip B. Madan, 1999, "Option Valuation Using the Fast Fourier Transform," Working paper, University of Maryland.

Casassus, J., Pierre Collin-Dufresne, Robert Goldstein, 2005, "Unspanned Stochastic Volatility and Fixed Income Derivatives Pricing," *Journal of Banking & Finance*, 29, 2723–2749.

Caverhill Andrew, 1994, "When Is the Short Rate Markovian?" *Mathematical Finance*, 4, 305–312.

Chacko, George, and Sanjiv R. Das, 2002, "Pricing Interest Rate Derivatives: A General Approach," *Review of Financial Studies*, 15(1), 195–241.

Chan, K. C., G. Andrew Karolyi, Francis A. Longstaff, and Anthony B. Sanders, 1992, "An Empirical Comparison of Alternative Models of the Short-Term Interest Rate," *The Journal of Finance*, 47(3), 1209–1227.

Chapman, David A., and Neil D. Pearson, 2000, "Is the Short Rate Drift Actually Nonlinear?" *The Journal of Finance*, 55(1), 355–388.

Chen, L., 1996, *Stochastic Mean and Stochastic Volatility: A Three-Factor Model of the Term Structure of Interest Rates and Its Application to the Pricing of Interest Rate Derivatives*, Blackwell Publishers, Oxford, U.K.

Chen, Li, Damir Filipovic, and H. Vincent Poor, 2004, "Quadratic Term Structure Models for Risk-free and Defaultable Rates," *Mathematical Finance*, 14(4), 515–536.

Chen, Ren-Raw, and Louis Scott, 1992, "Pricing Interest Rate Options in a Two-Factor Cox-Ingersoll-Ross Model of the Term Structure," *The Review of Financial Studies*, 5(4), 613–636.

Chourdakis, Kyriakos, 2004, Option Pricing using the Fractional FFT, Working paper, Queen Mary University.

Collin-Dufresne, Pierre, and Robert S. Goldstein, 2001a, "Stochastic Correlation and the Relative Pricing of Caps and Swaptions in a Generalized-Affine Framework," Working paper, Carnegie Mellon University.

Collin-Dufresne, Pierre, Robert S. Goldstein, 2001b, "Pricing Swaptions Within an Affine Framework," NBER Working paper.

Collin-Dufresne, Pierre, Robert S. Goldstein, 2002, "Do Bonds Span the Fixed Income Markets? Theory and Evidence for Unspanned Stochastic Volatility," *The Journal of Finance*, 57(4), 1685–1730.

Collin-Dufresne, Pierre, Robert S. Goldstein, and Christopher Jones, 2004, "Can Interest Rate Volatility be Extracted from the Cross Section of Bond Yields? An Investigation of Unspanned Stochastic Volatility," NBER Working Paper #10756.

Conley, T., L. P. Hansen, E. Luttmer, and J. Scheinkman, 1997, "Short-Term Interest Rates as Subordinated Diffusions," *Review of Financial Studies*, 10(3), 525–577.

Constantinides, George M., 1992, "A Theory of the Nominal Term Structure of Interest Rates," *The Review of Financial Studies*, 5(4), 531–552.

Courtadon, George, 1982, "The Pricing of Options on Default-Free Bonds," *The Journal of Financial and Quantitative Analysis*, 17(1), 75–100.

Cox, John C., Jonathan E. Ingersoll Jr., and Stephen A. Ross, 1980, "An Analysis of Variable Rate Loan Contracts," *The Journal of Finance*, 35(2), 389–403.

Cox, John C., Jonathan E. Ingersoll, Jr., and Stephen A. Ross, 1981, "A Re-Examination of Traditional Hypotheses about the Term Structure of Interest Rates," *The Journal of Finance*, 36(4), 769–799.

Cox John C., Jonathan E. Ingersoll Jr., and Stephen A. Ross, 1985, "A Theory of the Term Structure of Interest Rates," *Econometrica*, 53(2), 385–408.

Cox, John C., and Stephen A. Ross, 1976, "The Valuation of Options for Alternative Stochastic Processes," *Journal of Financial Economics*, 3(1), 145–166.

Dai Qiang, and Kenneth J. Singleton, 2000, "Specification Analysis of Affine Term Structure Models," *The Journal of Finance*, 55(5), 1943–1978.

Dai, Qiang, and Kenneth J. Singleton, 2002, "Expectation Puzzles, Time-Varying Risk Premia, and Affine Models of the Term Structure," *Journal of Financial Economics*, 63(3), 415–441.

Das, Sanjiv R., 1998, "On the Recursive Implementation of Term Structure Models," *Pecunia*, Summer, 45–49.

Das, Sanjiv R., 2002, "The Surprise Element: Jumps in Interest Rates," *Journal of Econometrics*, 106(1), 27–65.

Das, Sanjiv R., and Silverio Foresi, 1996, "Exact Solutions for Bond and Option Prices with Systematic Jump Risk," *Review of Derivatives Research*, 1(1), 7–24.

Debreu, Gerald, 1959, *Theory of Value: An Axiomatic Analysis of Economic Equilibrium*, Yale University Press.

Dothan, Uri L., 1978, "On the Term Structure of Interest Rates," *Journal of Financial Economics*, 6(1), 59–69.

Duarte, Jefferson, 2004, "Evaluating Alternative Risk Preferences in Affine Term Structure Models," *The Review of Financial Studies*, 17(2), 379–404.

Duffee, Gregory R., 2002, "Term Premia and Interest Rate Forecasts in Affine Models," *The Journal of Finance*, 57(1), 405–443.

Duffie, Darrell, 2001, *Dynamic Asset Pricing Theory*, Princeton University Press, NJ.

Duffie, Darrell, and Rui Kan, 1996, "A Yield-Factor Model of Interest Rates," *Mathematical Finance*, 6(4), 379–406.

Duffie, Darrell, Jun Pan, and Kenneth J. Singleton, 2000, "Transform Analysis and Option Pricing for Affine Jump-Diffusions," *Econometrica*, 68(6), 1343–1376.

Duffie, Darrell, and Kenneth J. Singleton, 1993, "Simulated Moments Estimation of Markov Models of Asset Prices," *Econometrica*, 61(4), 929–952.

Duffie, Darrell, and Kenneth J. Singleton, 1997, "An Econometric Model of the Term Structure of Interest-Rate Swap Yields," *The Journal of Finance*, 52-4, 1287–1321.

Duffie, Darrell, and Kenneth J. Singleton, 1999, "Modeling Term Structures of Defaultable Bonds," *The Review of Financial Studies*, 12(4), 687–720.

Duffie, Darrell, and Kenneth J. Singleton, 2003, *Credit Risk: Pricing, Measurement, and Management*, Princeton University Press.

Durham, J. Benson, 2005, "Jump-Diffusion Processes and Affine Term Structure Models: Additional Closed-Form Approximate Solutions, Distributional Assumptions for Jumps, and Parameter Estimates," Working paper, Division of Monetary Affairs, Board of Governors of the Federal Reserve System, Washington, DC.

Dybvig, Philip H., 1988, "Bond and Bond Option Pricing Based on the Current Term Structure," Working paper, Washington University.

Dybvig, Philip H., 1997, "Bond and Bond Option Pricing Based on the Current Term Structure," *Mathematics of Derivative Securities*, Eds. Michael A.H. Dempster and Stanley R. Pliska, Cambridge University Press, 271–293.

Dybvig, Philip H., Jonathan E. Ingersoll Jr., and Stephen A. Ross, 1996, "Long Forward and Zero-Coupon Rates Can Never Fall," *The Journal of Business*, 69(1), 1–25.

Fama, Eugene F., and Robert R. Bliss, 1987, "The Information in Long-Maturity Forward Rates," *The American Economic Review*, 77(4), 680–692.

Fama, Eugene F., and Kenneth R. French, 1993, "Common Risk Factors in the Returns on Stocks and Bonds," *Journal of Financial Economics*, 33, 3–56.

Fan, Rong, Anurag Gupta, and Peter Ritchken, 2003, "Hedging in the Possible Presence of Unspanned StochasticVolatility: Evidence from Swaption Markets," *The Journal of Finance*, 58(5), 2219–2248.

Gallant, A. R. and G. Tauchen, 1989, "Seminonparametric Estimation of Conditionally Constrained Heterogeneous Processes: Asset Pricing Applications," *Econometrica*, 57(5), 1091–1120.

Gallant, A. R. and G. Tauchen, 1996, "Which Moments to Match," *Econometric Theory*, 12(4), 657–681.

Geman, Helyette, 1989, "The Importance of the Forward Neutral Probability in a Stochastic Approach of Interest Rates," Working paper, ESSEC.

Geman, Helyette, El Karoui, J. C. Rochet, 1995, "Changes of Numeraire, Changes of Probability Measures and Option Pricing," *Journal of Applied Probability*, 32(2), 443–458.

Glasserman, P., and S. G. Kou, 2000, "The Term Structure of Simple Forward Rates with Jump Risk," Working paper, Columbia University.

Goldstein, Robert S., 2000, "The Term Structure of Interest Rates as a Random Field," *Review of Financial Studies*, 13, 365–384.

Han, Bing, 2004, "Stochastic Volatilities and Correlations of Bond Yields," Working Paper, McCombs School of Business, University of Texas, Austin.

Hansen, Lars Peter, and Scott F. Richard, 1987, "The Role of Conditioning Information in Deducing Testable Restrictions Implied by Dynamic Asset Pricing Models," *Econometrica*, 55(3), 587–613.

Harrison, J. Michael, and David M. Kreps, 1979, "Martingales and Arbitrage in Multiperiod Securities Markets," *Journal of Economic Theory*, 20(3), 381–408.

Harrison, J. Michael, and Stanley R. Pliska, 1981, "Martingales and Stochastic Integrals in the Theory of Continuous Trading," *Stochastic Processes and Their Applications*, 11, 215–260.

Harrison, J. Michael, and Stanley R. Pliska, 1983, "A Stochastic Calculus Model of Continuous Trading: Complete Markets," *Stochastic Processes and Their Applications*, 15, 313–316.

Heath, David, Robert Jarrow and Andrew Morton, 1990, "Bond Pricing and the Term Structure of Interest Rates: A Discrete-Time Approximation," *Journal of Financial and Quantitative Analysis*, 25, 419–440.

Heath, David, Robert Jarrow and Andrew Morton, 1992, "Bond Pricing and the Term Structure of Interest Rates: A New Methodology," *Econometrica*, 60(1), 77–105.

Heidari, Massoud, and Liuren Wu, 2003, "Are Interest Rate Derivatives Spanned by the Term Structure of Interest Rates?" *Journal of Fixed Income*, 13(1), 75–86.

Heston Steven, 1993, "A Closed-Form Solution for Options with Stochastic Volatility with Applications to Bond and Currency Options," *Review of Financial Studies*, 6, 327–343.

Ho, Thomas S. Y., and Sang-Bin Lee, 1986, "Term Structure Movements and the Pricing of Interest Rate Contingent Claims," *The Journal of Finance*, 41(5), 1011–1029.

Ho, Thomas S.Y., and Sang-Bin Lee, 2005, "A Multi-Factor Binomial Interest Rate Model with State Time Dependent Volatilities," Working paper, Thomas Ho Company.

Houweling, P., and T. Vorst, 2005, "Pricing Default Swaps: Empirical Evidence," *Journal of International Money and Finance*, 24, 1200–1225.

Hull, John, 1997, *Options, Futures, and other Derivatives*, Prentice Hall, 3rd Edition, NJ.

Hull, John, 2003, *Options, Futures, and other Derivatives*, Prentice Hall, 5th, Edition, NJ.

Hull, John, M. Predescu, Alan White, 2004, "The Relationship between Credit Default Swap Spreads, Bond Yields, and Credit Rating Announcements," *Journal of Banking and Finance*, 28(11).

Hull, John, and Alan White, 1990, "Pricing Interest Rate Derivative Securities," *The Review of Financial Studies*, 3(4), 573–592.

Hull, John, and Alan White, 1993, "One-Factor Interest-Rate Models and the Valuation of Interest-Rate Derivative Securities," *The Journal of Financial and Quantitative Analysis*, 28(2), 235–254.

Hull, John, and Alan White, 1994a, "Numerical Procedures for Implementing Term Structure Models I: Single-Factor Models," *The Journal of Derivatives*, 2(1), 7–16.

Hull, John, and Alan White, 1994b, "Numerical Procedures for Implementing Term Structure Models II: Two-Factor Models," *The Journal of Derivatives*, 2(2), 37–48.

Hull, John, and Alan White, 1996, "Using Hull-White Interest Rate Trees," *The Journal of Derivatives*, 3, 26–36.

Hull, John, and Alan White, 1999, "Forward Rate Volatilities, Swap Rate Volatilities, and the Implementation of the LIBOR Market Model," *Journal of Fixed Income*, 10(3), 46–62.

Hull, John, and Alan White, 2003, "The Valuation of Credit Default Swap Options," *Journal of Derivatives*, 10(3), 40–50.

Inui, Koji, and Masaaki Kijima, 1998, "A Markovian Framework in Multi-Factor Heath-Jarrow-Morton Models," *The Journal of Financial and Quantitative Analysis*, 33(3), 423–440.

Jackel, Peter, and Riccardo Rebonato, 2001, "Valuing American Options in the Presence of User-Defined Smiles and Time-Dependent Volatility: Scenario Analysis, Model Stress and Lower-Bound Pricing Applications," *Journal of Risk*, 4(1), 35–61.

Jagannathan, Ravi, Andrew Kaplin, and Steve G. Sun, 2003, "An Evaluation of Multi-Factor CIR Models Using LIBOR, Swap Rates and Swaptions," *Journal of Econometrics*, 116(1–2), 113–146.

Jamshidian, Farshid, 1989, "An Exact Bond Option Pricing Formula," *The Journal of Finance*, 44(1), 205–209.

Jamshidian, Farshid, 1997, "LIBOR and Swap Market Models and Measures," *Finance and Stochastics*, 1, 293–330.

Jarrow, Robert A., David Lando and Stuart M. Turnbull, 1997, "A Markov Model for the Term Structure of Credit Spreads," *The Review of Financial Studies*, 10(2), 481–523.

Jarrow, Robert, Haitao Li, and Feng Zhao, 2004, "Interest Rate Caps Smile Too! But Can the LIBOR Market Models Capture It?" Working paper, Cornell University.

Jarrow, Robert, Haitao Li, and Feng Zhao, 2007, "Interest Rate Caps Smile Too! But Can the LIBOR Market Models Capture It?" *Journal of Finance*, 62(1).

Jarrow, Robert, Stuart M. Turnbull, 1995, "Pricing Derivatives on Financial Securities Subject to Credit Risk," *The Journal of Finance*, 50(1), 53–85.

Jeffrey, Andrew, 1997, Asymptotic Maturity Behavior of Single Factor Heath-Jarrow-Morton Term Structure Models: A Note, Working paper, Yale School of Management.

Johannes, Michael, 2004, "The Statistical and Economic Role of Jumps in Continuous-Time Interest Rate Models," *Journal of Finance*, 59, 227–260.

Karoui, El, N. R. Myneni, and R. Viswanathan, 1992, "Arbitrage Pricing and Hedging of Interest Rate Claims with State Variables: I Theory," Working paper, University of Paris.

Kennedy, D. P., 1994, "The Term Structure of Interest Rates as a Gaussian Random Field," *Mathematical Finance*, 4, 247–258.

Kennedy, D. P., 1997, "Characterizing Gaussian Models of the Term Structure of Interest Rates," *Mathematical Finance*, 7, 107–118.

Lacey, Nelson J., and Sanjay K. Nawalkha, 1990, "*Closed-Form Duration Measures and Strategy Applications*," The Research Foundation of the Institute of Chartered Financial Analysts, Charlottesville, Virginia.

Lacey, Nelson J., and Sanjay K. Nawalkha, 1993, "Convexity, Risk, and Returns," *Journal of Fixed Income*, 3(3), 72–79.

Lando, David, 1998, "On Cox Processes and Credit Risky Securities," *Review of Derivatives Research*, 2(2), 99–120.

Lee, B. S., and B. F. Ingram, 1991, "Simulation Estimation of Time-Series Models," *Journal of Econometrics*, 47(2), 197–205.

Leippold, M. and L. Wu, 2003, "Design and Estimation of Quadratic Term Structure Models," *European Finance Review*, 7(1), 47–73.

Li, Anlong, Peter Ritchken, and L. Sankarasubramanian, 1995, Lattice Models for Pricing American Interest Rate Claims, *Journal of Finance*, 50(2), 719–737.

Li, Haitao, and Yuewu Xu, 2002, "Short Rate Dynamics and Regime Shifts," Working paper, Cornell University.

Li, Haitao, and Feng Zhao, "Unspanned Stochastic Volatility: Evidence from Hedging Interest Rate Derivatives," *Journal of Finance*, 61(1), 341–378.

Longstaff, Francis, Sanjay Mithal, and Eric Neis, 2003, "The Credit-Default Swap Market: Is Credit Protection Priced Correctly?" Working paper, University of California at Los Angeles.

Longstaff, Francis A., Pedro Santa-Clara, and Eduardo S. Schwartz, 2001, "The Relative Valuation of Caps and Swaptions: Theory and Empirical Evidence," *Journal of Finance*, 56, 2067–2109.

Longstaff, Francis A., and Eduardo S. Schwartz, 1992, "Interest Rate Volatility and the Term Structure: A Two-Factor General Equilibrium Model," *The Journal of Finance*, 47(4), 1259–1282.

Longstaff, Francis A., and Eduardo S. Schwartz, 1995, "A Simple Approach to Valuing Risky Fixed and Floating Rate Debt," *The Journal of Finance*, 50(3), 789–819.

Madan, Dilip B., and H. Unal, 1998, "Pricing the Risks of Default," *Review of Derivatives Research*, 2(2), 121–160.

Marris, D., 1999, "Financial Option Pricing and Skewed Volatility," MPhil Thesis, Statistical Laboratory, University of Cambridge.

Marsh, Terry A., and Eric R. Rosenfeld, 1983, "Stochastic Processes for Interest Rates and Equilibrium Bond Prices," *The Journal of Finance*, 38(2), 635–646.

Merton, Robert C., 1973, "Theory of Rational Option Pricing," *The Bell Journal of Economics and Management Science*, 4(1), 141–183.

Merton, Robert C., 1974, "On the Pricing of Corporate Debt: The Risk Structure of Interest Rates," *Journal of Finance*, 29, 449–470.

Merton, Robert C., 1976. "Option Pricing when Underlying Stock Returns Are Discontinuous," *Journal of Financial Economics*, 3, 125–144.

Miltersen, Kristian R., Klaus Sandmann, and Dieter Sondermann, 1997, "Closed-Form Solutions for Term Structure Derivatives with Log-Normal Interest Rates," *The Journal of Finance*, 52(1), 409–430.

Nawalkha, Sanjay K., 1995, "Face Value Convergence for Stochastic Bond Price Processes: A Note on Merton's Partial Equilibrium Option Pricing Model," *Journal of Banking and Finance*, 19(1), 153–164.

Nawalkha, Sanjay K., and Natalia A. Beliaeva, 2007a, "Efficient Trees for CIR and CEV Short Rate Models," *Journal of Alternative Investments*, forthcoming.

Nawalkha, Sanjay K., and Natalia A. Beliaeva, 2007b, "Pricing American Interest Rate Options Under Jump-Extended CIR and CEV Short Rate Models," Working paper, University of Massachusetts, Amherst.

Nawalkha, Sanjay K., Natalia A. Beliaeva, and Gloria M. Soto, 2007a, "Pricing Interest Rate Caps using Preference-Free Multi-Factor Affine-Jump Models," Working paper, University of Massachusetts, Amherst.

Nawalkha, Sanjay K., Natalia A. Beliaeva, and Gloria M. Soto, 2007b, "An Extension of the Jarrow, Li, and Zhao Model with Time-Homogeneous Volatility and Jump Risk Premiums," Working paper, University of Massachusetts, Amherst.

Nawalkha, Sanjay, K., Natalia A. Beliaeva, and Gloria M. Soto, 2007c, "Simple Formulas for Pricing Credit Default Swaps using Preference-Free Multifactor Affine and Quadratic Models," Working paper, University of Massachusetts, Amherst.

Nawalkha, Sanjay, K., Natalia A. Beliaeva, and Gloria M. Soto, 2007d, "A New Taxonomy of the Dynamic Term Structure Models," Working paper, University of Massachusetts, Amherst.

Nawalkha, Sanjay K., Natalia A. Beliaeva, and Gloria M. Soto, 2007e, *Credit Risk Modeling: The Fixed Income Valuation Course*, Work in Progress, Wiley Finance, John Wiley & Sons, Hoboken, NJ.

Nawalkha, Sanjay K., and Donald R. Chambers, 1999, *Interest Rate Risk Measurement and Management*, Institutional Investor, Euromoney, London.

Nawalkha, Sanjay, K., and Gloria M. Soto, 2007a, "Simple Formulas for Pricing Eurodollar/Euribor Futures using Preference-Free Multifactor Affine and Quadratic Models," Working paper, University of Massachusetts, Amherst.

Nawalkha, Sanjay, K., and Gloria M. Soto, 2007b, "An Extension of the Cumulant Expansion Method for Pricing Caps and Swaptions using Preference-Free Multifactor Affine and Quadratic Models," Working paper, University of Massachusetts, Amherst.

Nawalkha, Sanjay K., Gloria M. Soto, and Natalia A. Beliaeva, 2005, *Interest Rate Risk Modeling: The Fixed Income Valuation Course*, Wiley Finance, John Wiley and Sons, Hoboken, NJ.

Nawalkha, Sanjay K., and Jun Zhang, 2004, "Generating a Markovian Process for the Proportional Volatility HJM Model using the Forward Measure," Working Paper, University of Massachusetts, Amherst.

Nelson, Charles R., and Andrew F. Siegel, 1987, "Parsimonious Modeling of Yield Curves," *The Journal of Business*, 60(4), 473–489.

Nelson, Daniel B., and Krishna Ramaswamy, 1990, "Simple Binomial Processes as Diffusion Approximations in Financial Models," *The Review of Financial Studies*, 3(3), 393–430.

Pan, Jun, 2002, "The Jump-Risk Premia Implicit in Options: Evidence from an Integrated Time-Series Study," *Journal of Financial Economics*, 63(1), 3–50.

Pan, Jun, and Kenneth J. Singleton, 2005, "Default and Recovery Implicit in the Term Structure of Sovereign CDS Spreads," Working paper, Massachusetts Institute of Technology.

Piazzesi, Monika, 1998, "A Linear-Quadratic Jump-Diffusion Model with Scheduled and Unscheduled Announcements," Working paper, Stanford University.

Piazzesi, Monika, 2005, "Bond Yields and the Federal Reserve," *Journal of Political Economy*, 113(2), 311–344.

Pritsker, M., 1998, "Nonparametric Density Estimation and Tests of Continuous Time Interest Rate Models," *Review of Financial Studies*, 11(3), 449–487.

Rebonato Riccardo, 1998, *Interest Rate Option Models* 2nd edition, John Wiley and Sons, Hoboken, NJ.

Rebonato Riccardo, 1999a, "On the Simultaneous Calibration of Multi-Factor Log-Normal Interest-Rate Models to Black Volatilities and to the Correlation Matrix" *Journal of Computational Finance*, 2(4), 5–27.

Rebonato Riccardo, 1999b, "On the Pricing Implications of the Joint Log-Normality Assumption for the Cap and Swaption Markets," *Journal of Computational Finance*, 2(3), 30–52.

Rebonato Riccardo, 1999c, "Calibrating the BGM Model," *Risk*, 12, 74–79.

Rebonato Riccardo, 1999d, *Volatility and Correlation*, John Wiley and Sons, Hoboken, NJ.

Rebonato, Riccardo, 2002, *Modern Pricing of Interest-Rate Derivatives: The LIBOR Market Model and Beyond*, Princeton University Press, Princeton NJ.

Rebonato, Riccardo, and Ian Cooper, 1995, "The Limitations of Simple Two-Factor Interest Rate Models," *Journal of Financial Engineering*, 5, 1–16.

Ritchken, Peter, and L. Sankarasubramanian, 1995a, "Volatility Structures of Forward Rates and the Dynamics of the Term Structure," *Mathematical Finance*, 5, 55–72.

Ritchken, Peter, and L. Sankarasubramanian, 1995b, "The Importance of Forward Rate Volatility Structures in Pricing Interest Rate Sensitive Claims," *Journal of Derivatives*, 25–41.

Santa-Clara, Pedro, and Didier Sornette, "The Dynamics of the Forward Interest Rate Curve with Stochastic String Shocks," *Review of Financial Studies*, 14(1), 149–185.

Schaefer, Stephen M., and Eduardo S. Schwartz, 1987, "Time-Dependent Variance and the Pricing of Bond Options," *The Journal of Finance*, 42(5), 1113–1128.

Schoenmakers, John, and B. Coffey, 2000, "Stable Implied Calibration of a Multi-Factor LIBOR Model via a Semi-Parametric Correlation Structure," Working paper # 611, Weierstrass Institute, Berlin.

Schoenmakers, John, and B. Coffey, 2003, "Systematic Generation of the Correlation Structures for the LIBOR Market Model," *International Journal of Theoretical and Applied Finance*, 6(4), 1–13.

Scott, Louis, 1995, "The Valuation of Interest Rate Derivatives in a Multi-Factor Term Structure Model with Deterministic Components," Working paper, University of Georgia.

Sidenius, J., 2000, "LIBOR market models in practice," *Journal of Computational Finance*, 3(3), 5–26.

Stanton, R., 1997, "A Nonparametric Model of Term Structure Dynamics and the Market Price of Interest Rate Risk," *The Journal of Finance*, 52(5), 1973–2002.

Sufana, R., 2003, "The Wishart Autoregressive Process of Multivariate Stochastic Volatility," Working Paper, University of Toronto.

Thompson, Samuel, 2004, "Identifying Term Structure Volatility From the LIBOR-Swap Curve," Working Paper, Arrowstreet Capital, L.P.

Vasicek, Oldrich, 1977, "An Equilibrium Characterization of the Term Structure," *Journal of Financial Economics*, 5(2), 177–188.

About the CD-ROM

INTRODUCTION

This appendix provides you with information on the contents of the CD that accompanies this book. For the latest and greatest information, please refer to the ReadMe file located at the root of the CD.

SYSTEM REQUIREMENTS

- A computer with a processor running at 120 Mhz or faster
- At least 64 MB of total RAM installed on your computer; for best performance, we recommend at least 128 MB
  NOTE: Many popular spreadsheet programs are capable of reading Microsoft Excel files. However, users should be aware that a slight amount of formatting might be lost when using a program other than Microsoft Excel.

USING THE CD WITH WINDOWS

To install the items from the CD to your hard drive, follow these steps:

1. Insert the CD into your computer's CD-ROM drive.
2. The CD-ROM interface will appear. The interface provides a simple point-and-click way to explore the contents of the CD.

If the opening screen of the CD-ROM does not appear automatically, follow these steps to access the CD:

1. Click the Start button on the left end of the taskbar and then choose Run from the menu that pops up.
2. In the dialog box that appears, type *d:***start.exe**. (If your CD-ROM drive is not drive d, fill in the appropriate letter in place of *d*.) This brings up the CD Interface described in the preceding set of steps.

WHAT'S ON THE CD

The software consists of various Excel/VBA files that allow valuation of fixed income derivatives using interest rate trees for low-dimensional affine models and using analytical and quasi-analytical solutions for higher-dimensional affine, quadratic, and LIBOR market models. To avoid repetition, the Excel files are organized according to the "model" type, and not according to the chapters, which have overlapping content in some cases. The CD contains six files that are described as follows:

1. **File name: TSIR.xls** This file estimates the term structure of spot rates or zero-coupon yields given the input data on prices, maturities, coupons, and face values of individual bonds entered by the user. The term structures are estimated using both the McCulloch cubic-spline method and the Nelson and Siegel exponential method. The estimated term structures can be used to price new bonds with different maturity characteristics in this file or used as inputs in other files that require term structures for valuation purposes.

2. **File name: TREES.xls** This file allows valuation of bonds and European and American bond options by building trees for one-factor affine models. We give trees for both the time-homogeneous models (i.e., fundamental/single-plus models), and the time-inhomogeneous models (i.e., double-plus models).

3. **File name: ATSM.xls** This file allows valuation of bonds, interest rate swaps, Treasury futures, Eurodollar/Euribor futures, forward rate agreements, caps, floors, collars, European bond options, and European swaptions, using single-plus and double-plus simple affine term structure models (ATSMs) with up to six factors. Since the simple ATSMs nest a variety of one-, two-, and three-factor ATSMs (given in chapters 4, 6, 7, 8, and 9) outlined in Table 9.3 of the book, the solutions in this spreadsheet apply to all of these models. This spreadsheet also calculates covariances and correlations of changes in the instantaneous forward rates of different maturities.

4. **File name: QTSM.xls** This file allows valuation of bonds, interest rate swaps, Treasury futures, Eurodollar/Euribor futures, forward rate agreements, caps, floors, collars, European bond options, and European swaptions, using single-plus and double-plus $Q_3(N)$ models (given in Chapter 10) with up to six factors. This spreadsheet also calculates covariances and correlations of changes in the instantaneous forward rates of different maturities.

5. **File name: CDS.xls** This file allows valuation of default-free coupon bonds, risky coupon bonds, credit-default-swap (CDS) premiums, default-free yield-to-maturity (YTM), risky YTM, and the spread between the default-free YTM and risky YTM, using the reduced-form simple ATSM and $Q_3(N)$ frameworks (given in chapters 9 and 10, respectively), under the recovery-of-face-value (RFV) assumption. The simple ATSMs allow only square-root processes to capture the joint dynamics of the short rate and the default intensity.

6. **File name: LIBOR.xls** This file allows valuation of caps using the lognormal forward Libor model (LFM), and valuation of European swaptions using the lognormal forward swap model (LSM), as well as the LFM using a single

numeraire. The user has flexibility in entering the parameters of a time-homogeneous forward rate volatility function (i.e., function 4 in equation (12.65) with k(.) = 1, a constant, and the function h(.) defined by equation (12.66)), and two types of exogenously specified forward rate correlation functions (based on Schoenmakers and Coffey [2000, 2003]), given in equations (12.84) and (12.88) in Chapter 12.

Any additional software files, extensions of old files, and upgrades will be made available on www.fixedincomerisk.com/software.htm.

TROUBLESHOOTING

Your Windows Explorer may be set up so that files with .dll extensions are not displayed and some file name extensions are hidden. To change the settings of Windows Explorer proceed as follows:

1. In Windows Explorer, open the folder containing the files you want to view.
2. On the Tools menu, click Folder Options, and then click the View tab.
3. To view all hidden file types, click the "Show hidden files and folders" option. To see all the file name extensions, clear the "Hide file extensions for known file types" check box. Finally, click the Apply button.

The software is optimized for a screen area of $1,024 \times 768$ pixels or higher and requires Windows XP or later and Excel XP or later. Also, the Solver Add-in for Excel should be available for using the Excel files. If the Solver Add-in is unavailable, you will receive a message with instructions about loading the Solver; for further assistance see Help in your Excel program.

Finally, you must click Enable Macros when the Excel files are opened. Also, to allow macros to run in Excel, the security level must be set to either Medium or Low (Medium level is recommended). To set the security level: On the Tools menu, point to Macro, and then click Security. For information on macro security, see Help in your Excel program.

Updates to the software can be downloaded from the web site at http://www.fixedincomerisk.com.

CUSTOMER CARE

If you have trouble with the CD-ROM, please call the Wiley Product Technical Support phone number at (800) 762-2974. Outside the United States, call (317) 572-3994. You can also contact Wiley Product Technical Support at **http://support.wiley.com**. John Wiley & Sons will provide technical support only for installation and other general quality control items. For technical support on the applications themselves, consult the program's vendor or author.

To place additional orders or to request information about other Wiley products, please call (877) 762-2974.

Index

For more information about the CD-ROM, see the About the CD-ROM section on page 658.